CW01095867

ASHTON & REID
ON
CLUBS AND ASSOCIATIONS

Second edition

ASHTON & REID
ON
CLUBS AND ASSOCIATIONS

Second edition

David Ashton MA (Oxon) FCIArb
of Gray's Inn
Barrister • Chartered arbitrator •
Accredited mediator

and

Paul W Reid MA (Cantab)
of the Inner Temple
Barrister • Recorder of the Crown Court

JORDANS

2011

Published by
Jordan Publishing Limited
21 St Thomas Street
Bristol BS1 6JS

British Library Cataloguing-in-Publication Data

A catalogue record for this book is available from the British Library.

ISBN 978 1 84661 251 0

Typeset by Letterpart Ltd, Reigate, Surrey

Printed in Great Britain by CPI Antony Rowe, Chippenham and Eastbourne

FOREWORD TO THE FIRST EDITION

An up-to-date and comprehensive book on Club Law is long overdue. We have waited a long time, but the wait has been worthwhile.

The concept of the club is founded in the 17th century when like-minded persons came together in coffee houses for political and social ends. In the next century 'gentlemen's clubs' emerged, notably White's (probably the earliest) and The Garrick (of which I am a proud member). Sports clubs were not far behind, the Jockey Club, MCC and the Royal and Ancient immediately spring to mind. They became a peculiarly English institution with a distinctive ethos of 'clubability'. The members jealously and zealously regarded the association as 'their' club run by and for the members with an unincorporated structure and in an informal yet democratic manner. The concept worked so well that it attracted the attention of others who recognised the merits and advantages of a club and who were inspired to adopt the formula as a means of creating institutions with far wider purposes and pursuits. Hence the emergence of a whole spectrum of clubs, associations and societies which include, for example, working men's clubs, British Legion clubs, gaming clubs, societies devoted to hobbies and even fan clubs. In all, a total running into tens of thousands. A later development was the creation of a more complex creature, incorporated clubs registered under the Industrial and Provident Societies Act or the Companies Act.

It is immediately apparent that the authors have undertaken a monumental task to produce in one volume the law and practice relating to the whole spectrum. A glance at the list of statutes and statutory instruments alone reveals the complexity of the subject and the dedication required to tackle the subject. But we need not worry. How fortunate that the publishers chose to entrust the task into such safe hands. David Ashton in 1964 re-wrote the book on Club Law published by the Working Men's Club and Institute Union and in the course of many years in practice he has acted for or advised numerous clubs, ranging from top football clubs to the local angling club. For 17 years he was counsel to the Kennel Club. Paul Reid has developed a particular expertise in Club Law, having been for the last 15 years Standing Counsel to the National Golf Clubs' Advisory Association, in the course of which he has written over a thousand opinions for golf clubs on all aspects of law and practice.

The end result is one of the most impressive works of its type that I have ever encountered. It describes and explains the law and practice in an exemplary manner. The hallmark of this book is its lucidity, practicality and readability. Every club secretary of every club of every description must acquire a copy, keep it to hand and be ready to refer committees, officers and members to its contents. It would be remiss of lawyers in this field to be without it.

The Rt Hon Sir Philip Otton
20 Essex Street
London WC2R 3AL
February 2005

PREFACE TO THE SECOND EDITION

The subject matter of this book remains no less challenging than before. First, in the Bodleian Law Library in Oxford (and we assume elsewhere) books on club law are categorised as 'the law of persons' since they do not fit neatly into any other legal category, which gives some idea of the breadth of the subject matter of this book. Secondly, Professor Warburton in the second edition of her book on unincorporated associations in 1992 said that in the six years since her first edition the clarity of the law on this aspect had not improved. We echo that. Six years on from the first edition of this book we find that we are still sparring with that species of club which is at the heart of this book, namely, the unincorporated members' club, described as 'the most anomalous group of human beings that is known to the law': an entity which is not a legal person at common law but which is often treated as more than the aggregate of its members for the time being and which, as a further twist, has been given by statute a fiscal personality for tax purposes and a criminal personality for certain statutory offences. Thirdly, there has been a plethora of relevant legislation affecting the contents of this book since the first edition, all of it no doubt well-intentioned but in several instances overly complex and/or ineptly drafted (a good example being the Safeguarding Vulnerable Groups Act 2006, now put on hold by the coalition government).

Indeed, the authors recently came across a legal handbook where the two experienced barristerial editors in their preface had asked their readers to inform them of any errors of omission on the ground that 'such is the mighty flood of legislation nowadays that a vital twig floating on the stream could well be missed'. Take the Equality Act 2010 (Commencement No 4, Savings, Consequential, Transitional, Transitory and Incidental Provisions and Revocation) Order 2010 as an exemplar. The title says it all. The man on the Clapham omnibus would simply be amazed by the amount of annotation and footnotes which is required fully to understand this statutory instrument. The Order was issued on 20 September 2010 and we do not jest when we say that two days later the government, owing to an error of omission, issued an Amending Order, and in that short space of time it had already issued 19 statutory instruments relating to other matters. Nevertheless, it is our earnest hope that the number of missed twigs in this second edition has been kept to the minimum. The 'flood of legislation' comment does demonstrate, however, the need for guidance to all those persons concerned with responsibilities in a club, society or association as regards the legal framework in which these bodies operate, especially bearing in mind the observation of that learned judge, Sir Robert Megarry, that there are commonly many obscurities and uncertainties in this realm.

We are again very grateful to our colleagues at 13 KBW for their contribution in the compilation of this edition: Arthur Blake in relation to chapter 13 on judicial review and third party challenges to club decisions; John Clargo, of the chambers property team, in relation to chapter 14 on landlord and tenant; and Nigel Woodhouse, of the chambers employment team, in relation to chapter 15 on employment. Our especial thanks go to Reginald Nock, a practising tax barrister, who very kindly agreed to overhaul chapter 16 on taxation. We also thank once again Peter Thompson QC, a former member of 13 KBW who is now the Consultant Editor of Butterworth's *County Court Practice*, for reading and helpfully commenting on many revised chapters in draft.

The reader will observe that in order to make the text more readable we have called into existence, as in the first edition, the wholly fictitious town of Basset, being the county town of Bassetshire. We have peopled this town and county with characters named in the famous song of Widecombe Fair:

Tom Pearce, Tom Pearce, lend me your grey mare
All along, down along, out along lee
For I want to go to Widecombe Fair
With Bill Brewer, Jan Stewer, Peter Gurney,
Peter Davey, Daniel Whiddon, Harry Hawke,
Old Uncle Tom Cobley and all.

We have endeavoured to state the law as at 31 December 2010.

David Ashton
*Paul W Reid**
13 King's Bench Walk
Temple
London
EC4Y 7EN
February 2011

* Practising primarily out of Park Court Chambers, Leeds LS1 2SJ.

CONTENTS

TABLE OF CASES

References are to paragraph numbers.

TABLE OF STATUTES

References are to paragraph numbers.

TABLE OF STATUTORY INSTRUMENTS

References are to paragraph numbers.

LAW REPORT ABBREVIATIONS

A & E:	Adolphus & Ellis' Reports (1834–40)
AC:	Law Reports, Appeal Cases in the House of Lords and (from 2009) the Supreme Court (1865 to date)
ACSR:	Australian Corporations and Securities Reports (Australia) (1989 to date)
ACD:	Administrative Court Digest (2001 to date)
Admin LR:	Administrative Law Reports (1989 to date)
All ER:	All England Reports (1936 to date). All England Reports also compiles collections of earlier law reports.
ALR:	Australian Law Reports (1973 to date)
App Cas:	Law Reports, Appeal Cases in the House of Lords (1875 to 1890)
Atk:	Atkyn's Chancery Reports (1736–55)
B & Ald:	Barnewall & Adolphus' Kings Bench Reports (1817-22)
B & C:	Barnewall & Cresswell's King's Bench Reports (1822-30)
BCC:	British Company Law Cases (1983 to date)
BCLC:	Butterworth Company Law Cases (1983 to date)
Bos & P:	Bosanquet & Puller's Common Pleas Reports (1796–1804)
B & S:	Best and Smith's Queen's Bench Reports (1861–65)
BTC:	British Tax Cases (1983 to date)
Camp:	Campbell's Nisi Prius Reports (1808-16)
Car & P:	Carrington & Payne's Nisi Prius Reports (1823–41)
CB:	Common Bench Reports by Manning, Granger & Scott (1845-56)
CB(NS):	Common Bench Reports by Manning, Granger & Scott (New Series) (1856–65)
Ch:	Law Reports, Chancery Division (1891 to date)
Ch App:	Law Reports, Chancery Appeal cases (1865–75)
Ch D:	Law Reports, Chancery Division (1876–90)
CL:	Common Law Reports (1853–55)
CLR:	Commonwealth Law Reports (1903 to date) (Australia)
CLY:	Current Law Yearbook (1947 to date)
CMLR:	Common Market Law Reports (1962 to date)
COD:	Crown Office Digest (1988–2000)
Co Rep:	Coke's King's Bench Reports (1572-1616)

Cr App R:	Criminal Appeal Reports (1908 to date)
Crim LR:	Criminal Law Reports (1954 to date)
De GM & G:	De Gex Macnaghten & Gordon's Bankruptcy Reports (1851–57)
ECC:	European Commercial Cases
EG:	Estates Gazette (1858 to date)
EGLR:	Estates Gazette Law Reports (1985 to date)
EHRR:	European Human Rights Reports (1979 to date)
El & B:	Ellis & Blackburn's Queen's Bench Reports (1851–58)
ELR:	Education Law Reports (1994 to date)
ER:	English Reports (a compilation of earlier law reports from 1210 to 1865)
EWCA:	England & Wales Court of Appeal (2001 to date) (neutral citation)
EWHC:	England & Wales High Court (2001 to date) (neutral citation)
F & F:	Foster & Finlayson's Nisi Prius reports (1858–67)
FSR:	Fleet Street Reports of Patent Cases (1963 to date)
Guardian:	The Guardian newspaper
HL Cas:	Clark's House of Lords Cases (1847–66)
HLR:	Housing Law Reports (1967 to date)
ICR:	Law Reports, Industrial Cases Reports (1975 to date)
IR:	Irish Reports (1894 to date) (Ireland)
IRLR:	Industrial Relations Law Reports (1972 to date)
JP:	Justice of the Peace (Weekly Notes of Cases) (1887 to date)
JPL:	Journal of Planning and Environment Law (1973 to date)
KB	Law Reports, King's Bench Division (1901–52)
LGLR:	Local Government Law reports
LGR:	Knight's Local Government Reports (1903 to date)
LG Rev:	Local Government Review (1971 to date)
LJ Ch:	Law Journal Reports, Chancery, New Series (1831-1946)
LJ KB:	Law Journal Reports, King's Bench, New Series (1831-1946)
LJ MC:	Law Journal Reports, Magistrates' Cases, New Series (1831–96)
LJ QB:	Law Journal Reports, Queen's Bench, New Series (1837–1946)
Ll L Rep:	Lloyd's List Law Reports (1919-1950)
Lloyd's Rep:	Lloyd's List Law Reports (1951 to date)
LLR:	Licensing Law Reports
LR Eq:	Law Reports, Equity cases (1865–75)
LR HL:	Law Reports, English and Irish Appeals in the House of Lords (1866-75)
LR Ir:	Law Reports (Ireland) (1878–93)
LR PC:	Law Reports, Privy Council (1865-75)
LSG:	Law Society Gazette (1903 to date)
LS Gaz:	Law Society Gazette (1903 to date)
LT:	Law Times Reports (1859 to 1947)

LT Jo:	Law Times Reports Newspaper (1843 – 1965)
M & G:	Manning & Granger's Common Pleas Reports (1840–44)
M & W:	Meeson & Welsby's Exchequer Reports (1836–47)
NI:	Northern Ireland Law Reports (1925 to date)
NLJ:	New Law Journal (1965 to date)
NLJ Rep:	New Law Journal Reports
NSW LR:	New South Wales Law Reports (1880–1900 and 1971 to date) (Australia)
NZLR:	New Zealand Law Reports (1883 to date) (New Zealand)
PIQR:	Personal Injury and Quantum Reports (1992 to date)
P & CR:	Planning and Compensation Reports (1949 to date)
Price:	Price's Exchequer Reports (1814–24)
QB:	Law Reports, Queen's Bench Division (1890 to 1901 and 1952 to date)
QBD:	Law Reports, Queen's Bench Division (1875–90)
R:	Rettie's Session Cases, 4th series (1878–98) (Scotland)
RA:	Rating Appeals (1962 to date)
RPC:	Reports of Patent, Design and Trade Mark Cases (1884 to date)
RRC:	Ryde's Rating Cases (1956 to date)
RTR:	Road Traffic Reports (1970 to date)
RVR:	Rating & Valuation Reporter (1965 to date)
SC:	Session Cases (Scotland)
Sim (NS):	Simon's Vice-Chancellor's Reports, New Series (1850–52)
SJLB:	Solicitors' Journal Law Brief
SLT:	Scots Law Times (1893 to date) (Scotland)
Sol Jo:	Solicitors' Journal (1857 to date)
Stark:	Starkie's Nisi Prius Reports (1814–22)
STC:	Simon's Tax Cases (1973 to date)
Times:	The Times newspaper (1785 to date)
Times LR:	The Times newspaper reports published separately from the newspaper (1990 to date)
TC:	Reports of Tax Cases (1875 to date)
TLR:	Times Law Reports (1884–1952)
UKHL:	United Kingdom House of Lords (2001 to 2009) (neutral citation)
UKSC:	United Kingdom Supreme Court (2009 to date) (neutral citation)
UKUT:	United Kingdom Upper Tribunal (neutral citation)
VATTR:	Value Added Tax Tribunal Reports
VTD:	Value Added Tax Tribunal Decisions
WLR:	Weekly Law Reports (1953 to date)
WN:	Weekly Notes (1862–1952)
WR:	Weekly Reporter (1853–1906)
WTLR:	Wills and Trusts Law Reports

DICTIONARY DEFINITION OF A CLUB

CLUB *klub*, *n* a heavy tapering stick, knobbly or thick at one end, used to strike with; a cudgel; a bat used in certain games; an instrument for playing golf; a playing card with black trefoil pips; a combination, bunch; a clique, set; an association of persons for social, political, athletic or other ends; an association of persons who possess premises or facilities which all members may use; a clubhouse, or the premises occupied by a club; a nightclub. – *vt* to beat with a club; to use a heavy object as a club; to throw into confusion(*military*); to gather into a bunch; to combine. – *vi* (*esp* with *together*) to join together for some common end; to share in a common expense; to visit nightclubs. – *adj* **clubbable** or **clubable** sociable – *n* **clubbability** or **clubability**. – **club class** a class of seat on an aircraft between tourist class and first class; **club-face** the face of a golf club; **club-foot** a deformed foot; **club-haul** (*nautical*) to tack, *esp* in an emergency; **club-head** the head of a golf club; **clubhouse** a house for the accommodation of a club; **clubland** the area around St James's in London, where many of the old-established clubs are; **club-law** government by violence; **club-line** (*printing*) a short line at the end of a paragraph; **clubman** a member of a club or clubs; a frequenter of clubs; a man-about-town; **club moss** any primitive mosslike plant of the order Lycopodiales; **clubroom** the room in which a club meets; **clubroot** a fungal disease which attacks the roots of plants of the genus Cruciferae; **club sandwich** a sandwich of three slices of bread or toast, containing two fillings – **in the club** (*slang*) pregnant; **join the club** (*colloquial*) we are all in the same position; me too; **on the club** (*slang*) certified unfit to work. [Old Norse and Swedish *klubba*; same root as *clump*].

Taken from The Chambers Dictionary *1998*

Part 1:

THE FORMATION AND DISSOLUTION OF A CLUB

Chapter 1

FORMATION OF THE CLUB

1. THE LEGAL DEFINITION OF A CLUB

1.1 The essential criteria As may be seen from the dictionary definition of a club set out on the preceding page lx, the word 'club' has multifarious uses in the English language. Club law, not to be confused with club-law, is a concept generally recognised in English law and it is the aim of this book to elucidate the law and practice which govern this branch of the law.[1] The definition of a club for the purposes of club law needs explanation. Everyone has experience of or has heard about clubs. They come in all shapes and sizes: Arsenal Football Club, the Kennel Club, the Royal Automobile Club, the Garrick Club, the Acol Bridge Club, Haltwhistle & District Working Men's Club, the Caravan Club, the Royal and Ancient Golf Club of St Andrews and so on. Clubs' terminology to describe themselves is equally variegated: a club may for example be called an alliance, an association, a brotherhood, a centre, a circle, a federation, a fellowship, a forum, a fraternity, a fund, a guild, an institute, an institution, a league, a society or a union.[2] In its definition of a club the Chambers Dictionary talks of 'an association of persons for social, political, athletic or other ends; an association of persons who possess premises or facilities which all members may use'. But for the purposes of club law, however, this definition needs qualification. To be recognised as a club at law we consider that it must fulfil all of the following criteria:

(1) it must comprise two or more persons who are voluntarily bound together for an agreed and common purpose;[3]

---

1 See Megarry V-C's comment in *In re GKN Bolts & Nuts Ltd Sports and Social Club* [1982] 1 WLR 774 at 776, 'As is common in club cases, there are many obscurities and uncertainties, and some difficulty in the law.'

2 A trade union is an unincorporated members' club where the members are bound together by a contract of membership but trade unions are so specially regulated by statute as to form a separate class of their own, and are outside the scope of this book. A trade union has quasi-corporate status and is prohibited from registering as a company under the Companies Act 2006 or as a society under the Friendly Societies Act 1974 or under the Co-operative and Community Benefit Societies and Credit Unions Act 1965: s 10 of the Trade Union and Labour Relations (Consolidation) Act 1992.

3 *Conservative Central Office v Burrell* [1982] 1 WLR 522, CA, at 525 (a tax case). Freedom of association with others is enshrined in Article 11 of the European Convention on Human Rights enacted as part of the Human Rights Act 1998.

(2) it must exist for a lawful purpose other than simply for the purposes of trade or making a profit for its members;[4]
(3) it must not be of a temporary nature;[5]
(4) it must have a constitution or a set of rules which fairly regulates the conduct of its members towards each other;[6]
(5) there must be a defined process for the admission of members;[7]
(6) it must possess what can best be described as collegiality, that is, the process of making decisions or agreeing on actions shared by all the members.[8]

Although 'a village football team, with no constitution and a casual fluctuating membership, meeting on a Saturday morning on a rented pitch' was correctly described by the court in *R v L and F*[9] as an unincorporated association, it would not comprise an unincorporated members' club at law since it would not fulfil the third, fourth or fifth criteria nor probably the sixth criterion.

1.2 Clubs, societies and associations The reader will observe that the dictionary definition of a club cited in **1.1** above actually embodies the word 'association'. The Chambers Dictionary goes on to define an association as 'a society of persons joined to promote some object'. That the three generic words of clubs, societies and associations, are often used synonymously is amply demonstrated by the judgment of Lord Lindley cited in **1.10** below where he uses the three generic words interchangeably within his opening

---

4 *Kowloon Stock Exchange v Commissioner of Inland Revenue* [1985] 1 WLR 133, PC, at 139 (where the court held that the Stock Exchange was a not a club because it existed to aid the profit-making activities of its members); *Wise v Perpetual Trustee Co* [1903] AC 139, PC, at 149; *Flemying v Hector* (1836) 2 M & W 172; *Stafford Borough Council v Elkenford Ltd* [1977] 1 WLR 324, CA. The acquisition of gain which is incidental to the club's main activities is no bar to club status: *Carlisle and Silloth Golf Club v Smith* [1913] 3 KB 75, CA (green fees received from non-members); *Newton-le-Willows Cricket, Bowling, Tennis, Hockey and Rugby Union Football Club v Newton-le-Willows Urban District Council* [1966] RVR 120 (rental received from outside organisations for hire of the club's recreation hall). The fact too that a proprietor of a club intends to make profit does not undermine this criterion because the members of the club have no such intention for themselves.

5 See, for example, Licensing Act 1902, s 24(1); Shop Clubs Act 1902, s 2(b); Gaming Act 1968, ss 11(2) and 40(4)(c) and Sch 3, para 7(1); and Gambling Act 2005, ss 266 and 267.

6 *Conservative Central Office v Burrell* [1982] 1 WLR 522, CA, at 525. An anomalous position arises when a pressure group or organisation, seeking to avoid criminal or civil liability concerning its activities, denies that it has any separate existence as an unincorporated association: see *Oxford University v Webb* [2006] EWHC 2490 (QB) (Irwin J) ('Animal Liberation Front') and the cases therein cited. Here the courts have held that for injunctive purposes an unincorporated association may exist despite the lack of formality in its formation and management.

7 *Burrell's* case, at 525.

8 *Val de Lobo (Turismo) Limitada v Chandler* (unreported) 2 October 1997, per HH Judge Peter Crawford QC, sitting as a High Court Judge, in a reserved judgment. The fact that a proprietor takes the leading role in a proprietary club does not undermine this criterion in that the club's activities will be run in a collegiate way under the fourth criterion.

9 [2009] 1 All ER 786, CA.

ten words.[10] And it is a fact that the underlying legal principles are exactly the same, whatever the nomenclature, in each case *provided the said criteria are fulfilled.* Where confusion is often caused is the applicability or otherwise of the second criterion. There are, for example, many trade associations which do not qualify as a 'club' because they exist for the purposes of trade or profit.[11] The confusion is worse confounded by the loose use of the word 'club' in commercial circles when they are not clubs at all.[12] For the sake of simplicity we have used the word 'club' in the text, as far as possible, to include the whole spectrum of clubs, societies and associations.

2. HISTORICAL INTRODUCTION

1.3 The origin of clubs in the sense that we are using the word 'club' can be traced back in England to the mid seventeenth century. In Tudor times the breaking away from the Catholic Church put Henry VIII and, more so, Elizabeth I in a vulnerable position with regard to those disaffected parties who wanted to bring England back into the fold of Catholicism. Freedom of thought and speech coupled with an association of persons was perceived as a potentially destabilising or subversive threat to the monarchy and was not tolerated. The much feared Court of Star Chamber, an early Tudor court of law which evolved into a political weapon, played a major role in suppressing personal rights and the liberty of the subject until its summary abolition by the Long Parliament in 1641 under the Stuart king, Charles I. From then on, a much more relaxed attitude prevailed towards the peaceable association of persons.[13] The first coffee-house in London was introduced from Oxford in 1652 by a person known simply as Jacob the Jew, and the coffee-house rapidly took root; by 1663 there were over 80 coffee-houses in the City of London. These establishments were used by coteries in need of a regular meeting place, one such in nearby Westminster being Miles's coffee-house which was the venue of the Rota Club founded for political debate. In the mid 1650s there met in Oxford a group of scientific virtuosi who instituted an organised club (each member paying a weekly shilling towards its expenses) which later in 1662 coalesced into the Royal Society of London for the Improvement of Natural Knowledge, now known simply as the Royal Society. On 26 July 1660 Samuel Pepys recorded

---

10 See *British Diabetic Association v The Diabetic Society* [1995] 4 All ER 812 (a passing off action).

11 Eg a Protection & Indemnity Club ('P & I Club') which provides collective self-insurance to its shipowner members; or the Mid-Counties Co-operative Society which is part of the Co-operative movement ('the Co-op') which runs retail shops; or the Grain and Feed Trade Association ('GAFTA') which promotes international trade in grains, animal feedstuffs, pulses and rice. Investment clubs, where the primary purpose of the club is the acquisition of gain for its members, do not fall within the scope of this book.

12 See **1.49**.

13 Non-conformists and protestant dissenters, however, had to wait their turn until the Act of Toleration 1689 passed in the first year of the reign of William and Mary. Catholics had to wait much longer.

in his diary, 'we went to Wood's at the Pell Mell (our old house for clubbing) and there spent till ten at night'.

1.4 The eighteenth century saw a big increase in drinking and social clubs, which commonly met on a weekly basis at a tavern to eat or sing or debate, a well-known example being the Kit-Cat Club[14] of notable Whigs who used to meet at the Flask Tavern in Highgate, but many humbler clubs existed as well. At the same time, on a more intellectual level, in 1764 Dr Johnson, the celebrated lexicographer, founded in London the Literary Club, among whose members were Sir Joshua Reynolds the artist, Edward Gibbon the historian, Oliver Goldsmith the playwright, David Garrick the actor, and Adam Smith the economist. In 1836 and 1837 Charles Dickens published in serial form his famous novel called *The Posthumous Papers of the Pickwick Club* which dealt with certain members' various adventures around England.[15] In the nineteenth century, too, there grew up 'the gentleman's club' which was so characteristic of Victorian society and which earns a mention in the Chambers Dictionary under 'clubland' ('the area around St James's in London, where many of the old-established clubs are'). Although White's, the earliest, was established in 1693 as a chocolate-house which in the next century became a fashionable gentlemen's club, many of these clubs such as the Athenaeum, the Travellers and the Reform, were founded in the first half of the nineteenth century and were housed in grand edifices. The club had come of age. Since mid-Victorian times, helped by the country's then economic prosperity which resulted in people of all classes having more leisure time, there has been a proliferation of clubs, societies and associations of every description: artistic, literary, military, musical, occupational, political, social, sporting, theatrical and university. They now number a great many thousands. Up and down the country they exist, practically no town in England or Wales without its fair share of clubs, involving a very large segment of the population.

3. CLASSIFICATION OF CLUBS

1.5 For the purposes of this book clubs may be classified either as members' clubs or as proprietary clubs. Members' clubs as a classification has various sub-divisions:

(1) ***unincorporated members' clubs***;[16]

---

14 Named after a pudding-pie man called Christopher Catling, on whose premises the club had originally met.

15 The members in question were Mr Pickwick himself and Messrs Snodgrass, Tupman, and Winkle, who were obliged to report to the rest of the membership.

16 This category includes unincorporated institutions to which the provisions of the Literary and Scientific Institutions Act 1854 apply: see further **1.53**.

(2) ***working men's clubs*** registered under one of the Friendly Societies Acts;
(3) ***community clubs***, that is to say, industrial and provident societies, co-operative societies and community benefit societies registered under one of the Industrial and Provident Societies Acts or under the Co-operative and Community Benefit Societies and Credit Unions Act 1965;
(4) ***shop clubs*** registered under the Shop Clubs Act 1902;
(5) ***incorporated clubs*** registered under one of the Companies Acts.

1.6 The decision to form a club In the paragraphs below are set out the different characteristics of each mode of club. The choice is an important one to get right since it will have legal and financial consequences. Accordingly, what follows is an outline of the essential differences between the various types of club.

4. FORMATION OF MEMBERS' CLUBS

1.7 Unincorporated members' clubs By far the most common type of club is the unincorporated members' club. Their number is untold. Its undoubted popularity is because it is the easiest, cheapest and the most informal way of forming a club. Added to which is the twofold advantage, admittedly shared by all members' clubs, (1) the use of the concept of the trust whereby trustee members can hold and manage the club property and assets on behalf of all the members and (2) the favourable treatment which such clubs have received since 1902 under the Licensing Acts.[17] Many historic clubs such as the Jockey Club (founded 1750), the Royal and Ancient Golf Club of St Andrews (founded 1754) and the Marylebone Cricket Club ('MCC') (founded 1787) in their capacity as unincorporated members' clubs used to govern their own particular sport until the twentieth century when they handed over to more representative bodies. The latter two continue as unincorporated members' clubs, with the Jockey Club only lately being granted a royal charter in 1970. In the case of MCC it comprises some 18,000 full members, 4,000 associate members, owns valuable property in the shape of Lord's Cricket Ground and raises its own teams to play cricket at first class level. Such an organisational structure would not be tolerated unless it worked in practice.

1.8 An unincorporated association is a 'creature of contract'.[18] An unincorporated members' club comes within this category. The club itself is

---

17 The first Act which brought clubs within its purview was the Licensing Act 1902.

18 *Conservative Central Office v Burrell* [1982] 1 WLR 522, CA, at 527; *Baker v Jones* [1954] 1 WLR 1005, at 1009.

not a legal entity.[19] An unincorporated club comprises its members for the time being[20] and such a club has been described as 'the most anomalous group of human beings that is known to the law'.[21] In *Leahy v Attorney General for New South Wales*[22] Viscount Simmonds remarked on the esoteric nature of the unincorporated members' club:

> 'It arises out of the artificial and anomalous conception of an unincorporated society which, though it is not a separate entity in law, is yet for many purposes regarded as a continuing entity and, however inaccurately, as something other than an aggregate of its members.'

In *R v L and F*[23] (a criminal prosecution brought against two members of an unincorporated golf club for polluting a watercourse with oil from its storage tank) the Court of Appeal accepted[24] that an unincorporated association has no legal identity separate from its members but then continued:[25]

> 'As to fact, many unincorporated associations have in reality a substantial existence which is treated by all who deal with them as distinct from the mere sum of those who are for the time being members ... As to the law, it no longer treats every unincorporated association as simply a collective expression for its members and has not done so for well over a hundred years. A great array of varying provisions has been made by statute to endow different unincorporated associations with many of the characteristics of legal personality.'

The court referred to partnerships and trade unions by way of example but these entities are of a special nature and do not count as clubs, societies or associations in the sense that we are using this phrase.[26] Nonetheless, the comment about statutory endowment of legal personality is true. Our standpoint, however, is that the common law position has in no way changed over the last 100 years: a proposition recognised by the court itself when it said of an unincorporated association,[27] 'it is simply a group of individuals linked together by contract'.

1.9 The contract referred to in **1.8** is that which exists between the members themselves. The terms on which they contract with one another

---

[19] *Steele v Gourley and Davis* (1886) 3 TLR 118, at 119; *John v Rees* [1970] Ch 345, at 398 (Megarry J).

[20] *Gaiman v National Association for Mental Health* [1971] Ch 317, at 335 (Megarry J).

[21] *Feeney and Shannon v MacManus* [1937] IR 23, at 31 (Johnstone J) (concerning The General Post Office Dining Club in Dublin).

[22] [1959] AC 457 PC, at 477.

[23] [2009] 1 All ER 786.

[24] Ibid, at [12].

[25] Ibid, at [14] and [15].

[26] See footnote 2 above and Lord Lindley's dictum cited in **1.10**.

[27] [2009] 1 All ER 786, at [12].

are the rules of the club.[28] The consideration for such a contract is the member's subscription to the club.[29] In essence an unincorporated members' club is a club for members run by the members with no outside control: a great advantage. This in turn ensures privacy for the club's affairs as well as flexibility. It has been said that membership of a club is not merely a contract since membership often gives the member valuable proprietary and social rights.[30] On joining the club the member acquires both rights and liabilities as between himself and the other members.[31] The contractual rights are easily discernible because they comprise what are compendiously called the privileges of membership. The property rights are much less easily defined, and are discussed below.[32]

1.10 It is generally well known, and one of its major attractions, that in an unincorporated members' club the liability of the individual member is limited to his entrance fee (if any) and his subscriptions.[33] In *Wise v Perpetual Trustee Co Ltd*[34] Lord Lindley put the matter thus:

> 'Clubs are associations of a peculiar nature. They are societies the members of which are perpetually changing. They are not partnerships; they are not associations for gain; and the feature which distinguishes them from other societies is that no member as such becomes liable to pay to the funds of the society or to anyone else any money beyond the subscriptions required by the rules of the club to be paid so long as he remains a member. It is upon this fundamental condition, not usually expressed but understood by everyone, that clubs are formed; and this distinguishing feature has often been judicially recognised.'

1.11 On the other hand, the responsibility for transactions and activities carried on by the club rests normally with the managing committee. It is they to whom creditors or injured persons will look for payment of the

---

28 *In re Sick and Funeral Society of St John's Sunday School, Golcar* [1973] Ch 51 (Megarry J).

29 The *Golcar* case, op cit, at 59, save as between the founder members when the consideration would be the mutual promises to join the club when formed. In those rare clubs where no subscription is payable the consideration would be the mutual promises to abide by the agreed rules.

30 *John v Rees* [1970] Ch 345, at 397; *Rigby v Connol* (1880) 14 Ch D 482, CA; *Baird v Wells* (1890) 44 Ch D 661: see **8.2**; *Lee v Showmen's Guild of Great Britain* [1952] 2 QB 329, at 341–342 (Denning LJ).

31 The rights in question must be intended to be legally binding. Thus it has been held that the winner of a competition held by a golf club could not sue for his prize: *Lens v Devonshire Club* (1914) The Times, 4 December (Scrutton J), cited in *Wyatt v Kreglinger & Fernau* [1933] 1 KB 793, CA, at 806.

32 See **8.3**.

33 *In re St James Club* (1852) 2 de GM & G 383 at 387 and 390 (Lord St Leonards LC); *Steele v Gourley and Davis* (1887) 3 TLR 772 at 773 (Lord Esher MR).

34 [1903] AC 139, PC, at 149.

club's debts or compensation for injuries suffered on club premises.[35] This may have severe financial consequences for the members of the club who are also members of the committee[36] and may be seen as a serious disadvantage of an unincorporated members' club.

1.12 Getting started Surprising as it may seem, there is no authority as to what counts as the moment of birth of an unincorporated members' club. It has been said:

> 'In the case of a members' club the usual procedure will be for those wishing to establish the club to hold a meeting at which a resolution will be passed embodying the decision to bring the club into being'.[37]

However, this statement needs qualification. If there were no rules or only draft rules at the date of the resolution, it may be asked how the club could be in existence without there being rules agreed between all the founder members, or at least the basic rules so agreed. It is likely that the court would have to be satisfied that there was a valid and enforceable contract between the founder members before making a finding that the club existed. Thus a resolution to establish a club with rules to be formulated later will be an inchoate contract and will have no legal significance. The question is not simply an academic one. In the unreported case of *Hanuman v Guyanese Association for Racial Unity and Democracy* (1996)[38] the plaintiff unsuccessfully sued the officers of an unincorporated members' club for disbursements paid by him for the benefit of the association in setting up the association. The county court judge found as a fact[39] that the association did not come into being until all the expenditure had been made so that he held there was no contractual basis on which the association itself or its officers could be liable, and the Court of Appeal refused leave to appeal against that decision. Therefore it may be surmised that until all the criteria set out in **1.1** are satisfied, it cannot be safely assumed that an unincorporated members' club has been established.

1.13 Mutual societies: earlier legislation In the nineteenth and early twentieth centuries Parliament intervened to a limited and perhaps haphazard extent by permitting certain mutual societies. An early form of such society was the unincorporated friendly society[40] and in 1875 Parliament authorised a new species of mutual society called a working

---

35 As to liability of the committee, see **12.4** (in contract) and **12.27** (in tort).

36 As to protecting the committee, see **12.17** (as to contract) and **5.44** and **12.58** (as to tort).

37 *Daly's Club Law* (7th edn, 1979) p 10.

38 Reference LTA/96/5434/G: before Aldous and Phillips LJJ on 13 June 1996.

39 What facts the judge relied on to come to this conclusion do not appear from the Court of Appeal judgments.

40 The first Friendly Society Act was passed in 1793. It was predicated on the idea of members coming together for the purpose of an insurance business based on thrift and self-help.

men's club to be registered under the Friendly Societies Act 1875.[41] The consequence of registration was to formalise the constitution of the club and make it subject to the control of the Registrar of Friendly Societies. Meanwhile, Parliament had permitted certain members' clubs to be registered under the Industrial and Provident Societies Act 1852.[42] This registration also formalised the constitution of the club and made it subject to the control of the Registrar of Friendly Societies, but with one big difference: on registration the club acquired corporate status so that the club itself was now a legal person, which was a very significant step towards protecting the committee members of the club from liability. It should be added here that there are common features in the two extant statutory codes and in particular they prescribe a common system of accounting for clubs registered under either the Friendly Societies Act or the Industrial and Provident Societies Act.[43] It was observed in **1.21** of the first edition of this book that the title of 'industrial and provident society' was old and rather antiquated. Parliament thought so too and passed the Co-operative and Community Benefit Societies and Credit Unions Act 2010 which has changed the nomenclature of these societies and updated other aspects of such societies and unions without making any fundamental changes to their structure.

1.14 In 1902, Parliament had intervened to protect members of shop clubs (otherwise known as thrift funds) from compulsory membership at the instance of their employer. Shop clubs under the Shop Clubs Act 1902 (now repealed by the Wages Act 1986)[44] have only ever played a minor part in the history of clubs.

1.15 In 1992 the Friendly Societies Commission was set up to supplement the office of the Chief Registrar of Friendly Societies.[45] However, by the Financial Services and Markets Act 2000 the Treasury was empowered to transfer to itself or to the Financial Services Authority (1) the functions of the Friendly Societies Commission,[46] (2) the functions of the Chief and Assistant Registrar of Friendly Societies,[47] and (3) the functions concerning the registration of industrial and provident societies.[48] These transfers all took place in 2001 with the result that the Treasury has, in the main, the powers of making regulations and orders, while the Financial Services

41 Now Friendly Societies Act 1974, s 7(1)(d). A working men's club is not a friendly society as such since it does not fall within the statutory definition of a friendly society: ibid, s 7(1)(a).

42 Hitherto such clubs had been registered under the Friendly Societies Act.

43 See the Friendly and Industrial and Provident Societies Act 1968 (now re-named).

44 A *voluntary* shop club can still be formed: see **1.33**.

45 Friendly Societies Act 1992, s 1.

46 Financial Services and Markets Act 2000, s 334.

47 Ibid, s 335.

48 Ibid, s 338.

Authority has taken over the other functions and is now the regulating authority for working men's clubs and community clubs.[49]

1.16 Incorporated friendly societies In 1992[50] Parliament created a new form of friendly society, namely, an *incorporated* friendly society, with the intention that the Friendly Societies Act 1974, whilst not repealed, would become obsolete.[51] We have not dealt separately with these societies in this book because, like trade unions, they are of such a specialised nature that they fall outside its scope. They undoubtedly have some characteristics of a club in that they have a membership governed by rules[52] and by s 10 of the 1992 Act they can include social activities which are not inconsistent with their other permitted activities. But their main activities are business activities[53] and it is doubtful whether they satisfy the second criterion (existing for purposes other than trade or profit) or the sixth criterion (the need for collegiality).[54] It is interesting to see, however, that by s 65(4) of the Licensing Act 2003 incorporated friendly societies can apply for a club premises certificate, but this is only because s 65(5) has deeming provisions in their favour, which suggests that without them the incorporated friendly society would not be a qualifying club.

1.17 Working men's clubs The Friendly Societies Act 1875 defined working men's clubs as 'societies for purposes of social intercourse, mutual helpfulness, mental and moral improvement, and rational recreation'.[55] The Friendly Societies Act 1974 was the main consolidating Act relating to friendly societies until the passing of the Friendly Societies Act 1992. By this last-mentioned Act no further registration of working men's clubs may take

---

49 Financial Services and Markets Act 2000 (Mutual Societies) Order 2001, SI 2001/2617. The Chancellor of the Exchequer in a speech at the Mansion House in London on 16 June 2010 intimated that the government would be abolishing the Financial Services Authority ('FSA') in its present form. The Registrar of Friendly Societies, who was superseded by the FSA, was a more avuncular figure and better attuned to the role of regulation of clubs which by definition are not trading entities, and the FSA has not been comfortable in carrying out this regulatory role.

50 Friendly Societies Act 1992, s 5(1).

51 See the annotations to this Act by Ian Swinney, LLB in Current Law Statutes 1992, vol 3 p 40–6.

52 Friendly Societies Act 1992, Sch 3, para 5.

53 Ibid, Sch 2: class A is insurance business; class B is general business; and class C is business not falling within A or B.

54 Ian Swinney LLB in his annotations referred to in footnote 51 above says that, unlike the early societies which regarded playing a social role as an essential part of their function, modern friendly societies are formed to take advantage of tax-exempt status and are really to be regarded as insurance companies, albeit of a special type.

55 Friendly Societies Act 1875, s 8(4).

place under the 1974 Act,[56] but clubs already registered (whether under this or some earlier Friendly Societies Act) are permitted still to function under the aegis of the 1974 Act.[57]

1.18 The current Acts are the Friendly Societies Acts 1974 and 1992, together with the Co-operative and Community Benefit Societies and Credit Unions Act 1968 (formerly entitled the Friendly and Industrial and Provident Societies Act 1968).

1.19 The advantages of registration under the Friendly Societies Act are that it provides a structured and orderly framework for the club to carry on its activities.[58] The club must have rules binding on its members;[59] it must make annual returns to the regulating authority;[60] it must keep proper books of account;[61] and it may invest its funds;[62] it may make loans to its members;[63] and it may make charitable donations for the benefit of its members.[64] Although the club will remain a voluntary unincorporated members' club, registration under the Act means that the club's property vests in one or more trustees of the club[65] and legal proceedings concerning its property will be in the name of the club.[66] Registration also means that the club automatically has provisions governing the resolution of disputes[67] and what happens in the event of dissolution.[68]

---

56 Friendly Societies Act 1992, s 93(1). Section 7(1)(b)–(f) of the 1974 Act identifies the five non-friendly societies which may remain under the aegis of the 1974 Act. Of these five, only working men's clubs satisfy the essential criteria set out in **1.1** above.

57 Friendly Societies Act 1992, s 93(2) and Friendly Societies Act 1974, s 7(1) as amended by the 1992 Act, Sch 16, para 4(a). The number of working men's clubs is not easy to establish. The Financial Services Authority keeps no separate record of such clubs registered under the Friendly Societies Act. Many working men's clubs are unregistered and so count as unincorporated members' clubs. Many others were registered under one of the Industrial and Provident Societies Acts (the 1965 Act is now re-named) and so count as community clubs. The umbrella organisation, the Working Men's Club and Institute Union, represents some 2,000 working men's clubs out of its total membership of 3,000 clubs. Anecdotal evidence suggests that their number is falling and will continue to fall.

58 Friendly Societies Act 1974, s 7(2).

59 Ibid, s 22.

60 Ibid, s 43.

61 Ibid, s 29; Co-operative and Community Benefit Societies and Credit Unions Act 1968, s 1(1).

62 Friendly Societies Act 1974, s 46.

63 Ibid, s 48.

64 Ibid, s 52.

65 Ibid, ss 54 and 58. See further **5.19**.

66 Ibid, s 56. See further **18.12** and **18.30**.

67 Ibid, ss 77 and 79.

68 Ibid, ss 93 and 94.

1.20 Community clubs Lord Justice Mummery in *Co-operative Group (CWS) Ltd v Stansell Ltd*[69] explained the background to co-operative societies and industrial and provident societies:

> 'During the 19th century many bona fide co-operative societies and other industrial and provident societies were formed. Their purpose was to make profits from the personal participation and exertions of their members ("industrial") and to apply the profits in making provision for their members' future ("provident"). Acting together in a business-like and self-help way for the mutual benefit of members was a laudable activity encouraged and facilitated by legislators. There was a series of Industrial and Provident Societies Acts: 1852, 1862, 1867, 1876 and 1893. There were parallel developments and similar legislation governing friendly societies, building societies and trade unions. There are now about 8,300 industrial and provident societies. In general, they are subject to simpler procedures and less formal regulation than registered companies, which are governed by legislation of ever increasing complexity, much of it needed to protect the public.'

1.21 The focus of the original legislation was on the working class. An example in practice is the case of *Trebanog Working Men's Club and Institute Ltd v Macdonald*[70] where the club was registered under the Industrial and Provident Societies Acts 1893 to 1913 and where the object of the club was stated in its rules as being:

> 'to carry on the business of club proprietors, by providing for the use of its members, and for such associates … as are admitted to honorary membership, the means of social intercourse, mutual helpfulness, mental and moral improvement, rational recreation, and the other advantages of a club.'

Because of the attraction of incorporation the focus was widened under the subsequent Industrial and Provident Societies Acts to include all classes of persons (involving, for instance, golf, tennis and rugby clubs). Despite incorporation, these clubs remain in essence members' clubs.[71]

1.22 The current Acts are the Co-operative and Community Benefit Societies and Credit Unions Acts 1965, 1967 and 1968, and the Co-operative and Community Benefit Societies Acts 1975, 1978 and 2002 (all six of these acts included the words 'Industrial and Provident Societies' in their former title and should now be cited by their new title); the Co-operative and

---

69 [2006] 1 WLR 1704, CA, at 1707.

70 [1940] 1 KB 576, CA.

71 *Trebanog Working Men's Club and Institute Ltd v MacDonald* [1940] 1 KB 576; see Josling and Alexander, *The Law of Clubs* (6th edn, 1987), at p 190.

Community Benefit Societies Act 2003;[72] and the Co-operative and Community Benefit Societies and Credit Unions Act 2010.

1.23 A club may be registered under the 1965 Act for the purpose of carrying on any industry, business or trade if either (a) the club is a bona fide co-operative society[73] or (b) the club is conducted for the benefit of the community and there are special reasons why the club should be registered under the 1965 Act rather than as a company under the Companies Act.[74] (This explains the new title of the Act.) In either case membership is by ownership of at least one share;[75] the shares may be of any denomination and the overall number need not be limited but no individual member may have a total shareholding of more than £20,000.[76]

1.24 A bona fide co-operative society is not defined in the 1965 Act but it has two essential elements:[77] (1) the business of the society will be conducted for the mutual benefit of its members in such a way that the benefit mainly stems from their participation in its business, and (2) control of the society will under its rules be vested in the members equally and not in accordance with their financial interests in the society. Thus, for example, a registered society may be carrying the business of a social club as in the *Trebanog* case or the business of a tennis club as in *Addiscombe Garden Estates Ltd v Crabbe*.[78]

1.25 A community benefit society must be able to show that it will benefit persons other than their own members; that its business is in the interests of the community; and that it is suitable for registration because it is non-profit-making and its rules prohibit assets from being distributed amongst its members. A typical example will be a housing association which provides housing for various groups within the community. A football supporters' club is another example.

1.26 The advantages of registration under the 1965 Act are (1) that upon registration the club becomes a body corporate by its registered name, with perpetual succession and a common seal, the members having limited

---

72 The original title of the 2003 Act had referred to co-operatives rather than co-operative societies.

73 Co-operative and Community Benefit Societies and Credit Unions Act 1965, s 1(2)(a). This does not include a society whose object is to make a profit mainly by paying interest on money invested with the society: ibid, s 3.

74 Co-operative and Community Benefit Societies and Credit Unions Act 1965, s 1(2)(b) as amended by Companies Consolidation (Consequential Provisions) Act 1985, Sch 2.

75 Co-operative and Community Benefit Societies and Credit Unions Act 1965, s 6(1).

76 Co-operative and Community Benefit Societies and Credit Unions Act 1965, s 6(1), as amended by Industrial and Provident Societies Act (Increase in Shareholding Limit) Order 1994, SI 1994/341.

77 Per the Annual Report of the Chief Registrar 1989–90, paras 4.4 and 4.5.

78 [1958] 1 QB 513, CA.

liability as under the Companies Acts;[79] and (2) that upon registration all the property of the club will vest in the club itself.[80] Registration also has the advantages of providing a structured and orderly framework for the club to carry on its activities. The club must have rules binding on its members;[81] it must keep proper books of account;[82] it must make annual returns to the regulating authority;[83] it must display its latest balance sheet at its registered office;[84] and it may make advances to its members;[85] and it may invest its funds.[86] Registration also means that the club automatically has provisions governing the resolution of disputes[87] and what happens in the event of dissolution.[88]

1.27 The disadvantages of registration under the 1965 Act are the loss of club's control of its own affairs, the inflexibility of its rules and the loss of privacy appertaining to its affairs. For example, on this last point the club must supply upon request, free of charge, to every person interested in the funds of the club a copy of the latest annual return or audited balance sheet.[89]

1.28 Getting started To form a club, application is made to the Financial Services Authority who will provide the necessary paperwork.[90] A fee is payable. The application must be made by at least seven persons wanting to register a new club.[91] The word 'Limited' must be the last word of the name of the club, unless the Authority is satisfied that the club's objects are wholly charitable or benevolent.[92] If the club is a charity, it does not need to register with the Charity Commission.[93]

1.29 Credit unions These are self-help associations designed to provide their members with a source of low-cost credit. They are now regulated by

---

79 Co-operative and Community Benefit Societies and Credit Unions Act 1965, s 3, as amended by the schedule to the Co-operatives and Community Benefit Societies Act 2003.
80 Ibid, s 3.
81 Ibid, s 14.
82 Ibid, s 1(1).
83 Ibid, s 39.
84 Ibid, s 40.
85 Ibid, s 21.
86 Ibid, s 31.
87 Ibid, s 60.
88 Ibid, s 55.
89 Ibid, s 39(5) and Co-operative and Community Benefit Societies and Credit Unions Act 1968, s 11(5), as amended by the Friendly Societies Act 1974, Sch 11. There is no statutory definition of the expression 'person interested' and it is arguable that this would include a creditor of the club.
90 Information and a form may be obtained from the Financial Services Authority's (2010) website, www.fsa.gov.uk.
91 Co-operative and Community Benefit Societies and Credit Unions Act 1965, s 1(1)(b).
92 Ibid. s 5.
93 The club will be an exempt charity: Charities Act 1993, s 3, Sch 2.

the Credit Unions Act 1979 and the legislation referred to in **1.22**. Each credit union has a 'common bond'; this may be for people living or working in the same area, or for people working for the same employer, or for people who belong to the same association such as a church group or a trade union.[94] Although popular in many parts of the world they have never flourished in Great Britain to any great extent.[95] Credit unions are required to have proper membership rules[96] and they may be registered under the 1965 Act.[97] Therefore they may be regarded as a type of community club and so are not dealt with separately in this book. It is right to add, however, that the 1979 Act does contain provisions which apply solely to credit unions, such as a minimum membership of at least 21[98] and a maximum membership of 5,000,[99] although a credit union may obtain exemption from this last limit if the exemption is in the public interest and it does not jeopardise the existence of the common bond between the members. Thus, for instance, the Police Credit Union for police families has some 16,000 members. Since 2002 the Financial Services Authority has been the regulating authority for credit unions.[100]

1.30 Getting started According to the Association of British Credit Unions Limited setting up a credit union is a process that may take between one and three years from the idea of registration to the actual authorisation as a credit union.

1.31 Shop clubs A shop club or thrift fund is a club whereby a workman or employee connected with a workshop, factory, dock, shop or warehouse on the one hand and the employer on the other hand both make contributions to a savings club. In Victorian times employers often made the joining of such a club compulsory for the workman and the Shop Clubs Act 1902 was passed to regulate the situation. In future the employee could only be *compelled* to join such a club if (a) it was registered and certified under the Friendly Societies Act and (b) three-quarters of the work force desired the establishment of such a club.[101] An unregistered shop club, however, was and is permissible provided that membership thereof is *voluntary*.[102] Because of the development of trade union law and the advent

---

94 Credit Unions Act 1979, s 1(4)–(5).

95 Their numbers are in a state of flux. As at 30 September 2008 there were 508 credit unions registered in England, Wales and Scotland, a decrease of 24 from 2007. Yet the numbers of adult members is increasing. On 30 June 2007 there were 604,945 adult members in England, Wales and Scotland whereas on 30 June 2008 there were 661,640 (unaudited figure), an increase of 56,695. Source: Financial Services Authority Factsheet (undated, but published on its website in 2010).

96 Credit Unions Act 1979, s 4 and Sch 1.

97 Ibid. s 1(1).

98 Ibid, s 6(1).

99 Ibid, s 6(2).

100 Financial Services and Markets Act 2000, s 338(1)(f).

101 Shop Clubs Act 1902, s 2.

102 See *Balchin v Lord Ebury* (1903) 48 Sol Jo 83.

of national insurance contributions few clubs have taken advantage of the statutory provisions and, indeed, the 1902 Act was wholly repealed by the Wages Act 1986.

1.32 All shop clubs are unincorporated members' clubs. The schedule to the Shops Act 1902 governs the rules of the *registered* shop club and makes provision for such matters as the conditions under which a member becomes entitled to benefits;[103] the manner of altering the rules;[104] the investment of funds and the keeping of accounts;[105] the dissolution of the club;[106] and the calling for an investigation into the club's affairs.[107]

1.33 Getting started Since 1986 any *voluntary* new shop club (or similar) would no doubt be formed by the employer, with suitable rules, and the club would be treated like any other unincorporated members' club.

1.34 Incorporated clubs Incorporation of a club under the Companies Act has been available since 1855.[108] Companies in the United Kingdom are now regulated by the Companies Act 2006 which has the dubious distinction of the being the longest parliamentary act ever passed, with 1,300 sections and 16 schedules. It is generally agreed that one-third of the Act restates the law, one-third modifies it, and one-third is completely new. The Act provides a comprehensive code of company law. Because of its length, its complexity and the need for underlying regulations the Act was brought into force by stages and came fully into force on 1 October 2009.

1.35 At law an incorporated club is a very different creature from an unincorporated members' club. The club itself will be a legal person[109] distinct from the members themselves.[110] Despite incorporation, where the company is composed exclusively of all the members for the time being of a club, it will constitute a members' club since the incorporation will simply be 'a convenient instrument or medium for enabling the members to conduct … a club, the objects of which are immune from every taint of commerciality'.[111] Such an arrangement does not alter the relationship of the members amongst themselves. This will be the same as obtains in an unincorporated members' club, that is to say, the contractual relationship

---

103 Shop Clubs Act 1902, Sch, para ii: see Appendix 2.
104 Ibid, para iii.
105 Ibid, para v.
106 Ibid, para xi.
107 Ibid, para xii.
108 Limited liability under a company was first introduced in 1855 and there have been previous codifying or consolidating Acts in 1862, 1908, 1929, 1948 and 1985.
109 Companies Act 2006, s 16(2).
110 *Salomon v Salomon & Co Ltd* [1897] AC 22.
111 *IRC v Eccentric Club Ltd* [1924] 1 KB 390, CA, at 421 (Warrington LJ). The Eccentric Club, a social club, was a not-for-profit company limited by guarantee.

will be governed by the rules of the club. Incorporation with limited liability under the Companies Act 2006 takes one of two forms: either as a company limited by shares[112] or a company limited by guarantee.[113]

1.36 Company limited by shares This normally has working capital created by the issue of shares. Members invest their capital into the company by purchasing the shares in the expectation that a dividend will be paid in respect of those shares. Therefore these companies are usually formed with the idea of trade or profit in mind. In its constitutional document the company must state that the liability of its members is limited to the amount unpaid on the shares held by them.[114]

1.37 It is important to ensure that after incorporation provision is made for all the members of the club to become members of the company. This is because if there is a holding of the shares by non-members of the club, the club will cease to be a members' club but will become a proprietary club with the company as the proprietor.[115] Another area of difficulty, if shares of the company are held by non-members of the club, is the granting of a club premises certificate authorising the supply and sale of alcohol since such a club will be unable to fulfil the condition set out in s 63(2)(b) of the Licensing Act 2003 (rules and arrangements must benefit the club, not third parties).

1.38 If a prospective member wishes to join the company he will have to subscribe for one or more shares in the company, but usually restricted to *one* share. And shares may not be issued for less than their par (nominal) value.[116] It is possible for a club to issue penny shares at par value but a large authorised share capital would be required to allow for expansion of the membership, and the articles would have to remove the statutory rights of pre-emption which apply to new issues of shares and which require them first to be offered to existing shareholders.[117] More problems arise on the exit of the members from the club. A mechanism is required to cope with members leaving the club or being expelled. Shares cannot be cancelled without the consent of the court.[118] Shares can be bought back by the company but only by following the detailed procedure set out in the

---

112 Companies Act 2006, s 10.

113 Ibid, s 11.

114 Ibid, s 3(2). There was similar provision in earlier legislation, eg Companies Act 1985, s 1(2).

115 This is implicit from the judgment of Lord Evershed MR in *Automobile Proprietary Limited v Brown (VO)* [1955] 1 WLR 573, CA (concerning the Royal Automobile Club) where he refers to *Challoner v Robinson* [1908] 1 Ch 49, CA and *IRC v Eccentric Club Ltd* [1924] 1 KB 390, CA.

116 Companies Act 2006, s 542(1).

117 Ibid, s 561. A private company can exclude the shareholders' right of pre-emption: ibid, s 567(1).

118 Ibid, s 641.

Companies Act 2006,[119] and this would not be practicable as a means of dealing with a regular turnover of membership. A solution might be to issue redeemable shares provided there were some shares which were not redeemable.[120] The date of redemption would need to be fixed in the articles,[121] which would not create a suitably flexible method for dealing with members' resignations. A better solution would be a requirement that when a member left the club for any reason, another potential member would have to buy his share(s), alternatively the shares would have to be transferred into a holding trust or other similar entity. This last-mentioned transfer would not by itself remove the voting rights previously attached to the shares, so some provision would have to be included in the articles to accommodate the suspension of the rights attached to the 'floating' shares. Each retiring member must sign a stock transfer form and the directors would then have to approve the transfer to the new member.

1.39 Company limited by guarantee This is not allowed to have any share capital.[122] Accordingly, there is no question of any dividend being paid by the company to the members. Instead of buying shares the members of the company give a guarantee. In its constitutional document the company must state that the liability of its members is limited to such amount as the members undertake to contribute to the assets of the company in the event of its being wound up.[123] The amount of the guarantee must be specified in the statement of guarantee.[124] The amount of the guarantee is entirely a matter for the members of the company: it may be £1 or £10,000. It goes without saying that the larger the guarantee the more likely it is that traders will do business with the company, but many members feel that a substantial guarantee breaches the cardinal rule of a members' club that liability should be limited to the member's entrance fee and subscriptions. By way of example, under art 2 of the 2008 Model Articles for private companies limited by guarantee the liability is limited to £1.[125]

1.40 Where a club is incorporated as a company limited by guarantee, the members of the company will be the members of the club. A new member will simply apply to the company for membership in whatever form is required by the articles. Under article 21 of the 2008 Model Articles the form has to be approved by the directors. A member may withdraw from membership of the company by complying with the procedure laid down in the articles. Under art 22(1) of the 2008 Model Articles a member may

119 Companies Act 2006, Part 18, Chapters 1 and 4.

120 Ibid, s 684(4).

121 Ibid, s 685(4).

122 It was previously allowed but since 22 December 1980 no further companies limited by guarantee can be registered with a share capital: Companies Act 1980, s 1(2) and Companies Act 2006, s 5.

123 Ibid, s 3(3).

124 Ibid, s 11(3).

125 Companies (Model Articles) Regulations 2008, SI 2008/3229. See Appendix 7.

withdraw by giving 7 days' notice to the company in writing. Alternatively, the articles may provide for membership to be transferable, although it is advisable for clubs to make its membership non-transferable (for example, art 22(2) of the 2008 Model Articles stipulates that membership is not transferable). No pre-emption rights apply; and when a member leaves the company, the fact is simply noted in the register of members. Thus any change in the membership can be automatically reflected in the identity of the guarantors, so that there should never be any disparity between the membership of the company and the membership of the club. A company limited by guarantee may be entitled to charitable grants or awards from public funds,[126] whereas a company limited by shares would not be so entitled. A member's rights and liabilities under a company limited by guarantee are basically the same as under a company limited by shares (save as to those matters dealing with shares) and the same regime will apply to a director's duties.

1.41 A company limited by guarantee has a greater simplicity in its corporate structure than a company limited by shares. This is demonstrated by the fact that the 2008 Model Articles for companies limited by guarantee run to 39 articles whereas the 2008 Model Articles for companies limited by shares run to 53 articles. A clear example of this greater simplicity relates to the principles governing admission to and withdrawal (or expulsion) from membership of a company. The straightforward process described in **1.40** should be compared with the more complex admission procedures for companies limited by shares, the latter procedures being found in a combination of the articles of association, the Companies Acts, the common law applicable to companies and any shareholders' agreement.

1.42 **Private companies** The Companies Act 2006 went out of its way to simplify the corporate regime for small privately held companies. This will no doubt benefit a considerable number of clubs. Significant changes include:

(1) the company's articles of association have become its main constitutional document (this provision applies to all companies)[127] and any existing memorandum of association will be treated as part of its articles;[128]
(2) the company is no longer required to have a company secretary;[129]
(3) the company is no longer required to have an auditor;[130]
(4) the company is no longer required to hold an AGM;[131]

---

126 Where, for example, there is a ban on distribution of profits.
127 Companies Act 2006, s 17(a).
128 Ibid, s 28(1).
129 Ibid, s 270(1).
130 Ibid, s 485(1).
131 Ibid, s 336(1).

(5) the members are enabled to pass written resolutions without the need for a meeting;[132]
(6) the company can convene meetings at short notice where the consent is given by holders of 90% of the members having the right to attend and vote at the meeting.[133]

1.43 The perceived advantages of an incorporated club are:

(1) it protects the managing committee from liability in respect of the club's transactions and activities which result in a claim being made against the club: it is the club itself that will bear the responsibility;
(2) it relieves the committee member from being personally involved in any litigation concerning the club: the claim or defence will be in the name of the club;
(3) ownership of the club's property will reside in the club itself as opposed to the trustee members or ordinary members of the club;[134]
(4) because 'perpetual succession' is a consequence of separate legal personality, it enables gifts and bequests to be made to the club more easily, especially if the gift or bequest is intended to be for the benefit of future members as well as present members;
(5) borrowing is easier because companies can create 'floating charges' over their assets which means a creditor can secure a loan made to the company without hindering the use of the assets in the meantime.

1.44 One of the disadvantages of incorporation is that the club will be subject to the whole regimen of statutory control exercised through the courts. Further disadvantages are the costs and the hassle of complying with statutory obligations on an ongoing basis, for example, the filing of annual accounts at Companies House[135] or the notification of a change of company director.[136] This compliance requires both expenditure and diligence: for example, the omission of the club secretary to send to the registrar of companies in the prescribed form notification of a change of director could result in the prosecution of the company and its officers and their being fined, with a daily default fine for continued contravention.[137] Because of public regulation there is also some loss of privacy appertaining to the club's affairs.[138]

---

132 Companies Act 2006, s 288. The procedure for these resolutions is set out in ss 289–300. The required majority for passing these resolutions is a simple majority for an ordinary resolution (s 282) and a 75% majority for a special resolution (s 283).

133 Ibid, s 307(4)–(6).

134 As to trustees holding the club's property, see **5.19**, and **8.19**.

135 Companies Act 2006, s 854. The annual return with effect from 1 October 2009 'will become a lengthy and rather tedious document. It is far more complicated than the old one, which wasn't particularly easy to understand' (comment by Shipleys LLP, chartered accountants, in its house journal 'Shipshape – Summer 2009' p 4).

136 Ibid, s 167(1).

137 Ibid, s 167(4).

138 Eg relating to its membership list: see **5.88**.

1.45 Getting started To form a company, any two or more persons associated for a lawful purpose may, by subscribing their names to a memorandum of association and complying with the requirements of the Companies Act 2006 in respect of registration, form an incorporated company.[139] It is also common to purchase an 'off the shelf' company, where all the formalities have already been carried out, and to make suitable changes to the company name and its memorandum and articles of association. It is usual to employ a solicitor to make the necessary arrangements.

5. CHOOSING THE ESSENTIAL STRUCTURE

1.46 The crucial question whether the club should be an unincorporated members' club, a community club or an incorporated club has no simple, straightforward answer. The most one can say is that if ease of operation is the deciding factor, the unincorporated members' club is a well-tried and successful formula; if peace of mind is the deciding factor, a members' club registered under the Co-operative and Community Benefit Societies and Credit Unions Act 1965 or the Companies Act 2006 may be the answer; and if incorporation is decided upon, the better vehicle for a member's club is a company limited by guarantee rather than one limited by shares. A question which is often asked is whether an unincorporated club should become incorporated.[140] There is undoubtedly a trend towards this, especially in relation to large-scale clubs. However, if the club is in a healthy financial state and there is no need or intention to mortgage property or borrow monies, we consider that the statutory controls and obligations referred to in **1.44** will usually outweigh the benefits of incorporation. There may also be some tax implications in changing from an unincorporated status to an incorporated one.[141]

1.47 In *Co-operative Group (CWS) Ltd v Stansell Ltd*[142] Lord Justice Mummery cast an interesting sidelight on this question when he said that, in general, industrial and provident societies were subject to simpler procedures and less formal regulation than incorporated companies, which he pointed out are now governed by legislation of ever increasing complexity.[143] This would suggest that, if available, the formation of a community club might be a better proposition than an incorporated club.

---

139 Companies Act 2006, s 7.

140 Conversion into a company from an unincorporated members' club is no formality but a matter of substance: *Gaiman v National Association for Mental Health* [1971] Ch 317, at 335 (Megarry J). For one thing the directors of the company will have duties towards the company itself, not merely duties to the other members as in an unincorporated club.

141 See **16.19**.

142 [2006] 1 WLR 1704, CA.

143 Some measure of the disparity between the law relating to the formerly-called Industrial and Provident Societies Acts and that relating to the Companies Acts may be gleaned from

1.48 Statutory conversion Owing to the eventual demise of the Friendly Societies Act 1974, Parliament has encouraged working men's clubs to adopt a different structure. By special resolution such a club may determine to convert itself into a company under the Companies Act 2006,[144] or by the consent of the members duly obtained[145] a club may apply to the Financial Services Authority for registration as a community club under the Co-operative and Community Benefit Societies and Credit Unions Act 1965.[146] By ss 52 and 53 of this last-mentioned Act there has been since that date the power to convert from a community club into an incorporated club or *vice versa*. By the Co-operative and Community Benefit Societies and Credit Unions Act 2002 the government (a) amended the procedure whereby a community club may convert itself into an incorporated club[147] and (b) enabled the Treasury through secondary legislation to assimilate certain parts of mutual society law to company law.[148]

6. FORMATION OF PROPRIETARY CLUBS

1.49 It is important to distinguish a true proprietary club from a club which is referred to by a business man in his trading or business activities. In commerce the word 'club' is commonly used when a trader wants to target a particular segment of the public in order to offer persons favourable trading terms or to make a promotional offer. For example, Tesco plc, which operates a chain of grocery superstores, runs what it calls its Clubcard scheme; you apply to join its club by written application and once admitted the member obtains trading benefits from the club by way of discounted prices, etc. Such a club does not satisfy the criteria set out in **1.1**. Likewise, many book clubs, clothing clubs, and holiday clubs owned by proprietors do not qualify as true clubs because they would not satisfy these criteria, in particular the second criterion (not existing simply for trade or profit) and the sixth criterion (the need for collegiality). The distinction turns on the degree of control, both financial and physical, which the proprietor chooses to exercise over the members of the club, and in some cases the dividing line between a true proprietary club and a marketing device can be a fine one. As an example of a true proprietary club, one can take the Groucho Club in London, which is a social club with many members coming from

---

the fact that in *Halsbury's Laws of England* the former topic is dealt with in some 123 pages in vol 50 (5th edn, 2008) whereas the latter topic is dealt with in some 1,452 pages in vols 7(1) and 7(2) (4th edn, 2004) excluding the 2010 cumulative supplement.

144 Friendly Societies Act 1974, s 84(1).

145 Such consent must be obtained by the procedure required for a proposal to amend the rules of the club: ibid, s 84A(1).

146 Ibid, s 84A (inserted by the Friendly Societies Act 1992, Sch 16, paras 1 and 32).

147 Co-operative and Community Benefit Societies Act 2002, s 1.

148 Ibid, s 2. Consistent with this objective the Co-operative and Community Benefit Societies Act and Credit Unions Act 2010 has introduced into these societies and unions the disqualification provisions which are set out in the Company Directors Disqualification Act 1986: see **3.33**.

the media world. The club is owned by a proprietor who provides all the facilities and controls all the finances but there are proper club rules and, importantly, there is a membership committee comprising members of the club (plus one representative of the proprietor) which vets all applications for membership and which alone makes the decision whether to accept or reject the application.[149] A proprietor may protect the name of his club by a passing-off action.[150]

1.50 Nevertheless, a proprietary club is a very different legal concept from a members' club because the club will be owned by an outside person or company and the normal purpose of the club is for the proprietor to make a profit out of it.[151] To draw the distinction between members' clubs and proprietary clubs, the former are often referred to as *private* members' clubs.[152] The proprietor will own or provide the club premises, the furniture and the stock and will make them available to club members on such terms as he thinks fit.[153] The payment for the entitlement to use the facilities provided is the member's subscription.[154] When the period of the subscription expires the proprietor's obligations cease unless, and the exception needs emphasising, by consent of both parties the subscription is renewed. The relationship is solely one of contract between the proprietor on the one hand and the individual member on the other hand. There is no direct contractual relationship between the members themselves. The relationship between the member and his fellow-members will be a social one. The club, however, will not be eligible for a club premises certificate for licensing purposes. Nor is there any question of the members having any property rights in the club property.[155]

1.51 The liability for any debt or any transaction of the club will remain with the proprietor and so it will be he who will sue or be sued, not the members, in respect of club purchases or the conduct of its affairs. This position still applies where the proprietor has given the management of the club wholly or partly to a committee of members.

1.52 Getting started A proprietary club will come about either because a group of persons wish to form a members' club but do not have the money,

---

149 See *Challoner v Robinson* [1908] 1 Ch 49, CA describing the set up and running of a proprietary club, in this instance the United Artists Club (a distraint case).

150 *Ad-Lib Club Ltd v Granville* [1971] 2 All ER 300.

151 *Inland Revenue Commissioners v Eccentric Club Ltd* [1924] 1 KB 390, CA, at 421 (Warrington LJ).

152 See, for example, *John v Matthews* [1970] 2 QB 443, DC, at 447 E (Lord Parker CJ); *Charter v Race Relations Board* [1973] AC 868; and *Dockers' Labour Club and Institute Ltd v Race Relations Board* [1976] AC 285.

153 *Lyttelton v Blackburne* (1876) 45 LJCh 219; *Bowyer v Percy Supper Club Ltd* [1893] 2 QB 154, DC.

154 *Bowyer v Percy Supper Club Ltd* [1893] 2 QB 154, DC.

155 *Baird v Wells* (1890) 44 Ch D 661, at 676 (Stirling J): see **8.2**.

ability or inclination to own or run a club so that they entrust the task to a person or company to do it for them, or because a proprietor sees an opportunity in the market place for a members' club with facilities which he is able to provide.

7. FORMATION OF CLUBS AFFECTED BY STATUTORY PROVISIONS

1.53 Literary and scientific institutions Many of the learned societies and institutions of this country were incorporated by royal charter, whilst others have been incorporated under the Companies Acts. The majority, however, are not incorporated and count as unincorporated members' clubs. Whether incorporated or not, the provisions of the Literary and Scientific Institutions Act 1854 applies to every institution:[156]

> 'for the time being established for the promotion of science, literature, the fine arts, for adult instruction, the diffusion of useful knowledge, the foundation or maintenance of libraries or reading rooms for general use among the members or open to the public, of public museums and galleries of paintings and other works of art, collections of natural history, mechanical and philosophical inventions, instruments, or designs'.[157]

The Act deals with the nature, constitution, property, internal regulation and dissolution of the institution, and also with legal proceedings by or against the institution, and accords privileges and powers to the institution not normally enjoyed by private clubs and institutions.[158]

1.54 Other clubs More often than not clubs have specialised activities. Many of these clubs are regulated or part-regulated by statute, sometimes in order to control or restrict the club's activities and sometimes to the club's advantage or in order to help the club function efficiently. Set out in Appendix 6 is a list of some of the more common specialist clubs, indicating in broad terms which statutes are applicable to their activities. A number of

---

[156] Except the Royal Institution: s 33. Certain other institutions, such as the British Museum and the National Gallery, are governed by specific acts of Parliament and therefore fall outside the ambit of the 1854 Act.

[157] Ibid, s 33. The 1854 Act applies to institutions established before this Act. An early example of such an institution was the Russell Literary and Scientific Institution, founded in 1808 to provide a library and lectures on literary and scientific subjects for its members (*In re Russell Institution, Figgins v Baghino* [1898] 2 Ch D 72). Another early example, still flourishing, is the Roxburghe Club, founded in 1812 and devoted to printing unpublished documents and reprinting rare texts. Sections 18–33 of the Act appear in Appendix 1.

[158] *In re Russell Institution, Figgins v Baghino* [1898] 2 Ch D 72.

these clubs have a governing or central organisation to which the clubs belong and to whom the club can often turn in the event of a problem arising.

8. UMBRELLA ORGANISATIONS

1.55 There are several organisations in the United Kingdom which have a large number of clubs under their jurisdiction. Perhaps the best known is the Football Association. Under its aegis are 43 County Football Associations to which the astonishing number of some 37,500 football clubs are affiliated, involving about a million players. Other examples are Rotary International in Great Britain and Ireland which has over 1,800 clubs within this territory and some 59,000 club members, and the English Golf Union ('EGU') which has some 1,910 clubs belonging to its organisation and some 700,000 members. Sometimes the umbrella organisation like Rotary insists on all the clubs having a standard set of rules, others like EGU have clubs with as many different sets of rules as there are clubs. But all these clubs are genuine members' clubs and the same general principles of club law will be applicable to them as in the case of a single, free-standing members' club. A problem which can occur, however, is when a member of one club affiliated to an umbrella organisation is permitted entry as of right into another club as an associate; care has to be taken in relation to the rules of the host club and in connection with the Licensing Acts.[159]

9. THE CLUB AS A CHARITY

1.56 There may be occasions when it is suitable or desirable for a club or intended club to register as a charity. Historically charities existed to provide funds for deserving causes over an indefinite period of time. That historic reason is now coupled with tax advantages whereby the charity is better enabled financially to carry out its activities.[160] A well-known example is the Variety Club of Great Britain which is a company limited by guarantee and registered as a charity; whose members are in the world of show business; and which assists disabled and disadvantaged children. Charities are governed primarily by the Charities Act 1993 as amended and supplemented by the Charities Act 2006.[161] This last Act laid down two criteria which a club's activities must fulfil in order to become a charity: (1) they must fall within one or more of the 13 defined charitable purposes set

---

[159] Discussed at **9.34**.

[160] The advantages are discussed in **16.16**.

[161] See also Finance Act 2010, s 30 and Sch 6.

out in the Act[162] and (2) they must provide a benefit to the public.[163] There are 12 specific purposes and one general set of purposes at the end of the list:

(1) the prevention or relief of poverty;
(2) the advancement of education;
(3) the advancement of religion;
(4) the advancement of health or the saving of lives;
(5) the advancement of citizenship or community development;
(6) the advancement of the arts, culture, heritage or science;
(7) the advancement of amateur sport;
(8) the advancement of human rights, conflict resolution or reconciliation, or the promotion of religious or racial harmony or equality and diversity;
(9) the advancement of environmental protection or improvement;
(10) the relief of those in need by reason of youth, age, ill-health, disability, financial hardship or other disadvantage;
(11) the advancement of animal welfare;
(12) the promotion of the efficiency of the armed forces of the Crown,[164] or of the efficiency of the police, fire and rescue services or ambulance services;
(13) other purposes that are currently recognised as charitable or are in the spirit of any purposes currently recognised as charitable.

1.57 This last-mentioned set of purposes means that all existing charities will remain charities in accordance with the earlier permitted purposes,[165] namely, (a) the relief of poverty, (b) the advancement of education, (c) the advancement of religion, and (d) other purposes beneficial to the community not falling under the preceding heads.[166] Falling under head (d), for example, is the provision of facilities for recreation or other leisure-time occupation, if the facilities are provided in the interests of social welfare.[167] Under the old law the purposes identified in heads (a), (b) and (c) were presumed to be of a charitable nature. This presumption no longer exists; all charities must now prove that their activities are providing or will provide a benefit to the public.[168]

1.58 The object of the Act of 2006 is to give trustees greater flexibility and less bureaucracy in carrying out their tasks, especially where smaller

162 Charities Act 2006, s 2(2).
163 Ibid, s 3(1).
164 A curious purpose: some may look askance at a charitable gift to promote bigger and better weaponry.
165 See Statute of Uses 1601.
166 Charities Act 2006, s 2(4).
167 Recreational Charities Act 1958. It applies in particular to the provision of facilities at village halls, community centres and women's institutes.
168 Ibid, s 3(1).

charities are concerned, and to instigate easier ways for charities to make changes to their purposes, structures and administration. Several points may be noted. First, a new controlling body called the Charity Commission has been set up.[169] Previously, and perhaps surprisingly, the control lay with the Charity Commissioners who were individual persons. Secondly, a new legal entity, a charitable incorporated organisation, has been introduced: see **1.59**. Thirdly, a new tribunal, the Charity Tribunal, has been set up to act as 'the court of first instance' for appeals and applications in respect of certain decisions of the Charity Commission.[170] Previously any right of appeal lay to the High Court. Fourthly, trustees can now apply for relief from liability to the Charity Commission.[171] Previously trustees could only apply to the High Court for relief. Fifthly, the advice or guidance of the Charity Commission may now be sought in respect of administrative matters relating to the charity, such as the problem of charitable donations that can no longer be used as intended.[172]

1.59 Charitable incorporated organisations The Charities Act 2006 introduced a new corporate structure called the charitable incorporated organisation ('CIO'), created specifically to meet the needs of charities.[173] New charities and most existing ones are eligible to become or to convert to a CIO.[174] Hitherto an incorporated charity was subject to two sets of regulations, one as a charity and the other as a company. This innovation does away with the company law regulation; the CIO will be registered with the Charity Commission as a corporate body with limited liability. The CIOs were originally intended to come into being with the enactment of the Charities Act 2006 but secondary legislation was required to provide the detail on how CIOs would be established and operated, and this legislation has not yet been finalised. CIOs are likely to need three sets of regulations, namely, general regulations, insolvency and dissolution regulations and a Charity Tribunal amendment order. It is envisaged that CIOs will eventually be introduced some time in 2011.

1.60 Getting started The club must make an application to register with the Charities Commission, on its application form. A club will not be registered as a charity unless it has an income of more than £5,000 per annum. Some charities, such as universities, are *exempt* from registration

---

[169] Charities Act 1993, s 1A, inserted by Charities Act 2006, s 6.

[170] Ibid, s 2A, inserted by Charities Act 2006, s 8.

[171] Ibid, s 73D, inserted by Charities Act 2006, s 38.

[172] Ibid, s 29, as substituted by Charities Act 2006, s 24.

[173] Charities Act 2006, s 34 and Sch 7.

[174] See Part 8A of Charities Act 1993, inserted by Charities Act 2006, Sch 7. Exempt charities (i e exempt from registration with the Charity Commission) are ineligible; they are listed in Sch 2 to the 1993 Act, as amended by the 2006 Act; this list includes charitable societies registered under (a) the Friendly Societies Act 1974 or (b) the Co-operative and Community Benefit Societies and Credit Unions Act 1965. Societies registered under (b) may, however, convert to CIOs: Charities Act 1993, s 69G, inserted by Charities Act 2006.

and thus not subject to the Commission's supervisory powers; others are *excepted* from the need to register but remain subject to the Commission's jurisdiction.

10. THE CLUB AS A COMMUNITY INTEREST COMPANY

1.61 In 2004 the government introduced a new type of company called a community interest company ('CIC').[175] These companies are tailor-made for social enterprises whose activities are being carried on for the benefit of the community. There are currently (2010) over 3,000 CICs, some of which are clubs or associations which satisfy the criteria set out in **1.1**, such as the Scarborough Blind and Partially Sighted Society or the Lowerhouse Cricket Club in Lancashire, both of which now operate as CICs. CICs are formed under the Companies Act 2006 and are subject to that act and company law generally. The vehicle will either be a company limited by shares or limited by guarantee.[176] This form of structure may be preferred by clubs to charitable status because there is greater flexibility in terms of its activities; it is less regulated than a charity, being overseen by a Regulator;[177] and it is not managed by trustees but by directors who can receive reasonable remuneration.[178] Here the club's constitution will contain a statutory 'asset lock' which means that there are limits placed on the CIC's ability to make distributions to members or to make interest payments on debentures and debts.[179] An existing company may convert to a CIC[180] and so may an existing company which is already registered as a charity.[181] A CIC may convert to a registered society under the Co-operative and Community Benefit Societies and Credit Unions Act 1965 where it has put in place a restriction on the use of assets in accordance with the Community Benefit Societies (Restriction on Use of Assets) Regulations 2006.[182] A CIC continues in existence until it is dissolved[183] or converts to a charity.[184] If dissolved, the assets which remain after satisfaction of the company's liabilities will be transferred to another asset-locked body such as a different CIC or a charity, to be used for similar community purposes.[185]

---

175 Companies (Audit, Investigation and Community Enterprise) Act 2004, Part 2 (ss 26–63).
176 Ibid, s 26(2).
177 Ibid, s 27.
178 Ibid, ss 32(4)(e) and 45.
179 Ibid, s 30.
180 Companies (Audit, Investigation and Community Enterprise) Act 2004, s 38.
181 Ibid, s 39.
182 SI 2006/264. Co-operative and Community Benefit Societies and Credit Unions Act 1965, s 56, as amended by the Community Interest Company Regulations 2005, SI 2005/1778, reg 6A (this regulation was added by Community Interest Company (Amendment) Regulations 2009, SI 2009/1942).
183 Co-operative and Community Benefit Societies and Credit Unions Act 1965, s 53.
184 Ibid, s 54.
185 Ibid, s 31.

1.62 Getting started The formation and registration is similar to that of a limited company. Application is made to the CIC Regulator who will provide model memorandum and articles for the company to adopt or modify.

11. COMMUNITY AMATEUR SPORTS CLUBS

1.63 The Government recognised the important role that sports clubs play in promoting social and community inclusiveness and, in particular, promoting good health through regular exercise. But this contribution was not acknowledged by the tax system. It is an historical fact that the sports club sector has suffered from a lack of cash and a lack of adequate facilities, despite the many volunteers involved within the sector. Worse still, there has been a decline in participation of healthy sports which has added to the problems of local sports clubs. In 2002, therefore, the government introduced a package of tax advantages to support the community amateur sports club ('CASC').[186] The Corporation Tax Act 2010 has now restated their constitutional and tax position.[187]

1.64 First, there are distinctions to be noted. To qualify as a charity the club must promote the public's health by providing facilities for participation in amateur sport, and the club needs to register with the Charity Commission. To qualify as a community amateur sports club the club must provide as its main purpose facilities for, and promote participation in, one or more eligible sports, and the club needs to register with HM Revenue & Customs. In other words, in a charity the sports facilities are a means to an end, namely, the advancement of the community's good health, whereas in a CASC participation in the sport is the end in itself. One further distinction should be noted. A qualifying sport for charitable purposes may include a sport which exercises the mind only, such as chess;[188] in CASCs only physical sports are eligible because they are defined by reference to the relevant Sport Council's list.[189]

1.65 There are now (2010) some more than 5,000 registered CASCs. The decision to register should not be taken lightly, however, because once registered there is no power to de-register ('once a CASC, always a

---

[186] Finance Act 2002, s 58 and Sch 18.

[187] Corporation Tax Act 2010, ss 658 to 671. See **16.16**.

[188] This is because of the definition of 'sport' in s 2(3)(d) of the Charities Act 2006: 'Sports or games which promote health by involving physical or mental skill or exertion'.

[189] Corporation Tax Act 2010, s 661(1). The United Kingdom has four Sports Councils, respectively for England, Wales, Scotland and Northern Ireland. They apply the definition of sport ('all forms of physical activity') laid down by the Council of European Sports Charter 1993 (see Finance Act 2002, Sch 18, para 14 for the Sports Councils' authority). A complete list of eligible sports for England and Wales may be seen in Annex 1 to HMRC's detailed guidance on its (2010) website, www.hmrc.gov.uk/casc_guidance.htm.

CASC').[190] If the members have their eye on the main chance that a supermarket may come along and buy their club and grounds with the resulting profit to be divided amongst themselves, CASC is not a route which they should choose. A club is entitled to be registered as a CASC if it is, and required by its constitution to be, a club which:[191]

(1) is open to the whole community;
(2) is organised on an amateur basis;
(3) has as its main purpose the provision of facilities for, and the promotion of participation in, one or more eligible sports;
(4) meets the location condition;[192]
(5) meets the management condition.[193]

1.66 Open to the whole community A club is open to the whole community if:[194]

(1) membership is open to all without discrimination;
(2) its facilities are available to members without discrimination;
(3) its fees do not represent a significant obstacle to membership or use of its facilities.

A club is not prevented from being open to the whole community merely because it has different classes of membership depending on:[195]

(a) the age of the member;
(b) whether the member is a student;
(c) whether the member is paid wages;
(d) whether the member is a playing member;
(e) how far from the club the member lives; or
(f) merely because the club has restrictions on the days or times when different classes of membership have access to its facilities.

Discrimination in this context may be treated as that laid down by the Equality Act 2010 insofar as it is applicable to clubs,[196] save that

---

190 However, HM Revenue and Customs has the power to cancel the registration if a Revenue officer is satisfied that the club is no longer entitled to be registered as a CASC: Corporation Tax Act 2010, s 658(4)(b). This cancellation may have serious tax liability consequences.

191 Corporation Tax Act 2010, s 658(1).

192 Ibid, s 658(1)(d), added by Finance Act 2010, Sch 6(3), para 32, ie, the club is established in the UK or in some other territory specified in regulations made by HMRC and whose facilities are all located in the UK or in that other territory: Corporation Tax Act 2010, s 661A and Finance Act 2010, Sch 6, para 2(3).

193 Ibid, s 658(1)(e), added by the said schedule, para 31 ie, the club's managers are fit and proper persons to be managers of the club: ibid, s 661B.

194 Ibid, s 659(1).

195 Ibid, s 659(3).

196 See **4.19**.

discrimination on the ground of sex, age and disability may be taken into account as a necessary consequence of the requirement of a particular sport.[197]

1.67 Some examples may help. The club's emphasis must be on encouraging all members to participate regardless of their ability. The Basset Cricket Club might field a number of teams, ranging in ability from recreational and novice players up to a highly competitive standard. This would be acceptable as long as the overall emphasis was on participation. If the club only allowed participation at an elite level with other members in reality being spectators rather than players, this would not be acceptable. The club's subscription, charges or qualifying conditions for admission must not be set at such a level as to pose a significant obstacle to membership or the use of the club's facilities. Take dinghy sailing: even a basic second-hand boat and safety equipment costs several hundred pounds, so that if the Basset Sailing Club required all its members to have their own boat this would amount to a significant obstacle to membership. If the club, however, were to provide boats and equipment to new members at reasonable rates the obstacle would be removed. The club is not required to have its own premises or equipment to qualify as a CASC. The Basset Cycling Club which organised social and training rides and open competitions without owning premises would be eligible. Likewise, the Basset Swimming Club which had no facilities of its own but regularly hired the local authority's pool to hold swimming lessons and training sessions would be eligible.

1.68 Amateur status A club is organised on an amateur basis if:

(1) it is non-profit making, that is to say, any surplus income or gains are reinvested in the club and not distributed to any third parties;[198]
(2) it provides for members, and their guests only, the ordinary benefits of an amateur sports club;[199]
(3) its constitution provides for its net assets to be applied on its dissolution for approved sporting or charitable purposes.[200]

1.69 The ordinary benefits of an amateur sports club comprise:[201]

(a) the provision of sporting facilities;
(b) the reasonable provision and maintenance of club-owned sports equipment;

---

197 Corporation Tax Act 2010, s 659(2).
198 Ibid, s 660(1)(a)–(2). A club is not prevented from being non-profit making merely because it makes donations to charities or other CASCs: ibid, s 660(3).
199 Ibid, s 660(1)(b).
200 Ibid, s 660(1)(c).
201 Ibid, s 660(4).

(c) the provision of suitably qualified coaches;
(d) the provision, or reimbursement of the costs, of coaching courses;
(e) the provision of insurance cover;
(f) the provision of medical treatment;
(g) the reimbursement of reasonable travel expenses incurred by players and officials travelling to away matches;
(h) the reasonable provision of post-match refreshments for players and match officials;
(i) the sale and supply of food and drink as a social benefit which arises incidentally from the sporting purposes of the club.

The club is not prevented from providing the ordinary benefits of an amateur sports club merely because a member supplies goods and services to the club on an arm's length basis or because the club employs members of the club on an arm's length basis.[202]

1.70 On dissolution 'approved sporting or charitable purposes' means the purposes of the governing body of an eligible sport or of another CASC or of a charity where this particular application has been approved by the dissolving club's members in general meeting or by its governing body.[203]

1.71 The main purpose There is nothing wrong with a CASC having social members but their number must not be disproportionate to the number of playing members nor must the social activities of the club outweigh its playing activities.

1.72 Multi-sports club Some sports clubs provide facilities for more than one sport. In this event some thought needs to be given to the structure of the club since it affects the eligibility of CASC status. There is no problem if the club is an integrated single entity. If the club is a single entity with integrated sub-sections there is again no problem provided that the club consolidates into one set of club accounts the income and expenditure of all the integrated sub-sections. Where there is a lead club (which may own and manage the facilities) with independent affiliated clubs being allowed to use its facilities, no single club can be registered as a CASC to cover all of them and each individual club (including the lead club) must decide for itself whether to register as a CASC. Where there is a 'mother' club (which owns or rents the property and provides the facilities) with affiliated member clubs, the 'mother' club will be eligible as the single club to cover them all, provided that (a) the individual members of the affiliated clubs are entitled to become members of the 'mother' club, and (b) the 'mother' club itself actively promotes participation in eligible sports as opposed to being

---

202 Corporation Tax Act 2010, s 660(5).
203 Ibid, s 660(6)–(7).

merely a passive provider of premises and facilities. If the 'mother' club cannot satisfy the proviso, each affiliated club must decide for itself whether to register as a CASC.

1.73 Getting started The club should apply to an officer of Revenue and Customs to be registered as a CASC.[204] The officer must register the club if satisfied that the club is entitled to be registered.[205] The officer must notify the club of his decision either to register the club or to refusal to do so.[206] Revenue and Customs may publish the names and addresses of registered clubs.[207] An appeal lies to a tribunal against any decision made by the officer, if made within 30 days of the notification of the decision.[208]

---

204 Corporation Tax Act 2010, s 658(2).

205 Ibid, s 658(3).

206 Ibid, s 670(a)–(b).

207 Ibid, s 658(5).

208 Ibid, s 671.

Chapter 2

THE CLUB'S CONSTITUTION OR RULES

1. THE PRIMACY OF CLUB RULES

2.1 The club's set of rules is the bedrock of club law. A well-drawn set of rules[1] is crucial to the well-being and proper functioning of any club, no matter into what category the club falls. Rules should cater for all the exigencies which the club is likely to be confronted with. If a problem arises in a club, the first reaction of the committee or the members should be, 'What do the rules say about it?'[2] This does not mean to say that all sets of rules need to be complicated or minutely detailed. The extent of the rules depends on the extent of the club's activities. As a general proposition, rules should deal with matters of substance, not matters of procedure. Matters of detail or procedure can often be best dealt with in bye-laws or regulations if the need arises. It goes without saying that the rules should be expressed in clear and simple language, which does not need the training of a lawyer to expound what is the true meaning of any given rule.[3] Rules (and bye-laws) should always be dated so the members know when a particular rule or amendment came into force.

2.2 A paradigm of the need for well-drawn rules is the case of *Royal Society for the Prevention of Cruelty to Animals v Attorney-General and others*.[4] The Society went to court to obtain guidance on whether its membership policy and associated membership scheme were constitutional. The Society was founded in 1824 as an unincorporated association but was incorporated by a private Act of Parliament in 1932. The rules governing its members

---

1 It is possible to have a set of enforceable *oral* rules but a club with such rules would be a very small coterie of like-minded persons. A literary, mid-twentieth-century example was the Inklings, a club consisting of C S Lewis (*The Chronicles of Narnia*), J R R Tolkien (*The Lord of the Rings*), Nevill Coghill (modern verse translator of Chaucer's *The Canterbury Tales*) and Charles Williams of the Oxford University Press, who used to meet in C S Lewis' rooms at Magdalen College, Oxford and in the Eagle and Child public house in Oxford.

2 As long ago as 1836 in the case of *Flemyng v Hector* (1836) 2 M & W 172 (concerning the Westminster Reform Club) the courts were emphasising the importance of the club rules (Parke B at 184–185 and Alderson B at 187); *Lyttelton v Blackburne* (1876) 45 LJCh 219, at 222.

3 See Megarry J's comment in the *Re Sick and Funeral Society of St John's Sunday School, Golcar* case [1973] Ch 51, at 61, 'I have already observed that the rules are not well drafted, and I do not intend to explore all the difficulties discussed in argument'.

4 [2002] 1 WLR 448.

were made in 1932 and amended or altered in 1964, 1976, 1979, 1983, 1991 and 1997. Their confused state drove Mr Justice Lightman to conclude his judgment by saying:

> 'At the same time consideration should be given whether and how the rules should be amended generally so that they no longer represent a patchwork of amendments over the years with the inevitable construction difficulties to which such a patchwork gives rise and whether the society should adopt in their place a set of rules which are clear and consistent and enable it to function effectively.'

2. THE RULE-MAKERS

2.3 Members' clubs It is the responsibility of the members to decide upon and enact the rules. This is the direct consequence of the fourth criterion (the need for a set of rules) and the sixth criterion (the need for collegiality) set out in **1.1**. It is not uncommon, however, for the members to delegate some of their rule-making powers to a smaller group of members, for example, delegation to the committee to make bye-laws.[5] As may be seen below,[6] the power to make rules does not automatically or necessarily include the power to alter the rules.

2.4 Proprietary clubs Here the responsibility for the rules lies solely with the proprietor who must, in particular, ensure that his rules comply with that part of the fourth criterion which states that the rules must fairly regulate the conduct of the members towards each other, that is to say, they must pay due regard to the concept of collegiality.

3. STATUTORY INTERVENTION

2.5 Parliament has intervened several times to lay down a framework of rules governing the affairs of clubs, sometimes on a mandatory basis and at other times on a voluntary basis. Such intervention should be seen as beneficial.

2.6 Working men's clubs Section 7(2) of the Friendly Societies Act 1974 stipulates that the rules must contain those rules set out in Schedule 2 to the Act.[7]

---

5 See **2.23**.

6 See **2.44**.

7 See Appendix 5.

2.7 Community clubs Section 14 of the Co-operative and Community Benefit Societies and Credit Unions Act 1965 stipulates that the rules must contain those rules set out in Schedule 1 to the Act.[8]

2.8 Shop clubs Section 3 of the Shop Clubs Act 1902 stipulated that the rules must contain those rules set out in the Schedule to the Act.[9]

2.9 Literary and scientific institutions Section 24 of the Literary and Scientific Institutions Act 1854 gives the governing body express power to make bye-laws 'for the better governance of the institution, its members or officers and for the furtherance of its purpose and object'.[10]

2.10 Incorporated clubs Prior to 1 October 2009 companies were required to have as their constitutional documents an old-style memorandum of association and some articles of association,[11] often referred to simply as the memorandum and the articles. The old-style memorandum included the objects of the company which defined its powers. A company does not have power to act outside the scope of its objects.[12] From 1 October 2009 new companies will be incorporated under the Companies Act 2006. Under this Act companies will need a new-style memorandum of association and articles of association.[13] The new-style memorandum is a much reduced document and essentially it contains the names of the subscribers (the founder members) to the company and authentication that they have agreed to become members of the company.[14] Nothing else. This memorandum cannot be amended or updated. The company's continuing constitutional document will be the articles.

2.11 Any new company will not be required to list the objects of the company because from 1 October 2009 they will be *unrestricted*,[15] unless specifically restricted by the company's articles.[16] From 1 October 2009 those parts of the old-style memorandum (including the objects) of existing companies will be automatically deemed to be part of the company's articles.[17] The articles have been described as the company's internal rulebook.[18] Provided the articles (which must be contained in a single

---

8 See Appendix 4.

9 See Appendix 2.

10 See Appendix 1.

11 Companies Act 1985, ss 1(1) and 7(1).

12 *York Corporation v Henry Leetham & Sons Ltd* [1924] 1 Ch 557, at 573.

13 Companies Act 2006, ss 7(1)(a), 17 and 18(1).

14 Ibid, s 8(1).

15 Ibid, s 31(1).

16 Ibid, s 31(1).

17 Ibid, s 28(1).

18 For the important distinction between the company's 'rulebook' and the club's rulebook, see **2.39**.

document)[19] do not contain rules which are against the law, the members have complete freedom to choose which rules go into their company's articles. Successive Companies Acts have balanced the companies' freedom to make their own rules with the convenience of providing standardised model articles set out in legislation so that, as one commentator put it, companies do not have to re-invent the wheel. No company is obliged to adopt the model rules; a company may adopt some or all of the model articles[20] and, if it wants, the articles can be entirely bespoke rules but in this event it would be wise for the company to seek legal advice.

2.12 The model articles issued under the Companies Act 2006 respectively for private companies limited by shares and companies limited by guarantee ('the 2008 Model Articles') came into force on 1 October 2009.[21] Prior to this date the model articles which were in force were those commonly known as the Table A articles made under the Companies Act 1985.[22] It is important to note that these latter articles continue to apply to existing companies[23] unless they change their articles by special resolution,[24] at which point they will be obliged to take account of the provisions of the Companies Act 2006 affecting the constitution of the company.

2.13 Where a company is formed on or after 1 October 2009 it may choose to rely on the 2008 Model Articles without more ado. In this case the company does not need to register its articles at Companies House since these model articles will apply by default.[25] Where a new company files its own articles with Companies House after 1 October 2009 and subsequently the company finds that it has not made provision for a given set of circumstances the applicable rule in the 2008 Model Articles will apply by default.[26] It is to be noted that the 2008 Model Articles are considerably shorter than the 1985 ones because, for example, they do not duplicate procedural matters set out in the Companies Act 2006 itself, such as Part 13 of the Act (resolutions and meetings).

---

19 Companies Act 2006, s 18(3)(a).

20 Ibid, s 19(3).

21 Companies Act 2006, s 19(1), (2); Companies (Model Articles) Regulations 2008, SI 2008/3229: see Appendices 6 and 7.

22 Companies (Tables A to F) Regulations 1985, SI 1985/805, as amended in 2007 (SI 2007/2541 and SI 2007/2826) and 2008 (SI 2008/739) to take account of those provisions of the Companies Act 2006 already in force.

23 8(1) *Halsbury's Statutes* (4th edn, 2007 Reissue) p 280.

24 Companies Act 2006, s 21(1).

25 Ibid, s 20(1)(a).

26 Ibid, s 20(1)(b).

2.14 Licensing Act 1964 Sections 41 and 42 and Schedule 7[27] made qualification for a registration certificate dependant on the club's rules being compliant with these sections and this schedule. There is no similar provision in the Licensing Act 2003.

4. CONTENTS OF THE RULES

2.15 Express rules At the most basic level, the rules of the club should make provision for:

(1) the name of the club;
(2) the object and purposes of the club;
(3) the election or admission of members;
(4) the payment of subscriptions;
(5) the resignation of members;
(6) the suspension and expulsion of members;
(7) the management of club affairs;
(8) general meetings of the members;
(9) the alteration of the rules;
(10) the dissolution of the club.

2.16 For a complex organisation which, say, has a national identity and branches and perhaps a disciplinary role as well, the rules will need to be a lot more comprehensive and make provision accordingly. For example, the index to the constitution or rules of such a club might comprise the following:

General

(1) Name of the club[28]
(2) Object and purposes of the club[29]
(3) Charitable status [if any][30]
(4) Powers [if, say, it has a royal charter][31]
(5) Patron[32]
(6) President and Vice-Presidents[33]
(7) Other officers of the club[34]

---

27 See Appendix 3.
28 See **2.33**.
29 See **2.24**.
30 See **1.56**.
31 A royal charter stems from the royal prerogative (now exercised via the Privy Council) and was virtually the only way to create a corporate body before the advent of the Companies Acts. The charter will define the privileges and purposes of the body holding the charter.
32 See **5.4**.
33 See **5.6**.
34 See **5.7**.

(8) Trustees[35]

Membership

(9) Categories of member[36]
(10) Qualification for membership[37]
(11) Election of candidates[38]
(12) Privileges of membership[39]
(13) Entrance fee[40]
(14) Subscriptions[41]
(15) Resignation[42]
(16) Suspension and expulsion of members[43]
(17) Disciplinary proceedings[44]
(18) Restrictions on members[45]

Management

(19) Management of the club's affairs[46]
(20) Composition of the Council [the ruling body]
(21) Meetings of the Council
(22) Board of Management [the managing committee][47]
(23) Committees [sub-committees][48]
(24) Secretary General[49]
(25) Branches[50]
(26) Annual General Meeting[51]
(27) Special meetings[52]
(28) Notice to members[53]
(29) Procedure at general meetings[54]

---

35 See **5.19**.
36 See **4.6**.
37 See **4.3**.
38 See **4.2**.
39 See **4.27**.
40 See **4.28**.
41 See **4.28**.
42 See **7.2**.
43 See **7.26** and **7.8** respectively.
44 See **7.31**.
45 See **5.26**.
46 See **5.1**.
47 See **5.21**. For committee meetings, see **6.51**.
48 See **5.24**.
49 As to paid officials, see **5.10** and **5.11**.
50 See **5.20**.
51 See **6.2**.
52 See **6.5**.
53 See **6.9**.
54 See **6.19**.

Financial provisions

(30) Power to borrow monies[55]
(31) Accounts[56]
(32) Auditor[57]
(33) Investment manager[58]

Miscellaneous

(34) Bye-laws[59]
(35) Interpretation of the rules[60]
(36) Amendment of the rules[61]
(37) Dispute resolution[62]

Dissolution

(38) Dissolution of the club[63]
(39) Assets on dissolution.[64]

2.17 In deciding how detailed the rules should be or what special rules ought to be included, the members or their committee should think ahead as to what problems might arise in any particular area of the club's activity. For example, the players in a football club might find themselves outnumbered by the social members of the club. The social members are welcome because they generate cash at the club as well as camaraderie. But what if a developer offers to buy the club's playing field? The players are all against the offer but the social members are all in favour of it. The solution adopted by some sports clubs is to have a rule that states if any motion, which is put to the members at a general meeting, is prejudicial to the interests of the playing members, the non-playing members shall not be entitled to vote on it.[65] The authors do not necessarily recommend any such rule but it demonstrates the need for foresight when compiling the rules. If the rule is not there when it is needed, it may be too late to insert it as an amendment.[66]

---

55 See **5.59**.
56 See **5.11**.
57 See **5.18**.
58 See the second criterion set out in **1.1** and footnote 4 to that paragraph.
59 See **2.23**.
60 See **2.42**.
61 See **2.44**.
62 See **5.90** and **18.38**.
63 See **3.1**.
64 See **8.1**.
65 Such a rule would not contravene the Equality Act 2010 because it would not involve any of the protected characteristics: see **5.64**.
66 See *In re West Sussex Constabulary's Widows, Children and Benevolent (1930) Fund Trusts* [1971] Ch 1, at 9.

2.18 All clubs start out with the big advantage that candidates or applicants for membership must perforce join the club on its terms, not on their terms. If a candidate were to approach the secretary of the Basset Social Club and say, 'I would like to apply for membership of your club but I don't like the rule that says members must wear a red jacket in the clubhouse on Saturday evenings', the secretary would no doubt respond, 'In that case, don't bother to apply'. It is only once the member has joined the club that he is in a position to get the rule altered and of course he may find the great majority of the members are in favour of the red jacket rule.

2.19 Certain clubs are or were obliged by law to adopt as express rules those rules laid down by Parliament: see **2.6**, **2.7**, **2.8** and **2.14**.

2.20 **Gender rule** Nowadays most clubs are open to members of both sexes. It is sometimes said that the greatest contribution that 'this sceptred isle' has made to civilisation is the English language. Yet we have no pronoun or adjective which denotes a man *or* a woman. We are faced with 'he', 'him' and 'his' on the one hand and 'she', 'her' and 'hers' on the other hand. Rule-makers can get round this problem by referring to members, officers, and guests etc in the plural and thus using the words 'they', 'them' and 'their', which includes both sexes, but the use of the plural is not always appropriate. Section 6 of the Interpretation Act 1978 states that, unless the contrary intention appears, words importing the masculine gender include the feminine, but this law is not common knowledge so it is better to have an express rule to this effect. In this book we ask the reader to make the same inclusion where we refer to the male gender in the text.

2.21 **Implied rules** Many sets of club rules are drawn up informally and the members are content to express only the most important rules of membership, leaving the remaining details to be tacitly understood or worked out later. Subsequently, a problem or unexpected contingency occurs which reveals a deficiency in the rules. The question which then arises is whether the law will imply a term or terms to cover the deficiency. It is well settled that, generally speaking, the court will only imply a term in two situations: (1) to give business efficacy to the contract, and (2) to give force to the obvious but unexpressed intention of the parties to the contract.[67] Thus the club rules might stipulate that the member was to pay an annual subscription but omit to say when that subscription was due and payable. It would be easy in these circumstances to imply a term that the subscription was payable within a reasonable time of its being demanded. Similarly, it is unusual for the rules to say that the member shall behave in a proper and acceptable manner in the clubhouse but this obligation would be implied because it obviously represents the unexpressed intention of himself and his fellow members.

---

67 *Chitty on Contracts* (30th edn, 2008), at 13-004.

2.22 Customary rules On occasion a rule may be implied by custom or long usage by the members. The authors know of a case concerning a British Legion club where the club rules stipulated that in committee meetings the votes of abstainers were to be taken into account in calculating the requisite voting majority.[68] As an unwritten exception established over many years, where the committee held an expulsion meeting the chairman never voted on the expulsion motion (to demonstrate his independent role) and his vote was discounted when calculating the necessary two-thirds majority. This unwritten rule had the backing of the club's umbrella organisation. On one particular occasion the expulsion motion would have been defeated had the chairman's non-vote been counted as an abstention rather than discounted altogether. The club declared that the member had been duly expelled and we consider that the club probably came to the correct decision because the club was relying on a valid customary rule. It is important to note, however, that the customary rule must be notorious, certain and reasonable[69] and can only be incorporated into a contract provided that there is nothing in the express or necessarily implied terms to prevent such inclusion.[70] The hypothetical 'red jacket' rule referred to in **2.18** could, we surmise, be the subject of a customary rule.

2.23 Bye-laws and regulations Bye-laws (and regulations which is a synonymous category) are a form of subordinate legislation. In club law they exist for the purpose of governing the details or minutiae of internal management and administration of a club where it is unnecessary to burden the main rules with such matters. In the case of a members' club no term will be implied that the committee or the members in general meeting shall have power to make bye-laws unless, which is unlikely to occur in practice, *all* the members have consented to this course.[71] Therefore there must be express power in the rules to make bye-laws. An exception is a club to which the Literary and Scientific Institutions Act 1854 applies.[72] It is usual to give the power of making bye-laws to the managing committee; this has the advantage that they may be amended or altered as the circumstances require by the committee itself rather than by the more cumbersome procedure of amendment by the members in general meeting. The enabling rule should state for what purpose or purposes the bye-laws may be made. Bye-laws must be consistent with the main rules, nor should they contain matters of principle which usurp the function of the main rules. Nor must they be unduly oppressive of any minority of the club.[73] In order to ensure that bye-laws are sufficiently brought to the attention of the members, it is good practice to exhibit them on a notice board in the club premises.

---

68 See further **6.43**.

69 *Devonald v Rosser & Sons* [1906] 2 KB 728, at 743.

70 *London Export Corporation v Jubilee Coffee Roasting Co Ltd* [1958] 1 WLR 661, at 675.

71 The exception is based on the premise that, if all consent, the members' contract with each other will have been lawfully varied.

72 See **2.9**.

73 *Merrifield Ziegler & Co v Liverpool Cotton Association* [1911] 105 LT 97, at 104.

5. OBJECTS OF THE CLUB

2.24 Unincorporated members' clubs A club's objects clause should be stated in a suitably wide form to cover all the activities it may wish to pursue. This ensures that the club's funds and assets are expended in a proper manner. Because circumstances change over the years and the club's activities may take a new direction or have a new emphasis, a provision can be inserted in the objects clause which states that no one object is to predominate over another or the wording of the objects clause can be such that no one object prevails over another object.[74]

2.25 If the club's object was stated to be the provision of facilities for the playing of golf, would it matter if the club started spending its funds on the provision of facilities for the playing of squash? The answer is that it would matter, because the expenditure would have been unauthorised; the club's auditor might take exception to it and the committee who spent the money might be vulnerable to reimburse the club, unless *all* the members ratified the expenditure or unless the objects clause was amended with retrospective effect[75] to include the playing of squash.[76] Presumably in most cases the members would be aware of the expenditure on squash facilities and would be consenting to their committee spending the club's money in this way, so that no problem would arise in fact, but it is plainly not good practice to have the objects clause and the club expenditure out of kilter.

2.26 Working men's clubs A working men's club registered under a Friendly Societies Act must state in its rules the *whole* of the objects for which the club is established and the purposes for which the club's funds are to be applicable.[77]

2.27 It should be noted that it is not competent for a club registered under a Friendly Societies Act to convert itself into a company with objects more extensive or widely differing from the objects specified in the club rules,[78] although once converted it can exercise such powers of altering or enlarging its objects set out in its articles of association as the Companies Act 2006 permits.[79]

---

74 See **2.51** for an example of the advantage of a suitably wide objects clause.

75 As to retrospective alteration of the rules, see **2.47**.

76 See *Baker v Jones* [1954] 1 WLR 1005 (where the payments made by British Amateur Weightlifters' Association to solicitors to defend libel actions brought against some of its members were held illegal because there was no power in the rules to use the funds in this manner).

77 Friendly Societies Act 1974, Sch 2, para 3(1).

78 *Blythe v Birtley* [1910] 1 Ch 228, CA (alteration of memorandum of association).

79 The club must bear in mind, however, the need for the club to have an agreed and common purpose as required under the first criterion: see **1.1**.

2.28 Community clubs A club registered under the Co-operative and Community Benefit Societies and Credit Unions Act 1965 must state in its rules what its objects are.[80] There is no requirement to state in the rules the whole of the objects for which the club is established, as obtains in the case of clubs registered under the Friendly Societies Act. Thus the objects clause of the club can be drawn in a suitably wide form.

2.29 Shop clubs A club registered under the Shop Clubs Act 1902 must state in its rules the *whole* of the objects for which the club is established.[81]

2.30 Incorporated clubs Prior to 1 October 2009 the objects of the company would necessarily have been stated in the old-style memorandum of association. For companies incorporated on or after this date the new-style memorandum has become a formal document recording the position at the point of registration of the company and has nothing to do with the objects of the company.[82] An existing memorandum is now to be treated as part of the articles.[83] Unless the articles specifically restrict the objects of the company its objects are now unrestricted.[84] Accordingly, for clubs incorporated on or after 1 October 2009 we consider that it is essential for the club's objects to be stated in the company's articles, otherwise the first criterion (the need for an agreed and common purpose)[85] will not be met. To ensure the longevity of the objects clause in the articles the company can utilise the entrenchment provisions contained in s 22 of the Companies Act 2006.[86]

2.31 Literary and scientific institutions An institution (not having a royal charter nor established nor acting under an Act of Parliament) may alter, extend or abridge the purposes of the institution provided that three-fifths of the members present at a special meeting have agreed to this course.[87]

2.32 Proprietary clubs The objects clause will be drafted by the proprietor and insofar as the assets and funds of the club belong to the proprietor the objects clause is of less significance than in a members' club. Nevertheless, a proprietary club should concisely state what are the objects of the club so that the members are aware of the nature of the club they are applying to join.

---

80 Co-operative and Community Benefit Societies and Credit Unions Act 1965, Sch 1, para 2.
81 Shop Clubs Act 1902, Sch, para ii.
82 Companies Act 2006, s 8(1).
83 Ibid, s 28(1).
84 Ibid, s 31(1).
85 See **1.1**.
86 See **2.59**.
87 Literary and Scientific Institutions Act 1854, s 27: see Appendix 1.

2.33 Name of the club The stated objects should be fairly reflected in the name of the club. In an unreported case, *Re Claremont Liberal Club Limited* (1910),[88] registered under the Companies (Consolidation) Act 1908, the club applied in September 1910 to Mr Justice Swinfen Eady for sanction to extend its activities 'to work mines, promote companies, underwrite shares, and sell coal and coke'. The judge refused permission on the ground that in order to carry out these activities the club would first have to change its name to a general purposes company. There is, however, in practice little restriction on the choice of name. With regard to incorporated clubs the Secretary of State has the power to reject a name if he is of the opinion that it would constitute a criminal offence or is offensive.[89] With regard to community clubs the Financial Services Authority can refuse to register a name which in its opinion is undesirable.[90]

2.34 Certain guarantee companies and other private companies are entitled to omit the word 'Limited' from their name if (1) it is a charity, *or* (2) it already has exemption because the objects of the company are the promotion of commerce, art, science, education, religion, charity or any profession, *and* provided (a) it requires its profits (if any) to be applied in promoting its objects, (b) no dividend is paid to its members, and (c) on winding up its assets are transferred to another body with similar objects rather than distributed to the members.[91]

6. BINDING NATURE OF THE RULES

2.35 Unincorporated members' clubs The club rules are impliedly binding on each member as a matter of contract law.[92] It is, however, a wise precaution to state in every set of rules that on joining the club the member expressly agrees to be bound by the rules as may be made from time to time, and for the new member to be provided with a copy of the rules.[93] The importance of express rules is underlined by the fact that further rules, however desirable, will not be implied into club rules unless either they are necessary to give business efficacy to the contract of membership or because

88 Cited by B T Hall in his book on *Club Law* published in August 1915 by the Working Men's Club & Institute Union.

89 Companies Act 2006, s 53. Companies House has published guidance on name restrictions.

90 Co-operative and Community Benefit Societies and Credit Unions Acts 1965, s 5(1).

91 Companies Act 2006, ss 60–62.

92 *In re Sick and Funeral Society of St John's Sunday School, Golcar* [1973] Ch 51, at 60.

93 This is not essential as may be seen from *Raggett v Musgrave* [1827] 2 Car & P 556 (where the rules were accessible but not posted in the clubhouse or sent to the members, yet were still held to be binding on the members). And see *John v Rees* [1970] 1 Ch 345, at 388 (where Megarry J said, 'In the case of a club, if nobody can produce any evidence of a final resolution to adopt a particular set of rules, but on inquiry the officers would produce that set as being the rules upon which it is habitual for the club to act, then I do not think the member would be entitled to reject those rules merely because no resolution could be proved').

the implied term represents the obvious, but unexpressed, intention of the parties.[94] As will be seen, such rules as those dealing with expulsion of members[95] or amendment of the rules[96] will not be implied into the rules in the absence of express rules to this effect.

2.36 It is common for clubs to make it a rule that the elected candidate shall not be entitled to the privileges of membership until he has paid the entrance fee (if any) and his first subscription. In this event the election constitutes an offer of membership so that on notification of his election the candidate can reject the offer and decline membership because the contract is only complete when he had paid the entrance fee and the first subscription.[97] If there is no such rule the candidate's application is the offer and the acceptance is the notification of election.

2.37 Working men's clubs and community clubs By s 22(1)(b) of the Friendly Societies Act 1974 and by s 14(1) of the Co-operative and Community Benefit Societies and Credit Unions Act 1965 it is provided that the rules of clubs registered under these Acts are binding on the members. Under s 21 of the former Act and s 15(1) of the latter Act the club is obliged to provide a copy of the rules for a small fee to the member on demand.

2.38 Shop clubs The Shop Clubs Act 1902 is silent on the point but it is considered that the members are all impliedly bound by the rules of their particular club, especially as the Act mandatorily required each registered shop club to provide for certain fixed rules.

2.39 Incorporated clubs As stated in **2.11**, the articles of association are the company's internal rulebook. The company's articles are subject to the Companies Act 2006 and are legally binding on the company and its members.[98] The articles are chosen by the members and comprise a form of statutory contract between the company and the members in relation to their membership of the *company*.[99] But it must be clearly understood that these articles are not the same thing as the club's rulebook, although the two will of necessity overlap.[100] Therefore the club rules should always be set out in a separate and self-contained rulebook which will be binding on the members as a matter of contract law in relation to their membership of the *club*. If, however, there were to be any conflict between the articles and the club rules, the articles would prevail since they have statutory force under the Companies Acts. This rulebook can be authorised by the directors

---

94 *Chitty on Contracts* (30th edn, 2008), at 13-004.

95 See **7.8**.

96 See **2.44**.

97 *Re New University Club (Duty on Estate)* (1887) 18 QBD 720, at 727.

98 Companies Act 2006, s 18(1).

99 *Globalink Telecommunications Ltd v Wilmbury Ltd* [2003] 1 BCLC 145, at 154.

100 Josling and Alexander, *The Law of Clubs* (6th edn, 1987), at p 21.

under the articles: see for example art 5 of the 2008 Model Articles where the directors can make provision for delegation of their powers of management to committees and the members. Having a separate club rulebook means that the domestic arrangements of the club can be dealt with flexibly and at little expense, especially if the rules contain a power of amendment to be exercised by the managing committee of the club.[101]

2.40 Proprietary clubs The proprietor will set out the club rules as part of the contract between himself and the individual club member and these rules will bind the member as a matter of contract law. If the proprietary club is incorporated, it is likely that few of the members will have ready access to the company's memorandum and articles of association, so that it becomes all the more important that the rules are set out in a separate and self-contained rulebook. It is also a sensible practice for the rules to recite the proprietor's obligation to provide the members with facilities, and premises if applicable, at his own expense without liability on the part of the member save as to the subscription and other agreed charges.

2.41 On remission of subscription It might be thought that the remission of a member's subscription, say because he has fallen on hard times, might be considered simply as a valid act of management or as an acceptable act of kindness on the part of the committee. But the legal position is not as simple as that. It will be recalled from **1.8** that in a members' club the consideration for the promise whereby each member agrees to be bound by the rules of the club is the payment of his subscription. Without consideration contracts are not enforceable unless contained in a deed.[102] So if the committee remits on compassionate grounds the whole of the subscription, where is the consideration for the member's promise to be bound by the club rules for the period of that subscription? Could the excused member say, for example, that he was not bound for that period by any expulsion or suspension rule? We consider that the answer is in the negative because the consideration would probably be construed by courts in a different way. It is normally construed as a detriment to the promisee (the member), the detriment being the payment of the subscription. But consideration may consist of a benefit to the promisor (the club). In *Edmonds v Lawson*[103] the relationship between a pupil barrister (the promisee) and the members of her chambers (the promisor) was held to be contractual even though she paid no pupillage fee.[104] The requirement of consideration was satisfied because it was to the benefit of the barristers' chambers to

---

101 An alternative route, sometimes adopted if there is no separate club rule book, is to exclude the club rules from the articles and to deal with them under the company's bye-laws, such bye-laws being authorised by and promulgated under the articles and thereafter being amended as and when necessary by the directors.

102 *Chitty on Contracts* (30th edn, 2008), at 3-01.

103 [2000] QB 501.

104 See also *Modahl v British Athletic Federation Ltd (No 2)* [2002] 1 WLR 1192, CA, at [50]–[52] (Latham LJ).

have a pool of candidates from which to choose their members. Likewise, it can be cogently argued that it is of benefit to the club to retain an excused member, especially if he is a star player in a sports club or a committee member in a social club or simply considered a good club member whose presence in the club contributes to its well-being. Thus an excused member is still bound by club rules. Some clubs avoid this problem by giving the committee the express power to remit the whole or part of a subscription in the exercise of its discretion.

7. INTERPRETATION OF THE RULES

2.42 As to the manner in which club rules should be approached, in 1881 in *Dawkins v Antrobus*[105] Jessel MR said that the ordinary rules of construction were to apply as with any other contract. However, a hundred years later in 1982 the courts saw club rules in a different light. In *Re GKN Nuts & Bolts Ltd Sports and Social Club*[106] Megarry V-C said:

> 'In [club] cases the court usually has to take a broad sword to the problems, and eschew an unduly meticulous examination of the rules and resolutions. I am not, of course, saying these should be ignored; but usually there is a considerable degree of informality in the conduct of the affairs of such clubs, and I think that the courts have to be ready to allow general concepts of reasonableness, fairness and common sense to be given more than their usual weight when confronted by claims to the contrary which appear to be based on any strict interpretation and rigid application of the letter of the rules. In other words, allowance must be made for some play in the joints.'

This allowance for 'some play in the joints' is also reflected in modern and recent interpretation of contracts by the courts: the surrounding circumstances in the making of the contract and commercial common sense now play their part in its interpretation.[107] But a word of caution should be added. In the *GKN* case the Vice Chancellor emphasised at 783 the need for 'scrupulous observance of the rules' when it came to changing the property rights of members. The same scrupulous observance of the rules will be required when it comes to a question of suspension or expulsion of the member.[108] In addition, all rules must be construed in the context of the club's objects clause.

---

105 [1881] 17 Ch D 615, at 621.

106 [1982] 1 WLR 774, at 776.

107 *Mannai Investment Co Ltd v Eagle Star Assurance Co Ltd* [1997] 2 WLR 945, HL, per Lord Hoffmann; *Skanska Rashleigh Weatherfoil Ltd v Somerfield Stores Ltd* [2006] EWCA Civ 1732, per Neuberger LJ; *Chartbrook Ltd v Persimmon Homes Ltd* [2009] 1 AC 1101, per Lord Hoffmann.

108 See **7.10**.

2.43 It is in order for a club rule to state that if there is any dispute about the meaning or interpretation of a rule, the dispute shall be put to the committee for a ruling thereon. What the rule cannot go on to say is that the committee's decision is final with no recourse to the courts because this ouster of the court's jurisdiction is contrary to public policy and void.[109]

8. ALTERATION OF THE RULES

2.44 **Unincorporated members' clubs** It is of cardinal importance that the rules contain an express provision whereby the members are empowered to alter the club's rules (and bye-laws) by way of amendment, addition or revocation because when a member joins the club he does so on the terms of a contract set out in the rules at that point in time and such a contract cannot be subsequently varied without the consent of *all* the members.[110] No power to alter the rules will be implied into the contract. In *Harington v Sendall*[111] a member of the Oxford and Cambridge University Club, an unincorporated members' club, agreed to be bound by 'the following rules and regulations'. The club wished to raise its subscription rule from 8 guineas to 9 guineas and Mr Harington as a member objected. The court rejected the club's argument that as a social club it could not carry on at all unless there was an implied power to alter the rules as the necessities of the club might demand. The court also rejected the club's argument that Mr Harington had acquiesced in the rule change because he had never objected to other rule changes in the past. The case provides several object lessons: first, by a slight alteration in the language of the rules Mr Harington would have been bound by amendments of the rules, for example, the rules could easily have said that the member was bound by 'the rules and regulations as may be made from time to time'. Secondly, it is unwise to stipulate the amount of the subscription in the rule itself instead of adopting some general phrase, for example, 'such amount as may be determined by the members in a general meeting'. Thirdly, acquiescence may be difficult to prove.

2.45 On this last point, however, there may be occasions when acquiescence may be inferred from a lack of opposition or objection to the

---

109 *Lee v Showmen's Guild of Great Britain* [1952] 2 QB 329, CA, at 342 (Denning LJ); *Baker v Jones* [1954] 1 WLR 1005, at 1010. Such a rule would also offend against Article 6(1) of the European Convention on Human Rights (the Human Rights Act 1998 incorporated this convention into UK domestic law).

110 See *Dawkins v Antrobus* (1881) 17 Ch D 615, CA, at 621 (Jessel MR); *Harrington v Sendall* [1903] 1 Ch 921, at 927 (Joyce J); and *Re Tobacco Trade Benevolent Association* [1958] 3 All ER 353 where Harman J stated, at 355, 'This body [an unincorporated charity] started with no power to alter its rules, and such a body cannot alter its rules by its own motion except possibly by the concurrence of *every* member of the body' (emphasis added).

111 [1903] 1 Ch 921.

new rule. In *Abbatt v Treasury Solicitor*,[112] the unincorporated British Legion Club in 1954 affiliated to a different umbrella organisation, the Working Men's Club and Institute Union; changed its name to the Old Castle Club; adopted a new set of rules; registered under the Friendly Societies Act 1896; and conveyed its property to new trustees. In 1960 the club sold part of its land and the purchasers raised a query as to title. Here the Court of Appeal held on the facts that although the rules of the old club contained no express power to amend or alter them the members as a body had acquiesced in the rule changes, so that the new club was the same as the old one but 'dressed in different clothes'. In the course of his judgment at 1583 Lord Denning MR stated:

> 'It is true that the old rules contained no express power to amend or alter them. But I should have thought it was implied that the members could, on notice, by a simple majority in general meeting, amend or alter the rules. In any event, however, if at such a meeting a majority purport to amend or alter the rules, and the others take no objection to it, but instead by their conduct acquiesce in the change, then those rules become binding on all.'

It may be doubted, however, whether Lord Denning's first proposition as to the implied power of amendment accurately sets out the law in the light of clear authority contrary to this proposition.[113]

2.46 Since 1902[114] any club which supplies intoxicating liquor to its members or their guests has been required to register under the Licensing Acts, and in each case until the coming into operation in 2005 of the Licensing Act 2003 the club had to state the mode of altering its rules, so that the power to amend the rules is now a commonplace feature of club rules. There is no such requirement under the Licensing Act 2003; maybe the government thought that the provision of rules which included a power to amend was such an obvious fact of life for clubs that it no longer needed to spell it out expressly in the legislation. Nevertheless, if say an important constitutional change was required by a large majority of members, it would be a serious matter if there were no power of amendment contained in the rules and the club were unable to remedy the situation by unanimous consent or by acquiescence. This is because the ultimate remedy would be either to pass by the requisite majority a resolution to dissolve the club and distribute the assets or for the majority to resign en masse from the club in order to form a new one. This latter remedy will mean abandoning the existing club's assets to the minority of members who objected or abstained

---

112 [1969] 1 WLR 1575, CA.

113 See the cases cited in footnote 110 above. In the *Tobacco Trade* case, at 355 Mr Justice Harman in 1958 declined to infer acquiescence of a purported alteration which had taken place in 1871 and not objected to since that date.

114 See Licensing Act 1902, s 24.

on the vote to bring about the important constitutional change, and this abandonment might be an unacceptable solution to many members.

2.47 Retrospective amendment The question is sometimes asked whether the rules can be altered retrospectively. In *Dawkins v Antrobus*[115] Colonel Dawkins, a member of the Travellers Club, an unincorporated members' club, put a pamphlet about General Stephenson, another member of the club and a serving officer, in a wrapper endorsed on the outside 'Dishonourable conduct of Colonel (now Lieutenant-General) Stephenson' and sent it by post to his official address at the Horse Guards. For that conduct he was expelled from the club under an expulsion rule which existed at the time of the alleged misconduct but not when he had joined the club and the court held that Colonel Dawkins was bound by the inserted rule. Lord Justice Brett, at 632, commented that an expulsion rule could have no retrospective effect and this proposition is readily understandable both generally and in the context of that case. But whether all retrospective alterations are invalid is a different matter. We consider that in principle there is nothing objectionable in a retrospective rule provided that it is made by the members acting bona fide in the interests of the club as a whole. There is a presumption in statute law that legislation is not retrospective or retroactive, especially in relation to vested rights and obligations,[116] and a similar presumption should be made in club rules so that the occasions on which a retrospective rule would be appropriate are few and far between.[117]

2.48 Alteration to a fundamental rule The question arises whether a rule is so important or fundamental to the objects or nature of the club that it may not be subsequently altered without dissolving the club. The answer depends on the reaction of the members to such a rule change. There are three possible scenarios:

(1) all members agree to the change. There is no difficulty here as a new contract of membership will have been created;
(2) the dissenting member or members all resign.[118] This leaves the remaining membership free to operate under the rule change;
(3) the club may have to be dissolved. Suppose the Basset Dining Club was restricted to 25 male members whose raison d'être was the enjoyment of convivial small dinners with cigars and brandy. If there was a rule change whereby the membership was open to women or the membership limit was increased to 100, the only workable or fair solution might well be to dissolve the club.

---

115 (1881) 17 Ch D 615, CA.

116 See *Wilson v First County Trust (No 2)* [2003] 3 WLR 568, HL, especially the speech of Lord Rodger of Earlsferry at 618.

117 See the hypothetical example given in **2.25**.

118 As to the resigning member's unexpired subscription in this situation, see **4.34**.

2.49 The question which has to be addressed is what constitutes a fundamental rule. This is a question of fact in each case. So the example given in **2.48**(3) above might not in every circumstance amount to a change to a fundamental rule. Increasing the membership of the Basset Hockey Club from 25 to 100 or the enlargement of the membership to include women players as well as men players would be unlikely to be accepted by the court as a change to a *fundamental* rule since the essence of a hockey club would be the provision of playing facilities for an indeterminate number of players of either sex who wished to participate in the sport. In *Morgan v Driscoll*[119] the plaintiff was a priest who was a member of an unincorporated association known as the Secular Catholic Clergy Common Fund. Under its rules of 1861 an incapacitated member had an absolute right to an allowance from the fund. In 1918, under a rule permitting amendment, the association amended its rules to make the allowance discretionary. Mr Justice Sargent upheld the amendment as valid on the ground that it 'did not go to the foundation of the association and was not incompatible with the fundamental object of the association' which was to give financial aid to incapacitated clergymen. In *Doyle v White City Stadium*[120] Lord Hanworth MR concurred with this proposition and gave as an example of incompatibility an alteration of the rules whereby a society connected with boxing turned itself into a society for conducting horse-racing.

2.50 The next question which arises is whether a duly passed alteration to a fundamental rule actually binds those members who objected to it. The answer here is in the negative if it can be reasonably considered that the parties would not have contemplated any such alteration when the member joined the club. In *Hole v Garnsey*[121] the case concerned the liquidation of a society registered under the Industrial and Provident Societies Act 1893 and called the Wilts and Somerset Farmers Limited. The object of the society was to dispose of agricultural and dairy produce produced by its members. The rules contained a power of amendment (Rule 64) and a duly passed amendment required the members to take additional shares. The House of Lords held that the amended rule was not effective against members who had not assented to it. Lord Tomlin in his speech, at 500, stated:

> 'Does a power enabling a majority[122] to amend the rules justify as against a dissenting member any alteration whatever, where, as here, neither by the statute[123] nor by the rules themselves is any one rule expressed to be more fundamental and unalterable than any other?

---

119 (1922) 38 TLR 251.

120 [1935] 1 KB 110, CA, at 121.

121 [1930] AC 472.

122 In this instance a three-fourths majority.

123 In this instance the Industrial and Provident Societies Act 1893.

> The answer in my judgement must be in the negative. In construing such a power as this, it must, I think, be confined to such amendments as can be reasonably considered to have been within the contemplation of the parties when the contract was made, having regard to the nature and circumstances of the contract. I do not base this conclusion upon any narrow construction of the word 'amend' in Rule 64, but upon a broad general principle applicable to all such powers. If no such principle existed I see no reason why a dairy society in Wiltshire should not by the means of the exercise of [an amending] power find itself converted into a boot manufacturing society in Leicester with an obligation on the members to contribute funds to the new enterprise.'

2.51 But against this principle it should be remembered that, as Lord Sumner remarked at 491 in the case of *Hole v Garnsey*, the courts have gone far to support the autonomy of social clubs and their power to affect members by rules and regulations, passed regularly and in good faith. A striking example of this is the case of *Thellusson v Viscount Valentia*.[124] The Hurlingham Club was formed in 1868 with a power to amend the rules. The objects in Rule 2 read as follows: 'The club is instituted for the purpose of providing a ground for pigeon-shooting, polo, and other sports'. From inception pigeon-shooting was carried on at the club, prizes being given and competitions arranged by the committee. Polo and other sports had been carried on for a shorter period. The membership itself was divided into shooting and non-shooting members. In 1905 the majority of members duly passed a resolution discontinuing the sport of pigeon-shooting at the club, and a minority of members brought an action against the committee for a declaration that the resolution was null and void. The action failed because no particular sport was fundamental to the existence of the club, it being successfully argued by the club that its fundamental purpose was the association of its members for sporting activities.

2.52 But can a person remain a member of a club if he had in no way accepted a rule change which fundamentally altered the terms of his contract of membership? Let us take Lord Hanworth's example of a boxing club which by a duly passed amendment of the rules turned itself into a horse-racing society. Leaving aside the question of dissolution,[125] we consider that the answer lies in the member's election. He can either elect to resign or he can elect to remain a member.[126] If he chooses the latter course, he will have irrevocably acquiesced in the rule change, which will thus become binding on him. Payment of his next subscription would be conclusive evidence of his election to remain a member. What a member cannot do is to remain a member and simply assert that he was not bound by the alteration to the fundamental rule which he disagreed with.

---

124 [1907] 2 Ch 1, CA.

125 See **2.48**(3).

126 *Farnworth Finance Facilities v Attryde* [1970] 1 WLR 1053, CA, at 1059 (Lord Denning MR).

2.53 Once a rule has been validly amended or acquiesced in, it is binding on all the members, old and new, whether or not they voted against the amendment or took no part in the voting.[127] The fact that a duly passed alteration of the rules has not come to the member's attention or that he had received no actual notice of the alteration does not affect the validity of the rule.[128]

2.54 Amendment procedure It is good practice to state in the power to amend that any resolution to amend the rules shall either be the subject of a special meeting called specifically for that purpose or, if raised at the annual general meeting, notice in writing of the proposed resolution is to be given by the member at least 14 days prior to the holding of the AGM. It is to be noted that a rule which stipulates that an annual general meeting is to be held 'for general purposes' does not encompass a power to alter or amend the rules of the club.[129] It is also good practice to state in the power to amend that the resolution to amend the rules shall be carried by substantially more than a simple majority of the members present and entitled to vote at the meeting, say by a two-thirds majority.[130] If there is no such stipulation in the rules, it is considered that the resolution will be capable of being passed on a simple majority,[131] and this is perceived to be unsuitable because the rules should not be altered lightly and a substantial majority demonstrates that the amendment commands proper support in the club.

2.55 Working men's clubs, community clubs and shop clubs Clubs which are registered under one of the following three Acts are required by the relevant statute to make provision in their rules for the manner of 'making, altering or rescinding of rules', that is to say, in relation to working men's clubs the requirement is contained in para 4 of Sch 2 to the Friendly Societies Act 1974; in relation to community clubs it is contained in para 5 of Sch 1 to the Co-operative and Community Benefit Societies and Credit Unions Act 1965; and in relation to shop clubs it is contained in para iii of the Schedule to the Shop Clubs Act 1902. Under s 14(2) of the 1965 Act a member has to give his prior consent in writing if the rules are amended to require him to take or subscribe for further shares. No amendment of the above rules will be valid until it has been registered with the Financial

---

127 *Burke v Amalgamated Society of Dyers* [1906] 2 KB 583, at 591 (Lawrence LJ).

128 *Doyle v White City Stadium* [1935] 1 KB 110, CA, at 122 and 134. However, giving proper notice of the general meeting, at which the rule alteration is to be considered, is essential: see **6.8**.

129 *Harrington v Sendall* [1903] 1 Ch 921, at 926.

130 For example, s 4(2) of the Credit Unions Act 1979 stipulates that the rules of a credit union may not be amended except by a resolution passed by not less than two-thirds of the members present at a special meeting.

131 See further **6.41**.

Services Authority.[132] Any alteration of the rules, however, must be compatible with the declared objects of the club.

2.56 Literary and scientific institutions In clubs to which the Literary and Scientific Institutions Act 1854 applies[133] the members have a statutory right to alter, extend or abridge their rules in relation to the purpose or purposes for which the club was established[134] but if two-fifths of the members consider the alteration injurious to the club, they may apply within 3 months of the alteration being made to the Department of Trade and Industry which has power to conduct an inquiry and prevent the alteration if it considers it to be injurious to the club.[135] This statutory provision would appear to override any contrary provision contained in the club's rules.

2.57 Incorporated clubs The company has the ability to amend any of its articles of association at any time by special resolution[136] and the company cannot deprive itself of this power by a statement to this effect in the articles.[137] Any alteration of the articles must be compatible with the objects expressed in the memorandum or (since 1 October 2009) in the articles. Thus in *Re Cyclists' Touring Club*[138] the club was registered under s 23 of the Companies Act 1867 as an association not for profit and its object was to promote, assist and protect cyclists. A majority of the members resolved to change the name of the club to The Touring Club and to include among the persons to be assisted all tourists, including motorists. The court held that the proposed alteration was not possible since one of the stated objects of the club was to protect cyclists against motorists. Where a company amends its articles, it must give notice to the registrar of companies and no amendment will be effective until entry of that notice in the register.[139]

2.58 If, as is now usual, the club's rules are set out in a separate rulebook pursuant to the directors' exercise of their powers of management under the articles, a question might arise as to what would happen if the rulebook contained no power to alter the rules. It is submitted that the right answer would be for the directors of the company to authorise a new set of rules, this time making sure that the rules did contain an express power to alter the rules.

---

132 Friendly Societies Act 1974, s 18(1); Co-operative and Community Benefit Societies and Credit Unions Act 1965, s 10(1); and Co-operative and Community Benefit Societies and Credit Unions Act 1968, s 12(3).

133 See **1.53** for the categories of institution to which this Act applies.

134 Literary and Scientific Institutions Act 1854, s 27.

135 Ibid, s 28.

136 Companies Act 2006, s 21(1). For company resolutions, see **6.52**.

137 *Walker v London Tramways Co* (1879) 12 Ch D 705.

138 [1907] 1 Ch 269.

139 Companies Act 2006, s 31(2).

2.59 Entrenchment The old-style memorandum of association was the place where companies used to entrench those elements of their constitution which they did not wish to see altered.[140] Section 22 of the Companies Act 2006 has introduced a new entrenchment regime. Where the club is anxious to ensure, for instance, that its objects clause remains the same or that the club membership is eligible only to a category of defined persons, it can take advantage of this regime. The objects clause and members' eligibility will now appear in the articles, and the articles (as hitherto) can normally be altered by a special resolution which requires a 75% majority. Entrenchment allows companies to impose a higher hurdle than a 75% majority and/or to impose specific conditions before any entrenched provision is altered. Section 22(2), however, provides that entrenchment can only be introduced in one of two ways: on formation of the company or by unanimous agreement of the members. It was contemplated that the entrenchment provisions would come into force on 1 October 2009 but because concerns were raised that they might have unforeseen adverse consequences on certain members' rights the entrenchment provisions have been put on hold until further notice.[141]

2.60 Proprietary clubs If a proprietor is running a members' club, it is wise for him to insert in the club's rules a power to amend the rules because this avoids any argument as to precisely what powers of amendment the club and he respectively have at their disposal. The scope of the amending rule depends on the level of control he has chosen to exercise over the club. Many proprietors retain the sole right to amend the rules. A proprietor is entitled to and usually does offer membership on an annual basis so that on renewal he has the opportunity of amending the rules more to his liking since any contract he makes will be with each individual member, who is free to choose whether to accept or reject the offer of a new contract. We consider, however, that the proprietor could not have different rules for members of the same class since this would not be consistent with the fourth criterion (the need for fair rules) and the sixth criterion (the need for collegiality) referred to in **1.1**.

---

[140] Companies Act 1985, ss 4–6.

[141] See Companies Act 2006 and Limited Liability Partnerships (Transitional Provisions and Savings) (Amendment) Regulations 2009, SI 2009/2476, reg 2(1)–(2).

Chapter 3

DISSOLUTION OF THE CLUB

1. INTRODUCTION

3.1 It is a matter of concern that many clubs do not have adequate rules when it comes to dissolution of the club; especially is this so in unincorporated members' clubs. One does not need to look far for the reason, however. The rules are drafted at the beginning of the club's life when dissolution is not on the agenda. Nobody has thoughts of dissolution and the topic is often dismissed as irrelevant. But the fact of the matter is that proper provision in the rules dealing with dissolution is both practical and sensible and will avoid a potentially acrimonious or disastrous end to the club's life.

3.2 At the outset the rule makers need to ask themselves not only what problems they might envisage on the forced demise of the club on the grounds, say, of lack of money or lack of members but what outcome they would desire if the club was dissolved when fully solvent and was in possession or ownership of valuable property or assets. Express rules dealing with the event of dissolution is a far better solution than letting the general law of the land provide the answer in the absence of express rules. For example, in the case of *Abbatt v Treasury Solicitor*,[1] already referred to in **2.45**, the trustees of the new club contracted in 1960 to sell part of the land 'inherited' from the old club in 1954 for the sum of £300. The purchaser raised a query as to title. Who owned this land? It had belonged to the members of the old club but that club no longer existed. Did the members of the new club own it? No, said the judge, it belonged to the members of the old club who were members at the date of dissolution in 1954. Yes, said the appeal court, overruling the judge. The case involved four separate parties, namely, the trustees of the new club, the trustees of the old club, a representative of the members of the old club and the treasury solicitor, and outings in three different courts.[2] One of the options open to the court was to hold that the Crown owned the land as bona vacantia (that is, goods that

---

1 [1969] 1 WLR 1575, CA.

2 Ie proceedings in the Andover County Court, the High Court of Justice and the Court of Appeal.

were otherwise ownerless),[3] so that no member either of the old club or the new club owned the land, this being a worst-case scenario. The case vividly demonstrates the need for a proper rule on dissolution in every set of club rules.[4]

2. MERGER OF CLUBS

3.3 Unincorporated members' clubs The merger or amalgamation of clubs is a mild form of dissolution in that the original clubs will cease to exist but are in fact given a further lease of life by the inception of the merged club, which would be a new entity whether it be unincorporated or incorporated. The difficulties which can arise here are not ones of principle but ones of practicality. It is recommended that the two clubs jointly draw up a document headed 'Merger Principles' which sets out the basis of the proposed merger. Then each club should simultaneously but separately hold a dissolution meeting at which it will be resolved (1) by the requisite majority (eg a simple majority of those present at the meeting) that the club shall forthwith merge with the other club and (2) by the requisite majority (eg two-thirds of the members entitled to vote) that, provided the other club passes an identical resolution to merge, the present club be dissolved on a date to be agreed by the committee of the merged club. It is important that the resolutions are taken in the order and in the form indicated in case the other club is unwilling or unable to pass the same resolutions. If both clubs pass the two resolutions as anticipated, the two dissolution meetings should immediately be followed by a joint meeting at which the motion will be put that the new merged club should forthwith be formed. If passed, the next item on the agenda will be the date for the inaugural meeting of the merged club in order to put in hand the election of officers and members of the committee.

3.4 It is obviously desirable that the rules of the merged club be placed before the joint meeting and a resolution passed that they be adopted but this may not be possible because of the need for discussion, or further discussion, as to the form they will take or the two sets of existing rules may still need reconciliation on certain points. This does not matter because in the meantime the two existing clubs will continue to exist until such time as the new rules are agreed by the members, at which point in time the new committee can decide to dissolve the old clubs. The date of this dissolution can be taken as the legal date of birth of the new club.

---

3 See the headnote at 1575; *In re Trusts of the Brighton Cycling and Angling Club* (1953) *The Times*, April 29, CA (the assets of a club which had ceased to exist were declared bona vacantia to which the Crown was entitled).

4 Another good example of the need for dissolution rules is the case of *In re Sick and Funeral Society of St John's Sunday School, Golcar* [1973] 1 Ch 51.

3.5 If the members of the merged club wish their new club to be a community club or an incorporated club, it is best for the two unincorporated members' clubs first to merge and then to put in hand the process of conversion.

3.6 Working men's clubs and community clubs By special resolution of each of them, a working men's club may amalgamate with another working men's club, with or without dissolution or division of the funds of the two clubs.[5] On amalgamation the property in each becomes vested in the trustees of the new club without conveyance or transfer.[6] Likewise, a community club may pass a special statutory resolution to amalgamate with another community club, with or without dissolution or division of the funds of the two clubs.[7] On amalgamation the property in each becomes vested in the new club without the need for any conveyance other than that contained in the special resolution.[8] It would seem that on amalgamation of either type of club the Financial Services Authority will cancel the registrations of the two former clubs and the new club will be registered in their place.

3.7 Incorporated clubs The court has power to facilitate the amalgamation of companies under s 900 of the Companies Act 2006.[9] If the two incorporated clubs wish to establish a new incorporated club, the court may make provision for the dissolution of the existing clubs without winding them up[10] and may make provision for such other incidental, consequential and supplemental matters as are necessary to secure that the amalgamation is fully and effectively carried out.[11] Each of the existing clubs must deliver a copy of any relevant court order to the registrar of companies within 7 days of its being made.[12] On registration of the new company the registrar will issue a certificate of incorporation.[13]

3.8 Literary and scientific institutions An institution (not having a royal charter nor established nor acting under an Act of Parliament) may amalgamate, wholly or partly, with any other like institution provided that three-fifths of the members present at a special meeting have agreed to the proposition to amalgamate.[14]

---

5 Friendly Societies Act 1974, s 82(1). Amalgamation is to be distinguished from transfer of engagements: see **3.13**(1).

6 Friendly Societies Act 1974, ss 54(1) and 58.

7 Co-operative and Community Benefit Societies and Credit Unions Act 1965, s 50(1). Amalgamation is to be distinguished from transfer of engagements: see **3.14**(2).

8 Ibid, s 50(1).

9 Amalgamation is to be distinguished from transfer of the whole undertaking: see **3.17**(2).

10 Companies Act 2006, s 900(2)(d).

11 Ibid, s 900(2)(f).

12 Ibid, s 900(6).

13 Ibid, s 15(1).

14 Literary and Scientific Institutions Act 1854, s 27: see Appendix 1.

3. DISSOLUTION OF MEMBERS' CLUBS

3.9 Unincorporated members' clubs In the ordinary way the members of the club will need to pass a resolution to dissolve the club. It is common to stipulate in the rules that a resolution to dissolve the club may be passed, and only passed, at a general meeting specially convened to consider the resolution to dissolve and that a two-thirds or three-fourths majority of those present at the meeting and entitled to vote will be required before the resolution is carried. It is also usual practice to require a specified number of members to sign the requisition for this special meeting, and sometimes this is put at a higher figure than required for a requisition to consider business other than the dissolution of the club. If the club held a registration certificate under the Licensing Act 1964, the rules were required to fix a number of requisitionists which did not exceed 30 nor more than one-fifth of the total number of members entitled to attend and vote at a general meeting (whichever was the less).[15] There is no such rule requirement under the Licensing Act 2003.

3.10 The case of *In Re William Denby & Sons Ltd Sick and Benevolent Fund*[16] concerned an unregistered friendly society but what was said in that case would equally apply to an unincorporated members' club. Mr Justice Brightman said, at 978, that there were four situations where such a society could be treated as dissolved so as to render the unspent assets distributable in some direction:[17]

(1) the occurrence of an event upon the happening of which the rules prescribe dissolution;[18]
(2) where all the members, or the requisite majority, agree on dissolution;
(3) where the court orders dissolution in the exercise of its inherent jurisdiction;[19]
(4) where the substratum upon which the society was founded has gone.[20]

---

15 Licensing Act 1964, Sch 7, para 2(3).

16 [1971] 1 WLR 973.

17 It was pointed out by Lewison J in *Boyle v Collins* [2004] 2 BCLC 471 at [27] that 'Although it is convenient shorthand to speak of "the dissolution of a club" (or a fund), it is strictly inaccurate, since there is nothing to dissolve. All that has happened is that the members are no longer precluded from claiming their entitlement. Perhaps that is why in the *Denby* case Brightman J said that a club was "treated as dissolved".' This dictum is controversial; we submit that Viscount Simmonds in *Leahy v Attorney General for New South Wales* [1959] AC 457 (see **1.8**) was right when he said that an unincorporated members' club was for many purposes a continuing entity separate from its members, even though this is an undoubted legal anomaly.

18 *In re Printers and Transferrers Amalgamated Trades Protection Society* [1899] 2 Ch 184.

19 *In re Lead Co's Workmen's Fund Society* [1904] 2 Ch 196; *Keys v Boulter (No. 2)* [1972] 1 WLR 642, at 644 (Megarry J); *Re Witney Town Football and Social Club* [1994] 2 BCLC 487, at 491. The court here means the High Court of Justice as the county courts, being created by statute, have no inherent jurisdiction.

20 *In re Customs & Excise Officers' Mutual Guarantee Fund* [1917] 2 Ch 18 (guarantee fund otiose

3.11 In the case of *In re GKN Bolts & Nuts Ltd Sports and Social Club*[21] (an unincorporated members' club) Megarry V-C, at 779, elaborated on the fourth situation:

> 'As a matter of principle I would hold that it is perfectly possible for a club to be dissolved spontaneously ... Mere, or even a long period of, inactivity on the part of the members of the club does not mean that the club is defunct or dissolved. But inactivity coupled with other circumstances may demonstrate that all concerned regard the club as having ceased to have any purpose or function, and so no longer existing. Short inactivity coupled with strong circumstances or long inactivity coupled with weaker circumstances may equally suffice to draw the inference of non-existence. In all cases the question is whether, putting all the facts together, they carry sufficient conviction that the club is at an end and not merely dormant.'

By way of example it is worth setting out why in that case the Vice Chancellor, at 781, came to the conclusion that the club had become dissolved:

> 'On that date [18 December 1975] the position was that the club had ceased to operate as a club for several months. The picture was not one of mere activity alone; there were positive acts towards the winding up of the club. The sale of the club's stock of drinks was one instance, and others were the ending of the registration for VAT, and the dismissal of the steward. The cessation of any club activities, the ending of the use of the sports ground and the abandonment of preparing accounts or issuing membership cards were all in one sense examples of inactivity; but I think that there was in all probability some element of deliberation in these matters, and not a mere inertia ... However, the resolution to sell the sports ground [the club's last asset[22]] seems to me to conclude the matter.'

3.12 It is to be noted that the courts have no statutory jurisdiction under company or insolvency legislation to wind up an unincorporated members' club which is a social club[23] or probably any other type of unincorporated members' club:[24] see further **3.29**.

---

because officers' fidelity bonds no longer required); *Feeney and Shannon v MacManus* [1937] IR 23 (dining club's premises destroyed in the Irish uprising of 1916); *In re St Andrew's Allotment Association* [1969] 1 WLR 229 (sale of the land containing the allotments) cf *Re Stamford Working Men's Club* (1952) *The Times*, October 24 and (1953) *The Times*, April 29, CA.

21 [1982] 1 WLR 774.

22 So described by the judge himself.

23 *In re St James's Club* (1852) De GM & G 383, at 389; 6 Halsbury's Laws of England, (4th edn) at p 256.

24 *In re International Tin Council* [1989] 1 Ch 309, CA, at 330.

3.13 Working men's clubs The dissolution of this type of club may be carried out in the following ways:

(1) under s 82 of the Friendly Societies Act 1974, by the transfer of all the club's engagements to another club registered under the 1974 Act[25] or to a company under the Companies Act[26] or to an industrial and provident society.[27] In this event the registration of the club becomes void and must be cancelled by the Financial Services Authority;[28]
(2) under s 86 of the 1974 Act, by an instrument of dissolution approved by a special resolution of the club,[29] that is to say, by not less than three-quarters of the members entitled to vote at the meeting;[30]
(3) under s 87 of the 1974 Act,[31] by an order of the court on a petition for a compulsory winding up presented by the Financial Services Authority where it receives a report on the affairs of the club from an inspector by the Authority and it appears to the Authority that it is in the interests of the members of the club or of the public that the club should be wound up;
(4) under s 91 of the 1974 Act,[32] by the cancellation of the club's registration by the Financial Services Authority on the various grounds set out in this section, the most important of which are, in relation to clubs, where the club has wilfully and after notice from the Authority violated any of the provisions of the 1974 Act and where the club has ceased to exist;[33]
(5) under s 93 of the 1974 Act, upon the happening of any event declared by the rules to be the determination of the club (or branch);[34]
(6) under s 95A of the 1974 Act,[35] by an award of dissolution made by the Financial Services Authority after its investigation of the affairs of the club;[36]
(7) if unregistered, by order of the court under the court's inherent jurisdiction.[37]

---

25 Friendly Societies Act 1974, s 82(2) as amended by Friendly Societies Act 1992, Sch 16, para 29.
26 Ibid, s 82(3) as amended by the said para 29.
27 Ibid, s 82(3) as amended by the said para 29.
28 Ibid, s 82(5) as amended by the Friendly Societies Act 1992, Sch 22, Part 1.
29 Ibid, s 93(1)(b).
30 Ibid, s 86(1)(b).
31 As substituted by the Friendly Societies Act 1992, Sch 16, para 34.
32 Friendly Societies Act 1974, s 91(1) as amended by the Friendly Societies Act 1992, Sch 16, para 37.
33 As to whether a club has ceased to exist, see **3.11**.
34 Ibid, s 93(1)(a).
35 Inserted by Friendly Societies Act 1992, Sch 16, para 39.
36 Friendly Societies Act 1974, s 93(1)(c) as amended by Friendly Societies Act 1992, Sch 16, para 38.
37 *In re Lead Co's Workmen's Fund Society* [1904] 2 Ch 196; *Re William Denby & Sons Ltd Sick and Benevolent Fund* [1971] 1 WLR 973.

3.14 Community clubs The dissolution of this type of club may be carried out in the following ways:

(1) under s 16 of the Co-operative and Community Benefit Societies and Credit Unions Act 1965,[38] by the cancellation of the club's registration by the Financial Services Authority on the various grounds set out in this section, the most important of which are, in relation to clubs, where the membership has been reduced to fewer than three members and where the club has ceased to exist;[39]
(2) under s 51 of the 1965 Act, by the transfer of all the club's engagements to another club registered under the 1965 Act.[40] This transfer will result in the cancellation of the registration of the transferor club;
(3) under s 55(a) of the 1965 Act,[41] by being wound up in the same manner as a company registered under the Companies Acts: see **3.17**(1), **3.18** and **3.19**. It is considered, by analogy with company law, that a creditor or member of the club can also petition for the winding up of the club;[42]
(4) under s 55(b) of the 1965 Act, by the consent of not less than three-fourths of the members of the club testified by their signatures to the instrument of dissolution;[43]
(5) under s 56 of the 1965 Act,[44] by an order of the court on a petition presented by the Financial Services Authority on the ground that the club was registered before 26 July 1938 and that it appears the club is not a bona fide co-operative society and/or is not being conducted for the benefit of the community, and that it would be in the interests of investors or depositors or any other person that the club should be wound up.

3.15 Shop clubs By para xi of the Schedule to the Shop Clubs Act 1902 the rules of a shop club must contain a dissolution rule which states that there

---

38 As amended by Financial Services and Markets Act 2001 (Mutual Societies) Order 2001, SI 2001/2617, art 13 and Deregulation (Industrial and Provident Societies) Order 1996, SI 1996/1738, art 3(2).

39 As to whether a club has ceased to exist, see **3.10**.

40 In *Co-operative Group (CWS) Ltd v Stansell Ltd* [2006] 1 WLR 1704 the Court of Appeal held that a transfer of engagements transferred not only obligations and liabilities to third parties, as well as to members, without the need for novation (which would normally require the consent of such third parties) but also contractual rights and property, again without any need for third party consent.

41 As amended by the Insolvency Act 1986, Sch 14 and by the above-mentioned art 13. Special provisions apply to registered housing associations: see 50 Halsbury's Laws of England (5th edn, 2008) at para 2566, note 7.

42 See *In re Surrey Garden Village Trust Ltd* [1965] 1 WLR 974 (where certain members unsuccessfully petitioned for the winding up of an industrial and provident society; the petition was dismissed, not on the ground that the members had no standing to bring the petition, but on the ground that the petition was opposed by a considerable number of other members and was oppressive and an abuse of process).

43 The instrument has to comply with the provisions of s 58 of the 1965 Act.

44 As amended by Financial Services and Markets Act 2001 (Mutual Societies) Order 2001, art 13.

can be a voluntary dissolution of the club by consent of not less than five-sixths in value of the persons contributing to the funds of the club[45] and of every person for the time being entitled to benefit from the funds of the club (unless their claims be first satisfied or adequately provided for). Otherwise what is said about unincorporated members' clubs applies to these clubs.

3.16 Literary and scientific institutions The dissolution of a club to which the Literary and Scientific Institutions Act 1854 applies is governed by s 29 of that Act and is carried out by a resolution passed by three-fifths of its membership. Otherwise what is said about unincorporated members' clubs applies to these institutions, if they come within this category. In the event of any dispute on dissolution concerning the adjustment of its affairs, the matter must be referred to the local county court for the dispute to be resolved.

3.17 Incorporated clubs The dissolution of this type of club may be carried out in the following ways:

(1) by winding up the company.[46] A winding up is either voluntary or compulsory. In both compulsory and voluntary liquidation, dissolution of the company occurs automatically 3 months after the registration by the registrar of companies of the liquidator's final return at Companies House;[47]
(2) where the court makes an order sanctioning an arrangement whereby the whole undertaking of one company is transferred to another company[48] and the court orders the dissolution of the transferor company without winding up;[49]
(3) by the registrar of companies taking steps to dissolve a company which in his reasonable opinion is neither carrying on business nor in operation.[50] This process will entail the registrar ultimately publishing a notice in the London Gazette that at the expiration of 3 months the company's name will be struck off the register unless cause is shown to the contrary and that the company will be dissolved.[51] At the expiration of this period the registrar may strike the company's name

45 This would include the employer as contributor.
46 Insolvency Act 1986, s 73. On winding up a liquidator is appointed and the company will be in liquidation. It will be still in existence but unable to carry on any activity.
47 Ibid, s 201(1)–(2) for voluntary winding up and ibid, s 205(1)–(2) for compulsory winding up. Dissolving the company means removing its name from the Register of Companies with the result that the company will cease to be a legal person.
48 Companies Act 2006, s 900(2)(a).
49 Ibid, s 900(2)(d).
50 Ibid, s 1000(1).
51 Ibid, s 1000(3).

off the register,[52] and must then publish this fact in the London Gazette.[53] This dissolution does not depend on insolvency;

(4) by the directors, or a majority of them, applying to dissolve the company.[54] The directors apply on a prescribed form to strike the company's name from the register, and the registrar of companies will publish a notice in the London Gazette of his intention to strike the company's name from the register at the expiration of 3 months after the date of the notice, and inviting any person to show cause why this should not be done.[55] The registrar must publish a notice in the London Gazette that the company's name has been struck off,[56] and on publication the company will be dissolved.[57] This dissolution does not depend on insolvency.

3.18 Voluntary winding up There are two species of voluntary winding up, namely, members' voluntary and creditors' voluntary. In either case the members in general meeting must pass a resolution for voluntary winding up.[58] A members' voluntary winding up can only occur if the club is solvent, and this involves the directors making a statutory declaration of solvency that they have made a full enquiry into the company's affairs and have formed the opinion that the company will be able to pay its debts in full together with interest.[59] A creditors' voluntary winding up comes about because the directors are unable to make the declaration of solvency.[60]

3.19 Compulsory winding up The court has jurisdiction to wind up a company compulsorily on the seven grounds set out in s 122 of the Insolvency Act 1986 but the two grounds which are most likely to affect a club are:

(1) the company is unable to pay its debts;[61]
(2) the court is of the opinion that it is just and equitable that the company should be wound up.[62]

---

52 Companies Act 2006, s 1000(4).
53 Ibid, s 1000(5).
54 Ibid, s 1003 (1)-(2).
55 Ibid, s 1003(3).
56 Ibid, s 1003(4).
57 Ibid, s 1003(5).
58 Insolvency Act 1986, s 85(1).
59 Ibid, s 89(1).
60 Ibid, s 90.
61 Ibid, s 122(1)(f). The definition of inability to pay debts is set out in ibid, s 123: either the club cannot pay its debts as they fall due (the cash flow test) or the value of the club's assets is less than its liabilities, including contingent and prospective liabilities (the balance sheet test).
62 Ibid, s 122(1)(g).

An application for a compulsory winding-up order is by a petition presented to the court by the company or its directors or by a creditor or, in more limited circumstances, by a contributory (a member of the company).[63]

4. DISSOLUTION OF PROPRIETARY CLUBS

3.20 It is not strictly necessary for the rules of a proprietary club to deal with the question of dissolution of the club because of the nature of the contractual relationship between the proprietor and the club member. On the expiry of the period of the subscription, which no doubt will be the same date for all the members, the proprietor can simply say that he has decided to close down the club and the member will have no say in the matter. If he dissolves the club before the expiry of the period of the subscription, the individual member will have a claim in damages against the proprietor for the unexpired period of the subscription and for the loss of amenities during this period,[64] unless the rules expressly cater for this contingency. On the other hand, it is considered good practice for a proprietor to state in the club rules the situation as to dissolution of the club since this avoids argument if or when dissolution occurs.

5. MEMBERS' LIABILITY ON DISSOLUTION

3.21 Unincorporated members' clubs The members' liability, unless the rules otherwise provide, will be limited to the payment of their entrance fee (if any) and to their subscriptions.[65] As far as contracts entered into by the club are concerned, the residual liability of a committee member may well exceed his entrance fee and subscriptions.[66]

3.22 Working men's clubs Although the Friendly Societies Act 1974 is silent on the point,[67] it is considered that on dissolution the member's liability will be restricted to their subscriptions.[68] It is to be noted, however, that under s 87(3)[69] of the said Act the Financial Services Authority can direct the members or officers of the club to pay some or all of the expenses of the inspector's report referred to in **3.12**(3). As far as contracts entered

---

63 Insolvency Act 1986, s 124.

64 *Re Curzon Syndicate Ltd* (1920) 149 LT Jo 232. See **4.33** for a further discussion of this case.

65 *Wise v Perpetual Trustee Co* [1903] AC 139, PC at 149: see **1.10**.

66 See further **12.4**.

67 Unlike the Friendly Societies Act 1992 which limits the member's liability of an incorporated society to his subscriptions: Sch 3, para 8(1).

68 50 *Halsbury's Laws of England* (5th edn, 2008), at para 2167.

69 As substituted by Friendly Societies Act 1992, Sch 16, para 34.

into by the club are concerned, the residual liability of a committee member may well exceed their subscriptions.[70]

3.23 Community clubs If the club is wound up in pursuance of an order of the court or a members' resolution under the Insolvency Act 1986, the liability of a past or present member to contribute to the payment of the club's debts and liabilities or the expenses of winding up is as follows:

(1) no person who ceased to be a member not less than one year before the beginning of the winding up is liable to contribute anything;[71]
(2) no person is liable to contribute anything in respect of a debt or liability contracted after they ceased to be a member;[72]
(3) a non-member (ie a past member) is not liable to contribute anything unless it appears to the court that the contributions of the existing members are insufficient to satisfy the just demands on the club;[73]
(4) no contribution shall be required from any person exceeding the amount (if any) unpaid on shares in respect of which they are liable as a past or present member;[74]
(5) where withdrawable shares have been withdrawn, a person is taken to have ceased to be a member in respect of those shares as from the date of the notice or application for withdrawal.[75]

3.24 Shop clubs The schedule to the Act of 1902 is silent on this point and we consider that, unless the rules otherwise provide, the liability of members will be limited to their contribution to the funds of the club and, generally speaking, the members will be in the same position as a member of an unincorporated members' club.

3.25 Incorporated clubs The constitution of the company, whether limited by guarantee or by shares, must state that the liability of its members is limited.[76] Creditors therefore know that they cannot look to the whole property of the individual members to pay them but are restricted to the property of the company.[77] Section 74 of the Insolvency Act 1986 regulates the member's liability on the winding up of the company. Under this regime the members are obliged to 'contribute' to the company's assets, hence these members are known as contributories.

---

70 50 *Halsbury's Laws of England*, op cit, at para 2167. See further **12.4**.

71 Co-operative and Community Benefit Societies and Credit Unions Act 1965, s 57(a). On the other hand, the liability of a member does not cease on his death so that his estate will take over his liability: *In re United Service Share Purchase Society Ltd* [1909] 2 Ch 526.

72 Ibid, s 57(b).

73 Ibid, s 57(c).

74 Ibid, s 57(d).

75 Ibid, s 57(e).

76 Companies Act 2006, s 3.

77 *Gore-Browne on Companies* (45th edn, 2010), at 7[1].

3.26 Where the company is limited by guarantee, the member's liability is limited to such amount as the member undertakes to contribute to the assets of the company in the event of its being wound up.[78] The statement of guarantee[79] must state that each member undertakes that, if the company is wound up while they are a member or within one year after they cease to be a member, he will contribute as follows: (a) payment of the company's debts and liabilities contracted before they ceased to be a member, (b) payment of the costs, charges and expenses of the winding up, and (c) adjustment of the rights of the contributories among themselves.[80] The amount of the guarantee must be set forth in the company's constitution.[81] Past guarantors are only liable if the current guarantees do not meet the company's debts.[82]

3.27 Where the company is limited by shares, the constitution must state that the member's liability is limited to the amount, if any, unpaid on the shares held by them.[83] The maximum liability of present and past members is limited to the amount unpaid on the shares.[84]

3.28 Proprietary clubs The proprietor is solely responsible for the club's debts. The member of the club will have no liability to the club's creditors unless by a quite separate contract made between the member and the creditor he or she expressly assumes liability, for instance, by giving a guarantee in respect of the club's indebtedness to the club's bankers.

6. IMPACT OF INSOLVENCY LEGISLATION

3.29 Unincorporated members' clubs The Insolvency Act 1986 raises issues in relation to the affairs of an unincorporated members' club which need to be addressed. Sections 220 and 221 of the Insolvency Act 1986 empower the court to wind up compulsorily an 'unregistered company' which includes 'any association'. Under this regime the association can only be wound up if it is dissolved or has ceased to carry on business, or is unable to pay its debts, or the court is of the opinion that it would be just and equitable to wind up the association.[85] The question arises whether an unincorporated members' club is caught by these provisions. If it is, s 226 makes any contributory (ie the club member) liable to pay or contribute to the payment of any debt or liability of the club, the very antithesis of limited

78 Companies Act 2006, s 3(3). See Article 2 of 2008 Model Articles.
79 Now contained in the new-style memorandum of association: Companies Act 2006, s 11(2).
80 Ibid, s 11(3).
81 Ibid, s 11(3). The said Article 2 specifies a guarantee of £1.
82 Insolvency Act 1986, s 74(2)(a)–(c).
83 Companies Act 2006, s 3(2). See the said Article 2.
84 Insolvency Act 1986, s 74(2)(d).
85 Ibid, s 221(5).

liability and of course way beyond the member's entrance fee and annual subscriptions. Under previous but similar legislation the courts have held that an unincorporated members' club cannot be wound up as an unregistered company because the reference to the 'principal place of business'[86] of the unregistered company demonstrated that the winding-up regime had no applicability to any association which was not engaged in trade or commerce and which was not conducted for gain.[87]

3.30 An attempt by the creditors was made in *Re Witney Town Football and Social Club*[88] to wind up the club under s 221 on the ground that it was unable to pay its debts. This was a club of professional footballers founded in 1885 and it owned property of considerable value. It owed debts of about £30,000 to five creditors. Rule 2 of its rules stated: 'The club shall exist solely for the purpose of professional Association Football. The club will also provide various social amenities for its members'. The members numbered some 500 whose liability under the rules was restricted to their subscriptions. Rule 17 of its rules stated that 'upon dissolution of the club, all net assets shall be devoted to Association Football and not distributed between the members'. On appeal from the dismissal of the winding up petition, Mr Justice Morritt held that whether or not a club was 'an association' within the meaning of s 220 depended on the true construction of the rules rather than the size and activity of the club.[89] He decided that its rules were within the category of a normal club and as such the club was outside the statutory winding up provisions. The judge added, at 491, the comment that the club could still be wound up by the High Court under its inherent jurisdiction. This is of course quite a different matter from being wound up under the provisions of the Insolvency Act 1986 where a liquidator would be appointed, one of whose duties would be to receive proofs of debt from unsecured creditors.

3.31 **Working men's clubs and shop clubs** Their position is the same as an unincorporated members' club.

3.32 **Community clubs** It would seem by the insertion[90] of the reference to the Insolvency Act 1986 in s 55(a) of the Co-operative and Community Benefit Societies and Credit Unions Act 1965 that the legislature was contemplating that if the club was wound up under s 55 it would be subject

---

86 Now to be found in Insolvency Act 1986, s 221(3).

87 *Re St James Club* (1852) 2 De GM & G 383; *Re Bristol Athenaeum* (1890) 43 Ch D 236; *Re Russell Institution* [1898] 2 Ch 72, at 79. It is true that for landlord and tenant purposes the club does carry on a business (*Addiscombe Garden Estates v Crabbe* [1958] 1 QB 513, CA; *Coles v Samuel Smith Old Brewery (Tadcaster)* [2007] EWCA Civ 1461) but that is not the same thing as being engaged in trade or commerce which would be contrary to the second criterion referred to in **1.1**.

88 [1994] 2 BCLC 487.

89 So that the fact the club members were *professional* footballers was of no consequence.

90 See Insolvency Act 1986, Sch 14.

to the statutory insolvency regime, subject to the modification that any reference to the registrar of companies in the Insolvency Act 1986 shall now mean the Financial Services Authority.[91] However, since community clubs do not have directors, but officers only, it is plain that those parts of the Insolvency Act 1986 dealing with the liability of directors cannot apply to community clubs. It is to be noted, however, that the misfeasance and the fraudulent trading (but not the wrongful trading) referred to in **3.34** can be committed by an officer of the 'company' (ie the club) or by a person taking part in the management of the 'company'. This potential liability would thus not affect the ordinary club member.

3.33 Disqualification of officers and committee members Section 3 of the Co-operative and Community Benefit Societies and Credit Unions Act 2010 has enacted that the provisions relating to the disqualification of directors shall now apply to the officers and committee members of a club registered under the 1965 Act:[92] see **3.35**.

3.34 Incorporated clubs Leaving aside the limited liability of the members of the company (ie the ordinary members of the club), which is dealt with at **3.25**, members who are directors should be aware of the four situations where the director may become personally liable for the debts of the company or to contribute to the company's assets in the event of a winding up of the company. They are: (a) being made liable for misfeasance or breach of fiduciary or other duty;[93] (b) being made liable for fraudulent trading;[94] (c) being made liable for wrongful trading;[95] or (d) acting whilst disqualified as a director.[96] Liability for wrongful trading only arises in the context of an insolvent winding up.[97]

3.35 Disqualification of directors There is also the question of disqualifying a director under s 6 of the Company Directors Disqualification Act 1986 if in an insolvent liquidation he is found to be 'unfit' to be a director. Unfitness here can mean incompetence if (a) the director caused the company to trade whilst insolvent *and* (b) there was no reasonable

91 Co-operative and Community Benefit Societies and Credit Unions 1965, s 55(a)(i), amended by the Financial Services and Markets Act 2000 (Mutual Societies) Order 2001. (In fact the Insolvency Act 1986 makes no reference to the registrar of companies and Parliament must have overlooked this fact when substituting the Insolvency Act 1986 for the Companies Act 1948 in s 55(a)).

92 Achieved by inserting s 22E into the Company Directors Disqualification Act 1986, which procedure is subject to the modifications set out in s 3(4) of the 2010 Act.

93 Insolvency Act 1986, s 212.

94 Ibid, s 213.

95 Ibid, s 214.

96 Company Directors Disqualification Act 1986, s 15.

97 Insolvency Act 1986, s 214(2).

prospect of meeting creditors' claims.[98] Although in clubs a miscreant director and others who are caught by these provisions will be a shareholder or member of the company, it is their management, or lack of it, which gives rise to liability, not their membership of the company. Thus the ordinary club member will fall outside the ambit of these provisions.

3.36 Administration order There should also be mentioned the possibility of an administration order being made in respect of a company under the Insolvency Act 1986. The statutory objectives of administration are (a) rescuing the company as a going concern, or (b) achieving a better result for the company's creditors than would be likely if the company were wound up without first being in administration, or (c) realising property to make a distribution to one or more secured or preferential creditors.[99] Objective (a) must be given priority.[100] An application to the court for an administration order may be made by the company itself[101] or by the directors[102] or by one or more creditors of the company.[103] Alternatively, the company or the directors or a creditor holding a floating charge over the whole or substantially the whole of the company's property may appoint an administrator without court proceedings,[104] although such an appointment does not take effect until notice of the appointment is filed with the court.[105] Save in the case of a creditor exercising his floating charge,[106] the court cannot make an administration order without proof of the company's insolvency or the likelihood of its insolvency.[107] This administration process was devised in 1986 to help companies facing insolvency by giving them an opportunity to obtain an administration order with a view to entering into a voluntary arrangement with its creditors or, alternatively, to allow a more advantageous realisation of assets than would be effected on a winding up. It is therefore a half-way house on the road to liquidation.

3.37 Proprietary clubs If the proprietor is a company, the provisions of the Insolvency Act 1986, which are referred to in **3.34**, will apply to the directors of this company, not to the club's officers. The liquidator of the proprietor company, however, will be under a statutory duty to get in, realise and distribute the company's assets to the company's creditors,[108] so that the members of the club might find themselves with a new proprietor not to their liking, or with no club at all if the liquidator were to sell the club

---

98 *Secretary of State for Trade and Industry v Creegan* [2002] 1 BCLC 99, CA. In other words, merely trading insolvently is not enough on its own.

99 Insolvency Act 1986, Sch B1, para 3(1).

100 Ibid, Sch B1, para 3(3).

101 Ibid, Sch B1, para 12(1)(a).

102 Ibid, Sch B1, para 12(1)(b).

103 Ibid, Sch B1, para 12(1)(c).

104 Ibid, Sch B1, paras 14 and 22.

105 Ibid, Sch B1, paras 18, 19, 29 and 31.

106 Ibid, Sch B1, para 35.

107 Ibid, Sch B1, para 11(a).

108 Ibid, s 143(1).

premises with vacant possession. Any claim for damages against the company in respect of the unexpired portion of the subscription period will form the subject matter of a proof of debt lodged by the member as an unsecured creditor.[109]

3.38 If the proprietor is an individual person and he become bankrupt, his assets will, generally speaking, automatically vest in his trustee in bankruptcy[110] who, like the liquidator, will take steps to realise any asset for the benefit of the bankrupt's creditors,[111] with the same possible results as are mentioned in 3.37.

---

109 See *Re Curzon Syndicate Ltd* (1920) 140 LT Jo 232.

110 Insolvency Act 1986, s 306.

111 Ibid, s 324(1).

Part 2:

INTERNAL RELATIONSHIPS: THE CLUB AND ITS MEMBERS

Chapter 4

ADMISSION INTO THE CLUB

1. FORMAL PROCESS

4.1 A formal process of admitting members into a club is what distinguishes a club from an amorphous group of people who happen to come together for a particular occasion or event. The occasion or event may recur many times with the same people coming together but their gathering can in no wise be described as a club.[1] This formal process could in theory be very simple. The club rules could provide that the club was open to all those who supported its objects and that upon the payment of a specified sum the applicant for admission would be admitted into the club, for example, in *Woodford v Smith*[2] the printed application form was entitled 'Membership Form' and stated, 'I consent to my name being included in the list of members of the Fulham and Hammersmith Ratepayers' and Residents' Association, and I undertake to pay an annual subscription of £[x]'.

2. SELECTION PROCESS

4.2 In practice a club, of whatever nature, will want to ensure as far as possible that its members are congenial to one another so that a process of selection is introduced. A simple form of selection is to lay down that admission is by invitation only. And one commonly talks about the *election* of members to a club rather than admission of members. This ability to reject those persons who are, or apparently are, unsuitable or unacceptable to join a club has been an important factor in sustaining clubs over a long period of time. And, as a general proposition, a person cannot complain if he or she is refused membership of a club.[3] Different considerations will apply if the refusal is seen as an unlawful restraint of trade[4] or if the club is a community amateur sports club.[5] The advent of the Equality Act 2010, too,

---

1 *Stafford Borough Council v Elkenford Ltd* [1977] 1 WLR 324, CA.

2 [1970] 1 WLR 806.

3 *Nagle v Fielden* [1966] 2 WLR 1027, CA, at 1032 (where Lord Denning said, 'If a man applies to join a social club and is black-balled, he has no cause of action: because the members have made no contract with him. They can do as they like').

4 *Nagle v Fielden* op cit (concerning the Jockey Club's refusal to admit into membership a professional horse trainer who was a woman).

5 See **1.63**.

has considerably altered the landscape on this topic in that it was enacted to ensure that people are not *unfairly* excluded from clubs which they would like or are eligible to join, but are unable to do so because of the discrimination being exercised against them.

4.3 It is the normal practice in the great majority of members' clubs for the ordinary members to be elected and, where the club held a registration certificate under the Licensing Act 1964, this was compulsory.[6] The Licensing Act 2003, perhaps more properly, reverts to the language of admission.[7] The process of election can be either done by the members in general meeting or, since that is often an unwieldy procedure, is more commonly done by the committee which itself has been elected by the members. Whichever way is chosen, the procedure should appear in the rules. There is nothing improper or unusual in a club placing a maximum number on its membership[8] or laying down criteria or qualifications which the candidate must fulfil for admission into the club.[9] It is usual for the club to require a candidate to be proposed and seconded by one or more members of the club but there is no requirement at law that this should be the case; the rules may permit the candidate simply to apply to the club secretary who will refer the matter to the committee or the members, as the case may be, for their decision.

4.4 It used to be very common for social clubs to adopt the practice of black-balling, that is to say, stipulating in the rules that one or two black balls in the ballot box would result in the automatic rejection of any application for membership (the white balls signifying acceptance of the application). Nowadays if such a practice is adopted it is done with slips of paper. But the principle remains the same. The practice, however, must be expressly embodied in the rules since it introduces a special voting procedure which will override the normal rules as to voting majority (as to which see **6.41**).

4.5 In a proprietary club it is common for the proprietor to make the decision whether to admit the applicant without there being any election by the members. Sometimes, however, the proprietor establishes a membership committee to deal with applications for membership, in which case he

---

6 Licensing Act 1964, Sch 7, para 3(1).

7 Licensing Act 2003, s 62(2).

8 For example, the Kennel Club limits its ordinary membership to 1,500 and the Roxburghe Club (see footnote 157 to **1.53**) limits its membership to 40. This limitation on numbers would apply to a community amateur sports club, even though required to be 'open to the whole community' (see **1.66**) provided, we surmise, the restriction was a reasonable one.

9 For example, the Roxburghe Club restricts its membership to those who possess distinguished libraries or book collections or those who have scholarly interests in books; and the Oxford and Cambridge Club in London restricts its membership to those who have defined connections with Oxford and Cambridge Universities.

might retain a power of veto in respect of any particular application or he might insist on some representation on the committee.[10]

3. CATEGORIES OF MEMBERSHIP

4.6 The majority of clubs have more than one category of member and it is important to clarify in the rules what are the rights and obligations of each category of member.

4.7 **Ordinary members** In every club this class of member will form the vast majority of the membership since it is these members who in the ordinary course of events pay the entrance fee (if any) and the annual subscription which keeps the club afloat financially. They are often referred to in the rules as full members.[11]

4.8 It is customary for ordinary members to be annual members in the sense that their subscription is renewable on a yearly basis, but there are occasions when ordinary membership is offered for a longer term than one year. If a club wished to raise a certain sum of cash straightaway, it could offer a 5-year membership whereby the member paid his 5 years' subscriptions forthwith at a discounted rate. There is no legal requirement that all categories of member shall pay the same subscription or for the same period of time.

4.9 On occasion disputes arise as to whether or not somebody is a member of a club.[12] This should not present any problem in practice. The member's application is normally done on a written form provided by the club or done by written communication from the club secretary. It is commonplace, however, for these documents to be lost or misplaced. This does not matter because the best evidence of continuing membership is the demand for, and the payment of, the annual subscription. With regard to a community club, it is required to keep at its registered office the names and addresses of all it members[13] and the member may (but not usually) be issued with a share certificate. If the club is a company limited by shares or by guarantee, it too is required to keep at its registered office the names and addresses of all its members[14] and, in the former case, the member will be issued with a share certificate (usually a £1 ordinary share). With regard to a proprietary club, the proprietor will be wise to issue a club membership card both on admission to the club and on renewal of the annual

---

10 See the example given in **1.49**.

11 See *In Re GKN Nuts & Bolts Ltd Sports and Social Club* [1982] 1 WLR 774, at 784.

12 See, e g *Woodford v Smith* [1970] 1 WLR 806.

13 Co-operative and Community Benefit Societies and Credit Unions Act 1965, s 44(1)(a).

14 Companies Act 2006, ss 113 and 114.

subscription. In *Boyle v Collins*[15] (concerning a community club) Mr Justice Lewison commented that it most cases it would be obvious to the committee whether or not a particular person was a member of a club.

4.10 Life members Life membership is, as its name indicates, for the member's lifetime. It is offered on the same financial basis as the 5-year membership referred to in **4.8**. The life member will pay his subscriptions all in one go, discounted for the fact that the club is receiving a large part of the money in advance of the dates it would otherwise have become due. Life members invariably enjoy the full privileges of membership, save that no further subscriptions will become due from the member. Some clubs have a category of *honorary* life members awarded in recognition of their long membership of the club or their outstanding services to the club,[16] where the member is excused from any further subscription but is still able to participate fully in the activities of the club.

4.11 Life membership does not render the member immune from being suspended or expelled from the club, though no doubt due consideration would be given to the fact of life membership in dealing with the matter. A life member, like all other members, is entitled to resign from the club. A life member who resigned or was expelled would not be entitled to claim back any proportionate part of his life membership fee because the whole sum was paid on an earlier date as the consideration for being granted life membership. Care must be taken in the drafting of the rule relating to the club's ability to offer life membership. No further annual subscription may be demanded, but it may be that the club would wish to reserve the right to require all members, including life members, to pay a levy at some time in the future to cover, for example, an unexpected item of expenditure. If so, the rules would have to make express provision for such demand being made of life members.

4.12 Honorary members Honorary membership is usually offered to a member or non-member of the club as a reward for past services or assistance to the club or who by reason of his distinction or position or experience in the field of activity in which the club operates will be an ornament to the club or will be able to assist the club in some material way. It is common practice for the honorary numbers to be elected by the managing committee and their number restricted in the rules. These members do not pay any entrance fee or subscription. They enjoy the privileges of membership save that almost invariably they have no voting rights at general meetings and are ineligible for election to any office within the club. Their position should be clearly stated in the rules.

---

15 [2004] BCLC 471.

16 Some clubs award a vice-presidency as a mark of gratitude instead of an honorary life membership.

4.13 Junior members It is common, especially in sporting or recreational clubs, for there to be a junior section or a family section where the members are aged under 18 years.[17] The position with regard to junior members should be carefully spelt out in the rules.[18] The following are important points to bear in mind:

(1) a minor, that is, a person under 18, is not liable for any contract save contracts for necessaries[19] so that technically the junior member will not be liable for his subscription. Because of this it is essential that the parent or sponsor of the junior member countersigns the application form for membership in their capacity of contracting party;
(2) there is no defence of minority when it comes to the law of tort.[20] If, however, a junior member through negligence or wilfulness causes damage to club property or injury to someone on club property, he will be unlikely to have the financial resources to pay compensation. Therefore, on the same application form, it is a wise move to make the parent or sponsor expressly agree to make good any damage or injury caused by the junior member. The consideration for such agreement will be the granting of junior membership;
(3) a junior member should take no part in the running of the club and therefore the rules should spell out precisely what privileges or restrictions shall apply to junior membership;
(4) it is considered good practice for a junior member on attaining his majority to apply to become an ordinary (or full) member of the club in accordance with the established procedure set out in the rules.

4.14 Associate members This phrase is used in different senses:

(1) it is a form of membership which comes with fewer privileges than ordinary (or full) membership. In a few large or important clubs, the applicant may have to start his membership at this level and then progress to full membership;
(2) it is a form of reciprocal membership where the members of another club are admitted to the host club on a temporary basis because, say, the other club is shut for refurbishment or where, say, a cricket club

---

17 A person under the age of 18 but above the age of 16 may be a member of a community club if the rules so permit and may enjoy all the rights of a member, but may not be a committee member, trustee, manager or treasurer of the club: Co-operative and Community Benefit Societies and Credit Unions Act 1965, s 20, as amended by the Family Law Reform Act 1969, Sch 1.

18 An example of a junior membership rule is contained in Appendix 10.

19 *Chitty on Contracts* (30th edn, 2008), at 8-004. Necessaries are such things as relate to the person of the minor, e g necessary food, drink, clothing, lodging and medicine. Under s 3 of the Minors' Contracts Act 1987 the court has power to require the minor to transfer any property he has acquired under an unenforceable contract if it is just and equitable to make him do so.

20 *Clerk and Lindsell on Torts* (20th edn, 2010) at 5-49 to 5-53.

offers associate membership for the summer months to its neighbouring football club which shuts for these summer months;

(3) it is a form of membership used by umbrella organisations where the rules of the umbrella organisation and the rules of the host club permit entry into the host club of members of other affiliated clubs, albeit with restricted privileges. Here the associate will often pay the umbrella organisation a fee in order to exercise his rights as an associate member;

(4) it is a term of art used by s 67 of the Licensing Act 2003. In this context a person is an associate member of a club if in accordance with the rules of that club he is admitted to its premises as being a member of another club and that other club is a recognised club, that is to say, it is a club which satisfies conditions 1 to 3 of the general conditions set out in s 62 of the Act.[21]

In the light of the various uses of the phrase, 'associate member', it is important that the rules are explicit and clear on this topic. It should be added that often these members are simply referred to as associates.

4.15 Temporary members There is nothing to prevent a club from having in its rules a category of temporary members but it is a category which needs to be handled with care. The club members need to be satisfied that such a category will be of benefit to the club. The category must form only an insignificant proportion of the overall membership,[22] otherwise the club may cease to be a genuine members' club. It is a good practice for the rules to state that any temporary member shall be admitted only on the authority of, say, two members of the managing committee and that the temporary membership will only last for a limited period, say, 14 days. The rule can limit temporary membership to a particular occasion. Suppose the Basset Chess Club holds an annual chess tournament in Basset which lasts for one week and attracts Grandmasters and many chess devotees who have no associate member status; the rules or bye-laws can cater specifically for the admission of persons attending this event as temporary members for the week in which the tournament is held. The admission of temporary members is subject to the 2-day rule.[23] It should be added that if temporary members are admitted, they are entitled to enjoy all the facilities of the club, so that it would be wrong to exclude them from, say, participating in a club raffle or from a particular bar.

---

[21] See **9.11** for these conditions and **9.34** for the position of associate members under the Licensing Act 2003.

[22] This point was specifically dealt with under para 3(2) of Sch 7 of the Licensing Act 1964. There is no equivalent provision in the Licensing Act 2003 but a surfeit of temporary members will make it very difficult for a club to comply with the condition that it must be a club established and conducted in good faith as a club: s 62(4) of the 2003 Act.

[23] Licensing Act 2003, s 62(2).

4.16 Affiliates This term has been in the past and still is used as a synonym for a member of a society or an associate.[24] This is a recipe for confusion in club law. In this context it is best used as denoting a connection between the club and/or its members and another, larger group of clubs, all of which have a common interest or aims, and which does not necessarily involve the affiliates in any paying membership of the larger group. An example of affiliation used in this context is set out in Appendix 9 in the rules of the Bassetshire Hockey Umpires Association.

4. RESTRICTIONS ON RIGHT TO REJECT APPLICATIONS FOR MEMBERSHIP

4.17 Lawful discrimination By its nature a club almost invariably discriminates in its admission procedure. As described in **4.2**, the members of a club admit to membership those whom they find congenial by reason of mutual interests, sporting ability, adherence to a political persuasion or whatever. There is nothing to prevent the members of a club excluding applicants for membership for reasons which to an outside observer may seem completely unreasonable, provided such exclusion has not been prohibited by Parliament.

4.18 Lack of sports ability It probably goes without saying that a sports club is entitled to insist on a minimum standard of ability before considering an application for membership. An applicant for playing membership of the MCC cricket club is no doubt required to display a considerable standard of skill if he is to stand any chance of his application being accepted. Most private golf clubs, too, require an applicant for full membership either to have a recognised handicap or to be able to demonstrate a good knowledge of and ability in the game. On the other hand, a village cricket or soccer club may well not make such demands, on the basis that a place in a team can always be found for an enthusiast. The introduction of the community amateur sports club ('CASC')[25] has complicated the issue in that a club which applies to register as a CASC, or to receive lottery funding, must make its application procedure open to the whole community; the club may, however, refuse (or revoke) membership where it is likely to be contrary to the best interests of the sport or the good conduct and interests of the club.[26]

4.19 Unlawful discrimination: Equality Act 2010 Prior to the Equality Act 2010 ('EQA 2010'), which came into force, with minor exceptions, on 1

---

24 See the Oxford Shorter English Dictionary.

25 See **1.63**.

26 See the Detailed Guidance Notes published by HM Revenue & Customs on its (2010) website, http://www.hmrc.gov.uk/charities/casc/index.htm.

October 2010,[27] it was unlawful for a club to discriminate against a person on the grounds of race[28] or disability[29] or sexual orientation[30] when considering an application for membership but that was the extent of unlawful discrimination as far as clubs were concerned. This is another area where the existing piecemeal legislation has been consolidated into one Act of Parliament covering all aspects of discrimination, harassment and victimisation. For the first time clubs will now be subject to the full range of anti-discrimination legislation, and this will affect their admission procedures. The purpose of the Act is to protect certain personal characteristics from discrimination. Part 7 of EQA 2010 (ss 100–107) and Schs 15 and 16 deal specifically with 'associations' when it comes to admission into membership.

4.20 Application to clubs EQA 2010 applies to an 'association' which is defined as a body with at least 25 members[31] where access to membership is controlled by rules and which involves a process of selection.[32] Membership may be of any description,[33] eg full member, associate member or temporary member. The association itself may be incorporated or unincorporated[34] and may be a private club or a proprietary club.[35] The generic word 'body' is sufficiently wide to cover a club or a society or an association.

4.21 Protected characteristics The following are protected characteristics under EQA 2010 which affect associations:[36]

(1) age;
(2) disability;
(3) gender reassignment;
(4) pregnancy and maternity;
(5) race (which includes colour, nationality and ethnic or national origin[37]);
(6) religion or belief (or lack of belief);
(7) sex;

---

27 See the various Commencement Orders culminating in Equality Act 2010 (Commencement No 4, Savings, Consequential, Transitional, Transitory and Incidental Provisions and Revocation) Order 2010, SI 2010/2317.

28 Race Relations Act 1976, s 25.

29 Disability Discrimination (Private Clubs etc) Regulations 2005, SI 2005/3258, regs 7 and 8.

30 Equality Act (Sexual Orientation) Regulations 2007, SI 2007/1263, reg 16.

31 Equality Act 2010, s 107(2)(a). A Minister of the Crown may by order amend this number: ibid, s 107(3).

32 Ibid, s 107(2)(b).

33 Ibid, s 107(5).

34 Ibid, s 107(4)(a).

35 Ibid, s 107(4)(b). What the subsection actually says is that it does not matter whether the association is carried on for profit.

36 Ibid, ss 4 and 100(1).

37 Ibid, s 9(1)(b).

(8) sexual orientation.

Insofar as EQA 2010 applies to disabled persons seeking membership,[38] this imposes a duty on an association to consider taking the reasonable steps outlined in **5.71** when it comes to their applications for membership.

4.22 Single characteristic associations EQA 2010 permits by way of exception an association, whose purpose is to bring together persons with a shared protected characteristic such as that of nationality or sexual orientation or a particular disability, to continue to operate its admission procedures based on restricted membership.[39] Thus the Bassetshire Club may continue as a gentlemen's club by restricting its membership to those who share a protected characteristic, in this instance the male gender (a characteristic of sex). The club, however, cannot go on to restrict its membership to Christian men since that would be restricting its membership to two protected characteristics, namely, sex and religion. In other words, the club can restrict its membership to men (sex) *or* Christians (religion), but cannot impose a double restriction. Under EQA 2010 an association of blind persons can restrict its membership to blind persons and would not be required to admit to membership persons with another disability, say, deafness. It is unlawful, however, for any association to restrict its membership to people of a particular colour under the guise of the protection of the characteristic of race.[40] So the Basset Afro-Caribbean Society can restrict its membership to the Afro-Caribbean community provided it does not restrict its membership to black persons.[41]

4.23 Discrimination It is unlawful for an association to practise either direct or indirect discrimination when it comes to the arrangements for (a) deciding whom to admit to membership; or (b) in laying down the terms on which it is prepared to admit a person to membership; or (c) by not accepting a person's application for membership.[42]

- ***Direct discrimination*** takes place where because of a protected characteristic, or because of a combination of two protected characteristics, one person treats another person less favourably than he would treat others.[43] For example, the Basset Social Club may not refuse to accept membership applications from persons or charge them

---

38 Equality Act 2010, Sch 15, para 2(2)–(5).

39 Ibid, Sch 16, para 1(1). Special provisions relate to associations which are charities: ibid, ss 193 and 194.

40 Ibid, Sch 16, para 1(4).

41 This would, curiously, be an emanation of the now-banned colour bar. A classic example was *Dockers' Labour Club and Institute v Race Relations Board* [1976] AC 285 where the club operated an express colour bar to prevent coloured persons from entering into the club.

42 Equality Act 2010, s 101(1)(a)–(c).

43 Ibid, ss 13(1) and 14(1). Pregnancy and maternity are excluded from any combination: ibid, s 14(2).

a higher subscription rate simply because they are Muslims or because they are gay Christians. This is direct discrimination, in the former case, on the ground of religion and, in the latter case, on the combined ground of religion and sexual orientation. Or the Basset Golf Club, which has members of both sexes, may not lay down a rule of admission that female members may only play on certain days whereas male members may play at all times. This is direct discrimination on the ground of sex. A club may, however, discriminate on account of the applicant's age if this is justified, that is to say, the discrimination is a proportionate means of achieving a legitimate aim.[44] For example, the subscription of youngsters at the Basset Tennis Club may be set at a discounted rate to encourage their participation in the game of tennis at an early age.[45]

- ***Indirect discrimination*** takes place when a condition, rule, policy or practice applies to everyone but disadvantages people who share a protected characteristic.[46] The association must not thereby put that other person at a disadvantage when it comes to membership.[47] Indirect discrimination may be excused if the provision, criterion or practice can be shown to be a proportionate means of achieving a legitimate aim.[48] Take the example of a Jewish hockey player who wants to join the Basset Hockey Club where the trial for new players always takes place on a Saturday precluding his attendance. This could amount to indirect religious discrimination unless the practice was justified, for instance, no other day of the week was found to be satisfactory for a trial day. On the other hand, indirect discrimination which fairly applies across the board to all applicants will not be unlawful, so that the Basset Rugby Club could lawfully apply criteria for admission which excluded all those persons incapable of participating in the vigorous contact sport of rugby, even though these criteria resulted in indirect discrimination against disabled persons.[49]

4.24 Harassment It is unlawful for an association to harass a person who is seeking membership,[50] save EQA 2010 does not apply to harassment based on religion or belief or sexual orientation.[51] Harassment takes place in three situations:

---

[44] Equality Act 2010, s 13(2). By s 197 a Minister of the Crown may by order amend EQA 2010 relating to the topic of age.

[45] On the other hand, giving discounted subscriptions to older members on the ground of their age is more problematic under Equality Act 2010.

[46] Ibid, s 19(1)–(2).

[47] Ibid, s 19(2)(a)–(c).

[48] Ibid, s 19(2)(d).

[49] Ibid, s 15(1)(b).

[50] Ibid, s 101(4)(b).

[51] Ibid, s 103(2).

(a) where it involves unwanted conduct that has the purpose or effect of violating the applicant's dignity or creating a hostile, degrading, humiliating or offensive environment for the applicant;[52] or
(b) where the unwanted conduct is of a sexual nature and has the same purpose or effect as mentioned above;[53] or
(c) where the unwanted conduct is of a sexual nature or related to gender realignment or sex and has the same purpose or effect as mentioned above and, as a result of the applicant's rejection or submission, the other person treats the applicant less favourably than otherwise would have been the case.[54]

4.25 Victimisation It is unlawful for an association to victimise a person when it comes to the arrangements for deciding (a) whom it will admit to membership;[55] or (b) in laying down the terms on which it is prepared to admit a person to membership;[56] or (c) by not accepting a person's application for membership.[57] Victimisation takes place where one person subjects another person to a detriment because that other person does a protected act or (according to the former's belief) has done or may do a protected act.[58] A protected act means (i) bringing proceedings under EQA 2010; or (ii) giving evidence or information in connection with proceedings under EQA 2010; or (iii) doing any other thing for the purposes of or in connection with EQA 2010; or (iv) making an allegation against a specific person that they have contravened EQA 2010.[59]

4.26 Remedies for unlawful discrimination The county court has exclusive jurisdiction to determine a claim for a contravention under Part 7.[60] The court must sit with assessors unless the judge is satisfied that there are good reasons for not doing so.[61] Proceedings must be brought within 6 months of the date of the act to which the claim relates or within such other period as the county court thinks just and equitable.[62] As to proving the claim, if there are facts from which the court *can* decide, in the absence of other explanation, that a person about whom a complaint is made has contravened the provision concerned, the court *must* hold that the contravention did occur.[63] The county court has the power to grant any remedy which can be granted by the High Court in proceedings in tort or

---

52 Equlaity Act 2010, s 26(1).
53 Ibid, s 26(2).
54 Ibid, s 26(3).
55 Ibid, s 101(5)(a).
56 Ibid, s 101(5)(b).
57 Ibid, s 101(5)(c).
58 Ibid, s 27(1).
59 Ibid, s 27(2).
60 Ibid, ss 113(1) and 114(1)(d).
61 Ibid, s 114(7).
62 Ibid, s 118(1).
63 Ibid, s 136(2).

on a claim for judicial review.[64] An award of damages may include compensation for injured feelings (whether or not it includes compensation on any other basis).[65] The county court, however, must not grant an interim injunction or any remedy other than awarding damages or making a declaration unless it is satisfied that no criminal matter will be prejudiced by doing so.[66] If the county court is satisfied in a case of indirect discrimination that the offending provision, criterion or practice was not applied with the intention of discriminating against the claimant, the court must not award damages without first considering how else to dispose of the claim.[67]

5. PRIVILEGES OF MEMBERSHIP

4.27 Apart from being common practice not to allow a member any privileges until he has paid the entrance fee (if any) and his first subscription, in one instance there is a compulsory requirement for privileges to be deferred. Under the Licensing Act 2003 the club rules must state that a person may not be admitted to membership or, as a candidate for membership be admitted to any of the privileges of membership, without an interval of at least 2 days between his nomination or application for membership and his admission to such privileges.[68] The phrase, 'at least 2 days', means that it covers a period of 4 days (see **6.11**), so that an application for membership received on Monday morning will mean that the candidate or member cannot take advantage of the privileges until Thursday morning at the earliest.

6. ENTRANCE FEE AND SUBSCRIPTIONS

4.28 Overview Nearly all clubs charge an annual subscription, and perhaps ask for an entrance fee as well, since this is the obvious way of financing the club on a continuing basis. But this is not a requirement of law. In some old-established clubs one will occasionally find that the members do not pay a subscription as such but a levy is made on the members at the end of the club's financial year to cover the expenses incurred over the previous year.[69] The levy can therefore be treated as a kind of subscription, the first year's expenses being met out the entrance fees or some other capital sum.

---

64 Equality Act 2010, s 119(2).

65 Ibid, s 119(4).

66 Ibid, ss 114(6)(a) and 119(7).

67 Ibid, s 119(5)–(6).

68 Licensing Act 2003, s 62(2). This includes temporary members.

69 Oxford colleges, for example, still operate a similar system for their students, called battels, at the end of each term.

4.29 Insofar as the management of the club is in the hands of the committee, the usual course is for the committee to put forward or recommend to the members the amounts of the proposed subscription for the various categories of member for the coming year without any input from or consultation with the members. On the other hand, on democratic principles it is important that the committee is accountable to the members in this matter and that is why one of the invariable items on the agenda at an annual general meeting is the fixing of the entrance fee (if there is one) and the fixing of the annual subscription. If, for example, there is a sharp rise in the subscription rates, the committee will be obliged to justify their stewardship to the members over the past year which has necessitated the raising of the subscriptions, and this is an exercise to be welcomed. In some large clubs, especially if they contain an element of overseas membership, the members are content to let the committee decide on the annual rates of subscription. There is, however, nothing untoward in giving the committee the power (or a temporary power) to raise annual subscriptions by some agreed inflation factor or to increase the subscriptions by a limited amount, say not exceeding 5% of the previous year's subscriptions.

4.30 Payment by instalments It is not uncommon for clubs to allow members to pay their subscriptions by instalments. The committee needs to take care that any agreement as to credit is not regulated by the complex provisions of the Consumer Credit Act 1974 (as amended by the Consumer Credit Act 2006). If the payment is to be made by more than four instalments or if the member is charged interest on the principal sum outstanding, this will involve the club in obtaining a consumer credit licence. The answer lies in making sure that agreement is an exempt one, that is to say, the credit is for a fixed sum; the repayment instalments do not exceed four in number; and the repayment date is within 12 months beginning with the date of the credit agreement.[70]

4.31 Waiver of subscriptions There is in appropriate circumstances an implied power to waive the member's obligation to pay his subscription. In *Abbatt v Treasury Solicitor*[71] Mr Justice Pennycuick, at 569, put the matter thus:

> 'I should have thought that where it becomes impossible for the time being to carry on the activities of a club, e.g. as a result of destruction of the club premises, the trustees or committee must have an implied power to suspend or reduce subscriptions; and that if they do so –

---

70 Consumer Credit (Exempt Agreements) Order 1989, SI 1989/869, art 3(1)(a)(i). It is common to have a repayment date of 360 days.

71 [1969] 1 WLR 561.

whether by formal resolution or by conduct – it could not be fairly said that the full subscriptions become due for the purpose of an expulsive provision.'[72]

4.32 Arrears of subscription This is dealt with in **7.6** under the rubric of lapsed membership. In a literary and scientific institution a member who is in arrear with his subscription may be sued 'as a stranger'.[73] Further, if the member is in arrear with his subscription, he shall not be counted as a member or entitled to vote at any meeting of the institution.[74]

4.33 Refunds Problems are sometimes encountered where the club has been dissolved and recently joined members have complained that they are entitled to a refund in whole or in part of the entrance fee in addition to the unexpired portion of the subscription. We consider that no part of the entrance fee is refundable as it comprised the consideration for the ability to join the club in the first place and is in no wise carried forward into the period of membership. But the point may not be free from doubt. In *Re Curzon Syndicate Ltd*[75] one of the members was permitted to prove in the liquidation for the amount of her entrance fee when the proprietary club, the Ladies United Service Club, closed down. But special circumstances may have applied here. In 1917 Mrs H, who was the governing director of the company which owned the club, and who was personally the lessor of the club premises, posted in the clubhouse a notice, in reply to a rumour that the club was going to close down, stating that the club would be carried on permanently. On 25 March 1919 Mrs H obtained judgment against the company for arrears of rent and on the same day closed the club, with the notice still being in place. The law report does not indicate the date when the member paid her entrance fee or the date when she became a member, nor the basis of recovery of the entrance fee. The judge may have come to the conclusion that there was an implied term in any contract of membership entered into after the posting of the notice that the club would not shut down save on reasonable notice. That being so, the company was in breach of the implied term by instant closure, and accordingly the entrance fee was recoverable as an item of wasted expenditure.

4.34 Another problem which might occur is if a member resigned because the other members had passed by the requisite majority a fundamental rule change with which he disagreed (see **2.52**). Suppose the member had paid his annual subscription a few days before the rule change and he now elects to resign his membership. Can he claim back the unexpired portion of his subscription from the club or its members? Unfair as it may seem, we do

---

72 This dictum was not overruled or criticised when the case went to the Court of Appeal: [1969] 1 WLR 1575.

73 Literary and Scientific Institutions Act 1854, s 25.

74 Ibid, s 31.

75 (1920) 149 LT Jo 232 (Lawrence J).

not consider such recovery is possible, save in a proprietary club. In a members' club the will of the majority of the members is paramount. As against the dissenting member the majority could argue that they were not in breach of any term of the contract of membership since the rules gave the members an unfettered power to alter the rules, which power had been democratically and procedurally exercised in a bona fide manner. This would mean that if the dissenting member wished to resign, that was his undoubted right but such right was exercised of his own volition. And this argument might well succeed in court. Nonetheless, we have no doubt that the correct solution to this problem is for the club to make an ex gratia refund of the subscription or the relevant portion of it. In a proprietary club, however, we consider that there would be an implied term in the contract of membership made between the proprietor and the member that no fundamental change to the rules, which adversely affected the position of the members, would take place during the period of the annual subscription. This implied term is necessary to give business efficacy to the contract and is not unfair on the proprietor since at the end of such period he can alter the rules to suit himself, and this might entail a fundamental rule change not to the liking of the members. If a member does not wish to renew his subscription on these new terms, that is a matter for him, and the contractual relationship between the proprietor and the member will simply cease to exist.

7. GUESTS AND VISITORS

4.35 If there is no supply or sale of alcohol or regulated entertainment involved in the club's activities, the topic of admission of the members' guests or of visitors into the club's premises or to its meetings, does not need to be addressed in the rules or bye-laws. The difference between a guest and a visitor in this context is that a guest will be an invitee of the member whereas a visitor will be a member of the public. It will be a matter for the discretion of the committee or the members in general meeting to decide if or when they will admit guests or visitors to participate in the club's activities and on what terms admission will be permitted. If the club feels more comfortable in regulating the entry of such persons, there is nothing untoward in making bye-laws to cover the situation or insisting that any guest or visitor coming into the club has to sign the visitors' book or requiring a guest or visitor to pay an entry fee.

4.36 Guests and discrimination laws EQA 2010 affects the admission of guests, visitors and associate members into the club premises, and its provisions are dealt with in **5.68** as forming part of the club's management of its affairs.

4.37 Guests and licensing laws Where members' guests are admitted into the club which holds a club premises certificate the sale and supply of alcohol to them is a licensable activity under the Licensing Act 2003. But care has to be taken over the sale and supply of alcohol to guests, visitors and associate members under this Act and this is dealt with in **9.33** and **9.34**.

4.38 Guests and gambling laws Where the club holds a club machine permit or a club gaming permit, genuine guests may be admitted into the club under the Gambling Act 2005 and may use the authorised gaming machines or may participate in the authorised gaming: see **11.22** and **11.25**.

Chapter 5

MANAGEMENT OF THE CLUB'S AFFAIRS

1. INTRODUCTION

5.1 In the absence of any rule to the contrary all ordinary (ie full) members of a club would have an equal say in the management of an unincorporated members' club. This form of Athenian democracy is impractical although occasionally found. When the Pre-Raphaelite Brotherhood was founded in 1848 by six artists and a sculptor, this was in effect a club which ran on such lines.[1] But in practice a club of any size or longevity cannot function without delegation under the rules of the members' powers of management to officers of the club and to a managing committee.[2] This is true, whatever the legal nature of the members' club. As far as proprietary clubs are concerned, it is common for the proprietor to establish a committee to act as an intermediary between him and the members[3] since this set-up works to the mutual advantage of the proprietor and the members, although as a matter of contract law no such committee is necessary.

2. OFFICERS OF A MEMBERS' CLUB

5.2 It is normal for clubs to elect officers who have specified functions to perform but very small clubs can survive without them, for example, the Pre-Raphaelite Brotherhood referred to in the preceding paragraph or the Inklings referred to in **2.1**. Clubs registered under the mutual societies legislation must have officers;[4] and incorporated clubs must have directors.[5]

---

1 Its unity of purpose, overtly demonstrated by its logo 'PRB', lasted until about 1853 when they all went their own separate ways.

2 Other names are also used such as the executive committee or the general committee. In many clubs it will simply be called the committee. The Licensing Act 1964 refers to an *elective* committee. Although this is a correct use of the adjective, most club members would normally refer to an *elected* committee (in contrast to an appointed one).

3 Eg *Lyttelton v Blackburne* (1876) 45 LJ Ch 219 (The Junior Naval and Military Club).

4 Shop Clubs Act 1902, Sch, para iv; Co-operative and Community Benefit Societies and Credit Unions Act 1965, Sch 1, para 6; and Friendly Societies Act 1974, Sch 2, para 5.

5 Companies Act 2006, s 154.

5.3 Officers of a club fall into two categories; they are either honorary posts or managerial posts. Since the functions of most honorary officers are generally well known it is unusual to specify in the rules precisely what duties their post entails, but if any unusual or specific duties are required of them this should be expressly spelt out. On the other hand, with managerial officers it is good practice to state in the rules or the bye-laws, as and when necessary, what duties the post entails. It is not uncommon in small clubs for one person to hold more than one office, but to dispel any doubts on this point the rules sometimes indicate which offices may be held in tandem.

5.4 **Patron** The first two definitions of 'patron' in the Chambers Dictionary[6] are given as '[a] a protector; [b] a person, group or organization, etc which gives support, encouragement and often financial aid'. A patron of a club therefore tends to fall into one of two categories; (1) he or she is a person of high rank or eminence who formally supports the objects of the club and acts as its 'protector'[7] but is not a member of the club because this might otherwise impose duties and obligations on the patron which are unacceptable to him or her; or (2) they are a group of members in the club who give the necessary support and encouragement to other members of the club.

5.5 The formal patron commonly holds the post at pleasure. The appointment is usually in the hands of the managing committee and is or should be an uncontroversial appointment. In many clubs, however, a formal patron is considered an unnecessary or inappropriate embellishment and the group of members who comprise the patrons will be the president and vice-presidents. It is not uncommon for the rules to state 'The club shall be under the patronage of one President and as many Vice-Presidents as the Committee shall determine'. Unlike a formal patron, these patrons will have achieved their presidency or vice-presidency by an election process.

5.6 **Presidents** The presidency of a club is a non-executive post, unlike the chairmanship of the club, which involves managerial functions. We consider that combining the honorary office of president with the managerial office of chairman is incompatible and should not be countenanced. In many clubs the president performs an ambassadorial role, having previously given yeoman service to the club over a period of time. It is the president who will 'preside' at important functions such as the annual dinner. At the AGM the president, if he attends, will open the proceedings and then hand over to the chairman or secretary to deal with the formal part of the meeting. If the president is to be given any managerial duties,

6 Published 1998.

7 In classical Roman times a patron was a patrician who gave legal protection to a client in return for services.

these should be specified in the rules.[8] It is usual for a president to be supported by one or more vice-presidents. The vice-presidents themselves are usually elected to their office for the same reason as the president. They are a useful addition to a club because they form a pool of candidates for the presidency when the need arises and they can deputise for the president when he is absent. Unlike presidents, however, vice-presidents often take part in the running of a club so that, for example, the chairman of the club might well be a vice-president as well.

5.7 **Chairman** Unlike all the other officers, the word 'chairman' has a masculine connotation and it can be a sensitive issue in clubs. There seems to be no general practice and it is best left to the chair person to decide how he or she would like to be addressed or described. It is to be noted that s 319 of the Companies Act 2006 is headed 'Chairman of meeting' and that the 2008 Model Articles issued under the Companies Act 2006 refer to the chairman, not the chair. If the latter description is preferred, the word will commonly carry a capital 'C' to distinguish the person from the item of furniture. In this book we had to choose one or other word to describe this office in the text and we opted for 'chairman' as being the more dignified title.

5.8 One has to draw a distinction here between the chairman of the club and the chairman of the managing committee. Almost invariably they are one and the same person. The chairman of a club is one part of a triumvirate that often ensures that the club operates in an efficient way with the least fuss and bother, the other two members being the secretary and the treasurer. That this triumvirate commonly exists is because the managing committee, into whose hands the control of the club's affairs has been placed, is usually a much larger body which may well meet on a regular but infrequent basis. The chairman's main roles are, as his title suggests, the chairmanship of the members in general meeting and the chairmanship of the managing committee. The chairman is the senior and most influential member of the club who takes part in the running of the club and it is not uncommon for the secretary or treasurer (or employees of the club) to consult him about a club matter and, if possible, obtain a decision on the matter. There is nothing untoward about this procedure provided that any decision of substance taken by the chairman is reported to the committee at its next meeting and the chairman's decision is ratified by the committee.[9]

5.9 **Secretary** This is the officer who generally speaking will be in charge of the day-to-day running of the club. In many clubs he will be the honorary secretary. This may sound confusing as he does not hold an honorary office. The word 'honorary' in his title means that he receives no remuneration for

---

8 For example, the President of the Chartered Institute of Arbitrators, despite his ambassadorial role, is still required to make appointments of arbitrators.

9 See *R v Brent Health Authority, ex parte Francis* [1985] QB 869, at 878.

performing his duties. The secretary has various important administrative tasks: they are to maintain an up-to-date list of members and their addresses and their contact numbers; to collect subscriptions; to deal with club correspondence; to organise and attend general meetings of the club and prepare the agenda and minutes thereof; to liaise between the committee and the sub-committees; and to prepare a report on the club's activities since the last AGM and to circulate the same amongst the membership. If the club is a body corporate, the secretary or the person acting as secretary is the officer personally responsible for the payment of corporation tax by the club.[10]

5.10 If the secretary is a paid official, he will have a contract of employment in which his duties will be spelt out in the usual way.[11] In many clubs, especially golf clubs, a paid secretary is the most prominent figure of authority in the club.[12] Although he reports to the managing committee, in practice much of the day-to-day running of the club will be in his hands. A paid secretary should never be a member of the club because of possible conflicts of interest between his obligations to his employer (the club) and his obligations to his fellow members.

5.11 **Treasurer** This is an important officer who should keep and maintain the accounts of the club in good order. In particular, he is responsible for preparing the accounts for the members at the annual general meeting; this will involve at the minimum a balance sheet and a profit and loss account detailing the income and expenditure over the past year. The treasurer will be answerable to the managing committee during the year leading up to the annual general meeting. The treasurer will normally be an unpaid officer and thus will be the honorary treasurer. However, a big club may have a paid manager or finance director who deals with financial matters or who reports direct to a finance committee or the managing committee, so that the office of treasurer here takes on a more symbolic role.

5.12 In many clubs there needs to be liaison between the secretary and the treasurer to ensure that financial matters are properly handled. The treasurer will be under a duty to bank without delay in the club's name all moneys received from the secretary. It is the treasurer's task to see that club moneys are spent solely for club purposes but it is usually the secretary's duty to organise that payments are made on time, such as the renewal of insurance premiums or the payment of value added tax. If the club is not a

---

10 Taxes Management Act 1970, s 108 (1)–(3)(a), as amended by Companies Consolidation (Consequential Provisions) Act 1985, Sch 2 and Finance Act 1993, Sch 14, para 7. The officer is entitled to be indemnified by the club: ibid, s 108(2).

11 See Chapter 14 below for the topic of employment.

12 Because (a) he is always there; (b) he is not transitory like an elected officer; and (c) he is the person to whom correspondence and complaints are addressed.

body corporate, the treasurer or the person acting as treasurer is the officer personally responsible for the payment of corporation tax by the club.[13]

3. ELECTION AND TENURE OF OFFICERS

5.13 The president and vice-presidents are elected officers. Sometimes their tenure is annual, sometimes it is for a longer period but, unlike a formal patron, it is not good practice to grant these presidencies for an unlimited duration.[14] As to the mode of electing officers generally, practice varies; sometimes it is solely in the hands of the committee, sometimes it is solely in the hands of the members in general meeting and sometimes it is in the hands of the members but only on the recommendation of the committee, so that if the recommendation is rejected the members cannot proceed to elect their own candidate but must await a fresh recommendation from the committee. As for the chairman, in many clubs he is elected by the managing committee from one of its own number immediately after the annual general meeting. In other clubs the nomination for chairman is open to the whole membership and is part of the annual election of the officers and committee at the annual general meeting. As for the hon. secretary and the hon. treasurer, they are usually officers elected by the members but sometimes the rules stipulate that they too are to be elected by the committee from amongst its own number. It is important for the rules to be clear on these points. For the election of members of the committee, see **5.22**.

5.14 If the committee elects an officer from its own number, that committee member, say the treasurer, will remain in office until he is re-elected or replaced by another committee member by the vote of the *new* committee *after* the AGM. The treasurer would continue in office even though he was no longer on the committee because he was voted off the committee at the AGM or had stood down voluntarily. This is different from an officer who is elected by the members at the AGM. His office will expire *at* the AGM, at which point he may be re-elected or replaced by another member by the vote of the meeting.

5.15 Nomination Where the officers are elected by the members in general meeting the process of nomination should be dealt with in the rules. In a club of any size there is usually a rule calling for a proposer and seconder, often needing the signed consent of the nominee, and requiring the nomination to be lodged within a certain number of days before the annual general meeting. What happens if there are insufficient candidates to fill all

---

13 Taxes Management Act 1970, s 108(1)–(3)(b), amended as aforesaid. The officer is entitled to be indemnified by the club: ibid, s 108(2).

14 There are some very old established clubs where the President holds office for life.

the posts or a particular post such as the treasurership? A not uncommon occurrence in small clubs. Can the chairman of the meeting call for nominations from the floor of the meeting? As a matter of practicality we consider the answer to be in the affirmative. This ad hoc nomination may be against the rules but, if successfully voted upon, its legality will rest upon the acquiescence of those members who have attended the meeting and who are thus representing all the members of the club.[15] If the office remains unfilled after the AGM, the committee may have the power under the rules to co-opt a member to that office until the next AGM.[16] On the other hand, where the officers are elected by the committee from its own number, the process of election is often an informal matter which dispenses with the need for a written nomination or a proposer and seconder.

5.16 Voting A democratic voting system will almost inevitably be a complex affair if it is based on the premise that any person elected to an office should have at least 50% of the votes cast. It is of course a relatively simple matter if there are only two candidates because one of them will normally get more than 50% of the votes. The only difficulty here lies in what happens if there is a tie. The usual solution to this problem is to adopt the solution provided in parliamentary elections, that is, to decide the election by lot.[17] A contest between two candidates is necessarily run on the basis of 'first past the post'. The real difficulties arise when the 'first past the post' voting system is adopted and the contest is between three or more candidates. 'First past the post' often means (as in our national politics) that a candidate with a minority of votes is elected: a case of the tail wagging the dog. Despite its obvious deficiencies, we consider that for the vast majority of clubs 'first past the post' will be a satisfactory voting system because of its uncomplicated nature and the swiftness of the result.[18]

5.17 Contested elections of officers at general meetings are usually conducted by secret ballot. The secretary should prepare the ballot papers before the meeting with the names of the candidates arranged in alphabetical order. Candidates often prepare a short manifesto (say 150 words) which is circulated prior to the election meeting or sometimes the chairman at the meeting lets each candidate introduce themselves and say a few words in support of their candidature. The vote is taken by each member marking with a cross their choice of candidate on a ballot slip. The vote is then counted by the secretary or the scrutineers if appointed. Where

---

15 See *Prideaux' Directions to Churchwardens* (10th edn, 1835) cited in **6.36**.

16 See **5.25**.

17 See Representation of the People Act 1983, Sch 1, para 49. In *Fryer v Harris* (1955) *The Times*, July 30, where the votes were equally divided, the returning officer spun a coin to decide the election.

18 Another reason for using 'first past the post' is the dearth of candidates in many club elections. Far from having a surfeit of candidates, many clubs have difficulty in persuading members to become officers of the club.

the officers are elected by the committee from its own number, a secret ballot is desirable if there is to be a contested election for any particular office.

4. AUDITOR

5.18 If an unincorporated club is of any substance, it is common to appoint an auditor (usually an honorary auditor) to examine and officially verify the accounts of the club. Working men's clubs and community clubs must appoint an auditor[19] (and make rules accordingly)[20] although there is now a power for such clubs to opt out of an audit if certain conditions are met.[21] Companies must appoint an auditor,[22] unless they are private companies which can opt out of this requirement.[23] Companies must prepare audited accounts for each financial year,[24] unless they are small companies which are exempt from this obligation.[25] The auditor has an independent role to play and is not an officer of the club.

5. TRUSTEES

5.19 Where the club is unincorporated and holds assets and property, it is customary for trustees to be appointed according to the rules and for the assets and property to be vested in trustees on trust for the whole membership. Where such a club owns or leases land, this is a necessary requirement because property cannot be conveyed to or registered at the Land Registry in the name of a non-existent person. The trustees will invariably be full members of the club. In the case of a registered working men's club, there must be one or more trustees appointed by a resolution of a majority of members at a general meeting or in such other manner as the rules provide.[26] The appointment must be notified to the Financial Services

---

19 Co-operative and Community Benefit Societies and Credit Unions Act 1968, s 4.

20 Friendly Societies Act 1974, Sch 2, para 6; Co-operative and Community Benefit Societies and Credit Unions Act 1965, Sch 1, para 10.

21 Co-operative and Community Benefit Societies and Credit Unions Act 1968, s 4A; Deregulation (Industrial and Provident Societies) Order 1996, SI 1996/1738; Friendly and Industrial and Provident Societies Act 1968 (Audit Exemption) (Amendment) Order 2006, SI 2006/265, which assimilated the law with that relating to companies: see footnote 25 below for the exemption figures.

22 Companies Act 2006, ss 485 and 489.

23 Ibid, s 485(1).

24 Ibid, s 475.

25 Ibid, s 477. A small company is defined for this purpose as having an annual turnover of not more than £5.6 million and its balance sheet total for the financial year not being more than £2.8 million: s 477(2).

26 Friendly Societies Act 1974, s 24(1)–(2) as substituted by the Friendly Societies Act 1992. See, eg *Coles v Samuel Smith Old Brewery (Tadcaster)* [2007] EWCA Civ 1461 (where the

Authority.[27] In the case of an unincorporated literary or scientific institution, it is usual for assets and property to be vested in trustees but if none are appointed in respect of personal property, 'the money, securities for money, goods, chattels and personal effects' shall be vested in the governing body of the institution.[28] Trustees are often appointed where the club is incorporated under the Companies Acts or registered under the Co-operative and Community Benefit Societies and Credit Unions Act 1965 but technically this is not necessary because the club is a legal person and can hold assets and property in its own right. The question of trusteeship is further discussed in **8.24**.

6. BRANCHES AND SUB-CLUBS

5.20 A national association or a large club, say a multi-sports club, may have one or more branches or sub-clubs. The role of a branch is to represent the parent club in its own locality. The role of a sub-club is to support and implement the objects of the parent club. It is normal for the branch or sub-club to elect its own officers and committee and to manage its own affairs, but with its activities being subject to the ultimate control of the parent club. To this end it is essential that the rules of the branch or sub-club stipulate that there shall be an annual report made to the parent club accompanied by an audited financial statement relating to its finances. It is also normal practice for the branch or sub-club rules to state that any assets or moneys held by them shall be and remain in the beneficial ownership of the parent club. In this event these rules should stipulate that the members and officers of the branch or sub-club shall act as fiduciaries to the parent club in respect of such assets and moneys.

7. MANAGING COMMITTEE IN A MEMBERS' CLUB

5.21 **Overview** For the efficient management of the club it is this committee which has delegated to it the control and management of all the affairs of the club. It is therefore essential that the rules specify the composition, the powers and duties of this committee. Under the Literary and Scientific Institutions Act 1854, if no governing body is constituted on the establishment of the institution, the members themselves shall have the power to create their own governing body.[29] In some cases it is mandatory for the club to have a managing committee. Working men's clubs,

---

trustees of the Ward Green Working Men's Club obtained an order for specific performance against the brewery concerning an option to purchase the clubhouse).

27 Ibid, s 24(3)–(4).

28 Literary and Scientific Institutions Act 1854, s 20.

29 Ibid, s 32.

community clubs and shop clubs are all required to have this committee[30] and, where the club was the holder of a registration certificate under the Licensing Act 1964, the affairs of the club were required to be vested in such a committee. The Licensing Act 2003 is silent on the need for a managing committee, which is a pity, but its institution is now so widespread that it is perhaps no longer necessary to legislate for its existence. In this section we refer to the managing committee simply as the committee.

5.22 Election and tenure The election of the committee is necessarily set out in the rules. If the club held a registration certificate, para 4 of Sch 7 to the Licensing Act 1964 contained mandatory stipulations about the tenure and election of the committee. Even with the demise of this Act and the non-appearance of such stipulations in the Licensing Act 2003, we consider that para 4 embodies the best practice and should be followed in any event.[31] As to *tenure*, this may be for not less than 1 year but should not be more than 5 years. As to *election*, this should be held annually, and if all the elected members do not go out of office in every year, there should be fixed rules for determining those who are to retire. All the members of the club, who are entitled to vote at the election and are of not less than 2 years' standing, should be capable of being elected, subject to any provision for nomination and any provision prohibiting or restricting re-election. A rule whereby say a third shall retire each year can assist the continuity of management. It is usual to permit committee members to put themselves forward for re-election on the expiry of their term of office, subject sometimes to a maximum number of consecutive years which the member may serve in his elected capacity. What is said in **5.15** and **5.16** about nomination and voting relating to the election of officers applies equally to the election of committee members.

5.23 Bankruptcy of committee member A member who is bankrupt should not stand for election to the committee because, although technically eligible in an unincorporated members' club, committees enter into contracts and bankrupts may not obtain, alone or jointly with another person, credit for more than £500 or engage in club business without, in either case, disclosing their bankruptcy.[32] A bankrupt cannot be a company director or take part in the management of a company[33] which are additional reasons why in an incorporated club a bankrupt should not be elected to the committee. For the same reasons, a committee member who becomes bankrupt whilst a committee member should stand down from the committee.

---

30 Friendly Societies Act 1974, Sch 2, para 5; Co-operative and Community Benefit Societies and Credit Unions Act 1965, Sch 1, para 6; Shop Clubs Act 1902, Sch, para iv.

31 See Appendix 3.

32 Insolvency Act 1986, s 360(1)–(2); Insolvency Proceedings (Monetary Limits) (Amendment) Order 2004, SI 2004/547.

33 Company Directors Disqualification Act 1986, s 11.

5.24 Sub-committees It is possible for a club to have as many co-equal committees as it wants. But in practice it has been found be more satisfactory and efficient to have one main committee (the managing committee) with as many sub-committees as may be necessary, which are answerable to the managing committee.[34] The rules should state that all sub-committees shall conduct their business in accordance with directions from the committee and that they shall periodically report their proceedings to the committee for approval and ratification. If decisions made by the sub-committee, for example, those of a disciplinary sub-committee, are to have binding force on the members of the club, it is essential that the rules should spell out this power, emphasising that the decision is being made on behalf of the committee. It is usual for the rules to provide that members of all sub-committees shall retire automatically on the date on which the annual general meeting is held but to make them eligible for re-appointment by the committee immediately after the meeting if it sees fit to do so. The point of automatic retirement is that it gives the committee, whose composition may have substantially changed as a result of elections at the annual general meeting, the opportunity of re-constituting any sub-committee to assist it in the business of running the club.

5.25 Exercise of powers It is important to realise that members are delegating their powers of control to the *whole* committee and not to the individual members thereof.[35] Consequently it is essential that the rules state that the powers of the committee may be exercised by a quorate number of the committee, otherwise any decisions of committee must be taken by the whole committee.[36] Further, because it is an elected body we do not consider that that the committee would have the power to alter its composition without express power being given in the rules. Accordingly, the committee's co-option of a member on to the committee to give added weight or expertise or its filling of a casual vacancy on the committee for the remainder of the term of a committee member who, say, has resigned is not possible without this express power.[37] On the other hand, subject to any express rule to the contrary, the committee will be empowered to determine its own procedures as to how it will operate.[38] Pursuant to this power a committee can appoint a sub-committee or a working party or delegate a task to a particular officer or member of the club. Whenever the committee adopts procedures which involve sub-delegation, it is crucial that it requires the persons delegated to report their activities to the committee for

34 Licensing Act 1964, Sch 7, para 4(4) stated that a sub-committee shall be treated as an elective committee if its members were appointed by the managing committee and not less than two-thirds were members of the managing committee.

35 *Brown v Andrew* (1849) 18 LJ QB 153; *R v Liverpool City Council ex p Professional Association of Teachers* (1984) *The Times*, March 22.

36 See further **6.29**.

37 For clubs which held a registration certificate there was statutory power to fill a casual vacancy: Licensing Act 1964, Sch 7, para 4(5).

38 *Cassell v Inglis* [1916] 2 Ch 211, at 231. See **6.28** as to the effect of members' resolutions on the committee's powers of management.

approval and ratification, since ultimately the club's affairs are the responsibility of the committee and it is they who are answerable to the members.

5.26 Conflicts of interest In exercising its powers the committee should be astute in spotting potential conflicts of interest. The committee may decide that the roof of the clubhouse needs substantial repair and a building contractor who is a committee member volunteers to carry out the work for a reasonable price. The conflict arises because it is in the club's best interest to get the job well done for as low a price as possible and in the building contractor's best interest to ensure his 'reasonable price' is as profitable as possible. Any conflict should be dealt with by the committee either by having a policy of not dealing contractually with any club member or by making sure that all conflicts of interest are properly disclosed and that any decision on the subject matter of the conflict excludes the member when it is taken. In relation to community amateur sports clubs, special statutory provisions apply: a member may supply goods or services to the club or may be in paid employment with the club provided in each case the arrangements are conducted on an arm's length basis.[39]

5.27 Intervention by the court regarding internal matters The set of rules which contains the contract between the members is subject to the jurisdiction of the court in the same way as any other contract.[40] At one time it was considered that the courts only intervened in club cases to protect rights of property[41] but this view has since been rejected.[42] But there is still an important distinction to be made between questions of *ethics* as opposed to questions of *law*. In *Lee v Showmen's Guild of Great Britain*[43] (a trade union expulsion case) Lord Justice Romer at 350 put the matter thus:

> 'Two elements of importance distinguish those [club] cases from this [case]. First, by the rules in the club cases by which the members agreed to be bound it was expressly provided that the test of expulsion was whether "in the opinion of" the domestic forum the conduct of the member warranted it; and, secondly, the decisions on which the intervention of the courts was unsuccessfully sought were questions of ethics and not of law. Such questions are peculiarly within the province of the committee of a social club, and it is now well established that the courts will not interfere even with unreasonable

---

39 Corporation Tax Act 2010, s 660(5)(a)–(b).

40 *Lee v Showmen's Guild of Great Britain* [1952] 2 QB 329, at 341.

41 *Lyttelton v Blackburne* (1876) 45 LJ Ch 219, at 223 (a club case); *Rigby v Connol* (1880) 14 CH D 482, at 487 (Sir George Jessel MR) (a trade union case).

42 *Abbott v Sullivan* [1952] 1 KB 189, CA (a trade union case); *Amalgamated Society of Railway Servants v Osborne (No.2)* [1911] 1 Ch 540, CA, at 562 (a trade union case).

43 [1952] 2 QB 329, CA.

> decisions provided the committee have not acted dishonestly or in excess of jurisdiction in arriving at them.'[44]

Likewise, in *Richardson-Gardner v Fremantle*[45] (expulsion of the plaintiff-member by the committee of the Junior Carlton Club, a political club founded to support the Conservative Party) Lord Romilly MR at 85 stated:

> 'But in cases of this description all the court requires is to be satisfied that the persons who were summoned really exercised their judgment honestly. The court will not consider whether they did so rightly or wrongly.'

A high water mark of non-intervention is the case of *Weinberger v Inglis (No 2)*:[46] the House of Lords refused to interfere with the decision of the committee of the Stock Exchange where its sole reason for not re-electing the plaintiff as a member in 1917 was his German birth, even though he was a naturalised British subject who had been a member of the Stock Exchange without blemish for the previous 22 years.[47]

5.28 On the other hand, in *Lee's* case Lord Justice Denning emphasised that in club cases the courts now protect rights of contract. He stated, at 342:

> 'If a member is expelled by a committee in breach of contract, this court will grant a declaration that their action is ultra vires. It will also grant an injunction to prevent his expulsion if that is necessary to protect a proprietary right of his; or to protect him in his right to earn his livelihood: see *Amalgamated Society of Carpenters v Braithwaite* [1922] 2 AC 440; but it will not grant an injunction to give a member the right to enter a social club, unless there are proprietary rights attached to it, because it is too personal to be enforced: see *Baird v Wells* [1890] 44 Ch D 661.[48] That is, I think, the only relevance of rights of property in this connexion. It goes to the form of remedy, not to the right.'

5.29 In sum, we conclude that the courts will deal with any *breach of a term*, express or implied, in the contract of membership, which is alleged to have come about by or through the decision of the committee, in the same way as they would deal with any other breach of contract. In the event of a *non-breach of a term* of the contract of membership, the courts do not act as a

---

44 *Dawkins v Antrobus* (1881) 17 Ch D 615, CA, at 630 (Brett LJ: a very robust judgment); *Young v Imperial Ladies Club Ltd* [1920] 2 KB 523, CA, at 535 (Scrutton LJ); *Hole v Garnsey* [1930] AC 472, at 491 (Lord Sumner).

45 (1871) 24 LT 81.

46 [1919] AC 606.

47 As to livelihood claims, see *Braithwaite's* case in **5.28** and see further **13.9**.

48 See further **7.21** as to injunctive relief concerning expulsion from social clubs.

'court of appeal' from the committee's decision[49] but even if they can be persuaded to intervene they are unlikely to do so unless there has been some moral culpability where the decision is arrived at from fraud, personal hostility or bias.[50]

5.30 Vote of No Confidence On occasion there may come a time when the members have lost confidence in their committee to run the club acceptably or properly. This situation needs careful handling if the committee take the view that, despite what the members generally may think, their stewardship of the club's affairs is beneficial to the club. It must be remembered that the committee would have been elected for a finite period and so are entitled to stay in office until the next election. The easy answer therefore is to vote the committee out of office at the next election.

5.31 But the situation might be such that the members feel that they have to take action prior to the next election. The procedure would be for the members to requisition a special meeting in order to pass a Vote of No Confidence in the committee and a resolution calling upon the committee to resign forthwith. It is here that the members may encounter choppy waters. What happens if the secretary or the committee refuse or simply fail to call the duly requisitioned meeting? The answer is that the requisitionists themselves can convene the meeting.[51] But what happens if the committee then blithely ignore the Vote of No Confidence and the call to resign which, say, had been overwhelmingly passed at the meeting? The answer is for the members to treat the committee's refusal to act upon these resolutions as a ground for expulsion from the club. This in turn might produce another procedural hurdle caused by the fact that it is usually the committee who exercises the power of expulsion. However, the committee would not be able to exercise the power on this occasion since they would be the accused and the first rule of natural justice is that no-one can act as a judge in his own cause.[52] In any event the committee is ultimately answerable to the general body of members, so in these particular circumstances we consider that the power of expulsion would reside in the members generally who would thus be entitled to convene a special meeting to deal with what would undoubtedly be a critical situation in the club.

5.32 Statutory power to remove the committee It should be noted that clubs registered under the earlier legislation (that is, working men's clubs, community clubs and shop clubs) must make provision in their rules for the

---

49 *Young v Imperial Ladies Club Ltd* [1920] 2 KB 523, at 535 (Scutton LJ); *Lee v The Showmen's Guild of Great Britain* [1952] 2 QB 329, at 341 (Somervell LJ).

50 *Richardson-Gardner v Fremantle* (1871) 24 LT 81, at 85.

51 See **6.7**.

52 See **7.13**.

removal of the committee as well as rules for appointing it.[53] No doubt, as in an unincorporated members' club, the way of expressing dissatisfaction with the committee would be the passing of a Vote of No Confidence.

8. MANAGING COMMITTEE'S DUTY OF CARE TO MEMBERS

5.33 Overview Important questions arise as to what duty of care, if any, the committee members owe to the other members or to the club itself. If there is a duty of care, what is its ambit? How far will honesty and good faith be a sufficient discharge of their duties, bearing in mind that the committee members are occupying an unpaid post? How far does the law of agency apply? Are the committee members all jointly liable to the same extent or can the liability vary from member to member? It is rare for the precise relationship between the members and the committee to be spelt out in the rules. It is equally rare to come across a case where the club has sued its own committee so that there is a dearth of reported authority on the point.

5.34 It is well established that for the purposes of Part II of the Landlord and Tenant Act 1954 a club is carrying on a business.[54] Lord Reid in *Hedley Byrne & Co Ltd v Heller & Partners Ltd*[55] commented that one of the occasions on which the law imposes a care of duty is when there is a business connection between the parties as opposed to a purely social occasion.[56] We consider that in managing the club's affairs the committee member's relationship with his fellow members is not simply a social one; for example, he will be responsible (with others) for overseeing the financial welfare of the club. Further, it is self-evident that the committee members in carrying out their functions are not acting merely on behalf of themselves but on behalf of the other members of the club as well. Thus the nature and scope of any duty which the committee may owe to the club becomes a question of agency under the contract of membership.[57] An agent acts for a principal. In managing the club's affairs the first question which arises is who constitutes the committee's principal in any given case.

(1) ***Unincorporated members' club*** The difficulty in identifying the committee's principal lies in the fact that the club itself has no legal personality. It is tempting to say that the principal is the membership as a whole as opposed to some discrete part of it. But we do not think

53 Friendly Societies Act 1974, Sch 2, para 5; Co-operative and Community Benefit Societies and Credit Unions Act 1965, Sch 1, para 6; and Shop Clubs Act 1902, Sch, para iv.

54 *Addiscombe Garden Estates Ltd v Crabbe* [1958] 1 QB 513, CA (a tennis club); *Coles v Samuel Smith Old Brewery (Tadcaster)* [2007] EWCA Civ 1461, at [2] (a working men's club).

55 [1964] AC 465, at 482.

56 See *Chaudhry v Prabhakar* [1989] 1 WLR 29, CA, at 35 and 38.

57 *Flemyng v Hector* (1836) 2 M & W 172, at 180 (Abinger CB).

this reflects the reality of the situation. Owing to the unique and anomalous legal status of this type of club, we consider that the principal could potentially differ with each set of circumstances. Sometimes the principal might be the whole membership, at other times it might be a specific group of members or conceivably it might be a single member.[58] Suppose the members of the Basset Constitutional Club at their AGM discuss and resolve that the club should apply for the renewal of the lease of their clubhouse which is shortly due to expire. Nothing is said as to who should negotiate with the landlord. The committee thereupon undertake the task. Here we surmise that the principal would be the whole membership. Suppose, however, on another occasion the club's Wine Committee[59] requests the committee to put in hand the ordering of certain wines chosen by the Wine Committee for the forthcoming year and the committee proceed to deal with this task. Here we surmise that the principal would be the members of the Wine Committee. Or suppose the Secretary, as part of his remit of many years' standing, decides what new crockery and cutlery is required in the club's dining room but is too busy to deal with the order himself and requests the committee to deal with this task. Here we surmise that the principal would be the Secretary.

(2) ***Community club*** Here the simple and correct analysis is that the principal would be the club itself as it has a legal personality.[60] Accordingly, we consider that any duty as agent which might otherwise be owed jointly or severally by the committee to the members of the club *qua* principals under the contract of membership (see (1) above) would be subsumed into the overriding duty to the corporate club.

(3) ***Incorporated club*** The position is very similar to that of the community club, and the principal would be the club itself. The complication here is that the corporate club will have directors as well as a committee. The directors' principal will also be the club itself. This duplication of roles raises a potential conflict which is discussed in **5.47**.

5.35 Standard of care First, any decision by the committee must be taken for the benefit of the club as a whole and not for some section or faction thereof,[61] and this was and is supported by the Licensing Acts 1964 and 2003 because in each case the club had and has to be established and

---

[58] The case of *Campbell v Thompson and Shill* [1953] 2 WLR 656, referred to in **15.4**, is a reminder that there is no simple answer on this point.

[59] This would normally be a sub-committee but it is common for the word 'sub' to be omitted from the nomenclature of sub-committees.

[60] It was so held by HH Judge Charles Harris QC in a reserved judgment at the Oxford County Court in *Morris Motors Athletic and Social Club Ltd v Fraser* (unreported) 20 December 2006, where the claimant was a community club suing its former committee members. The club was set up by Lord Nuffield himself.

[61] *Woodford v Smith* [1970] 1 WLR 806, at 816; *Lambert v Addison* (1882) 46 LT 20, at 25; *Tanussi v Molli* (1886) 2 TLR 731 (concerning the Italian Couriers Club).

conducted in good faith as a club.[62] Secondly, a committee member will invariably be a gratuitous agent, that is to say, a person who receives no remuneration for acting as agent. This automatically distinguishes a committee member from a professional agent who is paid for his services. It used to be said that the duties of a gratuitous agent (whose liability lies in tort rather than contract) were different from a professional agent and that he was only liable for the care which he exercised in his own affairs.[63] This proposition is no longer tenable and the modern position is that the standard of care which is appropriate is that which might reasonably be expected in all the circumstances.[64] That is to say, the difference between a gratuitous agent and one who is paid is one of degree only.[65] So in considering the committee's standard of care in any given case one has to take into account the nature of the club and the sort of tasks its committee is expected to undertake. There is plainly a difference between a club such as the Kennel Club which is the leading organisation in the canine world and say the Basset Village Club which functions as a social club in the local village. The duties of the committee of the former club will be more various and more onerous than those of the latter club, and no doubt will involve much larger sums of money. As a matter of commonsense, too, one would expect a committee to give more forethought and greater attention to detail if it is concerned with a building project costing half a million pounds than if it is concerned with guest invitations to the club's annual dinner dance. On the question of the standard of care of a gratuitous agent, Lord Justice Stuart-Smith in *Chaudhry v Prabhakar*[66] said:

> 'Relevant circumstances would be the actual skill and experience that the agent had, though, if he had represented such skill and experience to be greater than it in fact is and the principal has relied on such representation, it seems to be reasonable to expect him to show that standard of skill and experience which he claims to possess. Moreover, the fact that the principal and agent are friends does not in my judgment affect the existence of the duty of care, though conceivably it may be a relevant circumstance in considering the degree or standard of care.'

5.36 Failure or omission to take action might on occasion amount to a breach of the duty of care. Take the case of the club's leasehold premises, the lease of which is about to expire, mentioned in **5.34**(1). Let us suppose that the members in general meeting had specifically authorised the committee to take steps to obtain the renewal of the lease. Shortly afterwards the landlord serves a Section 25 notice (a notice of termination of the tenancy) which requires the club as lessee to make an application to the court by the

---

62 Licensing Act 1964, s 41(2)(a) and Licensing Act 2003, s 62(4).
63 *Wilson v Brett* (1843) 11 M & W 113.
64 *Chaudhry v Prabhakar* [1989] 1 WLR 29, CA.
65 *Chitty on Contracts* (30th edn, 2008), at 31-118.
66 [1989] 1 WLR 29, CA, at 34.

termination date asking for a new tenancy.[67] The committee, however, fails to apply to the court either timeously or at all, and the club is unable to oppose the Section 25 notice, thereby causing the club to seek new premises. The members might well have a cause of action against the members of the committee for any loss or damage caused by their omission to make the necessary application. Therefore it behoves every committee member to attend committee meetings regularly and actively to participate in the running of the club's affairs. To this end it is a salutary and common rule that a committee member who is absent without an accepted apology from three consecutive committee meetings shall be deemed to have vacated office.

5.37 An illustration of this topic is the unreported case of *Morris Motors Athletic and Social Club v Fraser* (2006).[68] The claimant, a community club, sued the former members of its committee in negligence for ignoring the advice of the club's solicitor. The club had entered into an option agreement whereby part of its grounds would be sold to a developer for housing in return for which the developer promised to build a new clubhouse free of charge. The option was exercised by the developer who then required the club under the terms of the option agreement to enter into a tripartite agreement with the local council and the developer. The club's solicitor initially advised the committee that the club should not enter into this latter agreement for various technical reasons but eventually advised the committee that the right course was to sign it because, first, any valid reservations could be taken up with the local council so that the club would in no way prejudice its legal position by entering into the agreement and, secondly, any further delay in signing would inevitably result in court action against the club. The committee remained unhappy about signing the tripartite agreement and so did not cause the club to do this, whereupon the developer sued the club and obtained a court order compelling it to sign, which resulted in an expensive order for costs being made against the club. And HH Judge Charles Harris QC held the committee liable in damages in respect of those costs.

5.38 In the *Morris Motors Club* case all the committee's members accepted collective responsibility, but we surmise that this would not always be the case. Suppose one of the committee members had said in committee that it was imperative to sign the tripartite agreement now that the club solicitor had advised this course. And suppose his standpoint had been disregarded by the other committee members who continued to object to signing the agreement. We take the view that the dissenting member would have had a complete answer to the club's allegation that he had ignored the club solicitor's advice. Our view is in some measure supported by the case of

---

67 See further **14.16**.

68 See footnote 60 above. One of the authors acted as counsel in this case.

Todd v Emly[69] which is discussed in **12.5**. (This divergence of standpoint would no doubt have produced a conflict of interest amongst the defendants in the *Morris Motors Club* case, requiring the separate representation of the dissenting member). Finally, one needs to consider the situation where the committee member plays no active part in the conduct complained of. Suppose in the *Morris Motors Club* case a committee member was ill or abroad when the solicitor gave his advice to sign the tripartite agreement. Would that member have been able to say that he had no idea that the solicitor had changed his mind about his advice? If he could have established the facts, we consider that this would have been a viable defence. But we take a different view of the committee member who knowing of the solicitor's changed advice attends the committee meeting and simply abstains when the majority continue their objection to signing. This is because of his acquiescence in the ignoring of the advice by the majority of the committee.

9. MEMBERS' PERSONAL INJURY CLAIMS AGAINST THE CLUB

5.39 This topic involves the club's duty of care and needs to be addressed separately.

5.40 Members' clubs One starts off with the general proposition that at common law neither the managing committee of an unincorporated members' club nor a corporate members' club owes any duty in contract or in tort to the member that he will be safe in using the club premises because no member assumes such a responsibility towards his fellow members as an incidence of membership. As to contract, in *Shore v Ministry of Works*[70] the case (despite its name) concerned the Corsham Community Centre, an unincorporated members' club. The plaintiff-member was injured by a brick dislodged from the clubhouse roof whilst attending an entertainment at the club and she sued the committee for damages for breach of an implied warranty of her contract of membership that the premises were safe for the purposes for which she was admitted as a member of the club. Her action failed at first instance and on appeal because the court held that the contract contained no such implied warranty. As to tort, in *Robertson v Ridley*[71] the plaintiff was a member of the Sale and Ashton-on-Mersey Conservative Club, an unincorporated members' club. He was riding his motorcycle on the driveway which led away from the clubhouse when it struck a pothole, as a result of which that he fell off and was injured. He brought an action against the chairman and secretary of the club for damages in negligence and lost both at first instance and on appeal because

---

69 (1841) 7 M & W 427 and (1842) 8 M & W 505.

70 [1950] 2 All ER 228, CA.

71 [1989] 1 WLR 872, CA

the court held there was no liability at common law on a club or its members for the defective state of the club premises.

5.41 *Robertson v Ridley* is an example of Homer nodding[72] and is of doubtful authority despite being in the Court of Appeal. It is clear from the law report, at 873, that the plaintiff as part of his claim had sued the chairman and secretary for damages for breach of the common duty of care under s 2(2) of the Occupiers' Liability Act 1957.[73] By s 1(1) of this Act the common duty of care took the place of the duty of care at common law. Yet none of the three lords justices referred to the 1957 Act or mentioned the phrase, the common duty of care, in their judgments and all three of them relied on cases decided before 1957. It is to be noted that s 1(2) of the 1957 Act says that the substitution of the common duty of care 'shall not alter the rules of the common law as to the persons on whom a duty is imposed or to whom it is owed'. But that does not answer the question whether the duty of care imposed under the 1957 Act was to be equated with the duty of care (or lack of it) imposed at common law in this particular instance?[74] The long title of the 1957 Act said it was an Act to *amend* the law as to the liability of occupiers and it would seem strange if the two duties of care were synonymous. However, even if the two duties are different, an unresolved question remains whether a club member is a 'visitor' to his own club for the purposes of the 1957 Act: see **12.40**. Lastly, there is the question as to who counts as the occupier of a club. No problem arises with an incorporated club since it is a legal person, but some difficulty may arise over who constitutes the occupier of an unincorporated members' club: see **12.39**.

5.42 Aside from occupier's liability, in *Prole v Allen*[75] the plaintiff-member sued the committee and the club steward in negligence for injuries suffered when at night she fell down some unlighted steps at the exit of the club premises. The steward had switched off the light prior to the accident. The claim failed against the members of the committee on the ground that they owed the member no duty of care but succeeded against the steward because of the responsibility vested in him by all the members. Mr Justice Pritchard put the matter thus:

---

72 'Even Homer nods'. Horace *Ars Poetica* 359: *Indignor quandoque bonus dormitat Homerus.*

73 Wrongly categorised by the plaintiff at 873 as a breach of statutory duty. The section is set out in **12.37**.

74 In *Grice v Stourport Tennis, Hockey and Squash Club* (1997) CLY 3859 the plaintiff-member in gaining access to the clubhouse slipped and fell thereby injuring his back, and he then sued the unincorporated club in negligence. *Pace* the decision in *Robertson v Ridley*, the Court of Appeal allowed the plaintiff to amend his pleading to claim damages against (a) the trustees, (b) the chairman of the ground and premises committee, (c) the steward and (d) two members representing all the other members of the club. This case is unsatisfactory in that it too makes no mention of the Occupiers' Liability Act 1957.

75 [1950] 1 All ER 476.

'He was appointed by all the members, operating through the committee, and, in my judgment, he thereupon became the agent of each member to do reasonably carefully all those things which he was appointed to do, and in that way he came to owe a duty to each of the members to take reasonable care to carry out his duties without negligence.'

5.43 In *Jones v Northampton Borough Council*[76] the plaintiff, a member of the Shepherd Social Club, an unincorporated members' club, sued the council and Mr Owen, who was another member and the chairman of the club, for damages for an injury suffered when playing indoor football. Mr Owen had hired the pitch for a competition and was warned by the council that because of a leak in the roof the pitch contained a pool of water and that he would be entitled to cancel the hiring. Mr Owen chose to go ahead with the competition and the plaintiff was injured when an opponent slipped in the water and heavily collided with him. Mr Owen relied on *Robertson v Ridley* and *Prole v Allen* but was found guilty of negligence. Lord Justice Ralph Gibson, at 388, had this to say:

'The [two] cases relied on by [Mr Owen] were no more than examples of the rule that the mere fact of common ownership of a club, even coupled with membership of a committee on the part of a defendant, did not by itself give rise to a duty of care ... No doubt the nature of the relationship between members of a club would [often][77] be such that it would be impossible to find that one member had undertaken any responsibility to inspect, or to enquire, or to consider whether circumstances would or might give rise to a risk of injury. But there might be circumstances in which a member [or officer of the club or a member of the committee][78] acquired knowledge both of the actual danger and of the fact that, if a warning was not given, the members on whose behalf he had undertaken to perform a task would be exposed to a risk of injury. In such circumstances it was open to the court to find that a duty of care existed [to the injured member] and was broken.'

There then ensued the case of *Owen v Northampton Borough Council*[79] which concerned the apportionment of liability for Mr Jones' injury as between Mr Owen and the council. In his judgment Lord Justice Purchas stated:[80]

'The membership of a club, apart from wholly exceptional circumstances not relevant to this appeal, cannot have the effect of

---

76 [1990] Times LR 387, CA.

77 The lord justice added this word in the later case of *Owen v Northampton Borough Council* (1992) 156 LG Rev 23, CA.

78 See also on p 388.

79 (1992) 156 LG Rev 23, CA.

80 Ibid, at 31.

excluding ordinary liability in tort of the *Donoghue v Stevenson* type once a duty to take care as between neighbours is established.'[81]

5.44 Protection of the committee and the member Being in breach of the duty of care, whether at common law or under the common duty of care, constitutes the tort of negligence (a civil wrong) and the usual way of protecting tortfeasors against negligence claims is by suitable insurance. Whatever may be the legal position, it is plainly desirable that members of the committee and those members entrusted by the committee to carry out tasks on its behalf deserve protection from financial liability against personal injury claims made by the club's own members.

5.45 Proprietary clubs It would appear that, unlike in a members' club, the owner of a proprietary club does warrant to the member that his club premises are safe to use; this is because the owner will have admitted the member for reward.[82]

10. CONTROL BY DIRECTORS IN AN INCORPORATED CLUB

5.46 Overview All incorporated clubs must have directors[83] who will manage the business of the company.[84] It is a curious fact that the Companies Acts have never defined the office of director. Section 250 of the Companies Act 2006 states that a director 'includes any person occupying the position of director by whatever name called'. It is generally accepted that a director is a person who manages the affairs of the company for the benefit of himself and the shareholders or members of the company.[85] Most directors will be de jure directors, that is, properly appointed in accordance with the law and the company's articles. A few directors may be de facto directors, that is, persons who openly act as directors even though not validly appointed.[86] An even fewer number may be *shadow* directors, that is,

81 [1932] AC 562. 'Neighbour' is used in a technical sense: see **12.32**.

82 *Shore v Ministry of Works* [1950] 2 All ER 228, at 232 (Jenkins LJ).

83 Companies Act 2006, s 154. Private companies must have at least one director and other companies must have at least two directors. At least one director must be a natural person: ibid, s 155. It is highly inadvisable for any incorporated club to have a sole director.

84 Article 3 of the Companies (Model Articles) Regulations 2008, SI 2008/3229 and reg 70 of the Companies (Tables A to F) Regulations 1985, SI 1985/805.

85 *Re Forest of Dean Coalmining Co* (1879) 10 Ch D 451, at 453 (Jessel MR).

86 *Secretary of State for Trade and Industry v Hollier* [2007] BCC 11 (per Etherton J: the touchstone is whether the person in question is part of the corporate governing structure).

persons in accordance with whose directions or instructions the directors of the company are accustomed to act,[87] but who disclaim any role as a director.[88]

5.47 Most incorporated clubs will also have a managing committee, some or all of whom will be directors of the company. Where the membership of the committee does not coincide with the board of directors a potential problem can arise. Assume there are 12 members of the committee but only four of whom are directors. Will the eight committee members who are not directors be counted as directors? The answer is, alas, not a simple one. For certain provisions, eg insolvency of the company[89] or disqualification of directors,[90] the answer might be in the affirmative but it would all depend on the role which the non-director committee member actually played in the club's affairs. But except in the realm of insolvency of the club, the non-director committee member is very unlikely to be faced with personal liability of any sort arising under company law legislation.[91]

5.48 It is to be noted that, if this particular article is adopted, art 4 of the 2008 Model Rules[92] states that the members or shareholders of the company, as the case may be, may by special resolution direct the directors to take, or refrain from taking, specified action.

5.49 **Director's general duties** A director by virtue of his office owes, broadly speaking, two categories of duty towards the company itself: (1) fiduciary duties (that is, duties of good faith and honesty) and (2) duties of skill and care.[93] These duties are owed to the company, not to individual members of the club.[94] For the first time in the history of English company law the Companies Act 2006 replaced and codified the principal common law and equitable duties of directors. Traditional common law notions of corporate benefit have been cast aside and the new emphasis is on corporate social responsibility.[95] In summary the codified duties are as follows:

Directors must:

(1) act within their powers;[96]

---

87 Insolvency Act 1986, s 251; *Secretary of State for Trade and Industry v Deverell* [2000] 2 WLR 907, CA.

88 *In re Hydrodam (Corby) Ltd* [1994] 2 BCLC 180, at 183 (Millett J).

89 Ibid (a case of wrongful trading under Insolvency Act 1986, s 214).

90 *Re Lo-Line Electric Motors Ltd* [1988] BCLC 698, at 707 (Browne-Wilkinson V-C).

91 For civil liability to non-members or third parties, see Chapter 12 below.

92 See Appendices 7 and 8.

93 See, generally, *Gore-Browne on Companies* (45th edn, 2009), para 15[1].

94 *Percival v Wright* [1902] 2 Ch 421.

95 See eg Companies Act 2006, s 172(1)(d).

96 Ibid, s 171.

(2) promote the success of the company;[97]
(3) exercise independent judgment;[98]
(4) exercise reasonable care, skill and diligence;[99]
(5) avoid conflicts of interests;[100]
(6) not accept benefits from third parties;[101]
(7) declare an interest in a proposed transaction with the company.[102]

5.50 As to the standard of care, skill and diligence to be exercised, the Act lays down a twofold test:[103]

(1) the director must act with the general knowledge, skill and experience of a person carrying out the functions of that director (the objective test); and
(2) the director must bring to bear his actual knowledge, skill and experience when acting as director (the subjective test).

Insofar as the Companies Act 2006 does not purport to provide an exhaustive statement of the duties of directors, we cite the decision of Mr Justice Jonathan Parker in *In re Barings plc (No 6)*[104] where, at 489, he gave a helpful overview of what was expected of a director:

> '(i) Directors have, both collectively and individually, a continuing duty to acquire and maintain a sufficient knowledge and understanding of the company's business to enable them properly to discharge their duties as directors. (ii) Whilst directors are entitled (subject to the articles of association of the company) to delegate particular functions to those below them in the management chain, and to trust their competence and integrity to a reasonable extent,[105] the exercise of the power of delegation does not absolve a director from the duty to supervise the discharge of the delegated functions [which importantly includes a duty to monitor delegates in the performance of their delegated functions].[106] (iii) No rule of universal application can be formulated as to the duty referred to in (ii) above. The extent of the

97 Companies Act 2006, s 172.
98 Ibid, s 173.
99 Ibid, s 174(1).
100 Ibid, s 175.
101 Ibid, s 176.
102 Ibid, s 177.
103 Ibid, s 174(2).
104 [1999] 1 BCCL 433.
105 *Land Credit & Co of Ireland v Lord Fermoy* (1870) 5 Ch App 763 (a lawful delegation by the board of directors to a committee of directors pursuant to the articles). Where adopted, art 5 of the 2008 Model Rules (entitled 'Directors may delegate') states that, subject to the articles, the directors may delegate any of the powers which are conferred on them under the articles to a committee.
106 The words in square brackets were inserted by the Court of Appeal in *Hollins v Russell* [2003] 1 WLR 2487, at [196].

duty, and the question whether it has been discharged, must depend on the facts of each particular case, including the director's role in the management of the company.'

5.51 Club's and director's financial duties We surmise that the vast majority of clubs will come within the 'small company' regime,[107] that is to say, a company which in any given year satisfies two or more of the following criteria:

(1) its turnover is not more than £5.6 million;
(2) its balance sheet total is not more than £2.8 million;
(3) the number of employee is not more than 50.

The significance of this regime is that the incorporated club will be subject to a more lenient scheme of accounts and reports than otherwise would have been the case. Directors are responsible for ensuring that the company keeps adequate accounting records which disclose with reasonable accuracy at any time the financial position of the company.[108] The directors must not approve the annual accounts unless that they are satisfied that they give a true and fair view of the company's assets, liabilities, financial position and profit or loss.[109] The accounts must include a balance sheet as at the last day of the financial year and a profit and loss account.[110] The directors are under a duty to prepare a directors' report for each financial year of the company[111] which must give the names of the directors and state the principal activities of the company carried on in the course of the year.[112] Directors are also responsible for safeguarding the assets of the company[113] and hence for taking reasonable steps for the prevention and detection of fraud.[114]

5.52 Conflict of interest between the director and the members There is surprisingly little authority on this point given the opportunities for conflict which might arise. This is no doubt because the board of directors of the company will have overlapping membership with the management committee and they will both be pulling in the same direction. Occasions may sometimes arise, however, where the director's duties to the company may conflict with his duties to the members as a whole. Take the case of an obstreperous employee whom the members resolve in general meeting

---

107 Companies Act 2006, s 382.
108 Ibid, s 386.
109 Ibid, s 393.
110 Ibid, s 396.
111 Ibid, s 415.
112 Ibid, s 416.
113 *Selangor United Rubber Estates Ltd v Craddock (No.3)* [1968] 1 WLR 1555, at 1575.
114 In *In re Kingston Cotton Mill Company (No 2)* [1896] 2 Ch 279, CA, Lopes LJ said, at 288, of a company auditor: 'He is a watch-dog, not a bloodhound'. A similar remark could be made of a company director. It has elsewhere been remarked that a company director has 'a duty of curiosity'.

should be dismissed forthwith. Against this resolution a director must remember that under s 172(1)(b) of the Companies Act 2006 he is under a duty to have regard to the interests of the company's employees. In addition, the employee will almost certainly have contractual and statutory rights in connection with his employment, and these rights must be honoured. The director's duty to the company will weigh equally with his duty to the members.[115] If the director were to fail in his duty, the company could look to him for redress.

5.53 Inactive director An inactive executive director must not be confused with a non-executive director. Take the instance of the Duchess of Abercorn in *Young v Imperial Ladies Club Limited*,[116] who was excused by Lady Samuel, the chair of the executive committee, from attending any committee meeting because she was too busy elsewhere to attend such meetings. Suppose the duchess had been an executive director of the company as well as a committee member. And suppose on the same ground she was excused attendance at board meetings. Could the duchess have relied on this ground to justify non-performance of her duties as a director? The current answer is in the negative: the court would judge the director's performance in accordance with the tests set out in **5.50**.

5.54 Protecting the director The answer lies in suitable insurance. The reader is directed to **12.23**(1).

11. CONTROL BY PROPRIETOR IN A PROPRIETARY CLUB

5.55 The proprietor has full control of the club's affairs. If he makes provision for a committee, he will spell out what powers of management he is delegating to the committee, including the expenditure of the proprietor's money.

12. CASH BASIS OF A MEMBERS' CLUB

5.56 As we have seen,[117] when a member agrees to join a members' club, he is agreeing to pay the entrance fee (if any) and the annual subscription but nothing more. Absent any agreement (either within or without the rules) a member does not authorise his fellow members to pledge his credit

---

115 *Gaiman v National Association for Mental Health* [1971] Ch 317, at 335.

116 [1920] 1 KB 523, CA. See **7.10** for a discussion of this case.

117 See **1.10**.

in any club transaction.[118] It follows that the club should operate on a cash basis. In *Todd v Emly* Mr Baron Parke said:[119]

> 'The evidence shews that a fund was subscribed, which fund was to be administered by a committee. The committee can only be supposed to have agreed to do that which the subscribers to the club had power to do themselves to do, that is, to administer the fund as far as it went. They were not expected to deal on credit, except for such articles as it might be immediately necessary for them to have dealt with on credit. The making [of] purchases of what was necessary would be only what they ought to do according to the trust reposed in them, and these must be taken to be purchases for ready money, unless distinct evidence was given that they were authorised to enter into contracts on the part of the general body for the common purpose, and to deal on credit, so as to make one the agent of the other. It might be different, perhaps, in the case of hiring the servants of the establishment, where there must necessarily be credit for a certain period, because you cannot pay wages down[120] but as to butcher's meat, wine, furniture, and almost anything else, those may be ready money transactions.'

The cash-basis principle lies at the heart of an unincorporated members' club because it is the members of the committee who are liable for the club's debts, and they should not be put into the invidious position of financial risk in carrying out their duties, especially as their services are given free of charge for the benefit of the club as a whole. The club should therefore not operate a system of deficit budgeting. In any given year the expenditure should be forecast as accurately as possible and the annual subscription fixed accordingly (taking into account other sources of income such as investments and fund-raising activities). It is the duty of the committee member to keep a vigilant eye on expenditure to ensure that it will be met from existing club funds or from an authorised levy on the members or, if genuinely necessary and prudently entered into, from authorised borrowing such as a bank loan or overdraft.

5.57 Drawing cheques No officer of a club has an inherent right to sign cheques on behalf of the club. It is part of the committee's function to authorise those officers of the club who may sign cheques drawn on the club's account, unless the rules or bye-laws deal with this point. It is a sensible precaution to stipulate that all cheques must be signed by two officers of the club, but this can sometimes lead to unwise practices,[121] so the practice is now often adopted of permitting a sole signatory on the

---

[118] *Flemyng v Hector* [1836] 2 M & W 172 (Parke B, at 184 and Alderson B, at 187).

[119] (1841) 7 M & W 427 at 434. The case is further discussed at **12.5**.

[120] Ie you pay them in arrear.

[121] Eg one signatory signing all the cheques in blank and then handing over the cheque book to his co-signatory.

cheque provided that if the sum involved is in excess of a specified amount the cheque has to be counter-signed by a second signatory.

5.58 Using credit cards Clubs now commonly have the facility of credit cards issued by their bank. It is sometimes overlooked that if the committee members of an unincorporated members' club enter into a credit agreement for business purposes in a sum not exceeding £25,000,[122] this will be a regulated agreement within the Consumer Credit Act 1974 and thus protected by the Act, notwithstanding the facts that the club carries on a business and the credit is advanced for business purposes.[123] This situation arises because the Act protects a debtor which is an unincorporated body of persons (as well as an individual) in contrast to a corporate body which does not count as a consumer.[124] The credit may be in the form of fixed-sum credit such as a loan or a running account such as a bank overdraft provided in either case the credit limit of £25,000 is not exceeded.[125] Another benefit to an unincorporated members' club is that, where its committee has paid for goods or services via a credit card and subsequently has a claim against the supplier of goods or services in respect of a misrepresentation or a breach of contract, it will have a like claim against the creditor who supplied the finance.[126] Some banks now issue debit cards which carry the same degree of protection as credit cards.

13. POWER TO BORROW MONEYS

5.59 Unincorporated members' clubs These clubs have no inherent or implied power to borrow moneys; this is a concomitant of the club being run on a cash basis. Thus either the rules must contain an express power to borrow moneys or *all* the members of the club must consent to the borrowing in question. If there is an express power to borrow in the rules, it is essential to put some ceiling on the amount which may be borrowed without the consent of the members being first obtained in general meeting.

5.60 Literary and scientific institutions These institutions have no implied power to borrow for purposes which fall outside the activities described in s 33 of the Literary and Scientific Institutions Act 1854. In *Re Badger, Mansell v Viscount Cobham*[127] the Stourbridge Institute was established for the promotion of literature, science and art. It was managed by a council. At its premises was a much used billiard room and the

---

[122] Consumer Credit Act 1974, s 16B(1)(a), inserted by Consumer Credit Act 2006, s 4.
[123] *Chitty on Contracts* (30th edn, 2008), vol 2, at 38–033.
[124] Consumer Credit Act 1974, s 8(1) as amended by Consumer Credit Act 2006, s 2(1)(a); 1974 Act, s 189(1) as amended by 2006 Act, s 1(b).
[125] Consumer Credit Act 1974, s 10(1).
[126] Ibid, s 75(1).
[127] [1905] 1 Ch 568.

majority of the council resolved either to build a new room (its preferred option) or to repair the old room, but either course required the borrowing of money. There was no express power in the rules to borrow money. Mr Justice Buckley held that there was no implied power to borrow money to build a new billiard room since this was outside the purposes contemplated by the Act. He held, however, that under s 19 of the Act the council could call upon the trustees of the property to repair the existing room, in which case the trustees would have a charge on the property for moneys so expended and would be entitled to reimburse themselves if necessary by raising a mortgage on the institute's premises.[128]

5.61 Working men's clubs, community clubs and shop clubs None of these clubs has any inherent or implied right to borrow moneys. A shop club, it is envisaged, would not at any stage need to borrow moneys. On the other hand, it is considered that there would be nothing improper in a working men's club or a community club borrowing moneys if there was an express power in the rules authorising such borrowing in order to carry out the objects of the club.

5.62 Incorporated clubs In the absence of an express provision in the old-style memorandum or now in the articles, a power to borrow will not be implied 'unless it be properly incident to the course and conduct of the business for its proper purposes'.[129] Thus, generally speaking, any trading or commercial company will have an implied power to borrow moneys so long as borrowing was not prohibited by the old-style memorandum or now prohibited in the articles.[130] Insofar as clubs do not exist simply for trade purposes (see the second criterion referred to in **1.1**), it is considered that an incorporated club will not have any implied power to borrow moneys, necessitating an express power. If the old-style memorandum or the articles are silent on the point, the question arises whether the members of the company at a general meeting could pass a special resolution to permit, say, a specific item of borrowing to carry out some lawful transaction. The answer is in the negative because such borrowing would be ultra vires of the company; the company will first have to alter its articles to include a power of borrowing. Therefore the resolution would not become valid even if *all* the members assented, thus differentiating it from an unincorporated members' club. If the company has power to borrow, it will also have the power to give security.[131] As with an unincorporated members' club, it is essential to put some ceiling in the articles on the amount which may be borrowed without the consent of the members being first obtained in general meeting. It is also worth pointing out that in order to obtain a company loan a bank will often require a director of that

---

128 See also *Re Cleveland Literary and Philosophical Society's Land* [1931] 2 Ch 247.

129 *Blackburn Building Society v Cunliffe, Brooks & Co* (1882) 22 Ch D 61, at 70.

130 *Gore-Browne on Companies* (44th edn, 2004), 28[2], now complicated by the Financial Services and Markets Act 2000: see *Gore- Browne on Companies* (45th edn, 2010), 28[5]–[7].

131 *Re Patent File Co* [1870] 6 Ch App 83.

company to give a personal guarantee in respect of the loan, which immediately negates the principle of limited liability.

5.63 Proprietary clubs Any borrowing of money will be the proprietor's concern.

14. DISCRIMINATION IN MANAGING THE CLUB'S AFFAIRS

5.64 Overview In managing its affairs the club will be bound to comply with the provisions of the Equality Act 2010 ('EQA 2010').[132] The purpose of EQA 2010 is to protect certain personal characteristics, such as race and gender, from discrimination. Associations are specifically dealt with in Part 7 (ss 100–107) and Schs 15 and 16. Mention of EQA 2010 has already been made in connection with admission into membership of the club: see **4.19**. It applies to an 'association' as defined in **4.20**. The full list of protected characteristics is set out in **4.21**. There is a statutory exception to permit the existence of single characteristic associations: see **4.22**. Discrimination, harassment and victimisation are explained in **4.23**, **4.24** and **4.25**. The remedies available for unlawful discrimination are set out in **4.26**.

5.65 It is unlawful for an association to discriminate against a member or to victimise that member in the way it affords, or fails to afford, access to a benefit, facility or service which the club provides or by subjecting that member to some other detriment.[133] Suppose the Bassetshire Club has a strict dress code that male members are obliged to wear a tie and jacket when dining at the club in the evening. A member suffering from long-term psoriasis (a skin complaint) asks to be excused from this code when he comes to the club for dinner because the wearing of a collar and tie is extremely painful. The club refuses to grant any waiver. This would amount to direct disability discrimination. The club could insist, however, that if a waiver were granted the member should come smartly dressed.

5.66 Similar protection is given to associates.[134] An associate means a person who is not a member of the association but in accordance with the association's rules has some or all of the rights of membership as a result of being a member of another association.[135] It is to be noted that a single characteristic association, such as an association for deaf persons, can limit the rights of associates to persons sharing the same characteristic.[136]

---

132 See Equality Act 2010, ss 142 and 144.

133 Equality Act 2010, ss 101(2)(a) and (d), 101(6)(a) and (d).

134 Ibid, ss 101(3)(a) and (d), 101(7)(a) and (d).

135 Ibid, s 107(6).

136 Ibid, Sch 16, para 1(2).

5.67 It is unlawful for an association to harass a member or an associate.[137] EQA 2010 does not, however, apply to harassment of members or associates because of their religion or belief or because of their sexual orientation.[138]

5.68 Guests It is unlawful for an association to discriminate against a person or to victimise that person in the arrangements (a) for deciding whom to invite, or permit to be invited, as a guest; or (b) in laying down the terms on which it is prepared to invite a person, or permit a person to be invited, as a guest; or (c) by simply not inviting a person, or permitting that person to be invited, as a guest.[139] It is to be noted that a single characteristic association, such as an association for deaf persons, can limit the invitation of guests to persons sharing the same characteristic.[140]

5.69 Following on from that, it is unlawful for an association to discriminate against a guest actually invited by the association or invited with its permission (express or implied) or to victimise that guest in the way it affords, or fails to afford, access to a benefit, facility or service which the club provides or by subjecting that guest to some other detriment.[141] Examples are given in **5.65** and **5.72**. It is also unlawful for an association to harass a guest or potential guest[142] save that EQA 2010 does not apply to such harassment based on their religion or belief or their sexual orientation.[143]

5.70 Gender discrimination in sport EQA 2010 takes account of gender-affected activity, that is to say, sporting competitions where physical strength, stamina or physique are major factors in playing the sport or activity and where one sex would generally speaking be at a disadvantage in comparison with the other sex.[144] In these competitions it is lawful for the association to continue to organise separate competitions for men and women.[145] The Act also makes it lawful to restrict participation of a transsexual person in such competitions if this is necessary to secure fair competition or the safety of competitors.[146] Children in gender-affected activity are a special case. Younger children of both sexes can participate in the same activity; it is for the association to decide whether this is appropriate after taking into account the age and stage of development of the children who are likely to be competitors.[147]

---

137 Equality Act 2010, s 101(4)(a) and (c).

138 Ibid, s 103(2).

139 Ibid, ss 102(1)(a)-(c), 102(4)(a)–(c).

140 Ibid, Sch 16, para 1(3).

141 Ibid, s 102(2) and (5).

142 Ibid, s 102(3).

143 Ibid, s 103(2).

144 Ibid, s 195(3).

145 Ibid, s 195(1).

146 Ibid, s 195(2).

147 Ibid, s 195(4).

5.71 Disability discrimination: reasonable adjustments EQA 2010 imposes a duty on an association to take *reasonable steps* to make adjustments for disabled persons, whether they be members, associates or guests.[148] A disabled person is defined as a person who has a physical or mental impairment and the impairment has a substantial and long-term adverse effect on that person's ability to carry out normal day-to-day activities.[149] Long-term means the effect has lasted at least 12 months; or is likely to last that long; or is likely to last for the rest of the affected person's life; or is likely to recur.[150] Substantial means more than minor or trivial.[151] The duty comprises three requirements as follows:

(1) where the association's provision, criterion or practice puts a disabled person at a substantial[152] disadvantage relating to access to a benefit, facility or service, or when invited as a guest, in comparison with persons who are not disabled, the requirement is to take reasonable steps to avoid that disadvantage;[153]
(2) where a physical feature of its premises[154] puts a disabled person at a substantial disadvantage in comparison with persons who are not disabled, the requirement is to take reasonable steps: (a) to avoid that disadvantage; or (b) to adopt a reasonable alternative method (i) of affording access to the benefit, facility or service or (ii) of inviting persons as guests;[155]
(3) where a disabled person would, but for the provision of an auxiliary aid, be put at a substantial disadvantage relating to access to a benefit, facility or service, or when invited as a guest, in comparison with persons who are not disabled, the requirement is to take reasonable steps to provide the auxiliary aid.[156]

A failure to comply with any of these requirements is a failure to comply with the said duty[157] and the association thereby discriminates against a disabled person.[158]

5.72 As may be seen, EQA 2010 imposes a duty on the association to make arrangements for proper access to the association's benefits, facilities and services. Suppose the Basset Music Club with 75 members usually holds its annual dinner in an upstairs function room of a local restaurant. There is no

---

[148] Equality Act 2010, s 20(2)–(5) and (13) and Sch 15, para 2(2).
[149] Ibid, s 6(1)–(2) and Sch 1.
[150] Ibid, Sch 1, para 2.
[151] Ibid, s 212(1).
[152] Substantial means more than minor or trivial: ibid, s 212(1).
[153] Ibid, s 20(3) and Sch 15, para 2(4).
[154] This includes premises which the association occupies and other premises where the benefit, facility or service is being provided by the association: ibid, Sch 15, para 2(6).
[155] Ibid, s 20(4) and Sch 15, paras 2(3), (5) and (6).
[156] Ibid, s 20(5) and Sch 15, para 2(4).
[157] Ibid, s 21(1).
[158] Ibid, s 21(2).

lift to this room. A new member is disabled in that he has severe difficulty in climbing stairs. The club would be under a duty to consider changing the venue to a downstairs room because this would be a reasonable step to take by way of adjustment. On the other hand, if the great advantage of the upstairs function room for the Basset Music Club's annual dinner was the presence of a fine piano, the playing of which was an integral part of the event, we consider that this fact would excuse the club from altering its venue to a downstairs room which had no piano. The same considerations would apply if members' guests were invited to this dinner and one of the member's wives was confined to a wheelchair.[159] We add that EQA 2010 tempers the duty by saying that an association is not obliged to take any step which *fundamentally* alters the nature of the benefit, facility or service in question or the nature of the association itself.[160] Also, if meetings of the association take place in a member's or an associate's house, there is no obligation on the association to make any adjustment to a physical feature of that house.[161]

5.73 Disability discrimination regulations The Disability Discrimination (Private Clubs etc) Regulations 2005,[162] were repealed on 1 October 2010.[163] They were no longer necessary because they have been superseded by the provisions of EQA 2010. If required, however, regulations may be made under Sch 21 to EQA 2010.[164] One point does arise out of the repeal of the 2005 regulations. Under Part 3 of the 2005 Regulations the association's duty to make reasonable adjustments for the benefit of disabled persons in relation to any of its practices, policies or procedures or to any physical feature was expressed as follows: 'to take such steps as is reasonable *in all the circumstances*'. We consider that the italicised words meant that in appropriate circumstances affordability by the association could be taken into account when complying with its statutory duty. The italicised words no longer appear in the legislation and it is therefore an unresolved question whether failing to provide a reasonable adjustment can be justified on the grounds of affordability in appropriate circumstances or whether the only question to ask is whether the adjustment is a reasonable one to make. Finally, a difficulty may arise where the association is occupying its premises under a lease (or licence)[165] in that the association may not be entitled under the terms of the lease to make the necessary alterations to the premises in order to comply with its statutory obligations. In such a case the lease shall have the effect as if it provided for the tenant to be entitled to

---

159 Refusal in the first place to invite the disabled wife of a member to the club's annual dinner which was open to all members' partners would be discrimination under Equality Act 2010, s 102(1)(c) if based simply on the fact that she was a wheelchair user.

160 Ibid, Sch 15, para 2(7).

161 Ibid, Sch 15, para 2(8).

162 SI 2005/3258.

163 Equality Act 2010 (Disability) Regulations 2010, reg 15(2)(vii), SI 2010/2128.

164 Equality Act 2010, Sch 21, para 6.

165 Ibid, Sch 21, para 2(1)(a).

make the necessary alterations with the written consent of the landlord, such consent not to be unreasonably withheld.[166]

5.74 Health and safety EQA 2010 makes an exception relating to pregnant women members in that it is not discriminatory if the association restricts or denies them access to a benefit, facility or service in order to remove or reduce a risk to their health and safety.[167] This restriction or denial may be based on the association's reasonable belief.[168] An association may restrict or deny such access to members other than pregnant women based on the same reasonable belief.[169] Equivalent provision is made in relation to associates and guests.[170]

15. CHILDREN INVOLVED IN CLUB ACTIVITIES

5.75 A club has always had a duty at law to look after children and young people, whether members or non-members, who participate in club activities.[171] There is no doubt that such clubs should have a written child protection policy and clear procedures for responding to child protection concerns, and sports clubs in particular should have a Child Welfare Officer. In May 2009 the National Society for the Prevention of Cruelty to Children launched an on-line film called 'Play Sport Stay Safe'.[172] Its message was that children and young people may be vulnerable to physical abuse, sexual abuse, bullying, disability discrimination and racial discrimination when on club premises for sporting or other activity. Parliament has now taken the matter a stage further. Under the Safeguarding Vulnerable Groups Act 2006 there was established the Independent Safeguarding Authority ('ISA') and a Vetting and Barring Scheme brought into force with effect from 12 October 2009 whereby certain people with regular contact with children were required to register with ISA. However, the scheme ran into serious criticism and in June 2010 the coalition government halted further registration under the scheme with the intention of substantially remodelling it, but the extant regulations continue in force.[173] Because of this state of affairs, we give only a brief explanation of the scheme.

---

166 Equality Act 2010, Sch 21, para 3.
167 Ibid, Sch 16, para 2(3)(a), (4)(a).
168 Ibid, Sch 16, para 2(3)(b), (4)(b).
169 Ibid, Sch 16, para 2(3)(c)–(d), (4)(b)–(c).
170 Ibid, Sch 16, para 2(3), (4).
171 By virtue of its acting *in loco parentis*.
172 See www.nspcc.org.uk/inform/cpsu/cpsu_wda57648.html.
173 Viz. SIs 2008/16; 2008/474; 2009/1548; 2009/1797; 2010/1146; 2010/1154; 2010/1171. Convoluted and poorly drafted, this legislation has had to be amended several times in its short life.

5.76 The 2006 Act established a Children's Barred List[174] and a person included on that list commits an offence if he engages in regulated activity.[175] Activity is regulated activity where (a) it is carried out by the same person frequently,[176] that is, once or more a week[177] or is carried out by the same person on three or more days in a 30-day period[178] or takes place overnight, that is, between the hours of 2 am and 6 am,[179] and (b) the activity includes any form of teaching, training or instruction of children[180] or, in certain prescribed circumstances, driving a vehicle used only for the purpose of conveying children and the person supervising or caring for the children.[181] A child is a person who has not attained the age of 18 years.[182] The scheme applies to volunteers as well as to paid employees.[183] A provider of regulated activity includes both an unincorporated members' club and an incorporated club,[184] and the provider too has obligations under the scheme. A club will therefore need to check a person's ISA status before it allows that person to have the requisite contact with children. In particular, the club as the provider has the duty of giving information to ISA if it withdraws a person engaged in regulated activity on the ground of risk of harm to a child ('the harm test').[185] The London Voluntary Service Council has published guidance on this topic.[186]

16. DATA PROTECTION

5.77 Overview In conducting its affairs the club will be bound to comply with the provisions of the Data Protection Act 1998 ('DPA 1998').[187] It is a complex piece of legislation[188] which came into effect in 2000 and is underwritten by a body of subordinate legislation including the Privacy and Electronic Communications (EC Directive) Regulations 2003.[189] The Act

---

174 Safeguarding Vulnerable Groups Act 2006, s 2.

175 Ibid, s 7(1).

176 Ibid, Sch 4, Part 1, para 1(2)(a).

177 'Frequent' is not defined in the 2006 Act or in the regulations but see the guidance referred to in footnote 186 below.

178 Safeguarding Vulnerable Groups Act 2006, Sch 4, Part 3, para 10(1) as amended by Safeguarding Vulnerable Groups Act 2006 (Regulated Activity, Devolution and Miscellaneous Provisions) Order 2010, SI 2010/1154.

179 Safeguarding Vulnerable Groups Act 2006, Sch 4, Part 3, para 10(2)(a).

180 Ibid, Sch 4, Part 1, para 2(1)(a).

181 Ibid, Sch 4, Part 1, para 2(1)(f).

182 Ibid, s 60(1).

183 Ibid, Sch 4, Part 1, para 2(6).

184 Ibid, ss 6(2)(a) and 6(10).

185 Ibid, s 35(1). What comprises the harm test is set out in s 35(4).

186 Guidance on Developing a Policy for Safeguarding Children and Vulnerable Adults, June 2010.

187 Data Protection Act 1998, s 5(3).

188 In *Campbell v MGN Ltd* [2003] 2 WLR 80, CA, at 100, the trial judge (Morland J) had described the path to his conclusion as weaving his way through a thicket.

189 SI 2003/2426.

exists to provide protection for people's personal information and to allow others to use it in accordance with set statutory principles.

5.78 The primary objective of DPA 1998 is to protect an individual's right to privacy[190] and to protect the accuracy of his personal data held by others in a computerised form or in a similarly organised manual filing system.[191] Data here means information recorded in a form in which it can be processed by computer or other automatic equipment or processed by manual records held in a 'relevant filing system'.[192] Secondly, data means information about a living individual who can be identified from the data, and includes his name and address, his bank details and any expression of opinion about the individual and any indication of the intentions of the data controller[193] or any other person in respect of that individual[194] (for example, the committee's appraisal of the honesty of the club treasurer, or the club's intention to invite a member to resign his membership on the grounds of his unpopularity). Personal data may be processed fairly and lawfully if the data subject has given his consent[195] or if the club has a legitimate interest in using or storing the data (for example, a member's rudeness towards a club employee).[196] There are stricter rules for *sensitive* personal data which means information as to the racial or ethnic origin of the data subject, his political opinions, his religious beliefs, his physical or mental health, his sexual life, the commission of any offence by him, and his membership of a trade union.[197] Sensitive data may be processed fairly and lawfully if the data subject has given his *explicit* consent[198] or if the club has an essential need to use or store the data (for example, a member's violent behaviour towards a club employee which amounted to a criminal offence).[199] Sensitive data may also be processed if the following conditions are satisfied: (a) the processing is carried out in the course of the club's legitimate activities, (b) the club is not established or conducted for gain and it exists for political, philosophical, religious or trade-union purposes, (c) the processing relates only to club members or to those who have regular contact with the club in connection with its purposes, and (d) the sensitive personal data is not disclosed to a third party without the data subject's consent.[200]

---

190 The invasion of privacy engages Article 8 of the European Convention Human Rights, viz. the right to respect for one's private and family life, one's home and one's correspondence.

191 *Durant v Financial Services Authority* [2004] FSR 28, CA, at [4].

192 Data Protection Act 1998, s 1(1).

193 See **5.79** as to who counts as the data controller.

194 Data Protection Act 1998, s 1. Mere mention of the data subject in a document does not necessarily amount to personal data; it has to be information that affects his privacy, whether in his personal or family life or in his business or professional capacity (per Auld LJ, at [28] in *Durant's* case).

195 Ibid, Sch 2, para 1.

196 Ibid, Sch 2, para 3.

197 Ibid, s 2.

198 Ibid, Sch 3, para 1. That is to say, implied consent is not sufficient.

199 Ibid, Sch 3, para 2(1).

200 Ibid, Sch 3, para 4.

5.79 The data controller This means the person who, either alone or in common with other persons, determines the purposes for which and the manner in which any personal data is, or is to be, processed.[201] In a club this would normally be the secretary.

5.80 Data protection principles The eight principles are set out in Part I of Sch 1 to DPA 1998. They may be summarised as follows. All personal data must:

(1) be fairly and lawfully processed;
(2) be processed for a specified and lawful purpose;
(3) be adequate, relevant and not excessive;
(4) be accurate and, where necessary, kept up to date;
(5) not be kept for longer than necessary;
(6) be processed in accordance with the rights of the individual;
(7) be kept secure;
(8) not be transferred to a country outside the European Economic Area unless that country ensures an adequate level of protection for such data.

5.81 Exemptions Part IV of the Act lists the exemptions from compliance with the data protection principles. Areas of activity where exemptions are granted include:

(1) national security;[202]
(2) crime and taxation;[203]
(3) health, education and social work;[204]
(4) regulatory activity[205] eg data processed by the Director of Fair Trading in the course of his statutory functions;
(5) journalism, literature and art;[206]
(6) research, history and statistics.[207]

5.82 Data in a manual filing system An important point to note concerns the accessibility of manual data held in a 'relevant filing system'. In *Durant v Financial Services Authority*[208] Lord Justice Auld, at [48], had this to say about DPA 1998 in relation to manual records:

---

201 Data Protection Act 1998, s 1(1).
202 Ibid, s 28.
203 Ibid, s 29.
204 Ibid, s 30.
205 Ibid, s 31.
206 Ibid, s 32.
207 Ibid, s 33.
208 [2004] FSR 28, CA.

> 'It is plain … that Parliament intended to apply the Act to manual records only if they are of sufficient sophistication to provide the same or similar ready accessibility as a computerised filing system. That requires a filing system so referenced or indexed that it enables the data controller's employee responsible to identify at the outset of his search with reasonable certainty and speed the file or files in which the specific data relating to the person requesting the information is located and to locate the relevant information about him within the file or files, without having to do a manual search. To leave it to the searcher to leaf through files, possibly at great length and cost, and fruitlessly, to see whether it or they contain information relating to the person requesting information and whether that information is data within the Act … cannot have been intended by Parliament.'

This judicial pronouncement has the curious effect of seemingly encouraging a club to keep personal data on a casual and haphazard basis as a way of avoiding DPA 1998 but this would only be of assistance to a disorganised club. A properly run club now needs to computerise its records and thus clubs will have to face the fact that DPA 1998 will apply to them.

5.83 Member's access to data The club member as the data subject has the following rights of access to personal data:[209]

(1) to be informed by the data controller whether such data is being processed concerning him;
(2) if so, to be given a description of that data; the purposes for which it is being processed; and the identity of the recipients of that data;
(3) to be informed of the source of information available to the data controller;
(4) where the processing of personal data is carried out by automatic means (eg by computer) for the purpose of evaluating matters relating to him (eg his creditworthiness, his reliability or his conduct) and this processing has constituted, or is likely to constitute, the sole basis for any decision affecting him, to be informed by the data controller of the logic involved in that decision-taking.

5.84 The data controller is not obliged to supply any information unless he has received a request in writing from the data subject and has received a fee not exceeding the prescribed maximum, currently (2010) the sum of £2.00,[210] as he may require.[211] Where the data controller cannot comply with the request without disclosing information relating to another individual

---

209 Data Protection Act 1998, s 7(1). The court can order the data controller to comply with a request for information (ibid, s 7(9)) and the court can call for and look at documents before making its decision under s 7(1)(d): ibid, s 15(2) and see *Johnson v Medical Defence Union* [2005] 1 WLR 750.

210 Data Protection Act 1998, s 7(1), (2), and Data Protection (Subject Access) (Fees and

who can be identified from that information, he is not obliged to comply with the request unless either the other individual has consented or it is reasonable in all the circumstances to comply with the request without the consent of the other individual.[212] In assessing the reasonableness of dispensing with such consent the data controller must take into account any duty of confidentiality owed to the other individual.[213] On the other hand, the data controller is obliged to give the information requested if this is possible by redaction of or omission from the information the name or other identifying particulars of the other individual.[214] An example may help. Suppose at a committee meeting of the Basset Social Club a committee member proposes under the rules that Peter Gurney, a longstanding member of the club, be co-opted as a committee member but Harry Hawke, the club treasurer, opposes the motion on the ground that Mr Gurney is well-known at the club for being a troublemaker. The proposal is defeated and the matter is fully recorded in the minutes. Mr Gurney knows from his proposer that his co-option was to be discussed at the meeting. Can he now request the secretary as the data controller to supply him with the information about himself contained in those minutes? The secretary considers that the request is a legitimate one under DPA 1998. Let us assume that Mr Gurney may be a difficult person on occasion but it is wholly unfair and defamatory to describe him as a troublemaker. The proceedings of the committee are confidential to the committee members so a duty of confidentiality is owed to Mr Hawke. The secretary therefore approaches Mr Hawke to seek his consent to the information contained in the minutes about the co-option being communicated to Mr Gurney, but Mr Hawke refuses to give his consent because he is concerned about his own position. The short answer is that the secretary should supply to Mr Gurney a suitably redacted copy of the minutes or a relevant extract thereof, omitting from the text any reference to Mr Hawke's name or other particulars which might identify him. Since the confidentiality of the minutes belongs to the whole committee, it would be a wise move on the part of the data controller to consult the committee before releasing any information to the data subject.

5.85 Notification to the Commissioner Provided the club is processing and storing personal data for its own purposes and will not be divulging any personal data to outside third parties, there will be no need for the data controller to notify the Information Commissioner.[215] Thus it is thought that a large number of small clubs will be exempt from notification. Nevertheless, the Commissioner has power to enforce the Data Protection

Miscellaneous Provisions) Regulations 2000, SI 2000/191, amended by Data Protection (Subject Access) (Fees and Miscellaneous Provisions) (Amendment) Regulations 2001, SI 2001/3223.

211 Data Protection Act 1998, s 7(2).

212 Ibid, s 7(4).

213 Ibid, s 7(6)(a).

214 Ibid, s 7(5).

215 See ibid, ss 16–20 for the requirement of notification.

Principles against those who are exempt from notification.[216] This is done by way of an enforcement notice.[217] If the data controller is under a duty to notify, he must pay the annual notification fee, currently (2010) the sum of £35.[218]

5.86 Committee membership list The committee acts on behalf of all the members in managing the affairs of the club (see **5.34**). A principal will obviously be entitled to know who is his agent and how he may be contacted. The name and contact details of a committee member is personal data which is protected in the ordinary course of events. But we consider that the committee member impliedly consents to this data being released to the general membership on his joining the committee,[219] and a committee list should be circulated annually by the club. This consent does not include the release of sensitive personal data, such as the committee member's sexual orientation, which would require his express consent before being released to the general membership, nor does this consent extend to persons outside the membership of the club. This matter is best dealt with in the rules.

5.87 General membership list DPA 1998 has caused considerable confusion over the ability of a club to compile a list of members for circulation to the general membership. It is clear that on joining a club a member impliedly consents to the club holding his name, address and other contact details as part of a membership list; otherwise the club could not function as such. What is less clear is whether the member impliedly consents to his fellow members having these personal details. We take the robust view that insofar as collegiality is an essential criterion of a club,[220] the member does impliedly consent to his fellow members knowing who he is and how he may be contacted; otherwise one might ask why anyone would want to join a club in the first place if he desired to keep this information private.[221] A lack of a circulated membership list might on occasion have an adverse effect on the democratic running of the club. Suppose certain members of the Basset Social Club wanted to convene a

---

216 Data Protection Act, s 40(1). See also the annotation by Andrew Charlesworth LLB in Current Law Statutes 1998, vol 1, p 29–25.

217 Ibid, s 40(1).

218 Ibid, s 18; Data Protection (Notification and Notification Fees) Regulations 2000, SI 2000/188. The fee of £35 applies where the data controller is in Tier 1 (applicable to almost all clubs).

219 Or at any rate sufficient contact details: e g the release of the committee member's land line telephone number but not necessarily his mobile telephone number.

220 See **1.1**.

221 An issue could arise here under Article 8 of the European Convention on Human Rights. Names and addresses are in themselves neutral in this context. Their lawful use or disclosure depends on whether they are being used or disclosed in pursuit of a legitimate object and, if so, whether such use or disclosure is proportionate: *R (Robertson) v Wakefield Metropolitan District Council* [2002] QB 1052, at [29]–[35] (Maurice Kay J).

special meeting to pass a Vote of No Confidence[222] in the committee and under the rules this required a requisition of 30 members. Without a membership list the members' right to call the meeting might be stultified, especially if the secretary was unwilling to give the aggrieved members any help on this point.

5.88 We therefore consider that there should be a presumption in any club that a membership list will be provided to its members, and we see no reason why this matter should not be dealt with appropriately in the rules.[223] If the members were to conclude that there was an unacceptable risk that their confidential membership list, if circulated to all the members, might fall into the wrong hands or there were policy reasons for distributing a restricted membership list, for instance, one which omitted the addresses of junior members, these reservations can be the subject of discussion and, if required, resolutions at a general meeting, or they can be dealt with in the bye-laws. If a list is circulated, this will be on the clear understanding that its contents are protected by DPA 1998.

- ***Incorporated clubs*** We point out here that under the Companies Act 2006 the company is obliged to keep a register of members[224] which is available for inspection without charge by a member of the company and on payment of a prescribed fee by a member of the public,[225] in either case pursuant to a request stating the purpose for which the information is to be used.[226] The register must contain the name and address of each member[227] and, if the company has more than 50 members, it must be indexed.[228] The company has the right to go to court to prevent inspection of the register if it asserts that such inspection or the provision of a copy of the list of members is not being sought for a proper purpose.[229]

5.89 Membership data on club's website A website is now a commonplace, useful and, in many ways, economical means of providing information about the club and its activities and of communicating with the members and the outside world. Setting up a website involves registering a domain, web hosting and website designing, none of which comes cheaply. The club's website will be accessed via the World Wide Web, which is independent of the club and the use of which will be at the user's risk. Crucially, certain pages of the website, such as membership details, will be only available to club members who will have been issued with a User

---

222 See **5.30**.
223 See eg Rule 16 of the model rules in Appendix 10.
224 Companies Act 2006, s 113(1).
225 Ibid, s 116(1).
226 Ibid, s 116(3).
227 Ibid, s 113(2).
228 Ibid, s 115(1).
229 Ibid, s 117(3).

Name and a Password to log-in; use of this procedure will constitute an opt-in. The registration data and certain other information about the member will be subject to the club's privacy policy, which includes compliance with the data protection principles, and the website will be protected by intellectual property rights, including copyright. It will often have links to third party websites. It is important for the club to give notice on its website of the exclusion of liability on its part for any loss or damage arising out of any person's use of, or inability to use, the website or in respect of any negligent misstatement on the website.[230] The club's liability for defamatory statements published on the club's website is dealt with in **12.57**.

17. DEALING WITH INTERNAL DISPUTES

5.90 Introduction Many clubs are anxious that if a dispute arises between the club and its members or between the members themselves which relates to the club's rules or bye-laws or which concerns the affairs of the club, it should be dealt with privately, and thus the rules make provision for private dispute resolution, usually by mediation or arbitration. Under the rules the mediator or arbitrator may be either an internal or an external appointment. What happens, however, if the aggrieved member ignores the arbitration clause because he wants, say, the publicity of a court case and issues a claim form against the club? The answer is for the club to seek a stay of the court proceedings under s 9 of the Arbitration Act 1996. Such a stay is mandatory unless the arbitration agreement is null and void, inoperative or incapable of being performed. A further point to note is that an individual may waive his right of access to the courts under Article 6(1) of the European Convention on Human Rights[231] by entering into a contract in which he agrees to submit disputes to arbitration.[232]

5.91 Unincorporated members' clubs The rules must specifically deal with resolution of disputes since a contractual term to exclude recourse to the courts in the event of a dispute will be void on public policy grounds[233] unless accompanied by the provision of arbitration. If the rules are silent on the point, no term will be implied into them that the complaint or dispute must be dealt with internally, but the parties may by consent agree to some form of private dispute resolution and if the matter came to court the parties are now required to give consideration to resolving their dispute other than by litigation.[234]

---

230 See *Hedley Byrne & Co Ltd v Heller & Partners Ltd* [1964] AC 465.

231 The Human Rights Act 1998 incorporated this convention into UK domestic law.

232 *Deweer v Belgium* [1979–1980] EHRR 439, at [49].

233 *Lee v The Showmen's Guild of Great Britain* [1952] 2 QB 329, CA, at 342 (Denning LJ); *Baker v Jones* [1954] 1 WLR 1005, at 1010.

234 See **18.36**.

5.92 Working men's clubs Dispute settlement is a mandatory matter for the rules.[235] The Friendly Societies Act 1992 put in place substituted provisions as to how disputes are to be resolved.[236] Disputes shall be resolved by arbitration in the manner directed by the rules and, without derogating from this right to go to arbitration, the club may establish internal procedures for the resolution of complaints or the parties may consent to a reference to an adjudicator for investigation and settlement of the complaint.

5.93 Community clubs Unlike the Friendly Societies Act 1992, the Co-operative and Community Benefit Societies and Credit Unions Act 1965 does not make dispute settlement a mandatory matter for the rules. Instead, the Act regulates the position as follows: if the rules give directions as to the manner in which disputes are to be decided, this procedure must be adopted, unless the parties to the dispute by consent refer the matter to the county court.[237] Whichever procedure is adopted, any decision on the dispute shall be binding and conclusive on all parties without appeal and shall not be removable into any court of law or restrainable by injunction.[238] If the rules direct that the dispute shall be heard by justices in a magistrates' court, the parties to the dispute may by consent refer the matter to the county court.[239] If the rules are silent on the question of dispute settlement, or if no decision on the dispute is made within 40 days after application for a reference under the rules, any party to the dispute may apply to the county court or to a magistrates' court for a determination of the dispute.[240]

5.94 Shop clubs Dispute settlement is a mandatory matter for the rules.[241] No other statutory provision applies. The procedure laid down by the rules must be followed, although presumably it would be in order for the parties to the dispute mutually to consent to some other mode of dispute resolution.

5.95 Incorporated clubs The situation is the same as for an unincorporated members' club: see **5.91**. Any provision for resolution of the dispute

---

235 Friendly Societies Act 1974, s 7(2) and Sch 2, Part I(9).

236 Friendly Societies Act 1992, ss 80 and 81, replacing Friendly Societies Act 1974, ss 76–80.

237 Co-operative and Community Benefit Societies and Credit Unions Act 1965, s 60(1)(2), as amended by Friendly Societies Act 1992, s 83.

238 Co-operative and Community Benefit Societies and Credit Unions Act 1965, s 60(3). Parliamentary draftsmanship has gone awry here. In 1965 the original version of s 60 gave as an alternative to arbitration a determination of the dispute by the Chief Registrar of Friendly Societies. In 1992, in substituting the county court for the Chief Registrar, Parliament overlooked the prohibition that the decision was not to be removable to any court of law. The prohibition would still apply to decisions made via an internal procedure.

239 Ibid, s 60(5).

240 Ibid, s 60(6).

241 Shop Clubs Act 1902, Sch, para viii.

by some internal procedure or by mediation or arbitration must appear in the club rules or bye-laws or in the articles.

5.96 Proprietary clubs It is for the proprietor to frame a suitable rule dealing with resolution of disputes between the proprietor and the members. The situation is very similar to that of an unincorporated members' club.

Chapter 6

MEETINGS OF CLUB MEMBERS

1. INTRODUCTION

6.1 The holding of meetings of club members is an essential part of club life. Members' clubs incorporated under the Companies Acts in this respect have a distinct advantage over unincorporated members' clubs. They are much aided by the procedural rules set out in the Companies Act 2006 and, where applicable, in the Insolvency Act 1986. No such cushion is available to unincorporated members' clubs. Here it is crucial that these clubs have express rules which adequately deal with the convening and holding of meetings both of the members and of the committee. In the absence of any express rule, we consider that the members would almost certainly have an implied right to convene and hold meetings[1] but this would not be a satisfactory regime under which to function. On the other hand, working men's clubs, community clubs and shop clubs usually have adequate or sufficient rules covering the topic of meetings because in each case they are obliged by statute to make provision in their rules for the mode of holding meetings and the right of voting.[2]

2. ANNUAL GENERAL MEETING

6.2 Nowadays it is almost unheard of for the rules of a members' club not to make provision for the holding of an annual general meeting ('AGM'). It was a mandatory requirement where the club held a registration certificate under the Licensing Act 1964[3] and, although this requirement has not been carried through to the Licensing Act 2003, we consider that an absence of any procedure whereby an AGM is held would probably offend against the sixth criterion (the need for collegiality) referred to in **1.1**. Its importance lies in the fact that it provides the opportunity for the members to receive reports about the club activities during the preceding year and to discuss the way forward for the coming year. The main items of business of an AGM are: receiving reports from the secretary and the treasurer; receiving and, if thought fit, approving the club's accounts for the preceding financial

---

1 By reason of the sixth criterion (the need for collegiality) referred to in **1.1**.

2 Friendly Societies Act 1974, Sch 2, para 4; Co-operative and Community Benefit Societies and Credit Unions Act 1965, Sch 1, para 5; Shop Clubs Act 1902, Sch, para iii.

3 Licensing Act 1964, Sch 7, para 2(1).

year; electing the officers of the club and members of the committee; fixing the subscriptions; and transacting the general business of the club. The date of the AGM is often fixed in the rules by specifying an actual date (or sometimes the month) which must not be passed in each year without an AGM having been held. Commonly, too, the rules stipulate that an interval of more than 15 months must not elapse between successive AGMs, and this was a mandatory requirement where the club held a registration certificate.[4]

6.3 The item 'any other business' (often abbreviated to 'AOB') needs clarification. Its proper use at an AGM is to deal with points arising out of the *general* business of the club, that is, what has gone before in the other items on the agenda. Some rules draw a distinction between general and special business[5] by defining all business as special save those items regularly appearing on the AGM agenda, in order that the AOB item at the AGM cannot be abused. The AOB item at the AGM cannot be used to pass a specific proposal or to raise important matters unconnected with the general business of the club. On the other hand, the AOB item is a proper opportunity for members to put questions or observations to officers of the club. The dividing line between the proper use and the improper use of the AOB item is a fine one, and it ultimately falls to the chairman of the meeting to decide where to draw the line.

6.4 Some rules dealing with important matters state that such matters may only be dealt with 'at a meeting called for the purpose'. Can they be raised at an AGM? The answer is in the negative because an AGM is convened to conduct the general business of the club, which does not include special business such as amendment of the rules or dissolution of the club.[6] The doubt can easily be avoided by stating in the rule, 'at a *special* meeting called for the purpose'. However, it is common practice nowadays, in order to save time and money, for amendments to the rules, especially non-contentious ones, to be permitted at the AGM provided proper notice is given to the members. In this event, the item on the agenda will be marked 'Special business'.[7]

3. SPECIAL MEETINGS

6.5 These are meetings of the club members which deal with special business, that is to say, meetings which are called for a particular and stated purpose (or purposes) and which, generally speaking, cannot be dealt with

---

4 Licensing Act 1964, Sch 7, para 2(1).

5 Special business is not be confused with special resolutions, a term of art used in company law.

6 *Harington v Sendall* [1903] 1 Ch 921, at 926.

7 See the example given in Appendix 11.

at an AGM. Their correct legal name is a special general meeting or, in company law, an extraordinary general meeting (or EGM).[8] The only business that can be transacted at a special meeting is that business for which the meeting was called. There will therefore be no AOB item at the end of the agenda.

6.6 Special meetings are convened by order of the managing committee or on the requisition of the members. The rules should stipulate the number of members required for a valid requisition. Where a club held a registration certificate under the Licensing Act 1964, the rules had to specify a number not exceeding 30 or more than one-fifth of the total membership (whichever was the less).[9] This provision is not repeated in the Licensing Act 2003 but nevertheless it is considered a good working rule for all clubs. Membership here means ordinary members. If a club has fewer than 150 members, the specified number would necessarily be less than 30; for a club with 100 members a requisition by 20 members would suffice. The question arises whether a requisition can be made orally as well as in writing. Many rules talk in terms of a requisition *signed* by a specified number which presupposes a written document. A requisition is a formal demand and it may be doubted whether an oral demand would be valid.[10]

6.7 Failure to convene The question arises as to what happens if the committee (or the directors of an incorporated club) fail or refuse to convene a duly requisitioned meeting. In an incorporated club this difficulty is surmounted by s 305(1) of the Companies Act 2006 giving power to the requisitionists themselves to convene the meeting.[11] In a community club the difficulty is surmounted by giving power to the Financial Services Authority to call a special meeting upon the application of one-tenth of the membership of a registered society or, in the case of a society with more than 1,000 members, of 100 of those members.[12] In an unincorporated members' club which held a registration certificate the rules had to contain a provision that the members entitled to attend and vote at a general meeting would have the ability to summon a general meeting,[13] and we regard such a rule as imperative in all unincorporated members' clubs. However, in the absence of an express rule we consider that the

---

8 Regulation 36 of Table A Articles of Association: Companies (Tables A to F) Regulations 1985, SI 1985/805. Clubs commonly refer to their special meetings as EGMs.

9 Licensing Act 1964, Sch 7, para 2(3).

10 In the Chambers Dictionary (1998) the first definition of 'requisition' refers to a formal demand; the second definition refers to military supply; and the third definition is 'the *written* order for the supply of materials' (emphasis added).

11 The court may, on its own application or on the application of a director or a member entitled to vote at the meeting, order a meeting to be called, held and conducted in any manner the court thinks fit: Companies Act, 2006, s 306(2); and see *Re British Union for the Abolition of Vivisection* [1995] 2 BCLC 1 (where the court permitted proxy voting at a future EGM because the previously held EGM had degenerated into a near riot).

12 Co-operative and Community Benefit Societies and Credit Unions Act 1965, s 49(1)(b).

13 Licensing Act 1964, Sch 7, para 2(3). The Licensing Act 2003 contains no such requirement.

requisitionists themselves would have an implied right to convene such a meeting, otherwise it would render nugatory their collegiate rights. As a last resort the thwarted requisionists could apply to the court for relief.

4. INFORMAL MEETINGS

6.8 The committee may call at any time informal meetings of the members on any topic which is relevant to the expressed objects of the club. It follows that the vast majority of meetings of the members should not be classed as special meetings. For example, an invitation by the committee to all the members to discuss the club's blueprint for the better organisation of the club premises can be convened as a discussion group in order to sound out the members about its draft proposals. Generally speaking, it is only when a resolution is proposed to be put before the meeting which will be binding on all the members that the formalities of a special meeting are required.

5. NOTICE OF GENERAL MEETINGS

6.9 **Proper notice** There are two propositions which govern the convening of a general meeting of the members:

(1) the notice must be given timeously;[14]
(2) the notice must be given to every member who is entitled to attend and vote and who is not beyond summonable distance.[15]

6.10 To ensure their attendance each member should receive a notice which tells them (1) the date, (2) the time, (3) the place and (4) the nature of the business to be discussed or transacted. The rules should specify what length of notice a member will receive in respect of any particular type of meeting. A common period of notice is 14 days for a general meeting of the members and 21 days for an annual general meeting. In *Labouchere v Earl of Wharncliffe*[16] the plaintiff was a member of the Beefsteak Club, who had an altercation with another club member and then wrote a letter and articles about it in his magazine called Truth. A general meeting was called by the committee to consider the expulsion of the plaintiff and the resolution to expel him was carried. The rules required a fortnight's notice of the

---

14 *Labouchere v Earl of Wharncliffe* (1879) 13 Ch D 346.

15 *Smyth v Darley* (1849) 2 HL Cas 789, at 803 (Lord Campbell LC) (concerning the election of an officer, namely, the county treasurer of the city of Dublin); *Young v Imperial Ladies Club Ltd* [1920] 2 KB 523, CA, at 536 (Scrutton LJ) (concerning the expulsion of a member of a club); and *John v Rees* [1970] Ch 345, at 402 (Megarry J) (concerning the suspension of a local Labour Party).

16 (1879) 13 Ch D 346.

meeting. In the member's action against the club Sir George Jessel MR, at 352, had this to say about the time and manner of giving notice of meetings:

> 'In the present instance a meeting of the committee was held on the night of the 31st October, and concluded on the morning of the 1st November. That meeting decided to proceed in a very proper way, both by posting a notice in the coffee-room[17] of the club and by sending a circular to each of the members. So far as I am aware there is no common law [precept] for clubs as to the mode in which notices should be issued; and where no [club] rule prescribes a mode, it is within the general functions of a committee of a club to say how notices should be given on each particular occasion.
>
> Some matters connected with a club concern only those who habitually use it; and in connection with these matters, the posting of a notice in the coffee-room or the library is a very sensible plan to follow. But more important matters sometimes [arise] – matters relating, perhaps, to some organic change – matters connected with the general mode of conducting the club – matters connected with the conduct of a particular member; and in such cases it is only right to give notice by circular to those who do not habitually or daily use the club that these matters are coming on for consideration, in order that they may attend and take part in the discussion. When the latter course was adopted, the committee were bound to give a fortnight's notice. In this case the notice was for 14th November. If it was posted on 1st November, that would not be a fortnight's notice, and it was posted on the 1st November.'

The judge therefore held that, as the meeting was irregularly called, the committee had no power to expel Mr Labouchere.[18]

6.11 The computation of time has given rise to many disputes in the law. Suffice it to say that the general rule is that where the expression, '14 days' notice', is used the day of service is excluded,[19] so the judge in *Labouchere's* case was correct in saying the notice was one day short. The rule applies too if the fixed period of time is described as 'from' such-and-such a date.[20] It is otherwise if the fixed period of time is described as 'beginning with' such-and-such a date; here the first day is included.[21] If the notice prescribed is one of '14 clear days' or 'not less than 14 days', or 'at least 14

17 Many London clubs for historical reasons still call their dining room the coffee room. In *The Wind in the Willows* (published 1908) Mr Toad goes into the coffee-room of the Red Lion Hotel to have luncheon before driving off in another gentleman's motor-car.

18 Henry Labouchère was a journalist and Radical MP (1880–1906) who famously quipped, 'I do not object to Mr Gladstone always having the ace of trumps up his sleeve, only to his pretence that God put it there'.

19 *Zoan v Rouamba* [2000] 1 WLR 1509, CA, at [23], citing *Young v Higgon* [1840] 6 M & W 49.

20 Ibid, at [23], citing *Goldsmiths' Co v West Metropolitan Railway Co* [1904] 1 KB 1.

21 Ibid, at [24], citing *Hare v Gocher* [1962] 2 QB 641.

days', the last day has to be subtracted as well as the day of service when computing the period,[22] thus covering a period of 16 days. If the rules are silent on the question of notice, reasonable notice must be given. In incorporated clubs a general meeting of the company must be called by notice of at least 14 days,[23] although the articles may prescribe a longer period of notice[24] and insofar as annual general meetings are concerned it would be usual to specify at least 21 days' notice.[25] The Companies Act 2006 has adopted the 'clear day' rule for the notice of general meetings.[26]

6.12 The omission to give due notice of a meeting to even one member of a body, who is entitled to attend and vote[27] at the meeting and who is not beyond summonable distance, renders invalid the meeting and any decision thereat.[28] It is therefore a wise precaution to send out as a matter of course notice to all members whether or not they are thought to be within summonable distance. An invalid decision may in some circumstances be acquiesced in[29] or ratified[30] or the omission may be excusable.[31]

6.13 Non-receipt of notice If the two propositions referred to in **6.9** above were to be applied in their full rigour, this could be very inimical to organising valid meetings. First, although a member might well have a legitimate grievance if he did not receive, or received too late, notice of an important meeting, we consider that any request for the meeting to be reconvened should be refused if (a) the meeting was otherwise quorate and (b) the managing committee is satisfied that neither the aggrieved member's attendance at the meeting nor his vote thereat would have affected the outcome of any decision taken or any resolution passed.[32] Upon refusal the member's remedy would be to seek a court declaration that the meeting was invalid, an expensive and fruitless exercise if on reconvening the meeting the same result occurs. Secondly, the best and usual way of avoiding the consequences of failure to comply with these two propositions is to have the following express club rules:

---

22 *R v Turner* [1910] 1 KB 346, CA, at 359–360.

23 Companies Act 2006, s 307(1).

24 Ibid, s 307(3).

25 For public companies the AGM notice must be for at least 21 days: ibid, s 307(2)(a).

26 Ibid, s 360.

27 So that members without votes, such as honorary or junior members, need not be notified.

28 See the cases cited in footnote 15 above.

29 *Abbatt v Treasury Solicitor* [1969] 1 WLR 1575, CA, at 1583.

30 *In re Sick and Funeral Society of St John's Sunday School, Golcar* [1973] 1 Ch 51, at 57 (Megarry J).

31 *Young v Imperial Ladies Club Ltd* [1920] 2 KB 523, CA, at 536.

32 If more than one member is complaining about breaches of the two propositions, the committee must of course consider the cumulative effect of the absence of such members from the meeting.

(1) a rule which states that a sent notice shall be deemed to have been received by the member within a specified time of it being sent or delivered by whichever means was used by the club;[33]

(2) a rule which states that the accidental omission to give notice to one or more persons entitled to receive notice shall not invalidate the proceedings of the meeting in question. Incorporated clubs can rely on s 313 of the Companies Act 2006 which states that the accidental omission to give notice to one or more persons entitled to receive notice shall be disregarded.

6.14 Postal and electronic service The world has moved on and whereas formerly notice of meetings was always given in a hard copy format by post or personally, technological advances have decreed that electronic communication is the order of the day. The recognition of this state of affairs was reflected in the Electronic Communications Act 2000. The Companies Act 2006 laid down a new regime for notification of company meetings which we consider should be universally adopted for club meetings:

(1) Section 308 states the general rule. Notice of a general meeting of a company must be given:
   (a) in hard copy form, or
   (b) in electronic form, or
   (c) by means of a website

   or partly by one such means and partly by another.

(2) Section 1168 elaborates on the general rule:
   (i) a document is sent in hard copy form if it is sent in a paper copy or similar form capable of being read;
   (ii) a document is sent in electronic form if it is sent by electronic means (eg by e-mail or fax) or by some other means while in an electronic form (eg sending a disk by post);
   (iii) the recipient of a document in electronic form must be able to retain a copy of it;
   (iv) any sent document must be capable of being read with the naked eye;
   (v) to the extent that any document consists of images (eg photographs, pictures, maps, plans and drawings), the image must be capable of being seen with the naked eye.

6.15 It is, however, a cardinal principle that neither the club nor the member can be compelled to communicate electronically if they do not wish to do so. There must be mutual agreement. However, there is no doubt that electronic communication is not only much cheaper than postage but it is also swifter and absolves the secretary from a tedious administrative chore

---

33 On the other hand, a deeming provision might on occasion convert a valid notice into an invalid one so that the rule should add 'unless the contrary is shown': *Barclays Bank of Swaziland Ltd v Hahn* [1989] 1 WLR 506, HL.

in preparing and sending out letters. If electronic means of communicating notice of meetings are intended to be used in members' clubs, the rules must make specific provision for this. We add in parenthesis that by adding this facility the club does not preclude itself from communicating with its members by post or other means if it so wishes. Indeed, the rules need to cater for persons who do not have access to a computer, either by choice or for some other reason; otherwise the club will be impliedly stipulating that only those persons with a computer will be eligible for membership, and this must be wrong in principle. On the other hand, there is nothing untoward in the rules stipulating that if a member wishes to be contacted by the postal service to the exclusion of other means he must give express written notice of this fact to the secretary.

6.16 There are two means other than by hard copy by which documents can be made available to members: (1) by placing them on the club's website; and (2) by sending them electronically to the individual member. In adopting the first method the club will be offering to e-mail to members a hyperlink to web pages containing the document. In this event the club must decide the format to be used. If a document is posted to a website it should be available in basic HTML format so it can be read by browsers likely to be available to members such as Internet Explorer or Mozilla Firefox. In adopting the second method the club's usual method will be to e-mail the document by way of attachment. In this event the attachment should be in a technology likely to be available to members such as Microsoft Word or an Adobe pdf file.

6.17 Any e-mail address, telephone or fax number or any other 'address' supplied by the member for the transmission of electronic communication is normally protected by the Data Protection Act 1998 and is not covered by any statutory exemption. It should therefore not be released to third parties without the consent of the member[34] or pursuant to some statutory authority.[35]

6.18 It is perhaps necessary to point out that electronic communication, even where authorised by the rules, may not be the appropriate means of communication in particular circumstances. For example, if the club wished to investigate a complaint of serious misconduct made against a member, it would be very unwise to communicate with the member otherwise than by a posted letter marked 'private and confidential'. Likewise, it is considered good practice that when an important matter is to be discussed by the members either at the AGM or at a special meeting, especially where it involves the scrutiny of documents, communication should be made via the post.

---

34 See **5.78**.
35 See eg **5.81**.

6. ATTENDANCE AT MEETINGS

6.19 Here one must draw a distinction between private meetings of the club members and those meetings to which non-members or strangers are invited. In the latter case it is for the club to decide whom it shall invite, bearing in mind the rules of the club and, if applicable, the provisions of the Licensing Act 2003. Any particular stranger to whom the club objects, say a photographer from the local press, may be requested to leave and, if he refuses to go, he becomes a trespasser who may be ejected with the minimum of force as is reasonably necessary.[36]

6.20 Strangers have no right to attend private meetings of the club members and may only do so provided no objection is taken to their presence. Any objection to the presence of a stranger should be taken as a point of order at the outset of the meeting before any item on the agenda is discussed. Suppose the point of order is upheld by the chairman: is that the end of the matter? We consider that the answer is in the affirmative, even if the objection is made by one person only. The valid point of order should not be overruled by a consensus of the meeting, however large, expressing its desire for the stranger to remain. On the other hand, at a private meeting of the club the members could discuss as an item on the agenda whether to invite a stranger to attend a future private meeting for a particular purpose, for instance, an invitation to a solicitor to attend a committee meeting in order to give the committee advice and to answer questions about a problematic club trust fund. If the resolution was passed, the solicitor's subsequent attendance would not give rise to any point of order.

6.21 A member who is entitled to attend a meeting may not be suspended or expelled from a meeting, however truculent he is, provided his behaviour is not disorderly and does not obstruct the due processes of the meeting.[37] If the member is guilty of disorderly conduct he may temporarily be excluded or removed from the meeting, or he may be expelled therefrom.[38] It is the one of the chairman's duties to oversee this aspect of the meeting: see **6.24**.

7. AGENDA

6.22 The agenda for a general meeting is normally prepared by the secretary. A specimen agenda for an AGM may be found at Appendix 11.

---

36 *R v Chief Constable of Devon and Cornwall, ex p Central Electricity Generating Board* [1982] 1 QB 458, CA, at 478.

37 *Barton v Taylor* (1886) 11 App Cas 197, at 204 (concerning the New South Wales Assembly).

38 *Doyle v Falconer* (1865–1867) LR 1 PC 328, at 340 (concerning Dominican Legislative Assembly).

Formal motions which are proposed to be put to the meeting should be set out in full; this is especially important if the agenda is for a special meeting called for a particular purpose. It is improper to depart from the order in which the items are set down in the agenda unless a majority of the meeting agrees to the contrary.[39] The agenda for a committee meeting is sometimes prepared by the secretary, at other times by the committee chairman. It is good practice to try to keep the committee agenda running in the same order from meeting to meeting. It is important for an agenda to have an item 'Matters Arising', that is to say, arising out of the minutes of the last meeting.

8. CHAIRMAN OF MEETINGS

6.23 The chairman of the club by virtue of his office is the correct person to chair general meetings of club members. What happens in the absence of the duly appointed chairman? In all clubs one first has to look in the rules or bye-laws as to what, if anything, is said about the chairmanship of meetings. If the rules and bye-laws are silent and the chairman is absent from the meeting, the first task of the meeting will be to elect a chairman from those members present at the meeting. Commonly it is the secretary who deals with this situation; he should seek the nomination of a senior and respected member whom he thinks will control the meeting properly. This person does not necessarily have to be an officer of the club or a member of the committee. Once elected as chairman of the meeting, that person does not automatically cease to be the chairman if perchance the designated chairman were later to arrive at the meeting. This would depend on how far the meeting had progressed; in its early stages he might well stand down. In incorporated clubs this matter is regulated by statute. Section 319 of the Companies Act 2006 states that a member may be elected the chairman of a general meeting by a resolution of the company passed at that meeting but that this power is subject to any provision in the articles dealing with this topic. In existing companies formed before 1 October 2009 the question of chairmanship is dealt with in regs 42 and 43 of the Table A Regulations[40] and in companies formed on or after 1 October 2009 this question is dealt with in art 25 for companies limited by guarantee and in art 39 for companies limited by shares, each under their respective 2008 Model Articles.[41]

6.24 Chairman's duties The duties cast upon a chairman of a meeting are not only important but must be properly exercised to ensure a well-conducted meeting, remembering Mr Justice Megarry's dictum that,

39 *John v Rees* [1970] Ch 345, at 378.
40 SI 1985/805.
41 Companies (Model Articles) Regulations 2008, SI 2008/3229.

'Above all, [the chairman's] duty is to act not as dictator but as a servant of the members of the body, according to law'.[42] The chairman's duties may be summarised as follows:

(1) to check that the meeting has been properly convened;
(2) to ensure that a quorum of members is present;
(3) to welcome such guests or visitors as are permitted at the meeting;
(4) to adjourn the meeting to a larger meeting place if the chosen place is too small to accommodate the members present (if one is available)[43] or to adjourn the meeting to a later date at a different venue or, if necessary, to abandon the meeting;[44]
(5) to keep order and, if possible, to restore order if disorder breaks out and, in the latter event, to adjourn the meeting either for a short time or generally if his efforts to restore order are in vain;[45]
(6) to remain impartial throughout the meeting, and to stand down if he has a personal interest in the outcome of any motion;
(7) to rule on a point of order;[46]
(8) not to alter the order of the agenda unless a majority of the meeting agrees to this course;[47]
(9) not to introduce a motion of his own which is not on the agenda;[48]
(10) to see that speakers address the chair[49] and that questions are asked through the chair;
(11) to deal with amendments to motions in the correct order;[50]
(12) to ask the secretary, or he himself, to read out the precise motion which is being put to the meeting to be voted on;
(13) to oversee that voting procedures are conducted properly;
(14) to appoint tellers or scrutineers for the counting of votes;
(15) to declare the result of any vote on a motion.

---

42 *John v Rees* [1970] Ch 345, at 377.

43 In *Byng v London Life Association Ltd* [1990] Ch 170, CA, at 182. The court held at 183 that for a meeting to be validly constituted it is not necessary for all members to be physically present in the same room provided that proper audio/visual aids are used to enable the members in any overflow room to participate in the meeting.

44 *Byng's* case, at 187; *Mulholland v St Peter's, Roydon, Parochial Church Council* [1969] 1 WLR 1842, at 1848.

45 The duty to keep order was described by Megarry J as the first duty of a chairman in *John v Rees* [1970] Ch 345, at 382. The same case contains a detailed discussion of the chairman's power of adjournment in the event of disorder and how it should be exercised (at 379 onwards). If a chairman validly adjourns a meeting and leaves the chair, no-one else can replace the chairman and continue with the meeting.

46 *Re Indian Zoedone Co* (1884) 26 Ch D 70, at 77. A point of order may only relate to an alleged breach of procedural rules or raise a matter of law. It may be raised at any time and the chairman will hear and rule on it immediately.

47 *John v Rees* [1970] Ch 345, at 378.

48 Ibid, at 377.

49 He should curtail long speeches and prevent second speeches if others want to speak. If the chairman is speaking, or he rises to speak, he will take precedence over other speakers.

50 See **6.26**.

6.25 Adjournment Normally the power of adjournment is vested in the meeting.[51] The chairman cannot adjourn the meeting without its authority and, if he does so, the meeting may continue with a different chairman if necessary.[52] However, at common law the chairman has a residual power to adjourn a meeting if he cannot carry out his duty to ensure that all members, who are entitled to be heard and to vote, are given the opportunity to do so.[53] This power must be exercised on reasonable grounds, not simply in good faith.[54] If a meeting is adjourned for any reason, a fresh notice of the adjourned date does not have to be sent out to those members who did not attend the original meeting.[55] Those attending the meeting should be told by the chairman of the adjourned date, if this can be agreed there and then. In incorporated clubs, both under the 1985 Table A Regulations[56] and under the 2008 Model Articles,[57] where a meeting is adjourned for more than 14 days, at least 7 clear days' notice shall be given to *all* members specifying the time and place of the adjourned meeting, together with notice of the general nature of the business to be transacted. We consider that this practice should be adopted by all clubs. No business should be transacted at the adjourned meeting which could not have been transacted at the original meeting.

9. AMENDMENTS TO MOTIONS

6.26 Meetings consider motions. If the members at the meeting are 'moved' to vote in favour of a motion, the approved motion becomes a resolution whereby the members are 'resolved' to act in accordance with the motion. Experience shows that, unless properly handled, amendments to motions can cause havoc at a meeting. Sometimes the chairman is forewarned because the original motion and the proposed amendments are all set out in the agenda. The chairman does not have to take the amendments in the chronological order in which they were set down in the agenda; he should take them in the most logical order and he can prepare his thoughts on this before the meeting. Members, however, are entitled to propose amendments from the floor during the debate so long as they are within the scope of the motion of which notice was originally given.[58] Any amendment should be precisely formulated and not a simple contradiction or disagreement with the original motion because that is done by voting against the motion. It is far better if any proposed amendment is reduced to writing but provided its effect is made reasonably clear it may be submitted

---

51 *National Dwellings Society v Sykes* [1894] 3 Ch 159, at 162.

52 Ibid, at 162.

53 *Byng v London Life Association Ltd* [1990] Ch 170, CA, at 187–188.

54 *Byng's case*, at 189.

55 *Scadding v Lorant* (1851) 3 HL Cas 418, at 446.

56 Regulation 45.

57 Article 27 (companies limited by guarantee) and art 41 (companies limited by shares). These articles contain detailed provision about adjournment.

58 *Torbock v Lord Westbury* [1902] 2 Ch 871, at 874.

orally to the meeting.[59] If the proposed amendment is of an acceptable nature, it is customary for the chairman to ask for a seconder.[60] If found, the proposer, but not the seconder, should be allowed to speak in support of the amendment. The amendment is then discussed and the chairman, not the proposer, should sum up the situation if necessary. The amendment is then put to the vote, and if successful the amended motion now becomes the motion before the meeting and can itself be the subject of amendment. If unsuccessful, the original motion continues to be discussed.

6.27 In putting forward the proposed amendment to the meeting for the members to decide whether to accept or reject it, we consider that this item can be decided on a simple majority.[61] If the proposed amendment is accepted, then any substantive decision of the meeting thereafter must be on such majority as the rules require, for example, a two-thirds majority on a motion to alter the rules. In an incorporated club which has adopted the 2008 Model Articles, amendments to proposed resolutions are the subject of specific articles: art 33 for companies limited by guarantee and art 47 for companies limited by shares.

10. MEMBERS' RESOLUTIONS

6.28 A question sometimes arises how far a resolution passed by the members in general meeting is binding on the managing committee, Can the committee ignore the resolution? The answer depends on whether the resolution can be seen as an unwarranted derogation from the members' delegation of their managerial powers to the committee. If, as is the norm, under the rules they have delegated to the committee the control and management of all the affairs of the club, the members in general meeting cannot then proceed to pass any resolution which fetters or interferes with the proper exercise of the committee's powers of management. Any such resolution can be treated by the committee as a recommendation only, and it may give such weight to the recommendation as it thinks fit. Let us take the example of where the club has a club premises certificate, and the purchase and supply of alcohol is vested in the committee under the rules.[62] A resolution is passed by the members in general meeting to change the brewer who supplies the club. The committee would be within its rights to treat the resolution as a recommendation only and reject it, even if it had been carried by an overwhelming majority of the members. This rejection

---

59 *Henderson v Bank of Australasia* (1890) 45 Ch D 330, CA.

60 There is no legal requirement for a seconder (*Horbury Bridge Coal Iron and Waggon Co, Re* (1879) 11 Ch D 109, at 117) but the absence of a seconder goes to the chairman's discretion whether to accept the amendment: *Young v Sherman* (2001) 40 ACSR 12 (NSW Supreme Ct).

61 Unless, which is unlikely, the rules stipulate to the contrary.

62 Licensing Act 2003, s 64(2). The members may themselves manage the purchase and supply of alcohol in general meeting instead of the committee (ibid, s 64(2)), but except in a very small club this would not be a wise move.

may of course be based on some sound financial or contractual reason. If the members felt strongly enough about the rejection, however, their remedy would be either to requisition a special meeting to pass a vote of no confidence in the committee[63] or to vote the committee out of office at the next AGM elections.

11. QUORUM

6.29 A quorum is the number of persons who must be present at a general or committee meeting to constitute a valid meeting. It is crucial for the proper running of a club that a rule (or bye-law) deals with this point. In relation to general meetings of an unincorporated members' club and in the absence of such a rule, potentially all members would have to attend for a valid meeting to take place. In the Australian case of *Ball v Palsall*[64] Mr Justice Young had this to say, after reviewing the English authorities:

> 'Where the constitution of an unincorporated association makes no provision for a quorum for meetings of the association, in theory the business of that association can only be transacted when all the members are present; however, by consensual compact between the members some lesser number can be a quorum and in determining that lesser number, the activities of the members after the consensual compact was made are relevant.'

Evidence from the officers of a club that an unwritten rule as to quorum had been habitually used in the past could prove sufficient to justify a quorum less than the whole membership.[65]

6.30 It is good practice to avoid too small a number for a quorum for a general meeting of the members since this will prevent a clique from running the club.[66] This is an important point for incorporated clubs to remember because under s 318 of the Companies Act 2006 two members of the company can constitute a quorum for general meetings. Similarly, for companies formed before 1 October 2009, reg 40 of the 1985 Table A regulations laid down that two persons shall form a quorum at a general meeting. The answer for incorporated clubs is to adopt a special article which lays down an appropriate quorum for its general meetings.

6.31 One needs to draw a distinction between a quorum required to requisition a general meeting and, once convened, the quorum required for

---

63 See **5.30**.

64 (1987) 10 NSW LR 700, at 703.

65 *John v Rees* [1970] Ch 345, at 388.

66 At common law the minimum number for a quorum is two: *R v Secretary of State for the Environment ex p Hillingdon* [1986] 1 WLR 192.

a valid meeting to take place. The two quorums do not have to be the same number. If a club held a registration certificate, the quorum required for a valid requisition of a general meeting was not to exceed 30 or to be more than one-fifth of the total number of members entitled to attend meetings and vote thereat (whichever was the less)[67] and this is regarded as a good working rule for all clubs.[68] If a club has 300 members, one-fifth is 60, but the requisition would only require 30 signatures. However, it is perfectly in order for the rules to stipulate that the quorum for the meeting itself shall be a higher number, say 40 or 50. A question which also arises is whether a meeting has to be quorate at all times or only at the beginning of the meeting. Suppose several members left during the course of a meeting, and their leaving made the quorum insufficient. Could the meeting validly continue? The answer is in the negative because what is required is that the meeting must be quorate both at the beginning of the meeting when the chairman declares the meeting open, and when any decision is made during the meeting.[69] However, a member who left the meeting deliberately so as to remove the quorum cannot rely on the lack of quorum in challenging decisions made after his departure.[70] An apparent exception is the case of *Re Hartley Baird Ltd*[71] which concerned a company meeting. Mr Justice Wynn-Parry held that since the articles expressly stipulated for a quorum to be present at the *beginning* of the meeting, there was no requirement for a continuing quorum throughout the meeting.

6.32 Period of grace If there is no quorum at the scheduled start of a meeting in unincorporated members' clubs, it is customary to allow a short period of grace, say half an hour, to see if the required quorum can be established by latecomers. This is sometimes expressed in the rules or bye-laws but even if they are silent it is considered that it would be in the chairman's power to adjourn the start of the meeting for a short while for the benefit of those members who are present and who may have travelled a considerable distance to attend the meeting or have given up their leisure time to do so.[72] In incorporated clubs, reg 41 of the 1985 Table A Regulations and art 27(1) (for companies limited by guarantee) and art 41(1)(for companies limited by shares) of the 2008 Model Articles permit a period of grace of up to a half an hour if no quorum is present at the appointed time, after which time the meeting is automatically adjourned.

---

67 Licensing Act 1964, Sch 7, para 2(3).

68 Even though this rule has not been carried through to the Licensing Act 2003.

69 *Henderson v James Louttit and Co Ltd* (1894) 21 R 674, at 676 (Ct of Sess). Regulation 41 of the 1985 Table A Regulations, and art 27(1) (for companies limited by guarantee) and art 41(1) (for companies limited by shares) of the 2008 Model Articles are all to like effect.

70 *Ball v Pearsall* (1987) 10 NSW LR 700, at 705.

71 [1955] Ch 143.

72 See *John v Rees* [1970] Ch 345, at 383.

12. VOTING

6.33 There are four methods of voting which are used in club meetings:[73]

(1) by acclamation;
(2) by a show of hands;
(3) by poll;
(4) by ballot.

We add in parenthesis that there may come a time, sooner rather than later, when unincorporated members' clubs and other clubs apart than incorporated ones will adopt as part of their rules a similar procedure for transacting some of their business by way of written resolutions as outlined in **6.53**. This will obviate the need for face-to-face meetings because the whole process can be conducted electronically.

6.34 Acclamation Sometimes it is not necessary to put a motion to a formal vote since the chairman of the meeting will have sensed that the mood of the meeting does not require this step.[74]

6.35 Show of hands This is almost invariably the first method of voting at a meeting. If the meeting is large it is sensible to appoint scrutineers to help count the votes. The chairman can order a recount if necessary.[75] The chairman is entitled to vote along with the other members.[76] In incorporated clubs the voting must be decided on a show of hands under reg 46 of the 1985 Table A Regulations or under art 28 (for companies limited by guarantee) or art 30 (for companies limited by shares) of the 2008 Model Articles, unless a poll is duly demanded in accordance with the articles.

6.36 Poll A chairman may proceed to voting by poll without there first being a show of hands,[77] unless the rules stipulate that the first method of voting shall be by some other method of voting such as show of hands. A poll openly records the number of votes, either by an individual voting slip or by signing a voting list, and is a more accurate way of establishing the true vote. A member who is dissatisfied with the vote by show of hands can demand a poll as of right, unless there is a rule to the contrary.[78] Once a

---

73 A fifth way is voting by division (a method long used by Parliament but seldom if ever used by clubs).

74 *Re The Citizens Theatre Ltd* [1946] SC 14, at 18. This voting is often recorded in the minutes as 'Nem. Con.' This is shorthand for 'Nemine contradicente', i e with no one opposing. This is not the same thing as a unanimous decision in favour.

75 *Hickman v Kent or Romney Marsh Sheepbreeders' Association* (1920) 36 TLR 528, at 533.

76 *Nell v Longbottom* [1894] 1 QB 767, at 771.

77 *R v Rector of Birmingham* (1837) 7 A & E 254.

78 *Re Wimbledon Local Board* (1882) 8 QBD 459, CA.

valid request for a poll has been made, the result of any vote by a show of hands ceases to have effect.[79] A poll has to be taken of all the members entitled to vote.[80] This raises the question whether the poll is restricted to those attending the meeting or whether it means all the members of the club, which would normally necessitate the adjournment of the meeting. The answer is that the decision should be left to those attending the meeting. In *R v Rector of St Mary, Lambeth*[81] all the ratepayers of a large parish were entitled to vote in the election of the churchwardens and a meeting was duly convened. The election was conducted on a show of hands, and after the result several ratepayers demanded a poll of the whole parish, but the majority of the ratepayers at the meeting decided that it should be restricted to those present, and this decision was upheld by the Court of Exchequer Chamber. The court quoted an extract from *Prideaux' Directions to Churchwardens* (10th edn, 1835),[82] which neatly summarises why absent members cannot complain if they do not attend meetings: 'If persons properly qualified are duly assembled at the time and place appointed, the present include the absent, and the major part of the present include all the rest. For those who absent themselves after notice given, do it voluntarily, and therefore devolve their vote upon those who are present'.

6.37 Under reg 46 of the 1985 Table A Regulations and under the 2008 Model Articles a poll may be demanded *at* the meeting before or on the declaration of the vote by a show of hands.[83] In addition, under art 30(1)(a) (for companies limited by guarantee) or art 44(1)(a) (for companies limited by shares) of the 2008 Model Articles a poll may now be demanded *in advance of* the general meeting where the resolution is to be put to the vote. In this way the mandatory show-of-hands rule is not abolished but can be overridden. The 2008 Model Articles stipulate that any poll must be taken immediately so that, unlike at common law, there will be no question of adjourning the meeting, and this is a sensible stipulation. If the poll is used in conjunction with proxy voting, it should ensure a much greater involvement by all the members when it comes to making important decisions on special business, and is recommended for all categories of club, but is especially appropriate where the club has a large membership spread over a wide area which militates against personal attendance at meetings. A poll-cum-proxy procedure will, however, entail the rules being appropriately worded or amended in order to authorise it.

6.38 Ballot It is common for officers of a club to be elected by secret ballot at the annual general meeting, if the office is contested. The secretary should prepare the ballot papers before the meeting with the names of the

---

79 *R v Cooper* (1870) LR 5 QB 457.

80 *R v Rector of St Mary, Lambeth* (1838) 8 A & E 356.

81 (1838) 8 A & E 356.

82 The office of churchwarden had been, since the Reformation days, one of honour and responsibility, hence the numerous editions of Mr Prideaux' book.

83 2008 Model Articles, art 30(1)(b) (guarantee) or art 44(1)(b) (shares).

candidates arranged in alphabetical order. It is common for the candidates to prepare a short manifesto (say 150 words) which is circulated prior to the election meeting or for the chairman at the meeting to let each candidate introduce himself and say a few words in support of his candidature. The vote is taken by each member marking with a cross his choice of candidate. The vote is then counted by the secretary or by the scrutineers if appointed.

6.39 Proxies Where a member appoints another person to exercise all or any of his rights to attend, speak and vote at a general meeting, that person will act as the member's proxy. There is at common law no right to appoint proxies.[84] Therefore, apart from the Companies Act 2006, there must be an express rule permitting this mode of voting. On a show of hands, each member has one vote only even though they may be acting as proxy for several members.[85] This is because it is a counting of hands; nothing more. If a voter is unhappy with the outcome, he or she can demand a poll as of right and then all the proxy votes are taken into account.[86] The use of proxies under a poll is now commonplace. If the rules contain a right to demand a poll in advance of or at the general meeting, the club secretary will send out the proxy form with the notice of the meeting, to be returned via e-mail or post by a specified date before the meeting. A form of proxy is set out in Appendix 11. In incorporated clubs, the topic of proxies is dealt with in ss 324 to 331 of the Companies Act 2006. Broadly speaking, every member has a right to appoint a proxy who can speak and vote on his or her behalf at a company meeting.[87] The company's articles, however, may confer more extensive rights on members or proxies than are conferred by these sections.[88]

6.40 Equal voting rights The Equality Act 2010 has restored the position with regard to equal voting rights at general meetings which was set out (with limited exceptions) in para 2(4) of Sch 7 to the Licensing Act 1964. This paragraph was repealed by the Licensing Act 2003. Clubs must not now discriminate against members when it comes to voting at general meetings so that, for example, the Basset Golf Club could not give greater voting rights to its male members than to its female members since this would amount to sex discrimination.[89]

6.41 Voting majority This is another area where the rules need to make clear what majority is required for any resolution of the members to be binding on the membership as a whole. It has long been established that where the duties which are imposed on a corporation are of a public nature,

---

84 *Harben v Phillips* (1883) 23 Ch D 14; *Woodford v Smith* [1970] 1 WLR 806, at 810.

85 *Ernest v Loma Gold Mines Limited* [1896] 2 Ch 572, at 579 (Chitty J).

86 Ibid, at 579–580.

87 Companies Act 2006, s 324(1).

88 Ibid, s 331.

89 See **5.64** and **5.65**.

the will of the corporation may be expressed by a simple majority of the members, so that the act of the majority becomes the act of the corporation.[90] But in private bodies this rule does not apply uniformly across the board, for example, where a unanimous decision of the body is required.[91] Lord Denning MR in *Abbatt v Treasury Solicitor*[92] expressed the view that, absent an express rule in an unincorporated members' club, the members had an implied power to amend their rules by a simple majority, and by implication to make any other decision by this majority. Doubt has already been expressed as to the existence of this implied power of amendment[93] but this does not mean that the Master of the Rolls was wrong on the simple majority point, which has much to commend it for run-of-the-mill decisions.[94] A different voting majority may, however, be required for different classes of resolution. As a general rule a two-thirds voting majority for the more important resolutions has practical advantages over a three-quarters majority. It is normal practice for committees to adopt a simple majority when arriving at their decisions, save that in the case of an amendment of the bye-laws (if this is within the remit of the committee) it is advisable for the rules to stipulate a two-thirds majority.

6.42 In incorporated clubs an ordinary resolution at a general meeting of the company may be passed by a simple majority.[95] A special resolution at a general meeting requires a majority of not less than 75%.[96] The articles of association may prescribe what business of the company requires a special resolution, but a special resolution may also be required by law, for example, changing the name of the company[97] or amending its articles.[98]

6.43 In *Knowles v Zoological Society of London*[99] the society had over 7,000 fellows (members). In 1958 at a general meeting to confirm the adoption of new bye-laws, 1,788 fellows voted in favour whilst 1,227 voted against, 18 abstained and one vote was disallowed and the motion was passed by a simple majority at the meeting. The rules required confirmation by 'a majority of fellows entitled to vote'. Did this mean all the fellows of the society or only those present at the meeting? The Court of Appeal held the latter, but it is wiser if the rule states, 'a majority of members *present at the meeting and* entitled to vote'. The case also draws attention to the need, on

---

90 *Attorney General v Davy* (1741) 2 Atk 212; *Grindley v Barker* (1798) 1 Bos & P 229, at 236.

91 *Harington v Sendall* [1903] 1 Ch 921 (unincorporated members' club); *Perrott & Perrott Ltd v Stephenson* [1934] 1 Ch 171 (company).

92 [1969] 1 WLR 1575, at 1583.

93 See **2.45**.

94 *Warburton on Unincorporated Associations* (2nd edn, 1992) at p 28 supports the view that if the rules are silent as to the majority required to pass a resolution, a simple majority will be sufficient.

95 Companies Act 2006, s 282(1).

96 Ibid, s 283(1).

97 Ibid, s 77(1)(a).

98 Ibid, s 21(1).

99 [1959] 1 WLR 823, CA.

this form of wording, to count abstentions and wasted votes. Although members commonly think that by abstaining or wasting their vote they are remaining neutral, they are in fact assisting the opposition to the motion because their presence at the meeting will be taken into account in calculating the required majority. Similarly, abstainers would count towards the majority if the rule simply stated, 'a majority of the members present at the meeting'.[100] It would only be otherwise if the rule stated, 'a majority of those members present *and voting* at the meeting'. In this last event the number of abstainers would not be included in the calculation of the majority. Which form of wording should be used is a matter of preference for the individual club, but in view of the frequent confusion over the role of abstainers, some clubs may prefer to adopt this last-mentioned solution.

6.44 Casting vote Since the repeal of the Licensing Act 1964 it has once again become lawful to give the chairman of the meeting a casting vote in addition to his ordinary vote at general meetings of the members, and it is customary to do so. In incorporated clubs, reg 50 of the 1985 Table Regulations and art 13(1) of the Model Articles 2008[101] expressly give a casting vote to the chairman of the meeting, if the number of votes for and against a proposal is equal.

13. MINUTES

6.45 The concept behind the recording of minutes of a meeting is that the club has a 'fair and accurate' record of what has been decided or resolved. It thus saves argument at a later stage when recollection of the particular meeting has faded from the memory. The minutes should be as concise as the circumstances require. It is unusual for the minutes of general meetings to record speeches or arguments at the meeting.[102] The situation with regard to committee meetings is somewhat different. The Institute of Chartered Secretaries and Administrators in its publication, 'Good Boardroom Practice: A Code for Directors and Company Secretaries' states in Article 10 that the minutes of board meetings should 'record the decisions taken and give sufficient background to those decisions'.[103] For this purpose we consider that a board meeting can be equated with a committee meeting. In compiling the minutes a good test to adopt is to ask whether an absent member reading the minutes would fully understand what had been decided at the meeting.[104] The minutes should record the essential elements of the discussion and the full text of any resolution which was passed. They

---

[100] See, for example, s 4(2) of the Credit Unions Act 1979 where this form of words is stipulated.

[101] The same numbered article applies to both companies limited by guarantee and limited by shares.

[102] A separate document is sometimes created which records the meeting in more detail.

[103] The code is published on their (2010) website, www.icsa.org.uk.

[104] A specimen set of committee minutes may be found at Appendix 12.

should avoid comment and expressions of opinion. It is seldom helpful to record the proceedings in descriptive terms, such as 'Mr Brewer with some heat denounced the motion as a trick contrived for the purpose of expelling Mr Pearce', even if that is what he had said and the manner in which he had said it. No doubt Mr Brewer's opposition to the motion would mean his voting against it, which will be recorded, and this will be a sufficient recognition of his disapproval of the motion. Some committees maintain an Action List so that the progress of any matter can be monitored over a period of time. Another way of keeping track of a particular topic is to give it an individual number which can be carried forward from meeting to meeting. In incorporated clubs the company must keep for at least 10 years the minutes of all proceedings of general meetings.[105] These minutes must be open to the inspection of any member without charge.[106]

6.46 There are various methods of recording minutes but as a basic pattern they might be as follows:

> ***Method 1:***
>
> Mr Stewer attended before the committee re the charge of misconduct, namely, his rudeness to the President at the New Year's party.
>
> Resolved: that Mr Stewer be suspended from membership for three months. Voting for 9, against 3, abstention 1.

This method simply records, in the order in which they came before the meeting, each matter discussed and the eventual result. Another method is to record in addition all amendments, the names of movers and seconders, the fate of the various proposals and the ultimate result.

> ***Method 2:***
>
> Mr Stewer attended before the committee re the charge of misconduct, namely, his rudeness to the President at the New Year's party. Mr Stewer admitted the facts and apologised for his conduct. He then retired from the committee room.
>
> Mr Gurney moved (Mr Davey seconded) that he be reprimanded by the chairman of the club. Mr Whiddon moved (Mr Hawke seconded) as an amendment that he be expelled from the club. Voting for the amendment: for 5, against 8. Mr Cobley then moved a further amendment (Mr Brewer seconded) that Mr Stewer be suspended for three months. This amendment was carried and, on being put as the substantive motion, was carried by 9 votes in favour to 3 votes against, with one abstention.

---

[105] Companies Act 2006, s 355(1)–(2).

[106] Ibid, s 358(3).

Resolved: that Mr Stewer be suspended from membership for three months.

6.47 A problem can sometimes arise in meetings when a member insists that his viewpoint is recorded in the minutes, for example, he wants the reasons for his dissent recorded.[107] Is the secretary obliged to comply? The law is not clear on the secretary's duty in this regard but we do not think his duty goes that far. If the secretary (or minute-taker) has doubts about the propriety of recording any matter he should ask the chairman for a ruling.

6.48 **Signing minutes** The chairman of the meeting should sign the minutes of the previous meeting once the members who attended the meeting have approved their accuracy.[108] Once signed, the minutes must not be altered or corrected internally.[109] If the minutes need correction, the solution is to add an additional minute correcting the mistake and for the chairman to sign that addition, which will usually occur at the next meeting.

6.49 **Distribution** Minutes of general meetings should be supplied to the whole membership, whereas minutes of committee meetings are generally considered confidential to the committee members. In a company the directors' minute book is confidential to the directors because it contains the record of the private affairs of the company, a separate legal entity,[110] and by analogy this seems to apply to the committee's minute book, whether the club is incorporated or unincorporated. But the analogy cannot be pressed too far because in a members' club the committee is acting on behalf of the members collectively and the question might be asked why the members are disentitled from inspecting the minute book of its own committee. We submit that these minutes are prima facie confidential to the committee and should not be disclosed to any member except for good reason.[111] If it were otherwise the committee might be inhibited from doing its job properly, including the fear of a defamation claim. It is true that clubs do sometimes allow their members at or shortly before the AGM personally to inspect the committee's minute book for the preceding year (without allowing any copy to be taken thereof). This is a far cry from posting the minutes on the club's website or circulating them generally among the membership. The restricted disclosure at the AGM can at least be said to be supportive of confidentiality, whereas the latter procedures destroy it and should not be countenanced.

---

107 See the hypothetical example given in **5.36**.

108 If kept electronically, the minutes should be authenticated in some other manner.

109 *Re Cawley & Co* (1889) 42 Ch D 209, CA, at 226.

110 *Gore-Browne on Companies* (44th edn, 2004), 11[24].

111 See **5.84** for an example of disclosure pursuant to the Data Protection Act 1998.

6.50 Defamation We draw attention to the fact that meetings can sometimes generate allegations of defamation.[112] For there to be any liability in libel the statement containing the defamatory words must be published in writing to a third party. In the context of meetings this could arise in the circulation of minutes, or say in documents or e-mails circulated before, during and after the meeting. Club members should not be unduly worried on this score. They will in the ordinary course of events be protected by the defence of qualified privilege, that is to say, the member will normally have a legitimate interest in publishing the statement and the recipient will have a corresponding interest in receiving it. If protected by qualified privilege there is no liability, however negligent or inaccurate the statement, provided it was made honestly.

14. COMMITTEE MEETINGS

6.51 As mentioned in **5.25**, the managing committee is the master of its own procedures. However, in the absence of a quorum rule, the quorum for a committee will be the entire committee because the delegation of powers is not to the individual members of the committee but to the committee as a whole.[113] Such a quorum would be hopelessly impracticable. In these circumstances it would be for the committee to decide its own quorum for its meetings. The chairman of the club should chair meetings of the committee by virtue of his office. There should be provision for an alternative chairman if the designated chairman is absent.[114] If the rules are silent on the question of who should take the chair, it is up to the members present at the committee meeting themselves to choose their own chairman.[115] Otherwise the general rules of procedure for general meetings apply equally to committee meetings, although there is much greater informality in conducting the latter, for example, the date of the next committee meeting is commonly decided there and then at the end of a committee meeting; this new date must, of course, be circulated to those committee members who did not attend the original meeting. We would add that if through indolence or neglect or for any other reason, no committee meeting is convened when plainly it should have been, we consider that any member of the committee would probably have an inherent right to convene a committee meeting on reasonable notice; otherwise the management and control of the club's affairs would become rudderless, to the obvious detriment of the club.

---

112 For the topic of defamation see **12.52** and **12.63**.

113 *Brown v Andrew* (1849) 18 LJ QB 153; *R v Liverpool City Council ex p Professional Association of Teachers* (1984) *The Times*, March 22.

114 This is commonly done by making provision for a vice-chairman.

115 This would also apply to sub-committees where, more often than not, the chairman of the club would not be part of its composition.

15. STATUTORY REQUIREMENTS FOR INCORPORATED CLUBS

6.52 These clubs must comply with the provisions of the Companies Acts. For companies formed before 1 October 2009 the procedure of their meetings will be set out in their articles, that is to say, they are usually governed by the special provisions in the 1985 Table A regulations which are directed to the convening and holding of meetings (this includes notice, quorum, and voting etc). For companies formed on or after 1 October 2009 the Companies Act 2006 has adopted a different approach. Part 13 of this Act (ss 281–361) contains seven chapters which deal in depth with company resolutions and meetings, and therefore none of these provisions appear in the 2008 Model Articles. In a nutshell, the chapters relevant to clubs are those which deal with general provisions about resolutions (chapter 1); written resolutions (chapter 2; see **6.53**); resolutions at meetings (chapter 3); records of resolutions and meetings (chapter 6); and the computation of periods of notice (chapter 7). Some of the important provisions of these chapters are mentioned in the preceding paragraphs but a detailed discussion of them is outside the scope of this book.

6.53 Written resolutions These resolutions are governed by ss 288–300 of the Companies Act 2006. The procedure only applies to private companies,[116] but cannot be excluded by the company's articles.[117] Their importance lies in the fact that the procedure does away with face-to-face meetings but they may not be used to remove a director or auditor.[118] Directors[119] and members[120] may propose written resolutions. Resolutions may be passed by the same majority as for resolutions at meetings.[121] 'Written' does not necessarily mean in writing on hard copy; a written resolution may be proposed by e-mail or on the company's website.[122] Once the member has signified his agreement to the resolution he cannot revoke it.[123] The resolution must be passed within 28 days of the date of circulation; after this period it automatically lapses.[124]

116 Companies Act 2006, s 288(1).

117 Ibid, s 300.

118 Ibid, s 288(2).

119 Ibid, s 288(3)(a).

120 Ibid, s 288(3)(b).

121 Ibid, s 288(5). For voting majority see **6.41**. Under the Companies Act 1985 (as amended) the *unanimous* vote of *all* the members was required to pass a written resolution.

122 Ibid, ss 298 and 299.

123 Ibid, s 296(3).

124 Ibid, s 297(1)(b). The articles may specify a different period: ibid, s 297(1)(a).

16. MEETINGS OF MEMBERS IN PROPRIETARY CLUBS

6.54 General meetings of the members in a proprietary club are just as much an essential element as they are in a members' club. If therefore there was no provision for meetings (either for general or special business) in the club rules, it is doubtful whether the club would constitute a club at law, since the sixth criterion (the need for collegiality) referred to in **1.1** would not be fulfilled.

Chapter 7

CESSATION AND CURTAILMENT OF CLUB MEMBERSHIP

1. INTRODUCTION

7.1 This is a topic which has relevance to all clubs of whatever description. It is also an important topic for those members who find themselves at the wrong end of expulsion or suspension proceedings. If the committee of a members' club does not get the procedure right or makes a mess of the substantive hearing of the proceedings, the club will face the prospect of litigation being brought against it by the aggrieved party, with its attendant unpleasantness and with the risk of costs being awarded against the club. In proprietary clubs the practice varies; sometimes it is the proprietor who exercises the powers of expulsion and suspension and at other times the proprietor delegates these powers to the committee of the club.

2. RESIGNATION

7.2 **Express resignation** It will be recalled from **1.1** that the first criterion of a club is the voluntary nature of the association of the members who comprise the club. From this criterion follows the proposition that a member may at any time voluntarily retire from a club by his resignation or withdrawal from it. In *Finch v Oake*[1] Lord Justice Lindley, at 415, put the position as follows:

> 'What then is the position of a member who has paid his subscription of 10s 6d[2] for the current year? Can he withdraw from the association at any moment at his own pleasure, or can he withdraw only with the consent of his fellow members? In my opinion, when he has paid his subscription for the year he is under no obligation whatever to his fellow members. By paying his subscription he no doubt acquires certain rights and benefits. But what is there to prevent him from retiring from the association at any moment he wishes to do so? Absolutely nothing. In my opinion no acceptance of his resignation is

---

1 [1896] 1 Ch 409.

2 This was half a guinea in imperial coinage and 52.5 pence in decimal coinage.

required, though of course he cannot get back the 10s 6d which he has paid. The other members have no power to say that he shall not retire, and there is no law that a resignation which cannot be refused must be accepted before it can take effect. If therefore a member of this association chooses, even from mere caprice, to retire from it, he can do so at any time without the consent of the other members, and in order to become a member he must be re-elected.'[3]

7.3 This judicial statement needs some clarification:

(1) the right to resign is inherent and is not dependent on a club rule giving permission to resign. On the other hand, we see no reason why this right should not be regulated in the rules, for example, by stipulating that the resignation should be in writing or that it should be on 14 days' notice. For practical reasons a written notice of resignation creates finality and provides evidence to the potential benefit of both parties but the rules should not go so far as to forbid an oral resignation;

(2) no particular form of words is required to constitute a valid resignation. In the case of *In re Sick and Funeral Society of St John's Sunday School, Golcar*[4] Mr Justice Megarry had this to say:

> 'There can be no magic in the word "resign", nor in whether the resignation is written or oral. The essence of the matter seems to me to be whether the member has sufficiently manifested his decision to be a member no more. I cannot see why such a manifestation should not be by conduct instead of by words: the only question is whether the member's decision has been adequately conveyed to the society by words or deeds;'

(3) the need for re-election is important and was re-affirmed in the *Golcar* case, at 63. Could the committee waive the resignation as an act of management? We doubt so since the club will now be dealing with a non-member, and the members might take the objection that the re-election had occurred without the proper formalities being observed, such as the need for a proposer and seconder. It would be different if an express rule governed the position;[5]

(4) Lord Justice Lindley was being too dogmatic in saying that a member of a club owed 'no obligation whatever' to his fellow members. We consider that club members owe to one another various obligations or duties under the contract of membership. Some obligations such as the payment of subscriptions are express; others such as the requirement

---

3 See also *In re St James Club* (1852) 2 De G M & G 383, at 390.

4 [1973] 1 Ch 51, at 63.

5 *Lambert v Addison* (1882) 46 LT 20 (where the court upheld a bye-law, which permitted former members of the club to be re-admitted on paying arrears of subscription but without the formalities of an election and without paying the entrance fee).

to behave properly in the clubhouse are implied. The question arises whether the exercise of the undoubted right to resign could result in the member being in breach of his contract of membership. Suppose the Upper Basset Cricket Club had an outstanding opening batsman who had paid his annual subscription on 1 January. Could he without warning resign on 1 May and immediately join and play for the Lower Basset Cricket Club, their arch rivals? The answer is in the affirmative as a matter of contract law because a person makes no promise, express or implied, that he will continue as a member for the period of his paid-up subscription. The position may be different in practice because of the rules issued by the game's governing body or by the league in which the clubs are playing since such rules might prohibit the switching of clubs in this fashion.

7.4 Tacit resignation In the case of *In re Sick and Funeral Society of St John's Sunday School, Golcar*[6] the society became dissolved with surplus funds in hand and the question arose as to whom these funds should be distributed. The members were required to make weekly or quarterly payments by way of subscription to the sickness and funeral expenses fund. Certain members who had failed to make any payment for over 3 years now tried to pay their arrears of subscription in order to partake as members in the distribution. The question arose whether their failure had amounted to resignation, and Mr Justice Megarry held that it did so. The judge, at 62, had this to say on the topic:

> 'No reasonable man is likely to feel any real doubt about the intentions of a member of a society who for over three years has failed to make his weekly or quarterly payments, and has put forward not a word to suggest that this was due to some mistake, or that he did some acts which showed an intention to continue as a member. As I have indicated, among the many thousands of clubs and societies in the country there must be many cases of members whose membership has never been terminated in accordance with any provision in the rules, and yet who are regarded as still being members neither by themselves nor by the club or society. If their membership is said to have "lapsed", that may be another way of describing a tacit resignation. However it is described, it seems right that there should be such a doctrine, so that neither the member nor the club or society should be able to claim against the other on the basis that what has long been dead de facto still lives de jure. A moribund membership ought not to be capable of resurrection.'

7.5 Requested resignation What is the legal effect of a request by the committee to the member that he resign his membership? Can the refusal to comply with this request justify the termination of membership? In *Gaiman*

---

6 [1973] 1 Ch 51.

v National Association for Mental Health[7] the defendant association, which was a company limited by guarantee without share capital, had an article of association which read:

> 'Article 7 A member shall forthwith cease to be a member . . . (B) if he is requested by resolution of the council[8] to resign.'

There had been a recent influx of new members, all of whom were Scientologists and who fundamentally disagreed with the way the association was run. Under Article 7 the association duly requested the resignation of 302 of these members. Mr Justice Megarry held that, whilst the word 'resign' was somewhat of a euphemism, what terminated the membership was not the resignation but the request to resign. In other words, it was a *forced* resignation. The judge upheld the association's request as effectively terminating their membership. This had been done in accordance with the association's rules, which gave a right of appeal (which had been exercised), and in the honest belief that it was in the best interests of the association, but it was also done in contravention of the rules of natural justice. This case should be treated with considerable caution because the judge, at 335, specifically relied on the 'generous set of statutory rules governing companies and the rights of members' as enabling him to disapply the rules of natural justice in the field of company law with regard to that particular case.[9] In the ordinary course of events we consider that a forced resignation is tantamount to expulsion and no unincorporated members' club will succeed in upholding in court an expulsion dressed up as a resignation where there has been a disregard of the rules of natural justice.

- ***Invitation to resign*** All this is not to say that a genuine invitation to a member to resign his membership has no place in the options available to a managing committee in the event of unacceptable behaviour on the part of the member. A voluntary resignation has long been used as a beneficial face-saving device which has resolved many an awkward situation in a club.

3. LAPSED MEMBERSHIP

7.6 There is no implied term of the contract of membership that if a member fails to pay his subscription by the specified date, or within a reasonable time of it becoming due, his membership will lapse.[10] The club's primary remedy is to sue the member for the arrears of subscription. If the

---

7 [1971] Ch 317.

8 The governing body of the association.

9 The courts will normally apply the rules of natural justice in company law cases; see for example *Byrne v Kinematograph Society Renters Ltd* [1958] 1 WLR 762, at 784 (Harman J).

10 In a proprietary club arrears of subscription do not pose the same problem as in a

arrears are of long standing, say of at least one year or more, the club can argue that the member has repudiated his obligations under the contract of membership and it can then accept the repudiation which will discharge the contract.[11] This will have the effect of cancelling the membership but leaving the club with the ability to sue for the arrears of subscription. A neater solution is to have an express rule which states that in the event of a failure to pay the subscription within a specified period after it has become due the member's membership shall *automatically* lapse.[12] The rule can be made less draconian by stipulating in the rules (or in the bye-laws) that the member will receive in writing a reminder that his subscription is overdue and a warning that his membership will automatically lapse if the arrears are not paid by a certain date.

7.7 Where the membership has lapsed it is common practice to reinstate the member if he tenders the arrears and his current subscription. Is this reinstatement within the powers of the committee, considering that it is now dealing with a non-member? Does not the ex-member have to apply for re-election? Mr Justice Megarry in the *Golcar* case[13] said that lapse of membership could be described as 'tacit resignation'. Despite this dictum we consider that the committee would have power in appropriate circumstances to reinstate lapsed membership on the basis that a lapse is quite different from a resignation; the former comes about through the member's non-compliance with the rules relating to the payment of subscriptions, whereas the latter is a deliberate decision taken by the member. As the innocent party to the contract the club (or the committee on behalf of all the members) can waive the non-compliance with the subscription rule but it cannot undo the member's resignation decision which will have taken effect on notification to the club. An exception might be where the notice of resignation was required to be, say, on 14 days' notice. Here we consider that it could be withdrawn by mutual consent before the expiry of the 14-day period.

4. EXPULSION: MEMBERS' CLUBS

7.8 Need for express power If the rules of a members' club are silent on the topic of expulsion of a member of the club, no such power will be implied into the rules.[14] Provided there is provision to amend the rules, they would first have to be amended to give the club the necessary power to

members' club. This is because at the end of the subscription year the proprietor can simply refuse to renew the contract of membership with a defaulting member.

11 *In re Sick and Funeral Society of St John's Sunday School, Golcar* [1973] 1 Ch 51, at 62–63.

12 This will still leave the member liable for any arrears of subscription.

13 [1973] 1 Ch 51, at 62.

14 See *Dawkins v Antrobus* (1881) 17 Ch D 615, at 620 (Jessel MR at first instance). See **2.47** for the facts of this case.

expel a member.[15] In the absence of an expulsion rule it will not be possible as an alternative to convene a special meeting of all the members to discuss and then pass a resolution to expel a member. This is so even if every member of the club attended the meeting and voted unanimously for expulsion. The power to expel must always be expressly given in the rules.

7.9 The power to expel may be given to the membership as a whole but this is generally considered too cumbersome a procedure to be practical and so the power is usually devolved to the managing committee. A common (and proper) rule is one which states that the club shall have power to expel a member if his conduct, whether within the club premises *or elsewhere*, is injurious to the good name of the club or is such that in the opinion of the committee it renders him unfit to be a member.[16] It is also good practice for the rules to state that pending the hearing of any case or complaint against the member the committee shall have power to exclude the member from the club premises. This is not prejudging the case; it is simply an act of good management. This power of exclusion, however, must be expressly given in the rules.

7.10 Compliance with the rules It is essential that the procedure laid down by the rules is strictly followed, otherwise the expulsion will be declared void. In *Young v Imperial Ladies Club Limited*[17] a notice was issued convening a special meeting of the executive committee 'to report on and discuss the matter concerning Mrs Young and Mrs L', but no notice was sent to the Duchess of Abercorn who had previously indicated that owing to other calls on her time she would not be attending committee meetings. The committee met and decided to erase Mrs Young's name from the list of members. At first instance Mr Justice Roche held that as the rules had been substantially adhered to and as there was no breach of the rules of natural justice, the omission to notify the duchess of the meeting did not invalidate the proceedings of the committee. The Court of Appeal allowed Mrs Young's appeal on the grounds (1) that the omission to summon the absent member of the committee invalidated the proceedings of that body and (2) that the notice did not state the object of the meeting with sufficient particularity.

7.11 It should be noted, however, that what swayed the Court of Appeal was the insufficiency of the reason for not summoning the duchess, namely, her expressed unwillingness to attend committee meetings. There may be a valid reason for not summoning a committee member, such as his confinement to bed with a serious illness or the impossibility of his

15 *Dawkins v Antrobus* (1881) 17 Ch D 615, at 621.

16 Ibid, at 616; *Fisher v Keane* (1879) 11 Ch D 353, CA, at 358. And see *Hopkinson v Marquis of Exeter* (1867) LR 5 Eq 63 (court upheld expulsion of plaintiff from a political club, namely, the Conservative Club, for changing his political views).

17 [1920] 1 KB 81 and [1920] 1 KB 523, CA.

attendance at the meeting because of the distance he would have to travel.[18] However, far better would be an invariable practice to send out a notice to all committee members irrespective of whether it is known if this will result in their attendance.

7.12 So, too, the notice, which is given to the member summoning him before the committee, must comply strictly with the rules. A rule which provided for a notice of a certain number of days would not be complied with if it was given one day late; this non-compliance would then be fatal to any decision to expel the member.[19] If the rules are silent as to the length of notice to be given to the member for attendance on the committee, the notice must be of a reasonable length.

7.13 Rules of natural justice Subject to one caveat, in dealing with any case which concerns the possible expulsion of the member, it is important that the rules of natural justice are applied to the proceedings. A power of expulsion has been described as being of a quasi-judicial nature.[20] These rules are encapsulated in three propositions:[21]

(1) the right to be heard by an unbiased tribunal;[22]
(2) the right to have notice of the charges of misconduct;[23] and
(3) the right to be heard in answer to those charges.[24]

Any decision which was made in proceedings which did not operate these rules of natural justice will be invalid and liable to be set aside by the court.[25] The rules apply equally to an honorary member as to an ordinary member.[26] The caveat is that if the club were an incorporated one (which entails a large number of statutory rules governing the company and the

---

18 [1920] 1 KB 523, at 536. Contrast *P (a minor) v National Association of School Masters Union of Women Teachers (NASUWT)* [2003] 2 WLR 545, HL (where a union ballot was not invalidated by the accidental omission to send ballot papers to two members entitled to vote).

19 *Labouchere v Earl of Wharncliffe* (1879) 13 Ch D 346. See **6.10** for the facts of this case.

20 *Fisher v Keane* (1879) 11 Ch D 353, CA, at 360.

21 *Ridge v Baldwin* [1964] AC 40, at 132 (Lord Hodson).

22 *Nemo judex in causa sua* (No man should be a judge in his own cause): *R v Bow Street Metropolitan Stipendiary Magistrate ex parte Pinochet Ugarte* [2000] 1 AC 119, and [2001] 1 AC 147; *Re Medicaments and Related Class Goods* [2001] 1 WLR 700, at [37]–[38] (Lord Phillips MR). As to the test for bias, see **7.31**.

23 *Fisher v Keane* [1879] 11 Ch D 353, CA (where the plaintiff member had been suspended from membership of the Army and Navy Club without prior notice being given to him).

24 The *audi alteram partem* rule (Hear the other side): *R (X) v Chief Constable of West Midlands* [2004] 1 WLR 1518, at [113] to [132] (Wall J).

25 *Lee v Showmen's Guild of Great Britain* [1952] 2 QB 329, CA; *Fountaine v Chesterton* [1968] 112 Sol Jo 690 (cited in *John v Rees* [1970] Ch 345, at 398). Where the club rules expressly exclude the rules of natural justice (which would be very rare), such exclusion might well be unenforceable on the grounds of public policy: see Denning LJ in *Lee's* case, at 342.

26 *John v Rees* [1970] Ch 345, at 398.

rights of members) the court might not apply the rules of natural justice if there were sufficient indications that these rules were not to apply in any given case.[27]

7.14 The more serious the allegation being made against the accused, the stronger must be the evidence in support, although the civil burden of proof will continue to apply, namely, the balance of probabilities.[28] If the accused person requests that he be allowed legal representation and the rules do not provide for this contingency, this will be a matter of discretion for the club but in practice, depending on the nature or seriousness of the allegation, it is often advisable to permit such representation.[29] There is no rule that fairness always requires an oral hearing,[30] but if the committee allows such a procedure it should permit cross-examination of witnesses to take place.[31] A question which sometimes arises in practice is whether the committee, prior to a decision being made or a hearing taking place, is able to rely on different grounds for expulsion from those first communicated to the accused. Generally speaking, we consider the answer to be in the affirmative provided that the committee gives proper notice of the changed grounds.[32] It is a well established rule in contract law that if wrong or inadequate grounds are given for refusing to perform a contract a party may yet justify his refusal if there are facts in existence which would have provided proper grounds.[33] By a parity of reasoning the club would be entitled to rely on a later set of grounds in addition to or in lieu of its earlier ones. This rule, however, is subject to the qualification that the club may be precluded from setting up a different ground where by its conduct it would be unfair or unjust to allow the club to do this.[34]

7.15 Putting right errors Sometimes things go amiss and the managing committee or the appellate tribunal realise that mistakes have been made as to procedure or there has been non-compliance with the rules, and the question arises how to cure the problem. If looked at from the point of view of the member, he will on the face of things be entitled to go to court to obtain a declaration that the decision was invalid and of no legal effect by reason of the breach of the club rules or the rules of natural justice. That being so, the appellate tribunal (or the managing committee if there is no appellate tribunal) on being satisfied that the decision was defective as alleged, can simply remit the matter to the first instance tribunal without

27 *Gaiman v National Association for Mental Health* [1971] Ch 317, at 335; and see **7.5**.

28 *Re H* [1996] 1 All ER 1, HL, at 16 (Lord Nicholls).

29 A rule excluding legal representation at a hearing is not invalid as being contrary to natural justice: *Enderby Town Football Club v Football Association* [1971] Ch 591, CA.

30 *Local Government Board v Arlidge* [1915] AC 120, at 132; *R v Army Board* [1992] QB 169, CA, at 187.

31 *Bushell v Secretary of State for the Environment* [1981] AC 75 per Lord Edmund Davies at 116.

32 *Andrews v Mitchell* [1905] AC 78.

33 *Panchaud Frères SA v Etablissements General Grain Company* [1970] 1 Lloyd's Rep 53, CA, at 56.

34 Ibid, at 56–57.

going into the merits of the appeal. In other words, the slate is wiped clean and the expulsion process starts afresh.[35]

7.16 An alternative solution sometimes adopted is to let any appeal go ahead and simply have a complete re-hearing at the appellate level. This solution did not find favour with Mr Justice Megarry in *Leary v National Union of Vehicle Builders*[36] where, at 49, he stated:

> 'If one accepts the contention that a defect of natural justice in the trial body can be cured by the presence of natural justice in the appellate body, this has the result of depriving the member of his right of appeal from the expelling body. If the rule and the law combine to give a member the right to a fair trial and the right of appeal, why should he be told that he ought to be satisfied with an unjust trial and a fair appeal? … As a general rule … I hold that a failure of natural justice in the trial body cannot be cured by a sufficiency of natural justice in an appellate body.'

However, in *Calvin v Carr*[37] (which concerned the disqualification of a jockey imposed under the Rules of Racing of the Australian Jockey Club) Lord Wilberforce in the Privy Council considered that the above proposition was too broadly stated and went on, at 592, to say:

> 'First there are cases where the rules provide for a rehearing by the original body, or some fuller or enlarged form of it. The situation may be found in social clubs. It is not difficult in such cases to reach the conclusion that the first hearing is superseded by the second or, putting it in contractual terms, the parties are taken to have agreed to accept the decision of the hearing body, whether original or adjourned. … At the other extreme are cases where, after examination of the whole hearing structure, in the context of the particular activity to which it relates (trade union membership, planning, employment, etc) the conclusion is reached that a complainant has the right to nothing less than a fair hearing both at the original and at the appeal stage.'

Lord Wilberforce then mentioned, at 593, an intermediate class:

> '… the possibility that, intermediately, the conclusion to be reached, on the rules and on the contractual context, is that those who have joined in an organisation, or contract, should be taken to have agreed to accept what in the end is a fair decision, notwithstanding some initial defect. In their lordships' judgment such intermediate cases exist. In

---

35 *Leary v National Union of Vehicle Builders* [1971] 1 Ch 34, at 48E (Megarry J). In the same passage the judge said that there did not need to be a formal annulment of the first decision before starting afresh.

36 [1971] 1 Ch 34

37 [1980] AC 574, PC.

> them it is for the court, in the light of the agreements made, and in addition having regard to the course of the proceedings, to decide whether, at the end of the day, there has been a fair result, reached by fair methods, such as the parties should fairly be taken to have accepted when they joined the association. Naturally there may be instances when the defect is so flagrant, the consequences so severe, that the most perfect of appeals or re-hearings will not be sufficient to produce a just result.'

7.17 The subject was revisited by the Court of Appeal in *Modahl v British Athletic Federation Ltd*[38] (suspension from competitions of the claimant-athlete who alleged bias in the appointment of the disciplinary body) which applied the *Calvin* case in circumstances where the existence of an untainted appellate process had cured the alleged defect in the original disciplinary committee. In *Shrimpton v The General Council of the Bar*[39] the Bar's Disciplinary Tribunal suspended the appellant barrister from practice for 6 months for misconduct. He appealed to the Visitors to the Inns of Court whose number included three High Court judges (Lindsay, Blackburne and David Clarke JJ). The Bar Council conceded on the appeal that the original hearing was defective and a nullity because of the irregular composition of the disciplinary tribunal leading to potential bias. The Visitors followed the *Leary* case in allowing the appeal, and Mr Justice Lindsay in giving the judgment of the tribunal offered the following guidance on Lord Wilberforce's 'intermediate class':

> 'It would be material to the decision as to 'cure or no cure' in that intermediate class whether the appeal body performed its task without any predisposition and whether it had the means to make a fair and full enquiry: "for example where it has no material but a transcript of what was before the original body. In such case it would no doubt be right to quash the original decision".[40] In *Calvin* the Privy Council had particular regard not just to the applicable rules – concerned with horse racing in Australia – but with "the reality behind them"[41] namely the need in racing circles for speedy decisions on the issues without time for procedural refinements and of the rules having come to be accepted over the long history of Australian racing. Accordingly the Privy Council held that the (assumed) defects in the original decision were cured by the fair appeal.
>
> But the reality behind the Bar's Professional Code of Conduct is very different and it is thus easy to see an argument that in the professional-conduct environment the force of Megarry J's dictum [in *Leary*] is harder to resist than it was in *Calvin*. A tier of appeal would be

38 [2002] 1 WLR 1192.
39 [2005] EWHC 844.
40 Quoting *Calvin's* case, at 593.
41 Ibid, at 596.

denied to Mr Shrimpton who would be deprived of a hearing before a panel containing two lay members. The Visitors would become, in effect and at one and the same time both the tribunal of first instance and the final tribunal of appeal, an odd consequence, it would be said, of the nullity of the [original] decision.'

7.18 Good faith The decision to expel must be taken by the committee acting in good faith, that is, acting for the benefit of the club as a whole and not for some section or faction thereof,[42] and must of course come within the powers granted by the rules. Being an internal matter, and so long as the decision was honestly made within the rules[43] and, *semble*, was not so unreasonable as to be perverse, the court will not interfere with the committee's decision even if the court considered it was wrong.[44] On the other hand, it is highly unlikely that a court would accept as enforceable any rule which gave a power of expulsion which had retrospective effect;[45] such a rule would in any event be unacceptable to the membership at large.

7.19 Quorum and voting majority It is plain that the tribunal must be quorate when considering the issue of expulsion but it lends more weight to any decision if the relevant meeting is attended by a large number of the committee or members, as the case may be. It is normal practice to require that a decision to expel a member must be carried by at least a two-thirds majority of the members present at the meeting, and sometimes a three-quarters majority is preferred. The same voting majority should be used for any appellate process.

7.20 Remedies for wrongful expulsion If a member of a club has any complaint about the expulsion process or the end result of that process, his remedy is contractual, which will involve a claim for a declaration that the expulsion was wrongful[46] and/or an injunction to restore the claimant to membership and/or damages. It is now very unlikely that he will be entitled to seek a judicial review of the club's actions since this is a public law remedy.[47]

7.21 Injunction An injunction is an equitable remedy granted where damages would be an inadequate remedy. It is now underpinned by

---

42 *Woodford v Smith* [1970] 1 WLR 806, at 816; *Lambert v Addison* (1882) 46 LT 20, at 25; *Tanussi v Molli* (1886) 2 TLR 731 (concerning the Italian Couriers Club).

43 *Lyttelton v Blackburne* (1876) 45 LJ Ch 219, at 223.

44 See **5.27** and **5.29**.

45 *Dawkins v Antrobus* (1881) 17 Ch D 615, CA, at 632.

46 *Lee v Showmen's Guild of Great Britain* [1952] 2 QB 329, CA: see **5.28**.

47 *R v Disciplinary Committee of the Jockey Club, ex p Aga Khan* [1993] 1 WLR 909, CA, at 933 (Hoffmann LJ); see further **13.2** and **13.4**. See also *Law v National Greyhound Racing Club Ltd* [1983] 1 WLR 1302.

statute,[48] and is discretionary. This remedy can be used as a preventive measure if the facts warrant it.[49] But can the club refuse to reinstate the member on the ground that a right of membership is of such a personal nature that the court will not enforce it by way of specific performance or injunction? According to Lord Justice Denning in *Lee v Showmen's Guild of Great Britain*[50] a social club can put forward this argument and he cited the case of *Baird v Wells*[51] in support.[52] In fact, in the latter case Mr Justice Stirling, at 676, held that the bar to an injunction was the now discredited doctrine that the plaintiff had no proprietary right to protect rather than the right of membership being too personal to be enforced.[53] If the wrongfully expelled member desires it, it is common nowadays for reinstatement to be ordered by the court. Provided he acts without delay, and there is no real dispute as to the unlawfulness of the expulsion, the claimant can apply for an interim injunction to restore his membership. Because, however, an injunction is a discretionary remedy the court might be persuaded to refuse to grant an injunction, either interim or final, leaving the claimant to his remedy in damages. In *Glynn v Keele University*[54] the plaintiff, an undergraduate, was fined £10 and excluded for a year from residence on the university's campus by the university's vice-chancellor for appearing naked in the university precincts. This penalty was imposed without the undergraduate being given any opportunity to be heard on the matter. The plaintiff appealed but was absent abroad on the date listed for his appeal, and the appeal committee confirmed the penalty. The plaintiff sued the university claiming a declaration that the penalty was null and void, and damages. He applied for an interim injunction to restrain the university from excluding him from residence. The plaintiff did not dispute the facts on which the penalty was based. Pennycuick V-C held that the penalty was imposed in breach of the rules of natural justice but refused the injunction on the ground that the plaintiff had suffered no injustice.

7.22 Damages If an expulsion is declared unlawful or is set aside by the court, the claimant is restored to his original status and it will be as if there never had been any expulsion. This poses a conundrum. How can the claimant be compensated in damages for something which in the eyes of the law had never happened? On the face of things this would seem unjust on a person improperly deprived of his membership for the period between the date of expulsion and the date of restoration of membership or the date of declaration that the expulsion was invalid. In *Chamberlain v Boyd*,[55] the

---

48 Supreme Court Act 1981, s 37 (which applies in the county courts by virtue of the County Courts Act 1984, s 38).

49 *Lee v Showmen's Guild of Great Britain* [1952] 2 QB 329, CA, at 342.

50 [1952] 2 QB 329, at 342.

51 (1890) 44 Ch D 661.

52 See Denning LJ's judgment cited in **5.26**.

53 See Stirling J's judgment cited in **8.2** where the judge is dealing with members' proprietary rights.

54 [1971] 1 WLR 487.

55 (1883) 11 QBD 407.

plaintiff was an unsuccessful candidate for the Reform Club and brought a defamation action against a member who was alleged to have jeopardised his candidature by slanderous remarks. Lord Justice Bowen, at 415, cautiously observed:

> 'Possibly the membership of a club may be a matter of temporal advantage, and the deprivation of it may be an injury or damage of which the law will take cognisance.'

In *Collins v Lane, Cornish and Worcester Norton Sports Club Ltd*[56] the claimant, a retired police officer, was wrongfully expelled from the shooting club which was affiliated to the sports club, Mr Lane and Mr Cornish being respectively the chairman and secretary of the shooting club. Restoration of the claimant's membership did not arise. Basing themselves on *Chamberlain v Boyd* the Court of Appeal awarded the claimant the avowedly modest sum of £250 for deprivation of membership in the particular circumstances of that case. Lord Justice Beldam stated that by being deprived of his membership of the club in breach of the rules the claimant had lost something which was of value to him. The court rejected the club's submission that the claimant was entitled to no more than nominal damages. So whatever may have been the legal position in earlier times, we consider that it can now be taken as settled law that a wrongful expulsion will in appropriate circumstances result in an award of general damages for the loss of amenity during the period of wrongful exclusion from the club or for wrongful deprivation of membership if the exclusion is of a permanent nature. There seems little doubt too that if the claimant has been wrongfully expelled, he would be entitled to claim the unexpired portion of his subscription by way of special damages.

7.23 In *Morris Motors Athletic and Social Club Ltd v Fraser*[57] the defendants counterclaimed for wrongful suspension from the club for some 16 months, except for one defendant, Mr Butler, whose membership had been reinstated after 2 months. All the defendants had been members of the club for many years before their suspension. HH Judge Charles Harris QC in a reserved judgment awarded the defendants general damages for wrongful suspension and had this to say:

> 'Any approach to valuation is somewhat arbitrary. I do not think that the monthly [amenity] value of the club can sensibly be measured by the level of the subscription, which was one possibility. A St James club, at £1,000 per annum, perhaps provides rather fewer facilities for its members than the Morris Motors Athletic and Social Club does at a tiny fraction of the price. Both might be equally valuable a facility in the eyes of their members. However, given the lack of detail about how

56 [2003] LLR 19.

57 Unreported, Oxford County Court, 20 December 2006. See **5.37** for the facts of the claim against the defendants.

> much use the defendants in fact made of their club [save in the case of Mr Butler], it is clearly appropriate not to value their loss too highly. [The sum of] £10 a week for 16 months produces £640, which seems to me to be a reasonable sum in respect of all the defendants, save Mr Butler. I propose to award £650 to each of them. For Mr Butler £10 per week would only produce £80, a figure I consider too low for a man who used the club daily. I propose to award him £200.'

7.24 We point out that if the wrongfully expelled member is reinstated to membership, the *Morris Motors Club* case provides useful guidelines for evaluating his temporary exclusion from the club. If, however, the club successfully resists the reinstatement of the claimant's membership, the quantum of general damages for the wrongful expulsion will no doubt be increased to reflect this future loss of amenity, and may well include damages for loss of status, if the club is of some renown. The nature and surrounding circumstances of the wrongful expulsion will also be taken into account in assessing the general damages.

5. EXPULSION: PROPRIETARY CLUBS

7.25 The proprietor of a club is liable in damages for his act or the act of the committee in wrongfully expelling a member.[58] This is because the contract of membership contains an implied term that a member once admitted to membership shall not be excluded by the owner save in accordance with the rules, and damages will lie for any breach of this term.[59] As with members' clubs, the power to expel must be the subject of an express rule. A proprietor, however, has fewer problems on this score in that if, as is the norm, the membership is held on an annual basis, he has the option of simply refusing to renew the contract of membership on its expiry date.

6. SUSPENSION

7.26 Overview Everything said about expulsion applies with equal force to suspension.[60] Although the powers of expulsion and suspension usually go hand-in-hand in the rules, we consider that a power to expel would not

---

58 *Young v Ladies' Imperial Club Ltd* [1920] 1 KB 81, at 87.

59 *Abbott v Sullivan* [1952] 1 KB 189, CA, at 219. And see *Re Curzon Syndicate Ltd* (1920) 149 LT Jo 232 (where the proprietors of the Ladies United Services Club closed it without notice to the members. On the winding up of the company which owned the club, the members were held by Lawrence J to be entitled to prove in the liquidation for (a) the amount of the entrance fee (see **4.33**), (b) the unexpired portion of the subscription, and (c) damages for loss of the amenities of the club during the unexpired portion of the subscription).

60 *John v Rees* [1970] Ch 345, at 396.

of itself include the power to suspend. This is because suspension is of a different nature to expulsion and is not simply a paler version thereof. Accordingly, a power to suspend the member must be expressly given in the rules. It has been said that if the conduct complained of is of a serious nature it would be in order for the committee to suspend the member, even in the absence of a specific power of suspension, until a proper enquiry can be completed,[61] but this is doubtful because until a member is *proved* guilty of misconduct he is entitled to assert his innocence and thus enjoy the privileges of membership, subject to an authorised act of management such as excluding the member from the clubhouse pending the hearing of the case or complaint.

7.27 Consequences of suspension Suspending a member is shorthand for saying that the member loses all the privileges and rights of membership for the period of suspension. One of the privileges or rights of membership is the holding of office within the club or becoming a member of the committee. If the suspension occurs during a period of office, the member must stand down temporarily from that office. That much is clear. What is not so clear is whether a suspended member can be nominated or elected to an office or to the committee. We consider that as a matter of law this is possible because the suspended member still retains his membership.[62] Upon election, however, the suspended member will be unable to assume office and this might be highly inconvenient for the management of the affairs of the club as well as undesirable as a matter of principle. Consequently an express rule prohibiting nomination or election of a suspended member to any office or responsible position in the club is, we think, the proper solution to this problem.

7.28 Because the suspended member remains a member of the club he remains liable for his subscription or for any other authorised levy on the members. Can a suspended member still visit the club as a guest of another member? Most rules are silent on this point. We consider that the answer is in the negative because as a guest he would almost certainly be using the club's facilities in one way or another during his visit and his suspension has taken away this privilege; thus the change of status from member to guest cannot be used as a ploy to avoid the consequences of suspension.

7.29 Suspension should always be for a definite period, otherwise it may be tantamount to expulsion. It is common practice to limit suspension in the rules or in practice to a period not exceeding 12 months (or sometimes less)

---

[61] Josling & Alexander, *Law of Clubs* (6th edn, 1987), at p 40.

[62] We call to mind John Wilkes (1727–1797) who was first expelled from Parliament in 1763 but re-elected in 1768 and again three times in 1769 despite his repeated expulsions from Parliament for libelling the King and government in his newspaper, *North Briton*. The problem was that Parliament could not deny the validity of his candidature.

on the basis that if the member's conduct deserves suspension for a longer period than this, the correct remedy is expulsion from the club.

7.30 Partial suspension Can suspension take the form of partial suspension of the member's privileges? Rules never explicitly say this, merely that the club has the power to suspend the member. We take the view that as the greater includes the lesser there is nothing wrong in principle if the club deprives the member of some of his privileges of membership during the period of suspension rather than all his privileges. For example, the member may have been guilty of being unacceptably drunk at the club, in which case he might be banned from purchasing or drinking alcoholic drinks at the club bar for a period of some months whilst retaining the other privileges of membership. Could a similar ban on the member be imposed if he were found guilty of a drink/driving offence on his way home from the club? If the club had the usual rule that it could suspend the member for conduct which took place elsewhere than the club's premises and which was injurious to the good name of the club or rendered him unfit to be a member, we consider that a partial suspension based on a drink/driving offence would be upheld by the courts. If the member were convicted for a *second* time of a drink/driving offence we consider that the committee would be justified not simply in banning the member from the bar, but in imposing a full suspension, on the ground that drink/driving offences are not only criminal but amount to seriously anti-social behaviour.

7. DISCIPLINARY PROCEEDINGS

7.31 These do not form a separate category in the sense that everything which is said about expulsion and suspension applies equally to disciplinary proceedings brought by the club against its members. Practical problems concerning the appearance of bias can arise where the club's committee refers a disciplinary matter to a sub-committee for investigation, hearing and a report. When the matter comes back to the committee for decision the question arises whether those members who made the report are disqualified from sitting on the parent body. The test now favoured by the courts is whether 'the fair-minded and informed observer, having considered the facts, would conclude that there was a real possibility of bias'.[63] In clubs the members of the committee or any sub-committee are often well acquainted with the accused person. Thus a member who is a close friend of the accused will normally not think it proper to sit if a quorum can be formed without him.[64] On the other hand, it may be the administrative structure of the club is such that it is inevitable that the

63 *Porter v Magill* [2002] 2 AC 357, at [103] (Lord Hope).

64 *De Smith's Judicial Review* (6th edn 2007), at 10-43.

composition of the tribunal gives an appearance of bias. If this be the case, necessity constitutes an exception to the rule against bias.[65]

7.32 Disciplinary powers, like powers of expulsion and suspension, must be expressly granted in the club rules. Where disciplinary proceedings differ from expulsion or suspension proceedings is in the sanctions or penalties which are available to the disciplinary committee or tribunal. For example, on a complaint being proved, the Kennel Club has the power in appropriate cases to disqualify a member (and any non-member who agrees to submit to its rules) from judging or exhibiting at any dog show or competition, or to ban them from breeding dogs.[66] In addition, disciplinary proceedings often contain the power to fine a guilty party, a sanction not usually associated with expulsion or suspension. In *Bradley v The Jockey Club*[67] Mr Justice Richards, at [43], commented on the tribunal's role when imposing any penalty in disciplinary proceedings:

> 'Of course, the issue in the present case is not one of procedural fairness but concerns the proportionality of the penalty imposed … The test of proportionality requires the striking of a balance between competing considerations. The application of the test in the context of penalty will not necessarily produce just one right answer: there is no single "correct" decision. Different decision-makers may come up with different answers, all of them reached in an entirely proper application of the test. In the context of the European Convention on Human Rights it is recognised that, in determining whether an interference with fundamental rights is justified and, in particular, whether it is proportionate, the decision-maker has a discretionary area of judgment or margin of discretion. The decision is unlawful only if it falls outside the limits of that discretionary area of judgment.'

8. APPEALS

7.33 Many rules make provision for an appeal against expulsion or suspension or a disciplinary sanction. In the absence of exceptional circumstances or unless the rules say to the contrary, an appeal is a review of the first instance decision, not a complete re-hearing.[68] To this extent the appellate tribunal has a restricted role. It should not upset any original findings of fact unless there was no evidence to support that finding or

---

65 *De Smith's Judicial Review*, at 10-59. If the disciplinary sub-committee exercises power over *non-members* of the club by virtue, say, of some contract (e g as the Kennel Club does) or of some royal charter (e g as the Jockey Club did until 2007), it is important that its rules and procedures scrupulously avoid any unfairness or apparent bias.

66 See *Colgan v the Kennel Club* (Cooke J) (unreported) 26 October 2001, cited in *Bradley v the Jockey Club* [2004] EWHC (QB) 2164 at [71].

67 [2004] EWHC 2164 (QB), upheld on appeal: [2005] EWCA (Civ) 1065.

68 *Richardson v Ealing Borough Council* (2005) *The Times*, December 14, CA; see CPR r 52.11(1).

unless the finding was against the weight of the evidence as a whole.[69] It is also common for clubs to have no appeal procedure written into their rules. In this event, we consider that the committee would be acting within its managerial powers to permit an *ad hoc* appeal, if the circumstances warranted it. The appeal procedure can take several forms under the rules. Sometimes the rules cater for a specially constituted appellate tribunal; at other times the committee acts as the appellate tribunal or maybe the members in special meeting act as the appellate tribunal. If at all possible, the appellate tribunal should consist of different members from those who sat at first instance but this is not essential as a matter of law.[70] Some clubs include in their rules a provision whereby the appellant member is entitled to representation, legal or otherwise; we consider this to be a good practice and indeed clubs without such a provision in their rules should normally allow, on a concessionary basis, the attendance of a representative if this is requested.

9. BREACH OF BYE-LAWS

7.34 It is a common practice for clubs to impose a modest or reasonable fine if the member is either in substantial breach of the bye-laws or is a persistent offender in a small way.[71] The maximum fine should be stipulated in the rules or bye-laws. Although in the ordinary course of events dealing with a breach of the bye-laws is a much less serious matter than dealing with expulsion or suspension, which can terminate or curtail the member's privileges of membership, nevertheless the rules of natural justice as set out in **7.16** must be followed, albeit in a less formal way than with the expulsion or suspension process. We do not consider that a system of review or appeal is a necessary or desirable adjunct of giving the committee power to impose a fine for breach of the bye-laws.

10. REPRIMAND AND WARNING

7.35 A reprimand of a member by the committee over his misbehaviour in the club and/or a warning that such misbehaviour must not be repeated is on a different footing from expulsion or suspension because it does not involve any loss of the privileges of membership. The committee's powers in this respect are sometimes given expressly in the rules but, if not, we consider that as part of its management of the club's affairs the committee

69 *Bank of Credit and Commerce International (Overseas) Ltd v Akindele* [2001] Ch 437, CA, at 448.

70 *Leary v National Union of Vehicle Builders* [1971] 1 Ch 34, at 48; *Harrods Ltd v Harrodian School Ltd* [1996] RPC 697, CA, at 729 (Beldam LJ).

71 Under Literary and Scientific Institutions Act 1854, s 24, a literary or scientific institution may impose a reasonable pecuniary penalty for breach of its bye-laws provided that three-fifths of its members have confirmed this power at a special meeting.

would have an inherent right to reprimand or warn any member about the standard of his behaviour. As with the breach of bye-laws, we do not consider that a system of review or appeal is a necessary or desirable adjunct of the committee's power to reprimand or warn a member.

11. DISCRIMINATION AFFECTING MEMBERSHIP

7.36 Mention of the Equality Act 2010 has already been made in connection with admission into membership of the club (see **4.19**) and the management of the club's affairs (see **5.64**). The purpose of EQA 2010 is to protect certain personal characteristics, such as race and gender, from discrimination. The full list of protected characteristics is set out in **4.21**. Discrimination, harassment and victimisation are explained in **4.23**, **4.24** and **4.25**. The remedies available for unlawful discrimination are set out in **4.26**.

7.37 Loss of membership or associate rights The relevance of the Equality Act 2010 to this chapter is the further protection of those characteristics when it comes to the potential deprivation of membership or loss of rights, or the disadvantageous variation of the terms of membership or associateship. It is unlawful for a club to discriminate against a member or victimise that member in depriving him of membership or in varying his terms of membership.[72] Likewise, it is unlawful for a club to discriminate against an associate[73] or to victimise that associate in depriving him of or in varying his rights as an associate.[74]

---

[72] Equality Act 2010, s 101(2)(b)–(c), (6)(b)–(c).

[73] Defined in ibid, s 107(6): see **5.66**.

[74] Ibid, s 101(3)(b)–(c), (7)(b)–(c).

Chapter 8
OWNERSHIP OF THE CLUB'S PROPERTY

1. INTRODUCTION

8.1 Whereas no person would in the ordinary course of events join a club merely to see what assets he could acquire as a result of his membership, it is not an uncommon feature of clubs that during its lifetime or on its demise there arise questions of the true ownership of the club's assets. This may occur because a developer makes an attractive offer to purchase the club premises, thereby resulting in a windfall profit, or the club may founder through lack of members whilst retaining an undistributed fund of money. Those in charge of running the club therefore need to understand how the law works when it comes to the ownership of assets.

2. UNINCORPORATED MEMBERS' CLUBS

8.2 It is not always easy to discern where the legal and beneficial ownership lies in respect of assets and property held by these clubs. In *Baird v Wells*[1] (concerning the plaintiff's expulsion from membership by the decision of the committee of the Pelican Club, a proprietary club owned by the defendant) Mr Justice Stirling explained, at 675, why the members of members' clubs commonly have more than personal rights:

> 'In all cases of this nature, in which up to the present time an injunction has been granted, the [members'] club has been one of the ordinary kind, i.e. it has been possessed of property (such as a freehold or leasehold house, furniture, books, pictures, and money in the bank), which was vested in trustees upon trust to permit the members for the time being to have the personal use and enjoyment of the club-house and effects in and about it. But the interest of the members is not confined to that purely personal right. The members might, if they all agreed, put an end to the club; and in that case they would be entitled, after the debts and liabilities of the club were satisfied, to have the assets divided among them. In the present case the club, as such, has no property. The club-house and furniture belong to the Defendant Wells, and by him subscriptions are taken. He is not a trustee, but the owner, of the property.'

---

1 (1890) 14 Ch D 661.

Let us assume that the Basset Constitutional Club, an unincorporated members' club, is possessed of property such as is described by the judge. Who actually owns all this? The simple answer would appear to be the members of the club and, in the absence of any contrary indication, that would be the right answer. But this simple answer begs the question, on what legal basis is this ownership founded? It is this question which we try to answer below.

8.3 General propositions We consider that the following fourteen propositions can be established:

(1) in deciding any question of ownership, one must first look at the rules to see what they say on the subject.[2] Provided they are lawful,[3] express rules must be followed;

(2) the legal position is today governed solely by the law of contract[4] and not by the law of trusts or other equitable doctrine;[5]

(3) if the rules are silent on the question of ownership, the club's assets belong to the existing members of the club in common beneficial ownership;[6]

(4) this common ownership is neither a joint tenancy nor a tenancy in common so as to entitle the member to an immediate distributive share;[7]

(5) the member's interest in the club's assets lasts only so long as his membership lasts.[8] Once his membership ceases, for whatever reason, eg resignation, expulsion or death, his interest ceases;[9]

(6) a member's interest is not transmissible[10] nor does it pass to his estate when he dies, even though he was a member at the date of his death;[11]

(7) the members of the club can vary the rules as to ownership of assets, in the same way as any other contract may be validly varied, if the members are all agreed (or, if the rules so allow, by a majority vote);

---

2 *In re Bucks Constabulary Widows' and Orphans' Fund Friendly Society (No.2)* [1979] 1 WLR 936, at 943 (Walton J) (*'Bucks Widows' Fund'*).

3 That is to say, do not contain rules which offend, eg against the principles governing alienability or perpetuity.

4 *Bucks Widows' Fund*, at 952 and 953.

5 *In re Gillingham Bus Disaster Fund* [1958] Ch 300, at 314 (Harman J); *Tierney v Tough* [1914] 1 IR 142 (O'Connor MR).

6 *Murray v Johnstone* (1896) 23 R 981, at 990 (Lord Moncrieff); *Brown v Dale* (1878) 9 Ch D 78.

7 *In re Recher's Will Trusts* [1972] Ch 526 at 538 (Brightman J). See **8.6** and **8.26** for further reference to this case.

8 *Murray v Johnstone* (1896) 23 R 981, at 990.

9 *Bucks Widows' Fund*, at 943. Thus, in respect of a gift to existing members, on the death or resignation of an existing member, his share could not be severed but would accrue to the other members, even though such members included persons who had become members after the gift took effect: *Re Horley Town Football Club, Hunt v McLaren* (2006) WTLR 1817.

10 *In re St James' Club* (1852) 2 De GM & G 383, at 387 (Lord St Leonards LC).

11 *Murray v Johnstone* (1896) 23 R 981, at 990.

and provided there is in the ordinary course of events no private trust or trust for charitable purposes which hinders this process;[12]

(8) in the absence of any words which purport to impose a trust, any funds flowing into the club, eg by way of subscription, fund-raising or gift, would count as an accretion to the general funds of the club;[13]

(9) in the absence of any rule to the contrary, a term is implied into the contract subsisting between all the members that the club's surplus funds should on dissolution belong to the then existing members;[14]

(10) once a club ceases to function as a club, the right of a member to obtain realisation and distribution of the club property crystallises once and for all;[15]

(11) the distribution on dissolution should in principle be in equal shares to all persons who were members at the date of dissolution,[16] but could be on some other basis, if the rules or the facts warranted it;[17]

(12) where the rules have written into them some basis of inequality among the different classes of members in relation to their contractual burdens and benefits of membership (eg different rates of subscription for town and country members or different rates for senior and junior members), this inequality would normally follow into the distribution of surplus funds of the club on dissolution;[18]

(13) the managing committee or the club's trustees can in the course of their duties:[19]

   (a) put the club's assets at risk from creditors' claims under contracts made with the club;

   (b) cause third parties to obtain contractual or proprietary rights over the club's property, eg by the club taking out a mortgage;

   (c) declare with the consent of the members a valid trust in respect of some or all of the club's property;

---

12 *In re Recher's Will Trusts* [1972] Ch 526, at 539.

13 Ibid, at 539.

14 *Bucks Widows' Fund,* at 952.

15 *Abbatt v Treasury Solicitor* [1969] 1 WLR 561, at 567 (Pennycuick J: not overruled on this point).

16 *Bucks Widows' Fund,* at 952; *In re St Andrew's Allotment Association* [1969] 1 WLR 229 (Ungoed-Thomas J); *Feeney and Shannon v MacManus* [1937] IR 23, at 33 (Johnstone J). In the case of *In re the Sick and Funeral Society of St John's Sunday School, Golcar* [1973] Ch 51 ('*Golcar*') Megarry J said, at 60, that in principle there was no difference between the newest member of one year's standing and another member of 50 years' standing: 'Each has had what he had paid for: the newest member has had the benefits of membership for a year or so and the oldest member for 50 years. Why should the latter, who for his money has had the benefits of membership for 50 times as long as the former, get the further benefit of receiving 50 times as much in the winding up?'.

17 *In re GKN Bolts & Nuts Ltd (Automotive Division) Birmingham Works Sports & Social Club* [1982] 1 WLR 774 (Megarry V-C) (where only the full members were held entitled to participate in the surplus funds to the exclusion of other classes of member such as the honorary members and the temporary members).

18 The *Golcar* case (where a per capita basis was applied save for child members who were to receive a half share only because their contributions to the society were payable at half the adult rate).

19 *Bucks Widows' Fund,* at 940. See further **8.24** for trusteeship.

(14) if the club has become moribund, for example, because all the members have died or are untraceable, the assets will accrue to the Crown as bona vacantia, that is, treated as ownerless.[20]

8.4 If the club dwindles to one member it will cease to exist as a club[21] but we see no reason why the principles set out in propositions (1) to (13) in **8.3** should not apply to that one member in this terminal situation.

8.5 **Alienation of club property** Because each member has an interest in the club property there is no power for the committee of the club or for a majority of the members to dispose of club property against the wishes of a minority, unless it can be said that the disposal was authorised by the rules of the club and was consistent with the purposes of the club. This principle is well illustrated by the Scottish appellate case of *Murray v Johnstone*[22], which, it is submitted, would have equal application in English law. In that case a silver cup was presented to the curling clubs of Dumfriesshire and these clubs, which were unincorporated, framed rules under which the cup was to become the property of the club which won the cup twice in succession. In 1893 the Upper Annadale Club did so win and the members of that club at a subsequent general meeting resolved to present the cup to Mr Johnstone who was the club's star player. Mr Murray and four other members of the club brought an action against Mr Johnstone for the return of the cup to the club. The court granted the relief sought and Lord Moncrieff, at 990, stated the law as follows:

> 'But the question is, had a majority [of members] the powers to do so against the wishes of a substantial minority? I am of the opinion that it was beyond the powers of a majority of the club to alienate the trophy. In the present case if they [the members] had merely resolved that the cup should be held for the club by the defender [Mr Johnstone] as long as he remained a member, the resolution might have been justified as a reasonable act of management. But what is proposed is to alienate the club's property, and this I think cannot be done by the vote of the majority. In the course of argument it was urged that [on] this view it would be illegal for a majority of the members of a club to make a present out of the club funds to a secretary on his retiring, or to an old servant, or to present a medal or other prize to a member. Such a question seldom, if ever arises. If the gift proposed is substantial, it is usually made or eked out by private subscription among the members. If it is trifling, nobody objects. But if objection were taken by a minority, each case would depend upon its own circumstances, and fall to be decided according as the gift was or was not fairly authorised

---

20 *Bucks Widows' Fund*, at 942 and 943; *Cunnack v Edwards* [1896] 2 Ch 679, CA; *Re Trusts of the Brighton Cycling and Angling Club* (1953) *The Times*, April 29.

21 *Bucks Widows' Fund* at 943; see the first criterion at **1.1** above. A tontine society is different because here the last survivor automatically takes the benefits.

22 (1896) 23 R 981.

by the constitution and purposes of the club. Here what is proposed to be done is not to buy a prize or souvenir for the defender, but to present him with a valuable trophy, which was presented to the club as a body and intended to remain its property.'

8.6 Gifts and bequests to the club This is a topic which demonstrates one of the potential disadvantages of an unincorporated members' club. The general principles concerning such gifts or bequests were stated by Mr Justice Brightman in the case of *Re Recher's Will Trusts*.[23] In the course of his judgment, at 538, he gave some guidance on gifts and bequests to unincorporated associations:

> 'A trust for non-charitable purposes, as distinct from a trust for individuals, is clearly void because there is no beneficiary. It does not, however, follow that persons cannot band themselves together as an association or society, pay subscriptions and validly devote their funds in pursuit of some lawful non-charitable purpose. An obvious example is a members' social club. But it is not essential that the members should only intend to secure direct personal advantages to themselves. Or the association may be one which offers no personal benefit at all to the members, the funds of the association being applied exclusively to the pursuit of some outside purpose. Such an association of persons is bound, I would think, to have some sort of constitution; i.e. the rights and liabilities of the members will inevitably depend on some form of contract *inter se*, usually evidenced by a set of rules.'

8.7 Later in his judgment, at 539, Mr Justice Brightman explained how gifts and bequests could legitimately swell the coffers of an unincorporated association such as a members' club:

> 'The funds of such an association may, of course, be derived not only from the subscriptions of the contracting parties but also from donations from non-contracting parties[24] and legacies from persons who have died. In the case of a donation which is not accompanied by any words which purport to impose a trust, it seems to me that the gift takes effect in favour of the existing members of the association as an accretion to the funds which are the subject-matter of the contract which such members have made *inter se*, and falls to be dealt with in precisely the same way as the funds which the members themselves have subscribed. So, in the case of a legacy. In the absence of words

---

23 [1972] Ch 526.

24 See *Tierney v Tough* [1914] 1 IR 142 (O'Connor MR) (where the benefit society's fund was made up of contributions both from the canal company-employer) and from the boatmen-employees) and, on the society's dissolution, the employer's contributions were held to be absolute gifts to the society). It is surmised that this principle would apply in a shop club case or any similar set up involving both the employer and the employee where the object of the exercise was to confer financial benefits on the employee-members.

> which purport to impose a trust, the legacy is a gift to the members beneficially, not as joint tenants or as tenants in common so as to entitle each member to an immediate distributive share, but as an accretion to the funds which are the subject-matter of the contract which the members have made *inter se*.'

8.8 It may be gleaned from the above quotations that the problem arises when the gift or bequest to the club is made *subject to a trust*. A trust is necessary where (a) the club as beneficiary is not a legal person and (b) the donor intends that his gift shall benefit both present and future members, which is a common occurrence with clubs. This topic in relation to unincorporated members' clubs is by no means straightforward[25] and any donor would be well advised to seek legal advice before making a substantial gift or bequest to the club.

8.9 Built into the problem is the rule against perpetuity.[26] The law holds that private (ie non-charitable) trusts may not continue indefinitely.[27] The rule has two limbs: (a) the rulc against the remoteness of vesting (which affects 'people' trusts) and the rule against inalienability (which affects 'purpose' trusts).[28] The first limb prevents the vesting of the gift at too remote a time in the future and the second limb prevents the income of the trust being tied up for too long a time.

8.10 The Perpetuities and Accumulations Act 1964 helped unincorporated members' clubs under the first limb. The Act permitted the club in an instrument taking effect after 15 July 1964 to treat the gift as valid until such time as it became established that the vesting must occur after the end of the perpetuity period, that is, after a life in being plus 21 years, alternatively after a fixed term of 80 years (the 'wait and see' rule).[29] This meant that the gift would not fail for perpetuity but would vest in the current members who were ascertained within the perpetuity period.[30] The Perpetuities and Accumulations Act 2009 has taken the matter a stage further. In the case of instruments taking effect on or after 6 April 2010 the perpetuity period is 125 years and no other period.[31] This is so whether or not the instrument itself specifies a perpetuity period. As a result the common law perpetuity period (lives in being plus 21 years) has finally been swept away.[32] As to the second limb, the 2009 Act has substituted a narrower statutory restriction

---

25 See *Hayton & Mitchell on Trusts and Equitable Remedies* (13th edn 2010), at 5-71 to 5-88.

26 The rule against perpetuity is of general application, not limited to gifts or bequests made to unincorporated members' clubs.

27 *Hayton & Mitchell on Trusts and Equitable Remedies* (13th edn, 2010), at 7-62.

28 Ibid, at 7-62.

29 Perpetuities and Accumulations Act 1964, ss 1(1) and 3(1).

30 40(1) *Butterworths Encyclopaedia of Forms and Precedents* (5th edn, 2010 re-issue), at [706].

31 Perpetuities and Accumulations Act 2009, s 5(1); Perpetuities and Accumulations Act 2009 (Commencement) Order 2010, SI 2010/37.

32 *Butterworths Encyclopaedia* op cit, at [736].

against excessive accumulation. Generally speaking, the maximum accumulation period is now 21 years.[33]

8.11 Cy-près clause It has become increasingly common for the rules to state that in the event of a dissolution of the club the surplus assets (that is, the assets remaining after all the club's debts and liabilities have been met) should not be distributed to the members, which otherwise would be their entitlement,[34] but will be transferred or given to some club or other organisation having the same or similar objects as the dissolving club (generally known as a *cy-près* clause[35]). This is a very effective remedy against carpet-bagging members who simply wish to dissolve the club for mercenary reasons,[36] although no such rule can be entrenched immutably, unless the club is a charity[37] or a community amateur sports club.[38] Further, any lottery funding by the National Lottery is now contingent on the club having a *cy-près* type of dissolution clause in its rules.

8.12 Working men's clubs All property belonging to a working men's club, whether acquired before or after the club was registered, shall vest in trustees of the club for the use and benefit of the club and its members.[39] In *Re Blue Albion Cattle Society*[40] and *Re St Andrew's Allotment Association*[41] each judge postulated that in cases of friendly societies and mutual benefit societies the correct distribution of surplus assets on dissolution was based on a resulting trust, that is to say, based on the amounts contributed by each member, but Mr Justice Megarry in *In re the Sick and Funeral Society of St John's Sunday School, Golcar*[42] rejected this argument on the basis that membership of a club or association is primarily a matter of contract and that because the resulting trust is a concept of property law it was irrelevant to the division of a club's assets on dissolution. Accordingly, being unincorporated members' clubs, the legal position of working men's clubs is governed by the principles set out in **8.3**. We add that if the club is

---

33 Perpetuities and Accumulations Act 2009, s 14(4).

34 See **8.3**(9) above.

35 The *cy-près* doctrine at common law obtained where the charitable trust was impossible or impracticable to carry out and the court applied the charitable property as nearly as possible resembling the original trust: *Snell's Equity* (32nd edn, 2010), at 23–048. For statutory regulation of *cy-près* schemes in charities, see now Part IV of Charities Act 1993, as amended by Chapter 4 of the Charities Act 2006.

36 This became a particular concern of many golf clubs in the 1980s, at a time when there was a considerable increase in the value of clubs' land and premises, as a result of which many such clubs adopted a *cy-près* clause.

37 For the club as a charity, see **1.56**.

38 For the club as a CASC, see **1.63**.

39 Friendly Societies Act 1974, s 54.

40 (1966) *The Guardian*, May 28.

41 [1969] 1 WLR 229.

42 [1973] Ch 51, at 59.

registered under the Friendly Societies Act and becomes defunct through having no members any surplus funds will belong to the Crown as bona vacantia.[43]

8.13 Shop clubs A voluntary shop club is in the same position as an unincorporated members' club which is dealt with above. A registered shop club will still be an unincorporated members' club but some regulation of its position is contained in the schedule to the Shop Clubs Act 1902. The club's rules must provide for the investment of funds and a valuation of its assets and liabilities must take place at least once in every 5 years.[44]

3. INCORPORATED MEMBERS' CLUBS

8.14 Community clubs Being incorporated under one of the former Industrial and Provident Societies Acts or under the Co-operative and Community Benefit Societies and Credit Unions Act 1965 means that this type of club can hold assets and property in its own name as the legal and beneficial owner, although it is common for such assets and property to be vested in trustees for the use and benefit of the club and its members.[45] The club's rules will give some guidance as to the investment of funds and distribution of profits because these matters must be provided for in the rules.[46]

8.15 As stated in **1.23**, membership of a community club is by ownership of at least one share. The rules of the club regulate the shareholding and will state the limit on how many shares may be held, their nominal value and whether they are withdrawable or transferable.[47] If withdrawable, the rules must provide for the mode of withdrawal and the payment of the balance due on withdrawal.[48] If transferable, the rules must provide for the form of transfer.[49] There is no statutory requirement that a community club must issue a share certificate and generally speaking the rules seldom provide for this. A member has the right to nominate a person to become entitled at his death to his property in the club, and this may comprise shares, loans, deposits or otherwise.[50] The rules must make provision for the payment of

---

43 *Cunnack v Edwards* [1896] 2 Ch 679.

44 Shop Clubs Act 1902, Sch, paras v and x.

45 See *Addiscombe Garden Estates Ltd v Crabbe* [1958] 1 QB 513, CA as an example of a community club's property being held by trustees.

46 Co-operative and Community Benefit Societies and Credit Unions Act 1965, Sch 1, paras 12 and 14.

47 Co-operative and Community Benefit Societies and Credit Unions Act 1965, s 1(1)(b) and Sch 1, paras 7 and 9.

48 Ibid, Sch 1, para 9.

49 Ibid, Sch 1, para 9.

50 Ibid, s 23(1).

nominees.[51] There are statutory limits as to the amount of the nomination. Where the death has occurred or occurs after 4 August 1954 the limit is £1,500.[52]

8.16 The question of the beneficial ownership of the club's property on dissolution, as with an unincorporated members' club, is governed by the rules. Where the club is dissolved by a deed of dissolution,[53] the deed must state how it is intended to divide the funds and property of the club.[54]

8.17 Relatively straightforward facts can nevertheless throw up knotty problems on occasion. The case of *Boyle v Collins*[55] involved the Luton Labour Club and Institute Limited, a working men's club incorporated as a community club, and the issue was how to distribute its surplus assets among the members on dissolution. On 25 July 1997 the management committee and the property committee jointly met and suspended the club's activities with effect from 27 July 1997 because the club was trading insolvently and the entire management committee resigned, leaving only the property committee in place. There were three categories of members: life members, ordinary members and lady members. Under the rules life members were exempt from paying subscriptions but the ordinary and lady members were required to pay an annual subscription on 1 January. Subscriptions were sought for the year beginning 1 January 1997 but the club did not seek any subscriptions for the year beginning 1 January 1998. The property committee was authorised by the members to put in hand the sale of their main asset, the club premises, which was sold in August 1998 for a net sum of some £270,000. On 10 September 1999 the property committee voted to dissolve the club and on 31 March 2000 the Registrar of Friendly Societies cancelled the club's registration on the ground that the club had ceased to exist.[56] Under rule 11 if a member did not pay the subscription within 28 days of its becoming due he or she automatically ceased to be a member. Under rule 13 a person ceased to be a member on death. Under rule 28 on dissolution the club's assets were to be distributed among the members. Four members applied to the court to be appointed trustees of the club in order to administer the distribution of surplus assets to eligible members and three classes of member were represented as defendants, namely, (a) the life members, (b) the ordinary and lady

---

51 Co-operative and Community Benefit Societies and Credit Unions Act 1965, s 1(1)(b) and Sch 1, para 11.

52 Ibid, s 23(3)(c), as amended by the Administration of Estates (Small Payments)(Increase of Limit) Order 1975, SI 1975/1137, art 3(a). (Probably due to an oversight this limit was not increased to £5,000 with effect from 10 April 1984 under SI 1984/539 which updated a number of other statutes on this point). This nomination permits disposal on death without the necessity for probate or other proof of title.

53 See **3.14**(4).

54 Co-operative and Community Benefit Societies and Credit Unions Act 1965, s 58.

55 [2004] BCLC 471.

56 Co-operative and Community Benefit Societies and Credit Unions Act 1965, s 16(1)(a)(iii).

members and (c) the members who could not produce their membership card. Mr Justice Lewison held as follows:

(1) until cancellation of the registration on 31 March 2000 the club remained a legal entity and was not dissolved despite the earlier resolution to dissolve made on 10 September 1999. Consequently, up to 31 March 2000 the club was the beneficial owner of the club assets. Therefore distribution should take place as at this date, not the earlier date of the resolution[57] (this adversely affected the members identified in (3) below);
(2) rule 11 only applied whilst the club was actively functioning as a club. Thus the managing committee was acting within its implied powers of management when it suspended or waived the subscriptions due on 1 January 1998. Accordingly the eligible members were the life members and those members who had paid their subscriptions as at 31 December 1997;[58]
(3) because of rule 13, the 80 or so eligible members who had died before 31 March 2000 were not entitled to participate in the distribution;[59]
(4) a member did not become ineligible to participate in the distribution simply because he or she could not produce a membership card as stipulated by the committee; the rules were silent on the question of membership cards; and so proof of membership could be achieved by other means.

8.18 Clubs incorporated under Companies Acts A club incorporated under one of the Companies Acts has its own legal personality distinct from its members.[60] This separate personality means that the club itself can legally own property acquired through purchase or gift. A vital distinction has to be drawn between the member's contractual rights under his contract of membership and his statutory rights under the Companies Acts or the Insolvency Act 1986. In other words, we are here talking about *beneficial* ownership as opposed to *legal* ownership.

8.19 An incorporated club is still a members' club and the members' rights as between themselves are governed by the club rules.[61] Any express rules as to the ownership or distribution of the club's assets must be followed. The rules may provide for the company itself to hold the assets on trust for

---

57 Even cancellation of registration does not necessarily dissolve a community club; it can continue as an unregistered society, that is, as an unincorporated members' club: *Hole v Garnsey* [1930] AC 472, at 499 (Lord Tomlin).

58 There are conflicting cases on whether members in arrear with their subscriptions in an inactive club can participate in the distribution. In *Re Blue Albion Cattle Society* (1966) *The Guardian*, May 28, Cross J allowed participation provided they brought into account their arrears, whereas in *Re St Andrew's Allotment Association* [1969] 1 WLR 229, Ungoed-Thomas J disallowed participation by such members.

59 Presumably there was no question in this case of any rights of nomination: see **8.15**.

60 Companies Act 2006, s 16(3); *Salomon v Salomon & Co* [1897] AC 22.

61 See **1.35**.

the members or the company may appoint trustees to perform this task, and this trusteeship must be acted upon as a matter of law. Where the incorporated club's position differs from the unincorporated club is in the event that the rules of the incorporated club are silent as to the beneficial ownership of the club's assets.

8.20 Silence in the unincorporated members' club's rules will invoke the application of the propositions set out in **8.3** above. Silence in the incorporated members' club's rules will bring into play the principles of company law. The property of a company in no sense belongs to the members of the company[62] and it carries on its own business, not that of its members.[63] In the ordinary course of events the company is not a trustee of its property for its members.[64] In the absence of any trusteeship or contractual rights by virtue of the club rules, the members will have *no* property rights in the company's assets *at all*. Their tangible rights are limited to when the company is wound up. In the absence of contractual rights under the club rules, the position will be governed by the members' statutory rights under the Companies Acts and the Insolvency Act 1986, that is to say, if there are surplus assets once the company's debts and liabilities have all been paid, they will be distributed among the members of the company according to their rights and interests in the company.[65] This may result in the same distribution as would have occurred had the club been an unincorporated one. But this legal situation should awaken those running the club to the importance of having express contractual rules dealing with the ownership of the club's assets and, in particular, the need for trustees. Provided the trust was set up when the company was fully solvent,[66] a beneficiary under a bare trust of assets held by the company (or by the club's trustees) as trustee has a proprietary interest in those assets and is not relegated to the position of an unsecured creditor.[67] With a bare trust the property is ring-fenced in the event of the insolvent liquidation of the club because the basic principle is that only assets beneficially owned by the company fall to be administered and distributed to *unsecured* creditors in accordance with the winding-up legislation and rules.[68] The property would not of course be ring-fenced from a *secured* creditor such as a mortgagee or debenture holder if monies had been lent to the club on the security of the property.[69]

---

62 *Bank voor Handel en Scheepvaart NV v Slatford* [1953] 1 QB 248.

63 *Gramophone & Typewriter Co Ltd v Stanley* [1908] 2 KB 89.

64 *Butt v Kelsen* [1952] Ch 197, CA.

65 Insolvency Act 1986, ss 107, 143(1).

66 This eliminates the risk of the trust being set aside under whichever statutory régime is applicable on winding up.

67 *Gore-Browne on Companies* (45th edn, 2010), at 59[3].

68 Insolvency Act 1986, s 144(1). And see *Gore-Browne on Companies* (45th edn, 2010) at 59[3].

69 This mirrors the position of unincorporated clubs: see **8.3**(13)(b).

8.21 As with unincorporated members' clubs, if the incorporated club wishes to transfer or give its surplus assets to persons other than the members on dissolution of the club, then provision must be made for this eventuality in the articles or in the club rules. This is a common occurrence in companies limited by guarantee. We add here that the distribution of assets in any direction takes place on the winding up of the company. By the time the company is dissolved all assets should have been duly distributed. This is important because on dissolution of the company all undistributed property is deemed to be bona vacantia and belongs to the Crown.[70]

4. LITERARY AND SCIENTIFIC INSTITUTIONS

8.22 If the institution is unincorporated, during its lifetime its assets and property will be dealt with as any other unincorporated body. If incorporated under a royal charter (as a number have been), its trustees will no doubt hold the assets and property under a bare trust. If incorporated under the Companies Acts, its assets and property will be held either by trustees or by the institution itself. Upon dissolution, under s 30 of the Literary and Scientific Institutions Act 1854 any assets of the institution, which remain after the satisfaction of all its debts and liabilities, shall not be paid to or distributed among the members but shall be given to some other institution to be determined by the members at the time of the dissolution or, in default, to be determined by the judge of the county court of the district in which the principal building of the institution is situated.[71] An exception is where the institution is a joint stock company,[72] in which case the surplus assets may be distributed to the members.[73]

5. PROPRIETARY CLUBS

8.23 The proprietor is the sole owner of all the club's assets and property with the members having no interest in them.[74]

---

70 Companies Act 2006, s 1012.

71 Literary and Scientific Institutions Act 1854, ss 29, 30.

72 As defined in s 1041(1) of the Companies Act 2006. A joint stock company is one registered under one of the Joint Stock Companies Acts, a forerunner of the company limited by shares.

73 Literary and Scientific Institutions Act 1854, s 30; *Re Bristol Athenaeum* [1889] 43 Ch D 236 (held to be joint stock company); *Re Russell Institution* [1898] 2 Ch 72 (held not to be a joint stock company).

74 *Baird v Wells* (1890) 44 Ch D 661, at 676.

6. TRUSTEESHIP

8.24 Overview As trusteeship is a common occurrence in members' clubs, it is important for the members to understand the rudiments of this topic. An unincorporated members' club is not a legal person and cannot hold the legal title to property, such as land and buildings, in its own name.[75] Unless other arrangements are agreed, the legal ownership of these assets resides in the joint ownership of all the members who comprise the club for the time being. This would be impossibly inconvenient, hence the need for interposing a trust. But care needs to be taken over the choice of the other arrangements. In *Jarrott v Ackerly*[76] an unincorporated members' club called the Society of Automobile Mechanic Drivers of the United Kingdom, with a membership of over 2000, purported to take an underlease of premises. This was executed by one of the members, Charles Dawson, ostensibly acting on behalf of the club. The head lease was subsequently forfeited, and the club's trustees applied to the court for statutory relief under the Conveyancing and Law of Property Act 1892. Mr Justice Eve refused relief on the grounds (a) that the underlease purported to be made to lessees who had no legal status so there never was in fact any underlease, and (b) that in any event the trustees not being parties to the underlease had no right to sue as underlessees.

8.25 It may come as a surprise to the reader to learn that although well-established in English jurisprudence and much used for several centuries, there is as yet no agreed classification of trusts.[77] One way of looking at the situation is to put into a separate category *bare* (or simple) trusts and to treat all other trusts being *special* (or active) trusts.[78] There is said to be a bare trust whenever the trustee holds trust property in trust for an adult beneficiary absolutely.[79] The trustees will declare that they hold the club property upon trust for the (adult) members in accordance with the rules of the club[80] and as directed by the committee.[81] Under this arrangement the club's property is vested in the trustees under a bare trust for the members as a whole.[82] Here the trustees' control over the trust property is minimal and the beneficiaries' (members') control is paramount.[83] The trustees of a bare trust have no active duty to perform;[84]

---

75 *Hanbury and Martin on Modern Equity* (18th edn, 2009), at 14-014.

76 (1915) 113 LT 371.

77 48 *Halsbury's Laws of England* (4th edn, re-issue 2000), at para 524.

78 *Hanbury and Martin on Modern Equity* (18th edn, 2009), at 2-034.

79 Ibid, at 2-034.

80 *Bucks Widows' Fund* [1979] 1 WLR 936, at 939.

81 If the trust property is managed separately from the club's general assets, e g managed by a company whose shares are held on trust for the members, difficulties may arise because neither the managing committee nor the members in general meeting will have any direct control over the trustees' obligations.

82 Hayton and Marshall, *The Law of Trusts and Equitable Remedies* (11th edn, 2001), at p 215.

83 The beneficiaries have 'the entire economic interest in the asset': *Jerome v Kelly (Inspector of Taxes)* [2004] 1 WLR 1409, HL, at [2] (Lord Hoffmann).

they are merely the repository of the 'bare' legal title of the trust property and have at all times to comply with the directions of the beneficiaries acting through the committee.[85] And, indeed, the fact that the club property is vested in trustees on trust for the members is a quite separate matter and does not bear upon the contractual relationship as between the members themselves.[86] Thus it can be seen why a bare trust has to be distinguished from a special or active trust where the trustees are charged with the performance of substantial duties in respect of the control, management and disposition of the trust property, coupled with fiduciary duties owed to the beneficiaries.[87] A charitable trust established under **8.3**(13)(c) would count as a special trust as opposed to a bare trust. For practical reasons and by virtue of statute, in the case of land the number of trustees cannot exceed four.[88]

8.26 One other sort of trust needs briefly to be mentioned and that is a *purpose* trust. A trust may not be created simply for a purpose or object, that is, without ascertainable beneficiaries, unless it be charitable.[89] Thus in *Re Recher's Will Trusts*[90] a testatrix by her will dated 23 May 1957 gave a share of the residue of her estate to the London and Provincial Anti-Vivisection Society, an unincorporated association, which had ceased to exist on 1 January 1957. Mr Justice Brightman held that this would have been a valid bequest to the *members* of the society but for the fact that the society had been dissolved before the date of the gift. But if the testatrix had left the money on trust to the society for the *purpose* of advancing the cause of anti-vivisection the gift would have failed since it was a non-charitable purpose and could not be construed as a gift to any person.[91] (Under the Charities Act 2006 such a gift would now be construed as having a charitable purpose, namely, the advancement of animal welfare).[92]

8.27 The principal statute relating to trusts is the Trustee Act 1925, now augmented by the Trustee Act 2000.[93] It is usual to appoint more than one

---

84 *Snell's Equity* (32nd edn, 2010) at 27-027.

85 Gray, *Elements of Land Law* (4th edn, 2005), at 11.154–155; *Christie v Ovington* [1875] 1 Ch D 279, at 281.

86 *Bucks Widows' Fund*, at 952.

87 *Snell's Equity* (32nd edn, 2010) at 21-028.

88 Trustee Act 1925, s 34, as amended by the Trusts of Land and Appointment of Trustees Act 1996, Sch 3, para 3(9).

89 *Leahy v Attorney-General of New South Wales* [1959] AC 457, at 478 (Viscount Simmonds).

90 [1972] Ch 526.

91 But see *In re Lipinski's Will Trusts* [1976] 1 Ch 235 (Oliver J) (where the gift was not treated as a purpose trust but as an absolute gift to the members of an unincorporated, non-charitable association with a super-added (non-binding) direction as to how the money was to be used).

92 See **1.56**.

93 Other Acts are Variation of Trusts Act 1958; Trustee Investments Act 1961 (as amended); Trusts of Land and Appointment of Trustees Act 1996 (as amended); and Trustee Delegation Act 1999 (as amended).

trustee[94] and the number of trustees must not exceed four.[95] The club rules will also deal with the trustee's tenure of office and make provision in the event of his resignation from the club or his retirement from office or his death. Very commonly the rules will contain a provision that the members in general meeting may resolve to remove a trustee, and will contain a further provision that the committee is the nominated person under s 36 of the Trustee Act 1925 to appoint a new trustee.

8.28 Powers and duty of trustees The powers conferred by the Trustee Act 1925 are in addition to the powers conferred by the instrument creating the trust,[96] unless a contrary intention is shown.[97] Under the Trustee Act 2000 trustees enjoy a much wider general power of investment than hitherto.[98] This general power is in addition to powers conferred otherwise than by the Act[99] but, on the other hand, it is subject to any restriction or exclusion set out in the trust instrument itself.[100] The power is supported by a range of other powers whereby trustees can appoint agents,[101] nominees[102] and custodians,[103] whom they can remunerate,[104] and they have the ability to insure trust property.[105] The safeguard for beneficiaries lies in the statutory duty of care which applies to trustees in the exercise of these wider powers, that is to say, a duty to exercise such care and skill as is reasonable in the circumstances, having regard to any special knowledge or experience that they have or hold themselves out as having.[106] It should be noted, however, that the statutory duty of care only applies to the extent that the trust instrument permits this.[107] Accordingly, the club rules should make appropriate provision as to the powers of the trustees to invest the funds of the club and as to their duties in exercising those powers. The power of investment is sometimes exercised at the trustees' own discretion (with or without a cap on the value of the transaction) and sometimes on the direction of the committee.

---

94 Because a sole trustee cannot give a valid receipt for the proceeds of sale of land: Trustee Act 1925, s 14(2)(a), as inserted by the Trusts of Land and Appointment of Trustees Act 1996.

95 Trustee Act 1925, s 34(2)(a), as amended by the Trusts of Land and Appointment of Trustees Act 1996.

96 *Re Rees, Lloyds Bank Ltd v Rees* [1954] Ch 202.

97 *Re Turner's Will Trusts, District Bank Ltd v Turner* [1937] Ch 15.

98 The trustee may make any kind of investment that he could make if he were absolutely entitled to the asset of the trust: Trustee Act 2000, ss 3 and 8(3).

99 Trustee Act 2000, s 6(1)(a).

100 Ibid, s 6(1)(b).

101 Ibid, s 11.

102 Ibid, s 16.

103 Ibid, s 17. In other words, a power to appoint professional trustees.

104 Ibid, s 32.

105 Ibid, s 34.

106 Ibid, s 1(1).

107 Ibid, Sch 1, para 7.

8.29 Protecting the trustees Trustees will have a lien over the trust property against all costs, expenses and liabilities properly incurred as trustee.[108] It is essential, however, for the rules to make provision for the trustees to be indemnified against risk and expense out of club funds because the trustees cannot look to the members for an indemnity in the absence of such a rule.[109] The trustees of a literary or scientific institution who, by reason of their being the legal owner of the institution's building or premises, are liable for any payment of rates, tax, charges, costs and expenses, shall be indemnified by the governing body of the institution. In default of such indemnity the trustees are entitled to hold the building or premises as a security for their reimbursement and, to achieve this, may sell or mortgage the property.[110] The trustees of a charity may apply to the Charity Commission for relief from liability: see **1.58**.

---

108 Trustee Act 1925, s 30; *Re Beddoe* [1893] 1 Ch 547, at 548.

109 See *Snell's Equity* (32nd edn, 2010), at 7-03; *Wise v Perpetual Trustee Co Ltd* [1903] AC 139, at 149.

110 Literary and Scientific Institutions Act 1854, s 19.

Chapter 9

SUPPLY AND SALE OF ALCOHOL BY THE CLUB

1. INTRODUCTION

9.1 As mentioned in **1.7**, members' clubs have long enjoyed favourable treatment when it comes to the licensing laws. From 1964 until 2005, the commencement of the Licensing Act 2003 ('the 2003 Act'), the supply of alcohol[1] on club premises was regulated by Part 2 of the Licensing Act 1964 ('the 1964 Act') under a system which all are agreed worked reasonably well. However, the existing licensing laws were plainly in need of simplification and streamlining and the reform of the licensing procedures in 2003 repealed 22 Acts of Parliament and involved the consequential amendment of over 60 other Acts.[2] The 2003 Act radically changed the basis on which clubs are regulated in the supply and sale of alcohol. Because of the complex nature of the changes the 2003 Act did not come fully into force until November 2005.

9.2 **Summary of reform** To understand the radical nature of the reform it is worth summarising how the licensing landscape has changed:

(1) All licensable activities, which cover the sale and supply of alcohol, regulated entertainment, some sporting activities, late night refreshment licences, theatres and cinemas, (a) require an authorisation of some sort and (b) are brought into one licence at whatever venue. Hitherto there were six licensing regimes covering these matters;

(2) the authorisations called the club premises certificate and the premises licence attach to the *premises* to which they relate. Hitherto the registration certificate attached to the entity (eg the registration certificate of the Basset Rugby Club) and the justices' on-licence attached to the person (eg Bill Brewer, the licensee of the Basset Arms public house);

---

1 The 1964 Act referred to 'intoxicating liquor' (s 201(1)) whilst the 2003 Act refers to 'alcohol'. The former expression is technically correct in that the brewing industry refers to water as 'liquor' but is rather pedantic, whilst the latter expression is shorthand for the more accurate expression 'alcoholic drinks'. The meaning of alcohol is defined in s 191 of the 2003 Act as 'spirits, wine, beer, cider or any other fermented, distilled or spirituous liquor' with certain exceptions such as perfume and alcohol in confectionery.

2 Licensing Act 2003, Schs 6 and 7.

(3) the registration certificate has been abolished. In its place is the club premises certificate;
(4) the justices' on-licence has been abolished. In its place is the premises licence;
(5) the concepts of permitted hours, extended hours and special hours have been abolished.[3] In their place have come flexible hours to suit the individual premises;
(6) occasional licences and occasional permissions have been abolished. In their place have come temporary event notices which permit licensable activities on a temporary basis;
(7) the sale or supply of alcohol to children is now the same for clubs as other licensed premises.[4] It is a criminal offence to sell or supply alcohol to a person under the age of 18;[5]
(8) licensing by magistrates has been abolished. The licensing authority is now the local council.

9.3 One feature of club law should be noted. Parliament recognised that the supply of alcohol to a member in a members' club was not a sale, although the member had paid money to obtain it. The property of the club belonged to all the members in common, and what appeared at first sight to be a purchase by the member was no more than a reimbursement of club funds.[6] Accordingly, the 1964 Act prohibited the *supply* of alcohol to club members or their guests unless the club obtained a registration certificate from the magistrates' court.[7] Originally and on first renewal granted for one year, on the second or subsequent renewal the registration certificate could be granted for up to 10 years.[8] In the absence of objection, there was only limited scope for refusing to grant or renew a certificate[9] and this factor, coupled with its validity for 10 years, proved of great advantage to clubs.

9.4 **Transition** A more accurate description of the transitional provisions set out in Sch 8 to the 2003 Act would have been *conversion* provisions since they set out how existing registration certificates and on-licences were to be converted to club premises certificates and premises licences. The transitional period has passed into history and no longer need detain us.

---

3 Licensed drinking hours were first imposed in World War I to discourage excessive drinking by the civilian population.
4 A surprising lacuna in the 1964 Act.
5 Licensing Act 2003, s 146(1)–(3).
6 *Graff v Evans* (1882) 8 QBD 373, DC; *Trebanog Working Men's Club and Institute Ltd v MacDonald* [1940] 1 KB 576, DC.
7 Licensing Act 1964, ss 39(1) and 40(1).
8 Ibid, s 40(2) and (3).
9 Ibid, ss 45 and 46.

9.5 Objectives of the 2003 Act Unlike any previous licensing legislation the 2003 Act sets out objectives, which the licensing authorities must promote when carrying out their functions, namely:[10]

(1) the prevention of crime and disorder;
(2) public safety;
(3) the prevention of public nuisance;
(4) the protection of children from harm.

In addition, the licensing authority must have regard to the following in carrying out its functions:[11]

(5) its own published statement of licensing policy;[12]
(6) any guidance issued by the Secretary of State.[13]

9.6 The scheme of the 2003 Act is to define what are licensable activities and qualifying club activities and then to apply a statutory code to each of the main categories: Part 3 deals with the premises licence; Part 4 deals with the club premises certificate; Part 5 deals with permitted temporary activity. These three categories are called 'authorisations' in the 2003 Act. Part 6 deals with the personal licence.

2. LICENSABLE ACTIVITIES

9.7 The 2003 Act sets out the four categories:[14]

(1) the sale by retail of alcohol;
(2) the supply of alcohol by or on behalf of a club to, or to the order of, a member of the club;
(3) the provision of regulated entertainment;[15]
(4) the provision of late night refreshment.

---

10 Licensing Act 1964, s 4(2).
11 Ibid, s 4(3).
12 Ibid, s 5.
13 Licensing Act 1964, s 182. In licensing law nothing is writ in stone: on 28 July 2010 Ms Theresa May, the Home Secretary, proposed a raft of new measures to deal with problems arising from alcohol drinking.
14 Licensing Act 2003, s 1(1).
15 See **10.12**.

3. QUALIFYING CLUB ACTIVITIES

9.8 For the purposes of the above four categories the following are qualifying club activities:[16]

(1) the sale by retail of alcohol by or on behalf of a club to a guest of a member of the club for consumption on the premises where the sale takes place (ie a variant of **9.7**(1));
(2) the supply of alcohol by or on behalf of a club to, or to the order of, a member of the club (ie a repetition of **9.7**(2));
(3) the provision of regulated entertainment where that provision is by or on behalf of a club for (a) members of the club or (b) members of the club and their guests (ie a variant of **9.7**(3)).

4. AUTHORISATIONS

9.9 Authorisation is required for any licensable activity.[17] An authorisation is one of the following:[18]

(1) a club premises certificate;
(2) a premises licence;
(3) a temporary event notice.

The 2003 Act expressly allows persons to hold two or more authorisations at the same time.[19] For example, it is common to have a club premises certificate used in conjunction with temporary event notices, or occasionally a club premises certificate might be combined with a premises licence.

5. CLUB PREMISES CERTIFICATE

9.10 A club premises certificate will only be granted in respect of premises 'occupied by, and habitually used for the purposes of, a club'.[20] The certificate will declare that the club premises may be used for the qualifying club activities set out in the certificate.[21] This certificate has been specifically designed for members' clubs[22] and is likely to be the preferred option of the majority of clubs which wish to carry on the licensable activities set out in

16 Licensing Act 2003, s 1(2).
17 Ibid, s 2. It is an offence to carry on a licensable activity otherwise than under and in accordance with an authorisation under s 2: ibid, s 136(1).
18 Ibid, s 2(4).
19 Ibid, s 2(3).
20 Ibid, s 60(1)(a).
21 Ibid, s 1(2).
22 Ie excluding proprietary clubs.

9.7. Parliament has continued to treat members' clubs favourably under the 2003 Act, but it is fair to add that the supervision and control of the club's activities is undeniably stricter than under the 1964 Act. There is, too, a continuing downward trend in the number of clubs holding a certificate to supply or sell alcohol to its members and guests, as may be seen from the following data:[23]

- Prior to November 2005: some 23,500 clubs were holding a registration certificate;
- As at 31 March 2008: 17,069 clubs were holding a club premises certificate;
- As at 31 March 2009: 17,259 such clubs;
- As at 31 March 2010: 16,707 such clubs, with over 300 clubs having surrendered their certificate during the course of the year.

According to the Evidence and Analysis Unit of the Department for Culture, Media and Sport in its bulletin of 29 September 2010 the peak of club certificates was reached in 1983 and the number of club certificates is now at its lowest since 1950.

9.11 Qualifying club conditions To qualify for a club premises certificate a members' club must satisfy certain conditions.[24] There are five general conditions[25], and three additional conditions[26] if a club intends to supply alcohol, which the club must satisfy in order to qualify for a club premises certificate:

General:

(1) under the rules of the club a person may not be admitted to membership (or, as a candidate for membership be admitted to the privileges of membership) without an interval of at least 2 days between their nomination/application for membership and their admission as a member of the club;
(2) where the rules of the club permit persons to become members without prior nomination or application, those persons must not be admitted to the privileges of membership without an interval of at least 2 days between their becoming members and their admission to such privileges;
(3) the club is established and conducted in good faith as a club (see **9.12**);
(4) the club has at least 25 members;

[23] Sources: Department for Culture, Media and Sport, January 2005; UK Statistics Authority, 2008 and 2009; National Statistics Bulletin on Alcohol, Entertainment and Late Night Refreshment Licensing, England and Wales, April 2009 to March 2010, pp 10, 11 and 38, published by the Department for Culture, Media and Sport on 29 September 2010.
[24] Licensing Act 2003, ss 61 and 63.
[25] Ibid, s 62.
[26] Ibid, s 64.

(5) alcohol is not supplied, or intended to be supplied, to members on the premises except by or on behalf of the club.

Additional:

(6) insofar as the purchase of alcohol for the club, and its supply by the club, are not managed by the club in general meeting or by the general body of members, such purchase and supply are managed by an elected committee of members aged 18 years and over;[27]
(7) no arrangements have been made, or are intended to be made, for any person to receive at the expense of the club any commission, percentage or similar payment in connection with the purchase of alcohol by the club;
(8) no arrangements have been made, or are intended to be made, for any person directly or indirectly to derive pecuniary benefit from the supply of alcohol to club members and their guests except:
   (a) any benefit accruing to the club as a whole;
   (b) any benefit to a member deriving indirectly from profitable sales of alcohol at the club.

9.12 Test of good faith The matters to be taken into account in determining whether the club is established and conducted in good faith as a club are:[28]

(1) any arrangements restricting the club's freedom of purchase of alcohol;
(2) any provision in the rules, or arrangements, under which money or property of the club, or any gain arising from the carrying on of the club, is or may be applied other than for the benefit of the club as a whole or for charitable, benevolent or political purposes;[29]
(3) the arrangements for informing the membership about the club's finances;
(4) the state of the club's books of account and records;
(5) the nature of the premises occupied by the club.

If the licensing authority concludes that the club does not satisfy this test, it must give the club notice of the decision and the reasons for it.[30]

9.13 Advantages One commentator neatly summed up the situation: 'The Government has been anxious to retain the unique character of clubs in general and to ensure that they keep their sometimes quirky nature, whilst

---

27 It is unusual to let the general body of members have control of this aspect of the club's affairs.

28 Licensing Act 2003, s 63(2).

29 It is this provision which in particular ensures that the qualifying club must be a members' club rather than a proprietary club. This provision can also cause problems if the members' club is a company limited by shares which declares a dividend to its members.

30 Licensing Act 2003, s 63(3).

at the same time bringing them into the new regime with sufficient regulation to ensure that their special nature is not abused'.[31] Unlike other licensed premises, the holder of a club premises certificate enjoys the following advantages:

(1) there is no requirement for a member or employee of the club to hold a personal licence;
(2) there is no requirement to specify a designated premises supervisor in the licence;
(3) the police and authorised officers have no right of entry into club premises without a court order;[32]
(4) there are no police powers of immediate closure of the club premises, and they are excluded from the court's powers of closure of all licensed premises in a particular area.[33]

9.14 Application for certificate An application for a club premises certificate may be made by any qualifying club for 'any premises which are occupied by and habitually used for the purposes of the club'.[34] The application is made to the licensing authority in whose area the club premises are situated.[35] The detailed procedure is governed by Parts 3 and 4 of the Licensing Act 2003 (Premises Licences and Club Premises Certificates) Regulations 2005.[36] These regulations may be accessed in full by using the government (2010) website, www.opsi.gov.uk. Regulation 17 and Part A of Sch 9 require the club to make the prescribed declaration as to its being a qualifying club. Regulation 18 and Part B of Sch 9 require the club to apply for a club premises certificate in the prescribed form and to pay the prescribed fee. Regulation 21 permits the application to be made by electronic means. Regulations 25 and 26 prescribe the manner and timing of the advertisement of the application. Regulations 27 and 28 prescribe the notice to be given to each responsible authority for the area in which the premises are situated, that is to say, the police, the fire authority, the

---

31 Barker and Cavender, *Licensing – The New Law* (2003), at 8.1.4.

32 See **9.35**.

33 See **9.48** and **9.60**.

34 Licensing Act 2003, s 71(1).

35 Ibid, s 71(2). If the premises are situated in the areas of two or more licensing authorities the licensing authority is the one in whose area the greater or greatest part of premises is situated: ibid, s 68(3).

36 SI 2005/42, as augmented by the Licensing Act 2003 (Licensing Authority's Register) (Other Information) Regulations 2005, SI 2005/43; the Licensing Act 2003 (Fees) Regulations 2005, SI 2005/79; the Licensing Act 2003 (Premises Licences and Club Premises Certificates) (Miscellaneous Amendments) Regulations 2009, SI 2009/1809; and the Licensing Act 2003 (Premises Licences and Club Premises Certificates) (Amendment) (Electronic Applications) Regulations 2009, SI 2009/3159. See also the Licensing Act 2003 (Welsh Language Forms) Order 2007, SI 2007/805, which prescribes that Welsh and bilingual versions of the forms may be used when dealing with Welsh licensing authorities.

environmental health authority and the planning authority.[37] The application must be accompanied by:[38]

(1) a plan of the premises;
(2) a club operating schedule;
(3) a copy of the rules of the club.

9.15 Plan of premises Consideration should be given to the proper extent of the licensed premises. Premises mean 'any place'.[39] It is important that the extent is not too narrow, say restricted to the clubhouse and its immediate environs such as its lawns, forecourt and terrace or balcony, when it is known that social occasions take place elsewhere, for instance, a cricket club which has a marquee on the edge of its cricket ground during a festival or a golf club which has a drinks tent on the ninth or tenth tee or mobile refreshment facilities during a competition. The application must be accompanied by a scaled plan which shows all of the following details:[40]

(1) the extent of the boundary of the building, if relevant, and any external and internal walls of the building and, if different, the perimeter of the premises;
(2) the location of points of access to and egress from the premises;
(3) if different from (2), the location of escape routes from the premises;
(4) in a case where the premises are to be used for more than one licensable activity, the area within the premises used for each activity;
(5) fixed structures (including furniture) or similar objects temporarily in a fixed location (but not furniture) which may impact on the ability of individuals on the premises to use exits or escape routes without impediment;
(6) in a case where the premises include a stage or raised area, the location and height of each stage or area relative to the floor;
(7) in a case where the premises include any steps, stairs, elevators or lifts, the location of the steps, stairs, elevators or lifts;
(8) in the case where the premises include any room or rooms containing public conveniences, the location of the room or rooms;
(9) the location and type of any fire safety and any other safety equipment including, if applicable, marine safety equipment; and
(10) the location of a kitchen, if any, on the premises.

9.16 Inspection of premises Where a club applies for a club premises certificate or applies for a variation of a certificate or an application is made for a review of the certificate, authorised persons or the police may inspect the club premises within 14 days after the making of the application,

37 Licensing Act 2003, ss 69(4) and 71(6)(b).
38 Ibid, s 71(4).
39 Ibid, s 193. It also includes a vehicle, vessel or moveable structure.
40 Licensing Act 2003 (Premises Licences and Club Premises Certificates) Regulations 2005, reg 23.

provided that 48 hours' notice is given of the intended inspection.[41] The authorised persons are defined in s 69(2) of the 2003 Act and comprise an officer of the licensing authority, an inspector from the fire authority, a health and safety inspector, an environmental health inspector, an inspector or surveyor of ships (if a vessel is involved) and any other prescribed person.[42] The licensing authority can extend the 14-day period by up to seven days if the authorised person or the police constable had taken steps in good time to make the inspection but this had not proved possible within the time allowed.[43] In other words, the onus is very much on the inspecting authority to arrange the inspection in good time.

9.17 Club operating schedule This is a crucial document and must be in the prescribed form[44] and include a statement of the following matters:[45]

(1) the qualifying club activities to which the application relates;
(2) the times during which it is proposed that the activities are to take place;
(3) any other times during which it is proposed that the premises are to be open to members and their guests;
(4) if applicable, whether the supply of alcohol is proposed to be for consumption on the premises, or for both on and off the premises;
(5) the steps which it is proposed to take to promote the licensing objectives;
(6) such other matters as may be prescribed by the Secretary of State.

The contents of this schedule demonstrate the bringing together of all licensable activities in one comprehensive licence as mentioned in **9.2**(1), that is to say, the supply and sale of alcohol and the provision of regulated entertainment, which comprises entertainment and/or entertainment facilities.

9.18 Hours of operation The times during which alcohol is to be supplied on club premises must be specified in the Operating Schedule and can be whatever hours are required by the club, subject to the overriding provisions of the licensing objectives and in particular any objections by the police based on the crime prevention objective. Before applying for a club premises certificate, clubs should therefore examine their activities and decide what hours are appropriate.[46] There is no requirement that premises

---

41 Licensing Act 2003, s 96(1)–(4).

42 Ibid, s 69(2).

43 Ibid, s 96(7), (8).

44 Licensing Act 2003 (Premises Licences and Club Premises Certificates) Regulations 2005, Sch 9, Part 2 of Part B.

45 Licensing Act 2003, s 71(5).

46 One in ten registered clubs in the 9,000 sample were recorded as trading to midnight as at November 2007 (prior to transition this figure had been one in fifty) and the average closing time for the sampled clubs was 2356 hours, an increase of some 56 minutes over

have to be actually open during all the hours set out in the operating schedule. In many cases it may be appropriate to set out in the operating schedule later closing hours on Fridays and Saturdays, say half past midnight, and earlier closing hours, say 10.30 pm, on other days. In determining this timetable, it is plain that clubs have to be conscious of staff working hours and balance their interests against the undoubted advantage of the flexibility conferred by the availability of longer drinking hours. Once they are incorporated into this schedule the times become, so to speak, 'the permitted hours'. Managing committees need to be aware of the need to monitor the situation regarding opening hours, and members need to be conversant with opening hours, which should be published by notice in the clubhouse and/or set out in the bye-laws. If the bar steward is authorised to close the bar before the end of published opening hours, this fact should be made known to the members in order to avoid any argument with members who insist that they can go on drinking right to the end of the published hours.

9.19 Representations One of the purposes of proper advertisement of the application is to enable interested parties or responsible authorities to make representations to the licensing authority within 28 days after the application has been made to the licensing authority.[47]

(1) An 'interested party' is defined as a person or persons living in or being involved in a business in the vicinity of the club premises, or a body representing such persons;[48]
(2) A 'responsible authority' is defined as any of the following whose role covers the area in which the club premises are situated: the chief office of police, the fire authority, the health and safety authority, the local planning authority, and the environmental authority;[49]
(3) A representation will be relevant:
    (a) if it is concerned with the likely effect of the grant of the application upon the promotion of the licensing objectives;[50] and
    (b) if it is made by an interested party or responsible authority within the specified time and has not been withdrawn prior to the hearing,[51] and it is not considered frivolous or vexatious by the licensing authority.[52]

---

the previous average: see *Evaluation of the Licensing Act 2003*, App 3, published by the Department for Culture, Media and Sport, March 2008. Very few private clubs holding a club premises certificate have a 24-hour alcohol licence.

47 Licensing Act 2003 (Premises Licences and Club Premises Certificates) Regulations 2005, reg 22.

48 Licensing Act 2003, s 69(3).

49 Ibid, s 69(4). If the club premises are on a vessel, the responsible authorities are a navigation authority, the Environment Agency, and the British Waterways Board (or the Secretary of State): s 69(4)(h).

50 Ibid, s 85(5)(a).

51 Ibid, s 85(6)(a), (b).

52 Ibid, s 85(6).

9.20 Conditions on grant Conditions may be imposed on the certificate provided that they are consistent with the club operating schedule accompanying the application (which schedule itself has to comply with the licensing objectives),[53] or where they are required in relation to off-sales[54] or to the exhibition of films.[55] The certificate can be granted with different conditions that apply to the various areas of the club premises, or to different qualifying club activities, giving the authority maximum flexibility.[56]

9.21 Mandatory conditions The 2003 Act was amended in 2009 to permit the Secretary of State to prescribe up to nine mandatory conditions to be attached to the club premises certificate relating to the supply of alcohol to members and guests in club premises in order to promote the four licensing objectives.[57] The Licensing Act 2003 (Mandatory Licensing Conditions) Order 2010[58] came fully into force on 1 October 2010 and prescribes five such conditions. They may be summarised as follows:

(1) The 'responsible person' must take reasonable steps to ensure that staff on club premises do not carry out or arrange or participate in any 'irresponsible promotions':[59]
   (a) A responsible person means in relation to these mandatory conditions any member or officer of the club who is present in a capacity which enables him to prevent the supply of alcohol in question;
   (b) an irresponsible promotion means one of the following activities which are carried on for the purpose of encouraging the sale or supply of alcohol and where there is a significant risk of their leading or contributing to crime and disorder, or prejudice to public safety, or public nuisance, or harm to children:[60]
      (i) games which require or encourage drinking a quantity of alcohol within a time limit;
      (ii) games which require or encourage drinking as much alcohol as possible (whether or not within a time limit);
      (iii) provision of unlimited or unspecified quantities of alcohol either free or for a fixed or discounted fee to a group identified by a defined characteristic, for example, students at Basset University on a guided pub crawl;

---

53 Licensing Act 2003, s 72(2).

54 Ibid, s 73. See further **9.32**.

55 Ibid, s 74. The admission of children (ie those under 18) is subject to restrictions recommended by the licensing authority.

56 Ibid, s 72(10).

57 Ibid, ss 73A and 73B, inserted by Policing and Crime Act 2009, Sch 4, paras 3 and 4.

58 SI 2010/860.

59 Licensing Act 2003 (Mandatory Licensing Conditions) Order 2010, Sch, para 1(1).

60 Ibid, Sch, para 2.

(iv) provision of free or discounted alcohol or any other thing as a prize to encourage or reward the purchase and consumption of alcohol over a period of 24 hours;
(v) provision of free or discounted alcohol in relation to viewing on club premises of a sporting event where the provision is dependant on the outcome of the event or on the likelihood of something occurring or not occurring;
(vi) selling or supplying alcohol in association with promotional posters or flyers on, or in the vicinity of, club premises which can reasonably be said to condone, encourage or glamorise anti-social behaviour[61] or to refer to the effects of drunkenness in a favourable manner;

(2) the responsible person shall ensure that no alcohol is dispensed directly by one person into the mouth of another (other than where that other person is unable to drink without assistance by reason of a disability);[62]
(3) the responsible person shall ensure that free tap water is provided on request to members and guests where it is reasonably available;[63]
(4) the club shall ensure that an age verification policy applies to alcohol sold and supplied on the club premises. The policy must require members or guests who appear to the responsible person to be under the age of 18 (or such older age as may be specified in the policy) to produce on request, before being served with alcohol, identification bearing their photograph, date of birth and a holographic mark, such as is used on bank credit cards;[64]
(5) the responsible person shall ensure that the following alcoholic drinks are sold or supplied for consumption of the club premises in the following measures:
(a) beer or cider: ½ pint
(b) gin, rum, vodka or whisky: 25 ml or 35 ml
(c) still wine in a glass: 125 ml.

An exception applies where the alcoholic drinks are made up in advance ready for sale or supply in a securely closed container. The responsible person shall ensure the members and guests are made aware of these measures.[65]

---

61 Anti-social behaviour has the meaning given in Anti-Social Behaviour Act 2003, s 36: Licensing Act 2003 (Mandatory Licensing Conditions) Order 2010, Sch, para 2.

62 Ibid, Sch, para 2. Disability has the meaning given in Disability Discrimination Act 1995, s 1 (now repealed): ibid, Sch, para 2. This definition has, however, been repeated in the Equality Act 2010, s 6 (see **5.71**).

63 Licensing Act 2003 (Mandatory Licensing Conditions) Order 2010, Sch, para 3.

64 Ibid, Sch, para 4. Local authorities commonly impose as a condition the adoption of the Challenge 21 Scheme whereby persons who appear to be under the age of 21 are required to provide verification of their age in order to prevent under-age drinking, that is, the sale or supply of alcohol to persons under 18: see Licensing Act 2003, s 146.

65 Licensing Act 2003 (Mandatory Licensing Conditions) Order 2010, Sch, para 5.

9.22 Early morning alcohol restriction order The 2003 Act was further amended in 2010 to add ss 172A–172E,[66] which will come into force on a date appointed by the Secretary of State.[67] If considered necessary for the promotion of the licensing objectives, the licensing authority will have the power to make an early morning alcohol restriction order providing that (a) a club premises certificate or a premises licence granted by the authority or a temporary event notice given to the authority shall not have effect to the extent that they authorise the *sale* of alcohol between 3 am and 6 am, and (b) that a club premises certificate granted by the authority shall not have effect to the extent that it authorises the *supply* of alcohol by or on behalf of the club to, or to the order of, a member of the club between 3 am and 6 am.[68] The authority must advertise a proposed restriction order[69] and must hold a hearing to consider any representations.[70] The authority must publish any order which it makes[71] and may vary or revoke it.[72]

9.23 Form of certificate The club premises certificate shall be in the prescribed form[73] and must include:[74]

(1) the name and registered address of the club;
(2) the address to which the certificate relates;
(3) a plan of the premises;
(4) the qualifying club activities for which the premises may be used;
(5) any conditions to which the certificate is subject.

A summary of the certificate must also be issued in the prescribed form.[75]

9.24 Duty to keep and produce certificate and display summary[76] If the certificate authorises a qualifying club activity then the club secretary must ensure that the certificate (or a properly certified copy) is kept at the premises to which it relates and that a nominated person is responsible for it. That person must be:

(1) the secretary, or
(2) any member of the club, or
(3) any person who works at the premises for the purposes of the club.

---

66 Crime and Security Act 2010, s 55.
67 Ibid, s 59(1).
68 Licensing Act 2003, s 172A.
69 Ibid, s 172B(1).
70 Ibid, s 172B(2).
71 Ibid, s 172C.
72 Ibid, s 172D.
73 Licensing Act 2003 (Premises Licences and Club Premises Certificates) Regulations 2005, reg 35 and Sch 13, Part A.
74 Licensing Act 2003, s 78(2).
75 Licensing Act 2003 (Premises Licences and Club Premises Certificates) Regulations 2005, reg 36 and Sch 13, Part B.
76 Licensing Act 2003, s 94.

The licensing authority must be notified of the identity of the nominated person. The secretary commits an offence if he fails to do so without reasonable excuse.[77] The nominated person must ensure that the summary of the certificate, or a certified copy of the summary, is prominently displayed at the premises, together with a notice specifying the position which the nominated person holds at the club. He commits an offence if he fails to do so without reasonable excuse.[78]

9.25 Loss of certificate or summary Where the certificate or summary is lost, stolen, damaged or destroyed, the local authority must provide a certified copy, upon payment of a prescribed fee, if it is satisfied that the certificate or summary has thus become unavailable and that, if lost or stolen, the matter has been reported to the police.[79]

9.26 Change of name or address or rules of the club Where a club holds a club premises certificate, or has made an application for such a certificate which has not yet been determined, the club secretary must inform the licensing authority within 28 days of any change of name of the club or any alteration of its rules.[80] If the club holds such a certificate and ceases to use the registered address, it must inform the licensing authority as soon as reasonably practicable.[81]

9.27 Variation of certificate It is open to a club to apply for a variation of the club premises certificate at any time.[82] The variation process is governed by reg 20 and Sch 10 to the Licensing Act 2003 (Premises Licences and Club Premises Certificates) Regulations 2005 and shall be accompanied by the prescribed fee. The variation process has been made less costly and less time-consuming in relation to minor variations which do not affect promotion of the licensing objectives.[83] The application must be advertised and notified to various authorities.[84] The club will also be open to inspection by the police, fire authority or environmental health department.[85] The club must send to the licensing authority its club premises certificate, or an explanation of why the certificate is not

---

77 Licensing Act 2003, s 94(5).

78 Ibid, s 94(6).

79 Ibid, s 79.

80 Ibid, s 82.

81 Ibid, s 83.

82 Ibid, s 84(1).

83 Ibid, ss 86A, 86B and 86C, inserted by Legislative Reform (Minor Variations to Premises Licences and Club Premises Certificates) Order 2009, SI 2009/1772; and see Licensing Act 2003 (Premises Licences and Club Premises Certificates) (Miscellaneous Amendments) Order 2009, SI 2009/1809, prescribing amended forms, advertising requirements and fees relating to minor variations.

84 Licensing Act 2003, s 84(2) and (4).

85 Ibid, s 84(4) and s 71(6).

available.[86] If the licensing authority receives any relevant representations[87] a hearing must be held, unless all parties agree that this is not necessary.[88] If no relevant representation is received, the licensing authority must grant the variation sought,[89] and issue an amended certificate together with, if necessary, a new summary.[90] If relevant representations have been received and considered, the licensing authority may either modify the conditions of the certificate or reject the whole or part of the application.[91] The guiding principle, as elsewhere in the Act, is the promotion of the four licensing objectives set out in **9.5**.[92]

9.28 Review of certificate An interested party, a responsible authority, or a member of the club may apply at any time to a licensing authority for a review of the certificate.[93] The review will be based on the licensing objectives. If the local authority is both the licensing authority and a responsible authority it may, in its capacity as responsible authority, apply for a review and then determine the application in its capacity as licensing authority.[94] This is an interesting statutory avoidance of the first rule of natural justice which states that no person shall be a judge in his own cause, and gives rise to a situation which might provoke an application for judicial review if the application is not dealt with in a scrupulously fair manner by the licensing authority. The review process is governed by regs 20 and 29 and Sch 8 to the Licensing Act 2003 (Premises Licences and Club Premises Certificates) Regulations 2005. The licensing authority may at any time reject the application if it is satisfied that the ground for the application for review is not relevant to the licensing objectives; or if made by a party other than a responsible authority it is frivolous or vexatious; or it is a repetition of a ground unsuccessfully relied on in an earlier application and a reasonable time interval has not elapsed since the earlier occasion.[95] If the application for review is rejected the applicant must be informed on which ground the rejection has been based and, where the ground was that the application was frivolous or vexatious, the licensing authority must give reasons for its decision.[96] If, however, the application is not rejected by the licensing authority under s 87(4) it must hold a hearing to consider the

---

86 Licensing Act 2003, s 84(3).
87 As to relevant representation, see **9.19**(3).
88 Licensing Act 2003, s 85(3)(a).
89 Ibid, s 85(2).
90 Ibid, s 93(1).
91 Ibid, s 85(3), (4).
92 Ibid, s 85(3)(b).
93 Ibid, s 87(1). For the definition of an interested party and a responsible authority, see **9.19**(1).
94 Ibid, s 89.
95 Ibid, s 87(4), (5).
96 Ibid, s 87(6).

application and any relevant representations,[97] whereupon it may take such prescribed steps as it considers necessary to promote the licensing objectives.[98] The steps are:[99]

(1) to modify the conditions of the certificate;
(2) to exclude a qualifying club activity from the scope of the certificate;
(3) to suspend the certificate for a period not exceeding three months;[100]
(4) to withdraw the certificate.

9.29 Duration of certificate A club premises certificate will remain in force until it is surrendered; or withdrawn by the licensing authority following the failure of the club to continue as a qualifying club;[101] or after a review.

9.30 Surrender Where the club decides to surrender its club premises certificate it may give the licensing authority notice to that effect.[102] The notice must be accompanied by the certificate or, if not practicable, must be accompanied by a statement giving reasons for failure to produce it,[103] and the certificate lapses on receipt of the notice by the licensing authority.[104]

9.31 Withdrawal Where it appears to the licensing authority that a club in possession of a club premises certificate no longer satisfies the conditions for being a qualifying club in relation to a qualifying activity the authority must give notice to the club withdrawing the certificate insofar as it relates to that activity.[105] If the only condition not satisfied is that relating to the required minimum number of 25 members, the notice withdrawing the certificate must state that the withdrawal does not take effect until immediately after a period of 3 months following the date of the notice, and that it will not take effect if at the end of that period the club again has at least the required number of members.[106]

9.32 Off sales A club premises certificate may not authorise the supply of alcohol for consumption off the club premises unless it also authorises the supply of alcohol to members for consumption on the premises.[107] There are four mandatory conditions which will appear on the certificate:[108]

---

97 Licensing Act 2003, s 88(2). As to 'relevant representations', see **9.19**(3).
98 Ibid, s 88(3).
99 Ibid, s 88(4).
100 During which time the certificate has no effect: ibid, s 80(2).
101 Ibid, s 80(1).
102 Ibid, s 81(1).
103 Ibid, s 81(2).
104 Ibid, s 81(3).
105 Ibid, s 90(1).
106 Ibid, s 90(2).
107 Ibid, s 73(1).
108 Ibid, s 73(2), (3).

(1) the off-supply must be made at a time when the club is open for on-supply;
(2) the off-supply must be in a sealed container;
(3) the off-supply must be made to a club member in person; it may not be made to a member's guest;
(4) the club shall ensure that an age verification policy applies to alcohol supplied off the club premises. The policy must require members who appear to the responsible person to be under the age of 18 (or such older age as may be specified in the policy) to produce on request, before being served with alcohol, identification bearing their photograph, date of birth and a holographic mark.[109]

9.33 Guests and visitors The sale of alcohol to members' guests for consumption on the premises where the sale takes place is a licensable activity which is authorised by a club premises certificate.[110] Thus the guest may purchase an alcoholic drink not only for himself but for the member as well. The 2003 Act does not define what constitutes a guest but in order to protect the bona fides of the club it is plain that the person must be a genuine guest and this is a question of fact in each case. The position of guests is to be contrasted with that of visitors to the club. The latter are treated under the 2003 Act simply as members of the public, and they cannot themselves purchase or consume alcoholic drinks whilst on club premises (whatever it might say in the rules) unless the club holds a premises licence (see **9.37**) or the visitor is covered by a temporary event notice (see **9.49**).[111] Unlike the Licensing Act 1964, the admission of guests or visitors into a club under the 2003 Act is not dependant on the rules permitting this but nevertheless it is important that the rules regularise the admission of such persons into the club premises and, in particular, give the committee the power to exclude any guest or visitor in its absolute discretion.

9.34 Associate members Under s 67 of the 2003 Act any reference to a guest of a member includes a reference to an associate member of the club, and it also includes a guest of that associate member.[112] For the purposes of the 2003 Act a person is an 'associate member' if (a) in accordance with the rules of the host club he is admitted into the club premises as being a

---

[109] This condition was added by Licensing Act 2003 (Mandatory Licensing Conditions) Order 2010, art 3(2)–(3) and Sch, para 4. For 'responsible person' see **9.21**(1)(a).

[110] Licensing Act 2003, s 1(2)(b).

[111] The Licensing Act 1964 contained an important relaxation, now abolished. Under s 49 visitors could be admitted into the club premises and purchase alcoholic drinks for consumption on the club premises provided the club rules made provision for this and provided the club complied with certain restrictive conditions, such as notification to the chief officer of police. This admission of visitors could be done on a regular or frequent basis, thus providing the club with extra income.

[112] Licensing Act 2003, s 67(1).

member of another club, and (b) that other club is a 'recognised club'.[113] A recognised club is defined in s 193 as being a club which satisfies conditions (1), (2) and (3) of the general conditions in s 62.[114] Here it is essential that the rules deal with the admission of associate members because without an appropriate rule the associate member will not be able to attend the host club and purchase or consume an alcoholic drink on the club premises. Under this regime it is common for clubs to have collective reciprocal arrangements with other recognised clubs whereby the members of one club may be admitted as guests into the other club.

9.35 Police entry into club premises Where a justice of the peace is satisfied that there are reasonable grounds for believing that the club does not satisfy the conditions for being a qualified club in relation to any qualifying activity and that evidence to that effect may be obtained at the club's premises, he may issue a warrant authorising a constable to enter the premises, if necessary by force, in order to search them for that purpose.[115] The search must be made within 1 month of the date of the warrant, and a person entering under the authority of a warrant may seize and remove any documents relating to the business of the club.[116] On the other hand, there is no right of entry by the police or by an authorised officer[117] to enter club premises to see whether any licensable activity is being carried on in accordance with an authorisation, provided that the premises in question are covered by a club premises certificate and by no other authorisation.[118]

9.36 Community clubs, etc Co-operative societies and community benefit societies,[119] working men's clubs registered under the Friendly Societies Act and miners' welfare institutes[120] merit a special mention in the 2003 Act to ensure that they qualify as clubs within the legislation.[121] They must, however, meet the statutory requirements concerning their constitution and management.

---

113 Licensing Act 2003, s 67(2).

114 See **9.11**.

115 Licensing Act 2003, s 90(5).

116 Ibid, s 90(5) and (6).

117 Ie an officer of the licensing authority, an inspector appointed by the fire and rescue authority or a health and safety inspector: ibid, s 69(2).

118 Ibid, s 179(7).

119 Industrial and provident societies referred to in the 2003 Act changed their name under the Co-operative and Community Benefit Societies and Credit Unions Act 2010: see **1.13** and **1.22**.

120 At to the status of miners' welfare institutes, see footnote 6 to **11.3**.

121 Licensing Act 2003, ss 65 and 66.

6. PREMISES LICENCE

9.37 One of the persons who may apply for a premises licence is a recognised club.[122] As mentioned in footnote 111 to **9.33**, the relaxation contained in s 49 of the Licensing Act 1964 no longer exists. Generally speaking, if the club wishes to admit, or to continue to admit visitors, that is, members of the public, and to sell or supply alcoholic drinks to them, it has one of two options: either it will have to surrender its club premises certificate and apply for a premises licence or it will have to rely on the permitted allowance of 12 temporary event notices per year (see **9.49**). The premises licence will cover all the licensable activities set out in (1) to (4) in **9.7**,[123] and will thus include the sale of alcohol and/or the provision of regulated entertainment to visitors. However, there is no doubt that the premises licence is subject to a stricter and, by and large, a more costly system of regulation than operates under the club premises certificate; and it also requires the holder of a personal licence (see **9.61**). On the other hand, providing the club premises are suitable, there is a growing trend amongst members' clubs to consider the premises licence rather than the club premises certificate. The club premises certificate was created as the direct descendant of the club registration certificate but in some ways it lacks flexibility, especially with the loss of the section 49 facility. Club premises are often under-used during the weekdays and a premises licence creates a better opportunity for the club to diversify its activities on a regular or organised basis, such as the holding of dinners for outside societies, or the holding of a local bridge tournament, or the providing of the venue for meetings of outside organisations where alcoholic and other refreshments can be served after the meeting, and these activities in turn generate welcome income for the club. Lastly, combining a premises licence with a club premises certificate is occasionally feasible and can be advantageous. The authors know of a members' sports club built in 1928 which contains a ballroom with its own bar and catering facilities as part of its complex. The club has created separate access to the ballroom and obtained a premises licence restricted to this part of the club, so that it can be used for outside functions on a regular basis, whereas the remainder of these club premises is covered by a club premises certificate.

9.38 Application for licence The application may be made in respect of one or more licensable activities. The detailed procedure is governed by Parts 2 and 4 of the Licensing Act 2003 (Premises Licences and Club Premises Certificates) Regulations 2005.[124] These regulations may be accessed in full by using the government (2010) website, www.opsi.gov.uk. Regulation 9 and Sch 1 require details of the freeholder or leaseholder of the

---

[122] Licensing Act 2003, s 16(1)(c). A recognised club is defined in s 193 as meaning a club which satisfies conditions (1), (2) and (3) of the general conditions set out in s 62: see **9.11**.

[123] Ibid, s 16(1)(c).

[124] As augmented by the regulations referred to in footnote 36 above.

premises in question. Regulation 10 and Sch 2 require the club to apply for a premises licence in the prescribed form and to pay the prescribed fee. Regulation 21 permits the application to be made by electronic means. Regulations 25 and 26 prescribe the manner and timing of the advertisement of the application (as to representations see generally **9.19**). Regulations 27 and 28 prescribe the notice to be given to each responsible authority for the area in which the premises are situated, that is to say, the police, the fire authority, the environmental health authority and the planning authority. The application must be accompanied by:[125]

(1) a plan of the premises (see **9.15**);
(2) an operating schedule (see **9.17**);
(3) if the licensable activities include the supply of alcohol, a form of consent (in the prescribed form) given by the individual whom the applicant wishes to have specified as the premises supervisor.

9.39 Operating schedule This must be in the prescribed form[126] and include a statement of the following matters:[127]

(1) the licensable activities to which the application relates;
(2) the times during which it is proposed that these activities are to take place;
(3) any other times during which it is proposed that the premises are to be open to the public;
(4) where the applicant wishes the licence to have effect for a limited period, that period;
(5) where the activities include the supply of alcohol:
    (a) the prescribed information in respect of the individual whom the applicant wishes to have specified in the licence as the premises supervisor;
    (b) whether the supply is proposed to be for the consumption on the premises or off the premises or both;
(6) the steps which it is proposed to take to promote the licensing objectives;
(7) such other matters as may be prescribed.

9.40 Designated premises supervisor This is the individual person specified in the licence as the premises supervisor. He must hold a personal licence.[128] Supervision does not mean that the supervisor has to be present whenever alcohol is sold.[129] There are provisions to cater for the change in

---

125 Licensing Act 2003, s 17(3).
126 Licensing Act 2003 (Premises Licences and Club Premises Certificates) Regulations 2005, Sch 2.
127 Licensing Act 2003, s 17(4).
128 Ibid, s 19(3). See **9.61**.
129 See Barker and Cavender, *Licensing: the New Law* (2003), at 7.12.2.

the identity of the supervisor.[130] A holder of a personal licence, who is the applicant for a premises licence, does not have to be the designated supervisor of the premises to which the premises licence relates but he may be so.[131] The requirement for a designated premises supervisor has been relaxed in relation to community premises. These premises are defined as a church hall, chapel hall or other similar building; or a village hall, parish hall, community hall or other similar building[132] and they are now permitted to have an alternative mandatory condition that the managing committee of the community premises shall have responsibility for the supervision of alcohol sales in those premises instead of a designated premises supervisor.[133]

9.41 Mandatory conditions The 2003 Act, as enacted, imposes two mandatory conditions on the premises licence where it relates to the supply of alcohol:[134]

(1) no supply of alcohol may be made when there is no designated premises supervisor in respect of the premises licence, or at a time when the designated premises supervisor does not hold a personal licence or his personal licence has been suspended; and
(2) every supply of alcohol must be made or authorised by a person who holds a personal licence.

9.42 The 2003 Act was amended in 2009 to permit the Secretary of State to prescribe up to nine mandatory conditions to be attached to the premises licence relating to the supply of alcohol to members, guests and visitors on licensed premises in order to promote the four licensing objectives.[135] The Licensing Act 2003 (Mandatory Licensing Conditions) Order 2010 came fully into force on 1 October 2010 and prescribes five such conditions. These mandatory conditions are set out in **9.21**. A responsible person means in this context the holder of the premises licence or the designated premises supervisor (if any) or someone who is over the age of 18 who has been duly authorised by the premises licence holder or the supervisor to act as the responsible person. There are therefore *seven* mandatory conditions as regards the on-supply of alcohol. As regards off-sales, the only mandatory

---

130 An application to vary the supervisor may include a request that the variation of supervisor may take immediate effect because, eg he has died; in this event the variation will take effect when the application is received by the licensing authority: ibid, s 37. This replaces the old protection order which has been abolished.

131 Licensing Act 2003, s 15(2).

132 Ibid, s 193, as amended by the Legislative Reform (Supervision of Alcohol Sales in Church and Village Halls etc) Order 2009, SI 2009/1724, art 6.

133 Licensing Act 2003, s 25A, inserted by Legislative Reform (Supervision of Alcohol Sales in Church and Village Halls etc) Order 2009, art 3.

134 Licensing Act 2003, s 19.

135 Ibid, s 19A, inserted by Policing and Crime Act 2009, Sch 4, para 2.

condition, in addition to the original two, which applies to a premises licence is the age verification policy.[136]

9.43 Early morning alcohol restriction order This order applies to premises licences: see **9.22**.

9.44 Form of licence The premises licence shall be in the prescribed form[137] and must include:[138]

(1) the name and address of the holder of the personal licence;
(2) a plan of the licensed premises;
(3) if the licence is for a limited period, that period;
(4) the licensable activities for which the premises may be used;
(5) if the licensable activities include the supply of alcohol, the name and address of the individual (if any) who is the premises supervisor;
(6) the conditions subject to which the licence has effect.

A summary of the certificate must also be issued in the prescribed form.[139]

9.45 Variation of licence The variation process is governed by reg 12 and Sch 4 to the Licensing Act 2003 (Premises Licences and Club Premises Certificates) Regulations 2005 and shall be accompanied by the prescribed fee. The variation process has been made less costly and less time-consuming in relation to minor variations which do not affect promotion of the licensing objectives.[140] Where an application is made by a licence holder to vary the premises licence and the requirements as to advertisement, etc, of the application have been complied with, and in the absence of any relevant representations, the licensing authority must grant the application.[141] Application may also be made to vary the licence in order to specify a different individual as the premises supervisor.[142] Here the variation process is governed by reg 13 and Sch 5 to the 2005 regulations.

9.46 Review of licence A very similar set of provisions applies to the review of a premises licence as applies to a club premises certificate save that the persons who can make an application for review are restricted to an

136 Licensing Act 2003 (Mandatory Licensing Conditions) Order 2010, art 3(1), (3).
137 Licensing Act 2003 (Premises Licences and Club Premises Certificates) Regulations 2005, reg 33 and Sch 12, Part A.
138 Licensing Act 2003, s 24(1).
139 Licensing Act 2003 (Premises Licences and Club Premises Certificates) Regulations 2005, reg 34 and Sch 12, Part B.
140 Legislative Reform (Minor Variations to Premises Licences and Club Premises Certificates) Order 2009 and Licensing Act 2003 (Premises Licences and Club Premises Certificates) (Miscellaneous Amendments) Order 2009.
141 Licensing Act 2003, ss 34 and 35.
142 Ibid, s 37.

interested party or a responsible authority.[143] This review process is governed by regs 20 and 29 and Sch 8 to the Licensing Act 2003 (Premises Licences and Club Premises Certificates) Regulations 2005. To this standard review has been added a new summary review under the Licensing Act 2003 (Summary Review of Premises Licences) Regulations 2007 which relates to serious crime and disorder. This summary process is initiated by the police and is governed by regs 16A, 36A and 39A and Sch 8A to the Licensing Act 2003 (Premises Licences and Club Premises Certificates) Regulations 2005.

9.47 Duration of licence A premises licence has effect until it is revoked under s 52 (following an application for review), or on the expiry of any period to which the licence was expressed to be limited[144] or, in the case of a club, ceases to be a recognised club,[145] or it is surrendered.[146]

9.48 Police entry into and closure of licensed premises A constable or authorised officer[147] may enter any premises where a premises licence is in effect to see whether the premises are being, or are about to be, used for a licensable activity in accordance with an authorisation.[148] Such person may use reasonable force to obtain entry.[149] Where there is or expected to be disorder in a local area, the magistrates' court has power to close for 24 hours all premises in respect of which a premises licence has effect on the application of a police officer of the rank of superintendent or above.[150] In addition, a police officer of the rank of inspector or above may make for 24 hours a closure order of identified premises in respect of which a premises licence has effect if he reasonably believes that there is or will be disorder in the vicinity and closure is necessary for public safety or that a public nuisance is being caused by noise coming from the premises.[151]

7. TEMPORARY EVENT NOTICE

9.49 The temporary event notice is the third type of authorisation for licensable activities provided for under the 2003 Act.[152] The essence of this authorisation is that no actual permission is required for an individual over

---

143 See **9.28**. Here the relevant sections are Licensing Act 2003, ss 13, 51–53.

144 Ibid, s 26.

145 Ibid, s 27(1)(e). A recognised club is defined in s 193 as meaning a club which satisfies conditions (1)–(3) of the five general conditions set out in s 62: see **9.16**.

146 Ibid, s 28.

147 Defined as an officer of the licensing authority, an inspector appointed by the fire and rescue authority and a health and safety inspector: see ibid, s 179(6).

148 Ibid, s 179(1).

149 Ibid, s 179(3).

150 Ibid, s 160(1)(b) and (2).

151 Ibid, s 161(1), (2), (8).

152 Ibid, s 2(4)(c).

the age of 18 ('the premises user') to carry on one or more licensable activities on a temporary basis, that is to say, an event lasting up to 96 hours involving no more than 499 people.[153] The authorisation is subject to various conditions[154] and there are limits as to the number of temporary events which may be permitted.[155] Different limits apply depending on whether or not the premises user holds a personal licence.[156] By its nature an authorised temporary event arranged by a club is not confined to the club members. Although the premises in question would usually be the club premises, a temporary event notice can cover any premises.[157]

9.50 Functions organised by the club As an example, a club holds a club premises certificate and the secretary is approached by a non-member as to the possibility of holding a party for his family and friends on the club premises, with bar facilities and a band, to celebrate his son's 18th birthday. The club is agreeable to this arrangement (say, for sound financial reasons) so an individual must give the necessary notice to the licensing authority as the premises user.[158] In this instance the individual would be a club member nominated by the committee. It may be noted in passing that for the year ended 31 March 2010 some 122,500 temporary event notices were used in England and Wales; some 1,200 notices were withdrawn; some 250 notices were modified with police consent; and some 220 counter-notices were given by the licensing authority following police objection.[159] These figures show the popularity and smooth running of this type of authorisation.

9.51 A word of caution should be given here. Part 3 of Equality Act 2010 would apply to this situation. This part deals with services and public functions. In letting out its premises to members of the public the club will be a 'service-provider' and as such must not discriminate against[160] or harass[161] or victimise[162] a member of the public by not providing the required service or, for example, subjecting that person to some detriment.[163] 'Thus the club steward could not eject from the premises a breast-feeding mother who was a birthday party guest (this would be sex discrimination) nor could he ban a homosexual birthday party guest from using the gentlemen's lavatory (this would be sexual orientation discrimination).

153 Licensing Act 2003, s 100(1)–(5).
154 Ibid, s 98.
155 Ibid, s 107(4).
156 Ibid, s 107(2)(b).
157 Ibid, s 100(1).
158 Ibid, s 100(2).
159 Source: National Statistics Bulletin on Alcohol, Entertainment and Late Night Refreshment Licensing, England and Wales, April 2009 to March 2010, p 28, published by the Department for Culture, Media and Sport on 29 September 2010.
160 See **4.23**.
161 See **4.24**.
162 See **4.25**.
163 Equality Act 2010, s 29.

9.52 Service and acknowledgment of notice A temporary event notice must be given by an individual aged over 18 years.[164] The individual thereupon becomes the premises user for the purposes of the event.[165] The temporary event notice must be given (a) to the relevant licensing authority (in duplicate) and (b) the relevant chief officer of police[166] not later than 10 working days before the day on which the event period begins;[167] it must be in the prescribed form;[168] it must be accompanied by the prescribed fee;[169] and it must contain the following details:[170]

(1) the relevant licensable activities;
(2) the 'event period', i e the period (not exceeding 96 hours) during which the licensable activities will be carried on;
(3) the times of day during the event period when the licensable activities will be carried on;
(4) the maximum number of persons (which must be less than 500) which the premises user proposes will be on the premises at any one time;
(5) whether any supply of alcohol will be on or off the premises or both;
(6) such other matters as may be prescribed.

Where there is to be a supply of alcohol, the notice must make it a condition of using the premises that such supply is made by or under the authority of the premises user.[171] The licensing authority must acknowledge and return one of the two notices before the end of the first working day following the day on which it was received,[172] having marked an acknowledgment of receipt in the prescribed form.[173] The premises user may withdraw the notice not later than 24 hours before the event period.[174] This may be important because a notice duly withdrawn does not count towards the 24 hour restriction mentioned in the next paragraph.

9.53 Limit on number of notices No premises may be used more than 12 times in any one calendar year for a temporary event, with an overall maximum of 15 days in any one year on which temporary events may take

---

164 Licensing Act 2003, s 100(3).
165 Ibid, s 100(2).
166 This means the chief officer of police for the area in which the premises are situated or, where the premises are situated in two or more police areas, the chief officer of police for each area: ibid, s 104(5).
167 Ibid, ss 100(7)(a) and 104(1). A timeous application is essential; there is no power to abridge time. A working day is defined in ibid, s 193 as meaning any other day than a Saturday, a Sunday, Christmas Day, Good Friday or a day which is a bank holiday in England and Wales under the Banking and Financial Dealings Act 1971.
168 Licensing Act 2003, s 100(4).
169 Ibid, s 100(7)(b).
170 Ibid, s 100(5).
171 Ibid, s 100(6).
172 If the day or receipt was not a working day, the receipt must follow before the end of the second working day: ibid, s 102(1)(b).
173 Ibid, s 102(1) and (2).
174 Ibid, s 103(1).

place at any particular premises.[175] An important point to remember is that if the event period straddles 2 calendar years the restrictions apply separately in relation to those 2 years, that is to say, the event is counted twice, once in the first year and once in the second year.[176] Where a club holds a club premises certificate, and therefore no member or employee will hold a personal licence, a premises user may give up to five temporary event notices within the same year as the event specified in the notice.[177] Consequently three members of a club in possession of a club premises certificate could give the maximum of 12 temporary event notices where the temporary events are to take place on club premises. There must, however, be at least 24 hours' interval between event periods in respect of the same premises, where the notices are given by the same premises user or by an individual who is an associate of the premises user.[178] 'Associate' here means:[179]

(1) the spouse of the individual giving the notice;
(2) a child, parent, grandchild, grandparent, brother or sister of that individual;
(3) an agent or employee of that individual;
(4) the spouse of a person within category (2) or (3);
(5) living together as man and wife;
(6) in business together where that business relates to one or more licensable activities.

The Secretary of State may by order substitute different limits on the number of notices.[180]

9.54 Licensing authority's counter notice Where a licensing authority receives a temporary event notice and is satisfied that the provisions limiting the number of applications have been exceeded, it must give a counter notice in the prescribed form to the premises user.[181] This counter notice excuses the licensing authority from complying with the acknowledgment provisions referred to in **9.52**,[182] but the counter notice must be given not later than 24 hours before the beginning of the event period.[183] Where a counter notice is given, the licensing authority must send a copy of it to the chief officer of police.[184] The counter notice overrides the provisions relating to police objections.[185]

---

175 Licensing Act 2003, s 107(4) and (5). 'Year' means calendar year: s 107(13)(b).
176 Ibid, s 107(6).
177 Ibid, s 107(3)(b).
178 Ibid, s 101(a).
179 Ibid, s 101(2)–(4).
180 Ibid, s 107(12).
181 Ibid, s 107. As to the relevant limits, see **9.51** and **9.61**.
182 Ibid, s 102(3).
183 Ibid, s 107(8).
184 Ibid, s 107(11).
185 Ibid, ss 105(6)(b), 106(6) and 107(9).

9.55 Police's objection notice The premises user must also give a copy of the notice to the relevant chief officer of police[186] not later than 10 working days before the event period.[187] If, following receipt of the notice, the chief officer of police is satisfied that allowing the premises to be used as requested in the notice would undermine the crime prevention objective, he must give an 'objection notice' to the licensing authority and the proposed premises user, not later than 48 hours after he has received the temporary event notice.[188] The licensing authority must thereupon hold a hearing to consider the objection notice, unless all are agreed that this is unnecessary.[189] The licensing authority must decide either not to give a counter-notice or to give one (with reasons), preventing the temporary event from taking place.[190] Notice of this decision must be given (with reasons) to the premises user and also to the chief officer of police.[191]. The decision must be given at least 24 hours before the beginning of the event period.[192]

9.56 Modification of objection notice At any time before a hearing is held or dispensed with, the chief officer of police and the premises user may agree to modify the notice by making changes to the notice as served.[193] In this event the objection notice is treated as withdrawn.[194] A copy of the modified notice must be sent to the licensing authority by the chief officer of police.[195] If the premises are situated in more than one police area, every chief officer must consent to the modification.[196]

9.57 Duty to keep, display and produce temporary event notice The premises user must ensure that the notice is kept at the relevant premises in his custody or in the custody of a nominated person working at the premises.[197] He must also ensure that a copy of the (endorsed) notice is prominently displayed on these premises.[198] If he fails to comply without reasonable excuse, the premises user commits an offence.[199]

---

186 This means the chief officer of police for the area in which the premises are situated or, where the premises are situated in two or more police areas, the chief officer of police for each area.
187 Licensing Act 2003, s 104(1).
188 Ibid, s 104(2).
189 Ibid, s 105(2)(a).
190 Ibid, s 105(3).
191 Ibid, s 105(3).
192 Ibid, s 105(4).
193 Ibid, s 106(2).
194 Ibid, s 106(3)(a).
195 Ibid, s 106(4).
196 Ibid, s 106(5).
197 Ibid, s 109(3)(a).
198 Ibid, s 109(3)(b).
199 Ibid, s 109(4).

9.58 Loss of temporary event notice The local authority must provide a copy, upon payment of a fee, if the notice is lost, stolen, damaged or destroyed, when satisfied that the notice has thus become unavailable and that, if lost or stolen, the matter has been reported to the police.[200] The application for a replacement notice, however, must be made within 1 month of the event specified in the notice.[201]

9.59 Early morning alcohol restriction order This order applies to temporary event notices: see **9.22**.

9.60 Police entry into and closure of temporary event premises A constable or authorised officer[202] may enter club premises where a temporary event notice is in effect to see whether the premises are being, or are about to be, used for a licensable activity in accordance with an authorisation.[203] Such person may use reasonable force to obtain entry.[204] A constable or authorised officer also has power to enter at any reasonable time premises to which a temporary event notice relates to assess the likely effect of the notice on the promotion of the crime prevention objective.[205] Where there is or expected to be disorder in a local area, the magistrates' court has power to close for 24 hours all premises in respect of which a temporary event notice has effect in that area on the application of a police officer of the rank of superintendent or above.[206] In addition, a police officer of the rank of inspector or above may make for 24 hours a closure order of identified premises in respect of which a temporary event notice has effect if he reasonably believes that there is or will be disorder in the vicinity and closure is necessary for public safety or that a public nuisance is being caused by noise coming from the premises.[207]

8. PERSONAL LICENCE

9.61 A personal licence is a licence granted by a licensing authority to an individual enabling that person to supply, or to authorise the supply, of alcohol in accordance with a premises licence.[208] This supply can take place either by retail sale or via supply by or on behalf of a club to, or to the order of, a member of the club.[209] The ability to authorise the supply of alcohol is

---

200 Licensing Act 2003, s 110.

201 Ibid, s 110(2).

202 Defined as an officer of the licensing authority, an inspector appointed by the fire and rescue authority and a health and safety inspector: see ibid, s 179(6).

203 Ibid, s 179(1).

204 Ibid, s 179(3).

205 Ibid, s 108(1).

206 Ibid, s 160(1)(b) and (2).

207 Ibid, s 161(1), (2), (8).

208 Ibid, s 111(1).

209 Ibid, s 111(2).

important because, as stated in **9.40** above, there is no requirement in the 2003 Act that the designated premises supervisor, who must hold a personal licence, has to be present on all occasions when alcohol is sold or supplied. A person may only hold one personal licence at any one time.[210] A personal licence is initially granted for a period of 10 years and is renewable for 10 years at a time.[211]

9.62 Application for personal licence Application is made to the relevant licensing authority[212] and the procedure for determination is set out in s 120 of the 2003 Act. The salient points to note are that the licensing authority must grant the licence if it appears to it that:

(1) the applicant is aged 18 years or over;
(2) he possesses a licensing qualification[213] or is a person of a prescribed description;[214]
(3) no personal licence held by him has been forfeited in the period of 5 years ending with the day the application was made; and
(4) he has not been convicted of any relevant offence or any foreign offence.[215]

9.63 Continuing duty It should be noted that there is a continuing duty to notify the licensing authority of any relevant conviction or foreign conviction[216] or any change of name or address of the applicant.[217] If the holder of a personal licence is charged with a relevant offence, he must produce that licence to the court before which he appears or, if production is not practicable, he must notify the court of the existence of the personal licence, the identity of the licensing authority and the reasons why he cannot produce the licence.[218] Failure to do so is in itself an offence.[219] The court may, upon conviction of a personal licence holder for a relevant offence, order the forfeiture of the licence or its suspension for a period not exceeding 6 months,[220] and must notify the relevant licensing authority.[221]

---

210 Licensing Act 2003, s 118.
211 Ibid, s 115.
212 Ibid, s 117.
213 Defined in ibid, s 120(8).
214 See Licensing Act 2003 (Personal Licences) Regulations 2005, SI 2005/41, reg 3.
215 Licensing Act 2003, s 120(2). For the numerous 'relevant offences' see ibid, Sch 4, as amended by Licensing Act 2003 (Personal Licences: Relevant Offences) (Amendment) Order 2005, SI 2005/2366. 'Foreign offence' means an offence (other than a relevant offence) committed outside England and Wales: ibid, s 113(3).
216 Licensing Act 2003, ss 123 and 124.
217 Ibid, s 127.
218 Ibid, s 128.
219 Ibid, s 128(6).
220 Ibid, s 129.
221 Ibid, s 131. The licence holder is under a similar duty of notification: ibid, s 132.

9.64 Temporary event notices The holder of a personal licence may give up to 50 temporary event notices in any one year.[222] Apart from this, the same regime applies as set out in **9.49** to **9.60**.

9. PROPRIETARY CLUBS

9.65 Inevitably a proprietary club will require a premises licence, rather than a club premises certificate, as they will not meet the conditions for qualification in ss 62, 63 and 64 of the 2003 Act and will therefore not be a qualifying club within the meaning of the Act.

10. APPEALS

9.66 The appeals procedure is set out in the various paragraphs of Sch 5 to the 2003 Act. Part 1 of the schedule deals with premises licences, Part 2 deals with club premises certificates and Part 3 deals with 'Other Appeals'.

(1) ***Club premises certificate***: an appeal will lie for the following: rejection of application for club premises certificate under s 72 (para 10); rejection of variation application under s 85 (paras 10 and 12); a decision to impose conditions under s 72 (para 11); a decision on review under s 88 (para 13); and withdrawal of certificate under s 90 (para 14).
(2) ***Premises licence***: an appeal will lie amongst other things for the following: rejection of applications for a premises licence under s 18 (para 1); a decision to impose conditions under s 18 (para 2); rejection of variation application under ss 35 and 39 (paras 1, 4 and 5); transfer of licence under s 44 (para 6); a decision on the review under s 52 (para 8); and a decision on the summary review under s 53A(2)(b) (para 8A).[223] An appeal will also lie against the licensing authority's decision on a review of a premises licence under s 167 following the making of a closure order (para 18).
(3) ***Temporary event notice***: an appeal will lie where the chief officer of police gives notice of objection under s 104(2) (para 16(1)); and where the licensing authority gives a counter-notice under s 105(3) (para 16(2)).[224]
(4) ***Personal licence***: an appeal will lie amongst other things where the licensing authority rejects an application for a personal licence under ss 120 or 121 (para 17(1)); or revokes it under s 124(4) (para 17(4)).

---

222 Licensing Act 2003, s 107(2)(b).

223 Right of appeal added by Violent Crime Reduction Act 2006, s 22.

224 The chief officer of police may appeal if the authority decides *not* to give a counter-notice: Licensing Act 2003, Sch 5, para 16(3).

9.67 In all cases the appeal is to a magistrates' court.[225] The notice of appeal must be given within 21 days beginning with the day on which the appellant was notified by the licensing authority of the decision appealed against.[226] On appeal the magistrates' court may:[227]

(1) dismiss the appeal;
(2) substitute for the decision appealed against any other decision which could have been made by the licensing authority; or
(3) remit the case to the licensing authority to dispose of it in accordance with the direction of the court; and
(4) make such order as to costs which it thinks fit.

9.68 Closure of premises It is the magistrates' court itself which sanctions the closure order, so that the right of appeal against such an order is made to the Crown Court.[228] Notice of appeal must be given within 21 days beginning with the day on which the decision appealed against was made.[229]

11. FEES

9.69 The current (2010) fees are as follows:[230]

Chargeable bands (non-domestic rateable value):

A	B	C	D	E
£0–4,300	£4,301–£33,000	£33,001–£87,000	£87,001–£125,000	£125,001+
Club premises certificate:				
Conversion, new application and variation :				
£100	£190	£315	£450	£635
Annual charge:				
£70	£180	£295	£320	£350

Premises licence:

The fees are the same as set out above, save that for Band D a multiplier of 2 is applied and for Band E a multiplier of 3 is applied to the specified fee

---

[225] Licensing Act 2003, Sch 5, paras 9(1), 15(1), 16(4), 17(6) and 18(3), as amended by Courts Act 2003 (Consequential Provisions) Order 2005, SI 2005/886.

[226] Licensing Act 2003, Sch 5, paras 9(2), 15(2), 16(5), 17(7) and 18(5).

[227] Ibid, s 181(2).

[228] Ibid, s 166(1).

[229] Ibid, s 166(2).

[230] Licensing Act 2003 (Fees) Regulations 2005, SI 2005/79 as amended by Licensing Act 2003 (Premises Licences and Club Premises Certificates) (Miscellaneous Amendments) Regulations 2009.

where the premises are used exclusively or primarily for the supply of alcohol for consumption on the premises.

Other fees:

For a number of minor applications such as notification of a change of address or alteration of the rules and for copies of documentation, the fee is £10.50; for applications for a transfer of premises licence the fee is £23; for a temporary event notice the fee is £21.[231]

---

[231] A temporary event notice may contain more than one temporary event and a flat fee is chargeable which is not dependent on the number of events comprising the notice.

Chapter 10

ENTERTAINMENT PROVIDED BY THE CLUB

1. INTRODUCTION

10.1 Entertainments of various kinds are staged or provided by clubs, sometimes as part of a club's core activities, sometimes for the enjoyment of its members, and at other times to raise funds for the club. It is a sphere of activity which needs the club's attention because in putting on the entertainment other people's rights are often affected (we are here talking about copyright), and many entertainments are regulated by local government as a matter of public policy (we are here talking about the need for authorisation). The topic of entertainment was revisited by the Licensing Act 2003 with the result that much entertainment provided in clubs is now regulated by this Act, even though no alcohol is being supplied at the entertainment and even though no member of the public is present at the entertainment. The question of noise nuisance should also be borne in mind.[1] What is set out below applies to all clubs of whatever type they may be.

2. COPYRIGHT

10.2 What is protected Copyright protects original literary, dramatic, musical and artistic work; sound recordings, films, broadcasts and cable programmes; and typographical arrangements.[2] It is an economic and property right which enables the creator to earn money and is to be distinguished from his moral rights in the same material which protects his reputation. It is true to say that there is always a tension between copyright owners and those who wish to use works subject to copyright. (The growth of the internet has seriously exacerbated these tensions.) The width of copyright sometimes surprises lay people. For example, when a play has been published to the general public, people have been heard to ask why it cannot be performed without more ado. The answer is that if it is in copyright, the club must apply for performance rights, even for amateur productions. The principal act is the Copyright, Designs and Patents

1 See **10.28**.

2 Copyright, Designs and Patents Act 1988, s 1.

Act 1988 as amended by the Duration of Copyright and Rights in Performances Regulations 1995,[3] the Copyright and Related Rights Regulations 2003,[4] the Copyright, Designs and Patents Act 1988 (Amendment) Regulations 2010[5] and the Copyright Tribunal Rules 2010.[6]

10.3 Performance in public The performance of a work *in public* is an act restricted by the copyright in a literary, dramatic or musical work. There are various exceptions to this regime of copyright, such as fair dealing for the purposes of research or criticism or review.[7] Another important exception is that no breach of copyright takes place in domestic or quasi-domestic situations where a recording, for example, is played amongst family members.[8] The purpose of the copyright legislation is to protect the copyright owner in those situations where the listener or viewer would normally expect to have to pay for such entertainment. Hence the importance of the concept of performance in public. The question is solely one of fact. A members' club might be forgiven for thinking that performance limited to an audience of its own members (and their guests) was not a performance in public. But the club would be wrong: the factual situation has to be looked at from the copyright owner's point of view. Would the owner regard the audience as part of *his* public? If so, the performance is 'in public', even if as between the performers and the audience each side would regard the performance as being in private. Thus in *Harms (Incorporated) Ltd v Martans Club Ltd*[9] the performance of music by a dance band restricted to club members and their guests in a proprietary social club was held to be in public and in breach of copyright. An emphatic case is *Jennings v Stephens*[10] where the members of the Overstone and Sywell Dramatic Society gave an amateur performance of a play in a village hall solely in front of the members of the Duston Women's Institute. This performance was held to be in public and in breach of copyright.[11] Lord Justice Romer commented:[12]

---

3 SI 1995/3297.

4 SI 2003/2498.

5 SI 2010/2694.

6 SI 2010/791.

7 See Copyright, Designs and Patents Act 1988, Chapter III.

8 *Duck v Bates* [1884] 13 QBD 843, CA (performance of a dramatic work at Guy's Hospital where the audience comprised members of the staff and their friends held to be a quasi-domestic event); *Ernest Turner Electrical Instruments Ltd v Performing Right Society Ltd* [1943] Ch 167, CA, per Goddard LJ at 175.

9 [1927] 1 Ch 526.

10 [1936] 1 Ch 469, CA.

11 See also *Performing Right Society v Rangers Football Club Supporters Club* [1974] SLT 151, Ct of Sess (performance of musical works at football supporters' club held to be in public); *Ernest Turner Electrical Instruments Ltd v Performing Right Society Ltd* [1943] Ch 167, CA (music played to employees of a factory whilst they were working held to be a performance in public).

12 [1936] 1 Ch 469, CA, at 482.

> 'Suppose, for instance, that a number of people who are interested in the drama bound themselves together in a society or club for the purpose of providing by means of their subscription the performance before themselves from time to time of dramatic works. This must be something entirely outside their domestic lives and they would, in my opinion, attend performances merely as members of the public, and none the less because the section of the public which they represented may be limited by election [to the club].'

In the same case Lord Justice Greene said that the same result would have followed had the play been performed by members of the women's institute itself.[13]

10.4 Sound recording' exception As enacted, s 67 of the Copyright, Designs and Patents Act 1988 contained a provision that the playing of sound recordings on club premises did not amount to an infringement of copyright if the club was not established or conducted for profit and its objects were charitable or concerned with the advancement of religion or education or social welfare. Already modified, this exception is repealed with effect from 1 January 2011.[14] The playing of sounding recordings on club premises is to be governed by the full copyright regime.

10.5 Television and radio As originally enacted, s 72 of the Copyright, Designs and Patents Act 1988 contained a provision that the showing or playing of a broadcast in public did not amount to an infringement of copyright if it was not played to a paying audience. Since then the right to free public performance has been drastically cut down by amendment of the section.[15] The overall effect of the section as amended is that where a club has a television or radio playing for the benefit of the club members, the club will not only need a television-and-radio licence, but will be likely to need a licence from PRS for Music and a further licence from Phonographic Performances Limited, unless the programme being broadcast does not include (a) any literary, dramatic or musical works which are subject to copyright or (b) any commercially released sound recordings.[16]

10.6 Collecting Societies There is a good reason too why clubs need to take notice of copyright and that is because typically these days an author,

---

13 [1936] 1 Ch 469, CA, at 484.

14 Copyright, Designs and Patent Act 1988 (Amendment) Regulations 2010, SI 2010/2694, reg 3. See also reg 4(1) which repeals another sound recording exception under s 72(1B)(a) of the 1988 Act. The two regulations were passed to implement EU Directive 2006/115 dated 12 December 2006.

15 As a result of the Rental and Related Rights Directive, EU Directive 1992/100 and Information Society Directive, EU Directive 2003/29.

16 See *Copinger and Skone James on Copyright* (15th edn, 2004), para 9.200. (New edition scheduled for 2011).

composer or playwright or the recording company assign their copyright to a collecting society or authorise it to grant licences on their behalf to potential users and to enforce their rights against infringers. It is the collecting society who will negotiate and issue the licence and who will collect the royalties for distribution to the author or composer etc. A collecting society with a large handful of copyrights is in a powerful position to dictate the terms of the licence, and aggrieved persons can challenge the fees charged by complaining to the Copyright Tribunal.[17] A club which puts on dramatic or musical or video entertainment without checking whether a contractual licence from the copyright owner is required will sooner or later find itself in trouble. We should add that the copyright owner has exclusive rights to make adaptations of the original work,[18] so that for example editing a play or putting on an abridged version would not escape the copyright legislation.

10.7 In many instances there will be separate copyrights to contend with.[19] Take the playing of recorded songs in the clubhouse. The club may find that the copyright in the words of the songs belongs to one person, the songwriter; the copyright in the music belongs to another person, the composer; and the copyright in the recording itself belongs to a third person, the recording company. It was this diverse holding of the various copyrights that led to the formation of these one-stop-shops, and from an administrative point of view it makes the club secretary's job a lot easier to deal with a small number of bodies rather than a large collection of individual copyright owners. The downside of the situation is that the collecting societies are usually a lot more zealous in chasing people than would be the case with individual copyright owners.

10.8 There are now a number of collecting societies operating the United Kingdom. They are listed below, alphabetically, so that clubs are aware of the risks they take in ignoring copyright owners.

(1) *Artists' Collecting Society*: concerned with the collection royalties on behalf of British artists in the UK;
(2) *Association of United Recording Artists*: concerned with the exploitation of sound recordings embodying members' performances;
(3) *Authors' Licensing and Collecting Society*: administers the rights in literary and dramatic works on behalf of authors;
(4) *British Equity Collecting Society*: concerned with the collection, distribution and administration of performers' remuneration;
(5) *Compact Collections Ltd*: concerned with the collection of secondary television royalties for film and television content owners;

---

17 Copyright, Designs and Patents Act 1988, ss 145 and 149.

18 Ibid, ss 16(1)(e) and 21(1).

19 *Gramophone Co Ltd v Stephen Cawardine & Co* [1934] Ch 450.

(6) *Copyright Licensing Agency*: operates a collective licensing system for copying literary, dramatic, musical and artistic work using photocopying and other methods of multiple copying, such as scanning;
(7) *Design and Artists Copyright Society*: operates a collective licensing system for the copying the work of artists and other visual creators;
(8) *Performing Artists' Media Rights Association*: administers the performers' rights to receive payment for the exploitation of their commercially published sound recordings;
(9) *Phonographic Performance Limited*: licenses the performance in public of sound recordings owned or controlled by its members. (This licensing system overlaps with the PRS one);
(10) *PRS for Music*: licenses the right to perform in public, whether by performance, broadcast or other transmission, the musical works of its members who are songwriters, composers or music publishers. (This is an amalgamation of the former Performing Rights Society and the Mechanical Copyright Protection Society);
(11) *Video Performance Ltd*: concerned with the enforcement of rights in music videos where performed in public, including dubbing rights.

10.9 Duration of copyright and remedies for breach The copyright in any work, save sound recordings, lasts for the lifetime of the individual(s) who created the work, plus 70 years.[20] Companies may obtain the copyright by an assignment to them of the individual's rights. The copyright in sound recordings lasts simply for 50 years from first release.[21] The remedies for breach of copyright are damages, an injunction to prevent further breach, an account of profits made as a result of the breach and delivery up of the offending material.[22]

10.10 Apart from the above remedies, where copyright is infringed by the public performance of a literary or dramatic or musical work, a person who caused the work to be performed, played or shown is guilty of a criminal offence if he knew or had reason to believe that copyright would be infringed.[23] Performance in a club would constitute public performance.[24]

3. PUBLISHING BOOKS

10.11 The publisher of any printed book within the United Kingdom is obliged by statute to send a copy to the British Library Board within one

---

20 Copyright, Designs and Patents Act 1988, s 12 as substituted by the Duration of Copyright and Rights in Performances Regulations 1995, SI 1995/3297.

21 Copyright, Designs and Patents Act 1988, s 13A as amended by the regulations referred to in the previous footnote.

22 Ibid, ss 96 and 97.

23 Ibid, s 107(3).

24 See **10.3**.

month of publication and to certain other libraries on their request for a copy.[25] A book is widely defined: it includes any book, pamphlet or magazine, and any map, plan, chart or table.[26] By and large, club literature will not be subject to this obligation because the material is not 'published', that is to say, copies of the work are not issued to the public. However, it would be different if a club were to publish a history of the club which was available for sale in the local shops or if the club were to publish a booklet on the aims of the club or the facilities which it offered and made this booklet available generally. In these circumstances we consider that the statutory obligation would arise.

4. REGULATED ENTERTAINMENT

10.12 Overview The Licensing Act 2003 ('the 2003 Act') introduced a much simpler regime than had hitherto existed,[27] but one that brings more control over the club. The 2003 Act is concerned with what it calls regulated entertainment, which falls into two defined categories: (1) entertainment and (2) entertainment facilities. All licensable activities are required to be authorised,[28] and the provision of regulated entertainment is a licensable activity.[29] Although the supply of alcohol and the provision of entertainment often go hand-in-hand, they are treated as independent and separate matters under the 2003 Act. The provision of regulated entertainment by the club to its members and guests is a qualifying club activity for a club premises certificate.[30] Schedule 1 to the 2003 Act contains the detailed provisions which apply to regulated entertainment. As stated in **9.2(1)**, all authorisations relating to one set of premises are now contained in a single licensing document.

10.13 Categories of regulated entertainment There are eight categories of regulated entertainment which fall within the 2003 Act. The entertainment will be regulated where it takes place in the presence of (a) the members and guests of a qualifying club[31] or (b) a public audience[32] or (c) a private audience and a charge is made with a view to making a profit.[33] An audience includes spectators.[34] The obvious should be stated: all of the

---

25 Legal Deposit Libraries Act 2003, s 1.

26 Ibid, s 1(3).

27 The former regime depended on the distinction, now abolished, whether the entertainment was being provided to members of the public generally or whether it was restricted to a specified class of persons, such as club members and their guests. Only the former type of entertainment required a licence.

28 Licensing Act 2003, s 2.

29 Ibid, s 1(1).

30 Ibid, s 1(2)(c).

31 Ibid, Sch 1, para 1(2)(b).

32 Ibid, Sch 1, para 1(2)(a).

33 Ibid, Sch 1, para 1(2)(c).

34 Licensing Act 2003, Sch 1, para 2(2). Technically an audience *hears* and spectators *see* but

following events must be wholly or partly provided for the purpose of *entertaining* the persons present[35] so that, for example, a purely educational film would not require any authorisation.

(1) ***A performance of a play.***[36]
   (a) This means a performance of any dramatic piece, where the whole or a major proportion of it involves the playing of a role by one or more persons, who are actually present, by way of speech, singing or action (including improvisation).[37]
   (b) A rehearsal counts as a performance.[38]
   (c) The Minister stated in the House of Commons on 1 April 2003 that poetry readings and performances by stand-up comedians (which do not involve music) will not count as regulated entertainment.[39]

(2) ***An exhibition of a film.***[40]
   This means any exhibition of moving pictures.[41]

(3) ***An indoor sporting event.***[42]
   (a) This means any sporting event which takes place inside a building where the spectators are accommodated wholly inside that building.[43]
   (b) A sporting event means any contest, exhibition or display of any sport.[44]
   (c) Sport includes any game in which physical skill is the predominant factor or any form of physical recreation which is also engaged in for the purposes of competition or display.[45]
   (d) A building means any roofed structure (other than a structure a roof which may be open or closed) and includes a vehicle, vessel or moveable structure.[46]

(4) ***A boxing or wrestling entertainment.***[47]
   (a) This means any contest, exhibition or display of boxing or wrestling.[48]

---

the Chambers Dictionary (1998) defines an audience as 'an assembly of hearers or spectators' so perhaps the rider was unnecessary.

35 Licensing Act 2003, Sch 1, para 2(1).

36 Ibid, Sch 1, para 2(1)(a).

37 Ibid, Sch 1, para 14(1).

38 Ibid, Sch 1, para 14(2).

39 Hansard, HC Standing Committee D, col 62 (a statement probably covered by the rule in *Pepper v Hart* [1993] AC 593).

40 Licensing Act 2003, Sch 1, para 2(1)(b).

41 Ibid, Sch 1, para 15.

42 Ibid, Sch 1, para 2(1)(c).

43 Ibid, Sch 1, para 16(1).

44 Ibid, Sch 1, para 16(2).

45 Ibid, Sch 1, para 16(2).

46 Ibid, Sch 1, para 16(2).

47 Ibid, Sch 1, para 2(1)(d).

48 Ibid, Sch 1, para 17.

(b) The reason for this sport being in a separate category is that it will count as regulated entertainment whether it is carried on indoors or outdoors;

(5) ***A performance of live music.***[49]
For the purposes of this and the next category music includes vocal or instrumental music or any combination of the two.[50]

(6) ***Any playing of recorded music.***[51]
It is thought that on many occasions the 'incidental music' exemption will apply to this form of entertainment (see **10.20**(3) below);

(7) ***A performance of dance.***[52]

(8) ***Entertainment of a similar description to that falling within categories (5), (6) and (7).***[53]
Striptease would be an example within this category.

10.14 Categories of regulated entertainment facilities There are three categories of entertainment facilities which fall within the 2003 Act. The entertainment facilities will be regulated where they take place (a) in the presence of the members and guests of a qualifying club[54] or (b) in the presence of members of the public[55] or (c) privately and a charge is made with a view to making a profit.[56] Here no audience is involved because the facilities are provided to enable people to take an *active* part in the entertainment.[57]

(1) ***Making music.***[58]
   (a) Music includes vocal or instrumental music or any combination of the two.[59]
   (b) The definition is wide enough to cover karaoke activity.

(2) ***Dancing.***[60]
This would cover discotheque dancing.

(3) ***Entertainment of a similar description to that falling within the above-mentioned categories.***[61]

10.15 The Secretary of State has the power to amend both the descriptions of regulated entertainment and entertainment facilities.[62]

---

49 Licensing Act 2003, Sch 1, para 2(1)(e).
50 Ibid, Sch 1, para 18.
51 Ibid, Sch 1, para 2(1)(f).
52 Ibid, Sch 1, para 2(1)(g).
53 Ibid, Sch 1, para 2(1)(h).
54 Ibid, Sch 1, para 1(2)(b).
55 Ibid, Sch 1, para 1(2)(a).
56 Ibid, Sch 1, para 1(2)(c).
57 Ibid, Sch 1, para 3(1).
58 Ibid, Sch 1, para 3(2)(a).
59 Ibid, Sch 1 para 18.
60 Ibid, Sch 1, para 3(2)(b).
61 Ibid, Sch 1, para 3(2)(c).
62 Ibid, Sch 1, para 4.

10.16 Threshold test For entertainment or entertainment facilities to be regulated they must not only come within the above definitions but they must also satisfy two conditions.[63]

10.17 ***First condition***[64] The entertainment or entertainment facilities must be provided:

(1) wholly or partly to members of the public; or
(2) exclusively to members, or members and their guests, of a qualifying club;[65] or
(3) if neither of the above is applicable, for consideration and with a view to profit.

10.18 The consideration referred to means a payment of a charge by the persons enjoying the entertainment or facilities.[66] The profit must accrue to the organisers or managers of the entertainment or facilities[67] but excludes a disc jockey or musician who is not responsible for the organisation or management of the event.[68]

10.19 ***Second condition***[69] Premises must be made available for the purpose of enabling the entertainment to take place or for the purpose of providing the entertainment facilities.

10.20 Exemptions The 2003 Act then proceeds to enumerate the various exemptions to its regime.[70] The eight types of exemption are as follows:

(1) ***Films for advertising, informing or educating.***[71]
(2) ***Film exhibitions in museums and art galleries.***[72]
(3) ***Music incidental to non-regulated activities.***[73]
    (a) The provision of entertainment consisting of the performance of live music or the playing of recorded music is not regulated to the extent that it is incidental to some activity which itself is neither a regulated entertainment nor the provision of entertainment facilities.

---

63 Licensing Act 2003, Sch 1, para 1(1).
64 Ibid, Sch 1, para 1(2).
65 For the definition of a qualifying club see **9.11**.
66 Ibid, Sch 1, para 1(4)(a)(iii).
67 Ibid, Sch 1, para 1(4)(a)(i) and (ii).
68 Ibid, Sch 1, para 1(6).
69 Ibid, Sch 1, para 1(3).
70 Ibid, Sch 1, Part 2.
71 Ibid, Sch 1, para 5.
72 Ibid, Sch 1, para 6.
73 Ibid, Sch 1, para 7.

(b) The 2003 Act does not define the word 'incidental' which is no doubt used in its meaning of 'accompanying in a subordinate capacity'. An example would be a piano being played in the background in a club or restaurant.

(c) The exemption is also intended to preserve the relaxation contained in s 182 of the Licensing Act 1964 whereby live music and singing by 'not more than two performers' was permitted without any licence in premises of public entertainment (the so-called 'two-in-a-bar' rule). The music and singing here will be incidental to the main activity carried on in the bar of a club, namely, the provision of food and drink.

(4) ***Television and radio.***[74]

The normal use of a television and a radio is not regulated under the 2003 Act (their use is regulated by the Communications Act 2003).[75]

(5) ***Religious services.***[76]

This includes the provision of entertainment or entertainment facilities for purposes incidental to a religious meeting or service, such as a concert in aid of funds for a new church roof.

(6) ***Garden fetes.***[77]

(a) The provision of any entertainment or entertainment facilities at a garden fete or similar function or event (such as a bazaar or sale of work, but not a boot sale) is not regulated unless it is promoted with a view to applying the whole or part of its proceeds for the purposes of private gain.

(b) Private gain in this context has the same meaning as set out in s 19(3) of the Gambling Act 2005,[78] that is to say, there is no private gain despite the fact that one or more individuals obtain a benefit from the activity in question, provided the benefit occurs in the course of the activities of a non-commercial society.[79]

(c) The use of the word 'garden' would suggest that only outdoor functions or events can take the benefit of this exemption.

(7) ***Morris dancing.***[80]

Morris dancing (or similar) is not regulated where it is performed with unamplified, live music nor where facilities are provided to enable persons to take part in such dancing.

(8) ***Moving vehicles.***[81]

The provision of entertainment or entertainment facilities on a moving vehicle is not regulated. This exemption is no doubt intended to cater for street carnivals and the like.

---

74 Licensing Act 2003, Sch 1, para 8.

75 See **10.27**.

76 Licensing Act 2003, Sch 1, para 9.

77 Ibid, Sch 1, para 10.

78 Ibid, Sch 1, para 10(3) as amended by Gambling Act 2005, Sch 16, para 20(3).

79 See further **11.16**.

80 Ibid, Sch 1, para 11.

81 Ibid, Sch 1, para 12.

10.21 The above exemptions will only apply where there is no sale or supply of alcohol by the club when the entertainment or the entertainment facilities are being provided. If alcohol is available, then the appropriate authorisation will be needed, that is to say, a club premises certificate or a premises licence or a temporary event notice. It should also be noted that the *spontaneous* performance of music, singing or dancing does not amount to the provision of regulated entertainment and is not a licensable activity.[82]

5. PROCEDURES RELATING TO AUTHORISATIONS ETC

10.22 Since there is now one unified system of licensing which applies to both the sale and supply of alcohol and the provision of regulated entertainment and entertainment facilities, the reader is referred to Chapter 9 which deals with the necessary procedures:

(1) Licensable activities: see **9.7**.
(2) Qualifying club activities: see **9.8**.
(3) Authorisations: see **9.9**.
(4) Club premises certificate: see **9.10**.
(5) Premises licence: see **9.37**.
(6) Temporary event notice: see **9.49**.
(7) Personal licence: see **9.61**.
(8) Appeals: see **9.66**.
(9) Fees: see **9.69**.

10.23 Films: mandatory condition Where the club premises certificate or the premises licence authorises the exhibition of films, a mandatory condition must be included that the admission of children (viz. those under 18 years) to the film shall be restricted in accordance with the recommendations given by the British Board of Film Censors[83] or by the licensing authority itself.[84]

10.24 Plays: prohibited condition The licensing authority has no power to attach conditions to the club premises certificate or the premises licence which relate to the nature of the play or to the manner of its performance, unless they are justified as a matter of public safety.[85] We add here that

---

[82] National Statistics Bulletin on Alcohol, Entertainment and Late Night Refreshment Licensing, England and Wales, April 2009 to March 2010, p 39, published by the Department for Culture, Media and Sport on 29 October 2010.

[83] A body designated under s 4 of the Video Recordings Act 1984.

[84] Licensing Act 2003, ss 20 and 74.

[85] Ibid, ss 22 and 76.

where the artistic integrity of a performance makes it appropriate for a performer to smoke, that part of the premises where the performer smokes shall not be a smoke-free place.[86]

10.25 Statutory guidance As with the licensing of alcohol, the Secretary of State is under a duty to issue guidance as regards regulated entertainment[87] and the licensing authority must publish its own statement of licensing policy as regards regulated entertainment.[88]

10.26 Statistics Of the 16,707 members' clubs holding a club premises certificates as at 31 March 2010, 11,864 of them held an authorisation for regulated entertainment of some sort. The table below sets out the number of authorisations as at 31 March 2010 in respect of regulated entertainment and entertainment facilities.[89] Some clubs may of course feature in more than one category.

(1)	Plays:	1,972
(2)	Films:	2,583
(3)	Indoor sporting events:	4,408
(4)	Boxing and wrestling:	507
(5)	Live music:	8,445
(6)	Recorded music:	9,297
(7)	Performance of dance:	4,150
(8)	Entertainment similar to live music, recorded music or dance:	3,515
(9)	Facilities for making music:	4,471
(10)	Facilities for dancing:	6,973
(11)	Facilities for entertainment similar to making music or dancing:	3,011.

6. TELEVISION LICENCE

10.27 The club will need to obtain a television licence if it installs or uses any television receiving equipment,[90] such as a television set, computer,

---

86 Smoke-free (Exemptions and Vehicles) Regulations 2007 (SI 2007/765).

87 Licensing Act 2003, s 182.

88 Ibid, s 5.

89 Source: National Statistics Bulletin on Alcohol, Entertainment and Late Night Refreshment Licensing, England and Wales, April 2009 to March 2010, p 39, published by the Department for Culture, Media and Sport on 29 October 2010.

90 Communications Act 2003, s 363(1).

mobile phone, games console, digital box or DVD/VHS recorder.[91] The use in question will be the receiving of television programmes as they are being broadcast.[92] The licence will relate to a specified place,[93] such as the clubhouse, and thus it will cover all relevant equipment at that place which means, for example, the club can install and use two televisions under the one licence. The licence fee for colour television is set annually by the Secretary of State for Culture, Media and Sport and is currently (2010) the sum of £145.50.[94] The fee is payable to the BBC[95] and is collected by the corporation under its trading name of TV Licensing. Installing or using television receiving equipment without a licence is a criminal offence.[96] The BBC may obtain a warrant from the magistrates' court to enter premises where there are reasonable grounds for believing that television receiving equipment has been installed or is being used without a valid licence.[97] The separate radio licence was abolished in 1971. A television licence covers all of the BBC Network, regional and local radio in the UK, with the exception of the BBC World Service. If perchance the club has no television set but only a radio on its premises, it will need no licence.

7. NOISE NUISANCE

10.28 This is a recurrent problem in modern society on a crowded island.[98] The Environmental Protection Act 1990 allows the local authority to take action against individuals or companies who create a nuisance through pollution of some kind, and noise is now labelled a statutory nuisance, being a species of pollution.[99] If a complaint is made to the local authority, the environmental health officer is bound to investigate the complaint, and will try to resolve the matter amicably. The assessment of noise nuisance is based on whether it is 'reasonable', bearing in mind the locality, how often the noise occurs and how many people are affected. If the local authority thinks the noise is a statutory nuisance, it will serve an abatement notice which will set out what is required of the neighbour, for example, if the issue is loud music the club may be asked to stop the music outright; or it may be asked to play the music between set times only; or, whenever music is played, it may be asked to fit an appropriate noise limiting device. The local authority may also pass on information about the noise complaint to its licensing committee, who could use it on any review proceedings. If the abatement notice is not complied with, this may result in a prosecution

91 Communications Act 2003, s 368(1).
92 Ibid, s 368(3).
93 Communications (Television Licensing) Regulations 2004, SI 2004/692, Sch 2, para 4.
94 Communications (Television Licensing) (Amendment) Regulations 2010, SI 2010/640.
95 Communications Act 2003, s 365(2).
96 Ibid, s 363(2).
97 Ibid, s 366.
98 See *Kennaway v Thompson* [1981] QB 88, CA, at 94 (Lawton LJ).
99 Environmental Protection Act 1990, s 79(1)(g).

under the Act.[100] An unfortunate situation can arise where a newcomer moves into a property close to the club and then complains about loud music, whereas the previous owner had never made any complaint about the club's dances or playing of music despite having lived in the property for many years. The legal position is that the newcomer has the right to complain if on an objective basis the music amounts to noise nuisance. It is no answer at law to say that the club was there first or that the newcomer voluntarily came to the nuisance and so must accept the situation as he finds it,[101] although these facts may carry weight with the local authority in deciding what action to take under the Act.

---

[100] Environmental Protection Act 1990, s 80. If a club's premises were to be construed as business premises, the maximum fine is £20,000: s 80(6).

[101] *Sturges v Bridgman* (1879) 11 Ch D 852; *Shelfer v City of London Electric Lighting Co* [1895] 1 Ch 287 CA, at 315 (Lindley LJ).

Chapter 11

GAMING AND LOTTERIES RUN BY THE CLUB

1. INTRODUCTION

11.1 Gambling is probably an inherent human trait and is now tolerated by British governments rather than prohibited: the present scheme of governmental regulation is a compromise between toleration and prohibition.[1] This compromise suits the government because of the excise duties levied upon gaming and lotteries and it suits clubs because it provides a ready and welcome source of income for the club as well as pleasurable activity for the participants. Prior to 2005 the gambling legislation was a mish-mash of statutes enacted mainly in the 1960s and 1970s and was not only out of date but took no account of modern technology. The Gambling Act 2005 ('the 2005 Act') swept away virtually all the existing legislation on the topic. The new gambling regime laid down for clubs, however, is broadly similar in effect to the previous regime. The 2005 Act came into force in 2007.

11.2 The 2005 Act has 18 Parts with 18 accompanying schedules. Its objectives are threefold:[2] (1) to prevent gambling from being a source of crime, (2) to ensure that gambling is conducted in a fair and open way, and (3) to protect children and other vulnerable persons from harm or exploitation by gambling. There is a new regulatory body called the Gambling Commission[3] and its decisions may be taken to the Gambling Appeals Tribunal.[4] For the first time in a parliamentary act a specific part, namely, Part 12, has been dedicated to the regulation of gaming in clubs. This is a welcome simplification.

11.3 Gambling is defined in the 2005 Act as meaning gaming, lotteries and betting,[5] and we will deal with each topic in turn. Clubs themselves have

---

1 The rigour of the earlier law is demonstrated by *R v Ashton* [1852] 1 E & B 286 (a successful appeal against conviction concerning the playing of dominoes *without stakes* in a public house under the gaming acts then in force which rendered all games of chance unlawful except games of pure skill).

2 Gambling Act 2005, s 1.

3 Ibid, s 20.

4 Ibid, s 140 and Sch 8.

5 Ibid, s 3.

been divided into two categories, namely, members' clubs and commercial clubs.[6] Where the club needs authorisation in the form of a permit this has to be obtained from the local authority.[7]

11.4 Clubs defined A *members' club* must have (1) at least 25 members; (2) be established and conducted for the benefit of its members; (3) be established and conducted wholly or mainly for purposes other than gaming (unless the gaming is of the prescribed kind, namely, bridge and whist[8]); and (4) must not be operating on a temporary basis.[9] A *commercial club* is subject to the same conditions save that the second condition does not apply.[10] These clubs are called proprietary clubs in this book. It is to be noted that the Gambling 2005 Act uses a different definition of a club from that used by the Licensing Act 2003.[11]

11.5 Children defined A *child* means a person who is less than 16 years old.[12] A *young person* means a person who is less than 18 years old but who is not a child.[13]

11.6 Codes of Practice The Gambling Commission is under a duty to issue codes of practice about the manner in which facilities for gambling are provided.[14] Numerous guidelines have been published by the Commission which may be accessed using an internet search engine under the heading of 'Gambling Commission guidance'.

2. GAMING: AN OVERVIEW

11.7 Gaming is now statutorily defined as 'the playing of a game of chance for a prize'.[15] This excludes games of pure skill such as chess or draughts. A game of chance includes one which involves both chance and skill (such as

---

6 As with the previous legislation, the 2005 Act specifically mentions miners' welfare institutes as being within its ambit. These institutes are not clubs as defined in **1.1**, being associations established for social or recreational purposes where the association is managed by a group of miners' representatives or where it uses premises which are regulated under a charitable trust: Gambling Act 2005, s 268.

7 Ibid, s 2, thus copying the regime under the Licensing Act 2003.

8 Gambling Act 2005 (Gaming in Clubs) Regulations 2007, SI 2007/1942, reg. 2. Curiously, backgammon is not prescribed even though it is an equal-chance game of great antiquity and backgammon clubs do exist.

9 Gambling Act 2005, s 266.

10 Ibid, s 267.

11 See **9.11**.

12 Gambling Act 2005, s 45(1).

13 Ibid, s 45(2).

14 Ibid, s 24.

15 Ibid, s 6(1).

bridge, whist, backgammon or poker) but it does not include a sport.[16] A person plays a game of chance whether or not he risks losing anything at the game.[17] A prize means money or money's worth and includes both a prize provided by a person organising the gaming and the winnings of money staked.[18]

11.8 Equal-chance gaming does not involve playing or staking against a bank, such as in roulette, and the chances must be equally favourable to all participants.[19] Roulette is again a good example of an unequal-chance game because the croupier's wheel has a green '0' where no player wins to the obvious advantage of the bank. It matters not whether the bank is controlled or administered by a player.[20]

11.9 The 2005 Act starts off with the proposition that all gaming is unlawful unless it is run in accordance with a licence (eg a casino operating licence or a bingo operating licence) or it constitutes exempt gaming.[21]

3. EXEMPT EQUAL-CHANCE GAMING

11.10 Clubs are permitted to provide certain facilities for gaming on the club premises without the need for express authorisation. Members' clubs are not subject to gaming duty under their exempt gaming activities.[22]

11.11 Conditions To qualify for this exemption under Part 12 of the 2005 Act the club must comply with the following conditions:

(1) the facilities must be for equal chance gaming;[23]
(2) the following participation fees[24] apply where the club does not hold a club gaming permit:[25]
 (a) a maximum of £18 for the games of bridge or whist where no other gaming facilities are provided by the club on that date;
 (b) in all other cases, a maximum of £1 if the club is a members' club;

---

16 Gambling Act 2005, s 6(2).
17 Ibid, s 6(4)(a).
18 Ibid, s 6(5).
19 Ibid, s 8(2).
20 Ibid, s 8(2)(a). This statutory provision negates the argument that if the position of banker can be won or lost, or the position of banker circulates amongst the players, one can convert a game of unequal chance into a game of equal chance.
21 Ibid, s 33.
22 Finance Act 1997, s 10(3).
23 Gambling Act 2005, s 269(1).
24 A member's subscription does not count as a participation fee nor does any stake count as one: ibid, s 344(1)(c)–(d).
25 Gambling Act 2005 (Exempt Gaming in Clubs) Regulations 2007, SI 2007/1944, reg 4.

(c) in all other cases, a maximum of £3 if the club is a commercial club which holds a club machine permit;

(3) the following rules apply to the game of poker:[26]
(a) a player's stake for any one game must not exceed £10;
(b) a player's stakes for any one day must not exceed £250;
(c) a player's stakes for any one week must not exceed £1,000;
(d) the prize for any one game must not exceed £250;

(4) no amount is deducted or levied by the club or the person providing the gaming facilities from the sums staked or won;[27]

(5) a game played on one set of premises must not be linked with a game played on another set of premises (as sometimes happens in bingo);[28] a person may only participate in the gaming if he is a member of the club who became a member, or was nominated for membership, at least 48 hours before he participates.[29] This condition does not apply to commercial clubs.[30]

11.12 Prize gaming Part 13 of the 2005 Act authorises prize gaming. Prize gaming means that neither the nature nor the size of a prize played for is determined by reference to the number of players or the amount of the stakes.[31] This is a type of gaming where the organiser puts up the prizes in advance as distinct from gaming where the stakes of the participants make up the winnings. The definition of gaming in Part 1 covers any sort of gaming for prizes or winnings. Therefore, a provision in the 2005 Act which generally authorises gaming authorises prize gaming. Thus exempt equal-chance gaming in clubs includes prize gaming.

11.13 Conditions This gaming is subject to the following conditions:

(1) the chance to participate in a particular game must be acquired or gaming allocated on one day and in the place where the game is played;[32]

(2) the game must be played entirely on that day;[33]

(3) the participation fee charged for any one chance to win a prize in a game must not exceed £1, even if the chance provides the opportunity to win more than one prize;[34]

---

26 Gambling Act 2005 (Exempt Gaming in Clubs) Regulations 2007, SI 2007/1944, regs 2 and 3.

27 Gambling Act 2005, ss 269(3) and 270(3).

28 Ibid, ss 269(5) and 270(5).

29 Ibid, s 269(6)(a).

30 Ibid, s 269(6).

31 Ibid, ss 288, 293(3)(a).

32 Ibid, s 293(3)(a).

33 Ibid, s 293(3)(b).

34 Gambling Act 2005 (Limits on Prize Gaming) Regulations 2009, SI 2009/1272, regs 2(1)(a) and 2(2). For example, in a game of bingo the purchase of one game card (the chance) may

(4) the aggregate amount of the participation fees charged for any one chance to win a prize in a game must not exceed £500;[35]
(5) the limit for any one prize is £70 in money or value;[36]
(6) the aggregate of the prizes must not exceed £500 in money or value;[37]
(7) the result of the game must be made public where the game is played and as soon as reasonably practicable after the game is played and, in any event, on the day in which it is played;[38]
(8) participation in prize gaming shall not entitle the player to participate in any other gambling.[39]

4. NON-COMMERCIAL EQUAL-CHANCE GAMING

11.14 Part 14 of the 2005 Act contains an important addition to the exempt regime in that it exempts the club from the need to obtain any authorisation for equal-chance gaming and prize gaming where they take place at a non-commercial event.[40] The Act defines a non-commercial event as one where no sum raised by the event organisers[41] is appropriated for the purposes of private gain,[42] so that all sums are utilised for charitable purposes or for purposes benefiting the club as a whole. This type of gaming does not necessarily have to take place on club premises. So a club's whist drive or bingo session held at the local village hall to raise funds for the club would come within the ambit of this exemption.

11.15 Private gain Section 353(1) of the 2005 Act says that private gain is to be construed in accordance with s 19(3). Rather oddly this latter section gives no definition of private gain but simply describes a particular scenario which does *not* amount to private gain. To understand this oddity we need to go back to the case of *Payne v Bradley*.[43] There the receipt by a working men's club of the proceeds of bingo sessions organised by the club to meet its general expenses of maintaining the club was held by the House of Lords to be a private gain to the club and its members, and therefore illegal under

---

provide the player with three distinct opportunities to win a prize (one line, two lines, full house). The maximum fee remains at £1 because the game card constitutes a single chance to win one or more of several prizes.

35 Gambling Act 2005 (Limits on Prize Gaming) Regulations 2009, SI 2009/1272, reg 2(1)(b).

36 Ibid, regs 3(1)(a) and 3(2)(a).

37 Ibid, regs 3(1)(b) and 3(2)(b).

38 Gambling Act 2005, s 293(3)(c).

39 Ibid, s 293(5).

40 This mirrors the earlier legislation, namely, gaming at exempt entertainments under s 41 of the Gaming Act 1968 and amusements with prizes at exempt entertainments under s 15 of the Lotteries and Amusements Act 1976. Lotteries at exempt entertainments under s 3 of the 1976 Act are now covered by incidental non-commercial lotteries (see **11.45**).

41 This includes entrance fees, participation fees, sponsorship moneys and commission from traders: Gambling Act 2005, Sch 11, para 2.

42 Ibid, Sch 11, para 2.

43 [1962] AC 343.

the then gaming laws. This decision was reversed by the Gaming Act 1968 and the reversal is continued under the 2005 Act. Section 19(3) states that there is no private gain *despite the fact one or more individuals obtain a benefit from the gaming in question*,[44] provided this benefit occurs in the course of the activities of a non-commercial society. A non-commercial society is one which, as its name suggests, is established and conducted for charitable purposes or for non-commercial purposes (including participation in or support of sport, athletics and cultural activities).[45] The 2005 Act requires that both the money raised from the non-commercial event and the profits made from the gaming itself are not used for private gain. This means that if someone other than the club provides the facilities for gaming, they too must ensure that their profits go to good causes. On the other hand, persons not concerned with the gaming, such as caterers or suppliers of refreshment, are not caught by the no-private-gain rule.

11.16 Conditions for non-commercial equal-chance gaming This gaming must comply with the following conditions:

(1) participants are informed that the purpose of the gaming is to raise money for a specified purpose;[46]
(2) no profits from the gaming are applied to private gain.[47] Profits means the amount of the stakes together with moneys accruing to the organiser of the gaming minus the cost of prizes and other costs reasonably incurred in organising or providing facilities for the gaming;[48]
(3) the gaming must comply with the following rules:
   (a) the participation fee must not exceed £8 for any one game played at an event;[49]
   (b) the aggregate amount or value of the prizes in respect of all the games played at an event must not exceed £600;[50]
   (c) where two or more events are promoted on the same premises by the same person on the same day, the limits referred to in (a) and above shall apply;[51]

---

44 Eg because they are members of the club which is the beneficiary of the profits of the gaming.
45 Gambling Act 2005, s 19(1).
46 Ibid, s 300(2).
47 Ibid, s 300(3).
48 Ibid, s 300(8).
49 Gambling Act 2005 (Non-Commercial Equal-Chance Gaming) Regulations 2007, SI 2007/2041, reg 3(2).
50 Ibid, reg 3(3).
51 Ibid, reg 3(4).

(d) where a series of events other than described in (c) above takes place, the same limits apply, save that in respect of all the games played at the final event[52] the amount or value of the prizes may be increased up to £900;[53]

(4) the gaming does not take place at premises on which a premises licence has effect; or on a track at a time when activities are being carried on in reliance of a premises licence; or on premises when activities are being carried on in reliance of a temporary use notice;[54]

(5) the gaming is non-remote.[55]

11.17 Conditions for non-commercial prize gaming This gaming must comply with the same conditions as laid down for non-commercial equal-chance gaming (see **11.16**) except for the third condition which does not apply.[56]

11.18 Race nights These provide a useful example of how the exemption works in practice. In a race night the selection of the 'horse' to bet on is entirely dependent on chance. Often archive film is used without revealing the details of the race. A race night can be staged (a) as non-commercial equal-chance gaming where the chances are equally favourable to all participants and the players are not competing against a bank, or (b) as non-commercial prize gaming where the prizes are advertised in advance and do not depend on the number of people playing or the amount of the stakes (here the outcome of the 'race' determines the winner of the prize), or (c) as an incidental non-commercial lottery where the race night is not the only or main purpose of the non-commercial event (see **11.45**).

5. GAMING MACHINES

11.19 A gaming machine is now statutorily defined as being a machine which is designed or adapted for use by individuals to gamble, whether or

---

52 For there to be a final event, every player must have taken part in an earlier game of the series held on a previous day: Gambling Act 2005 (Non-Commercial Equal-Chance Gaming) Regulations 2007, SI 2007/2041, reg 6.

53 Ibid, reg 3(5).

54 Gambling Act 2005, s 300(6). Premises licences (as defined in ibid, s 150 eg a casino premises licence) are dealt with in Part 8 of the 2005 Act. Temporary use of premises is dealt with in Part 9 of the 2005 Act. A track means a horse-race course, dog track or other premises on which a race or other sporting event takes place: ibid, s 353(1).

55 Ibid, s 300. Remote gambling means gambling in which the participants use remote communication, including the internet, telephone, television or radio: ibid, s 4. Remote gambling requires a remote gambling licence under ibid, s 89.

56 Ibid, s 299.

not it can be used for other purposes.[57] Making a gaming machine available for use on club premises is an offence unless it is covered by the requisite exception, permit or licence.[58] Under the 2005 Act there are designated four classes of gaming machine, known as Categories A to D, with Category B being divided into five sub-categories.[59] The categories are defined as follows:[60]

(1) Category A: (not applicable to clubs);
(2) Category B:
B1/B2/B3: (not applicable to clubs);
B3A: it enables a person to participate in a lottery but not in any other form of gambling; it is made available for use by a members' club; the maximum charge for use is £1; the maximum prize value is £500; it does not fall within Category B4 nor within Category C or D;
B4: the maximum charge for use is £1; the maximum prize value is £250; it is not a Category C or D machine;
(3) Category C: the maximum charge for use is £1, the maximum prize value is £70; it is not a Category D machine;
(4) Category D:
money-prize machine: the maximum charge for use is 10 pence; the maximum prize value is £5;
non-money prize machine: the maximum charge for use is 30 pence; the maximum prize value is £8;
crane grab machine: the maximum charge for use is £1; the maximum prize value is £50;
coin pusher machine: the maximum charge for use is 10 pence; the maximum prize value is £15, of which no more than £8 may be a money prize;
penny fall machine: the same as for a coin pusher machine;
other machines: a machine is a Category D machine if the maximum charge for use is 10 pence and the maximum prize value is £8, of which no more than £5 may be money prize.

11.20 Exception: no-prize gaming machine A club commits no offence under the Act if it provides a gaming machine on the club premises which by its use does not give the individual the opportunity to win a prize.[61] The well known mechanical football game[62] which has two, and sometimes four, players at the controls is a gaming machine which comes into this category. Although put as an exception to the gaming machine regime, it is

57 Gambling Act 2005, s 235(1). This wide definition has meant that the 2005 Act has had to exclude various machines from the definition, such as a croupier's roulette wheel or a lottery ticket machine: see s 235(2).
58 Ibid, s 242.
59 Ibid, s 236.
60 Categories of Gaming Machine Regulations 2007, SI 2007/2158, as amended by Categories of Gaming Machine (Amendment) Regulations 2009, SI 2009/1502.
61 Gambling Act 2005, s 248.
62 At one time it was seen in a great many French cafés.

not a true exception because there is no element of gambling involved. Such machines are therefore not subject to any statutory control.

11.21 Exception: limited-prize gaming machine A club commits no offence under the 2005 Act if it provides a gaming machine on the club premises which by its use does not give the player the opportunity to win a prize in excess of the amount which he paid in order to use the machine.[63] These machines are sometimes known as play-again machines. Pinball and video-game machines come into this category. These machines are true gaming machines but need no express authorisation.

6. CLUB MACHINE PERMIT

11.22 A members' club and a commercial club may apply under Part 12 of the 2005 Act for this permit which authorises the holder to provide up to three gaming machines for use on club premises, being within Categories B3A, B4, C or D.[64]

11.23 Conditions The permit is subject to the following conditions:

(1) a person may only use the machine if he is a member of the club who became a member, or was nominated for membership, at least 48 hours before he uses the machine;[65]
(2) a person who is guest of a member may use the machine provided that he is a genuine guest, that is to say, he will not be treated as a guest if the member extending the invitation has no previous acquaintance with that person and invites him solely for the purpose of enabling him to take advantage of the gaming facilities;[66]
(3) no child or young person may use a Category B or C gaming machine on the club premises;[67]
(4) the holder of the permit must comply with any code of practice issued by the Gambling Commission concerning the location and operation of a gaming machine.[68]

---

63 Gambling Act 2005, s 249.
64 Ibid, s 273(2)(a); Categories of Gaming Machine Regulations 2007, SI 2007/2158, reg 6(4).
65 Gambling Act 2005, s 273(3)(a).
66 Ibid, s 271(4)(b). No regulations have been issued.
67 Ibid, s 273(4)(a).
68 Ibid, s 273(4)(b).

7. CLUB GAMING PERMIT

11.24 A members' club, but not a commercial club, may apply under Part 12 of the 2005 Act for this permit to authorise on the club premises the provision of (a) games of chance and (b) gaming machines.[69] This allows clubs to offer gaming facilities in addition to those available under the exempt gaming provisions. The permit authorises the club:[70]

(1) to make available up to three gaming machines, which must be within Categories B3A, B4, C or D;[71]
(2) to provide equal-chance gaming facilities which complies with all the conditions set out in **11.11** apart from the level of participation fees (where separate rules apply);
(3) to provide the facilities for prescribed games involving a bank or unequal chance games. The prescribed games are pontoon and chemin de fer.[72] It should be noted that the regulations exclude the game of blackjack and any version of pontoon which does not allow the bank to pass amongst the players.[73]

11.25 Conditions The permit is subject to the following conditions:

(1) the maximum fee for participation for any one day is £3 exclusive of VAT;[74]
(2) no amount is deducted or levied by the club or the person providing the gaming facilities otherwise than in accordance with regulations;[75]
(3) the public are excluded from any area where gaming is taking place.[76] The public means persons other than the members and their guests, the club staff and the persons providing the facilities;[77]
(4) a person may only participate in the gaming if he is a member of the club who became a member, or was nominated for membership, at least 48 hours before he participates;[78]
(5) a person who is a guest of a member may participate in the gaming[79] provided that he is a genuine guest, that is to say, he will not be treated as a guest if the member extending the invitation has no previous

---

[69] Gambling Act 2005, s 271(2)(a). This permit equates broadly to the former registration under Part II of the Gaming Act 1968.
[70] Gambling Act 2005, s 271(3).
[71] Categories of Gaming Machine Regulations 2007, SI 2007/2158, reg 6(4).
[72] Gambling Act 2005 (Club Gaming Permits) (Authorised Gaming) Regulations 2007, SI 2007/1945, reg 2(1).
[73] Ibid, reg 2(2).
[74] Ibid, reg 3(2). A day means a period of 24 hours beginning at midday: ibid, reg 3(3).
[75] Gambling Act 2005, s 271(4)(b). No regulations have been issued.
[76] Ibid, s 271(4)(c).
[77] Ibid, s 272(2).
[78] Ibid, s 269(6)(a).
[79] Ibid, s 271(6)(b).

acquaintance with that person and invites him solely for the purpose of enabling him to take advantage of the gaming facilities;[80]

(6) children and young persons are excluded from any area where the gaming is taking place;
(7) no child or young person may use a Category B or C gaming machine on the club premises;[81]
(8) the holder of the permit must comply with any code of practice issued by the Gambling Commission concerning the location and operation of a gaming machine.[82]

8. PROCEDURE FOR OBTAINING CLUB PERMITS

11.26 Schedule 12 of the 2005 Act contains detailed rules concerning the obtaining and regulation of club machine permits and club gaming permits. It should perhaps be noted that a club does not need an alcohol licence to apply for a club permit, although the two commonly go hand-in-hand.

11.27 Application[83] The club applies to the licensing authority in whose area the club premises are situated. A copy of the application must be sent to the Gambling Commission and to the local Chief Officer of Police.

The authority *must* refuse the application if:

(a) the applicant is not a club as defined;
(b) the club premises are wholly or mainly used by children or young persons.

The authority *may* refuse the application if:

(c) an offence under the Act or a breach of a permit has been committed by the club when providing gaming facilities;
(d) a permit held by the club has been cancelled within the previous 10 years;
(e) an objection has been lodged by the Commission or the police. If an objection is lodged, a hearing will take place unless all parties agree otherwise. Reasons must be given for rejecting the application.

---

80 Gambling Act 2005, s 272(4).

81 Ibid, s 271(7)(a).

82 Ibid, s 271(7)(b).

83 Gambling Act 2005, Sch 12, paras 1–9; Gambling Act 2005 (Club Gaming and Club Machine Permits) Regulations 2007, SI 2007/1834, as amended by Gambling Act 2005 (Club Gaming and Club Machine Permits) (Amendment) Regulations 2007, SI 2007/2689.

11.28 Fast-track application[84] Where the applicant is the holder of a club premises certificate under the Licensing Act 2003 there is no opportunity to objections to be made and the grounds for rejection are limited to ground (d) above and the fact that the club is conducting gaming other than which is prescribed. The reason for this provision is that the club will already have been through the licensing process in relation to its club premises certificate under the 2003 Act and to impose the full requirements of Sch 12 would be an unnecessary duplication.

11.29 Form of permit[85] The permit is in a prescribed form and the licensing authority maintains a register of permits. The club must keep the permit on the club premises. If the information in the permit ceases to be accurate the club must apply to have the permit varied. If the permit is lost or damaged the club may apply for a copy, for which a fee is payable. If the permit is lost or stolen, the club must report this fact to the police.

11.30 Duration and renewal[86] A permit will last for 10 years and can then be renewed by application made within the last 3 months of the 10-year period. On renewal the licensing authority has available the same grounds of refusal as set out in **11.27**. Where the permit was granted under the fast-track procedure, the permit lasts indefinitely until such time as the club premises certificate comes to an end. If the club as holder ceases to be a members' club or a commercial club, the permit shall lapse. The club may also surrender the permit by giving notice to the licensing authority.

11.31 Cancellation[87] The licensing authority may cancel a permit if it thinks that the club premises are used wholly or mainly by children and/or young persons or that an offence, or a breach of a condition of the permit, has been committed in the course of gaming activities carried on by the club. The licensing authority must give the club at least 21 days' notice of its intention to consider cancellation of the permit and consider any representations made by the club; a hearing will be held if the club requests one. The authority shall cancel the permit if the club fails to pay the annual fee, unless the failure was attributable to administrative error.

11.32 Forfeiture[88] Where a club or one of its officers is convicted of an offence under the Act, the court may order the forfeiture of the permit. Forfeiture may be suspended while an appeal is being brought against the conviction or against any order made on the conviction. It is for the court to notify the licensing authority of the order for forfeiture.

---

84 Gambling Act 2005, Sch 12, para 10.
85 Ibid, Sch 12, paras 11–16 and 26.
86 Gambling Act 2005, Sch 12, paras 17–20 and 24.
87 Ibid, Sch 12, paras 21 and 22.
88 Ibid, Sch 12, para 23.

11.33 Appeals[89] Where the licensing authority rejects an application for the issue or renewal of a permit or where it cancels the permit, the club may appeal to the local magistrates' court within 21 days of the receipt of the decision. An unsuccessful objector to the issue or renewal of a permit has a similar right of appeal.

11.34 Fees The fee payable for an application for a permit is £200 unless the club holds a club premises certificate, in which case it is £100.[90] On a renewal application, the same scale of fees applies.[91] After issue of the permit a first annual fee of £50 is payable and thereafter a further annual fee of £50 is payable.[92]

11.35 Inspection of premises Part 15 of the 2005 Act deals with the inspection of premises in connection with gambling activities.[93] As far as members' clubs are concerned, an authorised local authority officer may enter the club premises in respect of which an application has been made for a club gaming permit or a club machine permit for a purpose connected with the consideration of that application.[94] Furthermore, a constable or enforcement officer[95] may enter club premises to determine whether any gaming that is taking place, or about to take place, is doing so in accordance with the conditions laid down for exempt equal-chance gaming or is in accordance with its club gaming permit or its club machine permit.[96]

9. GAMING: A MISCELLANY

11.36 Bingo in members' clubs Under the 2005 Act bingo means any version of the game by whatever name it is described.[97] As with the Gaming Act 1968, the 2005 Act nowhere describes what bingo is. It is a game of equal chance played between a number (often a large number) of players. Each player is given a card with a series of numbers on it. The person in charge draws out of a bag or a special box (the tombola) a random number, or the number may be selected mechanically or electronically. The number is called out or displayed and if it corresponds to a number on the card, the player crosses out that number. The first person to cross out all or certain of

89 Gambling Act 2005, Sch 12, para 25.

90 Gambling Act 2005 (Club Gaming and Club Machine Permits) Regulations 2007, SI 2007/1834, reg 8.

91 Gambling Act 2005 (Club Gaming and Club Machine Permits) Regulations 2007, SI 2007/1834, reg 10.

92 Ibid, regs 12, 13 and 14.

93 See also Gambling Act 2005 (Inspection) (Provision of Information) Regulations 2007, SI 2007/319.

94 Gambling Act 2005, s 312(4).

95 Ie an employee or authorised agent of the Gambling Commission: ibid, s 303(1)–(2).

96 Ibid, s 312(1)–(3).

97 Ibid s 353(1).

the numbers makes known his completion and wins a prize. The game is generally now called bingo but is also known by the name of housey-housey or tombola.[98] Bingo is a game of equal chance and counts as exempt gaming provided (a) it complies with the conditions set out in **11.11** and (b) it does not amount to 'high turnover bingo' played during a 'high turnover period',[99] that is to say, where the total stakes or prizes for bingo games played at the club during any one period of 7 days exceed £2,000 in the course of 1 year beginning with the first day of the 7-day period.[100] If this limit is exceeded, the club must inform the Gambling Commission of this occurrence as soon as reasonably practicable.[101] The club must obtain a bingo operating licence under s 65(2)(b) of the 2005 Act before any further high turnover bingo takes place during that year.[102] There is one dispensation if the club applies for such a licence: there is no requirement for a personal licence holder which would otherwise apply.[103] Bingo may also be played as non-commercial equal-chance gaming (see **11.14**) or it may take place as an incidental non-commercial lottery (see **11.45**). It should be noted that small-scale bingo played in members' clubs has been exempt from bingo duty since 1992.[104]

11.37 Bingo operating licence If the playing of bingo in a club does not amount to exempt gaming, the alternative is to seek a bingo operating licence.[105] A non-remote bingo operating licence authorises the holder to make available for use one or more gaming machines of Category A to D.[106] Part 5 of the 2005 Act sets out the regulatory regime for controlling and monitoring the activities of bingo operators, the detailed provisions of which are outside the scope of this book. The holder of a bingo operating licence is required to pay an annual fee to the Gambling Commission,[107] and bingo duty is also payable.

11.38 Casino operating licence If a club for any reason is unable to take advantage of the exempt gaming provisions, the alternative is to seek a casino operating licence.[108] For the purposes of the 2005 Act 'casino' is defined as an arrangement whereby people are given the opportunity to

---

98 *Payne v Bradley* [1962] AC 343, at 354.

99 Gambling Act 2005, ss 269(1) and 275(1).

100 Ibid, s 275(2), (3), (4).

101 Gambling Act 2005, s 275(6).

102 Ibid, s 275(1).

103 Ibid, s 80(9).

104 Betting and Gaming Duties Act 1981, Sch 3, para 2, as amended by Finance (No 2) Act 1992, s 7(2). Small-scale bingo means that, on any one day, the winnings and the aggregated stakes do not exceed £500 or, within any one accounting period, the winnings and the aggregated stakes do not exceed £7,500: see the said Sch 3 (as amended).

105 Gambling Act 2005, s 91.

106 Ibid, s 68(5)(b).

107 Ibid, s 100.

108 Ibid, s 90.

participate in one or more casino games.[109] A casino game means a game of chance which is *not* equal-chance gaming.[110] Although the 2005 Act does not say so, we surmise that under a casino operating licence there can be no objection to the playing of equal-chance games. A non-remote casino operating licence authorises the holder to make available for use one or more gaming machines of Category A to D.[111] Part 5 of the 2005 Act sets out the regulatory regime for controlling and monitoring the activities of casino operators, the detailed provisions of which are outside the scope of this book. The holder of a casino operating licence is required to pay an annual fee to the Gambling Commission,[112] and gaming duty is also payable.

11.39 Temporary Use Notice Where an operating licence holder wishes to provide facilities for gambling temporarily on premises, he may give notice in writing (a 'temporary use notice') that he intends to use the premises for the provision of gambling.[113] It is rare for clubs to be the holders of an operating licence (an exception might be a large bingo club). The 2005 Act contemplates that premises which would normally be the subject of a temporary use notice are hotels, exhibition centres, entertainment venues and suchlike.

10. LOTTERIES: AN OVERVIEW

11.40 A lottery is now statutorily defined as meaning any arrangement whereby prizes are allocated by a process, which relies wholly on chance, to individual persons or to members of a class of persons who are required to pay in order to participate in the arrangement.[114] Thus if any merit or skill is involved in determining the distribution of prizes, this is not a lottery.[115] So a competition to guess the number of sweets in a jar or the weight of a pig is not a lottery. In the same vein neither the forecasting of the result of football matches[116] nor a competition to forecast the first four horses in a race[117] amounts to a lottery. On the other hand, it may safely be assumed that a club raffle (where one or more articles are distributed by lot) or a club sweepstake (where participants' stakes are pooled and horses or teams, etc are assigned by lot and prizes are awarded on the outcome of an event) will be a lottery.

---

109 Gambling Act 2005, s 7(1).
110 Ibid, s 7(2).
111 Ibid, s 68(5)(a).
112 Gambling Act 2005, s 100.
113 Ibid, Part 9 (ss 214–234) governs this topic.
114 Ibid, s 14(1), (2), (3).
115 *DPP v Bradfute and Associates Ltd* [1967] 2 QB 291, at 295 (Lord Parker LCJ).
116 *Moore v Elphick* [1945] 2 All ER 155.
117 *Stoddart v Sagar* [1895] 2 QB 474.

11.41 The clarity of the statutory definition is clouded by a further stipulation that a process which requires persons to exercise skill or judgement or to display knowledge shall be treated as relying wholly on chance if the process cannot reasonably be expected to prevent a significant proportion of persons lacking such skill, judgement or knowledge from participating in the lottery and/or winning prizes therein.[118] We consider that a significant proportion means a number worthy of note, that is to say, more than a minimal number but less than a substantial number. In *News of the World v Friend*[119] the House of Lords held that a 'spot the ball' competition in a newspaper was not unlawful as a lottery because of the skill required by the readers to put the ball in its most logical position, which was not necessarily its historical position. We surmise that today such a competition would be categorised as a lottery.

11.42 Continuing with the statutory definition, a prize includes any money, articles or services.[120] This is so whether or not the prize consists wholly or partly of moneys which have been paid, or articles or services which have been provided, by members of the class amongst whom the prize is allocated.[121] As to payment to participate in the lottery, any requirement to pay in order to discover whether a prize has been won or to take possession of a prize which has been allocated is treated as a payment to participate.[122]

11.43 The promotion of lotteries[123] is unlawful unless the lottery is of a type that is specifically permitted under the 2005 Act. There are two permitted types, namely, a lottery which is run in accordance with a licence under Part 5 (called a lottery operating licence) or it is an exempt lottery under Sch 11. There are four exempt lotteries under this schedule, three of which are likely to be used by clubs rather than a licensed lottery.

11.44 Exempt lotteries The three are as follows:

(1) incidental non-commercial lotteries;
(2) private society lotteries;
(3) small society lotteries.

---

[118] Gambling Act 2005, s 14(5).
[119] [1973] 1 WLR 248.
[120] Gambling Act 2005, s 14.
[121] Ibid, s 14(4)(b).
[122] Ibid, Sch 2, paras 6 and 7.
[123] What amounts to promotion is spelt out in detail in ibid, s 252.

11. INCIDENTAL NON-COMMERICAL LOTTERY

11.45 The nomenclature of this lottery is a good example of a transferred epithet because it is not the lottery which has to be non-commercial (the whole point of a club lottery is to raise money): it is the event, to which it is incidental, which has to be non-commercial.[124] Such a lottery might be a raffle which takes place at the club's annual dinner-dance held at a local hotel.

11.46 Conditions The terms on which such a lottery may be promoted are as follows:

(1) it must be 'incidental', that is to say, the lottery is a minor or subordinate event to the main event;[125]
(2) it must be promoted wholly for a purpose other than that of private gain;[126]
(3) from the proceeds of the lottery the promoters may deduct no more than £500 in respect of the costs of prizes[127] and no more than £100 in respect of costs incurred in organising the lottery;[128]
(4) there must be no rollover.[129] A rollover means an arrangement whereby the fact that a prize is not allocated or claimed in one lottery increases the value of the prizes available for allocation in another lottery;[130]
(5) no lottery ticket may be sold or supplied except on the premises where and while the event is taking place;[131]
(6) the results of the lottery must be made public while the event is taking place.[132]

11.47 Exception The promotion of this type of lottery shall not constitute a licensable activity under the Licensing Act 2003 by reason only that one or more of the prizes in the lottery or raffle consist of or include alcohol, provided the alcohol is in a sealed container.[133]

---

124 Gambling Act 2005, Sch 11, para 1(1)(a). See **11.14** as to the definition of a non-commercial event.

125 The 2005 Act does not define the word 'incidental' but neither did s 3 of the Lotteries and Amusements Act 1976 in legislating for 'small lotteries incidental to exempt entertainments'.

126 Gambling Act 2005, Sch 11, para 5. See **11.15** as to the definition of private gain.

127 Ibid, Sch 11, para 3; Gambling Act 2005 (Incidental Non-Commercial Lotteries) Regulations 2007, SI 2007/2040, reg 2(2).

128 Gambling Act 2005, Sch 11, para 4; the 2007 Regulations, reg 2(3).

129 Gambling Act 2005, Sch 11, para 6.

130 Ibid, s 256(1).

131 Ibid, Sch 11, para 7(1).

132 Ibid, Sch 11, para 7(2).

133 Licensing Act 2003, s 175, as substituted by Gambling Act 2005, Sch 16, para 20.

12. PRIVATE SOCIETY LOTTERY

11.48 A club which is established or conducted for purposes unconnected with gambling may promote a private society lottery if it is authorised in writing by the club's governing body and provided that each person to whom a ticket is sold (who may be a child or young person[134]) is either a member of the club or the sale takes place on the club premises.[135] Thus the word 'private' signifies that this is a lottery which excludes outsiders. This lottery is, however, of a more ambitious nature than the incidental non-commercial lottery described above.

11.49 Conditions The terms on which such a lottery may be promoted are as follows:

(1) the lottery may be promoted for any of the purposes for which the society is conducted;[136]
(2) no advertisement for the lottery may be displayed or distributed except on the society's premises, nor sent to any other premises;[137]
(3) promotion may only be by way of a ticket sold or supplied by the society. Each ticket must state the name and address of the promoting society; specify the class of persons to whom the society is willing to sell or supply tickets; and explain that no ticket is transferable;[138]
(4) the price for each ticket must be the same; it must be shown on the ticket; and it must be paid to the society before any person is given the ticket or any right in respect of membership of the class among whom prizes are to be allocated;[139]
(5) there must be no rollover.[140] Where, however, the prizes in a lottery are allocated by means of more than one draw (a common feature of this type of lottery in clubs), these draws will constitute a single lottery if the class of persons among whom the prizes are allocated remains the same.[141]

13. SMALL SOCIETY LOTTERY

11.50 This is another confusing nomenclature. The adjective 'small' qualifies the word 'lottery', not the word 'society'. This lottery has to be distinguished from a large lottery, as to which see **11.52**. This lottery is of

134 See Gambling Act 2005, s 56(1)(b).
135 Ibid, Sch 11, para 10.
136 Ibid, Sch 11, para 13.
137 Ibid, Sch 11, para 14.
138 Ibid, Sch 11, paras 15, 16 and 17.
139 Ibid, Sch 11, para 18.
140 Ibid, Sch 11, para 19. For the meaning of rollover, see **11.46**(4).
141 Ibid, s 256(2).

wider ambit than the private society lottery described above because members of the public may participate and it is therefore hedged about with more restrictions or conditions.

11.51 Conditions The terms on which such a lottery may be promoted are as follows:

(1) the lottery is being promoted by a non-commercial society,[142] for example, a members' club as defined in the 2005 Act;[143]
(2) the lottery is deemed to be a small lottery unless it constitutes a large lottery;[144]
(3) the lottery may be promoted for any of the purposes for which the society is conducted;[145]
(4) at least 20% of the proceeds of the lottery are applied to a purpose for which the society is conducted;[146]
(5) the maximum prize for a purchaser of a single ticket is £25,000;[147]
(6) no child should be invited or permitted to participate in the lottery.[148] A young person, however, can participate;[149]
(7) when a person purchases a ticket, he must receive a document[150] which:
    (a) identifies the promoting society;
    (b) states the price of the ticket;
    (c) states the name and address of the society member who is designated as having responsibility for the promotion of the lottery or, if there is one, of the external lottery manager;
    (d) states the date of the draw (or each draw) or enables the date of the draw (or each draw) to be determined;[151]
(8) the price for each ticket must be the same, and must be paid to the promoter of the lottery before any person is given the ticket or any right in respect of membership of the class among whom prizes are to be allocated;[152]

---

142 Gambling Act 2005, Sch 11, para 30(1)(a) and s 19(1). See **11.15** as to the definition of a non-commercial society.
143 See **11.4**.
144 Gambling Act 2005, Sch 11, para 31.
145 Ibid, Sch 11, para 32.
146 Ibid, Sch 11, para 33.
147 Ibid, Sch 11, para 34.
148 Ibid, s 56(1).
149 Ibid, s 56(2).
150 A document includes an electronic message which enables the recipient to retain the message electronically or to print it: ibid, Sch 11, para 36(2).
151 Ibid, Sch 11, para 36(1).
152 Ibid, Sch 11, para 37(1). The only payment required to become a member of a class is the price of a ticket: ibid, Sch 11, para 37(2).

(9) there may be a rollover[153] if each other lottery which may be affected by the rollover is itself a small society lottery promoted by or on behalf of the same society, subject to the maximum prize condition set out above;[154]

(10) the promoting society must throughout the period during which the lottery is promoted be registered with the local authority (see **11.53**);[155]

(11) the society must send to the local authority a statement containing certain specified matters (see **11.60**).[156]

11.52 Large lottery defined This means one of the following:[157]

(1) the arrangements for the lottery are such that its proceeds may exceed £20,000;

(2) the promotion of the lottery takes place at a time in a calendar year when the aggregate of the club's proceeds from society lotteries promoted wholly or partly during that year exceed £250,000;

(3) the arrangements for the lottery are such that, disregarding any other society lottery the sale of tickets for which is not concluded, it may become during its promotion a large lottery by virtue of the aggregate referred to in (2) above;

(4) if a lottery is a large lottery by reason of the rules set out in (1), (2) or (3) above ('the first lottery'), any other society lottery promoted by the society will be a large lottery if it is promoted wholly or partly:
   (a) after the beginning of the promotion of the first lottery and in the same calendar year as this promotion; or
   (b) in any of the 3 calendar years successively following the last calendar year during which the first lottery was promoted.

11.53 Registration of small society lottery Part 5 of Sch 11 to the 2005 Act contains detailed rules concerning registration with a local authority.

11.54 Local authority[158] In England this means a district council,[159] or the county council for a county with no district councils, or a London Borough Council, or the Common Council of the City of London, or the Council of the Isles of Scilly. In Wales this means a county council or a county borough council.

---

153 For the meaning of rollover, see **11.46**(4).
154 Gambling Act 2005, Sch 11, para 35(2). Ibid, Sch 11, para 35.
155 Ibid, Sch 11, para 38.
156 Ibid, Sch 11, para 39(1).
157 Ibid, Sch 11, para 31(2)–(5).
158 Ibid, Sch 11, para 41.
159 A borough council counts as a district council.

11.55 Application[160] The club applies to the local authority in whose area the club premises are situated, using a prescribed form and paying the prescribed fee, currently (2010) the sum of £40. The local authority is obliged to maintain a register of small society lotteries and to notify the Gambling Commission of the registration.

The authority *must* refuse the application if:

(a) within the previous 5 years an operating licence held by the club has been revoked;
(b) within the said period the club's application for an operating licence has been refused.

The authority *may* refuse the application if it thinks that:

(c) the club is not a non-commercial society;
(d) a person who will or may be connected with the promotion of the lottery has been convicted of a gambling offence;[161]
(e) information provided in or with the application is false or misleading.

The local authority may not refuse an application unless the club has been given the opportunity to make representations.

11.56 Revocation[162] The local authority may revoke a registration if it thinks that it would be obliged or permitted to refuse an application for the registration were it being made anew, that is, on the grounds set out in **11.55**. The revocation may take effect immediately or at the end of a specified period not exceeding 2 months from the date of revocation. The local authority may not revoke a registration unless the club has been given the opportunity to make representations.

11.57 Cancellation[163] The club can apply in writing to the local authority for the registration to be cancelled. The club's failure to pay the annual fee may lead to cancellation of the registration.

11.58 Appeals[164] If a local authority refuses an application or revokes a registration, the club may appeal to the local magistrates' court within 21 days of the receipt of the refusal or revocation.

---

160 Gambling Act 2005, Sch 11, paras 42–49.
161 Ibid, Sch 11, para 48(b) and Sch 7, para 1(a).
162 Ibid, Sch 11, para 50.
163 Ibid, Sch 11, paras 52, 53 and 54(3), (4).
164 Ibid, Sch 11, para 51.

11.59 Annual fee[165] The club is required to pay an annual fee to the local authority, currently (2010) the sum of £20.

11.60 Records[166] The club must send to the local authority a statement which sets out the arrangements for the lottery (including the dates on which tickets are available, the date of any draw and the arrangements for prizes including any rollover); the proceeds of the lottery; the amounts deducted for prizes and costs of organising the lottery; the amount applied to a club purpose; and what expenses (if any) were defrayed otherwise than by deduction from the proceeds. This statement must be sent to the local authority within 3 months of the draw, or the last draw, of the lottery. The statement must be signed by two adult members of the club appointed by the governing body of the club, and a copy of the appointment itself must accompany the statement. The local authority must retain the statement for at least 18 months and make it available to members of the public (for a reasonable fee). If the local authority thinks from the statement that the lottery in question is a large lottery, it shall notify the Gambling Commission of this fact.

11.61 Entry into club premises Where the club is registered with a local authority, an enforcement officer[167] or an authorised local authority officer may enter the club premises for the purpose of making enquiries in connection with a lottery promoted on behalf of the club.[168]

14. LOTTERIES: A MISCELLANY

11.62 Unclaimed prizes There are occasions when for a variety of reasons the club is unable to deliver the prize to the purchaser of a winning ticket. What happens to the prize? There is no problem if a rollover is permitted as in a small society lottery: the prize simply gets carried forward. In private society lotteries, which commonly have more than one draw, this problem is seldom encountered because they are in-house lotteries. An acute problem may arise in an incidental non-commercial lottery because the lottery winners have to be declared at the event itself, which is a one-off occasion, and the participants often comprise non-members of the club. Suppose the winner has gone home early feeling unwell and so is absent from the draw? Can the ticket be re-drawn? The answer is in the negative. The winner must be contacted. If this proves impossible after a reasonable attempt at locating the winner, there is no statutory answer. If the unclaimed prize is a sum of

---

165 Gambling Act 2005, Sch 11, para 54(1)–(2).

166 Ibid, Sch 11, paras 39 and 55.

167 Ie an employee or authorised agent of the Gambling Commission: Gambling Act 2005, s 303(1)–(2).

168 Ibid, s 314. See also Gambling Act 2005 (Inspection) (Provision of Information) Regulations 2007, SI 2007/319.

money, we suggest that the prize is allocated to the next lottery if feasible or that it simply becomes part of the club's general funds. If the prize is some tangible goods, for example, a bottle of whisky or a collection of pot plants, we suggest that the committee decides how best to dispose of the prize.

11.63 Lottery draw All participants must have an equal chance of winning. Clubs must therefore resist the temptation to draw the prizes in the reverse order of value or amount, a practice sometimes adopted to make the draw more exciting by leading up to the climax of the main prize. Doing this will wrongfully deprive the winner of a lesser prize of the chance of winning the main prize. Another point that requires consideration is the nature of prizes where the winning ticket is sold to a child or young person at say a club raffle which constitutes a private society lottery. Suppose one of the prizes is a box of cigars or a bottle of whisky: could this lawfully be won by a child or young person? We believe not,[169] and that the answer is to offer the winner a substitute prize of equal value.

11.64 Lottery operating licence If a club for any reason is unable to take advantage of the exempt lottery provisions the alternative is to seek a lottery operating licence.[170] Part 5 of the 2005 Act sets out the regulatory regime for controlling and monitoring the activities of lottery operators, the detailed provisions of which are outside the scope of this book. The holder of a lottery operating licence is required to pay an annual fee to the Gambling Commission,[171] and lottery duty is also payable.

15. BETTING

11.65 Betting is now statutorily defined[172] as making or accepting a bet on:

(1) the outcome of a race, competition or other event or process, or
(2) the likelihood of anything occurring or not occurring; or
(3) whether anything is or is not true.

The definition of betting has been extended to include prize competitions.[173]

---

169 The sale of tobacco is prohibited to someone under 18 years: Children and Young Persons Act 1933, s 7(1) as amended by Children and Young Persons (Protection from Tobacco etc) Order 2007, SI 2007/767; and the supply of alcohol by a member or officer of the club is prohibited to a person under 18: Licensing Act 2003, s 147(3)–(4).

170 Gambling Act 2005, s 98.

171 Ibid, s 100.

172 Ibid, s 9(1).

173 Ibid, s 11. A prize competition involves betting on an event or events of uncertain outcome but does not involve the deposit of a stake which is the norm in betting; here the participant is required to pay to enter the competition. Schedule 1 to the 2005 Act contains detailed provisions as to what is meant by payment to enter a prize competition.

11.66 It should be remembered that insofar as betting is concerned two key criminal offences under the 2005 Act are:

(1) providing facilities for gambling (which includes betting) unless a person holds an appropriate operating licence (that is, a betting operating licence) or unless an exception applies;[174]
(2) using premises for providing facilities for betting (whether making or accepting bets or by acting as a betting intermediary or providing other facilities for the making or accepting of bets) unless the use of the premises is authorised by a person holding a betting operating licence or unless an exception applies.[175]

11.67 It is axiomatic that no club will authorise any member to hold a betting operating licence in respect of its club premises and, unlike gaming or lotteries, no statutory exception applies to betting which takes place on club premises. Thus betting as such is an illegal activity on club premises.

16. CROSS-CATEGORY ACTIVITIES

11.68 Betting and gaming Gambling transactions where there is an overlap between betting and gaming are to be treated as gaming for the purposes of the 2005 Act,[176] unless the betting in question constitutes pool betting.[177] Roulette, for example, involves the placing of bets but in those clubs where this game is authorised it will not be treated as an illegal form of betting. So too a race night at the club does not involve illegal betting.

11.69 Betting and lotteries Where gambling transactions satisfy the definition of both a betting prize competition and a lottery, the arrangements are to be treated as betting[178] unless they constitute a lawful lottery.[179]

11.70 Gaming and lotteries Where gambling transactions satisfy the definitions of both games of chance and lotteries, the arrangements are to be treated as a game of chance[180] unless they constitute a lawful lottery.[181] An example of overlap involving race nights is given in **11.18**. Another example is the playing of bingo: see **11.36**.

---

174 Gambling Act 2005, ss 33–36.
175 Ibid, ss 37–40.
176 Ibid, s 16(3).
177 Ibid, s 16(2). Pool betting is defined in ibid, s 12.
178 Ibid, s 18(3).
179 Ibid, s 18(2).
180 Ibid, s 17(4).
181 Ibid, s 17(3).

17. PROPRIETARY CLUBS

11.71 General applicability of gambling law As stated above in **11.4**, proprietary clubs are described in the 2005 Act as commercial clubs. Such clubs are subject to the provisions of this Act. Commercial clubs come within the Part 12 regime except that they are not entitled to apply for a club gaming permit (see **11.22**). Commercial clubs are entitled to take advantage of the exempt lottery provisions relating to private society lotteries (see **11.48**) but not those relating to incidental non-commercial lotteries (see **11.45**) or small society lotteries (see **11.50**).[182] Large commercial clubs may of course wish to apply for a bingo operating licence (see **11.37**) or a casino operating licence (see **11.38**). These operating licences will require a premises licence under Part 8 of the 2005 Act to authorise the use of the club premises for gambling purposes.

182 Gambling Act 2005, Sch 11, paras 1(2), 10(2) and 30(1)(a).

Part 3:

EXTERNAL RELATIONSHIPS: THE CLUB AND THIRD PARTIES

Chapter 12

THE CLUB'S CIVIL LIABILITY TO THIRD PARTIES

PART A

CONTRACTS

1. INTRODUCTION

12.1 Whatever its nature and whatever its size, during the course of its lifetime a club is likely to be involved in contractual relationships of many sorts, either as purchaser of goods and services or perhaps as the provider for payment of services and facilities to outsiders. It is therefore crucial for those persons in charge of the club's affairs that they are aware of their rights and obligations when entering into a contract. What follows below is the legal situation looked at from the point of view of liability rather than entitlement. Two points need emphasising. First is the importance of the law of agency, especially in the realm of unincorporated members' clubs. Second is the desirability of recording agreements which have been made. It is common practice for people to enter into an agreement by telephone or by word of mouth since this is the way of the world and we have no quarrel with this procedure. But a note or letter, by post, fax or e-mail, which is sent straight afterwards and which *confirms* the agreement, will often prevent a dispute arising later on.

2. UNINCORPORATED MEMBERS' CLUBS: GENERAL PRINCIPLES OF LIABILITY

12.2 General propositions There are four general propositions to remember when considering the club's or the individual member's contractual liability to a third party:[1]

---

1 The converse situation, namely, pursuing the club's contractual entitlement in contract, is discussed in terms of procedure only, at **18.3**.

(1) the club is not a legal person;[2]
(2) no contract can exist without principal parties;
(3) the member's liability is normally limited to his entrance fee (if any) and his subscriptions;[3]
(4) whether the member can be held personally liable for contracts purporting to have been made on behalf of the club depends on the law of agency.[4]

12.3 No legal personality The consequence of lack of legal personality means that the club itself is unable to enter into any contract with a third party. Let us assume, however, that some members, eg the committee, have purported to act as agent for the club when making a contract. The law on this point is clear: if a person makes a contract on behalf of a non-legal person he may be held to have contracted in a *personal* capacity.[5] That is the nub of the problem.

12.4 The committee's prima facie liability The members of the managing committee, being in control of the club's affairs, are in the ordinary course of events personally liable for all contracts made by them on behalf of the club because they will be held to be the principals.[6] In this event the committee members will be liable to the full extent of the contract, not merely to the full extent of the club's funds.[7]

12.5 This status of principal leads to a point of considerable practical significance. It will be recalled that the committee must act unanimously unless (which is the norm) it is expressly authorised to act by a quorate number.[8] The question which arises is whether a committee member, who opposes or dissents from a decision of the majority, say, to enter into a contract with a particular third party, is liable to that third party if the committee defaults on its obligations under the contract. At first sight the answer would appear to be in the negative. In *Todd v Emly*[9] a wine merchant sued two committee members of the Alliance Club for the price of goods ordered by the steward. The plaintiff won at first instance but the appeal court, the Exchequer Chamber, ordered a re-trial. The plaintiff won the second trial but again the Exchequer Chamber ordered a re-trial.[10] Neither defendant had ordered the wine nor been present at any committee meeting

---

2 *Conservative and Unionist Central Office v Burrell* [1982] 1 WLR 522, CA, at 527.
3 *Wise v Perpetual Trustee Co Ltd* [1903] AC 139, PC, at 149.
4 *Maritime Stores Ltd v H P Marshall & Co Ltd* [1963] 1 Lloyd's Rep 602, at 608.
5 *Bradley Egg Farm Ltd v Clifford* [1943] 2 All ER 378, CA, at 386 (Scott LJ).
6 *Glenester v Hunter* (1831) 5 Car & P 62, at 65 (Tindal CJ); *Steele v Gourley and Davis* (1886) 3 TLR 772, at 773; *Bradley Egg Farms Ltd v Clifford* [1943] 2 All ER 378, CA, at 386.
7 *Pink v Scudamore* (1831) 5 Car & P 71.
8 See **5.25**.
9 (1841) 7 M & W 427.
10 (1841) 8 M & W 505. Sadly history does not relate what happened on the third trial.

when authority to place an order was given to the steward. On the second appeal Mr Baron Alderson stated in his judgment, at 510:

> 'In order to make the case out, and to establish the liability of the committee generally, the jury should be satisfied that what was done was not only within the knowledge of the committee generally but that it was in the particular knowledge of the two defendants.'

The same judge in the course of argument had stated at 508:

> 'It might be that the majority only gave authority, and that the defendants dissented from it. If so, I should think they only were liable who voted for it.'

The sting in the tail lies in what the court had said in its earlier judgments. Mr Baron Alderson stated, at 435, as follows:

> '… here the committee were authorised only to deal, as a body, for ready money. But at the same time, if any of the members of the committee choose not to contract for ready money, those members of the committee who have so contracted are liable upon their own contract, and the members who have not concurred in it are not liable, ***unless that be the common purpose for which the committee was appointed***.' (Emphasis added).

The 'common purpose' point was reiterated in the same appeal, at 434, by Mr Baron Parke:

> 'Then we come to the other, which is the main point of the case, and upon which it may be urged, that where parties enter into one common purpose of acting together, each of them has authority to bind the others to the extent of attaining that common purpose. But the defect of the plaintiff's case is, that there is no common purpose shewn, of dealing on credit for such articles as supplied in this case.'[11]

The 'common purpose' exception is likely in practice to mean that the dissenting member of the committee may well find himself potentially liable on a contract which he had neither agreed nor approved of and, depending on the nature or size of the contract, this state of affairs might involve his resignation from the committee.

12.6 Another question which can arise is whether a new member of the committee can be held liable in respect of authorised contracts made before his election. On the face of things, the answer is in the negative because the principals are fixed at the date when the contract was made and there is no such procedure as 'rolling substitutes' (unless the other party were to agree

---

11 See also the judge's remarks in the same case quoted in **5.56**.

to this, which would technically be known as novation). However, there are two points to be made: first, we consider that the new member may find himself liable on the contract because he has adopted it as his own. Take the example of the committee placing an order for building works in January; the new committee member is then elected in July; and in October as such member he votes in favour of a resolution to sue the builder for defective workmanship; the builder counterclaims against the club for the price of work done and materials supplied and obtains judgment on that counterclaim. In these circumstances the member is at risk of being treated as a principal on the contract and liable to the builder on his successful counterclaim.[12] Secondly, it follows that a member who resigns from the committee is still liable on those contracts which the committee had earlier entered into on behalf of the club when he was on the committee.[13]

12.7 The ordinary member's prima facie non-liability As stated in **1.10**, the general rule is that no member of the club is liable to pay to the club itself or to a third party any moneys beyond his entrance fee (if any) and his subscriptions. The rule, now almost universal, which vests the control of all the club's affairs in a managing committee would not by itself give to the committee the authority to make contracts on behalf of the members.[14] On the other hand, the rules of the club might expressly authorise the committee to make contracts on behalf of all the members; in this event the whole membership will be liable as principals on any authorised contract. This is a rule found in some early Victorian clubs, but an unwise one seldom if ever found in modern times.

12.8 Pledging the members' credit The committee of the club has no implied authority to pledge the credit of the members generally, for example, when ordering goods to be supplied[15] or work to be done[16] or when borrowing monies on debentures.[17] This is because the committee must be taken to know of and assent to the general proposition that an unincorporated members' club is run on a cash basis (see **5.56**). Consequent upon this lack of implied authority, if the committee enters into an authorised contract, its authority is restricted to spending the existing funds of the club.[18] It has been long established, however, that the committee has implied authority to pledge the members' credit when it comes to the

---

12 *Delauney v Strickland* (1818) 2 Stark 416 (Abbott LCJ) (concerning a member's liability to a third party in the General Service Club). See also **12.9**.

13 *Parr v Bradbury* (1885) 1 TLR 285 and 525, CA (continuing liability of a member under a debenture entered into before cessation of membership).

14 *Flemyng v Hector* (1836) 2 M & W 172, at 185 (Parke B).

15 See *Todd v Emly* (1841) 7 M & W 427, at 434; *Hawke v Cole* (1890) 62 LT 658.

16 *Flemyng v Hector* (1836) 2 M & W 172.

17 *Re St James Club* (1852) 2 De GM & G 383, at 390.

18 *Cockerell v Aucompte* (1857) 2 CB(NS) 440. However, this principle does not absolve the committee from full liability under the contract: see **12.4**.

employment of staff.[19] The member could of course, if he so wished, individually and expressly authorise the club or the committee to pledge his personal credit.[20]

12.9 Member's approbation Acquiescence in or tacit approbation of a club contract may be sufficient to establish liability against a member.[21] For example, in *Stansfield v Ridout*[22] the committee of the Beaconsfield Conservative Club in Battersea authorised the secretary to purchase beer from the plaintiff brewer. An action was brought against four members of the club, only one of whom was a member of the committee but all of whom had signed cheques for various goods ordered by the secretary, and all were held liable to the plaintiff. And in *Lee v Bissett*[23] a solicitor-member of the Naval and Military Club successfully sued certain members of the club in their personal capacity for his fees for work done on behalf of the club, the members in question being those who had previously each subscribed £60 to carry on the club, which was in financial straits, thereby enabling the club to employ the solicitor.

3. THE ROLE OF AGENCY

12.10 In an unincorporated members' club the committee as principal will commonly rely on one of the club's officers, such as the club secretary, or one of its employees to organise or enter into contracts on behalf of the club. The officer or employee will be acting as the committee's authorised agent. The general rule of the law of agency is that the contract of the agent is the contract of the principal,[24] so that the agent has power to bind and entitle his principal whilst he himself drops out of the transaction, incurring neither rights nor liabilities.[25] Proving the necessary agency is all-important in establishing liability against the principal. In an incorporated club, the club itself will be the principal and the committee members will here be acting as agents in the same way as the club's officers or employees, but the principles of agency are the same.

12.11 Agency is established in one of three ways: expressly, impliedly or ostensibly.[26] Express authority (also called actual authority) is where the principal gives the agent by means of spoken words or in writing the ability

---

19 *Todd v Emly* (1841) 7 M & W 427: see **5.56**.

20 *Overton v Hewett* (1886) 3 TLR 246, at 249 (Wills J).

21 *Steele v Gourley and Davis* (1886) 3 TLR 772, CA, at 773 (Lord Esher MR); *Earl of Mountcashell v Barber* (1853) 14 CB 53 (concerning a bank loan made to the managing committee of the Colonial Society).

22 (1889) 5 TLR 656.

23 (1856) 4 WR 233.

24 *Chitty on Contracts* (30th edn, 2008), at 31-084.

25 *Chitty*, op cit, at 31-001.

26 *Chitty*, op cit, at 31-020. There are numerous reported cases dealing with this topic.

to act on his behalf either generally or in relation to specific matters. Implied authority (sometimes called usual authority) is where the agent is put into a position to do whatever is ordinarily or necessarily incidental to the due performance of his express authority. Ostensible authority (also called apparent authority) is where the principal holds out the agent as having the requisite authority to act on his behalf[27] when in fact the agent had no such authority, or had limited authority only, which restriction was unknown to the other party.

12.12 Take the case of *Cockerell v Aucompte*[28] where the committee of an unincorporated coal club[29] expressly authorised the secretary to buy coal but did not furnish him with any cash funds to pay for it. The court held that the committee impliedly authorised the purchases on credit terms and, because the secretary was its duly appointed agent, the committee members were held liable to the coal merchant. Contrast it with the case of *Wood v Finch*[30], where a member and a trustee member of an unincorporated coal club, which was formed on the principle of buying coal wholesale on a cash basis out of members' paid-up subscriptions, were held not liable to the plaintiff coal merchant for the price of goods ordered by the club secretary on credit terms.

12.13 The committee (or the incorporated club) may clothe the agent with ostensible authority by holding him out as having proper authority to make a contract which pledges their credit.[31] Here each case has to be decided on its own facts leading sometimes to seemingly odd or inconsistent results:

(1) In the case of *Steele v Gourley and Davis*[32] (where the proprietary Empire Club became an unincorporated members' club called the New Empire Club) the butcher, in an action against two members of the committee, succeeded in recovering the price of meat supplied to the new unincorporated club but in the later case of *Overton v Hewett*[33], the fishmonger, in another action against all the members of the same committee, failed to recover the price of poultry supplied to the new unincorporated club, the difference being that in the first case the defendant committee members had by their conduct authorised the

---

27 It is important to note that it is not sufficient for the agent to represent the extent of his authority; the holding out must be done by the principal: *Armagas Ltd v Mundogas SA* [1986] AC 717, at 777.

28 (1857) 2 CB(NS) 440.

29 Such clubs were common in Victorian times. As befitted a justice of the peace, Charles Darwin was the honorary treasurer of the local coal club in the village of Downe in Kent.

30 (1861) 2 F & F 447.

31 See, eg *Pilot v Craze* (1884) 4 TLR 453 (where the manager of a five man committee organising a jubilee fête hired tents and flags; two stewards forming part of that committee were successfully sued for the hire charges).

32 (1886) 3 TLR 118, 669 and 772.

33 (1886) 3 TLR 246.

steward to purchase the goods whereas in the second case the plaintiff could not point to any such conduct on the part of the committee members.

(2) In the case of *Harper v Granville Smith*[34] (where the proprietary Salisbury Club became an unincorporated members' club called the New Salisbury Club) the wine merchant, in an action against a member of the committee, succeeded in recovering payment for champagne supplied to the new unincorporated club but a year later in the case of *Draper v Earl Manvers*[35] the milkman, in another action against a different member of the same committee, failed to recover the price of milk delivered to the new unincorporated club, the difference being that in the first case the committee member was aware of the transaction when the order was placed by the wine committee whereas in the second case the committee had under the rules delegated its purchasing function to a sub-committee and took no part in ordering the milk.[36]

12.14 A member who has authority to enter into a contract on behalf of the club or the committee may become personally liable if he signs the contract without expressing his agency.[37] However, parol evidence would generally be admissible to show that the club or the committee was the real principal.[38] When acting for the club or the committee, a member should always sign his own name on a document followed by the words of agency and then the principal's name: for example, 'Tom Pearce for and on behalf of the Basset Pony Club'.[39] In this way the member will be protected by the general rule of the law of agency set out in **12.10**. In *Rowntrees of London (Builders) Ltd v Screenwriters Club Ltd*[40] it was held that if the committee members want to displace the ordinary inference that the secretary or the steward orders goods on behalf of the club, as opposed to ordering them for his own personal use, evidence must be called by them to rebut the inference.

---

34 (1891) 7 TLR 284.

35 (1892) 9 TLR 73.

36 In other words, it can be surmised that the principals to the contract were the milkman and the members of the sub-committee: see **5.34**(1).

37 *Brandt (H O) Co v H N Morris & Co Ltd* [1917] 2 KB 784 at 793 CA (Viscount Reading CJ) ('when a man signs a contract in his own name he is prima facie a contracting party and liable, and there must be something very strong on the face of the instrument to shew that the liability does not attach to him').

38 *Fred Drughorn Ltd v Rederiaktiebolaget Transatalantic* [1919] AC 203.

39 When acting on behalf of an unincorporated members' club Tom Pearce should, strictly speaking, sign 'for and on behalf of the Committee of the Basset Pony Club' but it is now common for the signatory to state that the agency is on behalf of the club itself : see *R v L and F* [2009] 1 All ER 786, CA, cited in **1.8,** for the modern practice of giving unincorporated associations an informal personality.

40 (1953) 162 EG 352, CA.

12.15 Ratification In an unincorporated members' club a committee member may assume personal liability by ratifying an *unauthorised* contract made by an agent of the club.[41] A contract can only be ratified by the person on whose behalf the contract was purportedly made.[42] For ratification to take place the principal must know all the material circumstances.[43] Ratification may be inferred from silence or acquiescence.[44] Take the case of goods which are ordered by the club's agent without authority but which are used by the club members. Mere use of the goods by the members does not amount to ratification. But once the committee know about the true situation and acquiesce in it, it will have ratified the transaction in question. In an incorporated club ratification of an unauthorised contract by the club will normally take place via a director or the committee. Here ratification will not involve the director or the committee member in any personal liability, subject to (a) what is said about the director's duty in **12.21** and (b) any restriction of the committee's authority contained in the club rules.

12.16 Breach of warranty of authority If a member purports to make a contract on behalf of the club or the committeewhen he has no authority of any sort to make the contract, he will be liable in damages to the other party for breach of warranty of authority if the club or the committee rejects the contract.[45] On the other hand, if the club or the committee ratifies the unauthorised contract, the member will be exonerated from liability.[46] Yet again, if the other party knows or is put on enquiry that the member has no authority and the club or the committee rejects the contract, the member will have no personal liability towards that other party.[47]

4. PROTECTION OF THE COMMITTEE

12.17 It may be seen from **12.4** that the members of the managing committee in an unincorporated members' club are vulnerable to being held personally liable to the club's creditors and proper consideration should be given as to how these members may best be protected. There are various ways of doing this:

41 *Jones v Hope* (1880) 3 TLR 247 (note), CA, at 249 (Cotton LJ) (concerning the liability of the officers in an unincorporated volunteer corps to a wine merchant for goods supplied).

42 *Re Tiedemann & Ledermann Frères* [1899] 2 QB 66.

43 *De Bussche v Alt* (1878) 8 Ch D 286, CA, at 313.

44 *Bank Melli Iran v Barclays Bank DCO* (1951) 2 TLR 1057, at 1063.

45 *Collen v Wright* (1857) 7 E & B 30, affirmed on appeal (1857) 8 E & B 647 (a prime example of judicial law making: see Cockburn CJ's dissenting judgment at 658). The correct measure of damages flowing from this breach of warranty can raise a 'troublesome issue': *Habton Farms v Nimmo* [2003] 3 WLR 633, CA (where the Court of Appeal was divided on the issue of damages).

46 *Jones v Hope* (1880) 3 TLR 247 (note), CA, at 248; *Overton v Hewett* (1886) 3 TLR 246.

47 *Russo-Chinese Bank v Li Yau Sam* [1910] AC 174, PC. And see *Gore-Browne on Companies* (45th edn, 2010), at 8[19].

(1) ***Express exclusion or restriction of liability*** Exclusion or restriction of liability by contract is permissible. The committee can try to limit the liability of the committee members by persuading the other party to the contract to permit an express clause in the contract whereby the committee was only liable to the extent of the club's funds.[48] This might mean that the committee would have to divulge precisely what those funds were and the members as a whole might not look too kindly on such disclosure. Alternatively, the committee can by an express clause seek to exclude or restrict liability generally or to set a maximum limit on the amount of its liability. This may not be acceptable to the other party and in any event may be affected by the provisions of the Unfair Contract Terms Act 1977.[49] Where the other party to the contract enters a contract (a) as a consumer[50] or (b) on the club's 'written standard terms of business',[51] exclusion or restriction of liability (including quantum of loss)[52] on the club's part must satisfy the requirement of reasonableness.[53] It is to be noted that (b) is of considerably wider ambit than (a).

(2) ***Raising subscriptions*** Faced with a shortfall in funds wherewith to carry out the club's activities or to embark on a particular project, it is not only perfectly in order to call a special meeting to raise subscriptions generally or to have a one-off rise in the subscription or to make a levy on the members, but such a remedy is a classic way of overcoming a shortfall.[54] In appropriate cases the club might consider establishing a reserve or sinking fund. This is a specially designated account set aside by the club to meet any unexpected costs that may arise in the future as well as future costs of the upkeep or maintenance or improvement of the club premises.

(3) ***Lien*** If the committee has incurred personal liability by reason of entering into some authorised contract for the benefit of the club the committee will have a lien on the club property to the extent of their liability. The Irish case of *Minnit v Lord Talbot de Malahide*[55] is instructive on this point. The members of the Irish Farmers' Agricultural Club in general meeting authorised the committee to borrow £1,000 for building works to the club premises and for the provision of fittings and furniture. The committee raised the money on the security of guarantees given by certain members of the committee. This course of action was approved by the members in general meeting. The work was carried out and the fittings and furniture were provided. The work and goods were not fully paid for out of club

48 *De Vries v Corner* (1865) 13 LT 636.

49 Unfair Contract Terms Act 1977, ss 1(3)(a) and 3.

50 That is to say, the other party does not make the contract in the course of a business whereas the club does so: Unfair Contract Terms Act 1977, s 12(1). As to whether a club constitutes a business for this purpose, see **12.49**.

51 Unfair Contract Terms Act 1977, s 3(1).

52 Ibid, s 11(4).

53 Ibid, s 11; *Walker v Boyle* [1982] 1 WLR 495.

54 *Flemyng v Hector* (1836) 2 M & W 172, at 183 (Lord Abinger CB).

55 (1876) LR 1 Ir 143.

funds and the club failed, whereupon the guarantees were called upon and honoured. The club property was sold and the committee members were held entitled to reimbursement out of the proceeds of sale by virtue of their lien.[56]

(4) ***Indemnity*** Although it is considered unwise to give the members of the managing committee a blanket indemnity in the rules for any expenditure which they may incur in that capacity, there is nothing untoward or unusual in a more restricted rule which states that the members of the committee, the officers of the club, and the officials of the club shall be indemnified by the club out of club funds against any legal claim made against them in connection with the proper discharge of their duties.[57]

(5) ***Contribution*** Where a member of the committee has paid out moneys in respect of an authorised contract, he is entitled to a contribution from his fellow members of the committee,[58] but he will have no right to an indemnity from the members of the club[59] (in the absence of an express rule conferring an indemnity).

(6) ***Insurance*** Proper consideration should also be given to the obtaining of insurance in relation to all the activities of committee members. A prime example would be the case of *Bradley Egg Farm Ltd v Clifford*[60] where the defendants were the executive council of an unincorporated association called the Lancashire Utility Poultry Society. The Society entered into a contract with the plaintiff to carry out tests on its poultry. Its employee negligently caused damage to the poultry when carrying out the tests and the plaintiff successfully sued the members of the council for substantial damages. Failure to carry insurance in these circumstances would be foolish.

5. WORKING MEN'S CLUBS AND SHOP CLUBS

12.18 These clubs are not legal persons and so the principles set out in **12.2** to **12.17** are equally applicable to them.

---

56 In fact the proceeds of sale were insufficient and the committee members obtained a court order ((1881) LR 7 Ir 407) that they were entitled to an indemnity from the members as to the outstanding balance. This order would not be made today because of the definitive ruling in *Wise v Perpetual Trustee Co Ltd* [1903] AC 139, PC that the member's liability is in the ordinary course of events restricted to his entrance fee and subscriptions.

57 Mr J F Keeler MA BCL (Oxon) in an article entitled 'Contractual Actions for Damages against Unincorporated Bodies' (1971) 34 MLR 615, at p 616, suggests that committee members have an implied indemnity out of club funds for expenses properly incurred; sed quaere.

58 *Earl of Mountcashell v Barber* (1853) 14 CB 53, at 69.

59 *Wise v Perpetual Trustee Co Ltd* [1903] AC 139, PC at 149.

60 [1943] 2 All ER 378.

6. INCORPORATED CLUBS: GENERAL PRINCIPLES OF LIABILITY

12.19 The club itself is a legal person so that on the face of things contractual liability rests with the club itself. Neither the members of the club nor its committee will in the ordinary course of events be personally liable because of the general rule of agency law set out in **12.10** and, indeed, the constitution of the company is obliged to state that the members' liability is appropriately limited.[61] The club needs to understand the categories of an agent's authority set out in **12.11** and the principles of ratification and breach of warranty of authority set out in **12.15** and **12.16**.

12.20 Third party protection and director's liability As stated in **5.46** above, the ultimate control in an incorporated club rests with the directors. A director when acting for the company in contractual matters will be its agent in the same way as a committee member of an unincorporated members' club or a community club. Although a company has its own separate legal personality it has no ability to think or act for itself, so it can only act by resolution of its members in general meeting or by its agents.[62] And so the law of contract has applied adapted rules of agency whereby the company can be contractually bound.[63] Prior to the Companies Act 2006 there were various restrictions on a company's ability to act in a contractual capacity which were generally gathered together under the rubric of 'ultra vires' ('acting beyond its powers') and which meant that persons dealing with the company had to be on their guard as to whether they were entering into a valid contract with the company. This potential hazard was reduced by Parliament in 1985 and 1989, and Part 4 of the Companies Act 2006 (ss 39–52) carries that process further. The validity of a company's acts is not to be questioned on the ground of lack of capacity because of anything in the company's constitution. Any third party dealing with the company in good faith need not concern himself about whether the company is acting within its constitution. In other words, the power of the directors to bind the company is not to be constrained by the company's constitution. An exception to this rule relates to charities. Sections 39 and 40 (company's capacity and power of directors to bind company) do not apply to the transactions carried out by incorporated charities except where the third party either (a) did not know the company was a charity or (b) if he did, he gave full consideration for the transaction and did not know that the transaction was not permitted by the company's constitution or that it was beyond the powers of its directors.[64]

---

61 See **3.25**.

62 *Ferguson v Wilson* (1866–67) 2 Ch App 77, at 89.

63 See *Gore-Browne on Companies* (45th edn, 2010), at 7A[1] and chapter 8.

64 Companies Act 2006, s 42(1).

12.21 The director is under a legal duty to abide by the company's constitution.[65] This means that the director is required to abide by any restrictions set out in the constitution (that is, set out in the articles, which now include the old-style memorandum of association). For example, an article might state that a director may not enter into a contract on behalf of the company where the price payable by the company exceeds £50,000 without the prior consent of the members being given in general meeting. Suppose a director, without obtaining such consent, enters into a contract on behalf of the company with a third party where the price payable by the company is £75,000. This would normally have two consequences: (a) the company will be bound by the contract and (b) if the director's breach of duty causes the company loss or damage, he may find himself personally liable to make good the loss or damage.[66]

12.22 **Contract with non-existent company** A contract which purports to be made by or on behalf of a company at a time when the company has not been formed, has effect (subject to any agreement to the contrary) as one made with the person purporting to act for the company or as agent for it, and he is personally liable on the contract accordingly.[67] Problems can sometimes arise here on the formation of clubs.[68] In *Phonogram Ltd v Lane*[69] the court held that the person purporting to act for the company was liable personally, even though all parties were aware at the relevant time that no company was then in existence.

7. PROTECTION OF THE DIRECTOR

12.23 There are various ways in which a director may be relieved from liability which would otherwise fall on him for breach of duty:

(1) ***Insurance*** Any provision which purports to exempt a director of a company from liability that would otherwise attach to him in connection with any negligence, default, breach of duty or breach of trust in relation to the company is void.[70] But the company is permitted to purchase and maintain for the director's benefit insurance

---

65 Ibid, s 171.

66 See, e g Companies Act 2006, s 40(5).

67 Ibid, s 51(1).

68 See *Hanuman v Guyanese Association for Racial Unity and Democracy* (unreported) 13 June 1996, cited in **1.12**.

69 [1982] QB 938.

70 Companies Act 2006, s 232(1).

against such liability in relation to the company itself[71] and, equally important, to provide an indemnity against such liability in relation to third parties.[72]

(2) ***Ratification by ordinary resolution*** Some breaches of duty can be overlooked through the director's conduct being disclosed to the members in general meeting and ratified by the passing of an ordinary resolution. It is not always easy to draw the line as to what is ratifiable in this manner. Examples of ratifiable conduct are failing to disclose an interest in a contract to which the company is a party;[73] obtaining a secret profit in circumstances where there was no misappropriation or misapplication of company property;[74] and breach of the duties of skill and care.[75] On the other hand, breaches involving a failure of honesty of the director's part,[76] or involving a fraud on or oppression of the minority of shareholders[77] are not capable of being excused by this route.

(3) ***Ratification by the consent of all members*** The approval of the director's conduct by every member of the company, either before or after the breach of duty, will relieve the director in all cases from liability provided that the breach is not ultra vires the company and does not involve a fraud on its creditors.[78]

(4) ***Release by the court*** Under s 1157 of the Companies Act 2006 a director may be relieved from liability in certain defined circumstances. What the director has to prove is (1) that he acted honestly, (2) that he acted reasonably, and (3) that he ought fairly to be excused from liability. The third element involves the discretion of the court being exercised in the director's favour.[79] Any relief granted will be on such terms as the court thinks fit.

8. COMMUNITY CLUBS

12.24 The club itself is a legal person and to this extent its position is akin to that of an incorporated club when it comes to liability in contract to third parties. Neither the members of the club nor its committee will in the ordinary course of events be personally liable because of the general rule of agency law set out in **12.10**. The club needs to understand the categories of an agent's authority set out in **12.11** and the principles of ratification and

---

71 Ibid, s 233.

72 Ibid, s 234. This indemnity does not cover any fine imposed on the director or his legal costs where the director is convicted of a criminal offence: s 234(3).

73 *North-West Transportation Co v Beatty* [1902] AC 83.

74 *Regal (Hastings) Ltd v Gulliver* [1967] 2 AC 134 (Note), at 150 (case decided in 1941).

75 *Pavlides v Jensen* [1956] Ch 565, at 576.

76 *Mason v Harris* (1879) 11 Ch D 97, CA.

77 *Cook v Deeks* [1916] 1 AC 554, PC.

78 Companies Act 2006, s 239(6)(a); *Gore-Browne on Companies* (45th edn, 2010), at 17[3].

79 *Re J Franklin & Son Ltd* [1937] 4 All ER 43 in relation to an earlier enactment in identical terms.

breach of warranty of authority set out in **12.15** and **12.16**. The committee remains under a duty to observe any limitation on its powers flowing from the club's rules.[80] Where a third party deals in good faith with the club, the power of the committee to bind the club, or to authorise others to do so, shall be deemed to be free of any limitation under the club rules.[81] Finally, these clubs have no directors but officers and a committee instead,[82] so none of the statutory regime applicable to company directors is of relevance to these clubs. One further point needs to be mentioned. There is no equivalent of s 51 of the Companies Act 2006 which is applicable to community clubs (as to which section, see **12.22**). This means that, as with an unincorporated members' club,[83] a person purporting to deal contractually with a community club *before* its incorporation will have no remedy for goods supplied or services rendered, unless he can establish some collateral contract with a person connected with the club.[84]

9. PROPRIETARY CLUBS

12.25 Here any contract touching or concerning the club will be the liability of the proprietor insofar as third parties are involved, such as suppliers of goods to the club. An individual member of the club might, however, become personally liable if by some independent contract he became liable to the third party, such as signing a guarantee in favour of the proprietor's creditor, but nothing less than an independent contract will suffice to make the club member liable for the contractual affairs of the proprietor.

---

80 Co-operative and Community Benefit Societies and Credit Unions Act 1965, s 7A(3), added by Co-operative and Community Benefit Societies Act 2003, s 3.

81 Co-operative and Community Benefit Societies and Credit Unions Act 1965, s 7B(1), added as aforesaid.

82 'Officer' is defined as any treasurer, secretary, member of the committee, manager or servant other than a servant appointed by the committee and excludes an auditor: Co-operative and Community Benefit Societies and Credit Unions Act 1968, s 74, Sch 1.

83 See *Hanuman's* case quoted in footnote 68 above.

84 *Shanklin Pier Ltd v Detel Products Ltd* [1951] 2 KB 854. It is conceivable that in certain circumstances a claim may lie in unjust enrichment: *Chitty on Contracts* (30th edn, 2008), at 29-080.

PART B

TORTS

10. INTRODUCTION

12.26 A tort is a civil wrong (not arising in contract) in respect of which an action for damages or compensation lies. A club's liability in tort may arise either through the activities of its members or by virtue of its occupation or ownership of club premises. We are here dealing with situations where the club's activities impinge on the lives or well-being of third parties who are not members of the club. Any managing committee will or should know, often because of complaints, whether the activities of its members or the state of repair of the club property carry the risk of adversely affecting other people's well-being or enjoyment of life. As with agency in the law of contract, so here the doctrine of vicarious liability is an important factor which committees need to understand.

11. UNINCORPORATED MEMBERS' CLUBS: GENERAL PRINCIPLES OF LIABILITY

12.27 General propositions There are three general propositions to remember when considering a member's tortious liability to third parties:[85]

(1) the club is not a legal person;[86]
(2) the member, if he is the actual tortfeasor, will potentially be personally liable to the injured or aggrieved party;[87]
(3) the managing committee, as the managers and controllers of the club's affairs, will potentially be vicariously liable for the acts or omissions of those persons (whether employees or members of the club) who were acting in the course of their employment or acting in a manner authorised by the committee, and the members of the committee may thus become personally liable for the tort.[88]

---

85 The converse situation, namely, pursuing the club's remedy in tort, is discussed in terms of procedure only, at **18.3**.

86 *Conservative and Unionist Central Office v Burrell* [1982] 1 WLR 522, CA, at 527. Any judgment obtained against such a club will be set aside: *London Association for the Protection of Trade v Greenlands Ltd* [1916] 2 AC 15, at 20.

87 This includes authorising the tortious act as well as committing it: *Baker v Jones* [1954] 1 WLR 1005, at 1011).

88 *Jones v Northampton Borough Council* [1990] Times LR 387, CA, at 388.

12.28 Vicarious liability[89] A person is liable not only for the torts committed by himself but also for those which he has authorised or ratified.[90] Authorisation or ratification is not the same thing as vicarious liability, which has different parameters. In *Lister v Hesley Hall Ltd*[91] Lord Millett, at 243, said: 'Vicarious liability is a species of strict liability. It is not premised on any culpable act or omission on the part of the employer; an employer who is not personally at fault is made legally answerable for the fault of the employee'. The two most important classes of person for whose torts the managing committee may be vicariously liable are employees and independent contractors. As a generalisation, there is substantially less vicarious liability in relation to independent contractors as compared with employees, so it is important to ascertain into which category a person falls when he is retained or employed by the club.

12.29 Club's liability for torts of employee The exact nature of the relationship that exists between the members of the club and its employees is unclear. It is probably true to say that no contractual relationship exists because of the members' monetary liability being restricted to their entrance fees and subscriptions.[92] The position is almost certainly different in relation to the managing committee since they are in control of the club's affairs. However, being in control of the club's affairs is not the same thing as being in control of a person's work, which is one of the indicia that a person is an employee rather than an independent contractor.[93] The modern approach of the courts is to adopt a 'multiple' test where all aspects of the relationship are assessed before coming to the conclusion that a person is an employee.[94] In *Mattis v Pollock (trading as Flamingos Nightclub)*[95] (where a club owner was held liable for the violent acts of assault of his doorman) the Court of Appeal stated that the established test for vicarious liability required a broad approach: Was the employee's action so closely connected with what the employer authorised or expected of him in the performance of his employment that it would be fair and just to hold the employer vicariously liable for the damage sustained as a result of the employee's act?

12.30 Club's liability for torts of independent contractor The general rule is that if a person employs an independent contractor to do work on his

89 For the topic of vicarious liability generally, see *Clerk and Lindsell on Torts*, (20th edn, 2010), chapter 6.

90 *Ellis v Sheffield Gas Consumer's Co* (1853) 2 E & B 767.

91 [2002] 1 AC 215.

92 See *Clerk and Lindsell on Torts*, op cit, at 6-21. But see *Campbell v Thompson and Shill* [1953] 2 WLR 656 discussed at **15.4**.

93 *Mersey Docks and Harbour Board v Coggins and Griffith (London) Ltd* [1947] AC 1, at 17 (Lord Porter).

94 *Ready Mixed Concrete (South East) v Minister of Pensions and National Insurance* [1968] 2 QB 497, at 516; *Market Investigations Ltd v Minister of Social Security* [1969] 2 QB 173, at 185 where Cooke J posed a rule-of-thumb guide: 'Is the worker in business on his own account?' If he is, he will not be an employee.

95 [2003] 1 WLR 2158.

behalf, the employer is not responsible for any tort committed by the contractor or by the contractor's employees in the course of the execution of the work.[96] There are exceptions: if the law imposes a strict or absolute duty on the employer, the duty is said to be non-delegable and the employer will be liable for the torts committed by his independent contractor. Examples are statutory duties[97] or common law duties such as the duty to prevent the escape of fire.[98] (The common law categories of non-delegable duties are said to be not yet closed).[99] Another exception is where the employer engages an independent contractor to do work which is inherently dangerous or which involves a special risk of damage. Here the employer is under an absolute duty to take care and will be liable for the negligence or nuisance of his contractor.[100]

12.31 A further exception is where the defendant employs an independent contractor but is in breach of a *personal* duty to take care towards others. The case of *Brown v Lewis*[101] provides an interesting illustration of a committee's liability. The committee of the Blackburn Rovers Football Club had the power and duty to provide a spectators' stand. It needed repairing and the committee employed a workman to repair it. The stand was negligently repaired and collapsed, injuring the plaintiff. Although the law report is silent on the point, it would appear that the workman was an independent contractor. The committee was held liable, not because of the negligently carried out work, but because the committee had negligently chosen an incompetent person to carry out the work. This is therefore not a case of vicarious liability but a situation where the committee was held liable for breach of a personal duty of care to a third party.[102]

---

96 *D & F Estates Ltd v Church Commissioners for England* [1989] AC 177, at 208 (Lord Bridge).

97 *Gray v Pullen* (1864) 5 B & S 970 (defendant had statutory power to lay drains and a duty to reinstate the road after the drains were laid; the independent contractors negligently reinstated the road, for which the defendant was held liable).

98 *Balfour v Barty-King* [1957] 1 QB 496.

99 See *Clerk and Lindsell on Torts*, (20th edn, 2010), at 6–56.

100 *Honeywill & Stein Ltd v Larkin Bros Ltd* [1934] 1 KB 191 (negligence: dangerous flash photography used by contractor); *Matania v National Provincial Bank Ltd* [1936] 2 All ER 633, CA (nuisance: escape of dust and noise caused by building contractor carrying out structural alterations).

101 (1892) 12 TLR 455.

102 See two old cases in point: *Pinn v Rew* (1916) 32 TLR 451 (defendant farmer held *personally* liable for injury caused to a person on the highway by one of his animals being driven to his farm where he employed only one drover as an independent contractor when the situation plainly called for more than one drover), i e a culpable omission; and *M'Laughlin v Pryor* (1842) 4 M & G 48 (defendant held *personally* liable for injury caused to a passenger in a pony gig where he had hired a coach and four horses driven by two postillions as independent contractors but then gave them instructions which caused a collision with the gig), i e a culpable commission.

12. NEGLIGENCE, NUISANCE AND OTHER TORTS

12.32 Negligence and nuisance The torts which are most likely to be of concern to a club are negligence and nuisance. Negligence is the tort of widest application because it is based on conduct rather than the protection of a particular interest such as a right of way. As was said by Lord Macmillan in the celebrated case of *Donoghue v Stevenson*[103] (the snail-in-the-bottle-of-ginger-beer case), at 619, 'the categories of negligence are never closed'. In the same case Lord Atkin, at 580, made an oft-repeated statement of principle which is still applicable today:

> 'The rule that you are to love your neighbour becomes in law, you must not injure your neighbour; and the lawyer's question, who is my neighbour? receives a restricted reply. You must take reasonable care to avoid acts or omissions which you can reasonably foresee would be likely to injure your neighbour.'

To this principle, which involves the concepts of proximity and foreseeability, is now added a caveat that the court also has to be satisfied that the imposition of a duty of care must be fair, just and reasonable.[104] A further complication arises when a defendant is sued for causing pure economic loss; here the defendant's duty of care is dependent on his voluntary assumption of responsibility.[105]

12.33 On the other hand, the tort of nuisance is based on the interference by one occupier with the right in or enjoyment of land occupied by someone else. Two points should be noted: first, there must be an *escape* from the defendant's land to the claimant's land and, secondly, it is a tort directed to the protection of interests in land so that a claim for death or personal injuries arguably falls outside the scope of this tort.[106] The escape in question may be noise[107] or unpleasant smells,[108] or may simply be the causing of crowds to collect on your own land so that they spill over on to neighbouring land.[109] It is said to be a tort of strict liability but the exact

---

103 [1932] AC 562.

104 *Caparo Industries plc v Dickman* [1990] 2 AC 605, at 617.

105 *Customs & Excise Commissioners v Barclays Bank plc* [2007] 1 AC 181 (no duty of care owed by the bank to the claimant who had obtained a freezing injunction against the customers' bank accounts and where the bank, after receiving notice of the injunction, negligently permitted the customers to withdraw large sums of money from the accounts).

106 *Transco plc v Stockport Metropolitan Borough Council* [2004] 2 AC 1, at 10 (Lord Bingham).

107 *Bellamy v Wells* [1890] 60 LJ Ch 156 (the proprietary Pelican Club, with some 1,200 members, held liable to nearby residents for noisy crowds in the street emanating from the club which had been attracted by the boxing contests frequently held on the club premises late at night); *Soltau v De Held* (1851) 2 Sim (NS) 133 (ringing of church bells); *Hawley v Steele* (1877) 6 Ch D 521 (use of common land for rifle practice and firing); *Dunton v Dover* (1978) 76 LGR 87 (playground noise).

108 *Adams v Ursell* [1913] 1 Ch 269 (fried fish shop).

109 *Walker v Brewster* (1867) LR 5 Eq 25 (crowds gathered on the plaintiff's land caused by the

boundary between nuisance and negligence is now blurred because the modern tendency is to assimilate the two torts.[110]

12.34 Examples The situation is best understood through the medium of examples:

(1) An intriguing case, from a legal point of view, is *Miller v Jackson*.[111] The Lintz Cricket Club, an unincorporated members' club, in County Durham had been established about 1905. In about 1972 some new houses were lawfully built whose gardens abutted the cricket field. Cricket balls were hit into the gardens by batsmen. The club installed a high fence and then a higher fence but still eight or nine balls a year landed in the gardens or on the houses themselves. Mrs Miller sued the members of the club in negligence and nuisance and at first instance obtained an injunction to prevent cricket being played and damages as compensation. On appeal the presiding judge, Lord Denning MR, held that there was negligence sounding in damages but that the established playing of cricket on this particular ground did not constitute a nuisance and he said that no injunction should be granted because an injunction was not an available remedy in negligence; the second judge, Lord Justice Lane, held that there was both negligence and nuisance sounding in damages and that the injunction should continue; and the third judge, Lord Justice Cumming-Bruce, held that there was negligence and nuisance sounding in damages but that no injunction should be granted as a matter of discretion. So Mrs Miller got £400 and the injunction was discharged. An interesting point is that Mrs Miller came to the nuisance but this did not disqualify her from complaining about the club's activities,[112] although this fact could be taken into account when it came to the question of remedy.[113]

(2) The above case should be contrasted with *Bolton v Stone*[114] where Miss Stone had been hit on the head and injured by a cricket ball driven out of the ground of the Cheetham Cricket Club, an unincorporated members' club in Manchester, when she had just stepped out from her garden gate on to the highway. The evidence was that balls had been hit out of the ground some six times in 28 years. Miss Bolton sued the members of the club in negligence and nuisance. The risk of harm was foreseeable but the chances were very small and so the club argued that it was reasonable to ignore the risk. Miss Bolton

---

defendant holding fêtes on his neighbouring property); *Lyons, Son & Co v Gulliver* [1914] 1 Ch 631, CA (the defendant's theatre crowds obstructing highway access to plaintiff's nearby trading premises).

110 *British Road Services Ltd v Slater* [1964] 1 WLR 498, at 504 (Lord Parker CJ); *Goldman v Hargrave* [1967] 1 AC 645, at 657 (Lord Wilberforce). A recent example of this trend is the case of *Delaware Mansions Ltd v Westminster City Council* [2001] 1 AC 321: see **12.43**.

111 [1977] QB 966.

112 *Sturges v Bridgman* (1879) 11 Ch D 852.

113 *Kennaway v Thompson* [1981] QB 88, CA, at 91.

114 [1950] 1 KB 201, CA and [1951] AC 850.

won in the Court of Appeal on the basis that all the members of the club were liable in negligence as occupiers of the ground in failing to prevent balls being hit out the ground. The House of Lords allowed the appeal on the quite different basis that the committee of the club was not negligent in failing to take precautions to prevent such an accident.[115] Lord Reid in the case of *The Wagon Mound (No 2)*[116] attempted to clarify the position:

> 'What that decision [*Bolton v Stone*] decided was to recognise and give effect to the qualification that it is justifiable not to take steps to eliminate a real risk if it is small and if the circumstances are such that a reasonable man, careful of the safety of his neighbour, would think it right to neglect it.'

We regret that neither case gives clear guidance on a matter of practical importance to many clubs.

12.35 Further examples are:

(1) In *Castle v St Augustine's Links Ltd*[117] the plaintiff motorist's eye was seriously injured by a piece of glass from his windscreen which had been hit by a golf ball driven on to a busy highway from an adjoining golf links (such escape being a common occurrence) and he recovered damages in nuisance against the golf club.

(2) In *Hilder v Associated Portland Cement Manufacturers Ltd*[118] the defendant owned and occupied some grassland by its factory and allowed local children to play there. The boundary of this land was a low brick wall. Adjoining the land was a busy highway. A child kicked a ball over the wall which caused a rider to fall off his motorcycle and be killed. The defendant was held liable in negligence to the motorcyclist's widow.

(3) In the New Zealand case of *Evans v Waitemata District Pony Club*[119] all the club members were held liable in negligence for injuries caused to some paying spectators. The club had failed to provide a suitable number of convenient tethering places for the horses, and when two horses became frightened they broke free from their tether and started galloping wildly around the paddock.

---

115 See also the interesting argument of Miss Stone's counsel at [1951] AC 855, which relied on the strict variety of nuisance called *Rylands v Fletcher* liability (1868) LR 3 HL 330, but their lordships dismissed this argument out of hand, as Lord Denning MR observed in *Miller v Jackson*, at 979. We harbour some doubts as to the rightness of this summary dismissal.

116 [1967] 1 AC 617, at 641.

117 (1922) 38 TLR 615.

118 [1961] 1 WLR 1434.

119 [1972] NZLR 773.

(4) In *Kennaway v Thompson*[120] all the members of the Cotswold Motor Boat Racing Club were held liable in nuisance to a lakeside house owner in respect of their powerful and noisy racing boats on Whelford Lake.

(5) In *Tetley v Chitty*[121] all the members of the Medway Kart Club were held liable in nuisance for causing excessive noise to local residents from go-kart racing on Temple Marsh in Rochester, and the Medway Borough Council was held equally liable in nuisance because as landlord it had persisted in permitting the go-kart racing despite being warned about the noise nuisance.

(6) On the other hand, in *Blake v Galloway*[122] the defendant was held not liable in negligence for the claimant's serious eye injury caused by the throwing of a piece of tree bark during good-natured and high-spirited horseplay.[123] This was because of the tacit understanding that the claimant impliedly consented to a risk of a blow to any part of his body, provided the object was thrown 'without negligence and without intent to cause injury'.[124] In other words, there is still a duty of care in horseplay but to found liability the claimant has to prove 'recklessness or a very high degree of carelessness'.[125]

12.36 Access to club and nuisance It may be the case that the club has a right of way which is used as a means of access to the club. If the right is created by grant, the class of persons who are entitled to use it may be expressly defined or limited in the terms of the deed; but a grant of this nature must be construed, not strictly, but in accordance with the intention of the parties. Thus in *Baxendale v North Lambeth Liberal and Radical Club*[126] the court held that the right of way granted to the club was exercisable by all persons lawfully going to and from the club, which included the members of the club, the associate members, tradespeople and employees of the club, and that this user was reasonable. If there is an excessive use of the right of way, however, it may become an actionable nuisance.

12.37 Occupier's liability At common law an occupier's liability was based on the tort of negligence. In 1957 the Occupiers' Liability Act was passed whereby a 'common duty of care' was substituted for the common law rules.[127] Section 2 of the Act states:

---

120 [1981] QB 88, CA.
121 [1986] 1 All ER 663.
122 [2004] 1 WLR 2844, CA.
123 A friendly snowball fight would come into this category.
124 At [24] (Dyson LJ).
125 At [16] (Dyson LJ).
126 [1902] 2 Ch 427.
127 Occupiers' Liability Act 1957, s 1(1).

(1) An occupier of premises owes the same duty, the 'common duty of care', to all his visitors, except insofar as he is free to and does extend, restrict, modify or exclude his duty to any visitors by agreement or otherwise.
(2) The common duty of care is a duty to take such care to see that the visitor will be reasonably safe in using the premises for the purposes for which he is invited or permitted by the occupier to be there.

12.38 Who is an occupier The Act does not define an occupier and so the pre-1957 rules govern this point.[128] It includes owner-occupiers[129] and lessees[130] and other persons provided they have sufficient control over the premises to ensure their safety and to appreciate that a failure on their part to use care may result in injury to a person coming on them.[131] If the club were to hire out its premises for a particular occasion to a third party we consider that it would still remain the occupier for the purposes of the Act although, in the absence of an express term in the hiring, the club does not warrant the premises are suitable for the purpose for which they are hired.[132] Conversely, we consider that the club would not become the occupier of premises which it hired from someone else for its own club activities.

12.39 An unincorporated members' club cannot be held liable as occupier because it is not a legal person.[133] If the club premises are vested in trustees, it is they who will be treated as occupiers and who will be the defendants to any action.[134] But what happens in the case of a club which has no trustees but which is as a matter of fact in occupation of premises? The members as a whole may be considered the occupiers,[135] and Lord Justice Hutchison in *Hibernian Dance Club v Murray*[136] stated that there was a strong arguable basis for joining committee members of an unincorporated member's club in a representative capacity (ie on behalf of all the members) in a personal injuries claim based on occupiers' liability. But this basis raises many questions. If the whole membership is to be treated as the occupier, does this include the full member living permanently overseas in New York? If yes, this is bizarre. If no, would this member count temporarily as an occupier when he was staying at the club in England and a visitor was injured on the club premises? What about a member who lives in England but who is posted abroad for a 2-year tour of duty in Buenos Aires? Does he

---

[128] *Clerk and Lindsell on Torts* (20th edn, 2010) at 12–08.
[129] Ibid, 12–09.
[130] *Wheat v E Lacon & Co Ltd* [1966] AC 552, per Lord Denning at 577–579, but it excludes the landlord even if he has undertaken the obligation to repair. The landlord, however, may have other duties under the Defective Premises Act 1972: see **14.30**.
[131] See *Wheats'* case, above, at 579.
[132] *Wheeler v Trustees of St Mary's Hall, Chislehurst* (1989) *The Times*, October 10.
[133] *Verrall v Hackney Borough Council* [1983] QB 445, CA, at 461.
[134] *Clerk and Lindsell on Torts*, op cit, at 12–12.
[135] *Bolton v Stone* [1950] 1 KB 201, CA discussed in **12.34**(2).
[136] [1997] PIQR 46, at 55.

remain an occupier for that period? Or take another example. The MCC has some 18,000 full members and the club owns Lord's Cricket Ground.[137] Assuming there were no trustees, can it really be said that the ground is occupied by all 18,000 members? Given these vagaries and bearing in mind the House of Lord's dictum about the need for persons with sufficient control to ensure safety,[138] we submit that there is only one feasible answer, namely, that the occupation of club premises goes hand-in-hand with control of the club's affairs, and therefore the members of the committee in the ordinary course of events will be the occupiers in an unincorporated members' club.[139]

12.40 Who is a visitor The duty of care is owed to visitors but the Occupiers' Liability Act 1957 does not define a visitor and so the pre-1957 rules govern this point too. Visitors are those who would have been treated as invitees or licensees at common law. Permission to enter the club premises may be express or implied. Permission to enter may be given by an employee of the occupier but what if the employee had no authority to give permission to enter or, worse still, gave permission contrary to his instructions? The answer lies in the application of the rules relating to vicarious liability.[140] One curious point should be noted. An independent contractor (eg a builder) may be an occupier of club premises as well as the club itself.[141] Suppose the builder contrary to the club's instructions invites a person on to the premises who is then injured. Is that person a visitor or trespasser? The answer is that he will be a trespasser vis-à-vis the club but a visitor vis-à-vis the builder and liability will be decided accordingly.[142]

12.41 Whether a visitor remains a lawful visitor on club premises for the entirety of his stay can raise nice points of argument. A licence to enter is often a restricted one, that is, limited to those parts which it may be reasonably supposed the visitor will go. A visitor who strays into other parts of the club, say the kitchen, and is injured there may find himself without remedy,[143] although an involuntary or accidental straying will not convert a lawful visitor into a trespasser.[144] Further, a visit to a club would normally include an invitation to use the lavatory and a visitor remains a lawful visitor if he strays whilst making a reasonable search for it.[145] A

---

137 See **1.7**.

138 See **12.38**.

139 *Pace Clerk and Lindsell on Torts*, op cit, at 12–12 which states that the committee members in an unincorporated members' club do not have any liability as occupiers, citing in support *Robertson v Ridley* [1989] 1 WLR 872, CA, but the case is very weak authority for this proposition: see **5.41**.

140 See **12.28**.

141 *Wheat v E Lacon & Co Ltd* [1966] AC 552; *AMF International Ltd v Magnet Bowling Ltd* [1968] 1 WLR 1028, at 1052.

142 *Ferguson v Welsh* [1987] 1 WLR 1553.

143 *Lee v Luper* [1936] 3 All ER 817; *Mason v Langford* (1888) 4 TLR 407.

144 *Braithwaite v South Durham Steel Co* [1958] 1 WLR 986.

145 *Gould v McAuliffe* [1941] 2 All ER 527.

licence to enter can always be revoked, but a visitor does not become a trespasser until he has had a reasonable time in which to leave.[146]

12.42 Trespassers At common law a trespasser on to other people's property did so at his own risk.[147] But trespassers are not all malevolent and a rambler or a child might innocently wander on to someone's land and injure himself. So in 1984 another Occupiers' Liability Act was passed whereby a limited statutory duty of care replaced the common law rules. An occupier owes a duty of care to trespassers if (a) he is aware of any danger on his property or has reasonable grounds to believe it exists, (b) he knows or has reasonable grounds to believe that trespassers may be in the vicinity of the danger, and (c) the danger poses a risk against which he may reasonably be expected to offer some protection.[148]

12.43 Land and buildings adjoining highways An occupier of land and buildings which adjoin or are close to a highway has an obligation not to use his land, or to allow his land or buildings to get into such a condition, so as to amount to a nuisance.[149] Thus in *Tarry v Ashton*[150] the occupier of a building was held liable in nuisance when the lamp attached to the building and overhanging the pavement fell down and injured a passer-by. A tree on the occupier's land is not a nuisance merely because its branches overhang the highway,[151] but if the overhanging branches hinder or obstruct the reasonable use of the highway, this will be a nuisance.[152] The club may also be liable in nuisance for damage caused to neighbouring property by the encroaching roots of its tree; the principle here 'can be summed up in the proposition that, where there is a continuing nuisance of which the defendant knew or ought to have known, reasonable remedial expenditure may be recovered by the owner who has had to incur it'.[153]

12.44 Injuries at sport Many clubs are sports clubs whose activities include the playing of physically competitive sports such as rugby football. These activities should command the special attention of managing committees (and of course the attention of the governing bodies of the

---

146 *Robson v Hallett* [1967] 2 QB 939. And see *Stone v Taffe* [1974] 1 WLR 1575, CA.

147 *Robert Adie & Sons (Collieries) Ltd v Dumbrek* [1929] AC 358 (defendant had no liability to trespassing child killed by unguarded machinery). But see *British Railways Board v Herrington* [1972] AC 877 (where the House of Lords held that landowners did in fact owe a limited duty of care to trespassers).

148 Occupiers' Liability Act 1984, s 1(3). See the trio of trespassing swimmers' cases: *Ratcliff v McConnell* [1999] 1 WLR 670; *Donoghue v Folkestone Properties Ltd* [2003] QB 1008, CA; and *Tomlinson v Congleton Borough Council* [2003] 3 WLR 705, HL.

149 Eg see the cases of *Castle*, *Kennaway* and *Tetley* cited in **12.35**.

150 (1875–76) 1 QBD 314.

151 *Noble v Harrison* [1926] KB 332.

152 *Hale v Hants and Dorset Motor Services* [1947] 2 All ER 628.

153 *Delaware Mansions Ltd v Westminster City Council* [2002] 1 AC 321, at 335 (Lord Cooke of Thorndon).

sports in question). The sports rules will be framed so as to minimise the element of danger and the risk of physical injury. In *Vowles v Evans*[154] the claimant was an amateur rugby player with the Llanharan Rugby Football Club; he was playing in a match as hooker when the scrum collapsed, causing him serious injuries which rendered him paraplegic.[155] He sued the referee, the Welsh Rugby Union (who conceded they were vicariously liable for the referee whom they had appointed) and the chairman and secretary of his club. The referee and the Union were found guilty of negligence, but not the club. The Court of Appeal, upholding the judge, approved, at 1615, the general statement of law put forward by Gleeson CJ in an Australian case also involving rugby football, *Agar v Hyde*,[156] as follows:

> 'After all, opposing players can already sue each other for intentionally and negligently inflicted injuries;[157] they can sue the referee for negligent failure to enforce the rules; and the sports administrator that dons the mantle of an occupier assumes well established duties of care towards players, spectators and (in the case of golf clubs) neighbours. A duty of care is not negated merely because participation in the sport is voluntary.'

12.45 In *Smoldon v Whitworth*,[158] another case of an injured hooker, the Court of Appeal explained the nature of the referee's duty to the players; Lord Bingham of Cornhill CJ stated, at 138:

> 'The level of care required is that which is appropriate in all the circumstances, and the circumstances are of crucial importance. Full account must be taken of the factual context in which a referee exercises his functions, and he could not be properly held liable for errors of judgment, oversights or lapses of which any referee might be guilty in the context of a fast-moving and vigorous contest. The threshold of liability is a high one. It will not be easily crossed.'

The important message of the above cases is that clubs should make sure that referees and umpires who control their games and matches are properly trained, graded and appointed, and also properly insured in respect of their activities.

12.46 As regards the players themselves, the important message for the club is that it should instil into its membership a desire to win, but not to win at all costs, and club rules should be framed to cater for unacceptable

---

154 [2003] 1 WLR 1607, CA.

155 His primary complaint against the referee was his failure to insist on non-contestable scrummages on finding that there was no specialist prop forward to replace an injured prop forward.

156 (2000) 201 CLR 552.

157 *Condon v Basi* [1985] 1 WLR 866, CA.

158 [1997] PIQR 133.

behaviour in a game or competition. In contact sports the players consent to accidental injury, even if perhaps it causes serious injury, but players do not consent to deliberate or recklessly caused injury,[159] which may justifiably result in disciplinary action being taken by the club against the offending player.

12.47 Safety of spectators Apart from the question of the occupiers' liability[160] and the question of the safety of players[161], there is the allied question of spectators' safety which should command the attention of managing committees. One starts off with the proposition that spectators who come to watch sports or competitions will appreciate that watching may involve a risk that they may be injured. Although it may not be possible to eradicate every element of danger, spectators are entitled to assume that the club in permitting spectators has given proper thought to their safety. In *Hall v Brooklands Auto Racing Club*[162] the spectator-plaintiff was injured when two cars, travelling at some 100mph, nudged one another and caused one vehicle to somersault and fall into the spectators' enclosure. There was nothing wrong with the track or the barriers and no accident like it had happened in the 23 years of the existence of the defendant club owner. The plaintiff lost his action in negligence against the club. Likewise, in *Wooldridge v Sumner*[163] the spectator-plaintiff lost his action in negligence against the horseman of experience and skill in respect of injuries suffered when his galloping horse deviated from the course and knocked down the plaintiff.[164] In that case Lord Justice Sellers at 56 said:

> 'But provided the competition or game is being performed within the rules and the requirement of the sport and by a person of adequate skill and competence the spectator does not expect his safety to be regarded by a participant.'

That principle was expressed by Lord Justice Diplock in the same case at 68 as follows:

> 'A person attending a game or competition takes the risk of any damage caused to him by any act of a participant done in the course of and for the purpose of the game or competition notwithstanding that

---

159 *R v Barnes* [2005] 1 WLR 910, CCA; *R v Brown* [1994] 1 AC 212, at 262 and 265 (Lord Mustill). Boxing is an exception to the rule that it is unlawful to inflict *intentional* harm on one's opponent.

160 See **12.37**.

161 See **12.44**.

162 [1933] 1 KB 205, CA.

163 [1963] 2 QB 43, CA.

164 The plaintiff had also unsuccessfully sued the British Horse Society under the Occupier's Liability Act 1957.

such act may involve an error of judgment or a lapse of skill, unless the participant's conduct is such as to evince a reckless disregard of the spectator's safety.'[165]

Obtaining insurance to guard against the risk of injury to spectators is also sensible; the risk of injury may be small but the potential damages may be great and the smallness of the risk will no doubt be reflected in the amount of the insurance premium.

12.48 Exclusion of liability It will be recalled from **12.37** that an occupier can exclude or restrict his liability to his visitors 'by agreement or otherwise'. A suitably worded disclaimer of liability in an appropriate place or document, whereby the occupier gives explicit warning of a danger, may suffice in discharging the occupier's duty of care.[166] Exclusion of liability for negligence is permissible but may be subject to the restrictions set out in the Unfair Contract Terms Act 1977.[167] Business occupiers are prohibited from excluding or restricting their liability (including quantum of loss)[168] for death or personal injury[169] and can only exclude or restrict their liability for damage to a visitor's property if the contract or the notice satisfies the requirement of reasonableness.[170] Residential or private occupiers are exempt from these provisions, save where the visitor contracts on the occupier's 'written standard terms of business': here any exclusion or restriction of liability (including quantum of loss)[171] must satisfy the requirement of reasonableness.[172]

12.49 Whether a club is a business occupier may not always be an easy question to answer. The Act does not define what is a business. A members' club for landlord and tenant purposes carries on a business[173] but does not do so generally. On the other hand, a club could be carrying on a business in its role of providing goods or services to members of the public, for example, a railway preservation society, which is a members' club and which carries many members of the public for payment on its trains, would

---

165 See also *Wilks v Cheltenham Homeguard Motor Cycle and Light Car Club* [1971] 1 WLR 668, CA (where the spectator-plaintiff unsuccessfully sued a motorcyclist for negligently injuring him during a motorcycle scramble when the motorcyclist inexplicably left the course and went into the spectators).

166 *White v Blackmore* [1972] 2 QB 651, CA, at 670 (Buckley LJ) and 674 (Roskill LJ) (where the widow of a spectator, killed at a jalopy car racing circuit by reason of the defective arrangement of ropes fencing off the track, lost her action because of a notice absolving the organisers from liability for personal injury, fatal or otherwise, 'howsoever caused to spectators'). Lord Denning MR, at 659, delivered a powerful dissenting judgment.

167 Unfair Contract Terms Act 1977, s 1(3)(b). Despite its title the Act deals with exclusion of tortious liability as well as exclusion of contractual liability.

168 Ibid, s 11(4).

169 Unfair Contract Terms Act 1977, s 2(1).

170 Ibid, s 2(2).

171 Ibid, s 11(4).

172 Ibid, s 3(2).

173 *Addiscombe Garden Estates v Crabbe* [1958] 1 QB 513, CA.

to this extent be carrying on a business.[174] It may seem questionable whether the legislature was intending to include private clubs as business occupiers within the ambit of the Unfair Contract Terms Act 1977 but the point is plainly open to argument.[175]

12.50 Contributory negligence Where a club is found to be in breach of a duty of care, the fact that the claimant's own negligence contributed to the damage in question will result in an apportionment of damages according to the fault on either side.[176] In other words, the claimant will have failed to take reasonable care for his own well-being or safety and thus contributed to his own damage.[177] This doctrine will apply to cases in the tort of negligence[178] and in the tort of nuisance[179] but, generally speaking, it does not apply where the wrongdoing has been intentional.[180]

12.51 Dishonesty and fraud The question sometimes arises whether the club is liable for the dishonest or fraudulent acts of its employees. Suppose an employee goes into the club's changing room and steals a member's valuable watch. Is the club liable to make good the loss? As a general rule an employer is not liable for his employee's dishonest conduct unless the wrongful act was committed in the course of employment. But, it might be asked, how can theft ever be within the scope of anyone's employment? The answer at law lies in whether the goods have been entrusted to the employee for safe keeping: if yes, the theft was committed in the course of employment;[181] if no, the employee was acting outside his employment and the employer has no liability. Thus in the example of the stolen watch, if it had been the changing room attendant who stole the watch, the club would be liable to the owner, but if say it had been an opportunistic club chef it would escape liability. It should be pointed out that the employer's liability for the misconduct of his employee does not depend on showing that the employer in some way benefited from the dishonesty or fraud; the employer will be liable even if the employee intended solely to benefit himself.[182]

---

174 See Josling and Alexander, *The Law of Clubs* (6th edn, 1987), at p 99.

175 Here should be noted that if access to the premises is for recreational or educational purposes and loss or damage is suffered by reason of the dangerous state of the premises, this will not count as a business liability unless the access falls within the business purposes of the occupier: Unfair Contract Terms Act 1977, s 1(3), as amended by Occupiers' Liability Act 1984, s 2.

176 Law Reform (Contributory Negligence) Act 1945, s 1.

177 *Nance v British Columbia Railway* [1951] AC 601, PC, at 611 (Lord Simon).

178 *Clerk & Lindsell on Torts* (20th edn, 2010) at 3–45.

179 *Trevett v Lee* [1955] 1 WLR 113, CA, at 122 (Evershed MR).

180 *Clerk & Lindsell on Torts*, op cit, at 3–54 to 3–60.

181 *Morris v C W Martin & Sons Ltd* [1966] 1 QB 716 (dry cleaning employers held liable for theft of a fur coat entrusted to the employee for cleaning); *Nahhas v Pier House (Cheyne Walk) Management* (1984) *The Times*, February 10 (company held liable for thefts committed by its porter when he burgled a flat in the block using keys entrusted to his custody).

182 *Lloyd v Grace, Smith & Co* [1912] AC 716.

12.52 Defamation The tort of defamation consists of the unauthorised publication by the maker of libellous or slanderous statements to a third party. In broad terms the distinction between libel and slander is that libel is defamation in permanent form (eg written words) whereas slander is in transitory form (eg spoken words).[183] A defamatory statement is one which is untrue and likely to disparage in a substantial way a third person; in other words, it is the tort which protects one's reputation and good name. It is a branch of the law whose complexities and absurdities have often been criticised[184] and, despite attempts to rationalise and simplify it,[185] there is still a pressing need for the reform of the English libel laws.[186] What amounts to a defamatory statement is hard to pin down. Generally speaking, if the words complained of cause a person to be hated, despised or ridiculed, or cause others to shun or avoid him, or to lower him in the estimation of other, right-thinking persons, they can be said to be actionable statements.[187] But times change and whereas in 1846 it was held defamatory of a person to publish a statement that he had been blackballed on seeking admission to a club,[188] such a statement might not be considered defamatory today.[189] And in another old case, *Robinson v Jermyn*[190] it was held that it was not necessarily defamatory for the proprietors of the Cassino Club[191] in Southwold to post a notice in the club in that the two plaintiffs had been excluded from a particular room in the club, 'not being persons that the proprietors or the annual subscribers think it proper to associate with'. The court said that the notice did not mean that these persons were unfit for general society (which was the substance of the plaintiffs' allegation) but only unfit as members of that club.

12.53 What would happen if the club's secretary had circulated a written notice to the local newspapers that wrongly stated that the plaintiff had been expelled from membership of the club for misconduct?[192] In essence, a defence will lie if the defendant justifies the statement (that is, he agrees it is or may be defamatory but asserts that it is true and therefore not libellous);

---

183 *Gatley on Libel and Slander* (11th edn, 2008), at 1.6.

184 Eg *Morrell v International Thomson Publishing* [1989] 3 All ER 733, per May LJ at 734.

185 Eg *Lucas-Box v News Group Ltd* [1986] 1 WLR 147, CA; and the Defamation Act 1996.

186 See *British Chiropractic Association v Singh* [2010] EWCA Civ 350 (where the Court of Appeal criticised the law which allowed a professional body, which was a company limited by guarantee, to resort to libel litigation to silence a scientific writer instead of refuting him by scientific debate). On 9 July 2010 the Justice Minister, Lord McNally, said that the government would publish in early 2011 a draft bill for consultation reviewing the law of libel.

187 *Gatley on Libel and Slander*, op cit, at 1.8.

188 *O'Brien v Clement* [1846] 16 M & W 159.

189 *Gatley on Libel and Slander*, op cit, at 2.19.

190 (1814) 1 Price 11.

191 Cassino (or casino) was a popular card game in the early 19th century for four players in which players matched cards in hand with others exposed on the table and in which the ten of diamonds, known as the great cassino, was worth two points and the two of spades, known as the little cassino, was worth one point.

192 As happened in *Birne v National Sporting League* (1957) *The Times*, April 12.

or the defendant can make a plea of 'fair comment' (that is, he agrees the statement is or may be defamatory but the words complained of are honest opinion on a matter of public interest);[193] or the defendant can make a plea of privilege (that is, he agrees that the statement is or may be defamatory but he asserts that he had a legitimate interest or duty in publishing the statement and the person to whom it was communicated had a corresponding interest or duty to receive it). Unless it is covered by 'absolute' privilege, the privilege referred to is 'qualified' because it can be destroyed by malice (that is, knowingly abusing the privileged occasion; in effect an allegation of dishonesty against the maker of the statement). All these defences are highly technical. Also should be noted the offer to make amends introduced by the Defamation Act 1996 which came into effect on 28 February 2000 and which may now be pleaded by way of defence.[194]

12.54 The committee should beware of posting potentially contentious notices in the clubhouse, say that named members are defaulters in the payment of their subscriptions. This may well be a hostage to fortune since one or more of the non-payers may take umbrage and cause a row in the club or they may assert the notice is a defamatory and libellous statement. Notice of default is best sent direct to the home of the member in question so that there is no question of publication to third parties.[195] It is not unknown too for a mischievous or an aggrieved member to put up on a club notice board a derogatory statement, say, about a fellow member with whom he has fallen out or whom he thinks is carrying on an improper relationship with his wife. Let us assume the notice is both defamatory and libellous. Is the club or the committee in any way liable to the member who has been defamed? The answer is set out below.

12.55 An action for libel will not lie against an unincorporated members' club in its collective name since it does not constitute a legal person whereby it can publish or authorise the publication of a libel.[196] (For the same reason such a club cannot bring a libel action against somebody).[197] The persons who will be liable are those who authorised or directed its

---

193 *Joseph v Spiller* [2010] 3 WLR 1791, SC (where the court re-examined the ingredients of this defence). In *British Chiropractic Association v Singh* [2010] EWCA Civ 350, the Court of Appeal at [36] complained that the phrase 'fair comment' was misleading terminology and said that the defence should be renamed 'honest comment'; a view repeated by Lord Walker of Gestingthorpe in *Joseph v Spiller* at [130].

194 Defamation Act 1996, ss 2–4 and CPR PD53, paras 3.1–3.3.

195 If the rules stipulate that there will be automatic cessation of membership on the grounds of arrears of subscription (see, eg model rule 17(4) in Appendix 10), it would not be improper to post a notice in the clubhouse that a particular person had ceased to be a member since the members are entitled to know who are their fellow members at any given time, but it would be wise for the notice simply to state that the person had ceased to be a member without further elaboration.

196 *London Association for the Protection of Trade v Greenlands* [1916] AC 15.

197 *Electrical, Electronic, Telecommunication and Plumbing Union v Times Newspapers Ltd* [1980] QB 585.

publication.[198] In *Birne v National Sporting League*,[199] the plaintiff-bookmaker had been expelled from the league but wrongfully so. The secretary of the league published the fact of expulsion. The judge found the secretary had acted with malice on a privileged occasion and the committee and the proprietor of the league were held liable to the plaintiff because they had given the secretary a free hand and the principals were liable for the malice of their agent. On the other hand, in *Longdon-Griffiths v Smith*[200] the four trustees of the National Deposit Friendly Society published on a privileged occasion a report which was defamatory of the plaintiff, who was the society's general secretary. One of the trustees was actuated by malice. This did not destroy the privilege of the other three trustees. The case of *Egger v Viscount Chelmsford*[201] involved the Kennel Club, which is an unincorporated members' club. The secretary of the club's show regulations committee published a letter defamatory of the plaintiff. Here five members of the committee were held to have been actuated by malice but not the remaining four members whose defence of qualified privilege succeeded.[202] In addition, the secretary who wrote the letter was not guilty of malice and this was an independent defence since an innocent agent is not liable for the malice of his principal.

12.56 Suppose, however, the committee had no idea that the derogatory statement referred to in **12.55** had been put on the club notice board but it then becomes aware of it. Up to the time of its knowledge of the statement, the committee will have the defence of innocent dissemination.[203] But is the committee liable if it does nothing about it and lets it remain on the club notice board? The answer is that once the committee has become aware of the statement, it will have a reasonable opportunity to check its contents before deciding whether to remove the statement.[204] If the committee then decide to let it stay, and it subsequently turns out to be libellous, the committee will have been guilty of authorising its publication, and therefore liable to the defamed member.[205] The removal of the statement is the safest course if there is the slightest risk of its being defamatory.

12.57 Publication on the club's website Many clubs have websites which contain information about activities and persons within the club. It is for the committee to supervise and monitor the situation to ensure that the website is being used responsibly. If a statement on the website is defamatory neither the club nor its internet services provider (ISP) will be liable for the

---

198 *Mercantile Marine Service Association v Toms* [1916] 2 KB 243, CA, at 246–247.

199 (1957) *The Times*, April 12.

200 [1951] 1 KB 295.

201 [1965] 1 QB 248, CA.

202 It is important to realise that the four innocent committee members were not tortfeasors at all; the privilege attaches to the individual publisher, not to the publication.

203 Defamation Act 1996, s 1; *Gatley on Libel and Slander* (11th edn, 2008) at 6.20.

204 *Gatley on Libel and Slander*, op cit, at 6.26.

205 *Godfrey v Demon Internet Ltd* [2001] QB 201.

publication of the defamatory statement provided their role was entirely passive.[206] To establish liability against the club the claimant must show that the club knowingly authorised or sanctioned or participated in the publication of the defamatory statement.[207] The relevant knowledge may occur when the claimant notifies the club of the existence of the defamatory statement because being in charge of its own website the club has the power of removal of any offending subject matter.

13. PROTECTION OF THE COMMITTEE AND THE MEMBER

12.58 Protecting the committee The answer lies in insuring the committee against third party tortious liability. The insurance should include cover for the consequences of the fraudulent or dishonest conduct of the club members or its employees, where such consequences are visited upon the club itself and the club as a whole has played no part in the fraudulent or dishonest conduct.

12.59 Protecting the member There are occasions when it will be proper to spend club funds on insurance premiums to obtain insurance cover in order to protect the member against third party tortious liability. A clear example relates to the activities of members who are referees and umpires in sports clubs.[208] It would be a financial calamity for the member if as a rugby referee he was held liable in negligence in relation to a collapsed scrum which resulted in paraplegic injury to the hooker[209] and he then faced the prospect of paying the damages out of his own monies. Indeed, we consider that the committee might be in dereliction of its duties in managing the club's affairs if it failed to consider the insuring of its members against claims for negligence, especially if it was common knowledge that the members' activities, though lawful, entailed a risk of injury to persons or damage to property.

14. WORKING MEN'S CLUBS AND SHOP CLUBS

12.60 The member's liability in tort is the same as applies to an unincorporated members' club.

---

[206] Defamation Act 1996, s 1.

[207] *Bunt v Tilley* [2007] 1 WLR 1243.

[208] See Appendix 9 for a set of rules which gives an express power to the committee to insure the activities of its members.

[209] See *Vowles v Evans* [2003] 1 WLR 1607, CA cited in **12.44**.

15. INCORPORATED CLUBS: GENERAL PRINCIPLES OF LIABILITY

12.61 The principles of law set out in **12.27** to **12.57**, which apply to determine the tortious liability of the members of an unincorporated members' club, apply equally well to an incorporated club save in the following respects:

(1) the first proposition in **12.27** does not apply;
(2) the third proposition in **12.27** needs to be reformulated as follows:

> 'the club being a legal person, and to the exclusion of the members, will potentially be vicariously liable for the acts or omissions of those persons, whether employees or members of the club, who were acting in the course of their employment or acting in a manner authorised by the club';

(3) the legal personality of an incorporated club makes a substantial difference in defamation cases: see **12.63**.

12.62 Director's liability In normal situations it is the club which will be liable for any tort committed and the director will have no liability[210] but there are exceptions. The director will be personally liable (as well as the company) if he makes a fraudulent misrepresentation on behalf of the company.[211] And if a director exercises control other than through the board of directors, he may become a joint tortfeasor with the company.[212]

12.63 Defamation In *Electrical, Electronic, Telecommunication and Plumbing Union v Times Newspapers Ltd*[213] Mr Justice O'Connor put the legal position succinctly in respect of a corporate body suing for libel:

> 'So you have got to [have legal] personality which is capable of being defamed before a plaintiff can bring an action for libel. Of an individual there is no difficulty; so too a corporate body. That is an extensive term which is just as well to have in mind. Corporate bodies are of a very much wider variety than most people think. The obvious example with which we are all familiar is a limited company, but there are a wide variety of corporate bodies which have been set up by charter, by special Act of Parliament, by letters patent and so forth, and

---

210 *Williams v Natural Life Health Foods* [1998] 1 WLR 830, HL. See *Gore-Browne on Companies* (45th edn, 2010), at 7A[1] and 7[13]–[14] for a discussion on this topic.

211 *Standard Chartered Bank v Pakistan National Shipping Corporation (Nos 2 and 4)* [2003] 1 AC 959.

212 *MCA Records Inc v Charly Records Ltd* [2003] 1 BCLC 93, CA (director successfully sued on a personal basis for procuring breaches of copyright by his company).

213 [1980] QB 585, at 595.

> they all have corporate existence; and again, the law is clear, that a corporate body has a personality which can be defamed and it can bring an action in its own name for the libel on itself.'[214]

By the same reasoning an incorporated club can be sued for any libel which it has published or authorised to be published.

16. COMMUNITY CLUBS

12.64 Insofar as the club is a legal person, the member's liability in tort is akin to that of an incorporated club save that community clubs will have no directors, only officers and members.

17. PROPRIETARY CLUBS

12.65 Apart from the individual member who is the actual tortfeasor and liable as such (see the second proposition in **12.27**), it is the proprietor who shoulders the burden of vicarious liability, not the members or the committee of a proprietary club.

---

[214] See *British Chiropractic Association v Singh* [2010] EWCA Civ 350, at [10].

Chapter 13

THIRD PARTY CHALLENGES TO CLUB'S DECISIONS

1. INTRODUCTION

13.1 There are a number of occasions when a third party who is not a member of the club is affected by a decision taken by the club. The decision may adversely affect his standing in the community or his lifestyle or his means of livelihood, and he may therefore wish to challenge the club's decision. This is therefore an important topic which contains a number of complexities when trying to find the right answer to any given problem. This chapter applies to all clubs, no matter into what category they fall.

13.2 The Jockey Club, which was an unincorporated members' club until its incorporation by royal charter in 1970, controlled both flat and steeplechase horseracing throughout Great Britain until 2007. The club then permanently divested itself of its powers by giving them to an independent incorporated entity called British Horseracing Authority Limited which now governs and regulates the sport of horseracing. In the past the Jockey Club itself made the rules of horseracing; sanctioned the holding of race meetings; issued trainers' licences; and had disciplinary powers as the governing body of horseracing. The club provides useful examples of the various challenges made to its decisions by third parties and we surmise that they would still be of relevance to present-day challenges to the decisions of the British Horseracing Authority:

(1) In *Chapman v Ellesmere*[1] the plaintiff was a racing steward who acted under a licence from the Jockey Club. He was unable to sue the members of one of the club committees for defamation in respect of their publication of a report on his role in a particular race. This was because in accepting his licence he had agreed to rules under which the publication of such a report was specifically permitted.

(2) In *Russell v Duke of Norfolk*[2] the plaintiff was a trainer whose licence was withdrawn by the club's stewards 'in their absolute discretion'

1 [1932] 2 KB 431.

2 [1949] 1 All ER 109.

and then published the fact of withdrawal in its Racing Calendar. Mr Russell unsuccessfully sued for damages for breach of contract and libel.

(3) In *Nagle v Fielden*[3] the plaintiff was a very experienced woman trainer who was refused a trainer's licence based on the club's stewards' unfettered discretion but in reality because she was a woman. The court allowed her case to go to trial on the ground that the practice of refusing a trainer's licence to a woman might be void as being contrary to public policy. In *R v Jockey Club ex p RAM Racecourses*[4] Mr Justice Simon Brown commented, at 248, that since Mrs Nagle had no contract with the Jockey Club, it was not a case of an improper contract in restraint of trade but instead involved considerations of public law.

(4) In *R v Disciplinary Committee of the Jockey Club, ex p Massingberd-Mundy*[5] the applicant challenged the club's disciplinary committee's decision to remove his name from the list of those eligible to sit as chairmen of local panels of stewards. The court held that Mr Massingberd-Mundy enjoyed a non-renewable privilege which was a domestic decision not capable of judicial review, although Mr Justice Roch, at 224, did consider that if the Jockey Club's disputed decision did not arise, or not wholly arise, from contract, then judicial review might lie.

(5) In *R v the Jockey Club, ex p. RAM Racecourses Ltd*[6] the club accepted publicly a report it had commissioned that 60 additional fixtures should be made available in 1990 and 1991, including allocations to new racecourses. The applicant established a new racecourse and sought an allocation of 15 fixtures which the club declined to make. On an application for judicial review the court held that the applicant had no legitimate expectation of any allocation and dismissed the application, although Lord Justice Stuart-Smith, at 243, said he did not rule out such an application in appropriate circumstances, eg where the club had made an unambiguous statement to anyone seeking to open a new racecourse that they *would* be allocated a certain number of fixtures.

(6) In *R v Disciplinary Committee of the Jockey Club, ex p The Aga Khan*[7] the Aga Khan's winning filly was disqualified by the club's disciplinary committee and his trainer fined. The court held that the Aga Khan's legal position was governed by his contract with the Jockey Club and was a matter of private law not involving any public law principles, and so they dismissed his application for judicial review. Lord Justice Hoffmann, at 933, commented, 'I do not think one should try to patch up the remedies available against domestic bodies by pretending that they are organs of government'.

---

3 [1966] 2 QB 633, CA.

4 [1993] 2 All ER 225, CA.

5 [1993] 2 All ER 207, CA, a case decided in December 1989.

6 [1993] 2 All ER 225, CA, a case decided in March 1990.

7 [1993] 1 WLR 909, CA. Applied in another Jockey Club case, *R (Mullins) v Appeal Board of the Jockey Club (No 1)* [2006] ACD 2.

(7) In *Bradley v The Jockey Club*[8] the claimant had been a licensed and successful steeplechase jockey between 1982 and 1999, and was now carrying on business as a bloodstock agent. He was charged with providing confidential information whilst a jockey to a betting syndicate in breach of the Rules of Racing and he was disqualified as a jockey for several years by the club's Disciplinary Committee. The club's independent Appeal Board (whose panel consisted of judges, former judges or senior lawyers) dismissed his appeal. The disqualification meant the end of his career as a bloodstock agent, and Mr Bradley brought proceedings in the High Court on the basis that the penalty was disproportionate and unlawful. There was a dispute as to the jurisdiction of the court and Mr Justice Richards held that (a) the correspondence passing between Mr Bradley and the club in 2002 gave rise to a fresh contractual relationship and (b) whether the relationship between Mr Bradley and the club was contractual or non-contractual, the court had a *supervisory role* in checking to see if the tribunal had acted unfairly; or had misdirected itself; or had had no evidential basis for its decision. Mr Bradley's challenge was unsuccessful.

13.3 In challenging the decision the third party will be involved in one of three possible relationships:

(1) there exists an express contract between the club and the third party;
(2) the third party has consensually submitted to the jurisdiction of the club;
(3) no contract nor consensual submission exists as between the club and the third party.

As to the Jockey Club cases referred to in **13.2**, items (1), (2), (4) and (6) fell within the first category; item (7) fell within the first category, alternatively the second category; item (3) fell within the second category, alternatively the third category; and item (5) fell within the third category.

2. DECISIONS MADE UNDER AN EXPRESS CONTRACT

13.4 These present no difficulty from a legal point of view. If the decision which is being challenged arises in the course of a contract made between the club and the third party, the normal rules of the law of contract will apply. Here we are in the realm of private law rights. As the Court of Appeal said in the *Aga Khan* case,[9] if the third party has a contract with the club, he will normally be restricted to making his challenge under the terms of this contract, not in the wider realm of public law. And the courts do not

8 [2004] EWHC 2164 (QB).
9 [1993] 1 WLR 909.

exist as a 'court of appeal' at the behest of a third party in relation to unpalatable decisions made by the club.[10] The court will only intervene where the decision has involved some dishonesty, bias or caprice on the part of the club[11] or where the decision was plainly beyond the powers of the club.[12]

13.5 Rules of natural justice The rules of natural justice are set out in **7.13**. They indubitably apply to decisions made by the club which are challenged by the club member. Whether the court will intervene in a contractual or domestic dispute between the club and a third party if the latter complains of a breach of the rules of natural justice at the hands of the club is still an uncertain area of the law. The formal introduction into English law of the European Convention on Human Rights under the Human Rights Act 1998 is part of a process which by and large has made the courts more willing to entertain claims by third parties that the club has acted unfairly towards him. Various questions arise under this heading. In contesting the club's decision is the third party entitled to an oral hearing? Is the third party allowed legal representation? Is the club as decision maker obliged to give reasons for its decision? Has the decision maker departed from its usual practice or policy? How inflexible is that policy? Has the claimant a legitimate expectation that he will be consulted before the decision is made? And so on. In *Ridge v Baldwin*[13] the House of Lords said that the overall test was: What would a reasonable man consider to be fair in the particular circumstances? But this begs the question: What is fair? The answer would appear to be that if the liberty of the claimant or his livelihood or his property is at stake, the court is likely to require the rules of natural justice or, perhaps better expressed, the rules of fair play, to be properly observed so that there is even-handedness between the parties;[14] otherwise and subject to what is said in the last sentence of the previous paragraph the court is unlikely to intervene in contractual or domestic disputes between the club and a third party even if the rules of natural justice have not been observed.[15]

---

10 *Currie v Barton* (1988) *The Times*, February 12, CA.

11 *McInnes v Onslow-Fane* [1978] 1 WLR 1520, at 1535 (Megarry V-C).

12 *Davis v Carew-Pole* [1956] 2 All ER 524, at 527.

13 [1964] AC 40.

14 *Lau Liat Meng* [1968] AC 391; *Gaiman v National Association for Mental Health* [1971] 1 Ch 317, at 336; *R v Army Board of the Defence Council, ex p Anderson* [1992] QB 169; *R v Ministry of Defence, ex p Cunningham* [1998] COD 134, DC.

15 *Currie v Barton* (1988) *The Times*, February 12, CA (where a professional tennis player walked out of a county amateur competition because he objected to his ranking; the county tennis association thereupon banned the player from the amateur county team without first hearing him; the court held that the rules of natural justice did not apply because the ban did not affect his earning ability).

3. IMPLIED SUBMISSION TO THE CLUB'S JURISDICTION

13.6 In the absence of an express contract between the club and the third party, the consensual submission will be based on an implied contract which is to be inferred from the facts of any given case.[16] Let us take the example of some local amateur football clubs who join a particular league organised, say, by the county football association. No contract, written or oral, exists between the association and the individual players. The players will know (a) that their games are played according to certain rules, (b) that serious misconduct on the field is neither sporting nor acceptable behaviour amongst their fellow players, and (c) that breach of the rules or misconduct will or may result in some sanction being imposed on them. Assume the league rules make provision for disciplining a player found guilty of misconduct, but these rules, although generally available, have not been read by any of the players taking part in a particular game. In the course of this game a player deliberately assaults another player on the field causing him injury. The county association now summons the player to a disciplinary hearing. Can the accused player assert that the association has no power to discipline him? The answer lies in the ability of the association to prove the necessary consensual submission to its jurisdiction. In the ordinary course of events we consider that the association could reasonably draw the inference that, with his knowledge as indicated above, the accused player by his participation in the league's activities will have voluntarily submitted to its jurisdiction. Such inference is very unlikely to be overturned by the court. That the legal position is not clear-cut, however, is demonstrated by the dictum of Lord Justice Mance in *Modahl v British Athletics Federation Ltd*[17] when at [105] he said:

> 'As presently advised, I would prefer to view the claimant's submission in 1994 to the jurisdiction of the defendant's disciplinary committee (and thereafter to the independent appeal tribunal) as confirming the existence of a prior contract although, if necessary, I would regard it as the final step bringing one into existence.'

This dictum has the hallmarks of a circular argument and a dispute as to the club's jurisdiction might arise in any given situation. Assuming the club surmounts any jurisdictional hurdle, any challenge to the club's decision will be dealt with in accordance with the principles set out in **13.4** and **13.5**.

---

16 *Modahl v British Athletic Federation Ltd* [2002] 1 WLR 1192, CA (where Latham LJ reviewed the authorities on this point); *R (on the application of Sunspell Ltd (t/a Superlative Travel)) v Association of British Travel Agents* [2001] ACD 16 (Keene J).

17 [2002] 1 WLR 1192.

4. JUDICIAL REVIEW

13.7 Overview We are now dealing with the third category, that is, the third party has not consented to the club's jurisdiction because no contract, whether express or implied, exists to this effect between the club and the third party. Judicial review is the means by which the courts control administrative action by *public bodies*. It is a supervisory jurisdiction which reviews administrative action rather than being an appellate jurisdiction.[18] There are two essential elements which comprise a public body:

(1) it must have a 'public element' (which may take many different forms);[19] and
(2) it excludes those bodies whose sole source of power is by consensual submission to their jurisdiction.[20]

13.8 The courts will check that the claimant has sufficient standing or interest in making his claim. Judicial review may be appropriate even though there is a private law cause of action available, provided there is a sufficiently public issue involved.[21] Historically the courts have always been reluctant to interfere with domestic decisions made by clubs,[22] but this reluctance is on the wane.[23] Where, however, the claim falls into both public law and private law realms the claimant will have to justify his application for judicial review.[24] It is to be remembered that judicial review should be considered the remedy of last resort.[25]

13.9 Livelihood claims Judicial review will more readily be entertained by the court in respect of livelihood claims made by third parties. Restraint of trade, and its corollary the right to work,[26] have been the subject of much litigation. Suffice it to say, that the courts will always look askance at club rules which restrict the manner in which or the area in which a non-member may work. Prima facie such a restriction is void on grounds of public policy

---

18 *Smith v Nairn Golf Club* [2007] SLT 909, at 910 (petition for judicial review against committee's decision to suspend member for cheating in a match play competition).

19 *R (on the application of Beer (t/a Hammer Trout Farm)) v Hampshire Farmers Markets Ltd* [2004] 1 WLR 233, CA.

20 *R v Panel on Take-overs and Mergers, ex p Datafin plc* [1987] QB 815, at 838 (Donaldson MR).

21 *Andreou v Institute of Chartered Accountants in England and Wales* [1998] 1 All ER 14.

22 See **5.27**.

23 See, eg Simon Brown J's comment in *R v Jockey Club, ex p RAM Racecourses Ltd* [1993] 2 All ER 225, at 247.

24 Supreme Court Act 1981, s 31(3). Representative groups may have sufficient standing to warrant an application for judicial review: *R v Secretary of State for Social Services, ex p Child Poverty Action Group* [1990] 2 QB 540.

25 *R v Law Society, ex p Kingsley* [1996] COD 59.

26 There is no right to work as such under the European Convention on Human Rights, but its provisions do protect workplace activities and the European Court has emphasised the right to earn a livelihood: see Articles 4, 6, 8, 9, 10 and 11 of the Convention and see Starmer, *European Human Rights Law* (1999), at 28.1.

and a rule which is unreasonable or goes beyond what is necessary to protect the legitimate interests of the club will be struck down.[27]

(1) In *Breen v Amalgamated Engineering Union*[28] Lord Denning MR, at 200, laid down the modern approach to this issue.[29] Having referred to the need for statutory bodies to act fairly, he continued:

> 'Does all this apply to a domestic body? I think it does, at any rate when it is a body set up by one of the powerful associations which we see nowadays. Instances are readily to be found in the books, notably the Stock Exchange, the Jockey Club, the Football Association and innumerable trade unions. All these delegate power to committees. These committees are domestic bodies which control the destiny of thousands. They have quite as much power as the statutory bodies of which I have been speaking. They can make or mar a man by their decisions. Not only by expelling him from membership, but also by refusing to admit him as a member: or, it may be, by a refusal to [give him a] licence or to give their approval. Often their rules are framed so as to give them a discretion. They claim that it is an "unfettered discretion" with which the courts have no right to interfere. They go too far.'

(2) In *Nagle v Fielden*[30] (the woman trainer refused a trainer's licence by the Jockey Club) Lord Denning MR stated at 646:

> 'When an association, who have the governance of a trade, take it upon themselves to license persons to take part in it, then it is at least arguable that they are not at liberty to withdraw a man's licence – and thus put him out of business – without hearing him. Nor can they refuse a man a licence – and thus prevent him from carrying on his business – in their uncontrolled discretion. If they reject him arbitrarily or capriciously, there is ground for thinking that the court can intervene.'[31]

(3) In *Greig v Insole*[32] the International Cricket Conference and the Test and County Cricket Board, both unincorporated associations, proposed new rules which would have disqualified professional cricketers from playing international test cricket indefinitely if they played in matches organised by the World Series Cricket, a rival organisation set up by Kerry Packer. The player-plaintiff obtained a declaration that these

---

27 *Nordenfelt v Maxim Nordenfelt Guns and Ammunition Co. Ltd* [1894] AC 535; compare *Eastham v Newcastle United Football Club Ltd* [1964] Ch 413, at 437.

28 [1971] 2 QB 175.

29 See *Eastham v Newcastle United Football Club Ltd* [1964] Ch 413.

30 [1966] 2 QB 633.

31 See also *Enderby Town Football Club v Football Association* [1971] Ch 591, CA, at 606; *Modahl v British Athletic Federation Ltd* [2002] 1 WLR 1192, CA, at [36] (Latham LJ).

32 [1978] 1 WLR 302.

rules were ultra vires the Conference and the Board and were void as being in unreasonable restraint of trade.

(4) In *Newport Association Football Club v Football Association of Wales*[33] the defendant association passed a resolution banning Welsh clubs from playing in a league organised by the English Football Association. Certain clubs wished to continue paying in that league. The defendant then prohibited these clubs from playing home matches on their ground in Wales, causing them a loss of revenue. The clubs obtained a declaration that the sanction imposed was an unreasonable restraint of trade and obtained an interlocutory injunction allowing them to play home games in Wales.

13.10 Grounds of judicial review The grounds for holding the reviewed decision as invalid are normally (but not exclusively) grouped under the tripartite heading of illegality, irrationality and procedural impropriety.[34]

(1) ***Illegality*** This includes errors of law and breach of convention rights under the Human Rights Act 1998.
(2) ***Irrationality*** This includes *Wednesbury* unreasonableness, that is say, the decision is so unreasonable that no reasonable person could have come to it.[35]
(3) ***Procedural impropriety*** This includes bias on the part of the decision maker[36] and breach of the rules of natural justice (see **13.5**).

13.11 Pre-action Protocol The Pre-action Protocol for Judicial Review sets out a code of good practice and contains the steps which the parties should generally follow when making a claim for judicial review. In particular, the protocol requires that before making a claim the claimant should send a letter to the defendant, the purpose being to identify the issues in dispute and to establish whether litigation can be avoided. The court will ask the parties what steps they have taken to resolve the dispute, including why a complaints procedure or some other form of alternative dispute resolution has not been used.[37]

13.12 Time limits The claim form must be filed with the court promptly and in any event not later than 3 months after the grounds to make the claim first arose.[38] A claim form filed after the time limit must be accompanied by an application to extend the time limit.[39] The court will not

---

33 [1995] 2 All ER 87.
34 *Council of Civil Service Unions v Minister for the Civil Service* [1985] AC 374.
35 *Associated Picture Houses Ltd v Wednesbury Corporation* [1948] 1 KB 223, CA.
36 *R v Gough* [1993] AC 646.
37 *R (Cowl) v Plymouth City Council* [2002] 1 WLR 803, CA; Practice Statement (Administrative Court: Administration of Justice) [2002] 1 WLR 810.
38 CPR, r 54.5.
39 CPR PD 54, para 5.6(3). The power to extend the time limit is contained in CPR, r 3.1(2)(a).

extend the time limit without good reason,[40] such as sensible and reasonable behaviour by the claimant which has caused no prejudice to the defendant[41] or exhaustion of all alternative remedies by the claimant prior to commencing proceedings for judicial review.[42]

5. REMEDIES AVAILABLE

13.13 The private law remedies are declaration, injunction and damages.[43] The public law remedies are quashing orders, prohibiting orders and mandatory orders,[44] although in appropriate cases the public law remedies may encompass the private law remedies.[45] Private law rights are enforced in all the courts by way of the claim form procedure (see Chapter 18) whereas public law rights are enforced in the High Court of Justice by way of judicial review.

6. DISCRIMINATION CLAIMS AFFECTING LIVELIHOOD

13.14 A separate form of challenge lies in discrimination cases, now underpinned by the Equality Act 2010 (as to which, see generally **4.19**). Qualifying bodies must not discriminate against or victimise a person where that person needs a qualification or authorisation to practise or engage in a particular trade or profession.[46] Under this legislation Mrs Nagle today would have a statutory remedy against the British Horseracing Authority were it to refuse her a trainer's licence on the ground that she was a woman. In *British Judo Association v Petty*[47] the association refused to allow a woman referee to act as a referee in men's international competitions and this refusal was held to amount to unlawful sex discrimination under earlier legislation.[48]

---

40 *R v Warwickshire County Council, ex p Collymore* [1995] ELR 217.

41 *R v Commissioner for Local Administration, ex p Croydon London Borough Council* [1989] 1 All ER 1033).

42 *R v Rochdale Metropolitan Borough Council, ex p Cromer Ring Mill Ltd* [1982] 3 All ER 761.

43 *Roy v Kensington and Chelsea and Westminster Family Practitioner Committee* [1992] 1 AC 624 (declaration); *R v Secretary of State for Transport, ex p Factortame Ltd (No 2)* [1991] 1 AC 603 (injunction); *R v Secretary of State for Transport, ex p Factortame Ltd (No 5)* [2000] 1 AC 524 (damages).

44 Replacing the former prerogative writs of certiorari, prohibition and mandamus.

45 See Supreme Court Act 1981, ss 31(2) and 31(4).

46 Equality Act 2010, ss 53 and 54.

47 [1981] ICR 660, EAT.

48 Sex Discrimination Act 1975, s 13 (repealed and replaced by the Equality Act 2010). This case is still good law.

Chapter 14

LANDLORD AND TENANT RELATIONSHIPS INVOLVING THE CLUB

1. INTRODUCTION

14.1 Members' clubs are sometimes the owner of valuable freehold property, commonly their clubhouse and perhaps some surrounding land. Some clubs may have the opportunity to lease some part of their premises or property to a third party to produce income, on some occasions to a residential user, on other occasions to a business user. Other clubs may lease their club premises from a freeholder or from a landlord who himself has a superior landlord. Some clubs may want to house employees whose accommodation goes with the job. All of these clubs need to know the difference between a tenancy, a licence and a service occupancy agreement, and what sort of tenancy agreement or licence will best suit the club. Moreover, because of its activities a club holding a lease needs to know about business tenancies. A lease may contain 'the usual covenants' (promises) or it may contain common covenants or none at all, and the club needs to know what this means or entails. Over the centuries the common law has evolved many rules regulating the landlord and tenant relationship, such as the remedy of forfeiture, but Parliament throughout the twentieth century brought in more and more legislation modifying the common law rules as well as laying down statutory codes regulating residential tenancies both in the public and the private sector, and regulating business and agricultural tenancies. These codes usually had the aim of restricting the landlord's right to terminate a tenancy or, looked at from the tenant's angle, the aim of providing what is called 'security of tenure'. It has been remarked in relation to residential tenancies that, 'There is no doubt that the present situation is unnecessarily complicated and is overdue for reform'.[1] If in doubt as to its legal position, it is strongly recommended that a club should seek legal advice when taking or granting a lease of club property, or buying or selling leased property, in order to safeguard its assets and to understand fully its legal position.

14.2 We will first deal with tenancies generally, then with business tenancies followed by residential tenancies, and finally we will deal with licences.

---

1 *Blackstone's Civil Practice* 2004, ch 85, at 85.1.

2. LEASES

14.3 There are possible only two legal estates in land, freehold and leasehold estates. In legal language the former is called 'a fee simple absolute in possession' and is the greater estate and the latter is called 'a term of years absolute' and is the lesser estate.[2] In reality the freehold estate gives absolute ownership of land[3] whereas the leasehold estate creates an interest in land for a fixed period of time. A term of years is normally called a lease or a tenancy (which terms are interchangeable). A lease will either be a 'fixed term lease' or a 'periodic lease'. In the former the interest in land determines automatically when the fixed term has expired[4] whereas in the latter the interest in land continuously renews because the period reiterates until either the landlord or the tenant puts an end to it by a notice to quit. There is no doubt that the lease plays an important part in both the social and economic affairs of the country; hence the frequency with which the lease or tenancy is encountered in the business, residential and agricultural sectors.

14.4 With certain exceptions a lease must be created in a formal document,[5] the most important exception being a lease for a term not exceeding 3 years.[6] It is the essence of a lease that the tenant should be given exclusive possession of the property,[7] which differentiates it from a licence, although the dividing line between the two is sometimes a fine one.[8] A lease creates not only an estate in land (i e is binding against all the world) but is also a contract between the landlord and the tenant,[9] for example, the tenant's covenant to pay rent or the landlord's covenant to carry out structural repairs. Both the landlord and the tenant, unless prohibited by the terms of the lease, are able to sell their respective interests in a lease.

14.5 As to formalities, an unincorporated members' club cannot hold property in its own name.[10] This means that trustees must be appointed to hold property, both freehold and leasehold, belonging to the club. A literary

---

2 Law of Property Act 1925, s 1.

3 The briefest mention should be made of Part 1 of the Commonhold and Leasehold Reform Act 2002 (into force September 2004). Commonhold provides a vehicle for freehold ownership of buildings or land where there are common parts held by a commonhold association (i e the entity which owns the freehold of the common land). However, only a handful of commonholds have been registered at Land Registry (*Hansard*, HL Deb, col 169W (18 June 2008)).

4 Save where a statutory code provides for its continuation.

5 *Crago v Julian* [1992] 1 WLR 372, CA, at 376.

6 Law of Property Act 1925, ss 52(2)(d), 54(2)).

7 *Street v Mountford* [1985] AC 809.

8 See further **14.46**.

9 *City of London Corporation v Fell* [1994] 1 AC 458.

10 See **5.19**.

and scientific institution and a working men's club must hold all its property in trustees' names.[11] A community club and an incorporated club can hold property in their own names because they are legal persons, but it is common for it to be held in the name of specially appointed trustees.

3. COVENANTS IN LEASES

14.6 The covenants in a lease are the contractual promises made by the landlord to the tenant and vice versa. Generally speaking the parties are at liberty to agree whatever terms they see fit. They are binding between the original parties and until 1995 were generally enforceable by and against both original covenantors and their successors in title. Nowadays, however, the Landlord and Tenant (Covenants) Act 1995 provides for limits on the liability of a landlord or tenant who assigns his interest in a lease created on or after 1 January 1996. Previously, original parties to the lease may have retained contractual liabilities long after they ceased to have any connection with the land, even being liable to parties with whom they did not originally contract.[12]

14.7 Silent lease If the parties do not expressly make any provision, the following covenants will be automatically implied:

- *On the part of the landlord* (in addition to those specified at **14.29**): a covenant for quiet enjoyment;[13] a covenant not to derogate from grant;[14] a covenant that a furnished house is fit for human habitation at the time of the letting;[15] a covenant to take reasonable steps to keep in repair such facilities as are essential for the enjoyment of the demised premises and which are retained by the landlord as common parts of a building[16] or estate;[17] a covenant that a house is fit for human habitation at the time it is let and will be so kept by the landlord in a tenancy at a very low rent.[18]
- *On the part of the tenant*: a covenant to pay rent;[19] a covenant to pay rates and taxes not payable by the landlord[20] (eg rates or council tax); a

---

11 Literary and Scientific Institutions Act 1854, s 19; Friendly Societies Act 1974, s 54.

12 See *Spencer's Case* (1582) 5 Co Rep 16a; Law of Property Act 1925, ss 141 and 142.

13 *Budd Scott v Daniell* [1902] 2 KB 351.

14 *Harmer v Jumbil (Nigeria) Tin Areas Ltd* [1921] 1 Ch 200, CA.

15 *Smith v Marrable* (1843) 11 M & W 5.

16 *Liverpool City Council v Irwin* [1977] AC 239.

17 *King v South Northamptonshire DC* (1992) 64 P&CR 35, CA.

18 Housing Act 1985, s 8(1).

19 *Dean and Chapter of Rochester v Pierce* (1808) 1 Camp 466.

20 See eg Local Government Finance Act 1988, ss 6 and 43.

covenant not to commit waste;[21] where a landlord is obliged to repair the premises, a covenant to allow him to enter and view the state of repair.[22]

14.8 Usual covenants When an agreement is made that a lease shall be entered into on 'the usual covenants' the following are intended to be included:[23]

- *On the part of the landlord*: a covenant for quiet enjoyment of the leased property.
- *On the part of the tenant:* a covenant to pay rent; a covenant to pay tenant's rates and taxes; a covenant to keep the premises in repair and deliver them up in repair at the end of the term; a covenant to permit the landlord to enter and view the state of repair (if the landlord has undertaken any obligation to repair); a condition of re-entry for non-payment of rent (but not for breach of any other covenant).

14.9 Common covenants The following are commonly inserted into leases, with the concurrence of both parties: a lessee's covenant not to assign; a lessee's covenant not to carry on of certain trades or activities; and a proviso for forfeiture for breaches by the lessee of any covenant, whether for payment of rent or otherwise. It should be noted that a covenant not to assign, sub-let or part with possession may be an absolute undertaking or a qualified one. It is qualified where the prohibition is not to do these things without the landlord's consent. In this event, the covenant is subject to the proviso that the consent will not be unreasonably withheld.[24]

14.10 In the case of *Ranken v Hunt*[25] the Hoddlesden Working Men's Club's lease contained a covenant that its premises should not be used for 'sale of wine malt liquor or spirituous liquors'. The club rules provided for the purchase of such liquors and its distribution at fixed prices amongst the members, the profits being applied to the general purposes of the club. The court held that this distribution to the members was not a sale within the meaning of the covenant.[26]

---

21 Statute of Marlbridge 1267.

22 *Saner v Bilton* (1878) 7 Ch D 815; *Mint v Good* [1951] 1 KB 517. A landlord's right to enter may also arise pursuant to statute, eg Landlord and Tenant Act 1927, s 10 (business premises) and Landlord and Tenant Act 1986, s 11(6) (residential premises).

23 *Hampshire v Wickens* (1878) 7 Ch D 555.

24 Landlord and Tenant Act 1927, s 19(1). And see *Design Progression Ltd v Thurloe Properties Ltd* [2005] 1 WLR 1 (exemplary damages awarded to tenant in respect of landlord's breach of its statutory duty in relation to consent).

25 (1894) 38 Sol Jo 290, DC.

26 See further **9.3**.

14.11 Forfeiture Many leases contain an express right of (peaceable) re-entry or forfeiture by the landlord in the event of specified events, such as the tenant's breach of covenant (eg the covenant to repair) or the bankruptcy of the tenant. Forfeiture should be seen not as a method of termination of the lease but as a remedy or sanction against a defaulting tenant. Because it is a formidable remedy which can often result in termination of the lease, it has been regulated[27] by Parliament and the courts as follows:

(1) the landlord must expressly reserve the right to forfeit in the lease;
(2) the landlord must comply with strict procedural requirements;
(3) it is subject to strict rules of waiver;
(4) the tenant has extensive rights to apply to the court for relief from forfeiture.

14.12 The right to forfeit is not enforceable by action or otherwise unless and until the landlord serves on the tenant a notice:[28]

(1) specifying the event or breach complained of;
(2) if capable of remedy, requiring the tenant to remedy the breach;
(3) requiring the tenant to pay compensation for the breach.

The breach can be waived, for example, if, in a forfeiture concerning non-payment of rent, the landlord brings an action for arrears of rent.[29] Unless there are exceptional circumstances, relief from forfeiture in the case of failure to pay rent will almost invariably be granted if the tenant pays the arrears of rent plus costs before judgment is given.[30] In other cases, the tenant has the right to apply to the court for relief where it may grant or refuse relief on such terms as it thinks fit,[31] such as making an order for payment of compensation or granting an injunction to restrain future breaches. In deciding whether to grant relief, the court will take into account all the circumstances of the case, including the nature of the breach; its seriousness; the conduct of the parties; the value of the property; and what losses will be suffered by the tenant if relief is not granted.

4. BUSINESS TENANCIES

14.13 Introduction Even if the club has no cause to think about letting any part of its premises or property to a business user, there is one good reason

---

27 The Law Commission has said 'the law of forfeiture is in need of urgent reform' and has recommended a statutory scheme for the termination of tenancies following breach of covenant by the tenant (Law Com No 303, 2006).

28 Law of Property Act 1925, s 146.

29 *Dendy v Nicholl* (1858) 4 CB(NS) 376.

30 *Blackstone's Civil Practice 2008*, at 85.31.

31 Law of Property Act 1925, s 146(2).

why members' clubs need to know about business tenancies and that is the protection given by Part II of the Landlord and Tenant Act 1954[32] which by s 23(1) applies to the occupation by a tenant of premises for 'the purposes of business'.[33] Section 23(2) states:

> 'In [Part II] the expression 'business' includes a trade, profession or employment and includes any activity carried on by a body or persons, whether corporate or unincorporate.'

Thus in the leading case of *Addiscombe Garden Estates Ltd v Crabbe*[34], where the trustees of the Shirley Park Lawn Tennis Club, a community club, took a 'licence' of some tennis courts and a clubhouse, the Court of Appeal held (a) that although described as a licence the document should be construed as a tenancy agreement, and (b) that the club was carrying on a relevant activity in the shape of a lawn tennis club and thus came within the Act.[35] It is therefore surmised that virtually all those members' clubs which have a leasehold interest of their premises will have protection under Part II of the Landlord and Tenant Act 1954.[36]

14.14 Occupation of premises The club must occupy the premises in question by virtue of a tenancy, which can be either a fixed-term tenancy or a periodic one. A sub-tenancy is sufficient but not a tenancy at will[37] nor a licence.[38] The expression 'premises' is not defined in the 1954 Act but has been construed broadly: it includes a building or part of a building or simply land with no building on it. Thus in *Bracey v Read*[39] a tenancy of land without buildings, namely, some gallops on the Lambourn Downs used for training racehorses, was held to be a protected business tenancy.[40] Where the club property is held by trustees on trust for the members, the carrying on of the business by all or any of the beneficiaries (the members) is treated as equivalent to occupation by or the carrying on of business by the tenant.[41]

---

32 As substantially amended by the Regulatory Reform (Business Tenancies) (England & Wales) Order 2003, SI 2003/3096 ('the Reform Order 2003').

33 Landlord and Tenant Act 1954, s 23(1).

34 [1958] 1 QB 513, CA.

35 There are limits, however: see *Hillil Property v Narraine Pharmacy* (1980) 39 P&CR 67 (occupying premises to dump waste and rubbish not a protected activity); compare *Groveside Properties Ltd v Westminster Medical School* (1983) 267 EG 593 (where a tenancy of a flat for medical students was held to be not merely for residential purposes but to foster a collegiate spirit, thus counting as an activity for business purposes).

36 For a recent case, see *Coles v Samuel Smith Old Brewery (Tadcaster)* [2007] EWCA Civ 1461 at [2] where the tenancy of a working men's club was recognised as a business tenancy.

37 *Wheeler v Mercer* [1957] AC 416; *Manfield & Sons Ltd v Botchin* [1970] 2 QB 612.

38 Agreed by the parties in *National Car Parks Ltd v Trinity Development Co (Banbury) Ltd* [2002] 2 P&CR 253.

39 [1963] Ch 88.

40 On the other hand, agricultural tenancies are excluded from Part II of the 1954 Act: s 43(1)(a).

41 Landlord and Tenant Act 1954, s 41(1).

14.15 Security of tenure The security of tenure is achieved by the automatic continuation of the tenancy under s 24 of the 1954 Act and the tenant's right to apply to the court for a new tenancy of up to 15 years' duration.[42] The tenancy will not come to an end unless it is terminated in one of the statutory methods set out in the Act[43] or by the tenant's notice to quit or his surrender of the lease or by the landlord's forfeiture.[44] This means that the business tenancy will continue after the determination of a fixed-term tenancy (whether by effluxion of time or by the mere exercise of a landlord's break clause) and after the service of a landlord's notice to quit in respect of a periodic tenancy. The statutory methods are:

(1) by the landlord giving notice to terminate the tenancy under s 25;
(2) by the tenant making an application for a new tenancy under s 26;
(3) by the tenant giving notice to terminate the tenancy under s 27.

14.16 Section 25 notice The 'competent' landlord[45] must serve the notice in the prescribed form.[46] It must be served not more than 12 months nor less than 6 months before the date of termination specified in the notice.[47] The prescribed notice must:

(1) specify the date at which the tenancy is to come to an end (the 'termination date');[48]
(2) inform the tenant that if he wishes to ask the court for a new tenancy he must do so before the termination date unless, before that date, an agreement in writing to extend time is entered into;[49]
(3) state whether the landlord is or is not opposed to the grant of a new tenancy;[50]
(4) in a case where the landlord opposes the grant of a new tenancy, state the statutory grounds relied upon;[51]
(5) in a case where the landlord does not oppose the grant of a new tenancy, state the terms proposed for the new tenancy.[52]

---

42 Landlord and Tenant Act 1954, s 33. Previously the maximum term was 14 years. Fifteen makes quinquennial rent reviews easier.

43 Ibid, s 23(1).

44 Ibid, s 23(2).

45 Negotiation for a new tenancy will not be meaningful if, say, the immediate landlord is a leaseholder for a term which is only a few days longer than the tenant's interest, so the 1954 Act provides a mechanism for identifying the one landlord with whom the tenant should deal and who is called the competent landlord (s 44(1)).

46 See Forms 1 and 2 in the Landlord and Tenant Act 1954, Part II (Notices) Regulations 2004, SI 2004/1005.

47 Landlord and Tenant Act 1954, s 25(2).

48 Ibid, s 25(1).

49 Prior to 1 June 2004 a section 25 notice also required the tenant to serve a counter notice within 2 months stating whether the tenant did or did not intend to give up possession in accordance with the section 25 notice.

50 Landlord and Tenant Act 1954, s 25(6).

51 Ibid, s 25(7): see **14.19**.

52 Ibid, s 25(8) as inserted by arts 2 and 4 of the Regulatory Reform (Business Tenancies)

14.17 If there is a break clause in the tenancy, the club may find that the landlord will serve two notices, a section 25 notice and a break clause notice, each terminating the tenancy. It might be asked why one combined notice would not be sufficient. The answer is this: if the combined notice complies with the Act but does not fulfil the provisions of the break clause it will be of no effect and the tenancy will continue on a contractual basis, and the landlord will have to wait until the next break clause or until the tenancy expires; on the other hand, if the combined notice fulfils the provisions of the break clause but does not comply with the Act, the contractual tenancy will be brought to an end but will be automatically continued under s 24 of the Act until the landlord serves a valid section 25 notice.

14.18 If a landlord serves a section 25 notice but no application is made to the court for a new tenancy within the required time, namely, by the termination date referred to in **14.16**(1), the tenancy will come to an end on that date. A landlord may not serve a section 25 notice if the tenant has already served notice under s 26 or 27 (see **14.22** and **14.23**) or served notice to quit.[53]

14.19 **Grounds of opposition** Section 30(1) of the Act of 1954 provides seven grounds of opposition upon which the landlord can rely in opposing the application for a new tenancy:

Ground (a): the tenant's failure to comply with repairing obligations;

Ground (b): the tenant's persistent delay in paying rent;

Ground (c): the tenant's substantial breach of other obligations or his misuse or mismanagement of the premises;

Ground (d): suitable alternative accommodation is available;

Ground (e): the landlord requires the whole property for subsequent letting (this rarely arises in practice);

Ground (f): the landlord intends to demolish or reconstruct the premises (a common ground);

Ground (g): the landlord intends to occupy the premises himself either for business purposes or as his residence.

Under grounds (a), (b) and (c) the court has a discretion whether to grant or refuse a new tenancy. There is no discretion if the landlord establishes his opposition under grounds (d), (e), (f) and (g): no new tenancy will be granted. Ground (g) is not available to the landlord unless the landlord has

---

(England and Wales) Order 2003, SI 2003/3096. This presumably means realistic proposals: see *Mount Cook v Rosen* [2003] 1 EGLR 75 (where 'proposal' under the Leasehold Reform Housing & Urban Development Act 1993 was held to mean a realistic proposal which could be justified by expert valuation evidence).

53 Landlord and Tenant Act 1954, s 26(4).

owned his interest in the property for at least 5 years prior to the termination of the tenancy.[54] Under grounds (d), (e) and (f) the landlord may be able to satisfy the court that he can make good the ground of opposition at a date not later than 1 year after the date of termination specified in the section 25 notice and, if so, the court will make a declaration to this effect, and no new tenancy will be granted.[55] In relation to grounds (e), (f) and (g) the tenant may be entitled in certain circumstances to compensation for quitting the premises.[56]

14.20 Terms of the new tenancy If the tenant applies to the court for a new tenancy, its terms will be decided by the court if the parties cannot agree. They will include what property will be included the new tenancy,[57] its duration,[58] the rent[59]and other terms.[60] Between the service of a section 25 notice and the granting of a new tenancy there may be a considerable time interval and the existing rent will continue to be paid. If this rent was low the tenant had everything to gain by delay, so that since 1969 by s 24A of the 1954 Act[61] the landlord has been able to apply to the court for an interim rent to be determined which is reasonable for the tenant to pay. On the other hand, if the existing rent is higher than rents currently being obtained it is the landlord who gains by delay, so that with effect from 1 June 2004 the tenant can now apply to the court for a reasonable interim rent to be determined.[62]

14.21 It should be noted that with effect from 1 June 2004 the landlord as well as the tenant can apply for a new tenancy[63] and, conversely, that the landlord can apply for an order from the court that the current tenancy be determined and that no new tenancy be granted.[64] This means that the landlord's ground or grounds of opposition can be used as a springboard for an order for possession against the tenant. The landlord's application may be made as soon as he has served his section 25 notice or as soon as the

---

54 Landlord and Tenant Act 1954, s 30(2).

55 Ibid, s 31(2).

56 Ibid, s 37, as substituted by Law of Property Act 1969, and then amended by (a) Local Government, Planning and Land Act 1980, (b) Local Government and Housing Act 1989, (c) Local Government Finance (Miscellaneous Amendments and Repeal) Order 1990, SI 1990/1285, (d) the Reform Order 2003 and (e) Transfer of Tribunal Functions (Lands Tribunal and Miscellaneous Amendments) Order 2009, SI 2009/1307.

57 Landlord and Tenant Act 1954, s 32(1).

58 Ibid, s 33.

59 Ibid, s 34(1).

60 Ibid, s 35, eg including a break clause (*Leslie and Godwin Investments Ltd v Prudential Assurance Co Ltd* [1987] 2 EGLR 2) or excluding an option to purchase (*Kirkwood v Johnson* (1979) 38 P&CR 392).

61 Added by the Law of Property Act 1969.

62 Landlord and Tenant Act 1954, s 24A(1), as substituted by the Reform Order 2003, arts 1 and 18.

63 Ibid, s 24(1).

64 Ibid, s 29(2), as substituted by the Reform Order 2003, arts 2 and 5.

tenant has requested a new tenancy pursuant to a section 26 notice and the landlord has given a counter-notice under s 26(6).[65]

14.22 Section 26 notice Unless the landlord has already served a section 25 notice,[66] a tenant may take the initiative and serve during the contractual term or while the tenancy is continued by statute a notice under s 26 of the 1954 Act requesting a new tenancy. The effect of a section 26 notice is to terminate the tenant's current tenancy immediately before the date specified in the request for the beginning of the new tenancy.[67] The notice must be in the prescribed form[68] and must be served on the competent landlord.[69] Generally speaking, however, it may be unwise to serve a section 26 notice because, until it is known whether the landlord wishes to terminate the existing tenancy, it will not be in the interests of the tenant to request a new one; the existing tenancy will continue in any event under s 24 and very often will be on terms more favourable than those of a new tenancy, particularly at a time where rents are rising. If, on receiving a tenant's section 26 notice, the landlord does not want to grant a tenancy he must serve within 2 months a notice to that effect, stating the grounds upon which he will oppose any application for a new tenancy.[70]

14.23 Section 27 notice The tenant may not wish to apply for a new tenancy, in which case he may serve a notice on the landlord under s 27 of the 1954 Act. This provision only applies to fixed-term tenancies. The tenant must give notice in writing to the *immediate* landlord not later than 3 months before the date on which the tenancy would come to an end by effluxion of time.[71] Once the notice is given, s 24 will not apply and the tenancy will come to an end on its contractual date. If the contractual date has passed, so that the tenancy is being continued under s 24, the tenant can still give a section 27 notice: 3 months' notice in writing must be given to the immediate landlord and the notice must expire on a quarter day.[72] We add that a section 27 notice which is served before the tenant has been in occupation for a month is of no effect.[73] This is to prevent landlords granting tenancies on condition that a section 27 notice is served so as to circumvent the provisions for security of tenure.

14.24 Contracting out of the 1954 Act Originally any attempt by the landlord to contract out of the provisions of Part II of the Landlord and

---

65 Landlord and Tenant Act 1954, s 29(2).
66 Ibid, s 26(4).
67 Ibid, s 26(5).
68 The prescribed form is Form 3 in the Landlord and Tenant Act 1954, Part II (Notices) Regulations 2004.
69 Landlord and Tenant Act 1954, s 26(5).
70 Ibid, s 26(6). There is no prescribed form.
71 Ibid, s 27(1).
72 Ibid, s 27(2).
73 Ibid, s 27(1).

Tenant Act 1954 was rendered void,[74] but in 1969 the Act was amended to permit the court on the joint application of the parties to authorise the business tenancy to exclude the security provisions of the Act, or to approve a surrender.[75] In the event of the former, the application had to precede the grant of the tenancy.[76] From 1 June 2004 it is no longer be necessary to apply to the court for authorisation. The current procedure for contracting out requires the landlord to give a notice in writing to the tenant, urging the tenant to obtain independent legal advice before accepting a tenancy with no security provisions, and the tenant has to sign a declaration that this warning has been given.[77]

5. RESIDENTIAL TENANCIES

14.25 In the private sector there are two statutory codes, one under the Rent Act 1977 and the other under the Housing Act 1988 as amended by the Housing Act 1996, the main difference being the high level of security granted to the tenant under the former code and the much lower level of security which is possible under the latter.

14.26 Rent Act 1977 This Act was the last in a series of Acts which commenced in 1915 in order to restrict rents in the face of a housing shortage in the First World War and which together are generally known as 'the Rent Acts'. It will generally only apply to tenancies created before 15 January 1989 and so they are becoming increasingly scarce. In view of this, it is likely that a club will be concerned only with the residential situation under the Housing Acts 1988 to 2004 and in particular with the form of tenancy called the assured shorthold tenancy. We can therefore limit our discussion to saying that a tenant with security of tenure under the Rent Act 1977 becomes a regulated tenant. Initially, while his contractual tenancy (which may be a fixed term of many years or periodic from, say, week to week) is extant he is known as a 'protected tenant'. Thereafter, once any contractual tenancy has been determined, he has what is frequently described as a personal status of irremovability[78] and is known as a 'statutory tenant'.[79] In order to obtain possession of property occupied by a regulated tenant the contractual tenancy must first be terminated (eg on the expiry of a fixed term tenancy or by the service of a landlord's notice to quit in relation to a periodic tenancy) so as to render the tenant a statutory

---

74 Landlord and Tenant Act 1954, s 38(1).

75 By adding a new s 38(4): Law of Property Act 1969, s 15 and Sch 1 (now repealed).

76 *Essexcrest Ltd v Evenlex Ltd* [1988] 1 EGLR 69.

77 Landlord and Tenant Act 1954, s 38A, added by the Reform Order 2003, art 22(1). If the declaration is made less than 14 days before the tenancy commences, the declaration must be in the form of a statutory declaration made before another solicitor retained for the sole purpose of administering the oath: the Reform Order 2003, Sch 2.

78 A phrase first coined by Lush J in argument in *Keeves v Dean* [1924] 1 KB 685.

79 Rent Act 1977, s 2(1).

tenant. Then the landlord must further obtain an order of the court. Save for certain limited cases, a court will only make an order for possession if the landlord persuades the court that it is reasonable to make an order[80] and either (1) suitable alternative accommodation is available for the tenant[81] or (2) one or more of the permitted statutory grounds for obtaining possession is made out. Regulated tenants (whether protected or statutory) are popularly referred to as 'Rent Act tenants' or 'sitting tenants'.

14.27 Housing Act 1988 The Housing Act 1988 created an assured tenancy (generally referred to as an 'assured tenancy' or a 'fully assured tenancy') and a sub-species called an assured shorthold tenancy (generally referred to as an 'AST'), the latter having much less security than the former. One of the specific reasons for enacting the Housing Act 1988 was to create a residential tenancy with limited security of tenure. It was thought that the prospect of landlords finding themselves lumbered with tenants who were very difficult to remove had led to a shortage of rental properties coming on to the market. Originally the only way of creating an AST was by serving a valid section 20 notice (which set out important information for the tenant) *before* the agreement was entered into. In the absence of a valid notice the tenancy defaulted to a fully assured tenancy. The procedure was frequently forgotten or incorrectly observed and many landlords found themselves with assured tenants who were hard to remove, contrary to the legislative purpose. Consequently, since 28 February 1997 the default tenancy has been the AST and it will not be a fully assured tenancy unless the landlord serves a notice in the prescribed form on the tenant either before or during the course of the tenancy to the effect that the tenancy is a fully assured tenancy.[82] The difference between the two tenancies is considerable in practice. On the one hand, with a fully assured tenancy the landlord can only obtain possession by proving either (1) that one or more of the mandatory grounds in Sch 2 to the Housing Act 1988 is made out, or (2) that one or more of the discretionary grounds in that schedule is made out and that it is reasonable to make an order and, in either event, that a notice under s 8 specifying the relevant ground and the particulars thereof has been served on the tenant.[83] On the other hand, with an AST the landlord can obtain possession simply by showing (a) that the tenancy has come to an end and (b) that the tenant has been given proper notice requiring possession. Hence the AST has become very popular with landlords.

14.28 To qualify as an assured tenant (whether shorthold or not), the tenant must be an individual[84] and he must occupy the dwelling as his only

---

80 Rent Act 1977, s 98(1).

81 Ibid, s 98(1).

82 Housing Act 1988, s 19A and Sch 2A, para 1.

83 Examples of the grounds are given in **14.31**.

84 Housing Act 1988, s 1(1)(a). If it is a joint tenancy, each tenant must be an individual but only one of them need satisfy the occupation test.

or principal home.[85] Because ASTs may be created informally, there is now an obligation[86] on the landlord to provide a written statement of certain essential terms which have not been evidenced in writing, as follows:[87]

(1) the date on which the tenancy began;
(2) the amount of rent payable and the dates on which it is payable;
(3) any term providing for the review of rent;
(4) in the case of a fixed-term tenancy, the length of that term.

14.29 Terms of the tenancy By and large the parties are free to enter into an assured tenancy on whatever terms they agree.[88] The tenancy itself may be for a fixed term, e g for 6 months or a year, or a periodic tenancy, e g from week to week or from month to month. In addition, there are statutorily implied terms that the tenant will give the landlord access to the dwelling-house to enable him to execute repairs thereat[89] and that he will not without the consent of the landlord assign the tenancy or sub-let or part with possession of the whole or any part of the dwelling.[90] Most importantly, s 11 of the Landlord and Tenant Act 1985 (which applies to leases of dwelling houses for a term of less than 7 years[91]) imposes general repairing obligations on the landlord. In brief, the landlord must keep in repair the structure and exterior of the dwelling-house and keep in repair and proper working order the installations for the supply of water, gas, electricity and sanitation at the property. It is not possible to contract out of these statutory provisions.[92]

14.30 Landlord's general liability for defects A landlord is not an occupier and had no liability at common law for any defect in the property which he had leased to anyone other than the tenant.[93] Here again Parliament stepped in and passed the Defective Premises Act 1972 which provides a statutory remedy against the landlord in certain cases. Section 3 abolished the common law rule by virtue of which vendors and lessors of land were held immune from liability for negligence in building or other work carried out on the land before the sale or letting. Section 4 now

---

85 A stricter test than under s 2 of the Rent Act 1977 (where the tenant has merely to occupy the dwelling-house as his residence).

86 If a tenant asks for such a statement, the failure to provide it is a criminal offence: Housing Act 1988, s 20A(1) and (4).

87 Housing Act 1988, s 20A inserted by the Housing Act 1996.

88 See **14.7** as to implied terms.

89 Housing Act 1988, s 16.

90 Ibid, s 15. Generally in leases where there is a restriction on assigning without consent a landlord is not allowed to withhold consent unreasonably (Landlord and Tenant Act 1927, s 19(1)). However, he is allowed to do so in respect of an assured tenancy (Housing Act 1988, s 15(2)).

91 Landlord and Tenant Act 1985, s 13.

92 Ibid, s 12.

93 *Cavalier v Pope* [1906] AC 428. The position is different in relation to common parts of a multi-tenanted building (e g staircases) which are not let to tenants.

imposes a duty of care on a landlord for relevant defects[94] in the state of the premises which he has let and where he has an obligation or right to remedy such defects. The duty is to take such care as is reasonable in all the circumstances to see that the tenant and all those who might be affected by the defect are reasonably safe from personal injury or damage to their property.[95] This duty arises when the landlord knows about the defect (whether because he has been told by the tenant or for any other reason) or ought in all the circumstances to have known about it.[96]

14.31 Security of tenure: fully assured tenancy The only method by which a landlord can obtain possession, other than by the tenant voluntarily leaving, is by obtaining an order from the court establishing one or more of the statutory grounds set out in Sch 2 to the Act.[97] In essence the relevant grounds, as far as clubs are concerned, are as follows:

Mandatory grounds:

- holiday lettings out of season;[98]
- fixed term tenancies for a term of less than 12 months;[99]
- the landlord's intention to demolish, reconstruct or carry out substantial works in respect of the whole or part of the dwelling-house;[100]
- inherited periodic tenancy;[101]
- serious rent arrears.[102]

Discretionary grounds:

- the availability of suitable alternative accommodation;[103]
- some rent arrears;[104]
- persistent rent arrears;[105]

---

94 This means things which are in disrepair rather than inherently unsafe (*Alker v Collingwood Housing Association* [2007] 1 WLR 2230, CA (where no liability lay in respect of non-safety glass in a door which had been lawfully installed and which was in good repair).

95 Defective Premises Act 1972, s 4(1).

96 Ibid, s 4(2).

97 Housing Act 1988, ss 5 and 7. It should be noted that when a fixed term assured tenancy comes to an end a landlord is not entitled to possession because a statutory periodic assured tenancy immediately arises (Housing Act 1988, s 5(2)).

98 Ground 3.

99 Ground 4.

100 Ground 6.

101 Ground 7.

102 Ground 8.

103 Ground 9.

104 Ground 10.

105 Ground 11. This ground would apply where there were no actual arrears on the date when proceedings are commenced but the tenant has been persistently late in paying his rent on the due date.

- breach of tenant's obligation under the tenancy other than arrears of rent;[106]
- deterioration of the premises through acts of waste or through the neglect or default of the tenant;[107]
- causing a nuisance or annoyance to adjoining occupiers or using the premises for immoral or illegal purposes;[108]
- ill-treatment of the furniture provided by the landlord;[109]
- recovery of possession against a former employee where the premises were let to him in consequence of that employment;[110]
- tenancy induced by false statement of the tenant.[111]

They are called discretionary grounds because the landlord must additionally satisfy the court that it is reasonable to make an order for possession,[112] in contrast to the position with the mandatory grounds which, if established, generally compel the court to make an order.[113] It should be noted too that during the currency of a fixed term, it is only open to the landlord to seek possession on one or more of the statutory grounds *which involve the tenant's default* and where there is a term of the tenancy which allows the landlord to re-enter or put an early end to the tenancy for breach of covenant.[114] Once the fixed term has expired or in the case where the tenancy has always been periodic, then any of the statutory grounds may be relied upon.

14.32 Security of tenure: assured shorthold tenancy[115] An AST can now be for a fixed term of less than 6 months[116] or paradoxically for a term (greatly) exceeding 6 months[117] or it may be a periodic tenancy. With effect from 28 February 1997, even though the tenancy may strictly be for a term of less than 6 months, the landlord will effectively be granting a 6-month tenancy in that he will not be able recover possession before the expiry of that period. *This 6-month period is the extent of the tenant's security.* The time starts running from the grant of the original tenancy, even if the tenancy has been extended by the landlord.[118] Because the AST is a species of assured tenancy, it is open to the landlord to seek possession on the statutory grounds in the same way as for fully assured tenants (see **14.31** above).

---

106 Ground 12.

107 Ground 13.

108 Ground 14. Note that the conduct complained of under this ground need not be that of the tenant but may be that of someone else residing in, or even visiting, the dwelling house.

109 Ground 15.

110 Ground 16.

111 Ground 17.

112 Housing Act 1988, s 7(4).

113 Ibid, s 7(3).

114 Ibid, s 7(6).

115 The text is dealing with tenancies created after 28 February 1997. Somewhat different rules apply for tenancies created before 28 February 1997.

116 Hitherto an assured shorthold tenancy had to be for a term certain of not less than 6 months: Housing Act 1988, s 20(1).

117 Although in practice this would very rarely happen.

118 Housing Act 1988, s 21(5) as inserted by Housing Act 1996, s 99.

Additionally and most importantly, the landlord can obtain possession without establishing fault simply by giving at least 2 months' notice requiring possession in accordance with either s 21(1)(a) or 21(4)(a) of the Housing Act 1988 depending on whether the AST is for a fixed term or periodic.[119] This notice can be given so as to expire at the end of the initial 6-month period.

14.33 Succession There is a limited right to succession under an assured tenancy (including an AST). Only the tenant's spouse or, since 2004, civil partner, is capable of succeeding to the tenancy and only one succession is permitted.[120] If the deceased tenant was already a successor, there will be no further right of succession.[121] It should be noted here that both a fixed-term and a periodic assured tenancy form part of the deceased tenant's estate and can therefore be passed to a third party under a will or under the rules of intestacy. This new tenant, however, may be unknown to the landlord and an undesirable tenant, to boot; hence the need for the mandatory ground for possession under Ground 7.

14.34 Excluded tenancies For various policy reasons the Housing Act 1988 excludes from protection certain categories of tenancy, the relevant ones being, as far as clubs are concerned, as follows:

- High rent accommodation where the rent payable exceeds £100,000 per year;[122]
- a tenancy where no rent is payable;[123]
- very low rent accommodation where the rent payable is less than £1,000 per year in London or £250 per year elsewhere;[124]
- agricultural land exceeding 2 acres in extent let together with a dwelling-house;[125]
- lettings to students;[126]
- holiday lettings;[127]
- agricultural holdings;[128] and
- business tenancies.[129]

---

119 See **14.37**.

120 Housing Act 1988, s 17, as amended by the Civil Partnership Act 2004. A common law husband or wife is in the same position as a spouse or civil partner: s 17(4). And see also *Ghaidan v Godin-Mendoza* [2003] Ch 380, CA.

121 Ibid, s 17(1)(c).

122 Housing Act 1988, Sch 1, para 2; Assured Tenancies (Amendment) (England) Order 2010, SI 2010/908, art 3(2). This Order came into force on 1 October 2010 and applies to England only.

123 Housing Act 1988, Sch 1, para 3.

124 Ibid, Sch 1, para 3A.

125 Ibid, Sch 1, para 6.

126 Ibid, Sch 1, para 8.

127 Ibid, Sch 1, para 9.

128 Ibid, Sch 1, para 7.

129 Ibid, Sch 1, para 4.

14.35 Recovery of possession If the tenancy is a fixed-term one and the fixed term expires with the tenant still in occupation, the tenancy simply becomes a statutory periodic tenancy,[130], the terms of which are the same as under the contractual fixed-term tenancy.[131] If the tenancy is a periodic one in the first place or becomes one and the landlord serves a notice to quit, this will be of no legal effect and the periodic tenancy continues on the same terms.[132] Accordingly, there are only two ways of recovering possession:

(1) the tenant leaves voluntarily;
(2) the landlord obtains a court order for possession.

14.36 Court order: fully assured tenancy The landlord can only recover possession by establishing one or more of the statutory grounds for possession as set out in **14.31**. In all cases he should first serve a notice complying with s 8 of the Housing Act 1988 specifying the ground(s) of possession relied upon and specifying sufficient particulars to show the ground is made out.[133] Once the section 8 notice has been served and the time specified in the notice has expired, the landlord may then commence possession proceedings. In the event of a mandatory ground being established the order for possession will follow as a matter of course,[134] and in the event of a discretionary ground being established the court will make an order for possession only if it is reasonable to do so.[135]

14.37 Court order: assured shorthold tenancy The landlord may follow the section 8 notice route in the same way and in the same circumstances as for a fully assured tenancy. Over and above this route, he can simply give at least 2 months' notice in accordance with s 21.

(1) If it is a *fixed-term* tenancy, the court will make an order for possession where:
    (a) the term has expired, and no further tenancy is in existence except a periodic AST following on from the expiry date;[136] and
    (b) the tenant has been given not less than 2 months' notice[137] in writing that possession of the dwelling-house is required by the landlord;[138] and

---

130 Housing Act 1988, s 5(2).
131 Ibid, s 5(3)(e).
132 Ibid, s 5(1).
133 Standard forms are available from various legal stationers and can be obtained on-line at www.oyez.co.uk.
134 Housing Act 1988, s 7(3).
135 Ibid, s 7(4).
136 Ibid, s 21(1)(a).
137 In practice, many landlords serve such a notice at the same time as granting the tenancy.
138 Ibid, s 21(1)(b) as amended by the Housing Act 1996, s 98.

(c) the order for possession will not take effect earlier than 6 months after the beginning of the tenancy (or the beginning of the original tenancy if the order sought relates to a replacement tenancy).[139]

(2) If it is a *periodic* tenancy, the court will make an order for possession where:
   (a) the tenant has been given a notice in writing stating that possession is required on a date specified therein (being the last day of a period and not earlier than 2 months after the notice is given);[140] and
   (b) the date specified must be no earlier than the earliest date on which the tenancy could have been brought to an end by a notice to quit, had a notice to quit been served on the same day as the said notice;[141] and
   (c) the order for possession will not take effect earlier than 6 months after the beginning of the tenancy (or the beginning of the original tenancy if the order sought relates to a replacement tenancy).[142]

This notice referred to in (1)(b) and (2)(b) above is not a notice to quit so the common law technicalities do not apply[143] but even so it is important to comply with the provisions of s 21 of the Housing Act 1988 when giving such a notice, otherwise the notice will be invalid and of no effect.[144] Since there may be a risk of arithmetical error in giving the precise expiry date of a periodic tenancy, it is wise to use a general formula in the notice, such as:

> 'Possession is required of [the property], which you hold as tenant, at the end of the period of your tenancy which will end after the expiry of two months from the service upon you of this notice.'[145]

14.38 Tenancy Deposit Schemes Since 6 April 2007 legislation has been in force[146] to protect deposits paid to landlords under assured shorthold tenancies and to regulate disputes in relation thereto. There are two different deposit schemes. First, a custodial scheme[147] whereby the landlord pays the deposit to the scheme administrator to hold in a separate account until the determination of the tenancy. Secondly, an insurance scheme[148] whereby the landlord retains the deposit subject to undertaking to the scheme administrator to comply with the administrator's directions, such as to pay the deposit to the administrator in the event of a dispute as to whether the deposit should be returned to the tenant at the end of the

---

139 Housing Act 1988, s 21(5) as inserted by the Housing Act 1996, s 99.
140 Ibid, s 21(4)(a).
141 Ibid, s 21(4)(b).
142 Ibid, s 21(5) as inserted by the Housing Act 1996, s 99.
143 *Fernandez v McDonald* [2004] 1 WLR 1027, CA, at 1033.
144 Ibid.
145 *Notting Hill Trust v Roomus* [2006] 1 WLR 1375, CA, at 1379.
146 Housing Act 2004, ss 212–215.
147 Ibid, Sch 10, para 1(2).
148 Ibid, Sch 10, para 1(3).

tenancy. The administrator must insure against the risk of the landlord failing so to comply. In either case the landlord must notify the tenant about the scheme and its procedures.[149] If a landlord takes a deposit but fails to comply with the deposit scheme procedures a court may order him to return the deposit and pay the tenant a sum equal to three times the deposit.[150]

6. DISCRIMINATION IN LANDLORD AND TENANT MATTERS

14.39 The provisions of the Equality Act 2010 ('EQA 2010') as they impact generally on joining, managing and leaving a club have been considered elsewhere in the book.[151] Part 4 (ss 32–38) deals specifically with the disposal, management and occupation of premises and their potential impact on the club as landlord or tenant will now be considered.

14.40 Disposing of property A person having the right to dispose of premises[152] may not discriminate against[153] or victimise[154] another person:

(1) as to the terms upon which he offers to dispose of the premises to that other;[155]
(2) by not disposing of them to that other;[156]
(3) in his treatment of that other with respect to things done in relation to persons seeking premises.[157]

Thus a landlord may not refuse to let premises to a potential tenant on the ground that the applicant is the Basset Gay & Lesbian Society. This would amount to sexual orientation discrimination. Similarly, if the Basset Gay & Lesbian Society did successfully obtain a tenancy of the premises but later wished to sublet part, they would not be able to offer that part at a higher price to the Basset Afro-Caribbean Society than to any other potential assignee. This would amount to racial discrimination.

---

149 Housing Act 2004, s 213(5) and Housing (Tenancy Deposit) (Prescribed Information) Order 2007, SI 2007/797.
150 Housing Act 2004, s 214(3) and (4).
151 See **4.19**, **5.64**, **6.40**, **7.37**and **9.51**.
152 See Equality Act 2010, s 38(3)–(6).
153 Ibid, s 33(1). See further **4.23**.
154 Ibid, s 33(4). See further **4.25**.
155 Ibid, s 33(1)(a).
156 Ibid, s 33(1)(b).
157 Ibid, s 33(1)(c).

14.41 Part 4 of EQA 2010 does not apply to the protected characteristics of age, marriage or civil partnership so that a landlord could decline to let premises to the Basset Darby & Joan Club without being in breach of Part 4.

14.42 In addition to the bar on discrimination and victimisation, a person having a right to dispose of premises may not harass another in connection with anything done in relation to the occupation or disposal of those premises.[158] It is to be noted that for the purposes of harassment EQA 2010 excludes pregnancy and maternity[159] and that for the purposes of harassment in relation to premises EQA 2010 also excludes religion or belief and sexual orientation.[160]

14.43 Managing property This brings its own set of rules. A person who manages premises may not discriminate against or vicitimise another who occupies the premises.[161] This may occur:

(1) by the way in which the occupant is allowed to make use of a benefit or facility or by the occupant not being allowed to use it at all;[162]
(2) by evicting the occupant or taking steps to secure their eviction;[163]
(3) by subjecting the occupant to any other detriment.[164]

Suppose the landlord owned premises divided into two parts with some shared accommodation and he let the premises to two different clubs, the Basset Parent & Toddler Club and the Basset Start Again Club whose members had successfully undergone gender reassignment surgery. The landlord would not be able to prevent members of the latter club using the common toilet facilities which were available for use by the former club nor could he restrict their use by the latter club to certain times of the day. In both instances this would amount to gender reassignment discrimination.

14.44 A manager of premises is also prohibited from harassing an occupant of premises or someone who applies for premises.[165] Religion or belief and sexual orientation are excluded characteristics for the purposes of harassment in relation to the management of premises.[166]

14.45 Disability discrimination and occupation There is a general duty upon associations in relation to the making of reasonable adjustments for

158 Equality Act 2010, s 33(3). See further **4.24**.
159 Ibid, s 26(5).
160 Ibid, s 33(6).
161 Ibid, s 35(1).
162 Ibid, s 35(1)(a).
163 Ibid, s 35(1)(b).
164 Ibid, s 35(1)(c).
165 Ibid, s 35(2).
166 Ibid, s 35(4).

disabled persons.[167] EQA 2010 makes specific provision in relation to premises[168] and in particular places a duty to make these reasonable adjustments on a landlord[169] or proposed landlord[170] and a person responsible for common parts.[171] There need not in fact be a letting or proposed letting since a right to occupy suffices to impose the duty,[172] so this means a landlord will include a licensor. It is to be noted that the Disability Discrimination (Premises) Regulations 2006[173] were revoked on 1 October 2010[174] as they were no longer necessary, being superseded by the provisions of EQA 2010.

7. LICENCES

14.46 Introduction The basic distinction between a lease (or tenancy) and a licence is that under the former the tenant has exclusive possession of premises and can exclude all the world (including the landlord) whereas under the latter he has no such possession,[175] that is to say, the landlord retains a degree of control over the occupied premises. Broadly speaking, there are two situations where a club will come across a licence, the first being when it is itself a licensee of another person and the other is when it acts as employer. An example of the first category is where a cricket club is the freehold owner of the club premises and the surrounding cricket field which it uses during the summer months but allows another club in the winter months, say a hockey or soccer club, to occupy the premises with all its facilities under a licence. An example of the second category is where a golf club employs a groundsman to look after its golf course and provides on-site accommodation for the employee.

14.47 Club as licensee What will be involved is a contractual licence, a form of contract enforceable by both the licensor and the licensee,[176] and in many ways this will not differ much from a tenancy agreement. The big difference is the lack of security, especially at the end of the licence. In order to continue at the same premises the club will of necessity have to re-negotiate a new licence on the best terms that it can obtain. It is also important for a club to ensure that it obtains a contractual licence because of

---

167 As to which, see **5.71**.
168 Equality Act 2010, s 36 and Sch 4.
169 Ibid, s 36(1)(a) and 2(a); see also s 36(1)(d) and (5)(a).
170 Ibid, s 36(1)(b) and 3(a).
171 Ibid, s 36(1)(d).
172 Ibid, s 36(7).
173 SI 2006/887.
174 Equality Act 2010 (Disability) Regulations 2010, SI 2010/2128, reg 15(2)(viii).
175 *Street v Mountford* [1985] AC 809.
176 *Verrall v Great Yarmouth Council* [1980] 3 WLR 258, CA; *Tanner v Tanner* [1975] 1 WLR 1346, CA.

the licensor's power at common law to revoke a *bare* licence at any time.[177] If the club negotiates a fixed-term contractual licence or an express period of notice in a contractual licence without a fixed term it will avoid having to argue that it has 'a licence coupled with an equity', that is to say, asking the court to imply a negative contractual term in restraint of revocation before the expiry of the contractual period of the licence; albeit today the courts are much more willing to imply such a term than hitherto.[178] A contractual licence held by the club will be held sometimes in the name of trustees and at other times in the name of the club.[179]

14.48 Club as licensor Since the advent of the commonly used assured shorthold tenancy in 1989 and particularly since it became the default residential tenancy in 1997, the need for landlords to think of devices to avoid the much greater security of tenure enjoyed by regulated tenants under the Rent Acts and by fully assured tenants under the Housing Act 1988 has to a large extent evaporated. The device usually relied on was the licence which gives no security of tenure and where the landlord can obtain a court order for possession without having to rely on any statutory ground or without giving any reason. Many of these so-called licences were exposed in the courts as shams because although on their face they were described as licences the occupants in fact had exclusive possession and were thus tenants.[180] However, there is a further type of occupant, namely a service occupant, who is neither a tenant nor a licensee, a classic example being the caretaker of premises. If the club employee is genuinely required to occupy the premises or it is necessary for him to do so for the better performance of his duties, then the employee will be neither a licensee nor a tenant (even if he has exclusive possession) but rather a service occupier. This is because the law treats the occupation as being that of the employer rather than the employee and the employee's right to occupy the premises terminates with their employment.[181] Although the label which the parties put on the transaction is not definitive,[182] it is still important to use the right terminology when granting a licence, and words like 'the payment of rent' should be avoided when granting a licence.

14.49 Protection from eviction At common law when a tenancy or licence comes to an end the landlord or licensor is entitled to re-enter and take possession of the premises. However, the Protection from Eviction Act 1977

---

177 *Thompson v Park* [1944 KB 408, CA. *Wood v Leadbitter* [1845] 13 M & W 838. Albeit that the licensee will be entitled to a 'period of grace' in which to pack up and go. In some cases this may be a long time. In *Henrietta Barnet School v Hampstead Garden Suburb* [1995] EGCS 55, 8 months was considered insufficient time for a school to relocate.

178 *Chandler v Kerley* [1978] 1 WLR 693, CA, per Lord Scarman at 697 ('where the parties have contracted for a licence, equity today will provide an equitable remedy to protect the legal right').

179 See **14.5**.

180 See eg *Antoniades v Villiers* [1990] 1 AC 417.

181 *Glasgow Corpn v Johnstone* [1965] AC 609; *Norris v Checksfield* [1991] 1 WLR 1241.

182 *Crancour v Da Silvaesa* [1986] 1 EGLR 81, CA.

provides a measure of assistance to those residential occupiers who are not protected under the Rent Act 1977 or the Housing Act 1988, and to licensees who have no other statutory protection once their contractual entitlement to occupy has come to an end. For example, if a residential tenancy or licence has come to an end and the occupier continues to reside in the premises, it will be a criminal offence to deprive the occupier of possession save through a court order[183] or unlawfully to harass him.[184] The fact that criminal proceedings are taken under the 1977 Act will not prejudice the right of the occupier to seek a civil remedy against the landlord or licensor, such as damages for a breach of the covenant for quiet enjoyment.[185] It should also be noted that, in addition to damages at common law, a residential tenant may be able to claim very substantial damages for unlawful eviction under ss 27 and 28 of the Housing Act 1988.

8. PROPRIETARY CLUBS

14.50 Whether the proprietor is the freehold or leasehold owner of the club premises, the club will be either the licensee of the proprietor if it is a separate entity or the proprietor himself will be in occupation of the premises. In either event there will be no question of the club having protection under Part II of the Landlord and Tenant Act 1954 nor will the club have any landlord and tenant relationship with the proprietor's employees.

---

183 Protection from Eviction Act 1977, s 3(1).
184 Ibid, ss 1(2) and (3).
185 Ibid, s 1(5).

Chapter 15

THE CLUB'S EMPLOYMENT OF THIRD PARTIES

1. OVERVIEW

15.1 Clubs are frequently employers of staff. This employment brings in its wake a whole raft of statutory law and regulation. The potential liability of employing a significant number of staff is such that it has led one writer[1] to advocate that this factor alone should make an unincorporated members' club give careful thought to some form of corporate status as a protection from liability. We do not dissent from the proposition that such a club should give careful thought to this topic, but instead our emphasis would be that the employment of staff requires the managing committee to pay close attention to employment law if the club is to avoid its potential exposure to liability. The Department for Education and Employment and the Department for Business, Innovation & Skills produce a large number of free explanatory leaflets which deal with specific areas of employment law (eg unfair dismissal or redundancy payments) which are helpful to lawyers and non-lawyers alike to understand the position. The following paragraphs are intended to give an outline of the main areas of employment law which clubs of whatever type are likely to encounter when employing staff.[2]

15.2 What is employment This point has already been touched upon when considering the club's liability for torts.[3] The distinction here is between a contract *of* service (or a contract of employment in modern parlance) under which an employee will work and a contract *for* services under which an independent contractor (or self-employed person) will provide services to the employer. There is no one simple test for discerning the difference between an employee and a self-employed person. The label which the parties themselves give to the relationship is not decisive; one has to look at the reality of the situation and all the terms of the contract will be looked at objectively in order to arrive at the right answer.[4] The following are generally considered to be essential to a contract of employment:

---

1 *Warburton on Unincorporated Associations* (2nd edn, 1992) p 92.

2 See *Harvey on Industrial Relations and Employment Law* (loose-leaf) for detailed guidance.

3 See **12.29**.

4 *Carmichael v National Power plc* [1999] 1 WLR 2042, HL, at 2049C (Lord Hoffmann).

(1) an obligation on the employee to work personally;[5]
(2) a mutuality of obligation (usually an obligation on the part of the employer to make work available and a corresponding obligation on the employee to carry out the work);[6]
(3) a right by the employer to exercise a degree of control over the way in which the work is carried out.[7]

15.3 If these minimum requirements are met, other factors, such as stipulations as to hours of work, whether holiday pay is paid, who provides the tools and equipment, who bears the loss and how the contract is terminated, are looked at to see whether the contract can properly be characterised as one of employment.[8] By way of an example, a professional at a golf club may well satisfy the essential requirements of a contract of employment but the unusually relaxed terms under which golf professionals tend to work might mean that he could not be properly characterised as an employee. The distinction is significant because the more important statutory rights do not apply to a contract for services.

15.4 Who is the employer In the case of community and incorporated clubs the question poses no problem because the club has a separate existence from its members. This problem arises in the case of unincorporated clubs which have no legal personality. In the ordinary course of events the managing committee would be the employer as it is they who control the affairs of the club.[9] It is true that in *Campbell v Thompson and Shill*[10] Mr Justice Pritchard held that the employer of the plaintiff, a cleaner, was the whole membership of 2,500 of the City Livery Club but such a decision is very unlikely to be repeated today.

2. CONTRACT OF EMPLOYMENT

15.5 Notwithstanding the weight of statutory intervention the contract of employment remains the basis of the relationship between the employer and the employee. Although a contract of employment may be either written or oral or partly both, it is better practice for the employer to provide the employee with a contract in writing. The written contract should identify such parts of the staff handbook or other document as to which the employer wishes to give contractual effect.

---

5 *Express & Echo Publications Ltd v Tanton* [1999] IRLR 367; cf *Macfarlane v Glasgow CC* [2001] IRLR 7.

6 *Carmichael v National Power plc* [1999] 1 WLR 2042, HL.

7 *Ready Mixed Concrete v Minister of Pensions and National Insurance* [1968] 2 QB 497.

8 *Hall v Lorimer* [1994] ICR 218.

9 *Affleck v Newcastle Mind* [1999] 1 ICR 852 EAT, at 854 (Morrison J).

10 [1953] 2 WLR 656.

15.6 The employer must in any event give the employee a written statement of particulars of certain terms of his contract not later than 2 months after the beginning of the employment.[11] There is an obviously sound reason for this requirement. When disputes arise or are referred to an employment tribunal, it is essential that each side knows what its rights and obligations are and many a time the first area of dispute is what was agreed between the parties. The following statutory particulars must be set down:[12]

(1) the names of the employer and the employee;
(2) the date when the employment began;
(3) the date on which the employee's *continuous* employment began;[13]
(4) the scale or rate of remuneration, or the method of calculating the remuneration;
(5) the interval at which remuneration is: paid (eg weekly, monthly);
(6) the terms and conditions relating to hours of work;
(7) any terms relating to:
   (a) holidays
   (b) sick pay
   (c) pensions;
(8) the length of notice the employee is obliged to give and entitled to receive to terminate the contract of employment;
(9) the job title or a brief description of the employee's work;
(10) where the employment is not intended to be permanent, the period for which it is expected to continue or, if it is for a fixed term, the date when it is to end;
(11) either the place of work or, where the employee is required or permitted to work at various places, an indication of those places and the employer's address;
(12) any collective agreements which directly affect the terms and conditions of the employment;
(13) where the employee is required to work outside the UK for more than a month, certain further particulars like the currency of remuneration;
(14) any disciplinary rules applicable to the employee (or referring to some accessible document containing these rules);
(15) the identity of the person:
   (a) to whom the employee can apply if he is dissatisfied with any disciplinary decision or any decision to dismiss him;
   (b) to whom the employee can apply for the purpose of seeking redress of any grievance relating to his employment and the manner in which such application should be made (or referring to some accessible document containing the procedure).[14]

---

11 Employment Rights Act 1996, s 1(1).
12 Ibid, s 1(3)–(5).
13 As to continuous employment, see **15.9**.
14 As to items (1) to (13), see the Employment Rights Act 1996, s 1(3)–(5). As to items (14) and (15) see s 3 of this Act, as amended by s 35 of the Employment Act 2002. Items (14) and (15) do not apply to procedures relating to health and safety: Employment Rights Act 1996,

15.7 It is not compulsory for the contract of employment to set forth the terms and conditions relating to *all* the above items. What is required is *notice* of any terms agreed. One matter of importance which should always be in writing is an adequate job description so that both sides know precisely what is expected of the employee in carrying out his employment. If the contract does not include any particular item, eg no contractual pension is provided, the statement should say so.[15] It also has to be understood that the statutory written statement is not the contract of employment itself nor conclusive evidence of it,[16] but in many cases the employer and employee will be content to treat this statement as evidence of a binding contract of employment. Likewise a written contract can itself be relied upon as the statement of particulars so long as it includes all the necessary statutory information.

15.8 Implied terms In addition to the terms expressly agreed between the parties, there are terms which may be implied into the contract of employment on the grounds either that they reflect the obvious (albeit unexpressed) intention of the parties; or that they are necessary to give business efficacy to the contract; or that they reflect the usual (ie 'reasonable, certain and notorious'), custom and practice of the particular employer; or that they are implied by virtue of a specific statutory provision. Examples of terms commonly implied into contracts of employment are:

(1) on the part of the employee, that he will carry out his duties with due diligence and care; that he will obey lawful and reasonable orders; that he will serve his employer with fidelity and in good faith; and that he will not disclose confidential information;[17]
(2) on the part of the employer, that he will not without reasonable and proper cause conduct himself in a manner calculated or likely to destroy or seriously damage the relationship of trust and confidence which exists between employer and employee.[18]

A term will not be implied if to do so would contradict an express term of the contract.[19]

15.9 Continuous employment This is a concept which is important for many of the statutory employment rights, such as the right to claim a redundancy payment or compensation for unfair dismissal, which are conferred only on those employees who have accrued a sufficient period of

---

s 3(2). The Employment Act 2002, s 36 abolished the exemption whereby an employer with fewer than 20 employees did not need to inform employees of disciplinary procedures.

15 Employment Rights Acts 1996, s 2(1).

16 *Robertson v British Gas Corporation* [1983] ICR 351, CA.

17 *Chitty on Contracts* (30th edn, 2008) at 39-055 to 39-073.

18 *Malik v Bank of Credit and Commerce International SA* [1998] AC 20.

19 *Duke of Westminster v Guild* [1985] QB 688, CA, at 700.

continuous employment. There are technical rules (outside the scope of this book) as to what does and does not count as continuous employment. Broadly speaking, any week during the whole or part of which the employee's relationship was governed by a contract of employment counts towards continuous employment.[20] Periods of part-time employment, irrespective of the number of hours worked per week, still count in the computation of continuous employment. Continuity will not be broken by periods of maternity leave, sickness absence, or absence due to a temporary cessation of work.[21]

15.10 Continuity is preserved if an employee is transferred to an 'associated employer', eg a subsidiary or sister company of the previous employer,[22] or if the transfer is the result of a 'transfer of undertaking', eg on the purchase of the previous employer's business.[23] Likewise, the death of an employer does not break continuity nor does a change in partners, personal representatives or trustees.[24] Where the employee in an unincorporated members' club is employed by the managing committee (as is the norm) any change in the composition of the committee has no bearing on the continuity of the employment.[25] Thus would remain the case even if the *entire* committee was replaced at one particular election.

15.11 Part-time employees Part-time workers have the right not to be treated less favourably than comparable full-time workers whether as regards the terms of their contract or by being subjected to a detriment. In determining whether a part-time worker has been treated less favourably, where appropriate a pro rata principle is applied (eg in relation to pay and other benefits). If the employee establishes less favourable treatment, then the burden moves to the employer to justify it on objective grounds. This protection is particularly relevant to employees' contractual benefits such as membership of a bonus scheme or an occupational pension scheme. Employers should be careful not to exclude part-time workers from membership of such schemes unless there are proper reasons for doing so.[26]

15.12 Fixed-term employees Fixed-term employees are employed under a contract which is due to terminate on the expiry of a specific term; on the completion of a particular task; or on the occurrence or non-occurrence of a specific event other than normal retirement age. As with part-time workers, fixed-term employees have the right not to be treated less favourably than

---

20 Employment Rights Act 1996, s 212(1).
21 Even if there is no contract of employment in existence during these periods: ibid, s 212(3).
22 Ibid, s 218(6).
23 Ibid, s 218(2).
24 Ibid, s 218(4) and (5).
25 *Affleck v Newcastle Mind* [1999] 1 ICR 852 EAT, at 854.
26 See the Part-Time Workers (Prevention of Less Favourable Treatment) Regulations 2000, SI 2000/1551.

comparable permanent employees whether as regards the terms of their employment or by being subjected to a detriment. In determining whether a fixed-term employee has been treated less favourably, where appropriate a pro rata principle is applied. If the employee establishes less favourable treatment, then the burden moves to the employer to justify it on objective grounds. Treatment can be justified on the grounds that the terms of the fixed-term contract taken as a whole are at least as favourable as those of the comparable permanent employee.[27]

15.13 Both part-time and fixed-term employees can present a complaint of less favourable treatment to the Employment Tribunal within 3 months of the date of the less favourable treatment. This period can be extended if the tribunal thinks it just and equitable to do so. The tribunal may make a declaration as to the parties' rights; make an order for compensation; or make recommendations to reduce or obviate the effect of the less favourable treatment.[28]

3. PAY

15.14 The question of pay is primarily governed by the terms of the contract of employment, the particulars of which must form part of the statutory written particulars.[29] Some important payment rights, however, are regulated by statute and these rights are discussed below.

15.15 Minimum wage From 1 October 2010 the minimum wage for those aged 21 years and over is £5.93 per hour, for those aged 18 to 20 years it is £4.92 per hour and for those aged under 18 years who are no longer of compulsory school age[30] it s £3.64 per hour.[31] The employer must maintain records of hours worked and payments made. The employee may request inspection of these records and ask for a copy of them.[32]

15.16 Holiday pay An employee has a statutory right of up to 5.6 working weeks' paid annual leave (basic and additional) subject to an aggregate

---

27 See the Fixed-term Employees (Prevention of Less Favourable Treatment) Regulations 2002, SI 2002/2034.

28 Health and Safety at Work etc Act 1974, s 47(1).

29 See **15.6**.

30 In England and Wales a person is no longer of compulsory school age after the last Friday of June of the school year in which their 16th birthday occurs.

31 National Minimum Wage Regulations 1999 (Amendment) Regulations 2010, SI 2010/1901, regs 3 and 5.

32 See the National Minimum Wage Act 1998, s 10 and the National Minimum Wage Regulations 1999, SI 1999/584, as amended.

maximum of 28 working days a year.[33] There is no continuous-employment requirement to qualify for this right but during the first year of employment leave is deemed to accrue at the rate of one-twelfth of the annual entitlement at the beginning of each month of employment, and the entitlement to take leave is limited during the first year to the amount of leave that is deemed to have accrued under this formula at the time of taking the leave, less any leave already taken. The employee is entitled to be paid for any period of leave at the rate of 1 week's pay for each week of leave. If the contractual holiday rights are more generous than the statutory rights, the contractual rights will apply. Bank Holidays should count as paid holiday days.[34] An employer cannot contract out of the holiday pay provisions.[35]

15.17 Sick pay If there is no sick pay entitlement under the contract of employment the employee may be entitled to statutory sick pay. Generally speaking, the entitlement is 28 weeks. In order to qualify for statutory sick pay the employee must have 4 or more consecutive days of sickness during which he is too ill to work; he must notify his employer of his absence; and he must supply evidence of his incapacity to work.[36] Certain categories of employee are excluded from the entitlement to statutory sick pay, most notably those whose average weekly earnings are less than the weekly lower earnings limit for paying national insurance contributions, presently (2010) £97 per week.[37] The amount of statutory sick pay is currently (2010) £79.15 per week. If an employer refuses to pay statutory sick pay the employee can ask for written reasons for that decision.[38] The employee can then appeal to HMRC who will consider whether he is so entitled.[39]

15.18 Maternity pay In order to qualify for statutory maternity pay the employee must have been continuously employed by her employer for at least 26 weeks ending with the week immediately preceding the 14th week before her expected week of confinement ('EWCo'). In addition, her normal weekly earnings for the period of 8 weeks ending with the week immediately preceding the 14th week before EWCo must not be less than the lower limit for the payment of national insurance contributions,

---

33 Working Time Regulations 1998, SI 1998/1833, as amended, regs 13(1) and 13A. Thus, e g 5 working days per week x 5.6 holiday weeks = 28 days paid holiday.

34 *Tucker v British Leyland Motor Corporation Ltd* [1978] IRLR 493, at 496.

35 Working Time Regulations 1998, as amended, reg 35.

36 Social Security Contributions and Benefits Act 1992, ss 151–152; Social Security Administration Act 1992, s 14; and Statutory Sick Pay (General) Regulations 1982, SI 1982/894, as amended, reg 7.

37 Social Security Contributions and Benefits Act 1992, as amended, Sch 11; Social Security Act 1985, s 18(2); and the Statutory Sick Pay (General) Regulations 1982, SI 1982/894, as amended.

38 Social Security Administration 1992, s 14(3).

39 Statutory Sick Pay and Statutory Maternity Pay (Decisions) Regulations 1999, SI 1999/776.

presently (2010) £97 per week; and she must still be pregnant at the 11th week before her EWCo, or have had the baby at that time.[40]

15.19 The employee is entitled to statutory maternity pay for 39 weeks commencing when the employee, having given proper notice, stops work. This start may not be earlier than the 11th week before EWCo nor later than the week immediately following the week of confinement.[41] This means that the employee, if she wishes, can continue to work until the date of confinement and not lose her entitlement to statutory maternity pay. The notice in question is 28 days.[42] The employee must provide a maternity certificate signed by a doctor or midwife as evidence of her pregnancy and of the expected date of confinement.[43] The amount of statutory maternity pay is currently (2010) as follows: for the first 6 weeks of the maternity-pay period it is nine-tenths of the employee's normal weekly earnings for the period of 8 weeks immediately preceding the 14th week before EWCo.[44] Thereafter it is a payment of £124.88 per week or 90% of the woman's normal earnings, whichever is the lesser sum.

15.20 Deductions Deductions may be made from wages either because it is required by statute (eg an attachment of earnings order); or it is permitted by the terms of the contract of employment; or the employee has given his prior written consent to the deduction.[45] If the deduction is made pursuant to a term of the contract of employment, that term must have been shown to the employee (or, if not in writing, its effect notified in writing) before the deduction is made.[46] Wages in this context include any bonus, commission, holiday pay, statutory sick pay and statutory maternity pay.[47] Excluded from the definition of wages are, for example, payments in respect of expenses incurred by the employee in carrying out his job; payments by way of pension; and redundancy payments.[48] The employee's remedy for wrongful deductions is to make a complaint to the employment tribunal within 3 months of the deduction being made.[49]

---

40 Social Security Contributions and Benefits Act 1992, s 164(1)–(2).

41 Ibid, s 165, as amended by SI 1994/1230, reg 3 and by SI 1986/1960, reg 2 (itself amended by SI 1994/1367, reg 2); Employment Act 2002, s 18.

42 Employment Act 2002, s 20.

43 Social Security Administration Act 1992, s 15.

44 Social Security Contributions and Benefits Act 1992, s 166, as amended by SI 1994/1367, reg 6.

45 Employment Rights Act 1996, ss 13(1), 15(1).

46 Ibid, ss 14 and 15.

47 Ibid, s 27(1).

48 Ibid, s 27(2).

49 Ibid, s 23. There is a discretionary power to extend this time limit if the tribunal is satisfied that it was not reasonably practicable to present the claim within the 3-month period: s 23(4).

15.21 PAYE and NIC The wages of the club's employees are subject to income tax.[50] The employee's tax will be deducted at source under the Pay as You Earn scheme.[51] National Insurance Contributions, in effect another form of taxation, are payable by the club as employer and by the employee.[52]

4. MATERNITY AND OTHER LEAVE

15.22 Maternity leave Female employees have a statutory entitlement to maternity leave[53] and maternity pay.[54] If their contract of employment also includes a contractual entitlement to maternity leave and maternity pay then they can chose whichever scheme is more favourable. The statutory scheme is both detailed and oddly complex. Its main provisions are set out below.

15.23 ***Compulsory maternity leave*** An employer must not allow an employee to work for at least two weeks commencing with the day on which childbirth occurs.[55]

15.24 ***Ordinary maternity leave*** An employee is entitled to ordinary maternity leave ('OML') of 26 weeks. Her OML starts on the earliest of the following dates:

(1) the date notified by the employee as the date on which she intends her period of OML to commence (which must be no earlier than the beginning of the 11th week before the expected week of childbirth ('EWCh');
(2) the first day on which the employee is absent from work wholly or partly because of pregnancy or childbirth after the beginning of the fourth week before EWCh; or
(3) the day after the day on which childbirth occurs.[56]

An employee's entitlement to OML is conditional upon her giving her employer proper notice of her OML.[57] Having received such notice, the

---

50 Income Tax (Earnings and Pensions) Act 2003, Part 2 (ss 3–61J). The Act imposes a charge to tax on employment income. This system broadly retains the effect of the former Schedule E tax on emoluments.

51 Ibid, Part 11 (ss 682–712).

52 National Insurance Contributions and Statutory Payments Act 2004.

53 Employment Rights Act 1996, ss 71–75.

54 Social Security Contributions and Benefits Act 1992, as amended by Employment Act 2002 and Work and Families Act 2006. The main regulations are Statutory Maternity Pay (General) Regulations 1986, SI 1986/1960.

55 Employment Rights Act 1996, s 72.

56 Maternity and Parental Leave Regulations 1999, SI 1999/3312, as amended, reg 6.

57 Ibid, as amended, reg 4.

employer must confirm when the employee's OML (or, if applicable, her additional maternity leave) is due to end. The employee must give 28 days notice if she intends to return early.[58]

15.25 At the end of her OML an employee is entitled to return to her previous job unless during her OML she has been made redundant. She is entitled to return on terms and conditions no less favourable than those that she would have enjoyed had she not been absent, eg with the benefit of any pay rises awarded during her absence.[59]

15.26 ***Additional maternity leave*** An employee is entitled to an additional maternity leave ('AML') of 26 weeks commencing at the end of her OML.[60] At the end of her AML, unless she has been made redundant, she is entitled to return to her previous job or, if that is not reasonably practicable, to another job which is both suitable and appropriate.[61] That new job must itself be on terms and conditions not less favourable than those which would have applied had she not been absent.[62]

15.27 **Paternity leave** In order to qualify the employee must have been continuously employed for at least 26 weeks ending with the week immediately preceding the 14th week before EWCo. The employee must be either the child's father and have, or expect to have, responsibility for the child's upbringing; or be married to or be the partner of the child's mother and have the main responsibility for the upbringing of the child. The employee is entitled to 2 weeks paid leave for each child. Currently (2010) the pay is the lower of £124.88 or 90% the employee's average weekly earnings.[63] The leave may be taken during the period of 56 days commencing with the child's birth or the first day of EWCo. As with maternity leave, the employee's entitlement is conditional upon him giving the proper notice. At the end of his leave the employee is entitled to return to the same job (or, if that is not reasonably practicable, to another job which is suitable and appropriate) on the same terms and conditions as if he had not taken leave. An employer cannot contract out of the obligation to provide paternity leave and pay.[64]

15.28 **Parental leave** An employee who has been continuously employed for a year and has or expects to have responsibility for a child is entitled to

---

58 Maternity and Parental Leave Regulations 1999, SI 1999/3312, reg 11(1).
59 Ibid, reg18A.
60 Ibid, regs 5 to 7.
61 Ibid, reg 18A.
62 Ibid, reg 18(2).
63 Statutory Maternity Pay (General) Regulations 1986, SI 1986/1960: figure substituted by Social Security Benefits Up-rating Order 2010, SI 2010/793, art 10.
64 See the Paternity and Adoption Leave Regulations 2002, SI 2002/2788.

13 weeks unpaid parental leave for each child (18 weeks if the child is disabled). This leave should ordinarily be taken before the child's fifth birthday.[65]

15.29 Time off work Employees have additional rights to take time off work in a variety of situations including:

(1) time off with pay for the purpose of trade union official duties; or for ante-natal appointments; or to enable an employee under notice of redundancy to look for alternative employment;[66]
(2) time off without pay for the purpose of trade union activities and representation; or for public duties (eg sitting as a magistrate).[67]

5. RIGHT NOT TO SUFFER DETRIMENT

15.30 An employee's primary statutory rights, eg to maternity leave, paternity leave, etc are in most cases reinforced by a corresponding secondary right not to be subjected to a detriment for exercising the primary right.[68] In addition, there are particular activities which do not involve the exercise of a statutory right but which Parliament has chosen to protect by a right not to be subjected to a detriment for carrying out the activity, as are set out below. An employee who has been unlawfully subjected to a detriment at work can present a complaint to the employment tribunal if he does so within 3 months beginning with the date on which the detriment occurred or within such further period as the tribunal considers reasonable if it was not reasonably practicable for the complaint to be presented within the 3 month period. The tribunal will declare the claim to be well founded and may award such compensation as it considers just and equitable in all the circumstances.

15.31 Trade union activities It is unlawful for an employer to subject his employee to a detriment for membership of, or for taking part in the activities of, a trade union.[69] It should be noted that the purpose of a particular course of action by the employer is determined by the object which the employer desires to achieve rather than the consequences of that course of action.

---

65 See the Maternity and Parental Leave Regulations 1999, as amended, regs 13–20.

66 Trade Union and Labour Relations (Consolidation) Act 1992, s 168; Employment Relations Act 1999, ss 52, 55.

67 Trade Union and Labour Relations (Consolidation) Act 1992, s 170; Employment Relations Act 1999, s 50.

68 Eg Maternity and Parental Leave Regulations 1999, SI 1999/3312, as amended, reg 19; Paternity and Adoption Leave Regulations 2002, SI 2002/2788, reg 28.

69 Trade Union and Labour Relations (Consolidation) Act 1992, s 146.

15.32 Health and safety activities An employee has a right not to suffer detriment on grounds connected with health and safety.[70] This protection applies particularly to employees who are carrying out health and safety duties assigned to them; or who are health and safety representatives; or who in the absence of a health and safety representative bring health and safety issues to the attention of their employers and are subjected to a detriment as a result.

15.33 'Whistleblowing' An employee has the right not to suffer detriment because he has made a public interest disclosure. These provisions apply to employees who make protected disclosures of qualifying information.[71] 'Qualifying information' is information which in the reasonable belief of the employee tends to show that there has been or is likely to be a crime; a breach of other legal obligation; a miscarriage of justice; a danger to health and safety; or damage to the environment; or to show that one of the above matters has been or is likely to be deliberately concealed.[72] The disclosure of this information to an employer in good faith is 'protected'. Disclosure in good faith to certain prescribed persons, eg HMRC and the Health and Safety Executive is 'protected' if the employee reasonably believes that the information is relevant to the prescribed person and that it is true. Disclosure in good faith to other third parties is 'protected' if the employee reasonably believes that the information is true; the disclosure is not made for personal gain; the disclosure is reasonable; and there has been prior disclosure to the employer. Disclosure to third parties without prior disclosure to the employer is 'protected' only in more limited circumstances.[73]

6. HEALTH AND SAFETY AT WORK

15.34 An employer is under a common law duty to have regard to the safety of his employees. Statutory obligations have also been imposed on the employer, mainly by the Health and Safety at Work etc Act 1974 and the regulations published under it. Breach of the provisions of the 1974 Act and the regulations thereunder gives rise to criminal liability[74] and breach of these regulations which causes injury or damage gives rise to civil liability.[75] Any provision in the contract of employment excluding liability for breaches of the said regulations is void.[76]

70 Employment Rights Act 1996, s 44.
71 Ibid, s 43A and 43B, both sections added by Public Interest Disclosure Act 1998, s 1.
72 Employment Rights Act 1996, s 43B.
73 Ibid, ss 43C to 43H, all sections added by Public Interest Disclosure Act 1998, s 1.
74 Health and Safety at Work etc Act 1974, s 33.
75 Ibid, s 47(2).
76 Ibid, s 47(5).

15.35 Broadly speaking, the 1974 Act contains provisions which correspond to the general common law duty imposed on an employer to take reasonable care of the safety of its employee. In addition, the Act imposes more specific duties. For example, where an employer employs five or more employees,[77] the employer must prepare (and revise, if necessary) a written statement of its general policy with respect to the health and safety of its employees, which is to be displayed on an easily accessible notice board.[78] In addition, information as to health, safety and welfare must be given to employees by means of posters and leaflets approved and published by the Health and Safety Executive.[79]

15.36 In many respects the employer's common law duties have been rendered obsolete by regulations published over the last 20 years to implement the various EU Directives relating to health and safety at work. These common law and statutory duties may be summarised as follows:[80]

(1) ***Safe place of work***
The employer is under a common law duty to provide a reasonably safe place of work and means of access to work. The Workplace (Health, Safety and Welfare) Regulations 1992 now impose a statutory duty to ensure that workplaces are made and kept in an efficient state, efficient working order and good repair.[81] The regulations also include a range of specific requirements relating to lighting, cleanliness, room dimensions, arrangement of workstations, spillages and obstructions on floors etc.[82]

(2) ***Safe system of work***
At common law the employer's duty is to take reasonable steps to provide a system which will be reasonably safe, having regard to the nature of the work being carried out. Long established practice is usually regarded as strong evidence that the system being operated is a reasonable one.[83] Providing a safe system of work by itself is not sufficient. The employer must take such steps as are reasonably practicable to *implement* the system. The system must also now comply with such regulations as relate to the work being undertaken. There are a myriad of regulations covering such topics as noise at work, handling dangerous substances, construction work and asbestos.[84] The following regulations are likely to have most practical significance for clubs:

---

77 See the Employers' Health and Safety Policy Statements (Exception) Regulations 1975, SI 1975/1584.

78 Health and Safety at Work etc Act 1974, s 2(3).

79 See the Health and Safety Information for Employees Regulations 1989, SI 1989/682.

80 See *Munkman on Employers' Liability* (15th edn, 2009) for more detailed guidance.

81 See Workplace (Health, Safety and Welfare) Regulations 1992, SI 1992/3004, reg 5.

82 Ibid, regs 8–12.

83 *General Cleaning Contractors Ltd v Christmas* [1953] AC 180, at 195.

84 The complete and annotated health and safety regulations are to be found in *Redgrave's Health and Safety* (7th edn, forthcoming).

(a) the Management of Health and Safety at Work Regulations 1999.[85] These regulations require employers to put in place a proper health and safety procedure. In particular regulation 3 requires employers to carry out risk assessments of the work to be undertaken by their employees;

(b) the Manual Handling Operations Regulations 1992.[86] These regulations require employers inter alia to take steps to reduce the risk of injury from manual handling operations to the lowest level reasonably practicable. Manual handling operations are widely defined to include most manual tasks but the regulations particularly apply to lifting;

(c) the Health and Safety (Display Screen Equipment) Regulations 1992.[87] These regulations require employers to ensure that the workstations of employees who use computers are properly set up so as to reduce the risk of their developing conditions such as repetitive strain injuries.

(3) ***Safe equipment and materials***

At common law an employer's duty is to take reasonable steps to provide equipment, materials and clothing which allow the employee to carry out his work in safety. The Provision and Use of Work Equipment Regulations 1998 now impose on employers a statutory duty to ensure that work equipment is suitable for the purposes for which it was provided and that the equipment is maintained in an efficient state, in efficient working order and in good repair.[88] The regulations also include a range of specific requirements relating to such matters as training, lighting, dangerous parts, etc.[89] The Personal Protective Equipment at Work Regulations 1992[90] impose similar obligations in relation to protective equipment, eg gloves, hats, goggles, etc.

(4) ***Competent fellow employees***

The employer's duty is to provide competent fellow employees. So the known inadequacy of a particular employee should not be tolerated. In addition, under the doctrine of vicarious liability[91] the employer is liable for the acts of his employee if they are committed in the course of his employment, so that the negligent act of one employee towards another employee causing injury will render the employer liable to the injured employee. Any term in the contract of employment excluding this liability is void.[92]

---

85 SI 1999/3242.

86 SI 1992/2793. See especially reg 4.

87 SI 1992/2792.

88 SI 1998/2306. See regs 4 and 5.

89 Ibid, regs 9, 11 and 21.

90 SI 1992/2966.

91 See **12.28**.

92 Law Reform (Personal Injuries) Act 1948, s 1(3) (which Act abolished the doctrine of common employment).

15.37 If an employee establishes a breach of his employer's common law or statutory duties then the employee is entitled to damages for his injury and for the past and future losses consequent upon the injury. These damages will be reduced by the extent to which the employee's negligence (if any) contributed to his injury.[93]

15.38 Compulsory insurance Every employer carrying on a business[94] must maintain insurance, under one or more approved policies with an authorised insurer, against liability for bodily injury or diseases sustained by employees arising out of and in the course of their employment in Great Britain.[95] The sum insured must not be less than £5 million in respect of any one occurrence.[96] The insurer's annual certificate must be displayed at every place where the employer carries on business and be easily seen and read by every person employed there.

7. TERMINATION OF THE CONTRACT OF EMPLOYMENT

15.39 Modes of termination The contract may be terminated in various ways:

(1) ***By mutual agreement.***
(2) ***By expiry of the fixed term of employment***: in certain circumstances this expiry may qualify for compensation for unfair dismissal or a redundancy payment.
(3) ***By frustration of the contract***:
    (a) frustration occurs where the performance of the contract becomes impossible or substantially different from the contract contemplated at the outset by the parties through some unforeseen event and through no fault of the parties;[97]
    (b) termination of the contract is automatic, so there can be no claim for unfair or wrongful dismissal or for a redundancy payment.
(4) ***By notice of dismissal given by the employer:*** the contract of employment should always contain the length of notice the employee is entitled to receive when his employment is being terminated. If the contract is silent, the employee is entitled to reasonable notice.[98] The length of notice, however, must not be less than the statutory minimum,[99] namely:

---

93 See generally *Munkman on Employers' Liability* (15th edn, 2009).
94 This would almost invariably include a club employing staff.
95 Employers' Liability (Compulsory Insurance) Act 1969.
96 Employers' Liability (Compulsory Insurance) Regulations 1998, SI 1998/2573.
97 *Williams v Watsons Luxury Coaches Ltd* [1990] ICR 536 (illness); *FC Shepherd & Co Ltd v Jerrom* [1986] ICR 802 (custodial prison sentence).
98 *Reda v Flag Ltd* [2002] 1 IRLR 747.
99 Employment Rights Act 1996, s 12.

(a) one week for an employee who has been continuously employed for 1 month or more but less than 2 years;
(b) 1 week for every year of employment for an employee who has been continuously employed for 2 years or more but less than 12 years;
(c) not less than 12 weeks for an employee who has been continuously employed for 12 years or more.

(5) ***By notice of resignation given by the employee***:
(a) an employee may resign with or without notice. The statutory minimum period of notice is one week where the employee has been employed for 1 month or more[100] but the contractual period of notice is frequently longer than this. Failure to give proper notice is a breach of contract on the employee's part;
(b) if an employee resigns on notice, it is often over some disagreement with his employer; hence it is wise to let the period of notice be worked with the employee at home rather at work.

(6) ***Summary dismissal by the employer***: Most contracts of employment give the employer an express right to dismiss an employee without notice for gross misconduct. Such contracts usually contain a list of examples of gross misconduct such as violent or abusive behaviour, dishonesty, wilful disobedience of a lawful order or persistent misconduct;

(7) ***By the other party's acceptance of a serious repudiatory breach of the contract of employment on the part of the employer or employee***:
(a) it is essential that the breach is accepted by the innocent party as determining the contract. Acceptance of the breach, however, will be readily inferred. Acceptance by the employee will mean in many cases that the employee can assert that he was constructively dismissed by the employer;
(b) this mode of termination includes summary dismissal of the employee without notice or wages in lieu of notice, for example, serious misconduct involving wilful disobedience to a lawful order or theft of the employer's property or drunkenness whilst on duty;
(c) when an employee is sacked for whatever reason, on notice or summarily, it is always a wise practice to insist that the employee forthwith leaves the employer's premises as the employer does not want disgruntled employees to upset the rest of the workforce. If the dismissal is on notice, it is worth paying wages in lieu of notice.

15.40 Wrongful dismissal An employee who is dismissed by his employer in breach of the contractual terms agreed between them is entitled to bring a claim for damages in the courts where the limitation period for bringing a claim is 6 years from the date of dismissal[101] or in the employment tribunal

---

[100] Employment Rights Act 1996, s 86(2).
[101] Limitation Act 1980, s 6.

where the claim must be brought within 3 months (and where the tribunal does not have jurisdiction to award damages in excess of £25,000).[102] This claim is quite distinct from the statutory remedy of compensation for unfair dismissal. The measure of damages for wrongful dismissal is the amount which the employee would have received had the employer complied with his contractual and statutory obligations.[103] This will include loss of pay and related benefits such as the provision of a motor car. No damages will be awarded for injured feelings or distress caused by the dismissal.[104]

15.41 Unfair dismissal Compensation for unfair dismissal was first introduced in 1971 and is now governed by the Employment Rights Act 1996. Under this Act the employee has the right not to be unfairly dismissed. In a nutshell, the club employer who dismisses an employee without good reason or without following a fair procedure is vulnerable to a claim for unfair dismissal being bought against it in the employment tribunal.[105] Generally speaking, any term in the contract of employment restricting the right to bring an unfair dismissal claim is void.[106]

15.42 In order to bring a claim the employee must satisfy the following pre-conditions:

(1) that he was employed under a contract of employment;[107]
(2) that he was dismissed as defined by the Act;[108]
(3) that his period of continuous employment was of sufficient length for him to bring a claim.[109]

15.43 ***Dismissal*** This means:

(a) the contract of employment was terminated by the employer with or without notice; or
(b) where the contract was for a fixed term, that term had expired without the contract of employment being renewed;[110] or
(c) the contract was terminated by the employee with or without notice because of the employer's conduct (ie a case of constructive dismissal).

---

102 See the Employment Tribunals' Extension of Jurisdiction (England and Wales) Order 1994, SI 1994/1623.

103 *Laverack v Woods of Colchester* [1967] 1 QB 278; cf *Clark v BET plc* [1997] IRLR 348.

104 *Bliss v South East Thames Regional Health Authority* [1987] ICR 700, CA.

105 See, for example, *Warnes v Cheriton Oddfellows Social Club* [1993] IRLR 58.

106 Employment Rights Act 1996, s 203(1).

107 Ibid, ss 94(1) and 230(1).

108 Ibid, s 95(1).

109 Ibid, s 108(1).

110 The Employment Relations Act 1999, s 18(1) repealed the provisions of the Employment Rights Act 1996 which had permitted agreements to exclude unfair dismissal provisions in fixed-term contracts.

15.44 ***Qualifying period*** This is now 1 year[111] but subject to certain exceptions. No qualifying period is necessary, for example, where the reason or principal reason for the dismissal was a maternity-related reason;[112] or was a health-and-safety reason;[113] or was because of the employee's assertion of a statutory right;[114] or was a reason connected with the assertion of rights under the minimum wage legislation.[115] In order to calculate the qualifying period one needs to know the effective date of termination of the employment: in most cases this will be the date when the employee ceases work, but where the employment is terminated by notice the effective date will be the date on which the notice expires, and where the employee is engaged under a contract for a fixed term the effective date will be the date on which the term expires.[116]

15.45 Reasons for dismissal Once the dismissal has been established it is for the employer to show what was the reason or principal reason for the dismissal. If there is a dispute as to the reason, the employer has the onus of proving the reason.[117] It is important to note that the employer cannot at the employment tribunal rely on facts which he discovered *after* the dismissal to justify it, although this may affect the level of compensation.[118]

15.46 ***Acceptable reasons*** for the dismissal are:[119]

(1) *capability*: reasons relating to the capability or qualifications of the employee for performing work of the kind which he was employed to do. As to capability, it is essential for the employer to show what was required of the employee and that the employee was informed accordingly;
(2) *misconduct*: the misconduct of the employee relied on must be sufficiently serious to warrant dismissal or, if of less serious kind, there must be repetitive misbehaviour;[120]

---

111 The Unfair Dismissal and Statement of Reasons for Dismissal (Variation of Qualifying Period) Order 1999, SI 1999/1436.
112 Employment Rights Act 1996, s 108(3)(b).
113 Ibid, s 108(3)(c).
114 Ibid, s 108(3)(g).
115 Ibid, s 108(3)(gg).
116 Ibid, s 97(1).
117 *Maund v Penwith District Council* [1984] ICR 143.
118 *W Devis & Sons Ltd v Atkins* [1977] ICR 662. This is contrary to the common law where in an action for wrongful dismissal the employer can justify the dismissal by facts subsequently discovered: *Bell v Lever Bros* [1932] AC 161. If an *internal* appeal is heard in respect of the dismissal, the employer may rely at the appeal hearing on facts subsequently discovered: *West Midlands Co-operative Society Ltd v Tipton* [1986] ICR 192, HL.
119 Employment Rights Act 1996, s 98(1), (2).
120 *Auguste Noel Ltd v Curtis* [1990] ICR 604, EAT.

(3) *retirement*:[121] unlike the other potentially fair reasons for dismissal, a retirement dismissal will either be automatically unfair or fair in accordance with the provisions of Employment Rights Act 1996, s 98ZG;[122]
(4) *redundancy*: the employee was redundant;[123]
(5) *illegality*: the employee could not continue to work in the position which he held without contravention (on his part or the employer's part) of a duty or restriction imposed by or under an enactment;
(6) *'some other substantial reason'*: for example, a 'substantial reason' could be the necessary reorganisation of the business of the club,[124] or the imposition of necessary economies in running the club,[125] in circumstances which do not quite satisfy the statutory definition of redundancy. In practice employment tribunals uphold dismissals for 'some other substantial reason' only in rare cases.

15.47 Fairness of the dismissal Some reasons for dismissal are automatically deemed unfair. Generally speaking, these deeming provisions apply to employees who have been dismissed for exercising any of the primary employment rights or for carrying out any of the protected activities referred to in **15.30**. For example, in *Maziak v City Restaurants*,[126] which concerned a health-and-safety dismissal, it was held that Mr Maziak's dismissal was automatically unfair where he refused to cook food which he considered to be a hazard to public health. This was because under s 100(1)(e) of the Employment Rights Act 1996 he had been dismissed for 'taking steps to protect other persons from danger'. It did not matter that the 'other persons' were his co-employees.

15.48 If the reason for dismissal was an acceptable one, it is then for the employment tribunal to decide, except where the reason is retirement, whether it was fair or unfair in all the circumstances (including the size and administrative resources of the employer's undertaking).[127] Neither side has any evidentiary burden in this enquiry.[128] In deciding whether a dismissal is fair or unfair the tribunal must consider whether the dismissal fell within 'the range of reasonable responses'.[129] So, for example, in a capability dismissal the tribunal is likely to enquire whether the employer had available other, more suitable work for the employee or whether the

---

121 Employment Rights Act 1996, ss 98(2)(ba), 98ZA–98ZG.

122 From 6 April 2011 no new notices of retirement under the statutory retirement process may be issued and from 1 October 2011 employers will not be able to rely on the default retirement age to dismiss employees: see the government's consultation document, 'Phasing Out the Default Retirement Age', July 2010.

123 For the topic of redundancy see **15.52**.

124 See *Hollister v National Farmers' Union* [1979] ICR 542.

125 See *Durrant and Cheshire v Clariston Clothing Co Ltd* [1974] IRLR 360.

126 [1999] IRLR 780, EAT.

127 Employment Rights Act 1996, s 98(4).

128 *Foley v Post Office; HSBC Bank (formerly Midland Bank) v Madden* [2000] IRLR 827.

129 See *Foley's* case.

employer had considered an offer to train the employee up to the required standard. In misconduct dismissals the tribunal will take into account whether the employer had adopted a fair procedure in dismissing the employee;[130] a common failure is the omission to give any warnings about poor performance before the dismissal. Hence the importance of giving the employee a proper job description in the first place. The rules of natural justice operate here: the employee must be told of the alleged misconduct and given a proper opportunity to defend the allegation or explain his behaviour, and the employer must act in good faith in dealing with the matter. Furthermore, the employer should be satisfied that during the course of the process he has carried out a reasonable investigation of the issues raised.[131]

15.49 It should be noted that the right to be accompanied to any disciplinary meeting by either a work colleague or union representative[132] is a free standing statutory right. A breach of this right does not mean that the dismissal is deemed to be automatically unfair.

15.50 Remedies for unfair dismissal This in itself is a complex area where commonly changes take place, such as the raising of the ceiling of compensation, so that the club would be well advised to take professional advice on this topic. An employee who has been unfairly dismissed can present a complaint to the employment tribunal within 3 months beginning with the effective date of termination or within such further period as the tribunal considers reasonable if it was not reasonably practicable to present the complaint within the 3-month period.[133] Where the employment tribunal upholds the complaint of unfair dismissal, it may make any of the following orders:

(1) *an order for reinstatement*:[134] this is defined as an order that the employer shall treat the complainant in all respects as if he had not been dismissed. This order is rarely made;
(2) *an order for re-engagement*:[135] this is defined as an order that the complainant be engaged by the employer in employment comparable to that from which he was dismissed or other suitable employment. This means the employee will not get his old job back. This order is rarely made;

---

130 *Lock v Connell Estate Agents* [1994] IRLR 444.
131 Employment Act 2002, ss 29, 31, 32; and the Employment Act (Dispute Resolution) Regulations 2004, SI 2004/752.
132 Employment Relations Act 1999, s 10.
133 Employment Rights Act 1996, s 111(2).
134 Ibid, ss 114, 116(1).
135 Ibid, ss 115 and 116(2).

(3) *a basic award*:[136] where the tribunal makes an award of compensation it must consist of a basic award and a compensatory award.[137] These two awards are the ones most commonly made. The maximum amount is currently (2010) the sum of £11,400.[138] The amount of the award is based on the employee's age, length of continuous employment and gross average wage (subject to a current [2010] maximum of £380 per week which will increase to £400 per week on 1 February 2011).[139] The award is essentially calculated in the same way as a redundancy payment;

(4) *a compensatory award*:[140] the maximum amount is currently (2010) the sum of £65,300[141] and from 1 February 2011 will be £68,400.[142] The amount of the award may take into account past and future loss of earnings, loss of benefits, loss of pension rights, and loss of statutory rights.[143] The employee's duty to take reasonable steps to mitigate his loss generally determines the period for which he is awarded compensation. Thus a tribunal is unlikely to compensate the employee for any period beyond the date by which he should have found alternative employment. Furthermore, if the tribunal finds that the employee had been unfairly dismissed merely because the employer had failed to follow the proper procedure then the tribunal may discount any compensatory award to reflect the chance that the employee would still have been dismissed even if the proper procedure had been followed.[144] The level of compensatory awards is so fact specific that it is not possible to give guidance on likely awards, save to say that the two most important factors are income and mitigation.

(5) *an additional award*:[145] an additional award of compensation is made where the order for reinstatement or re-engagement has not been complied with.

15.51 When a tribunal makes no order for reinstatement or re-engagement but instead awards compensation:

---

136 Employment Rights Act 1996, s 119.

137 Ibid, s 118(1).

138 The basic award is one week's compensation for every year of employment (limited to a maximum of 20 years), but this rises to one-and-a-half weeks' compensation where the employee is not below the age of 41: ibid, ss 119 and 227(1). Hence 30 weeks times £380 equals £11,400.

139 Employment Rights (Increase of Limits) Order 2010, SI 2010/2926.

140 Employment Rights Act 1996, s 123(1).

141 There are certain exceptions where no maxima apply: ibid, s 124(1A), inserted by Employment Relations Act 1999, s 37, namely, dismissal by virtue of health and safety matters, whistleblowing or trade union activity.

142 Employment Rights (Increase of Limits) Order 2010, above.

143 A conventional figure of £350 is often awarded under this last head.

144 See *Polkey v AE Dayton Services* [1988] AC 344.

145 Employment Rights Act 1996, s 117.

(1) if the tribunal finds that the dismissal was caused or contributed to by any blameworthy conduct on the part of the employee then the tribunal will reduce the award by such proportion as it considers just and equitable having regard to that finding;[146]
(2) if the tribunal considers it just and equitable it has a discretion to increase any award to an employee by up to 25% if it appears to the tribunal that the employer has unreasonably failed to comply with the ACAS Code of Practice on Disciplinary and Grievance Procedures.[147]

15.52 Redundancy Redundancy payments were first introduced in 1965 and are now governed by the Employment Rights Act 1996. Subject to limited exceptions, any provision in the contract of employment excluding or limiting the right to a redundancy payment is void.[148] These payments are made in certain circumstances where the employee has lost his job. The employer also has a duty to consult the employees' representatives where it is proposing to dismiss as redundant at least 20 employees within a period of 90 days or less.[149] A person is made redundant if the dismissal was wholly or mainly attributable to:[150]

(1) the fact that the employer has ceased, or intends to cease, to carry on the business for the purposes of which the employee was employed, alternatively to carry on such business in the place where the employee was employed; or
(2) the fact that the requirements of that business for employees to carry out work of a particular kind have ceased or diminished, or are expected to cease or diminish; alternatively have so ceased or diminished in the place where the employee was employed by the employer.

15.53 The employee must satisfy the same pre-conditions as set out in **15.42** above in relation to claims for unfair dismissal, save that the reason for dismissal must of course be redundancy and save that the qualifying period of continuous employment is 2 years ending with the relevant date.[151] The 'relevant date' corresponds to the 'effective date of termination' in claims for unfair dismissal.[152] An employee who commences employment before his eighteenth birthday is treated as if his employment had commenced on that date.[153] The amount of the redundancy payment is

146 Employment Rights Act 1996, s 123(6).
147 Employment Act 2008, s 3 which came into force on 6 April 2009.
148 Employment Rights Act 1996, s 203(1).
149 Trade Union and Labour Relations (Consolidation) Act 1992, s 188, as amended by the Collective Redundancies and Transfer of Undertakings (Protection of Employment) (Amendment) Regulations 1999, SI 1999/1925, reg 3.
150 Trade Union and Labour Relations (Consolidation) Act 1992, s 139(1).
151 Employment Rights Act 1996, s 155.
152 Ibid, s 145.
153 Ibid, s 211(2).

based on the employee's age, length of continuous employment and gross average wage[154] (subject to a current [2010] maximum of £380 per week which will increase to £400 per week on 1 February 2011).[155] This means that the maximum redundancy payment is £11,400.[156]

15.54 Certain employees are not entitled to a redundancy payment. They include:

(1) an employee who has been offered suitable alternative employment and has unreasonably refused the offer;[157]
(2) an employee who is dismissed for misconduct.[158]

15.55 An employee is not entitled to a redundancy payment unless within 6 months of the 'relevant date' he has made a written claim to his employer for such a payment or he has presented a claim for unfair dismissal to the employment tribunal.[159] It is important to note that where the reason for dismissal is redundancy, the employer may be liable for a claim for unfair dismissal *in addition* to the redundancy payment if the employer has acted unfairly towards him in dismissing him for redundancy.[160]

8. DISCRIMINATION IN EMPLOYMENT

15.56 **Overview** One of the primary purposes of the Equality Act 2010 ('EQA 2010') was to codify and bring together in one Act all the anti-discrimination law. EQA 2010 has therefore replaced the Equal Pay Act 1970, the Sex Discrimination Act 1975, the Race Relations Act 1976, the Disability Discrimination Act 1995, the Employment Equality (Sexual Orientation) Regulations, the Employment Equality (Religion or Belief) Regulations 2003 and the Employment Equality (Age) Regulations 2006. The provisions of EQA 2010 as they impact generally on joining, managing and leaving a club and their effect on landlord and tenant relationships

154 Employment Rights Act 1996, ss 119 and 227(1).
155 Employment Rights (Increase of Limits) Order 2010, SI 2010/2926.
156 See footnote 138 above.
157 Employment Rights Act 1996, s 141.
158 Ibid, s 140.
159 Ibid, s 164(1).
160 Ibid, ss 98(4), 105.

involving the club have been considered elsewhere in the book.[161] Unlike these other aspects, equality in employment law is not a new concept for clubs to grasp.

15.57 Most of EQA 2010 came into force on 1 October 2010.[162] The purpose of EQA 2010 is to protect certain personal characteristics, such as race and gender, from discrimination. The list of eight protected characteristics is set out in **4.21**, to which must be added for employment purposes a ninth protected characteristic, namely, marriage and civil partnership. As to this last characteristic, it should be noted that a person has the protected characteristic of marriage or civil partneship if the person is married or is a civil partner;[163] single people are not protected by EQA 2010 against discrimination in this context. Discrimination, harassment and victimisation are defined and explained in **4.23, 4.24** and **4.25**.

15.58 Part 5 (ss 39–83) of EQA 2010, together with Schs 6–9, deal with work and employment and may be summarised as follows:

(1) it is unlawful for employers to discriminate against, harass or victimise a person at work or in employment services;[164]
(2) it contains provisions relating to equal pay between men and women;[165]
(3) it deals with pregnancy and maternity pay;[166]
(4) it is unlawful for an employment contract to prevent an employee disclosing his or her pay;[167]
(5) it contains a power to require private sector employers to publish information relating to the gender pay gap;[168]
(6) it restricts the circumstances in which potential employees can be asked questions about disability or health.[169]

15.59 The anti-discrimination provision referred to in (1) above is a primary purpose of Part 5. It is unlawful for employers:

---

161 See **4.19, 5.64, 6.40, 7.37, 9.51** and **14.39**.

162 Equality Act 2010 (Commencement No 4, Savings, Consequential, Transitional, Transitory and Incidental Provisions and Revocation) Order 2010, SI 2010/2317. Any discriminatory act relied on by an employee which occurred wholly before 1 October 2010 will be covered by the earlier legislation.

163 Equality Act 2010, s 8(1).

164 Equality Act 2010, ss 39–40.

165 Ibid, ss 64–71.

166 Ibid, ss 72–76.

167 Ibid, s 77.

168 Ibid, s 78.

169 Ibid, s 60.

(1) to discriminate against or victimise job applicants in deciding to whom to offer employment, the terms upon which employment is offered or by not offering them employment;[170]
(2) to discriminate against or victimise employees as to terms of employment, access (or by not affording access) to opportunities for promotion, transfer or training or for receiving any other benefit, facility or service, by dismissing them or subjecting them to any other detriment;[171]
(3) to harass job applicants or employees;[172]
(4) to discriminate against disabled job applicants or employees by failing to comply with a duty to make reasonable adjustments.[173]

15.60 Employer's vicarious liability In the realm of employment employers are liable for anything done by their employees except where the employer can show that reasonable steps had been taken to prevent the employee from doing that thing or from doing anything of that description.[174]

15.61 Direct discrimination The prohibition against direct discrimination applies to all protected characteristics but for work-related pregnancy and maternity discrimination the test is whether the woman has been treated 'unfavourably', rather than 'less favourably', reflecting the fact that there is no need for a woman complaining of pregnancy or maternity discrimination to compare her treatment to that afforded to a comparator.[175] In relation to other protected characteristics, a comparator is needed, and like must be compared with like, with there being no material difference between the circumstances relating to each case.[176] If there is no actual comparator a hypothetical comparator may be used.[177] There are limited exceptions, most notably where a particular protected characteristic is a requirement for the work, and the person to whom it is applied does not meet the requirement or, save in the case of sex, the employer has reasonable grounds for not being satisfied that this person meets it.[178] The requirement must be crucial to the post, and not merely one of several important factors. It must not be a sham or pretext and applying the requirement must be proportionate means of achieving a legitimate aim.[179] For example, we consider that it would lawful for a drama club to employ a professional black actor to play the part of Othello in order to give

---

170 Equality Act 2010, s 39(1), (3).
171 Ibid, s 39(2), (4).
172 Ibid, s 40(1).
173 Ibid, s 39(5).
174 Ibid, s 109.
175 Ibid, s 18.
176 Ibid, s 23.
177 By virtue of ibid, s 13 defining discrimination as treatment that is less favourable than a person "would treat others".
178 Ibid, Sch 9, para 1(a) and (c)
179 Ibid, Sch 9, para 1(b).

authenticity to its production of the play, or for an art club or camera club to employ a Chinese model for the purpose of learning painting or photography.

15.62 Indirect discrimination This can be justified if it is a proportionate means of achieving a legitimate aim.[180] Disability and age discrimination can be justified on this basis.[181]

15.63 Harassment The prohibition against harassment applies to all protected characteristics except for pregnancy and maternity, and marriage and civil partnership.[182] Employees can now complain about behaviour that they find offensive even if it is not directed at them and the complainant need not possess the relevant characteristic themselves.[183] Employers are also potentially liable for harassment of employees by third parties such as customers or clients who are not fellow employees.[184] Employers are only liable when harassment has occurred on at least two previous occasions; they were not aware that it had taken place; and they had not taken reasonable steps to prevent it from happening again.[185] Third party harassment applies to all protected characteristics except pregnancy and maternity, or marriage and civil partnership.[186]

15.64 Victimisation The prohibition against victimisation applies to all protected characteristics. There is no longer a need to compare treatment with that of a person who has not brought proceedings, etc under the Act.[187] An employee is not protected from victimisation if they have given false evidence or information, or made a false allegation, in bad faith.[188]

15.65 Disability discrimination The reader is referred to **5.71** and to Sch 8 to EQA 2010. There is no longer a need to show that any of a specified list of capacities (eg memory, speech, dexterity, mobility and so on) is affected.[189] In 2006 the Secretary of State issued 'Guidance on matters to be taken into account in determining questions relating to the definition of disability' and this continues in force until replaced by new guidance.[190] An important

---

[180] Equality Act 2010, s 19.

[181] Ibid, s 13(2).

[182] Ibid, s 26(5).

[183] By virtue of ibid, s 26(1) defining harassment as "unwanted conduct related to a relevant protected characteristic".

[184] Ibid, s 40(2).

[185] Ibid, s 40(1).

[186] Ibid, s 26(5).

[187] Because there is no requirement in ibid, s 27(1) that the detriment be less favourable treatment.

[188] Ibid, s 27(3).

[189] Because Disability Discrimination Act 1995, Sch 1, para 4 has not been reproduced in Equality Act 2010.

[190] Equality Act 2010 (Commencement No 4, Savings, Consequential, Transitional, Transitory

reform of EQA 2010 is that on recruitment it limits the making of enquiries and therefore helps to tackle the disincentive effect that an employer making such enquiries can have on a disabled applicant when applying for a job. It is not improper for an employer merely to ask a job applicant generally about his or her health, although making use of the answers may amount to disability discrimination.[191] Applicants may be asked on an application form whether they have a disability which requires the employer to make adjustments to the recruitment process, for example, the applicant has a speech impairment which requires more time for interview. Or take the case of an applicant applying for a job as a general assistant in the Basset Weightlifting Club. The job requires the manual lifting and handling of heavy weights. The club's committee in interviewing the applicant would be permitted to ask questions about his health to establish whether he was able to do the job (with reasonable adjustments for a disabled applicant, if required).[192] The committee would not be entitled to ask the applicant *other* health-related questions until he was offered a job.[193]

15.66 Remedy (protected characteristics) A person must bring a claim in the employment tribunal within 3 months of the alleged conduct taking place or within such other period as the employment tribunal thinks just and equitable.[194] Where the conduct continues over a period of time, time starts to run at the end of that period.[195] Where it consists of a failure to do something, time starts to run when the person decides not to do the thing in question.[196] An employment tribunal can make a declaration regarding the rights of the complainant and/or the respondent;[197] order compensation to be paid,[198] including damages for injury to feelings;[199] and make appropriate recommendations.[200] The measure of compensation is that which applies in tort claims, namely, compensation which puts the claimant in the same position, as far as possible, as he or she would have been in if the unlawful act had not taken place.[201] Where a tribunal makes a recommendation it does not have to be aimed solely at reducing the negative impact on the individual claimant who brought the successful claim, but can be aimed at reducing that impact on the workforce as a whole[202] (this is a new power). The recommendation must state that the

---

and Incidental Provisions and Revocation) Order 2010, SI 2010/2317, art 13. The Government Equalities Office has published for consultation a revised draft of the above-mentioned guidance. The consultation closed on 31 October 2010.

191 Equality Act 2010, s 60(3).

192 Ibid, s 60(6).

193 Ibid, s 60(1)(a).

194 Ibid, s 123(1).

195 Ibid, s 123(3)(a).

196 Ibid, s 123(3)(b).

197 Ibid, s 124(2)(a).

198 Ibid, s 124(2)(b).

199 Ibid, ss 124(6) and 119(4).

200 Ibid, s 124(2)(c).

201 Ibid, s 124(6).

202 Ibid, s 124(3)(b).

employer should take specific action within a specified period of time.[203] In any case where a recommendation, which is made for the benefit of the individual claimant only, is not complied with, a tribunal has the power to award compensation or increase any award already made.[204] In any case of indirect discrimination where the employer proves that there was no intention to treat the claimant unfavourably, a tribunal must not award compensation unless it first considers whether to make a declaration or recommendation.[205]

15.67 Where the employer asks an impermissible question on recruitment and rejects the applicant, and the applicant then makes a claim to the employment tribunal for direct disability discrimination, it will be for the employer to show that it had not discriminated against the applicant.[206]

15.68 Equal pay Unequal pay between men and women is another form of discrimination. EQA 2010 (and its predecessor, the Equal Pay Act 1970) covers both men and women although most complainants are women. EQA 2010 applies to all club employees whether full-time or part-time nor is there any qualifying period of employment before the Act applies. Replicating the 1970 Act, an employer under EQA 2010 must pay women and men doing equal work the same amount and give them the same contractual benefits.[207] Every contract of employment is to be treated as if it contains a sex equality clause which has the effect of ensuring that pay and all other contractual terms are no worse for a person of the opposite sex where they are doing equal work.[208] The sex equality clause applies to all the terms of the contract including wages and salary, non-discretionary bonuses, holiday pay, sick pay, overtime and non-monetary terms such as a gym membership which the employee is entitled to under their contract of employment. But what happens in relation to non-contractual pay and benefits, such as a purely discretionary bonus or promotion? The answer is that an employee cannot rely upon the sex equality clause but instead has to establish discrimination based on the protected characteristic of sex. We add that if an occupational pension scheme does not include a sex equality rule, it is to be treated as including one.[209]

15.69 There are three kinds of equal work:[210] (a) like work, (b) work rated equivalent and (c) work of equal value. All of these require the complainant to compare themselves with a person of the opposite sex in the same

---

203 Equality Act 2010, s 124(3).
204 Ibid, s 124(7).
205 Ibid, ss 124(4) and (5).
206 Ibid, s 60(5).
207 Ibid, s 65.
208 Ibid, s 66.
209 Ibid, s 67(1).
210 Ibid, s 65.

employment (the comparator). There needs to be a specific comparator, not merely a hypothetical one.[211] The comparator does not have to be contemporaneously employed with the applicant.[212] In deciding whether the work done by the man and the woman is 'like work', a broad approach should be adopted. Thus in *Capper Pass Ltd v Lawton*[213] a cook in a directors' dining room was held to be engaged on like work as the assistant chefs in the company's factory canteen. A person can only claim that work is 'rated equivalent' if there has been a completed job evaluation study which has concluded that this is so. A claim based on work of 'equal value' is likely to require the support of complex expert evidence to prove the necessary equivalence.

15.70 Defence of material factor As a general rule, if the work of an employee and a comparator of the opposite sex is equal, but their terms are not, the sex equality clause takes effect. If, however, the employer can show that the difference in terms is (a) due to a material factor which is relevant and significant and (b) does not directly or indirectly discriminate against the employee because of his or her sex, then a sex equality clause or rule will not apply.[214] Thus in *Benveniste v University of Southampton*[215] a woman employee was on a lower rate of pay than existing male colleagues owing to financial constraints imposed on the university. This amounted to a material factor. But once these constraints had been removed the employer had no defence to her claim for equal pay. In relation to indirect discrimination, unless the employer can show that the material factor is a proportionate means of achieving a legitimate aim it will not succeed in the material factor defence.[216]

15.71 Pay secrecy clauses EQA 2010 renders pay secrecy clauses in bonus schemes and employment contracts unenforceable in relation to the sharing of information between employees for the purpose of finding out whether, or to what extent, there is a connection between pay and having (or not having) a protected characteristic. Such discussions are protected acts and are subject to protection from victimisation.[217]

15.72 Remedy (equal pay) An employment tribunal may hear and decide claims relating to a sex equality clause or rule.[218] A claim for breach of a sex

---

211 *Alabaster v Woolwich plc and Secretary of State for Social Security* [2000] IRLR 754, EAT but EQA 2010, s 71 now allows claims to be brought where a person can show evidence of direct sex discrimination but is unable to gain the benefit of a sex equality clause due to the absence of a comparator doing equal work.

212 Equality Act 2010, s 64(2).

213 [1977] ICR 83, EAT.

214 Equality Act 2010, s 69.

215 [1989] ICR 617. A case decided under the Equal Pay Act 1970 but still good law.

216 Equality Act 2010, s 69(1)(b).

217 Ibid, s 77.

218 Ibid, s 127(1).

equality clause or rule, or an application for a declaration about the effect of such a clause or rule, must normally be brought within 6 months of the end of the employment contract.[219] Where the employer conceals a qualifying fact[220] from the claimant, time runs from the day on which the employee discovered, or could with reasonable diligence have discovered, the qualifying fact.[221] In an incapacity case the 6 months runs from the day on which the employee ceased to have the incapacity.[222] EQA 2010 does not prevent the civil courts from considering a contractual claim relating to a sex equality clause or rule but the court has the power to strike out such a claim if it would be more convenient for an employment tribunal to deal with it, or it may refer the question to the tribunal and stay the legal proceedings in the meantime.[223] The court or tribunal can make a declaration clarifying the rights of the parties.[224] The court or tribunal can also order an award by way of arrears of pay or damages.[225] The standard period used for calculating the award is 6 years dating back from when the proceedings were instituted.[226] Special provisions for calculating the award apply for claims involving concealment and/or incapacity.[227]

9. REFERENCES

15.73 Checking references It is important that the club as the employer makes proper inquiries as to the new employee's character and previous career, especially if the nature of the job involves the custody of or access to the members' property. If the employee turns out to be dishonest, the failure to make these inquiries may render the club liable in negligence if the dishonesty results in the loss of the member's property.[228]

15.74 Generally speaking, the employer has no obligation to give a reference to a departing employee,[229] but usually does so. It is essential that the reference is honestly and accurately given,[230] because the old employer may lay himself open to a tortious claim for negligent misstatement at the suit of the new employer if, in his desire to see the back of a troublesome

---

219 Equality Act 2010, s 129(3).
220 Defined in ibid, s 130(6).
221 Ibid, s 129(3).
222 Ibid, s 129(3).
223 Ibid, s 128.
224 Ibid, s 132((2)(a).
225 Ibid, s 132(2)(b).
226 Ibid, s 132(4).
227 Ibid, s 135.
228 *Williams v Curzon Syndicate Ltd* (1919) 35 TLR 475, CA (where the Ladies United Services Club was held liable for the dishonesty of its night porter who stole a member's jewellery lodged in its custody); *De Parrell v Walker* (1932) 49 TLR 37.
229 The failure to give a reference may amount to victimisation: *Coote v Granada Hospitality* [1999] ICR 100, ECJ and *Coote v Granada Hospitality (No 2)* [1999] IRLR 452, EAT.
230 *Bartholomew v London Borough of Hackney* [1999] IRLR 246, CA.

employee, he paints too rosy a picture of the employee's character and capabilities. On the other hand, if a reference is given, the employer owes a contractual duty of care to the employee to see that the reference is not misleading or negligently inaccurate because, if it is, he may be liable to the employee if the latter thereby suffers damage.[231] If a reference turns out to be inaccurate, the employer will not liable to the employee for defamation of character if it was given honestly and in the belief that the information was correct.[232] It is good practice to mark the letter and the envelope in which it is sent 'Private and confidential'.

15.75 The old employer may be asked specific questions about the employee but if a general reference is required, it should normally deal with the positions held by the employee and his competence and length of service; his honesty; his reasons for leaving; and other personal characteristics such as his good/poor time-keeping or his few/many days of absence from work through sickness.

15.76 Criminal Records Bureau This is an agency of the Home Office. It was established under Part V of the Police Act 1997 and launched in 2002. It enables organisations in the voluntary sector such as clubs to make safer recruitment decisions by identifying candidates who may be unsuitable for certain work, especially that which involves children and vulnerable adults. Organisations must be registered to have access to disclosure. An umbrella organisation can do this for other organisations which are not registered. Successful job applicants apply for a Standard or Enhanced Check (it is the applicant, not the employer, who applies because of the provisions of the Data Protection Act 1998). Employee applicants pay a fee, but the service is free to volunteers.

---

231 *Spring v Guardian Assurance plc* [1994] ICR 596, HL; *Cox v Sun Alliance Life Ltd* [2001] IRLR 458, CA.

232 The employer will be protected by the defence of qualified privilege: *Hodgson v Scarlett* (1818) 1 B & Ald 232. For the topic of defamation see **12.52** and **12.63**.

Chapter 16

THE CLUB'S LIABILITY FOR TAX AND NON-DOMESTIC RATES

1. INTRODUCTION

16.1 The law and practice relating to taxation is not only complex but constantly changing. The full range of taxes is potentially applicable to clubs, unincorporated associations and similar vehicles. This range includes corporation tax which is a direct tax upon 'profits' or 'gains' of a company or deemed company, although this liability may depend upon whether the transactions are with members or non-members. There will be the usual charges to tax upon acquisitions of goods and services from third parties, such as value added tax ('VAT'), or upon acquisitions of land, such as stamp duty land tax. Taxation issues are frequently made more difficult by deeming provisions in the legislation, for example, many clubs are unincorporate bodies but may be deemed to be corporate bodies for certain tax purposes.[1] Although it depends on its nature,[2] it is almost inevitable that some part of the activities of a members' club will result in a liability to tax which will necessitate the submission of a return and payment to HM Revenue and Customs ('HMRC'). This has two important practical implications for the committee or other body managing the affairs of the club, namely:

(1) a general awareness of the possible areas of liability to taxation. This is a highly technical area and the following comments are merely indications of the issues that need to be addressed; and
(2) an understanding of the need to file returns and pay tax which by legislation may be the personal responsibility of the officers of the club with the possibility of an indemnity should the club have sufficient resources.

There is no substitute for retaining the services of a qualified accountant or tax adviser in relation to the affairs of a members' club, even if they are not complicated. This is important in practice since the tax legislation may identify particular officers or employees of the club as being responsible under penalty for ensuring that returns are filed and tax paid.[3]

---

1 Finance Act 2003, s 100(1); Corporation Tax Act 2010, s 1121(1).
2 Eg *International Gymnastics School v C&E* (Lon/91/186).
3 See **5.9** (secretary's liability) and **5.12** (treasurer's liability).

2. DIRECT TAXATION

16.2 Corporation tax Corporation tax is charged upon the profits and gains of a company.[4] An unincorporated members' club comes within the definition of 'company' for the purposes of the Corporation Tax Act 2009 and the Corporation Tax Act 2010.[5] This means that, notwithstanding the fact that such a club has no legal personality,[6] the liability to tax is that of the club itself rather than the individual members who comprise the club.[7] In other words, odd though it may seem, as a matter of tax law the club has a fiscal personality.

16.3 Mutual trading Clubs as 'companies' are taxable on their profits, that is, their relevant receipts less allowable expenses.[8] For profits to arise, the club must be carrying on a 'trade' and, broadly speaking, it is not possible to trade with oneself so as to generate a 'profit'. This is the principle known as 'mutual trading' and such activities tend to be outside the tax regime, which is helpful to a club if it is applicable. Mutual trading occurs where several persons combine together and contribute to a common fund for the financing of their venture or object and where they have no dealings or relations with an outside body; in these circumstances any surplus which is returned to these persons (or to which they become entitled) is not profit which is chargeable to tax.[9] However, a charge to tax can arise upon 'profits' arising from dealings with non-members. This gives rise to difficulties in computation and record keeping where a club deals with both members and non-members, including the guests of non-members.

16.4 A members' club is an example of a mutual undertaking.[10] The necessary quality of mutuality which removes a club from the category of trader must be genuine, and there must be a reasonable relationship between what the member contributes and what he may expect to

4 Taxable profits on business transactions and chargeable capital gains are all now computed as corporation tax: see e g Corporation Tax Act 2010, s 1071(5).

5 Corporation Tax Act 2010, s 1121(1); but see *Conservative and Unionist Central Office v Burrell* [1982] 1 WLR 522, CA (where the Conservative Party was held to be a political movement rather than an unincorporated association).

6 See **1.8**.

7 *Worthing Rugby Football Club Trustees v IRC* [1985] 1 WLR 409 (liability of unincorporated members' club for corporation tax and development land tax).

8 The charge to tax does not apply to subscription income since this is not within the basic charging provisions: *Carlisle and Settle Golf Club v Smith* [1913] 3 KB 75, CA, at 79; but different issues arise in relation to VAT: see **16.26**.

9 Corporation Tax Act 2010, s 1070; *Jones v South-West Lancashire Coal Owners Association* [1927] AC 827.

10 *IRC v Eccentric Club Ltd* [1924] 1 KB 390, CA.

withdraw from the common fund, that is to say, a reasonable relationship between his liabilities and his rights.[11] The mutual trading rules do not apply to certain property activities.[12]

16.5 There can still be mutuality where the members' club carries on its business through the structure of a company provided that the identity of the club members is the same as the company membership.[13] An incorporated club which is a company limited by shares will not be treated as a proprietary club by HMRC if:[14]

(1) the members of the club and the shareholders of the company are intended to be identical bodies;[15]
(2) there is only one class of share;
(3) no dividend is payable to the members.

16.6 Different issues arise in relation to the supply of goods or services by the club to non-members. The moment the club steps outside the circle of self-trading, ie dealing solely with persons who are members, it will become liable to tax.[16] This, however, is not an easy circle to define. The permutations are numerous giving rise to grey or debatable areas: you may have a member purchasing a pint of beer and a sandwich in the bar for himself, or buying a round of drinks for himself and other members and their guests after a round of golf; or a member buying lunch for himself his family, not all of whom may be members or a non-member of that family ordering a cup of coffee whilst awaiting the member to arrive; or the club dealing with a non-member in relation to golf green fees or with a visiting society; or a wedding or birthday party taking place on the club's premises where members and non-members alike attend the function.[17]

16.7 In general, members' clubs will be liable to tax on non-mutual trading activities such as those with non-members; on interest received from

---

11 *Fletcher v Income Tax Commissioner* [1972] AC 414, PC (where a members' club called The Doctor's Cave Bathing Club owned a beach in Jamaica and changed its rules to permit 'hotel members' to join the club; held that the relationship between the ordinary members and the hotel members was in reality a trading relationship giving rise to a tax liability).

12 Income Tax (Trading and Other Income) Act 2005, s 321.

13 *IRC v Eccentric Club Ltd* [1924] 1 KB 390, CA; *Fletcher's case; Westbourne Supporters v Brennan* [1995] STC (SCD) 137.

14 See Revenue Business Income Manual 24255.

15 Fluctuations due to death, resignation and expulsion are generally ignored.

16 *Carlisle and Silloth Golf Club v Smith* [1913] 3 KB 75, CA (where the club was assessable for income tax in respect of visitors' green fees); *Carnoustie Golf Course v IRC* 1929 SC 419.

17 The issues may be different where the club does not itself operate the relevant function but delegates this to an independent party such as entering into separate arrangements with a caterer who conducts his own business on the club premises but who benefits from reduced costs such as not having to pay rent for the kitchen or the equipment, thus providing an indirect subsidy from the club to members and non-members who utilise such facilities.

investments or deposits of money such as bank accounts; on dividends and rents; on gains from the disposal of assets; and on capital sums derived from an asset. Income from sponsorship is also liable to tax; but voluntary payments to preserve the club may not be taxable.[18] The computation of this income or gain is calculated upon normal principles of taxation, but having applied these general principles, which can include anti-avoidance legislation,[19] they may be influenced by the need to allocate costs of goods and services, including the wages and salaries of employees of the club, between dealings with members and dealings with non-members.

16.8 On the issue of dealing with members' clubs, in December 1997[20] the Inland Revenue published a booklet entitled 'Clubs, Societies and Voluntary Associations' in which it stated:

> 'If members use the club's premises or facilities for personal events, such as a private party, and a separate charge is made, the money the club receives will be classed as income which is liable to corporation tax. However, a proportion of any running costs incurred may be allowed against it.'[21]

It might be asked why such a party is not mutual trading. Let us assume that we are talking about the Basset Rugby Football Club and it is one member's party to celebrate his Silver Wedding to which he and his wife invite both members and non-members alike. The club charges the member a fee for the hire of the room and for its facilities. The answer to the question is that the income is being derived from the member in his *personal* capacity rather then his capacity as member of the club, and this is partly evidenced by the nature of the function and partly by the fact that some guests may be present not as guests of the club member but as guests of the member's wife who is not a club member.[22] Therefore the income has to be declared for tax purposes. However, it all depends on the factual circumstances. Suppose another member of the same club held a private party at the club (for which the club charged him a fee) to celebrate his selection for England at an international match at Twickenham and invited only members to the function. We would regard this function as a species of mutual trading. Would it make any difference if this member said that that each invited

---

18 *IRC v Falkirk Ice Rink* [1975] STC 434; Revenue Business Income Manual 41810.

19 See e g *Eastham v Leigh London and Provincial Properties Ltd* [1971] Ch 871, CA.

20 Although somewhat dated, this still provides useful guidance of a general nature.

21 This will involve not only the separate identification of the receipts from the event but also the identification and allocation of the 'costs' of the event where these are not specific to the event. Some 'cash' may be specific such as the fees paid to waiters or bar staff (although separate issues may arise where premium rates or overtime are being paid). However, there may also be issues as to general 'overheads' because these may frequently be provided for out of the members' subscriptions.

22 As to guests: see Revenue Business Income Manual 24360. Where there are mixed receipts from members and guests and where there are non-exclusive areas i e parts of the club premises not restricted to members: see Revenue Business Income Manual 24455.

member could bring one guest with him to join in the celebration? We consider that the party would still remain as an item of mutual trading because the presence of the guests would make no difference to the fact that the member was acting in his capacity of club member in holding the party.[23]

16.9 Corporation tax is not payable on commissions paid to the club for permission to install vending or fruit machines on the club premises.[24] There is also a possible exclusion from the tax charge for receipts where the services are not operated on a commercial basis or are provided to members at a lower price than that charged to non-members.[25]

16.10 The club's accounts In addition to the records required for tax and other purposes, (including evidence for the allocation of receipts and payments between different activities which have taxable implications, such as mutual trading or recovery of VAT and input tax), there are for incorporated clubs prescribed detailed requirements as to the form and contents of accounts under the Companies Act 2006. This is not the case with community clubs registered under the Co-operative and Community Benefit Societies and Credit Unions Act 1965. The Financial Services Authority issues guidance on what type of information it considers should be included in the accounts of a registered club. It is prudent that this guidance should be followed by unincorporated members' clubs too. The overriding consideration is that the accounts must give a true and fair view of the financial and trading position of the club.[26] This last consideration means that the club should comply with all major Statements of Standard Accounting Practice (SSAPs) and Financial Reporting Standards (FRSs) issued by the Institute of Chartered Accountants. The principles set out in the SSAPs and FRSs are considered in the guidance notes issued by the Financial Services Authority and are too detailed to be set out here. If the club qualifies on account of its small size, it may be able to prepare its accounts under the Financial Reporting Standard for Smaller Entities (FRSSE). The main advantage of applying this standard is the exemption from complying with FRS 3 (Reporting Financial Performance).

16.11 In the ordinary course of events all the provisions of FRS 3 will be applicable to clubs. Therefore, at a minimum, there should be a statement regarding the recognised gains and losses at the bottom of the profit and loss account; a statement on continuing activities; and a reconciliation of members' funds in the balance sheet notes. A more detailed account will be necessary in certain circumstances, for example, if there has been a revaluation of the club's property in the financial year. In addition, the

---

23 It is assumed that the club rules permit guests in the circumstances outlined.

24 See Revenue Business Income Manual 24315.

25 See Revenue Interpretation RI 177.

26 FRS 18 Accounting Policies.

accounts will be crucial records when dealing with HMRC. Increasingly the taxation treatment is based upon the accounts of the taxpayer and the treatment in the accounts may influence the taxable treatment[27] and may affect the nature of any payments or receipts for tax purposes,[28] especially in the context of repairs and alterations to the club premises. They may also influence the computation of the mutual trading elements.[29]

16.12 Returns to HMRC Corporation tax on taxable income, such as investment income and profits from trading with non-members, has to be paid within 9 months of the end of each accounting period or, if later, within 30 days after the assessment is issued.[30] Subject to the relaxation where the amounts involved are already small,[31] members' clubs, whether incorporated or unincorporated, come within the corporation tax self-assessment scheme[32] and Form CT 600[33] has to be submitted to HMRC within 12 months of the end of each 12-month accounting period.[34] The booklet IR46 contains an example of how a club should complete this form. Where an unincorporated club is permitted to file a set of accounts for a period in excess of 18 months, for example, on its formation, it must file its Pay and File return within 30 months from the date of commencement of the period for which the accounts are made up.[35] Thus if a club was formed on 1 January 2010 and prepared its first set of accounts for a period of 24 months up to 31 December 2011, it would be required to complete its first Pay and File return by 30 June 2012. There are substantial penalties for failure to comply with the obligation of making a return.[36]

16.13 Payment of corporation tax The nil starting rate of corporation tax[37] has been abolished.[38] From 1 April 2006 all companies with taxable profits are liable to tax at a rate in force for the relevant period. There had been concern that many small clubs which previously had no tax liability now have to complete company tax returns, and pay corporation tax on very small amounts of income as a result of the abolition of the nil rate. Such income is often a negligible amount of bank interest but there is no de minimis rule for liability to corporation tax or where there has been an issue of a notice to file a return, even if it is uneconomic for HMRC to process the

27 *Johnston v Britannia Airways* [1994] STC 763.
28 See eg *Odeon Associated Theatres Ltd v Jones* (1973) Ch 288 CA, distinguishing *Law Shipping Co Ltd v IRC* [1924] SC 74.
29 *Worsley Brewery v IRC* (1932) 17 TC 349; *Albion Rovers v IRC* (1951) 33 TC 331.
30 Taxes Management Act 1970, s 59E (as inserted by s 30 of the Finance Act 1998) and the Corporation Tax (Instalment Payments) Regulations 1998, SI 1998/3175, as amended.
31 See **16.10**.
32 Finance Act 1998, s 117(1) and Sch 18. This system came into effect on 1 July 1999.
33 See also Form CT 416 (Clubs).
34 Finance Act 1998, Sch 18, para 14(1)(a).
35 Ibid, Sch 18, para 14(1)(c).
36 Ibid, Sch 18, paras 17 and 18.
37 £0 to £10,000 gross profits.
38 Finance Act 2006, s 26.

return. HMRC may be prepared to agree a relaxation; this needs to be clarified by the club with the relevant HMRC Tax Office.[39]

16.14 Mutual societies Working men's clubs registered under one of the Friendly Societies Acts are treated in the same way as unincorporated members' clubs when it comes to the question of taxation but because of their structure can automatically claim the benefit of mutual trading when computing their profits. They are not, however, entitled to the tax exemptions granted to friendly societies since they do not count as friendly societies as such.[40] Community clubs registered under one of the Industrial and Provident Societies Acts or under the Co-operative and Community Benefit Societies and Credit Unions Act 1965 are usually eligible to claim the benefit of mutual trading and, in some respects, are more favourably treated than unincorporated members' clubs. These registered clubs are treated as companies for the purposes of the tax regime[41] and taxable at the rates in force from time to time.[42] The current rate (2010) is 28 per cent.[43] It should be added that any share interest or loan interest paid by a community club to a member is subject to income tax on the member's part.[44] The payment, however, is to be made without deduction of tax, where the recipient's usual abode is within the United Kingdom.[45]

16.15 Charitable bodies Charities do not enjoy general exemption from income or corporation tax[46] but instead have the benefit of particular exemptions. These exemptions are now contained in Part 11 of the Corporation Tax Act 2010 (ss 466 to 517). This part deals with the incidence of corporation tax on charitable bodies. Community amateur sports clubs ('CASC') are governed by reference to the general law but are deemed to be 'charities' for many tax purposes and so are dealt with in this section.[47] CASCs may also be treated as charities for the purpose of inheritance.[48]

16.16 ***Tax advantages***

- ***Charities*** Historically charities existed to provide funds for deserving causes over an indefinite period of time. That historic reason is now

---

[39] See Revenue Business Income Manual 23110. HMRC have previously indicated that a relaxation might be considered if the annual corporate tax liability of a club, whether incorporate or unincorporate, is not expected to exceed £100.

[40] Friendly Societies Act 1974, s 7(1)(a).

[41] Taxes Management Act 1970, s 118(1) as amended by Corporation Tax Act 2010. Community clubs are not 'close' companies: s 442 of the latter Act.

[42] Finance Act 1972, s 96, as amended.

[43] Finance (No 2) Act 2010, s 1.

[44] Income Tax (Trading and Other Income) Act 2005, s 379(1).

[45] Income Tax Act 2007, s 887(1).

[46] *Brighton College v Marriott* [1925] 1 KB 312, at 317 (Pollock MR).

[47] See **1.63** and Appendix 13.

[48] See Revenue Inheritance Tax Manual 11139, and see the HMRC list on its (2010) website.

coupled with tax advantages whereby the charity is better enabled financially to carry out its activities. In summary they are as follows:

(1) a favourable tax position to attract donations;[49]
(2) tax repayment under the Gift Aid scheme;
(3) exemption from corporation taxation on:
(a) profits from charitable trade,[50]
  (b) profits from fund-raising events,
  (c) profits from lotteries,
  (d) property income,
  (e) investment income,
  (f) certain miscellaneous income,
  provided in all cases the profit or income is applied to charitable purposes only;
(4) entitlement to 80% relief from non-domestic rates;[51]
(5) entitlement to certain VAT advantages.[52]

- *CASCs* Clubs that are registered as CASCs are able to claim the following tax reliefs:
  (1) tax repayment under the Gift Aid scheme;
  (2) exemption from corporation tax on:[53]
    (a) UK trading income where such income does not exceed £30,000 in any 12 month accounting period,
    (b) UK property income where such income does not exceed £20,000 in any 12 month accounting period,
    (c) interest income and Gift Aid income,
    (d) chargeable gains,
    provided that in each case the income is applied to qualifying purposes, that is to say, providing facilities for and promoting participation in one or more eligible sports;[54]
  (3) entitlement to 80% exemption from non-domestic rates;[55]
  (4) entitlement to certain VAT advantages.[56]

---

49 See Corporation Tax Act 2010, Part 6 entitled 'Charitable Donation Relief' (ss 189–217); and Income Tax Act 2007, Chapter 2 of Part 8 entitled 'Gift Aid' (ss 413–430) which concerns tax relief on gifts of money made to charities by individuals. Tax relief is sometimes made by HMRC concession. But note *IRC v National Book League* [1957] Ch 488, CA, where facilities or benefits were received in respect of the charitable donation, which negated the tax relief.

50 As regards non-charitable 'trading' activities, it may be advantageous to carry out these activities through a trading subsidiary company which can then donate its profits tax free to the charity thereby cancelling its own taxation charge. See Revenue Business Income Manual 24325.

51 See **16.49** and **16.51**.

52 See **16.27 and 16.36**.

53 Corporation Tax Act 2010, ss 662–665.

54 Ibid, s 661(3).

55 See **16.49** and **16.51**.

56 See **16.28** and **16.30**.

16.17 Proprietary clubs These clubs are invariably run on commercial lines and the proprietor of the club, whether a company or an individual, will be subject to the usual incidence of taxation in respect of net profits made in running the club.

3. CAPITAL AND CHARGEABLE GAINS

16.18 Prima facie a club is liable to tax upon any gains, or entitled to relief for losses, incurred upon the disposal of relevant assets.[57] Such gains or losses will be computed on the general principles of tax law including many of the reliefs such as roll-over relief[58] if a suitable qualifying asset is acquired within the prescribed timeframe. There may also be eligibility for capital allowances.[59]

16.19 Tax implications of incorporating an unincorporated club It has been said that the incorporation of an unincorporated members' club provides a good example of a common theme in fiscal law, namely, what should be a straightforward exercise turns out to have complex tax implications.[60] The difficulties and factors to take into consideration in making the decision whether to incorporate arise over the following: the transfer of property; the question of whether the incorporation involves a taxable distribution by either the old club or the new club; a charge to capital gains tax or a relief such as the application of roll-over relief; the treatment of capital equipment; the imposition of stamp duty and stamp duty land tax; and the incidence of taxation on a solvent winding up of the club. A major issue will be the implications of VAT where the incorporating club was a registered taxable person or whether the treatment as a transfer of a going concern applies. Each transaction will depend very largely upon its own facts and circumstances. Consequently a fuller discussion of this topic is beyond the scope of this book.[61]

4. CLUB SUBSCRIPTION AS A DEDUCTIBLE ITEM

16.20 It is sometimes asked whether a member's subscription is deductible in computing his liability to income tax. For an item of expense to be deductible it must have been incurred wholly and exclusively in the course

---

57 See Revenue Capital Tax Manual 40100.

58 Taxation of Chargeable Gains Act 1992, ss 152–162A.

59 Capital Allowances Act 2001.

60 See Francis Fitzpatrick in his article *Incorporating an Unincorporated Association* in the Tax Journal 30 September 1993. Whilst certain taxes considered in this article such as stamp taxes and national insurance may have changed, the overall discussion remains helpful.

61 See Revenue Business Income Manual 24240 and 24400.

of business. Thus in *Brown v Bullock*[62] the plaintiff-taxpayer was appointed the bank manager of the Pall Mall branch of the Midland Bank. Like his predecessors for the past 40 years he joined the Devonshire Club in St James at the *insistence* of his employers, in order to foster local contacts and his business relationship with the bank's customers. The Court of Appeal held that in order to be deductible the test was whether the duties of the office or employment necessitated the incurring of the particular outlay, irrespective of what the employer had prescribed, and on this test the club subscription was not deductible. A hard but probably correct decision.[63] However, in *Elwood v Utitz*[64] the managing director of a Northern Ireland company was required to go to London from time to time and he joined two London clubs solely for the purpose of overnight accommodation and using their business facilities instead of staying at a suitable hotel which was the more expensive option. The Northern Ireland Court of Appeal distinguished the *Brown v Bullock* case and allowed the club subscriptions as a necessary expense and therefore a deductible item.

5. INDIRECT TAXATION

16.21 Value added tax The main type of indirect taxation which a club will encounter is value added tax ('VAT'), which is currently[65] imposed at 20% on the purchase of many goods and services by a club and upon certain receipts by the club in respect of its activities. The principal act is the Value Added Tax Act 1994.[66] This form of taxation is simple in concept but complex in its practical application. VAT causes a lot more problems for clubs than does direct taxation because no allowance is made for the concept of mutual trading.[67] Thus the supply of goods or services by a members' club to its own members can be subject to VAT even if the profits generated by this supply are not subject to corporation tax by reason of the mutual trading principle,[68] and complex rules apply to the subscriptions of members.[69] The general principles relating to VAT, as set out above, will apply to the proprietor of a proprietary club.

---

62 [1961] 1 WLR 1095, CA; see also *Emms v Revenue and Customs Commissioners* [2008] STC (SCD) 618.

63 Harman LJ found some of the arguments of the Crown so distasteful that he declined to give a judgment but agreed in dismissing the taxpayer's appeal.

64 [1966] 42 TC 482.

65 Finance (No 2) Act 2010, s 3(1). This rate will take effect in January 2011.

66 As much amended and supplemented by numerous regulations.

67 *Carlton Lodge Club v Custom and Excise Commissioners* [1975] 1 WLR 66.

68 Ibid. But see *Customs & Excise Commissioners v Professional Footballers' Association (Enterprises) Ltd* [1993] 1 WLR 153, HL (where it was held that no separate output tax was payable on the cost of trophies presented at a dinner where the dinner tickets included VAT, since the price of the ticket included the provision of trophies).

69 See **16.25**.

16.22 Basic principle The basic principle is that each supplier, whether wholesaler or retailer, must add VAT at the appropriate rate at the time of the supply to the price of goods or services supplied by way of business[70] and clubs are deemed to carry on a business.[71] It is important to ensure that the VAT position is properly dealt with since the price received is treated as including the tax even though not expressly charged.[72] It is essentially the club's risk if the tax is not properly dealt with.[73] It will be charged to the club upon its acquisition such as the rent of its premises, or its purchases of goods for onward sale to the members. The club may also have to charge VAT on the supplies it makes whether to members or third parties. This VAT charge is called an 'output' and is subject to certain relaxations generally for small transactions. The supplier must give a VAT receipt and must account to HMRC, usually on a quarterly basis, for the amount collected. In making his return to HMRC the supplier is entitled to deduct from the tax received upon supplies (known as 'output tax') the VAT charges which he has paid in his capacity of recipient of taxable goods and services (known as 'input tax'). This may entitle the club to a tax refund. Some items are zero-rated and other items are exempt.

16.23 Compulsory registration Under s 94(2)(a) of the Value Added Tax Act 1994 the definition of 'business'[74] includes the provision by a club, association or organisation (for a subscription or other consideration) of the facilities or advantages available to a member.[75] A club has to register with HMRC for VAT purposes once it supplies taxable goods or services to its members and/or third parties in excess of the threshold in force at any given time; this is currently (2010) the sum of £70,000.[76]

16.24 Vountary registration If the club is not registered, it is not a taxable person entitled to recover the VAT charged upon its rent or its purchases of goods and services. A club may choose to register below the current threshold and might consider doing so if its inputs equal or exceed its outputs, that is to say, the club supplies taxable goods or services of a

---

70 Value Added Tax Act 1994, s 4(1); *Hostgilt Ltd v Megahart Ltd* [1999] STC 141.

71 Ibid, s 94(2)

72 Ibid, s 19.

73 See, eg *Hostgilt Ltd v Megahart Ltd*[1999] STC 141; *Wynn Realisations Ltd v Vogue Holdings Inc* [1999] STC 524; *Higher Education Statistics v Customs and Excise* [2000] STC 332; *Basildon Rugby Union Football Club v Customs and Excise Commissioners* [1988] VTD 3239.

74 This, however, has to be interpreted by reference to European Directives; these refer to economic activities and can be extremely wide: see *Customs and Excise Commissioners v Lord Fisher* [1981] STC 238.

75 A purely voluntarily body is not carrying on business for VAT purposes: *Greater London Red Cross Blood Transfusion Services v Customs and Excise Commissioners* [1983] VATTR 241 but the mere fact that the activity is a public service is not inconsistent with the carrying on of a business. This still applies if the voluntary body requires reimbursement of expenses, as did the blood donor service. Schedule 9 to the Value Added Tax Act 1994 sets out the list of exempt supplies and of goods and services.

76 Value Added Tax Act 1994, Sch 1, para 1(1); Value Added Tax (Increase of Registration Limits) Order 2010, SI 2010/920.

relatively small value but needs to buy taxable goods or services of an equal or greater value or it is subject to VAT on its rent. However, the nature of its supplies to members and third parties where these are exempt may restrict the recovery of input tax.[77] HMRC have a duty to register a person if he makes a voluntary request to be registered and he satisfies certain conditions.[78] Once registered, HMRC may cancel the registration if a person ceases to make taxable supplies or the value of those supplies does not exceed £68,000 in any one year.[79]

16.25 Value added tax on subscriptions In general, club subscriptions are subject to VAT.[80] However, subscriptions may entitle a member to rights or benefit beyond mere membership and in such circumstances part of the subscription may be exempt from VAT.[81] 'Partial exemption' is a complex question of the nature of the relationship between the member and the club and is discussed in the next paragraph.

16.26 Club subscriptions provide a good example of how the simple concept has got mired in technicalities. The following propositions should be borne in mind:

(1) If the subscription covers nothing more than the bare membership of the club, the subscription will be subject to VAT. This is because the subscription is the consideration for the privileges of membership, and such privileges would fall to be treated as 'a supply of services'.[82] In this situation the club will no doubt be charging its members an economic rate for its facilities and the provision of food and drink and relying of the mutual trading principle to avoid corporation tax on its profits.
(2) If (which is a common occurrence) the subscription covers to a greater or lesser extent the provision of facilities to its members, the subscription has to be analysed to ascertain what proportion of the subscription covers the supply of taxable goods and services (other than zero-rated or exempt supplies) and VAT will be need to be added to that proportion of the subscription. In *Commissioners of Customs and Excise v The Automobile Association*[83] the member's annual subscription to the AA contained a package of benefits, such as a free handbook, a free magazine and free legal advice, and the VAT Tribunal, upheld by the Divisional Court, held that the subscription had to be 'dissected' to

---

77 Value Added Tax Act 1994, s 24; Value Added Tax Regulations 1995, SI 1995/2518, Part XIV.

78 Value Added Tax Act 1994, Sch 1, para 9.

79 For deregistration, see ibid, Sch 1, paras 3, 4 and 13.

80 Ibid, s 94(2).

81 Ibid, s 24; Value Added Tax Regulations 1995, Part XIV and should be the subject of consultation and negotiation with HMRC.

82 Value Added Tax Act 1994, ss 4(1), 5(2)(b) and Sch 4.

83 [1974] 1 WLR 1477, CA.

see which elements in it attracted VAT. Thus the AA Handbook and its magazine would be zero-rated and its legal advice service would be taxable at the standard rate. The court held that it was irrelevant that the package might vary from time to time. In *Trewby v Customs and Excise Commissioners*[84] the court held that the subscription to a country club did not include any share of an interest in the club's land, which would have been an exempt supply.

(3) If the subscription contains an element of donation, as it might well do in the case of a subscription to a charitable organisation such as the Variety Club of Great Britain, the donation element will not attract VAT.[85]

16.27 VAT Exemptions and reliefs Many transactions fall outside the scope of positive and zero rates of tax. However, there is no general relief for supplies made by public bodies or organisations for charitable or welfare purposes. It is necessary to search for a specific exemption for the particular activity. These reliefs take a variety of forms and the nature of the relief can have different consequences.[86] For example, a supply by the club may be zero-rated which does not restrict the extent of the credit for the tax on inputs. Alternatively, the supply may be 'exempt', ie not chargeable to VAT, but this will restrict the credit for input tax.[87] Special arrangements may be negotiated with HMRC but such arrangements should be reviewed from time to time so that they accurately reflect changes in the nature or structure of the club's activities.[88] However, in some cases wholly related to land it may be possible to waive the exemption by exercising the option to tax.[89]

16.28 Exemption for sports services Article 13(A)(1)(m) of the Sixth Council Directive[90] stipulated that sports services provided by a non-profit making organisation were to be the subject of a compulsory exemption. This took effect on 1 January 1990 and the exemption is now enacted into domestic law.[91] This exemption will apply even where the club makes a 'profit' on the services. In *Kennemer Golf and Country Club v Staatssecetaris van Financiën*[92] a substantial proportion of the income of the golf club in the Netherlands was derived from day membership fees paid by non-members for the use of the course and associated facilities. The club regularly made an operating surplus which was paid into a reserve fund for

---

84 [1976] 1 WLR 932, CA.

85 Customs and Excise Note No 701.

86 On occasion a club may make a supply which is 'outside the scope' of the tax – see Value Added Tax Act 1994, s 24.

87 *HMRC v London Clubs Management* [2010] STC 2789.

88 See eg *GUS Merchandise Corporation v Customs and Excise Commissioners (No 2)* [1995] STC 279.

89 Value Added Tax Act 1994, Sch 10, as amended.

90 Directive 77/388/EEC.

91 Value Added Tax Act 1994, Sch 9, Group 10.

92 [2002] QB 1252.

non-annually-recurring expenditure. The European Court of Justice held that VAT was not payable on the fees provided that the surplus was not distributed to the club members as profits.[93]

16.29 Exemption for cultural services Article 13(A)(1)(n) of the above-mentioned Directive stipulated that cultural services provided by a non-profit making organisation were to be the subject of a compulsory exemption.[94] This exemption is now enacted into domestic law.[95] In *Zoological Society of London v Customs and Excise Commissioners*[96] the society, a non-profit-making body, operated London Zoo and Whipsnade Wild Animal Park. The society was governed by a council, management boards and committees, none of whose members received any remuneration, but it also had paid employees including directors who attended meetings of the governing bodies. The society claimed exemption from VAT in respect of non-members' day subscriptions and the admission charges to the zoos on the ground that it was supplying cultural services. The European Court of Justice upheld this claim, despite the fact that the society had paid employees; this was because the society was being 'managed and administered on an essentially voluntary basis'.[97]

16.30 Exemption for fund-raising events This is covered by Group 12 of Sch 9 to the Value Added Tax Act 1994. The exemption applies to (a) the supply of goods and services by a charity (or charities) in connection with a fund-raising event organised for charitable purposes and whose primary purpose is to raise money,[98] or (b) the supply of goods and services by a qualifying body in connection with a fund-raising event organised exclusively for its own benefit and whose primary purpose is the raising of money.[99] A 'qualifying body' means the following:[100]

(1) any non-profit making body listed in Item 1 of Group 9: this includes a professional association; an association whose the primary purpose is the advancement of a particular branch of knowledge or the fostering

---

93 The English tax authority, Customs and Excise, complied with the Sixth Directive by issuing VAT Notice 701/45/94 on 1 April 1994. This gave rise to refunds of VAT which had been levied since 1 January 1990, and caused an ancillary problem as to whom the refunds belonged. Although it may seem unjust to the member who had provided the money for the tax, the answer is that the refunds belonged to the club because it was the club which had actually paid the tax with its own monies. It therefore lay with the club to decide what to do with the refund, whether to reimburse the member or to put the monies into its general funds.

94 Sixth Council Directive, op cit, art 13(A)(1)(n).

95 Value Added Tax 1994, Sch 9, Group 13.

96 [2002] QB 1252.

97 Sixth Council Directive, art 13(A)(2)(a).

98 Value Added Tax Act 1994, Sch 9, Group 12, Item 1.

99 Ibid, Sch 9, Group 12, Item 2.

100 Ibid, Sch 9, Group 12, as amended by Value Added Tax (Fund-Raising Events by Charities and Other Qualifying Bodies) Order 2000, SI 2000/801, art 3.

of professional expertise; and a body whose objects are in the public domain and are of a political, religious, patriotic, philosophical, philanthropic or civic nature;

(2) any non-profit making body listed in Item 1 of Group 10: this includes any body whose principal purpose is the provision of facilities for persons to take part in sport or physical education;

(3) any non-profit making body listed in Item 2 of Group 13: this means any body which controls the right of admission to a museum, gallery, art exhibition or zoo or to a theatrical, musical or choreographic performance of a cultural nature.

On the other hand, the exemption only applies where the primary purpose is fund-raising. The club therefore has to be careful that HMRC do not have grounds for saying that the event is a social occasion where the fund-raising is of lesser significance.[101]

16.31 Input recovery The implementation of exemptions to cover the income sources of a non-profit-making club can have an adverse impact on input recovery, so the club needs to consider whether it is acting prudently in claiming exemptions. This is particularly so where the club is embarking on a large capital project, such as an extension to the clubhouse, where input tax will be payable on many goods and services in connection with the project. The design of the building and its intended use may be crucial to the availability of the credit for the VAT on the goods and services supplied to the club. Careful structuring of the project, for example, the allocation of certain parts of the premises to separate taxable purposes, such as the location of separate members' and visitors' dressing rooms, can increase the recovery of the input tax on building works, and on repairs and rents, thereby reducing the overall costs to the club. Where the club is making a mixture of supplies, ie some taxable and some not, there is considerable scope to improve the recovery of input tax by negotiation with HMRC.

16.32 Taxable supplies The following points need to be borne in mind by committees to ensure compliance with VAT obligations. HMRC publish guidance notices in respect of all the following topics.

- *Bar sales and catering charges*[102] Food and drink is standard-rated where it is supplied in the course of catering; this includes food and drink supplied for consumption on the premises and hot take-away food. Premises means the whole clubhouse or its grounds.
- *Admission charges* These are normally standard-rated.
- *Bingo* The payment of VAT depends on whether cash bingo or prize bingo is played. It also depends on whether the club premises are

[101] As was held in the case of the *Blaydon Rugby Football Club* (VAT Tribunal ref: 13901).

[102] See eg *Carlton Lodge v Customs and Excise Commissioners* [1974] STC 507.

licensed under the Gambling Act 2005. Admission charges are standard-rated save for certain fund-raising events.

- *Discos, dances, socials and similar events* Admission charges are standard-rated save for certain fund-raising events. The club is accountable on the gross amount of taxable supplies, not simply on the net amount, that is to say, the club cannot offset the expenses of the event when calculating the amount of taxable supplies.
- *Gaming machines* All receipts from gaming machines are standard-rated.[103]
- *Lotteries, raffles, etc* Income from lotteries, raffles, totes, instant bingo tickets and the like is exempt.
- *Sponsorship and advertising services* Fees recovered by the club from sponsors may not be taxable as a business activity,[104] whereas advertising fees may be taxable, and there can be a fine line between the two.
- *Letting room on hire* Income from letting a room or hall on hire is exempt provided that:
  (1) the hirer has exclusive use of the room and hall during the period of hire;
  (2) the room is not designed or equipped for sport or physical recreation;
  (3) the club has not 'opted to tax' the building in which the room or hall is situated.[105] This exemption covers facilities within or next to the room or hall, such as a kitchen or bar, and covers those fixtures and fittings which form part of the hire, such as the lighting and sound equipment.[106]

16.33 Computation issues Although zero-rating and exemption mean that the output is not subject to tax, this is a crucial difference between these two principles. Input tax can be offset against zero-rated supplies which may entitle the club to a refund. On the other hand, the input tax cannot be set off against exempt activities.[107]

- ***Zero-rated supplies*** Schedule 8 to the Value Added Tax Act 1994 sets out the zero-rated supplies of goods and services. The schedule is divided into groups. The groups that are likely to be of interest to clubs are: books; caravans and houseboats; charities; clothing and footwear; construction of buildings; drugs, medicines and aids for the handicapped; food (which includes drink but excludes snack foods, eg potato crisps, and excludes drink charged with excise duty);

103 See the case of *Moorthorpe Empire Working Men's Club* (VAT Tribunal ref 1127) where the club kept no proper records of its receipts from gaming machines and the Tribunal upheld an estimated assessment by Customs and Excise in the sum of £24,405 in respect of the undeclared receipts.

104 Customs & Excise Notice 701/41/02.

105 See further **16.34**.

106 Customs & Excise Notice 700 (the Vat Guide) and Notice 742 (Land and Property).

107 See Value Added Tax Act 1994, s 24; Value Added Tax Regulations 1995.

protected buildings; sewerage services and water; talking books for the blind and handicapped and wireless sets for the blind; and transport.

- ***Exempt activities*** Schedule 9 to the Value Added Tax Act 1994 sets out the exempt activities. The schedule is divided into groups. The groups that are likely to be of interest to clubs are: betting, gaming and lotteries; education; fund-raising events by charities and other qualifying bodies; health and welfare; insurance; the grant of any interest or right over land (there are many exceptions in this group); postal services; and sports, sports competitions and physical education.
- ***Partial exemption*** It is unlikely that a club will be carrying on totally taxable or totally exempt activities. It is common for clubs to be carrying on a mixture of taxable supplies (which includes zero-rated ones) and exempt activities. The position as to partial exemption can be complicated and is best solved by negotiation with HMRC. The basic principle in the absence of any special arrangement is one of direct attribution.[108] For example, where there is an acquisition of food or catering equipment which is related to the club's catering activities, these activities may be wholly taxable, in which case the whole of the input tax on the acquisition would be recoverable. Many supplies, however, such as overheads, will not be directly identifiable with totally taxable or totally exempt activities. Here it is necessary to apportion the input tax between the various supplies. Sometimes it is possible to make the apportionment by reference to the relative parts of the club turnover or by reference to the square footage of the club premises or to the activities carried on. Where a special arrangement is agreed with HMRC, detailed records may be required.

16.34 Rent issues A common problem is the rent and other outgoings, such as repairs to the club's premises, which can amount to a large proportion of its costs. Frequently, where a club has a lease or tenancy and pays a rent for all or part of its premises, such rent will be subject to VAT because the landlord will have exercised the option to tax.[109] Such input tax on the rent may be available as a credit against the tax on its supplies (output tax). However, where there are exempt activities, eg in relation to subscriptions, the club's ability to deduct input tax from its output tax is restricted. We mention this example because of a trap where part of the premises are sublet. Subletting is prima facie an *exempt* activity and the club could easily lose part of the input tax charged upon its own rent. It is, therefore, essential that the club exercises the option to tax in this situation so that subletting and other activities are subject to VAT, with the result that the input tax credit on its own rent will not be restricted.[110]

---

108 Value Added Tax Act 1994, s 26; Value Added Tax Regulations 1995, Part XIV.

109 Value Added Tax Act 1994, Sch 10 (as amended).

110 Ibid, s 24; Value Added Tax Regulations 1995, Part XIV.

16.35 Benefits to employees Further problems arise over the provision of accommodation and other benefits by the club to its employees. For example, a club may provide a flat (which may or may not be part of the club premises) or it may provide the employee with a car or meals or refreshments. (These benefits in kind may attract income tax which will be dealt with by the club through PAYE and NIC).[111] What arises here is the question of VAT. Again, this can be a complex area which has no simple answer and is best resolved by negotiation with the HMRC, because each situation depends on its own facts. As an example, an issue could arise whether the employee's accommodation was simply residential (exempt activity) or whether it was necessary for the performance of his work (taxable supply). Or take the club's installation and provision of a telephone service in the employee's flat. Does this constitute a social amenity or is it necessary equipment for the employee's job? If the latter, it will probably be a business expense, enabling recovery of the input tax paid by the club.

16.36 Charitable bodies Value added tax is only chargeable on the supply of goods and services when the supply is in the course of a business carried on by the charity, as opposed to the supply of goods or services relating to objects of the charity when it is exempt.[112] The supply of certain goods or services by a charity is zero-rated, such as the supply by a charity of goods donated to it for sale or the sale of donated goods by a taxable person who has agreed in writing to give all the profits of the sale to the charity.[113] Building or repair work to charitable premises qualifies for special rates if suitably certified,[114] but it may be the obligation of the charity rather than the builder to produce the certificate.

16.37 The administration of VAT If the club has a turnover in taxable supplies exceeding the threshold[115] or chooses to register for VAT it needs to understand its obligations which are set out in summary form below:

(1) *Registered name* The registration may be in the name of the club, association or organisation and no account shall be taken of any change in its members.[116]
(2) *Identification* Every person registered for VAT will receive a VAT number. Constitutional arrangements may be important here. Suppose that the Basset Town Sports Club operates three separate sections, say cricket, hockey and tennis. Are these all separate 'taxable persons'? The answer is that they may be counted as separate entities if each section

---

111 See Income Tax (Earnings and Pensions) Act 2003, Part 3.

112 *Yoga for Health Foundation v Customs and Excise Commissioners* [1984] STC 360.

113 Value Added Tax Act 1994, s 30 (as amended).

114 Ibid, Sch 8, Group 5.

115 *Watchet Bowling Club v Customs and Excise Commissioners* [1980] VTD 1026; *Dartford Golf Club v Custom and Excise Commissioners* [1983] VTD 1576.

116 Value Added Tax Act 1994, s 46.

is managed by its own committee and operates its own bank account, so that the sections are wholly or in substantial part financially independent of one another.

(3) *Responsible persons* Anything required to be done for VAT purposes is the joint and several liability of every member holding office as president, chairman, treasurer, secretary or any similar officer of the club.[117] In default, the persons liable will be every member holding office as a member of a committee.[118] In default of this last provision, every member of the club will be liable.[119]

(4) *Records* Every taxable person must keep such records as HMRC by regulations require[120] and these may include tax invoices to support a claim to recover input tax. These records must be kept for 6 years.[121] However, these rules for computation and recordkeeping are modified for 'retailers', ie persons such as clubs whose transactions are predominantly for cash,[122] when 'special schemes' may apply which should be negotiated with HMRC. Where such arrangements apply, it is essential that the agreed accounts and records are preserved.

(5) *VAT returns* The standard accounting period is 3 months[123] although special rules apply where there is a large turnover[124] or where the taxpayer is in a recovery situation, ie his recoverable input tax exceeds his output tax on a regular basis.[125] In order to stagger the quarter days the Customs and Excise Commissioners divided occupations into groups. Clubs in general fall within Group 2 under Classification 28 (Miscellaneous Services) and under Trade Codes 8822, 8829 and 8870 or, in the case of gaming clubs, Trade Code 8830. The quarter days for clubs are the last days of January, April, July and October. Not later than the end of the month following the quarter day (eg by 28 February for the quarter day of 31 January) the taxable person must make a return on a prescribed form, showing the amount of tax due from or to him. At the same time he must pay any tax which is due to HMRC.[126]

With effect from 1 April 2010 it is mandatory for all registered taxpayers with an annual turnover of £100,000 or more, together with any newly registered taxpayer (regardless of their turnover), to submit their returns on-line and to pay electronically.[127]

---

117 Value Added Tax Regulations 1995, regs 7 and 10.

118 Note that this says *a* committee, not *the* committee.

119 This is an astonishingly draconian default measure, bearing in mind that the member's liability is normally limited to his entrance fee and his subscriptions (*Wise v Perpetual Trustee Co* [1903] AC 139) but, we surmise, it is unlikely to be invoked in practice.

120 Value Added Tax Act 1994, Sch 11, para 6(1).

121 Ibid, Sch 11, para 6(3).

122 Ibid, Sch 11.

123 Value Added Tax Regulations 1995, SI 1995/2518, reg 25.

124 Value Added Tax Act 1994, s 30; Value Added Tax Regulations 1995, Part IX.

125 Value Added Tax Regulations 1995, reg 25 proviso.

126 Ibid, reg 32

127 Ibid, reg 25A, authorised by Finance Act 2003, s 204(1).

(6) *Tax point* The above compliance requirements are related to the tax point, ie the date on which the taxable supply is deemed to accrue. There are detailed rules for identifying the date which needs to be carefully investigated. This is essentially the date of the supply of the goods or services such as delivery; but this is modified where a VAT invoice is issued.[128] However, special rules apply where cash is paid or there are 'retail arrangements'. In these cases the tax point is the payment of cash[129] when there are also special schemes for calculating the tax and record keeping.

6. STAMP DUTY LAND TAX[130]

16.38 Many clubs have club premises or land upon which they carry out their activities or provide accommodation for their employees. Stamp duty land tax was introduced in 2003 and is a tax levied upon the acquisition of chargeable interests in land.[131] These interests include[132] purchases of land; the grant or renewal of leases, including rent reviews; the holding over of expired leases pursuant to Landlord and Tenant Act 1954; variation of leases; and other rights over land other than a licence to occupy the land. It is a transaction tax because it does not depend on there being any document or instrument effecting the transaction.[133] It replaced stamp duty which was a documentary tax. The tax applies to transactions carried out by companies. A company is defined as including any body corporate or any unincorporated association.[134] It therefore applies to all clubs. There are many parties who are already in potential difficulties because they have entered into transactions that do not require documentation and have thereby incurred a charge to stamp duty land tax, but they have not made the necessary returns or paid the amount of tax due, making themselves liable to extensive penalties and interest.[135] Clubs therefore need to take careful stock of this situation.

---

128 Value Added Tax Act 1994, ss 30 and 83.

129 *Higher Education Statistics v Customs and Excise Commissioners* [2000] STC 332.

130 Clubs are also liable to stamp duty and stamp duty reserve tax upon the acquisition of chargeable shares and marketable securities. This will be relatively rare except in cases where a club wishes to invest surplus funds to build up a sinking fund or other resources for the long-term replacement of assets There is also stamp duty relief for charities (Finance Act 1982, s 129).

131 Finance Act 2003, ss 42(1), 43 and 48(1).

132 See ibid, Sch 17A.

133 Ibid, s 42(2)(a).

134 Finance Act 2003, s 100(1).

135 Ibid, Sch 10.

7. NON-DOMESTIC RATES

16.39 Introduction Every club, however small, which occupies premises will need to understand the legal position concerning its liability for non-domestic rates, commonly called business rates. Rates is a property tax and is levied by local government. The imposition of rates is carried out by the local authority in whose area the club property is situated.

16.40 Basic principle The basis on which non-domestic rates operates is (1) the occupation of business property and (2) the amount chargeable on the rateable value of that property[136]. Property is defined as domestic if, broadly speaking, it is wholly used for the purposes of living accommodation.[137] It follows from this definition that premises occupied by any club will be non-domestic and therefore subject to the non-domestic rating regime.

16.41 Occupation This basis is well settled. There are four necessary ingredients in rateable occupation. They are:[138]

(1) there must be actual occupation of the hereditament ('hereditament' is the technical term for a unit of occupation);[139]
(2) there must be exclusive occupation for the particular purposes of the possessor occupier;
(3) the occupation must be of some value or benefit to the possessor;
(4) the occupation must not be for too transient a period.

16.42 In every case the necessary degree of occupation is a question of fact, not a question of legal title to the property.[140] As is common with legal concepts there is a grey area which can give rise to difficulty. It is plain that, at one end of the scale, a club which uses a club room or hall belonging to someone else, say once a week or once a month is not liable for rates. It is equally plain that, at the other end, a club which is the freeholder or leaseholder of club premises that are regularly used week in and week out is liable for rates. It is the cases which fall in the middle which need to be more carefully analysed. An instructive comparison can be made between the cases of *Peak (VO) v Burley Golf Club*[141] and *Pennard Golf Club v Richards*

---

136 Local Government Finance Act 1988, s 43(1)–(2).

137 Ibid, s 66(1)(a). For Wales see also Non-Domestic Rating (Definition of Domestic Property) Order 2010, SI 2010/682.

138 *Laing v Kingswood Assessment Committee* [1949] 1 KB 344, CA, approved by the House of Lords in *London County Council v Wilkins (VO)* [1957] AC 362.

139 Local Government Finance Act 1988, s 64; *Gilbert (VO) v S Hickinbottom & Sons Ltd* [1956] 2 QB 40.

140 *Holywell Union v Halkyn District Mines Drainage Co* [1895] AC 117.

141 [1960] 1 WLR 568.

(VO)[142]. In the former case the club was held not liable for rates on its golf course where non-members were entitled as of right to play there without paying green fees to the club. On the other hand, in the latter case the club was held liable to pay rates on its golf course even though non-members had access over it by means of rights of way. The distinction between the two cases depends on the *exclusivity* of the occupation: in the former case the club members were sharing their occupation of the golf course with outsiders whereas in the latter case the club members' occupation was not diminished by the fact that outsiders had the ability to walk across their land.

16.43 The fact that the club holds the club premises on a licence or a tenancy will not exempt the club from paying rates.[143] If a club has exclusive use of part of premises it will be liable for rates on that part.[144] A club can still be the occupier of premises even though the licensor has occasional use of them as of right and has possession of a key to the premises.[145]

16.44 Occupiers' liability With regard to unincorporated members' clubs it is the actual occupiers who are liable to pay the rates, that is to say, the trustees of the club if the property is vested in them or the managing committee if there are no trustees.[146] It can never be the club itself which is in occupation.[147] Individual members of an unincorporated members' club are not in the ordinary course of events liable for rates,[148] but if the club were of a sufficiently small size the members might collectively be held liable for rates as joint occupiers of the premises.[149] This liability might arise even though the assessment is on one occupier only.[150] Working men's clubs registered under one of the Friendly Societies Acts will automatically have trustees of the club's property who are responsible for the payment of rates. With regard to community clubs and incorporated clubs, as legal persons

---

142 [1976] RA 203.

143 *R v Green* [1829] 9 B & C 203 (occupants of almshouses); *Case (VO) v British Railways Board* [1972] 16 RRC 123, CA, at 147 (where a staff association was held liable for rates in respect of club premises held on a licence, terminable on short notice, from the employer).

144 *O'Reilly v Cock* [1981] 260 EG 293.

145 *Squibb v Vale of White Horse District Council and Central Electricity Generating Board* [1982] RA 271.

146 *Verrall v Hackney London Borough Council* [1983] QB 445, CA, at 461 (May LJ).

147 Ibid, at 461.

148 Ibid, at 462 (where Mr Verrall, a prominent member and officer of the National Front, an unincorporated association, was held not liable for rates because he was not in actual occupation of the hereditament).

149 *Westminster City Council v Tomlin* [1990] 1 All ER 920, CA (where Mr Tomlin and seven others formed an unincorporated association called the Guild of Transcultural Studies and occupied the former Cambodian Embassy as trespassers. The rating assessment was on Mr Tomlin alone but it was held on the facts that all eight were liable for rates as joint occupiers).

150 See the *Tomlin* case cited in the last footnote.

they will be liable for rates unless the property is vested in trustees when it is they who are liable. The proprietor of a proprietary club is the person liable for rates.

16.45 Rateable value The rateable value of a property is the amount which it might reasonably be expected to let from year to year on the following assumptions: (a) the property was vacant and to let,(b) the tenant undertook to pay all usual tenant's rates and taxes, and (c) the tenant undertook to bear the cost of repairs and insurance and other expenses necessary to maintain the property in a state to command that rent.[151] Generally speaking, the rent for rating purposes is based on a hypothetical tenancy.[152] There is no uniform method of valuation.[153] Various methods of valuation are applied in order to arrive at the hypothetical rent. These include making reference to the actual rent of the hereditament; or to comparable rents; or in their absence to the assessment of comparable hereditaments; or to the profits of the hereditament; or to the costs of its construction.[154] In the absence of rental evidence of value, the accounts, receipts or profits of the occupier of the property may be relevant.[155] Where there is a strong demand for the same kind of use of similar property the rateable value will be same, whether the club in question is making full or scant use of the premises and irrespective of whether the club is rich or poor. On the other hand, if the occupier is the only possible tenant of the property, his ability to pay is a relevant consideration. On this basis a club's ability to pay has been considered as relevant in a number of cases before the Lands Tribunal and the valuation adjusted accordingly.[156] In *Avondale Lawn Tennis Club v Murton (VO)*[157]the Lands Tribunal adopted what had been earlier stated by way of principle in *Sheffield & Hallamshire Lawn Tennis Club Ltd v Elliott (VO)*:[158]

---

[151] Local Government Finance Act 1988, Sch 6, para 2(1) as amended by Local Government and Housing Act 1989 and Rating (Valuation) Act 1999.

[152] See *R v West Middlesex Waterworks* [1859] 28 LJMC 135, at 137 (case decided under previous rating legislation). And see *Tomlinson (VO) v Plymouth Argyle Football Club Ltd* [1960] 6 RRC 173, CA, at 179 (Lord Evershed MR): 'The question is not what would be a fair rent for the landlord, real or hypothetical, to ask but what would be a reasonable rent for a hypothetical tenant and a hypothetical landlord to agree between them'. This inevitably means a compromise of some sort.

[153] 39(1B) *Halsbury's Laws of England* (4th edn 2008) at 112.

[154] Ibid, at 87.

[155] *March (VO) v Gravesend and Northfleet Football Club Ltd* [1959] 4 RRC 299 (Lands Tribunal); *Tomlinson (VO) v Plymouth Argyle Football Club Co Ltd* (cited above) (valuation by reference to gate receipts was rejected).

[156] See *Tomlinson (VO) v Plymouth Argyle Football Club Co Ltd* (cited above); *Hitchin Town Football Club v Wallace (VO)* [1961] RVR 462; *Sussex Motor Yacht Club Ltd v Gilmore (VO)* [1966] RA 43; *Heaton Cricket Club v Westwood (VO)* [1959] 5 RRC 98; *Addington Community Association v Croydon Corporation and Gudgion (VO)* [1967] 13 RRC 126 (community hall) and *Downe Village Residents' Association v Valentine (VO)* [1976] RA 117 (village hall).

[157] [1976[RRC 308, at 312.

[158] [1966] RA 370.

'The club is not a competitive profit-making concern and the accounts of its finances, designed to keep it efficient and solvent, cannot be taken as a direct guide to the determination of the rent the hypothetical tenant could reasonably expected to pay, and in the absence of rental evidence the accepted or undisputed assessments on the comparable hereditaments in the district must be regarded as the principal guide to the annual value of the subject property. I do not however ignore the accounts entirely because they do offer some help in considering the burden of outgoings incurred by a club of this size and age'.

16.46 Rating lists It is a sensible practice for the club to try to agree its valuation with the valuation officer. Once the valuation officer's valuation has taken place the resulting rateable value is entered in a rating list. There is a statutory duty imposed on valuation officers to compile and maintain central and local non-domestic rating lists.[159] This duty required the compilation of rating lists for 1 April 1990 and at five-year intervals thereafter.[160] The club as a person aggrieved[161] may make a proposal to alter a rating list at any time before the day on which the next list is compiled.[162] The proposal must be made by notice in writing served on the valuation officer; it must state grounds for the proposal; and in certain cases it must state the reasons for believing that those grounds exist.[163] There are 15 wide-ranging grounds for seeking an alteration to a rating list.[164] If agreement cannot be reached, or the club wishes to appeal against the valuation officer's decision, the club can take the matter to the Valuation Tribunal for England.[165] Appeals from this tribunal now go to the Upper Tribunal which has superseded the Lands Tribunal.[166]

16.47 Chargeable amount The rateable value is the unit of assessment and the rate is now a multiplier set annually by the Secretary of State which, generally speaking, is uniform across the country.[167] Prior to 1 April 2008

---

159 Local Government Finance Act 1988, s 41(1).

160 Ibid, s 41(2).

161 As to the meaning of 'a person aggrieved' see *Arsenal Football Club v Smith* [1977] AC 1. An unincorporated members' club is, as a matter of practice, regarded as a person aggrieved: see *Warburton on Unincorporated Associations* (2nd edn, 1992) p 57; and see *R v L and F* [2009] 1 All ER 786, CA, cited in **1.8**.

162 Non-Domestic Rating (Alteration of Lists and Appeals) (England) Regulations 2009, SI 2009/2268, reg 5(1). Similar provisions apply to Wales: SI 2005/758.

163 Ibid, reg 6(1). Similar provisions apply to Wales: SI 2005/758. See 39(1B) *Halsbury's Laws of England* (4th edn, 2008) at 131.

164 Ibid, reg 4(1). The grounds are enumerated in 39(1B) *Halsbury's Laws of England*, op cit, at 130.

165 Ibid, reg 20. The Valuation Tribunal for England was set up in 2007. It replaced the 56 valuation tribunals then operating in England.

166 See ibid, reg 21.

167 *Ryde on Rating and Council Tax* (14th edn, Supp 54, 2010), at E3. Hitherto the rate had been set locally.

too there were separate formulae for occupied and unoccupied hereditaments; the latter paid only half of the amount of the former. They now pay the same rate.[168]

16.48 Relief from rates The position is governed by the Local Government Finance Act 1988 and the Non-Domestic Rating (Discretionary Relief) Regulations 1989 as amended.[169] Some relief is mandatory, and other relief is discretionary. Many members' clubs are eligible for rating relief of some sort.

16.49 Mandatory relief The position is as follows:

(1) *Charities* Their liability for non-domestic rates is reduced to one-fifth of the sum otherwise due.[170] This relief is subject to two qualifications:
   (a) the ratepayer must be a charity;
   (b) the hereditament must be wholly or mainly used for charitable purposes.[171]

   Registration under the Charities Act 1993 is conclusive proof that a club is charitable.[172] If not so registered, the club is entitled to the relief if it can satisfy the rating authority that it is established for charitable purposes.[173] The right to charity relief may be established by proceedings in the High Court for a declaration[174] or by resisting proceedings in the magistrates' court brought by the rating authority for non-payment of rates.[175]
(2) *Community amateur sports clubs* If registered, their liability for non-domestic rates is reduced to one-fifth of the sum otherwise due provided the hereditament is used wholly or mainly for the purposes of the club.[176]
(3) *Facilities for the disabled* The hereditament is exempt from non-domestic rates to the extent that it consists of property used wholly for the provision of facilities for training, or keeping suitably occupied,

---

[168] *Ryde on Rating and Council Tax*, op cit, at E3. In relation to charities and CASCs, unoccupied hereditaments are zero-rated: Local Government Finance Act 1988, s 45A, added by Rating (Empty Properties) Act 2007.

[169] SI 1989/1059.

[170] Local Government Finance Act 1988, s 43(5).

[171] Ibid, s 43(6)(a).

[172] *Wynn v Skegness UDC* [1967] 1 WLR 52 (case decided under the former Rating and Valuation Act 1961); Charities Act 1993, ss 4 and 96.

[173] *Over Seventies Housing Association v Westminster City Council* [1974] RA 247.

[174] *Oxfam v Birmingham City District Council* [1976] AC 126.

[175] *Royal Society for the Protection of Birds v Hornsea UDC* [1975] RA 26, DC. It is considered that both procedures (viz. declaration and resisting proceedings) are still available under the Act of 1988: see 39(1B) *Halsbury's Laws of England* (4th edn, 2008) at 72.

[176] Local Government Finance Act 1988, s 43(6)(b).

persons who are disabled or who are or have been suffering from illness; or for the provision of welfare services for disabled persons.[177]

(4) *Small business rate relief* The scheme works as follows:[178]
   (a) the hereditament (with minor exceptions) is the only non-domestic one occupied by the ratepayer in England;
   (b) eligible ratepayers with a rateable value of less than £6,000 will receive 50% relief;
   (c) eligible ratepayers with a rateable value between £6,001 and £12,000 will receive relief on a sliding scale from 50% to 0%;
   (d) eligible ratepayers with a rateable value between £12,001 and £25,499 in Greater London or £17,999 outside Greater London will have their rates liability calculated using the small business non-domestic rating multiplier instead of the national non-domestic multiplier.

   The level of this relief has been temporarily increased between 1 October 2010 and 30 September 2011,with the result that eligible ratepayers with a rateable value of less than £6,000 will receive relief at 100%, i e will pay no rates.[179]

Some clubs which do not come within the first three categories may be able to take advantage of this fourth category.

16.50 Discretionary relief The billing authority has a discretion whether to grant rating relief provided two conditions are satisfied:[180]

(a) the ratepayer comes within the eligible category on the chargeable day;
(b) there is in force a decision of the billing authority that this discretionary relief should operate.

The amount of relief can be less than is otherwise chargeable or it can be nil.[181]

16.51 The eligible organisations are:

(1) *Charities* The billing authority can grant relief over and above the 80% mandatory relief if the hereditament is used wholly or mainly for charitable purposes.[182]

---

177 Local Government Finance Act 1988, s 51, Sch 5, paras 16, 20, 21. Paragraph 16 defines what is meant by 'facilities', 'disabled' and 'illness'.

178 Non-Domestic Rating (Small Business Rate Relief) (England) Order 2004, SI 2004/3315, as amended by SI 2009/354 and SI 2009/3175. The figures were set in April 2010 and will be current until 2015.

179 Non-Domestic Rating (Small Business Rate Relief) (England) (Amendment) Order 2010, SI 2010/1655.

180 Local Government Finance Act 1988, s 47(3).

181 Ibid, s 47(4). See *Ryde on Rating and Council Tax* (14th edn, Supp 54, 2010) at E102,

182 Ibid, s 47(2)(a)

(2) *Community amateur sports clubs* If registered, the billing authority can grant relief over and above the 80% mandatory relief if the hereditament is used wholly or mainly for the purposes of the club.[183]

(3) *Institutions with eligible main objects and not for profit* This covers institutions and other organisations not established or conducted for profit and whose main objects are charitable or otherwise philanthropic or religious or concerned with education, social welfare, science, literature or the fine arts. A club is not to be taken as established or conducted for profit merely because it makes a financial surplus from investments or activities.[184] 'Education' in this context includes dramatic societies.[185] 'Social welfare' means the needs of the community which, as a matter of social ethics, ought to be met in the attainment of some acceptable standard.[186] 'Fine art' has been held not to include commercial photography[187] or folk dancing.[188]

(4) *Recreational clubs not for profit* This covers clubs, societies or other organisations not established or conducted for profit and whose premises are wholly or mainly used for the purposes of recreation. This appears to be a very wide category in respect of which there is no case law. The Oxford Shorter English Dictionary defines recreation as 'the action of recreating (oneself or another), or fact of being recreated, by some pleasant occupation, pastime or amusement'. There is no requirement that the recreation must be open-air recreation nor is it confined to games of physical sport.[189] It would seem that the making of a charge for admission to the recreation does not disqualify the hereditament from this relief.[190]

16.52 Enforcement If the rate demand is not paid, the billing authority must send a reminder notice to the ratepayer.[191] In default of payment, the

---

183 Local Government Finance Act 1988, s 47(2)(ba).

184 *National Deposit Friendly Society Trustees v Skegness UDC* [1958] AC 293 (surplus from investments); *North of England Zoological Society v Chester RDC* [1959] 1 WLR 773, CA (surplus from operations); *Ladbroke Park Golf Club Ltd v Stratford- on-Avon RDC* [1957] 1 RRC 202 (bar 'profits' in a members' club).

185 *Newport Playgoers' Society v Newport County Borough Council* [1957] 1 RRC 279; *Trustees of Stoke-on-Trent Repertory Players v Stoke-on-Trent Corporation* [1957] 1 RRC 279.

186 *National Deposit Friendly Society Trustees v Skegness UDC* [1959] AC 293, at 314. It has been suggested that a club concerned with social welfare is probably a charitable organisation within the meaning of the Recreational Charities Act 1958: see Warburton in [1980] *The Conveyancer and Property Lawyer* 173.

187 *Royal Photographic Society of Great Britain v City of Westminster and Cane (VO)* [1957] 2 RRC 169. This decision may be right on its facts but we consider that the stance adopted by the tribunal may be somewhat out of date: the famous Getty Museum in Los Angeles exhibits not only paintings but photographs as part of its collection. Many people think that black-and-white photography is an art form in itself.

188 *O'Sullivan v English Folk Dance and Song Society* [1955] 1 WLR 907.

189 *Ryde on Rating and Council Tax* (14th edn, Supp 54, 2010) at D369.

190 Ibid, at D369.

191 Non-Domestic Rating (Collection and Enforcement) (Local Lists) Regulations 1989, SI 1989/1058, as amended, reg 11(1).

authority may apply to a magistrates' court for a liability order.[192] If a liability order is made and not complied with, the authority may levy a distress on the ratepayer's property.[193]

[192] Non-Domestic Rating (Collection and Enforcement) (Local Lists) Regulations 1989, SI 1989/1058, reg 12(1).

[193] Ibid, reg 14(1). Deferral of payment may be possible under Non-Domestic Rating (Deferred Payments) (England) Regulations 2009, SI 2009/1597. Similar provisions apply to Wales: SI 2009/2154.

Chapter 17

THE CLUB'S RESPONSIBILITY FOR CRIME

1. INTRODUCTION

17.1 One definition of a law is an authorised enactment backed by a sanction. We live in a society where the rule of law is paramount. Almost all our activities as individuals are governed by laws, and everyone without exception must obey the law. To break the law commonly involves the commission of a crime, that is to say, an act punishable by the state. Clubs are subject to this regime. In the preceding chapters of this book we have discussed the activities of the club, whether it be the setting up of the club in the first place, its admission of members, the management of its affairs and the carrying on the business of a club, or the payment of its taxes. These activities are by definition set in a legal framework. In the background of all this discussion is the criminal law; it is the silent underpinning of the legal framework. It is true that clubs in the ordinary course of their activities usually manage to steer clear of brushes with the criminal law, but in a highly regulated society, sometimes embracing offences of strict liability, such avoidance is not always possible. It is important therefore that the club management has some understanding of this branch of the law. If the club or its members are involved in any accusations of criminal activity, the first thing to do is to contact a local solicitor for help and advice.

2. UNINCORPORATE BODIES

17.2 Overview Unincorporate bodies are not legal persons in the eyes of the common law and it is self-evident that an entity which is not a legal person cannot be guilty of a crime under such law. In *Attorney General v Able*,[1] which concerned the Voluntary Euthanasia Society Mr Justice Woolf, at 810, said, 'It must be remembered that [the society] is an unincorporated body and there can be no question of the society committing an offence'. It should be added for the sake of completeness that it is equally self-evident that a member of a club as an individual is subject to the criminal law in the same way as every other citizen. So the question arises in what way, if any, can an unincorporated body and its members be held criminally liable for

---

1 [1984] QB 795.

activities carried on by the club or for things which occur on the club's property. The starting point is that by Sch 1 to the Interpretation Act 1978 a person 'includes a body of persons corporate or unincorporate'. Section 5 of this Act says that 'unless a contrary intention appears' words are to be construed in accordance with Sch 1. It follows as an all-important principle that an unincorporate body is capable of being prosecuted under statute.[2]

17.3 The law relating to the criminal responsibility of unincorporated associations was restated by the Court of Appeal in *R v L and F*.[3] In that case an oil storage tank, the boiler and the connecting pipework were owned by and situated on land occupied by a golf club, an unincorporated members' club with some 900 members. An underground pipe taking oil from the tank to the boiler was fractured during work carried out by the club's independent building contractors, and the oil escaped and polluted a nearby watercourse. The Environment Agency prosecuted two members, the chairman and treasurer of the club, under s 85 of the Water Resources Act 1991 which states, 'A person contravenes this section if he causes or knowingly permits any poisonous, noxious or polluting matter … to enter any controlled waters'.[4] On conviction on indictment a person is liable to imprisonment for up to 2 years and/or to an unlimited fine. The judge at Taunton Crown Court ruled that the two members could not be convicted without personal culpability, of which the prosecution conceded there was none. On the other hand, the judge indicated that the club was liable to be prosecuted. The prosecution appealed against the judge's ruling concerning the two members on the ground that the alleged offence was one of strict liability.

17.4 The Court of Appeal said, at [24], that under statute there could be five different provisions relating to the criminal liability of an unincorporated association:

(1) it might stipulate that the association shall be prosecuted in its own name *and* that the members shall not be prosecuted;
(2) it might limit the criminal liability of members to cases where they have personal culpability ('officers' liability clauses');
(3) it might make any fine payable from the funds of the association, as distinct from those of any member personally;
(4) it might provide for the rules of service applicable to corporations to be adapted to unincorporated associations; and
(5) it might apply s 33 of the Criminal Justice Act 1925 and Sch 3 to the Magistrates' Courts Act 1980, which are provisions for the taking of

---

2 *R v W Stevenson & Sons (a partnership)* [2008] 2 Cr App R 14 (p 187).

3 [2009] 1 All ER 786.

4 In *National Rivers Authority v Empress Car Co (Abertillery) Ltd* [1999] 2 AC 22 it was held that, generally speaking, simply maintaining a storage tank was in itself sufficient to satisfy the test of 'causing or knowingly permitting', i e it was a case of strict liability.

pleas, the conduct or mode of trial proceedings, committal for trial and the like, where a defendant is a corporation.

17.5 Unincorporated members' clubs It follows that there are three routes which may be available to a prosecutor when prosecuting such a club under a statute:

(1) he can bring a prosecution against the club itself;
(2) he can prosecute the officers of the club under an 'officers' liability clause';
(3) he can prosecute the members of the club.

17.6 Prosecuting the club The question which had to be decided in *R v L and F* was whether the Water Resources Act 1991 did demonstrate that contrary intention referred to in **17.2**. The Court of Appeal, taking a different view from the prosecutor, came to the conclusion that no contrary intention could be deduced from the 1991 Act and therefore the Environment Agency was at liberty to prosecute the club. But no hard and fast rule can be applied, as the court said, at [22]:

> 'Notwithstanding the generality of the definition in Schedule 1 to the Interpretation Act 1978, there is no doubt that several statutes do make specific provision for the criminal liability of unincorporated associations. However, on inspection, these provisions vary so greatly that there is no settled policy which can be discerned from them, and we find it impossible to draw from them any general proposition that there is a form of enactment which is to be expected if an unincorporated association is to be criminally liable, and of which the absence signals a contrary intention for the purposes of section 5 of the Interpretation Act 1978.'

So each statute has to be examined to ascertain the answer as to what criminal liability attaches to the club and/or its members. We add that the Court of Appeal was at pains to point out, at [30], that their decision was limited to the strict liability offence in question and did not encompass those offences where intention or foresight was required to prove the offence:

> 'We do not for a moment consider any offence which involves any element of *mens rea*, which would be likely to raise quite different questions because of the personal and individual nature of a guilty mind. In such a case, it may well be that a contrary intention appears.'

17.7 Prosecuting the officers In some statutes relating to the criminal liability of unincorporate bodies they contain what is called an 'officers' liability clause' whereby criminal liability is extended to individuals in cases of personal culpability. For example, s 76(6) of the Health Act 2006 states:

> 'If an offence committed by an unincorporated association (other than a partnership) is proved –
>
> (a) to have been committed with the consent or connivance of an officer of the association or a member of its governing body, or
> (b) to be attributable to any neglect on the part of such an officer or member,
>
> the officer or member as well as the association is guilty of the offence and liable to be proceeded against and punished accordingly.'

The 'officers' liability clause' leaves no doubt that in specified cases the officers or members of the governing body of an unincorporate body can be prosecuted in respect of the aiding and abetting, or the conniving, of an offence or because of some neglect on their part. For example, the Water Resources Act 1991 contained no officers' liability clause so that no criminal liability could arise via this route in *R v L and F*.

17.8 Prosecuting the members In *R v L and F* the judge held that in the absence of an officers' liability clause and in the absence of personal culpability on their part *no* individual member could be prosecuted. The Court of Appeal reversed this ruling and held that *all 900* members were guilty of the offence. Why did the Court of Appeal come to this surprising decision? Their justification, at [33] and [34], was as follows:

> 'It is a necessary consequence of the different nature of an unincorporated association that all its members remain jointly and severally liable for its actions done within their authority. *In the present case, the 900-odd members of the club were indeed all maintainers of the tank* and, on the law as explained in *Empress Car Co* [1999] 2 AC 22 all [are] guilty of the strict liability offence of causing the leakage. This is not vicarious liability for the offence of the club, as was suggested in argument before the judge. Vicarious liability, when it exists, arises out of the employment by the defendant of another person to act for him. There is no sense in which the chairman, treasurer, or any other member of this club employed the club to do anything for them. The criminal liability of the members of the club, including the chairman and the treasurer, is primary liability, not vicarious liability. It arises because, as *Empress Car Co* holds, *each person jointly maintains the tank and has thus caused the leak*.' (emphasis added)

On what basis were the 900 members the maintainers of the storage tank? The Court of Appeal did not explain this. There could a factual basis for such a finding. First, the rules of the club might expressly make all the members the maintainers of the tank, although this is very unlikely, and was not something the court relied on. Secondly, all the members might be the occupiers of the club premises and thus be maintainers of the tank. This is a possibility because, for example, the Court of Appeal in *Bolton v Stone*[5] held that all the members of a cricket club were in occupation of their cricket ground[6] but there are serious problems with this approach.[7] We do not think it can be said that membership of a golf club in itself confers occupancy rights in relation to the club's property, and no evidence was given to the court from which it could infer occupation by all 900 members. Thirdly, all the members might be in control of the club's affairs and thus be maintainers of the tank. This might be a feasible proposition in a club of 9 members or even of 90 members, but is almost inconceivable in a club of 900 members. The club's affairs *under the rules* would be managed by its committee (and presumably were so in this case) and therefore anything done in relation to the tank would not fall within the authority of the members generally.[8] It would be the committee members alone of the general membership who would be maintainers of the tank, and thus liable to prosecution for a strict liability offence. So regrettably we take the view that neither the judge nor the Court of Appeal gave the right answer.

17.9 One other specific point arises out of *R v L and F*. The Court of Appeal, at [29], stated that the natural defendant was the landowner or, in ordinary language, the club. The members' golf club was to be defined on the day of the escape of the oil so that it excluded anyone who had joined since that date but it included any member who had subsequently left the club 'or died'. The court then went on to mention the relevance of the means of the defendant on conviction. But we cannot believe that the court intended to include dead members in any prosecution, and that the reference to them was an oversight.

17.10 There are several oddities arising from the restated law in *R v L and F* which suggest that the subject will have to be revisited by the courts or Parliament in due course:

(1) the members of an unincorporated members' club would appear to have a greater criminal liability than at civil law in respect of the same circumstances.[9] If the Environment Agency had sued the golf club and its members for damages caused by the escaped oil, the members would not have been found liable as a matter of primary liability

---

5 [1950] 1 KB 201, CA.

6 See **12.34**(2).

7 See **12.39**.

8 See, e g **5.1**, **5.21** and **6.28**.

9 *Archbold, Criminal Pleadings, Evidence and Practice* (2011 edn) at 1–145 submits that individual members of a club should be liable to prosecution only where it can be shown that the club's lapse was due to their act or default.

without negligence or fault on their part, whether the agency had sued in the tort of negligence or in the tort of nuisance;[10]

(2) if there is an 'officers' liability clause' in the statute (which commonly will follow the form or substance set out in s 76(6) of the Health Act 2006), the officers of the club and the members of the managing committee will ironically have less liability than the ordinary member since their liability will not be of the strict variety but will only arise on some personal culpability;

(3) if there had been an 'officers' liability clause' in the Water Resources Act 1991, could the committee member of the golf club have resisted the strict criminal liability in his capacity as an ordinary member by relying on his lesser liability under the officers' liability clause, or would the prosecutor have had the choice under which heading to prosecute the committee member?

(4) the members of an unincorporated member's club have potentially greater criminal liability than their counterparts in a members' club which is a company or some other variety of corporation. This curious distinction was pointed out by the court in *R v L and F*, at [33], without comment or criticism.

3. CORPORATE BODIES

17.11 Corporate bodies, such as community clubs and incorporated clubs, are legal persons and so can be prosecuted and fined, or committed for sentence to the Crown Court.[11] None of the difficulties which arise with unincorporate bodies as discussed above are applicable here.

4. VICARIOUS LIABILITY

17.12 Overview A problem arises when a person, who may or may not be a member of the club, commits a criminal offence in the course of his activities on behalf of the club. Who in the club, apart from the wrongdoer himself, can be held responsible? The answer lies in the doctrine of vicarious liability.[12] First, in relation to *members*, the club will not be liable for a criminal offence simply because it has been committed by a member. In an unincorporated members' club it is the managing committee and the officers who will in many instances be facing liability. In a corporate club, whether the act of an agent (member) is to be attributed to the club is to be decided on the issue of the closeness of the relationship between the agent

---

10 See **12.32**.

11 *R v Tyler and the International Commercial Co Ltd* [1891] 2 QB 588; Magistrates' Court Act 1980, s 38.

12 See *Archbold, Criminal Pleadings, Evidence and Practice* (2011 edn) paras 1–140 and 17–25 et seq.

and the club. The guilty mind of an agent who is not closely identified with the management of the club will not render it liable, whereas the guilty mind of a member-director or a member-manager will do so.[13] Secondly, in relation to *employees,* a club whether corporate or unincorporate may be held liable for the criminal consequences of the acts and omissions of its employees who were acting within the course of their employment, regardless of whether those employees can be said to be exercising the controlling mind of the club.[14]

17.13 Knowledge No hard and fast rule can be laid down as to when the committee or officers might be held liable. At common law a person can be held liable for 'aiding and abetting' a crime where he is not the principal offender. It is normally the case that offences are committed only when the accused *knowingly* does something which the criminal law forbids him to do. The lack of knowledge does not always allow the principal to escape liability where an employee or subordinate has committed the offence without the knowledge or connivance of the principal.[15] This is because of the operation of the doctrine of vicarious liability. Consider the following trilogy of unlawful drinking cases.[16] In *Vane v Yiannopoullos*[17] the licensee of a restaurant was physically present in the premises and actively in control when, unbeknown to him, an employee committed the offence of serving intoxicating liquor to customers who had not ordered a meal. The House of Lords upheld his acquittal of knowingly selling to persons to whom he was not permitted by the conditions of his licence to sell,[18] on the basis that he had no knowledge of the commission of the offence. Lord Reid said that there was a long-standing distinction between, on the one hand, the vicarious liability of a licensee for the acts done without his knowledge by an employee to whom he has delegated the entire management of the premises and, on the other hand, his non-liability for such acts done while he himself retains the general supervision of the premises. In *R v Winson*[19] the licensee of a licensed club took no active part in the running of the club and delegated this task to a manager who unlawfully permitted alcohol to be sold to persons who had not been members for 48 hours.[20] The licensee was convicted of knowingly selling alcohol unlawfully. And in *Anderton v Rogers*[21] alcohol was unlawfully sold to a non-member of an unincorporated

---

13 *H L Bolton (Engineering) Co Ltd v T J Graham and Sons Ltd* [1957] 1 QB 159 CA, at 172 (Denning LJ); *John Henshall Quarries Ltd v Harvey* [1965] 2 QB 233, DC.

14 *National Rivers Authority v Alfred McAlpine Homes (East) Ltd* [1994] 4 All ER 286 (company held liable for the conduct of its employees who caused pollution of a controlled water supply).

15 *Mousell Bros Ltd v London and North Western Railway Co* [1917] 2 KB 836, at 844 (Viscount Reading CJ).

16 Licensing offences are now largely dealt with under Part 7 of the Licensing Act 2003, but the question of 'knowledge' is still relevant.

17 [1965] AC 486.

18 Contrary to the Licensing Act 1961, s 22(1).

19 [1969] 1 QB 371, CCA.

20 Contrary to the Licensing Act 1964, s 161(1).

21 [1981] Crim LR 404.

club.[22] The members of the committee were unaware of this fact yet were convicted of knowingly selling alcohol unlawfully.

17.14 Part of the reason why the accused were found guilty in the two last-mentioned cases was because knowledge does not only include actual knowledge but also includes deliberately shutting one's eyes or mind to an obvious means of knowledge.[23] Thus simply appointing a manager of a club and leaving him to get on with the job will not normally exonerate the committee from criminal liability, as Lord Reid stated in the case of *Vane*. The committee will be expected to put in place proper procedures for managing and supervising the activities being carried on at the club.[24] In *Linnett v Metropolitan Police Commissioner*[25] an absentee licensee of a public house was convicted of 'knowingly permitting disorderly conduct' where he had left control of the premises to another, who had in fact knowingly permitted the conduct complained of. Lord Goddard CJ, at 295, said:

> 'If the manager chooses to delegate the carrying on of the business to another, whether or not that other is his servant, then what that other does or what he knows must be imputed to the person who put the other into that position.'

The members of committee would not, however, be responsible for the criminal acts of a stranger or third party who committed an offence on club premises without their knowledge or in their absence.[26]

17.15 Strict liability and due diligence These days the committee or the club as employer will have to take cognisance of many statutory obligations set out in various Acts of Parliament which regulate club activity, for example, the Licensing Act 2003, the Gambling Act 2005, the Weights and Measures Act 1985, and the Health and Safety legislation. The obligations are often offences of strict liability, that is to say, the offence can be committed without any fault of the part of the committee or the club. As Lord Parker LCJ said in *John Henshall (Quarries) Ltd v Harvey*,[27] 'There is no doubt that in the case of absolute offences, as they are sometimes called, a master, whether an individual or a company, is criminally liable for the acts of any servant acting within the scope of his authority'.[28] In some statutes Parliament has permitted a defence of due diligence whereby the accused can escape liability if he can prove that he took all reasonable steps to

22 Contrary to the Licensing Act 1964, s 160(1).

23 *Goodwin v Baldwin* (1974) *The Times*, 2 February; *Buxton v Chief Constable of Northumbria* [1983] 148 JP Jo 9; *Oxford v Lincoln* (1982) *The Times*, 1 March.

24 *R v Souter* [1971] 1 WLR 1187.

25 [1946] KB 290.

26 *Taylor v Speed* [1979] Crim LR 114.

27 [1965] 2 QB 233, DC, at 239.

28 For 'master' read 'employer' and for 'servant' read 'employee'. The world has moved on since 1965.

ensure compliance with his statutory obligation: see, for example, s 139(1) of the Licensing Act 2003 discussed in **17.20**. In the case of an incorporated club reliance on this defence may be more difficult to achieve because the state of mind of an employee or member who is a ruling officer of the company may be attributed to the company.[29] In an unincorporated members' club, the knowledge of one individual member will not be attributed to another individual member. It follows from this fact that if the committee member as principal is acquitted under the 'due diligence' defence in relation to a *non* strict-liability offence, the employee or the member, who will have been the perpetrator of the offence, will likewise be acquitted.[30]

5. STATUTES WHERE CRIMINAL LIABILITY MAY FALL ON THE CLUB

17.16 Constitutional matters: criminal offences In setting up the club and then dealing with formal matters thereafter, the officers and the managing committee of a club which derives its constitutional powers wholly or in part from some statute must as a matter of course comply with the provisions of the statute in question. Failure to comply with certain provisions may involve the club, its officers and its governing body in prosecution for criminal offences. A detailed discussion of the individual offences is beyond the scope of this book but we point out below where some of the offences are described:

- *Literary and Scientific Institutions Act 1854*: s 26.
- *Co-operative and Community Benefit Societies and Credit Unions Act 1965*: ss 61–66.
- *Friendly Societies Act 1974*: ss 98–101.
- *Charities Act 1993:* ss 49, 68ZB and 95.
- *Data Protection Act 1998:* ss 21(1)–(2), 22(6), 47(1)–(2), 54A(6),[31] 55(3)–(5) and 56(5).
- *Companies Act 2006:* Part 36 (ss 1121–1133).

17.17 Managerial matters: criminal offences In carrying out its activities it is not unlikely that a club will be confronted on occasion with the criminal law and the case of *R v L and F*[32] described in **17.3** is a good example of how this may come about. Set out below are some areas where criminal responsibility may intrude into the club's life.

---

29 *Coupe v Guyett* [1973] 1 WLR 669, DC, at 675 (Lord Widgery CJ).
30 Ibid (a prosecution under the Trade Descriptions Act 1968).
31 Section added by Crime (International Co-operation) Act 2003, s 81.
32 [2009] 1 All ER 786, CA.

17.18 Licensing The Licensing Act 2003 created a whole range of new offences, most of which are contained in Part 7 of the Act, under the heading of 'Unauthorised licensable activities'. It is important that the members of the committee supplying or selling alcohol to members and guests familiarise themselves with the licensing offences, which fall into three categories:

(1) offences relating to the management of the licensable activity (ss 136–138);
(2) offences relating to the premises where the licensable activities are being carried on (ss 140–153);
(3) offences arising from the various duties connected with the application process.

Examples of the third category are (a) the offence under s 96 of obstructing an 'authorised person'[33] in the exercise of the power to enter and inspect club premises on an application for a premises certificate, and (b) the offence under s 108 of obstructing an 'authorised officer'[34] (rather than an authorised person) in the execution of his right to enter premises to which a temporary event notice relates in order 'to assess the likely effect of the notice on the promotion of the crime prevention objective'.[35] Indeed, it may be said that, wherever there is a right is conferred on the licensing authority or a duty imposed on the person carrying on the licensable activity, obstruction of the licensing authority in the exercise of its rights or the failure to fulfil the imposed duty, will render that person liable to prosecution for a summary offence.

17.19 If an offence under the 2003 Act has been committed by a club (whether incorporated or unincorporated) and it is shown to have been committed with the consent or connivance of an officer of the club or a member of its governing body,[36] or to be attributable to his neglect,[37] that officer or member is also guilty of the offence.[38]

17.20 ***The defence of due diligence*** This is provided by s 139 of the Licensing Act 2003. Where a person (this includes a club)[39] is charged with

---

33 Licensing Act 2003, s 69(2): that is, an officer of the licensing authority, an inspector appointed under the Fire Precautions Act 1971 or the Health and Safety at Work etc Act 1974, and an environmental health inspector.

34 Licensing Act 2003, s 108(5): that is, an officer of the licensing authority.

35 Ibid, s 108(3).

36 See *A-G's Reference (No 1 of 1995)* [1996] 1 WLR 970.

37 See *Huckerby v Elliott* [1970] 1 All ER 189, DC (which concerned the New Embassy Club owned by a limited company and where the defendant's conviction was quashed because the prosecution had not proved that the offence of using the premises without a gaming licence was attributable to her neglect, she having properly relied on another director).

38 Licensing Act 2003, s 187.

39 Ibid, s 146(2).

(a) carrying on an unauthorised licensable activity;[40] or (b) exposing alcohol for unauthorised sale;[41] or (c) keeping alcohol on premises for unauthorised sale;[42] it is a defence if (1) his act was due to a mistake, or to reliance on information given to him, or to an act or omission by another person, or to some other cause beyond his control;[43] and (2) he took all reasonable precautions and exercised all due diligence to avoid committing the offence. Another example where the defence of due diligence applies is on a charge of selling alcohol to a child (ie a person under the age of 18 years).[44] It is also a defence to this particular offence that the person charged had a reasonable belief that the individual concerned was over 18.[45] Similar provisions apply to the offence of supplying liqueur confectionery to a person under the age of 16.[46]

17.21 ***Personal liability of club member*** An important point to note is that in the case of the offences of:

(a) allowing disorderly conduct on premises covered by a club premises certificate;[47]
(b) selling alcohol to a person who is drunk;[48]
(c) keeping smuggled goods;[49]
(d) breach of the prohibition of unaccompanied children in certain premises;[50]
(e) allowing the sale of alcohol to children;[51]
(f) consumption of alcohol by children;[52]
(g) delivering alcohol to children;[53] and
(h) the prohibition of unsupervised sales by children,[54]

an offence is committed by any member or officer of the club who is present at the premises at the time of the offence in question in a capacity which enables him to prevent it.[55]

---

40 Licensing Act 2003, s 136.
41 Ibid, s 137.
42 Ibid, s 138.
43 Ibid, s 139(1)(a).
44 Ibid, s 146(6).
45 Ibid, s 146(4).
46 Ibid, s 148.
47 Ibid, s 140(2)(c).
48 Ibid, s 141(2)(c).
49 Ibid, s 144(2)(c).
50 Ibid, s 145(3)(c).
51 Ibid, s 147(4)(b).
52 Ibid, s 150(3)(b).
53 Ibid, s 151(5)(b).
54 Ibid, s 153(4)(b).
55 See also the similar duty imposed under the Licensing Act 2003 (Mandatory Licensing Conditions) Order 2010, SI 2010/860, referred to at **9.21**(1)(a).

This provision is contained in each of the sections creating these offences, and means that any club member present at the time when the prohibited conduct is taking place, and knowing it is taking place, will potentially be guilty of an offence. The courts, however, will find themselves with the task of deciding in individual cases whether the person charged was present in a *capacity* which enabled him to prevent the conduct in question. Does this imply an element of formal control over the club activities at the relevant time? On the face of it, we think not. Theoretically any adult club member could be said to have some responsibility for ensuring the lawful running of his own club, and consequently to be present in the requisite capacity. What, then, of the club member who is quietly minding his own business in a corner of the bar when he notices someone who plainly looks under the age of 18 going up to the bar and ordering an alcoholic drink which is supplied to him, and then he sees this person consuming the drink at the bar? Let us assume this supply and consumption of alcohol constitute criminal offences.[56] The member's natural instinct might be to shrug his shoulders and to continue to mind his own business, but under the 2003 Act he could be held to be present in a capacity which enabled him to prevent the unlawful conduct. By his inaction he may find himself guilty of a criminal offence.

17.22 ***Club rules*** These are commonly altered, often for minor corrections, improvements or additions. Every alteration, however small, must be notified by the club secretary to the licensing authority within 28 days following the day on which the alteration was made,[57] in default of which the secretary commits an offence.[58]

17.23 Gambling Parts 3 and 4 of the Gambling Act 2005 contain general offences concerning the provision of gambling facilities and the use of premises in connection therewith. The basic mechanism for ensuring compliance with the gambling regime is the creation of an offence under s 33 that the provision of gambling facilities and the use of premises in connection therewith shall be an offence unless either (a) the gambling activity is licensed and/or conducted within the terms of the licence or (b) an exemption applies under s 33(2), the relevant ones for clubs being exempt equal-chance gaming (see **11.10**) and non-commercial equal-chance gaming (see **11.14**). The 2005 Act contains other specific offences, for example, ss 53–55 concerning the employment of a child (but not a young person) in gaming activities; and ss 258–263 concerning the promotion and conduct of lotteries.

---

56 See Licensing Act 2003, ss 147 and 150.
57 Ibid, s 82(4).
58 Ibid, s 82(6).

17.24 Landlord and Tenant Whereas the Rent Act 1977 contains a number of offences in relation to the operation of controlled tenancies,[59] the Housing Act 1988 contains only one offence in relation to assured tenancies, namely, the landlord's failure to give a written statement to the tenant of the terms of his tenancy.[60] The Protection from Eviction Act 1977 continues in force and this act contains criminal offences in the event of breach.[61]

17.25 Health and safety The club's duty as employer towards its employees is discussed at **15.34**. The sanction for breaking the law here is primarily contained in s 33 of the Health and Safety at Work etc Act 1974 which has created various offences for breach of the Act itself and in some cases for breach of the regulations issued thereunder. Following concern that many breaches of health and safety legislation did not result in serious enough penalties, the Health and Safety (Offences) Act 2008 was enacted which has substantially increased the maximum penalties.[62] For example, the maximum fines are increased for offences triable summarily from £5,000 to £20,000 and more offences are now potentially punishable with imprisonment for up to 12 months. Offences triable on indictment are now punishable by fine and/or imprisonment of up to 2 years.

17.26 ***Smoking ban*** Part 1 of the Health Act 2006 was enacted to protect the health of the public by imposing a ban on smoking in public places and workplaces. This part of the Act came into force on 1 July 2007. Premises are to be smoke-free if (a) they are enclosed or substantially enclosed[63] and (b) they are open to the public[64] or comprise a shared workplace.[65] The phrase 'open to the public' means that the public or a section of the public has access to the premises in question, whether by invitation or not or whether on payment or not.[66] This definition therefore includes club members attending their club premises since they will count as a section of the public.[67] There are certain exemptions, one of which is a designated bedroom in a members' club,[68] provided the room is clearly marked as a bedroom where smoking is permitted.[69] Apart from this exemption, no other exemption is permitted in respect of premises where a club premises

---

59 Rent Act 1977, ss 57(5), 81(4), 92(2), 94(5), 95(2)–(3), 119(2), 120(2), 122(2) and 124(1).

60 Housing Act 1988, s 20A(4), added by Housing Act 1996, s 97.

61 Protection from Eviction Act 1977, s 1, as amended by Housing Act 1988, s 29.

62 Health and Safety at Work etc Act 1974, Sch 3A, inserted by Health and Safety (Offences) Act 2008, s 1.

63 Health Act 2006, s 2(4). For the definition of 'substantially enclosed' see Smoke-free (Premises and Enforcement) Regulations 2006, SI 2006/3368, reg 2.

64 Ibid, s 2(1) and (3). For the definition of 'substantially enclosed' see Smoke-free (Premises and Enforcement) Regulations 2006, SI 2006/3368, reg 2.

65 Health Act 2006, s 2(2)–(3).

66 Ibid, s 2(7).

67 See *Jennings v Stephens* [1936] 1 Ch 469, CA, at 482, cited in **10.3**.

68 Smoke-free (Exemptions and Vehicles) Regulations 2007, SI 2007/765, reg 4(1).

69 Ibid, reg 4(2)(f).

certificate or a premises licence has effect.[70] The club as occupier or its managing committee is required to put up a 'No Smoking' sign at the entrance to the club premises.[71] An offence is committed by a person who smokes in a smoke-free place[72] and an offence is committed by a person who controls or is concerned in the management of smoke-free premises if he fails to stop someone smoking in a smoke-free place.[73] Enforcement is carried out by the local council[74] and it is an offence to obstruct an authorised officer of the enforcement authority acting in the exercise of his functions under the Act.[75]

17.27 Revenue offences In addition to the many penalties imposed for filing incorrect corporation tax returns or failing to file them when required, the powers of HM Revenue and Customs ('HMRC') are in some cases backed by criminal sanctions. There are severe penalties imposed for knowingly preparing or assisting the preparation of an incorrect tax return[76] and the Court of Appeal in *Saunders v Edwards*[77] indicated that supplying false information to HMRC or deliberately manipulating values or figures with a view to reducing the tax bill could involve a wide range of criminal offences. These will include forgery in putting forward the tax return as being a genuine document, fraud by making knowingly false statements and statutory offences such as false accounting.[78] HMRC are given wide powers to call for information in the form of written records or oral statements and have power to enter upon premises and seize documents. It is generally regarded as more effective from the point of view of HMRC simply to raise an estimated assessment which puts the onus on the taxpayer to produce documentation to challenge it. In general, HMRC would prefer to have corporation tax paid together with any penalties and interest and there is a tendency not to prosecute provided that a reasonable settlement can be obtained as regards unpaid corporation tax and penalties. This requires full and frank disclosure of all relevant material by the taxpayer. In relation to value added tax ('VAT') there is a tendency for HMRC to take the view that a criminal prosecution should take priority over an appeal to an appropriate VAT tribunal. This means that there may be a prosecution before the taxpayer has established that there is no incorrect return or that the correct amount of VAT has been paid. If the correct amount of VAT can be established as having been paid then there is, prima facie, no criminal offence and, should HMRC wish to press for a prosecution while there is a dispute as to liability, this should be

---

70 Health Act 2006, s 3(3).

71 Ibid, s 6(1); Smoke-free (Signs) Regulations 2007, SI 2007/923, reg 2. The sign must include the prescribed no-smoking symbol.

72 Health Act 2006, s 7(2).

73 Ibid, s 8(4).

74 Ibid, s 10; Smoke-free (Premises and Enforcement) Regulations 2007, reg 3.

75 Health Act 2006, s 11.

76 See www.hmrc.gov.uk/about/new-penalties/

77 [1987] 1 WLR 1116, CA, at 1133.

78 Fraud Act 2006; Theft Act 1968, s 17.

strenuously resisted since a criminal trial in front of a jury is not necessarily the most efficient vehicle for determining whether there is a liability to tax.

6. ALTERNATIVE CIVIL SANCTIONS

17.28 A development took place in relation to offences under the Regulatory Reform and Sanctions Act 2008 which came fully into force on 6 April 2009. The government decided it was more efficient to let certain regulators impose civil sanctions in certain areas of activity rather than prosecutions being launched against offenders. A new statutory body called the Local Better Regulation Office was set up[79] which, together with the designated regulators,[80] has been given the power to impose by notice certain sanctions in lieu of prosecution. Broadly speaking the sanctions are:[81]

(1) the payment of a fixed monetary penalty in respect of a relevant offence;
(2) the requirement to take steps to secure that the offence does not continue or recur; and
(3) the requirement to take steps within a specified period to secure that the position, so far as is possible, is restored to what it had been, had the offence not been committed.

17.29 The regulators which may involve clubs are the Environment Agency, the Financial Services Authority, the Food Standards Agency, the Gambling Commission, the Health and Safety Executive, the Information Commissioner and the Office of Fair Trading. The relevant offences are those contained in a statute in respect of which the regulator has an enforcement function[82] and which existed at the date of the enactment of the 2008 Act.[83] The Act lists the qualifying statutes where these sanctions may be imposed[84] and one of the qualifying statutes is the Health and Safety at Work etc Act 1974. The regulator has to be satisfied beyond reasonable doubt that the offence has been committed.[85] The monetary penalty in relation to a summary offence must not exceed the maximum sum which could be imposed on conviction.[86] Where a sanction is imposed, the offender is protected from prosecution until such time as the notice

79 In July 2010 the coalition government said the continuance of this body was under review.

80 Regulatory Enforcement and Sanctions Act 2008, s 37(1) and Sch 5.

81 Ibid, s 42(1) and (3).

82 See, for example, the case of *R v L and F* [2009] 1 All ER 786, CA discussed in **17.3** concerning the Environment Agency and the prosecution of a golf club.

83 Regulatory Enforcement and Sanctions Act 2008, s 38(1).

84 Ibid, s 37(2) and Sch 6.

85 Ibid, s 42(2).

86 Ibid, s 42(6).

expires.[87] The penalty procedure is subject to appeal to a tribunal.[88] It is envisaged by the government that the use of alternative civil sanctions will improve the level of compliance with health and safety and other important legislation.

7. SERIOUS OFFENCES

17.30 Corporate manslaughter Under the Corporate Manslaughter and Corporate Homicide Act 2007 there was created a new statutory offence of corporate manslaughter[89] to act as a stand-alone provision for prosecuting organisations and to complement offences primarily aimed at individuals. Under this Act an offence is committed (a) where the way in which an organisation's activities are managed or organised causes a person's death and (b) which amounts to a gross breach of the duty of care owed by that organisation.[90] The organisations to which this Act applies are (1) a corporation; (2) a body listed in Sch 1 to the Act which hitherto had been immune, such as a government department; (3) a police force; and (4) a partnership, or a trade union or employers' association, which is an employer.[91] By a curious lacuna no other unincorporated association, such as an unincorporated members' club, appears in the definition of an organisation. The Secretary of State, however, has the power to extend by order the categories of organisation to which the Act applies.[92] Thus an incorporated club in its capacity as employer might encounter this Act in relation to the death of an employee which concerned the provision of a safe system of work for that employee.

17.31 Serious crime prevention orders Under the Serious Crime Act 2007 a new form of civil injunctive order was created, called a serious crime prevention order, which is aimed at preventing serious crime. The High Court may make the order if it is satisfied that a person has been involved in serious crime and it has reasonable grounds to believe that the order will protect the public by preventing, restricting or disrupting involvement by that person in serious crime.[93] Serious crime is defined in Sch 1 to the Act and covers obvious offences such as drugs trafficking, armed robbery, prostitution and money laundering, and somewhat less obvious offences such as false accounting under the Theft Act 1968, certain intellectual property offences under the Copyright, Designs and Patents Act 1988 and specified offences under the Salmon and Freshwater Fisheries Act 1975, the Wildlife and Countryside Act 1981 and the Environmental Protection

---

87 Regulatory Enforcement and Sanctions Act 2008, s 41.
88 Ibid, s 54.
89 To be called corporate homicide in Scotland.
90 Corporate Manslaughter and Corporate Homicide Act 2007, s 1(1).
91 Ibid, s 1(2).
92 Ibid, s 21.
93 Serious Crime Act 2007, s 1.

Act 1990. A person who without reasonable excuse fails to comply with a serious crime prevention order commits an offence.[94] A serious crime prevention order may be made against a body corporate and therefore it may be convicted of the offence.[95] If the offence was committed with the consent or connivance of an officer of the body corporate, he too may be convicted of the offence.[96] In relation to unincorporated associations, a serious prevention crime order must be made in the name of the association and not in that of any of its members.[97] The order will continue in force even if the membership changes, unless all the persons who were members at the date of the order leave the association, at which point in time the order ceases to have effect.[98] If the association is convicted, the fine is to be paid out of the association's funds.[99] If the offence was committed with the consent or connivance of an officer of the association, he too may be convicted of the offence.[100]

---

94 Serious Crime Act 2007, s 25(1).
95 Ibid, s 30(2).
96 Ibid, s 30(2).
97 Ibid, s 32(1).
98 Ibid, s 30(2).
99 Ibid, s 32(6).
100 Ibid, s 32(7).

Part 4:

CLUBS AS PARTIES IN CIVIL PROCEEDINGS

Chapter 18

THE CLUB'S INVOLVEMENT IN CIVIL PROCEEDINGS

1. INTRODUCTION

18.1 It will be a fortunate club that can avoid disputes altogether either as claimant or as defendant. It is therefore necessary for every club to know how to bring and defend court proceedings in respect of any civil claim made by or against it.[1] This chapter therefore deals with matters of procedure, not with the substantive matter of any claim or dispute which is dealt with elsewhere in the book. The current rules are the Civil Procedure Rules ('CPR')[2] and they govern the practice and procedure in the county courts, the High Court of Justice and the civil division of the Court of Appeal. An important innovation was the introduction of the overriding objective[3] by which the court is enabled to deal with cases justly, expeditiously and fairly. 'Justly' means ensuring that the parties are on an equal footing; saving expense; and applying the concept of proportionality. The parties themselves have a duty to help the court to further the overriding objective.[4] In October 2009 the Supreme Court replaced the House of Lords as the highest appellate court in the land.[5]

18.2 If the club is involved in any litigation of any substance, whether as claimant or defendant, it is a wise move to call a special meeting of the members to obtain their express sanction for the litigation and to confirm that the costs of the litigation shall be borne out of club funds. It is recommended that this procedure should be followed even if the committee

---

1 Criminal responsibility is the subject matter of Chapter 17.

2 SI 1998/3132 (followed by numerous amending statutory instruments). As at 2010 some small parts of the Rules of the Supreme Court (RSC) still remain in force but the process of assimilation into the CPR will no doubt continue.

3 CPR, r 1.1(1) and (2).

4 CPR, r 1.3.

5 The High Court of Parliament has existed for hundreds of years, and was abolished as an appellate court in the legal reforms of 1873, hence the High Court of Justice and the Court of Appeal were together described as the *Supreme Court*. Three years later in 1876 the House of Lords was reinstated as the final appellate court, leaving this (now erroneous) description in place. The creation of a new Supreme Court in 2009 as the highest court in the land reflects better on the constitution as it separates a body with legislative powers from a body with judicial powers. The new judges are styled Justices of the Supreme Court; previously from 1876 they had been called Lords of Appeal in Ordinary (or colloquially Law Lords).

or the trustees, as the case may be, are empowered under the rules, either generally or specifically, to conduct litigation on behalf of the club. If the trustees, the officers of the club or other named members, sue or are sued as individuals representing the club, the special meeting should further confirm that those members will be indemnified out of club funds against all liabilities arising from the proceedings.

2. PURSUING CLAIMS

18.3 Unincorporated members' clubs Proceedings cannot be brought in the name of the club because it is not a legal person.[6] The action must therefore be brought either in the names of the individual members, on the basis of their personal rights (where they exist) or in the name of one or more members as representing all or some relevant part of the membership such as the managing committee.[7]

18.4 Pre-action Protocols The CPR uses the word 'protocol' to mean a document which outlines the steps parties should make in order to provide information to, and seek information from, each other about a prospective legal claim.[8] The purpose of a protocol is to promote settlement of disputes, thereby avoiding litigation.[9] Certain protocols have been approved by the Rules Committee[10] which, together with the CPR Practice Direction-Protocols, must be complied with. In those claims not covered by an approved protocol, the court will expect the parties to act reasonably in exchanging information and documents relevant to the claim before any action is begun.[11] This would normally include:[12]

(1) the claimant writing a letter to give details of the claim, enclosing copies of essential documents relied on;[13]
(2) the defendant acknowledging the letter within 21 days of receipt;[14]
(3) the defendant giving within a reasonable time a detailed written response, stating which part of the claim is accepted and which part is disputed, and giving reasons for disputing any part and enclosing essential documents on which the defendant relies;[15]

---

6 *London Association for Protection of Trade v Greenlands Ltd* [1916] 2 AC 15.
7 See **18.5**.
8 CPR Practice Direction – Protocols, para 1.3.
9 Ibid, para 1.4.
10 Namely, claims for clinical negligence, construction and engineering disputes, defamation, disease and illness, housing disrepair, judicial review, personal injury, possession based on rent arrears and professional negligence: ibid, para 5.1.
11 Ibid, para 4.1.
12 Ibid, para 4.2.
13 Ibid, para 4.3(b).
14 Ibid, para 4.4.
15 Ibid, paras 4.5 and 4.6(a)(b).

(4) the parties conducting genuine negotiations with a view to settling any valid claim economically and without court proceedings, and making proposals for settlement of that part of the claim which is accepted.[16]

Non-compliance with an applicable protocol will expose the defaulting party to sanctions which are imposed by the court under CPR Practice Direction–Protocols, para 2.3 and which relate to the issue of costs or the quantum of interest on damages.

18.5 Representative action This is governed by CPR, r 19.6. Where more than one person has the same interest in a claim the claim may be begun, or the court may order its continuance, by one or more of the persons who have the same interest as representatives of any other persons having the same interest. In club cases it is usual for one or more of the important officers to perform the representative role. The words, 'the same interest in a claim', appearing in r 19.6 are to be construed so as to give effect to the overriding objective of the CPR. In *National Bank of Greece SA v Outhwaite 317 Syndicate at Lloyd's*[17] it was held that it was proper to bring proceedings against one individual as representative of all members of the 39 Lloyd's syndicates which had subscribed to a particular insurance policy, even though the selected individual was only a member of one of the syndicates, there being no leading underwriter clause in the policy. Had the situation been reversed, namely, had the Outhwaite 317 Syndicate been suing the National Bank of Greece, the same principle would have applied. Further, it is no bar to a representative action that the exact natures of the interest represented differ somewhat; the procedural rule is not to be treated as a rigid matter of principle but as a flexible tool of convenience in the administration of justice.[18]

18.6 It is not possible for the sake of convenience for a club to name *any* individual or individuals it chooses as representing the club in an action which the club intends to bring. It follows from this proposition that the persons selected as acting on behalf of the club in a representative capacity must be properly named and properly described in the claim form.[19] For example, it should state 'Peter Davey, Daniel Whiddon and Harry Hawke as representing themselves and all other members of the Basset Pony Club' (on the basis that Mr Davey was the chairman of the club, Mr Whiddon was its secretary and Mr Hawke was its treasurer). Any exception must be explicitly spelt out. So that if the committee on behalf of the club was bringing an action against Tom Pearce, who was a club member, for defective saddlery supplied to the club the claim form should read, 'Peter

16 CPR Practice Direction – Protocols, para 4.5(a).

17 [2001] Lloyd's Rep IR 652.

18 *John v Rees* [1970] Ch 345, at 370 (Megarry J) (where there was a clear common interest between all the club members in having the issue resolved, but the members themselves were far from united in the way they wished it to be resolved).

19 *Adams v Naylor* [1946] AC 543.

Davey, Daniel Whiddon and Harry Hawke as representing themselves and all other members of the Basset Pony Club except the Defendant herein [Tom Pearce]'.[20] The claimant does not need to obtain the court's permission to issue a claim form as a representative of other claimants, but the court retains a power to order that a particular person may not act as a representative.[21] A person suing in a representative capacity does not need to obtain the consent of those he is authorised to represent,[22] even though they will be bound by the result of the case. As far as unincorporated members' clubs are concerned, this statement needs qualification, bearing in mind the contractual (ie consensual) basis of membership. If, as would be the norm, the members have put the control of the club's affairs into the hands of a managing committee, the members as a whole are thereby impliedly giving their consent to the committee bringing a representative action on behalf of the club and this implied consent will override the opposition of individual members.

18.7 The representative claimant is fully empowered to choose how to run the litigation on behalf of the class.[23] The represented persons are not parties to the litigation so that, for example, disclosure of documents can only be ordered against them as non-parties under CPR, r 31.17[24] and the represented parties are not liable for costs.[25] Unless the court otherwise directs, any judgment or order given in the claim in which a party is acting as a representative claimant is (a) binding on all those persons represented in the claim but (b) may only be enforced by or against a person who is not a party to the claim with the permission of the court.[26]

18.8 Service of documents A party must give an address for service within the jurisdiction, including a full postcode, where all documents to be served by any method other than personal service must be served.[27] A party who resides, or carries on business, within the jurisdiction and who does not give the business address of his solicitor as his address for service, must give his residence or place of business as his address for service.[28] This means that if the club occupies premises where it carries on its activities, it should give the address of the club as its address for service. If the club has no such premises, the address should be given of one of the individual persons representing the club as claimant, say the secretary.[29]

---

20 *Harrison v Abergavenny* [1887] 3 TLR 324; *Woodford v Smith* [1971] 1 WLR 806 (Megarry J), at 810–811.

21 CPR, r 19.6(2).

22 *Atkin's Court Forms* (2009 issue), vol 36, para 44; *Howells v Dominion Insurance Co Ltd* [2005] EWHC 552 (QB) at [8].

23 Blackstone's Civil Practice 2011, at [14.62].

24 *Ventouris v Mountain (The Italia Express) (No.1)* [1990] 1 WLR 607.

25 *Markt & Co Ltd v Knight Steamship Co Ltd* [1910] 2 KB 1021, at 1039.

26 CPR, r 19.6(4).

27 CPR, r 6.5(2).

28 CPR, r 6.5(3).

29 CPR, r 6.5(6).

18.9 Trustees If the property of the club is vested in trustees, and the claim touches or concerns this property, the proper claimants in any action will be the trustees acting on behalf of all the members of the club. Under CPR, r 19.7A(1) where proceedings are brought by trustees, it is not necessary to join the club members as persons having a beneficial interest. The trustees automatically represent this class of person, and the beneficiaries will be bound by any judgment or order given or made in the claim, unless the court orders otherwise in the same or some other proceedings.[30]

18.10 Charities If the club is a charity, special provisions apply. No 'charity proceedings' (being proceedings with respect to the administration of the trust of the charity)[31] shall be entertained or proceeded with in any court in England or Wales unless authorised by the Charity Commission[32] and no authority will be given where in its opinion the case can be dealt with by the Commission under the powers of the Charities Act 1993.[33] If the Commission refuses to give its authority, leave to take proceedings may be obtained from a judge of the Chancery Division of the High Court.[34]

18.11 Literary and scientific institutions If unincorporated, the position is governed by s 21 of the Literary and Scientific Institutions Act 1854.[35] The institution can sue in the name of the president, chairman, principal secretary or clerk, as determined by the institute's rules and regulations. In default of such determination the governing body shall appoint an appropriate person to sue on behalf of the institution. If incorporated, the position will be the same as for an incorporated members' club (see **18.15**).[36]

18.12 Working men's clubs The club cannot bring a claim in its own name because it is an unincorporated members' club. However, under the Friendly Societies Acts the appointment of officers and trustees of the club is a mandatory provision of the rules.[37] The trustees of the club, or any officers authorised by the rules, may bring, or may cause to be brought, any action or other legal proceedings in any court 'touching or concerning any property, right or claim' belonging to the club; and they may sue in their proper names without any other description than the title of their office.[38] Legal proceedings shall not abate or be discontinued by the death,

---

30 CPR, r 19.7A(2).

31 Charities Act 1993, s 33(8).

32 Ibid, s 33(2), as amended by Charities Act 2006, Sch 8; *Muman v Nagasena* [2000] 1 WLR 299, CA.

33 Ibid, s 33(3), as amended by the said Sch 8.

34 Ibid, s 33(5), as amended by the said Sch 8.

35 See Appendix 1.

36 The opening words of s 21 concerning those incorporated institutions not entitled to sue can now be disregarded in the light of the Interpretation Act 1978, s 5 and Sch 1.

37 Friendly Societies Act 1974, s 7(2) and Sch 2, Part I(5).

38 Ibid, s 103(1).

resignation or removal from office of any officer.[39] Where proceedings are to be taken against a trustee of the club, the other trustees of the club may bring the requisite proceedings in their name.[40] If the club has no solicitor acting for it, the club should give as its address for service of documents its place where it carries on its activities or, if it has no such place, the address of one of the trustees.[41]

18.13 Community clubs The club is a body corporate and may sue in its own name in respect of any claim it may wish to bring.[42] If the club has no solicitor acting for it, the club should give as its address for service of documents its place where it carries on its activities[43] or, if it has no such place, the address of some person holding a senior position within the club such as the president, chairman, treasurer or secretary.[44]

18.14 Shop clubs The club is an unincorporated members' club and the same considerations apply as set out at **18.3**.

18.15 Incorporated clubs The club is a legal person[45] and may sue in its own name in respect of any claim it may wish to bring. If the club has no solicitor acting for it, the club should give as its address for service of documents its place where it carries on its activities[46] or, if it has no such place, the address of some person holding a senior position within the company such as a director, manager or other officer of the company.[47] As an alternative the company can nominate its registered office under the Companies Act.[48]

18.16 Proprietary clubs Any claim against a third party concerning the club's affairs will be brought by the proprietor and will be of no concern to the members. If unincorporated, the proprietor should sue in his own name[49] or, if incorporated, should sue in the club's corporate name.

18.17 Simple claims For a club which has a corporate personality and which wishes to bring a money claim or a possession claim against someone without using a lawyer, it should contemplate using Money Claim Online (see www.moneyclaim.gov.uk) or Possession Claim Online (see www.

39 Friendly Societies Act 1974, s 103(3).
40 Ibid, s 103(7).
41 CPR, r 6.5(2) and (6).
42 Co-operative and Community Benefit Societies and Credit Unions Act 1965, s 3.
43 CPR, r 6.5(2) and (6).
44 CPR, r 6.4(4) and PD 6, paras 6.1 and 6.2.
45 Interpretation Act 1978, s 5 and Sch 1.
46 CPR, r 6.5(2) and (6).
47 CPR, r 6.4(4) and PD 6, paras 6.1 and 6.2.
48 CPR, r 6.2(2); Companies Act 2006, s 1139(1).
49 *Firmin and Sons Ltd v International Club* (1889) 5 TLR 694.

possessionclaim.gov.uk) which is run as a government service on the website. This can be a simple, convenient and secure way of obtaining a judgment or possession on a claim. However, the service is run via the county court and its enforcement procedures can on occasion be slow or frustrating.[50] Because of the more complex nature of representative actions, this procedure is probably not suitable for unincorporated members' clubs.

3. DEFENDING CLAIMS

18.18 Unincorporated members' clubs The club itself cannot be sued because it is not a legal person.[51] The courts will, however, on occasion if necessary permit an unincorporated association to be joined as a defendant if it is a 'sufficiently identifiable group'[52] but this comes with an important caveat expressed by Mr Justice Gross in *EDO MBM Technology Ltd v Campaign to Smash EDO*:[53]

> 'Immensely attractive though it is to resolve problems of identification of individuals by way of joining unincorporated associations into legal proceedings, it is not possible to do so unless, at the least, there are before the Court individuals capable of being sued as representatives of the association in question.'

18.19 It is essential for the club to ensure that, when sued, the right persons have been joined as defendants to any action either personally or in a representative capacity. CPR, r 19.6 applies equally to proceedings brought *against* the club as proceedings brought *by* the club. Suppose the claim against the club is for damages for noise nuisance caused by the club members on six consecutive Saturday nights. It will be no good describing the defendants as 'all the members of the Basset Social Club' since this is too vague and, anyway, some of the members may have joined the club after the six Saturdays in question. Nor is it good enough to describe the defendants as 'Some of the members of the Basset Social Club' because, once again, this is too vague a description.[54] The solution is for the class of defendants to be defined by reference to the date (or dates) on which the cause of action arose, as happened in the case of *Campbell v Thompson*[55] where the court ordered the writ to be amended so that the defendants were described as 'H R Thompson and C G Surtees Shill on their own behalf and

---

50 *Blackstone's Civil Practice 2011*, at [76.1].

51 *John v Rees* [1970] Ch 345, at 398 (Megarry J).

52 *Huntingdon Life Sciences Group plc v Stop Huntingdon Animal Cruelty* [2005] EWHC 2233 (QB), at [27] (Gibbs J).

53 [2005] EWHC 837 (QB), at [43].

54 *Markt & Co Ltd v Knight SS Co Ltd* [1910] 2 KB 1021, CA.

55 [1953] 1 WLR 656.

on behalf of all the other members of the City Livery Club on June 29, 1949', which was the date of the alleged accident.[56]

18.20 Or take another example. Suppose a claim against the Basset Social Club is made by the local wine merchant for the price of goods sold and delivered pursuant to an order given by the club secretary, Daniel Whiddon. The claim might be framed against the secretary that he was personally liable. His defence might be that he was simply acting as the disclosed agent of the committee and therefore was not personally liable. So it is likely that the claim form would cite the defendant as being 'Daniel Whiddon on his own behalf and on behalf of all the committee members of the Basset Social Club'. But this description might be inaccurate if the goods had been sold before some of the members had joined the committee.[57] So it might be necessary to describe the defendant with reference to the date of the order, namely, 'Daniel Whiddon on his own behalf and behalf of all the committee members of the Basset Social Club as at 15 March 2010'.

18.21 Employment tribunal cases It is to be noted that the practice in employment tribunals differs from that in the civil courts because of the greater informality and the strict timetable which applies in the tribunal. In *Nazir v Asim*[58] the Employment Appeal Tribunal said that employees generally cannot be expected to know the special legal position of unincorporated associations and to work out precisely who their employer might be and therefore it was acceptable for an employee simply to name the unincorporated association as the respondent to the claim, this practice being consistent with reg 4 of the Employment Tribunals (Constitution and Rules of Procedure) Regulations 2004.[59] (This permitted informality, however, may lead to problems of enforcement later on).

18.22 Acknowledgment of service Despite the radical overhaul of the procedural rules in 1998, the present position as far as unincorporated members' clubs are concerned is far from satisfactory. CPR Part 6 deals with the service of the claim form and CPR Part 10 deals with the acknowledgment of service of that form. The acknowledgment is a very important document because the failure to file it may result in a default judgment against the person being sued.[60] What the current rules omit is any provision dealing with service on unincorporated associations (except partnerships) and what to do if the claim form is not capable of being

---

56 This was, unusually, a personal injury action against all the members of an unincorporated members' club: see **15.4**. See also *Irish Shipping Ltd v Commercial Assurance plc* [1991] 2 QB 206, CA (plaintiff permitted to sue two insurers as representing 77 insurers involving 77 separate but identical contracts of marine insurance but with differing proportions of liability for each insurer).

57 See *Roche v Sherrington* [1982] 1 WLR 599.

58 [2010] ICR 1225, EAT.

59 SI 2004/1861.

60 CPR, r 10.2.

responded to. In the 1999 edition of the *Supreme Court Practice* appeared the following helpful note:[61] '*Unincorporated club.* If sued in the name of the club, acknowledgment of service may be given for the members of the committee as such, but a members' club cannot acknowledge service in the club's name, and should not be so sued'. What happens, however, if the local wine merchant does issue a claim form against 'the Basset Social Club', an unincorporated members' club, for goods sold and delivered? Such a claim form will be wholly irregular in that the claimant has sued a non-existent person but it is not a nullity and so is capable of amendment to join a proper party.[62] Thus it would not be a wise move to ignore the claim form, except perhaps where the limitation period was about to expire. The better way forward is to serve, using Form N9, an acknowledgment of service saying, 'The Basset Social Club is an unincorporated members' club and should not have been sued. This acknowledgment of service is filed by Peter Davey, Daniel Whiddon and Harry Hawke for and on behalf of the committee of the Basset Social Club. We do not propose to take any further step in this action until the defendant has been properly identified.'

18.23 If the defects in the claim form are less serious, for example, the claimant had misspelt Mr Davey's name or Mr Whiddon was no longer a member of the club and had been replaced on the committee by Mr Brewer, but otherwise the claim form was correctly suing the committee of the club, the club should deal with the problem under CPR PD 10, para 5.2. In the acknowledgment of service the club should state the correct name of the defendant followed by the incorrect name: 'Peter Davey, Bill Brewer and Harry Hawke for and on behalf of the committee of the Basset Social Club, described in the claim form as Peter Davy, Daniel Whiddon and Harry Hawke for and on behalf of the committee of the Basset Social Club'. Then it will be up to the claimant to amend his claim form (normally at his expense) so that the proper defendants are before the court. Any person wrongly sued in a representative capacity may apply to the court for a direction that he is not to act as a representative.[63] On the other hand, the claimant does not need the permission of the court to bring an action against named defendants as representatives[64] and, indeed, people can be appointed against their own will to defend on behalf of others.[65]

18.24 Enforcement of judgment in representative action The enforcement provisions in a representative action are set out in CPR, r 19.6(4) which states:

---

61 Vol 1, para 12/L/2, p 135.

62 *Hibernian Dance Club v Murray* [1997] PIQR P46, CA.

63 CPR, r 19.6(2) and (3).

64 *Andrews v Salmon* (1888) WN 102 (Kay J) (where the plaintiff had been expelled from the Randolph Churchill Conservative Club in Wanstead and without their consent he brought an action against the chairman of the committee and the hon. secretary as representing all the members of the club; and this procedure was upheld by the court).

65 *Wood v McCarthy* [1893] 1 QB 775.

> 'Unless the court otherwise directs any judgment or order given in a claim in which a party is acting as a representative under this rule:
>
> (a) is binding on all persons represented in the claim; but
> (b) may only be enforced by or against a person who is not a party to the claim with the permission of the court.'

What needs to be stated here is that under the former Rules of the Supreme Court[66] the member of a club, who was a non-party but represented in the action, was entitled *as of right* to dispute his liability when it came to enforcement against himself. This is no longer the case. The represented member now has to rely on the *discretion* of the court in opposing enforcement. This means that the club should take especial care in ensuring that in defending representative proceedings the defendants in the action are precisely and accurately defined as to whom is being represented.

18.25 The case of *Howells v Dominion Insurance Co Ltd*[67] is a good illustration in point. The Hemel Hempstead Football and Sports Club took out an insurance policy where the insured persons were all the members of the club. There was a serious fire at the club and the club claimed under the policy, and the insurers made interim payments of some £52,000. The insurers then repudiated the policy on the ground of material non-disclosure. Mr Howells, the chairman, and Mr Kelly, the secretary, in a representative action on behalf of all the members sued the insurers for a declaration that the policy was valid, and the insurers counterclaimed for the return of the interim payments. At the trial the club lost on its claim and the insurers won on its counterclaim. The insurers later sought to enforce its judgment against all the members. The members sought to avoid enforcement on the ground that their liability was limited to their subscriptions.[68] Mrs Justice Cox rejected this argument because this was not a case of the members being liable for the club's debt but a situation where all the members were party to the contract of insurance. She thus remitted the case to the Master for him to consider whether or not, in the exercise of his discretion, to enforce the judgment against individual members having regard to whatever special circumstances might exist in relation to each of them.[69]

18.26 Enforcement of costs orders It may be possible for a costs order to be enforced against the bank account standing in the name of an unincorporated members' club. In *Huntingdon Life Sciences Group plc v Stop Huntingdon Animal Cruelty*[70] Mr Justice Mackay allowed the claimant to enforce a costs order against the bank account of the eleventh defendant,

---

66 RSC Order 15, r 12(5).
67 [2005] EWCA 552 (Admin).
68 *Wise v Perpetual Trustee Co* [1903] AC 139, PC, at 149.
69 At [41].
70 [2005] EWHC 2233.

London Animal Action, an unincorporated association, without indentifying or naming any individual member of the association connected with the account, whereas permission had previously been given to enforce the court orders against *the members* of the association, not against the association itself.[71] This may therefore be regarded as a rather surprising decision. On the other hand, it is still good law that in a representative action the represented parties, not being parties to the action, are not individually liable for the costs of the action.[72] In exceptional circumstances costs may be awarded against non-parties.[73]

18.27 Trustees What is said in **18.9** applies equally to the situation where claims are brought against trustees.

18.28 Charities If the club is a charity, proceedings may be brought against it by suing an officer of the charity, for example, 'the President of the Basset Orphan Fund', or alternatively the charity's trustees may be named as parties.[74] Otherwise, what is said in **18.10** with regard to bringing claims applies equally to defending claims.

18.29 Literary and scientific institutions If unincorporated, the position is governed by s 21 of the Literary and Scientific Institutions Act 1854.[75] The same provisions which apply for suing apply equally where the institution is being sued: see **18.11**. In addition, if the claimant applies to the institution for a person to be nominated as defendant to his claim and the institution fails to make any such nomination, the claimant will be entitled to sue the president or the chairman as representing the institution. If a claimant obtains judgment against the person named as the defendant on behalf of the institution, its enforcement shall not be made against that person but only against the property of the institution. If incorporated, the position will be the same as for an incorporated club (see **18.33**).[76]

18.30 Working men's clubs The position is governed by s 103(1) of the Friendly Societies Act 1974. The same provisions which apply for suing apply equally where the club is being sued: see **18.12**.

---

71 See [2005] EWHC 2233, at [3].

72 *Moon v Atherton* [1972] 2 QB 435, CA, at 441; *Howells and Kelly v Dominion Insurance Co Ltd* [2005] EWCA 552 (QB), at [39].

73 *Howells v Dominion Insurance Co Ltd* [2005] EWCA 552 (Admin), at [39].

74 *Muman v Nagasena* [2000] 1 WLR 299, CA.

75 See Appendix 1.

76 The opening words of s 21 concerning incorporated institutions not entitled to be sued can now be disregarded in the light of the Interpretation Act 1978, s 5, Sch 1.

18.31 Community clubs The club is a body corporate[77] and should be sued in its own name.

18.32 Shop clubs The club is an unincorporated member's club and the same considerations apply in respect of defending claims as set out in **18.14**.

18.33 Incorporated clubs The club is a legal person[78] and should be sued in its own name.

18.34 Proprietary clubs In any matter concerning the club's affairs, the claimant will proceed against the proprietor, whether he is an individual or it is a company, and it is the proprietor who has the burden of defending the claim and meeting any liability as a result of such claim.

4. LIMITATION

18.35 At common law there was no time limit on bringing a claim against another person, and for public policy reasons the ability to bring an action has for several centuries been regulated by statute. The principal Act now in force is the Limitation Act 1980.[79] Deciding on a period of limitation is by definition an arbitrary process, so what counts is not the spirit of the law but the letter of the law. This topic is therefore replete with legal learning and decided cases on the various issues which have arisen over the years. What follows is necessarily a very brief outline of the law relating to limitation.

18.36 As with its predecessors, the 1980 Act mostly bars the remedy, not the substantive right,[80] so that any limitation defence must be expressly pleaded. Most of the ordinary periods of limitation are calculated from the date on which the cause of action accrued:

One year limit: Actions for libel, slander and malicious falsehood.[81]

---

77 Co-operative and Community Benefit Societies and Credit Unions Act 1965, s 3.

78 Interpretation Act 1978, s 5, Sch 1.

79 The 1980 Act consolidated the Limitation Acts of 1939, 1963, 1975 and the Limitation Amendment Act 1980.

80 See 28 *Halsbury's Laws* (4th edn, reissue) 856. In civil law jurisdictions it is normally the right which is extinguished.

81 Limitation Act 1980, s 4A.

Three year limit:	Actions for negligence, nuisance and breach of duty (whether arising in tort or in contract or by statute) where the damages claimed by the claimant consist of or include damages in respect of personal injuries.[82]
Six year limit:	Most actions founded on tort[83] and contract[84] and actions to recover arrears of rent.[85]
Twelve year limit:	Actions upon specialties[86] and actions to recover land.[87]

18.37 Extension of time limits The 1980 Act also provides for the extension and exclusion of certain periods of limitation. Where the claimant was under a disability at the time when the cause of action accrued, ie was a minor or of unsound mind, the action may be brought at any time before the expiration of 6 years from the date when he ceased to be under a disability or died (whichever first occurred), notwithstanding that the ordinary period of limitation has expired.[88] Where the action is based on the fraud of the defendant[89] or where any fact relevant to the claimant's right of action has been deliberately concealed by the defendant,[90] the period of limitation does not begin to run until the claimant has discovered the fraud or concealment or could have done so with reasonable diligence.[91] The court also has the discretion to exclude the time limit for libel, slander and malicious falsehood[92] and the time limit for actions in respect of personal injuries and death.[93] The Latent Damage Act 1996 inserted new ss 14A and 14B into the Limitation Act 1980 under which special time limits were introduced for actions for damages in the tort of negligence (other than actions for personal injuries) where the facts relevant to the cause of action were not known at the date when the cause of action accrued, subject to an overriding time limit of 15 years.[94]

---

82 Limitation Act 1980, ss 11 and 11A(4)–(7).

83 Ibid, s 2, but note the special time limit in the case of theft (s 4).

84 Ibid, s 5, but note the special time limit for actions in respect of certain loans (s 6). In particular, where money is repayable on demand, the limitation period will not begin to run in favour of the borrower until the lender has made a written demand for repayment.

85 Ibid, s 19.

86 Ibid, s 8. A specialty is a signed contract contained in a deed. The additional need for sealing was abolished by the Law of Property (Miscellaneous Provisions) Act 1989, s 1.

87 Limitation Act 1980, s 15.

88 Ibid, ss 28 and 28A. See, e g *Headford v Bristol and District Health Authority* [1995] 6 Med LR 1, CA (where the action was brought 28 years after the events complained of).

89 Limitation Act 1980, s 32(1)(a).

90 Ibid, s 32(1)(b).

91 Ibid, s 32(1). The case of *Sheldon v RHM Outhwaite (Underwriting Agencies) Ltd* [1996] AC 102 is a classic example of the difficulties in interpreting correctly the provisions of the 1980 Act: see the speech of Lord Nicholls of Birkenhead at 152.

92 Limitation Act 1980, s 32A.

93 Ibid, s 33.

94 The extended time limit under s 14A only applies to claims in negligence framed in tort, not to claims in negligence framed in contract: *Société Commerciale de Réassurance v ERAS (International) Ltd* [1992] 2 All ER 82, CA. This is a curious distinction, which turned on the

5. ALTERNATIVE DISPUTE RESOLUTION

18.38 Introduction Civil litigation is expensive. It is time-consuming for lawyers to investigate a dispute before proceedings are issued and thereafter to prepare for the trial once they are issued. And time costs money. On the other hand, we live in a complex society and acting as one's own lawyer is often an unwise activity. Despite the advent of the Civil Procedure Rules and better case management of litigation by the courts, high costs are endemic in properly conducted litigation.[95] Furthermore, litigation takes place in the public domain and for members' clubs it is often appropriate that clubs should consider ways of resolving disputes privately and confidentially rather than by litigation.[96] Indeed, in *Halsey v Milton Keynes General NHS Trust*[97] the Court of Appeal emphasised that those members of the legal profession who conduct litigation should routinely consider with their clients whether their disputes were suitable for alternative dispute resolution (or ADR as it is commonly called).[98] The Court of Appeal did add, however, that the court's role was to encourage but not to compel the parties to go to ADR.[99] All the pre-action protocols have been revised to strengthen the provisions dealing with the consideration of ADR in preference to litigation. What follows is an outline of alternative dispute resolution which is available. It must be remembered, however, that there is no one-size-fits-all solution to the problem of resolving disputes if an alternative is sought to litigation. Every dispute needs to be assessed individually to ascertain the best way forward. A further point to note is that an individual may waive his right of access to the courts under Article 6(1) of the European Convention on Human Rights[100] by entering into a contract in which he agrees to submit disputes to arbitration.[101]

---

words, 'an action for damages in negligence', and which demonstrates the legalistic approach of the courts in this branch of the law.

95 Lord Justice Jackson delivered in December 2009 his *Review of Civil Litigation Costs: Final Report* wherein he stated, 'In some areas of civil litigation costs are disproportionate and impede access to justice. I therefore propose a coherent package of interlocking reforms, designed to control costs and promote access to justice.'

96 See **5.90** as regards internal disputes.

97 [2004] 1 WLR 3002, CA.

98 We consider that a more appropriate nomenclature might be *private* dispute resolution to distinguish it from litigation which is controlled by the state.

99 *Halsey* at [11]. A party's unreasonable refusal to go to ADR carries the risk of an adverse order for costs at the costs stage of the litigation: at [13]. See also footnote 101 below.

100 The Human Rights Act 1998 incorporated this convention into UK domestic law.

101 *Deweer v Belgium* [1979–1980] EHRR 439, at [49]. See further Joined Cases C-317/08 and C-320/08 *Rosalba Alassini v Telecom Italia SpA* (ECJ) where Attorney General Kokott stated in her Opinion of 19 November 2009 at [58] that *mandatory* out-of-court dispute resolution before resort to judicial proceedings does not offend against Art 6 provided the procedure is transparent, simple and inexpensive; is proportionate; and has a legitimate objective. This would appear to sanction compulsory mediation.

18.39 Arbitration Almost any dispute that can be resolved by litigation can be settled by arbitration. Arbitration was practised in classical times.[102] Domestic arbitration is now governed by the Arbitration Act 1996. The arbitrator's decision is final and legally binding. There is very little scope for appealing to the court. The process is confidential, and is generally more flexible and simpler than litigation and contains a power to cap costs.[103] It can in suitable cases be conducted on documents only. One serious downside is that no third party procedure is available so that, for example, if pursuant to an arbitration clause a builder in an arbitration was claiming moneys from a club in respect of additional building works, the club would not be entitled to bring into the arbitration its surveyor or architect as a third party on the ground that it was through their negligence that these additional works were incurred. This is because arbitration is a consensual procedure, and the surveyor or architect might not consent to being joined in the arbitration and the builder himself might object to the presence of an additional party. As to costs generally, they are in the discretion of the arbitrator, subject to any agreement between the parties,[104] and as a matter of general principle they should follow the event.[105] The parties are, however, jointly and severally liable to pay the arbitrator's reasonable fees and expenses.[106]

18.40 An agreement to arbitrate under the provisions of the Arbitration Act 1996 must be in writing.[107] Although arbitration is a consensual process in that parties cannot be compelled to go to arbitration unless they have agreed to resolve their dispute by this means, the process may become compulsory where a valid agreement to arbitrate is in existence. Accordingly, if one party to an arbitration agreement brings legal proceedings against another party, that other party can obtain from the court a mandatory stay of the legal proceedings to allow the arbitration to take place.[108] An exception to the mandatory stay is where the court is satisfied that the arbitration agreement is 'null and void, inoperative or incapable of being performed'.[109] If the club is incorporated, a conflict can arise between the obligation to go to arbitration and the right to go to court. In *Exeter Football Club Ltd v Football Conference Ltd*[110] the claimant was a

---

102 See, e g *Ancient Greek Arbitration* by Prof. Derek Roebuck published by Holo Books (2001) describing arbitration and mediation from the time of Homer to Cleopatra.

103 Arbitration Act 1996, s 65.

104 Ibid, s 61(1).

105 Ibid, s 61(2).

106 Ibid, s 28(1).

107 Ibid, s 5. It is possible to have a valid oral arbitration agreement at common law (see *Bernstein's Handbook of Arbitration and Dispute Resolution Practice* (4th edn, 2003), at 2–113) but it is not governed by the 1996 Act and may lead to difficulties of procedure and enforcement; the answer is to convert the oral agreement into a written one.

108 Arbitration Act 1996, s 9. The procedure for making the application for a stay is set out in CPR Part 62 and the application should be made to the court dealing with the legal proceedings.

109 Ibid, s 9(4).

110 [2004] 1 WLR 2910.

company limited by shares and was a member of the defendant, a company limited by guarantee. Both were parties to an arbitration agreement which provided that disputes between them would be referred to arbitration. The court held that the statutory rights conferred on shareholders and members of a company to apply to the court for relief were inalienable and could not be diminished or removed by a contract to resolve the dispute by arbitration, so that the court had a discretion whether or not to stay the court proceedings despite the mandatory nature of s 9(4) of the Arbitration Act 1996. And the court refused to order a stay in the circumstances of the case.

18.41 Mediation Mediation (and conciliation) shares many of the characteristics of arbitration and take place where the parties agree to use a neutral person to help solve the dispute. Mediation is a confidential process. The mediator, however, is not a judge or arbitrator but a 'facilitator' who helps the parties to reach their own solution. In other words, it is a controlled negotiating process. One of mediation's crucial ingredients is the mediator's ability to talk to each side privately (on a strictly confidential basis). Another advantage of mediation is that the parties are looking for a commercial solution rather than deciding precise legal rights and obligations which litigation and arbitration are required to do. A successful facilitative mediation will therefore invariably involve the disputants in a compromise. A mediation involving a complex set of facts can often be dealt with in one full day's mediation, and so this procedure has the potential to save great expense in appropriate cases. Mediation can accommodate third party participation if the parties are agreeable to this course. Mediation is not legally binding or enforceable through the courts unless the parties agree to be bound by the decision reached with the mediator. As to costs, if the mediation is successful they will be absorbed into the settlement agreement. If unsuccessful, it is common for each side to agree to bear their own costs and to share the payment of the mediator's fees and expenses.

18.42 Med-Arb Sometimes a combined mediation and arbitration process takes place. The parties agree to mediate first to see if they can come to some agreed resolution of their dispute. If this does not prove possible, the parties move on to arbitration where a binding decision will be handed down. This process has considerable merit. However, a point of practical difficulty can arise as to whether the same person can be both the mediator and the arbitrator. Mediators very frequently see the parties separately, something which would be wholly irregular in arbitration (or litigation) since it would be a departure from due process or a breach of the rules of natural justice. There is a school of thought that says it is impossible to combine the two roles of mediator and arbitrator in the same dispute. If two separate professionals are involved, however, this inevitably increases the costs of resolving the dispute. A clear and express agreement between the parties is required if the same person is to act as mediator and then as arbitrator. As to costs, if the mediation is unsuccessful, it is sometimes agreed that each side will bear their own costs in any event and at other times that they will be costs in the arbitration, to be dealt with by the arbitrator, subject in either event to the parties sharing, or sharing initially, the payment of the mediator's fees and expense.

18.43 Adjudication Adjudicators too have been around for a long time. They are persons appointed to resolve a dispute with a legally binding decision but in a less formal manner than an arbitrator. For example, complaints by members of friendly societies may be referred to an adjudicator under s 81(1)(b) of the Friendly Societies Act 1992. Recently in the UK adjudication is a process which has been introduced into the construction industry to expedite resolution of disputes where litigation or arbitration might otherwise cause expensive contractual delays. There is a statutory right to have a dispute under a construction contract resolved by adjudication[111] and this process is governed by Part II of the Housing Grants, Construction and Regeneration Act 1996. It is intended to provide a swift, summary, interim means of resolving disputes as to payments which is binding on the parties until the dispute is finally resolved by litigation or arbitration.[112] The parties may, however, agree that the adjudication will be the final process. To keep the process short and simple no reasons need be given for the adjudication, unless the parties agree (which they often do) that reasons should be given.[113] Each party is jointly and severally liable to the adjudicator for the payment of such reasonable amount as he may determine by way of his fees and expenses, and the adjudicator has power to apportion this payment as between the parties.[114] Otherwise the adjudicator has no power to order costs against any party. The information and documents provided to the adjudicator are to be treated as confidential if the party supplying the same has indicated their confidentiality to him, except to the extent it is necessary for the purposes of, or in connection with, the adjudication.[115]

18.44 Expert determination Here the parties agree as a matter of contract that the dispute shall be resolved by an expert, who will almost invariably be an expert in the subject matter of the dispute, and that his decision will be legally binding on both parties. Once again no reasons are normally given for the determination unless the parties agree that they should be given. This process can in appropriate cases provide a quick and efficacious resolution to the dispute. As to costs, this is a matter for agreement between

---

111 Arbitration Act 1996, s 108(1).

112 *RJT Consulting Engineers Ltd v DM Engineering (Northern Ireland) Ltd* [2002] 1 WLR 2344, CA; see also the Scheme for Construction Contracts (England and Wales) Regulations 1998, SI 1998/649.

113 Ibid, reg 22.

114 Ibid, reg 11.

115 Ibid, reg 18.

the parties, but the expert will no doubt seek a prior agreement with the parties that they will be jointly and severally liable for his reasonable fees and expenses.

18.45 Early neutral evaluation This is where an independent neutral appraises the case and gives an assessment of the parties' chances of success if litigation were to be pursued. It has the advantage of giving both parties a realistic assessment of the costs and potential gains from litigation. This evaluation is a confidential process. As to costs, this is a matter for agreement between the parties, but the neutral will no doubt seek a prior agreement with the parties that they will be jointly and severally liable for his reasonable fees and expenses.

APPENDICES

Appendix 1

LITERARY AND SCIENTIFIC INSTITUTIONS ACT 1854, SS 18 TO 33

(As Amended)

****

18 Trustees may sell or exchange lands or buildings; or may let

If it shall be deemed advisable to sell any land or building not previously part of the possessions of the Duchy of Lancaster or Cornwall held in trust for any institution, or to exchange the same for any other site, the trustees in whom the legal estate in the said land or building shall be vested may, by the direction or with the consent of the governing body of the said institution, if any such there be, sell the said land or building, or part thereof, or exchange the same for other land or building suitable to the purposes of their trust, and receive on any exchange any sum of money by way of effecting an equality, and apply the money arising from such sale or given on such exchange in the purchase of another site, or in the improvement of other premises used or to be used for the purposes of such trust; and such trustees may, with like direction to consent, let portions of the premises belonging to the institution not required for the purposes thereof, for such term, and under such covenants or agreements, as shall be deemed by such governing body to be expedient, and apply the rents thereof to the benefit of the institution.

19 Trustees to be indemnified from charges; in default thereof empowered to mortgage or sell the premises

The trustees of such institution who, by reason of their being the legal owner of the building premises, shall become liable to the payment of any rate, tax, charge, costs, or expenses, shall be indemnified and kept harmless by the governing body thereof from the same, and in default of such indemnity shall be entitled to hold the said building or premises and other property vested in them as a security for their reimbursement and indemnification and, if necessity shall arise, may mortgage or sell the same, or part thereof, free from the trust of the institution, and apply the amount obtained by such mortgage or sale to their reimbursement, and the balance (if any) to the benefit of the institution, subject to the restrictions hereinbefore contained with regard to lands given and lands belonging to the Duchies aforesaid.

20 Property of institution, how to be vested

Where any institution shall be incorporated, and have no provision applicable to the personal property of such institution, and in all cases where the institution shall not be incorporated, the money, securities for money, goods, chattels, and personal effects belonging to the said institution, and not vested in trustees, shall be deemed to be vested for the time being in the governing body of such institution, and in all proceedings, civil and criminal, may be described as the monies, securities, goods, chattels, and effects of the governing body of such institution, by their proper title.

21 How suits by and against institutions to be brought

Any institution incorporated which shall not be entitled to sue and be sued by any corporate name, and every institution not incorporated, may sue or be sued in the name of the president, chairman, principal secretary, or clerk, as shall be determined by the rules and regulations of the institution, and, in default of such determination, in the name of such person as shall be appointed by the governing body for the occasion: Provided, that it shall be competent for any person having a claim or demand against the institution to sue the president or chairman thereof, if, on application to the governing body, some other officer or person be not nominated to be the defendant.

22 (*repealed*)

Amendments –Repealed by Statute Law (Repeals) Act 1986.

23 How judgment to be enforced against

If a judgment shall be recovered against the person or officer named on behalf of the institution, such judgment shall not be put in force against the goods, chattels, or lands, or against the body of such persons or officer, but against the property of the institution; shall be issued, setting forth the judgment recovered, the fact of the party against whom it shall have been recovered having sued or having been sued, as the case may be, on behalf of the institution only, and requiring to have the judgment enforced against the property of the institution.

Amendments –Statute Law (Repeals) Act 1986.

24 Institution may make byelaws to be enforced

In any institution the governing body, if not otherwise legally empowered to do so, may, at any meeting specially convened according to its regulations, make any byelaw for the better governance of the institution, its members or officer, and for the furtherance of its purpose and object, and may impose a reasonable pecuniary penalty for the breach thereof, which penalty, when accrued, may be recovered in any local court of the district wherein the defendant shall inhabit or the institution shall be situated, as the governing body thereof shall deem expedient: Provided always, that no pecuniary penalty imposed by any byelaw for the breach thereof shall be recoverable unless the byelaw shall have been confirmed by the votes of three fifths of the members present at a meeting specially convened for the purpose.

25 Members liable to be sued as strangers

Any member who may be in arrear of his subscription according to the rules of the institution, or may be or shall possess himself to detain any property of the institution in a manner or for a time contrary to such rules, or shall injure or destroy the property of the institution, may be sued in the manner hereinbefore provided: but if the defendant shall be successful in any action or other proceeding at the instance of the institution, and shall be adjudged to recover his costs, he may elect to proceed to recover the same from the officer in whose name the suit shall be brought, or from the institution, and in the latter case shall have process against the property of the said institution in the manner above described.

26 Members guilty of offences punishable as strangers

Any member of the institution who shall wilfully and maliciously, or wilfully and unlawfully, destroy or injure the property of such institution, whereby the funds of the institution may be exposed to loss, shall be subject to the same prosecution, and if convicted shall be liable to be punished in like manner, as any person not a member would be subject and liable to in respect of the like offence.

Amendment –Larceny Act 1916; Forgery Act 1913.

27 Institution enabled to alter, extend, or abridge their purposes

Whenever it shall appear to the governing body of any institution (not having a Royal Charter, nor established nor acting under any Act of Parliament,) which has been established for any particular purpose or purposes that it is advisable to alter, extend, or abridge such purpose, or to amalgamate such institution, either wholly or partially, with any such institution or institutions, such governing body may submit the proposition to their members in a written or printed report, and may convene a special meeting for the consideration thereof according to the regulations of the institution; but no such proposition shall be carried into effect unless such report shall have been delivered or sent by post to every member ten days previous to the special meeting convened by the governing body for the consideration thereof, nor unless such proposition shall have been agreed to by the votes of three-fifths of the members present at such meeting, and confirmed by the votes of three-fifths of the members present at a second special meeting convened by the governing body at an interval of one month after the former meeting.

28 Power to Board of Trade to suspend such alteration, if applied to by two-fifths dissentients

If any members of the institution, being not less than two-fifths in number, consider that the proposition so carried is calculated to prove injurious to the institution, they may, within three months after the confirmation thereof, make application in writing to the Lords Committee of her Majesty's Privy Council for Trade and Foreign Plantations, who, at their discretion, shall entertain the application, and if, after due inquiry, they shall decide that the proposition is then calculated to prove injurious to the institution, the same shall not be then carried into effect; but such decision shall not prevent the members of such institution from reconsidering the same proposition on a future occasion.

29 Provision for the dissolution of institutions and adjustment of their affairs

Any number not less than three-fifths of the members of any institution may determine that it shall be dissolved, and thereupon it shall be dissolved forthwith, or at the time then agreed upon, and all necessary steps shall be taken for the disposal and settlement of the property of the institution, its claims and liabilities, according to the rules of the said institution, applicable thereto, if any, and if not, then as the governing body shall find expedient: Provided, that in the event of any dispute arising among the said governing body, or the members of the institution, the adjustment of its affairs shall be referred to the judge of the county court of the district in which the principal building of the institution shall be situated, and he shall make such order or orders in the matter as he shall deem requisite, or if he find it necessary, shall direct that proceedings shall be taken in the Court of Chancery for the adjustment of the affairs of the institution.

30 Upon a dissolution, no member to receive profit – Proviso for joint-stock companies

If upon the dissolution of any institution there shall remain, after the satisfaction of all its debts and liabilities, and property whatsoever, the same shall not be paid to or distributed among the members of the said institution or any of them, but shall be given to some other institution, to be determined by the members at the time of the dissolution, or in default thereof by the judge of the county court aforesaid: Provided, however, that this clause shall not apply to any institution which shall have been founded or established by the contributions of shareholders in the nature of a joint stock company.

31 Who is a member

For the purposes of this Act, a member of an institution shall be a person who, having been admitted therein according to the riles and regulations thereof, shall have paid a subscription, or shall have signed the roll or list of members thereof: but in all proceedings under this Act no person shall be entitled to vote or be counted as a member whose current subscription shall be in arrear at the time.

32 The governing body defined

The governing body of the institution shall be the council, directors, committee, or other body to whom, by Act of Parliament, charter, or the rules and regulations or the institution, the management of its affairs is entrusted; and if no such body shall have been constituted on the establishment of the institution, it shall be competent for the members thereof, upon due notice, to create for itself a governing body to act for the institution thenceforth.

33 To what institutions the Act shall apply

The Act shall apply to every institution for the time being established for the promotion of science, literature, for fine arts, for adult instruction, the diffusion of useful knowledge, the foundation or maintenance of libraries or reading rooms for general use among the members or open to the public, or public museums and galleries of paintings and other works of art, collections of natural history, mechanical and philosophical inventions, instruments, or designs: Provided, the Royal Institution shall be exempt from the operation of this Act.

Amendments –Statute Law (Repeals) Act 1973.

Appendix 2

SHOP CLUBS ACT 1902, SCHEDULE

NOTE – this Act was repealed by the Wages Act 1986

Section 3

Schedule
Regulations as to certification under this Act

The rules of a shop club or thrift fund (herein-after termed "the society") shall provide for the following matters –

i. The name and place of office of the society.
ii. The whole of the objects for which the society is to be established, the purposes for which the finds thereof shall be applicable, the terms of admission of members the conditions under which any member may become entitled to any benefit assured thereby, and the fines and forfeitures to be imposed on any member and the consequences of non-payment of any subscription or fine.
iii. The mode of holding meetings and right of voting, and the manner of making, altering and rescinding rules.
iv. The appointment and removal of a committee of management (by whatever name), of a treasurer and other officers, and of trustees.
v. The investment of the funds, the keeping of the accounts, and the audit of the same once a year at least.
vi. Annual returns to the registrar of the receipts, funds, effects and expenditure and numbers of members of the society.
vii. The inspection of the books of the society by every person having an interest in the funds of the society.
viii. The manner in which disputes shall be settled.
ix. The keeping separate accounts of all moneys received or paid on account of every particular fund or benefit assured for which a separate table of contributions payable shall have been adopted, and the keeping separate account of the expenses of management and of all contributions on account thereof.
x. A valuation once at least in every five years of the assets and liabilities of the society, including the estimated risks and contributions.
xi. The voluntary dissolution of the society by consent of not less than five-sixths in value of the persons contributing to the funds of the society, and of every person for the time being entitled to any benefit from the funds of the society, unless his claim be first satisfied or adequately provided for.
xii. The right of one-fifth of the total number of members, or of one hundred members in the case of a society of one thousand members and not exceeding ten thousand, or of five hundred members in the case of a society of more than ten thousand members, to apply to the chief registrar, or, in any case of societies registered and doing business exclusively in Scotland or Ireland, to the assistant registrar

for Scotland or Ireland, for an investigation of the affairs of the society or for winding up the same.

Appendix 3

LICENSING ACT 1964, SCH 7

NOTE – this Act was repealed by the Licensing Act 2003

****

Sections 41 and 42

Schedule 7
Provisions as to club rules

1 Management of club

The affairs of the club, in matters not reserved for the club in general meeting or otherwise for the decision of the general body of members, must, under the rules, be managed by one or more elective committees; and one committee must be a general committee, charged with the general management of those affairs in matters not assigned to special committees.

2 General meetings

(1) There must, under the rules, be a general meeting of the club at least once in every year, and fifteen months must not elapse without a general meeting.

(2) The general committee must be capable of summoning a general meeting at any time on reasonable notice.

(3) Any members entitled to attend and vote at a general meeting must be capable of summoning one or requiring one to be summoned at any time on reasonable notice, if a specified number of them join to do so, and the number required must not be more than thirty nor more than one-fifth of the total number of the members so entitled.

(4) At a general meeting the voting must be confined to members, and all members entitled to use the club premises must be entitled to vote, and must have equal voting rights, except that –

(a) the rules may exclude from voting, either generally or on particular matters, members below a specified age (not greater than twenty-one), women if the club is primarily a men's club, and men if the club is primarily a women's club, and

(b) if the club is primarily a club for persons qualified by service or past service, or by any particular service or past service, in Her Majesty's forces, the rules may exclude persons not qualified from voting, either generally or on particular matters; and

(c) if the rules make special provision for family membership or family subscriptions or any similar provision, the rules may exclude from voting, either generally or on particular matters, all or any of the persons taking the benefit of that provision as being members of a person's family, other than that person.

3 Membership

(1) Ordinary members must, under the rules, be elected either by the club in general meeting or by an elective committee, or by an elective committee with other members of the club added to it for the purpose; and the names and address of any person proposed for election must, for not less than two days before the election, be prominently displayed in the club premises or principal club premises in a part frequented by the members.

(2) The rules must not make any such provision for the admission of persons to membership otherwise than as ordinary members (or in accordance with the rules required for ordinary members by sub-paragraph (1) of this paragraph) is likely to result in the number of members so admitted being significant in proportion to the total membership.

4 Meaning of "elective committee"

(1) In this Schedule "elective committee" means, subject to the following provisions of this paragraph, a committee consisting of members of the club who are elected to the committee by the club in accordance with sub-paragraph (8) of this paragraph for a period of not less than one year nor more than five years, and paragraph 2(4) of this Schedule shall apply to voting at the election as it applies to voting at general meetings.

(2) Elections to the committee must be held annually, and if all the elected members do not go out of office in every year, there must be fixed rules for determining, those that are to; and all members of the club entitled to vote at the election and of not less than two years' standing, must be equally capable of being elected (subject only to any provision made for nomination by members of the club and to any provision prohibiting or restricting re-election) and, if nomination is required, must have equal rights to nominate persons for election.

(3) Except in the case of a committee with less than four members, or of a committee concerned with the purchase for the club or with the supply by the club of intoxicating liquor, a committee of which not less than two-thirds of the members are members of the club elected to the committee in accordance with sub-paragraphs (1) and (2) of this paragraph shall be treated as an elective committee.

(4) A sub-committee of an elective committee shall also be treated as an elective committee if its members are appointed by the committee and not less than two-thirds of them (or, in the case of a sub-committee having less than four members, or concerned with the purchase for the club or with the supply by the club of intoxicating liquor, all of them) are members of the committee elected to the committee in accordance with sub-paragraphs (1) and (2) of this paragraph who go out of office in the sub-committee on ceasing to be members of the committee.

(5) For the purposes of this paragraph a person who on a casual vacancy is appointed to fill the place of a member of an elective committee for the remainder of his term and no longer shall, however appointed, be treated as elected in accordance with sub-paragraphs (1) and (2) of this paragraph if the person whose place he fills was so elected or is to be treated as having been so elected.

Appendix 4

CO-OPERATIVE AND COMMUNITY BENEFIT SOCIETIES AND CREDIT UNIONS ACT 1965, SCH 1

****

Section 1

Schedule 1

Matters to be provided for in society's rules

1

The name of the society, which shall comply with the requirements of section 5 of this Act.

2

The objects of the society.

3

The place which is to be the registered office of the society to which all communications and notices to the society may be addressed.

4

The terms of admission of the members, including any society or company investing funds in the society under the provisions of this Act.

5

The mode of holding meetings, the scale and right of voting, and the mode of making, altering or rescinding rules.

6

The appointment and removal of a committee, by whatever name, and of managers or other officers and their respective powers and remuneration.

7

Determination in accordance with section 6 of this Act of the maximum amount of the interest in the shares of the society which may be held by any member otherwise than by virtue of section 6(1)(a), (b) or (c) of this Act.

8

Determination whether the society may contract loans or receive moneys on deposit subject to the provisions of this Act from members or others; and, if so, under what conditions, under what security, and to what limits of amount.

9

Determination whether the shares or any of them shall be transferable, and provision for the form of transfer and registration of the shares, and for the consent of the committee thereto; determination whether the shares or any of them shall be withdrawable, and provision for the mode of withdrawal and for payment of the balance due thereon on withdrawing from the society.

10

Provision for the audit of accounts by one or more [auditors appointed by the society in accordance with the requirements of [Part 42 of the Companies Act 2006 or] *the Friendly and Industrial and Provident Societies Act 1968* [Co-operative and Community Benefit Societies and Credit Unions Act 1968]].

11

Determination whether and, if so, how members may withdraw from the society, and provision for the claims of the representatives of deceased members, or the trustees of the property of bankrupt members or, in Scotland, members whose estate has been sequestrated, and for the payment of nominees.

12

The mode of application of profits of the society.

13

If the society is to have a common seal, provision for its custody and use.

14

Determination whether and, if so, by what authority, and in what manner, any part of the society's funds may be invested.

Amendments –Friendly and Industrial and Provident Societies Act 1968; SI 2008/948; SI 2008/948; Co-operatives and Community Benefit Societies Act 2003, s 5(7).

Prospective Amendment –Para 10: words "Friendly and Industrial and Provident Societies Act 1968" in italics repealed and subsequent words in square brackets substituted by virtue of the Co-operative and Community Benefit Societies and Credit Unions Act 2010, s 2. Date in force: to be appointed: see the Co-operative and Community Benefit Societies and Credit Unions Act 2010, s 8(2), (3).

Appendix 5

FRIENDLY SOCIETIES ACT 1974, SCH 2

****

Section 7(2)

Schedule 2
Matters to be provided for by the rules of societies registered under this act

PART I
PROVISIONS APPLICABLE TO ALL SOCIETIES

1

The name of the society.

2

The place which is to be the registered office of the society, to which all communications and notices may be addressed.

3

(1) Subject to sub-paragraph (2) and (3) below, the whole of the objects for which the society is to be established, the purposes for which the funds thereof shall be applicable, the terms of admission of members the conditions under which any member may become entitled to any benefit assured by the society, and forfeitures to be imposed on any member and the consequences of non-payment of any subscription.

(2) Nothing in sub-paragraph (1) above shall require the inclusion in the rules of a registered society of tables relating to the benefits payable to or in respect of any members of the society in pursuance of group insurance business.

(3) Nothing is sub-paragraph (1) above shall prevent a registered friendly society from specifying in its rules the manner in which the conditions under which any member may become entitled to any benefit assured by the society are to be determined, instead of specifying the conditions.themselves.

4

The mode of holding meetings and right of voting, and the manner of making, altering or rescinding rules.

5

The appointment and removal of a committee of management (by whatever name), of a treasurer and other officers and of trustees and, in the case of a society with branches, the composition and powers of the central body and the conditions under which a branch may secede from the society.

6

The investment of the funds, the keeping of the accounts and the audit of the accounts at least once a year.

7

Annual returns to the Authority relating to the affairs and numbers of members of the society.

8

The inspection of the books of the society by every person having an interest in the funds of the society.

9

The manner in which disputes shall be settled.

10

In the case of dividing societies, a provision for meeting all claims upon the society existing at the time of division before any such division takes place.

11

(1) For the avoidance of doubt it is hereby declared that nothing in paragraph 3 above requires the rules of a society to contain tables in accordance with which obligations to provide benefits to members have been undertaken or policies of assurance have been issued by the society, if the rules of the society provide that no further obligations may be undertaken or (as the case may be) no further policies may be issued in accordance with any such tables.

(2) Subject to sub-paragraph (1) above and sub-paragraph (3) below, the tables which the rules of a registered society are required to contain by virtue of paragraph 3 above and any tables contained in the rules of a branch shall, in the case of a society or branch which proposes to carry on long-term business, be tables which, in so far as they relate to that business, have been certified by a qualified actuary.

(2A) In sub-paragraph (2) "long-term business" has the meaning given by section 117(2) of the Friendly Societies Act 1992.

(3) Sub-paragraph (2) above does not apply:

(a) to a society first registered before 26th July 1968, nor
(b) to a branch of such a society, nor
(c) to a society formed by the amalgamation of two or more such societies.

Amendments –Friendly Societies Act 1992; SI 2007/2617; Para 7: repealed in relation to registered friendly societies by the Friendly Societies Act 1992; SI 2001/3649.

Appendix 6

STATUTES AFFECTING CLUB ACTIVITIES

[Note: The under-mentioned list is not intended to comprise an exhaustive list of relevant statutes. In many cases only part of the statute is relevant to the club activity in question].

(1) Agricultural societies

Eg farmers' clubs; landowners' associations; growers' associations

Agriculture Acts 1947–1993

Agricultural Marketing Act 1983

Cereals Marketing Act 1965

Deer Act 1991

Dogs (Protection of Livestock Act) 1953

Food Act 1984

Food and Environment Protection Act 1985

Forestry Acts 1967–1991

Highways Act 1980

Highways (Amendment) Act 1986

Hill Farming Acts 1946, 1954 and 1985

Livestock Rearing Act 1951

Protection of Badgers Act 1992

Transport Act 1968

Weeds Act 1959

Wildlife and Countryside Act 1981

(2) Allotment societies

Agriculture Act 1947 and 1970

Allotments Acts 1922-1950

Land Settlement (Facilities) Act 1919

Small Holdings and Allotment Acts 1908 and 1926

(3) Angling and fishing clubs

Conservation of Seals Act 1970

Countryside Act 1968

Diseases of Fish Acts 1937 and 1983

Fisheries Act 1891–1981

Fishery Limits Act 1964 and 1976

Import of Live Fish (England and Wales) Act 1980

Rivers (Prevention of Pollution) Acts 1951 and 1961

Salmon Act 1986

Salmon and Freshwater Fisheries Act 1975

Sea Fish (Conservation) Acts 1967 and 1992

Sea Fisheries (Wildlife Conservation) Act 1992

Theft Act 1968

Water Act 1973

Water Acts 1945–1989

Water Resources Acts 1963–1991

(4) Animal- or bird-related clubs

Eg canine societies, pigeon fanciers' clubs, poultry clubs

Animal Boarding Establishment Act 1963

Animal Health Acts 1981 and 2002

Animal Health and Welfare Act 1984

Animals Act 1971

Animals (Cruel Poisons) Act 1962

Animals (Scientific Procedures) Act 1986

Birds (Registration Charges) Act 1997

Breeding of Dogs Acts 1973 and 1991

Dangerous Dogs Acts 1989 and 1991

Destructive Imported Animals Act 1932

Docking and Nicking of Horses Act 1949

Dogs Acts 1871–1906

Dogs (Amendment) Act 1928

Dogs (Fouling of Land) Act 1996

Endangered Species (Import and Export) Act 1976

Highways Acts 1980

Metropolitan Police Act 1839

Pet Animals Acts 1951

Pet Animals Act 1951 (Amendment) Act 1983

Prevention of Damage by Rabbits Act 1939

Protection of Animals Acts 1911

Protection of Animals (Amendment) Act 2000

Protection of Animals (Anaesthetics) Acts 1954 and 1964

Protection of Animals (Penalties) Act 1987

Wildlife and Countryside Act 1981

(5) Archaeological societies

Eg treasure-hunters' clubs[1]

Coroners Act 1988

National Heritage Acts 1980–2002

Protection of Military Remains Act 1986

Protection of Wrecks Act 1973

Treasure Act 1996

(6) Camping & caravan clubs

Caravan Sites Act 1968

Caravan Sites and Control of Development 1960

Countryside and Rights of Way Act 2000

National Parks and Access to the Countryside Act 1949 (as amended)

(7) Cycling clubs

Cycle Tracks Act 1984

Road Traffic Act 1988

(8) Drama clubs

Eg theatre clubs, dramatic and operatic societies

Copyright, Designs and Patents Act 1988

Environmental Protection Act 1990

Fire Precautions Act 1971

Licensing Act 2003

Occupiers' Liability Acts 1957 & 1984

Restriction of Offensive Weapons Acts 1959 and 1961

Theatres Trust Act 1976

(9) Film clubs

Cinemas Act 1985

Cinematograph Films (Animals) Act 1937

Films Act 1985

Licensing Act 2003

Video Recordings Acts 1984, 1993 and 2010

(10) Flying clubs

Aviation and Maritime Security Act 1990

---

1 An example of this type of club appeared in the Times newspaper of 26 July 1973, at p 18.

Aviation (Offences) Act 2003

Civil Aviation Act 1982 and 2006

Civil Aviation (Amendment) Act 1996

Customs and Excise Management Act 1979

Railways and Transport Safety Act 2003

Transport Act 2000

(11) Golf clubs

Countryside and Rights of Way Act 2000

Occupiers' Liability Acts 1957 and 1984

Trees Act 1970

Water Acts 1945–1989

Water Resources Acts 1963–1991

(12) Holiday clubs

Eg time-sharing clubs

Financial Services Act 1986

Timeshare Act 1992

Trade Descriptions Act 1968

(13) Horticultural societies

Eg garden clubs, flower-arranging societies

Farm and Garden Chemicals Act 1967

Horticulture Act 1960

Horticulture Produce Act 1986

Horticulture Produce (Sales on Commission) Act 1926

Horticulture (Special Payments) Act 1974

Plant Health Act 1967

Plant Varieties Act 1997

Plant Varieties and Seeds Act 1964

(14) Hunting clubs

Eg fox-hunting clubs, staghounds clubs

Deer Act 1991

Hares Preservation Act 1892

Hunting Act 2004[2]

Wild Creatures and Forest Laws Act 1971

---

2 The hunting of wild animals with dogs was abolished with effect from 18 February 2005, with certain exceptions such as the hunting of rats and rabbits.

Welfare of Animals at Slaughter Act 1991

Wildlife and Countryside Act 1981

(15) Motor racing and motor cycling clubs

Motor Cycle Noise Act 1987

Noise Act 1996

Noise and Statutory Nuisance Act 1993

Road Traffic Act 1988

Road Traffic (Temporary Restrictions) Act 1991

Road Traffic Regulation (Special Events) Act 1994

Transport Acts 1962–2000

(16) Musical societies

Eg concert clubs, discotheque clubs, ballroom-dancing clubs

Copyright Designs and Patents Act 1988

Fire Precautions Act 1971

Licensing Act 2003

Occupiers' Liability Acts 1957 and 1984

(17) Nature clubs

Eg birdwatching clubs, field societies, conservation societies

Nature Conservancy Council Act 1973

Wild Creatures and Forest Laws Act 1971

Wild Mammals (Protection) Act 1996

Wildlife and Countryside Acts 1981

Wildlife and Countryside (Amendment) Act 1991

Wildlife and Countryside (Service of Notices) Act 1985

(18) Political clubs

Eg national party associations, (non-party) ratepayers' associations, (non-party) residents' associations

Finance (No 2) Act 1983

Political Parties, Elections and Referendums Act 2000

Representation of the People Acts 1983–2000

(19) Preservation societies

Eg railway and canal preservation societies[3]

Ancient Monuments and Archaeological Areas Act 1979

British Waterways Act 1995

Canals Protection (London) Act 1898

Historic Buildings and Ancient Monuments Act 1953

National Heritage Acts 1980–2002

Railway Heritage Act 1996

(20) Radio clubs

Wireless Telegraphy Act 2006

(21) Rambling associations

Commons Acts 1876–2006

Commons Registration Act 1965

Countryside Act 1968

Countryside and Rights of Way Act 2000

Dogs (Protection of Livestock) Act 1953

Forestry Act 1967

Highways Acts 1980 and 1986

Marine and Coastal Access Act 2009

National Parks and Access to Countryside Act 1949

Open Spaces Act 1906

(22) Riding clubs

Eg pony clubs

Animal Health Acts 1981 and 2002

Docking and Nicking of Horses Act 1949

Farriers Registration Acts 1975 and 1977

Horses (Protective Headgear for Young Riders) Act 1990

Protection against Cruel Tethering Act 1988

Riding Establishments Acts 1964 and 1970

(23) Sailing clubs

Eg yacht clubs

Coast Protection Act 1949

---

3 There are many private and local Acts of Parliament governing railways and canals which may be relevant in any given case.

Countryside Act 1968

Customs and Excise Management Act 1979

Docks and Harbours Act 1966

Harbours Act 1964

Marine Insurance Act 1906

Marine Safety Act 2003

Merchant Shipping Acts 1988 and 1995

Merchant Shipping and Maritime Security Act 1997

Pilotage Act 1987

Railways and Transport Safety Act 2003

(24) Shooting clubs

Eg rifle clubs, clay pigeon shooting clubs, shooting syndicates

Firearms Act 1968

Firearms (Amendment) Act 1997

Firearms (Amendment) (No 2) Act 1997

Game Acts 1831 and 1970

Game Laws (Amendment) Act 1960

Game Licences Act 1860

Ground Game Acts 1880

Ground Game (Amendment) Act 1906

Gun Barrel Proof Acts 1868–1978

Hares Act 1848

Hares Preservation Act 1892

Theft Act 1968

Wild Creatures and Forest Laws Act 1971

Wildlife and Countryside Act 1981

(25) Sports clubs (other than golf clubs)

Activity Centres (Young Persons Safety) Act 1995

Fire Safety and Safety of Places of Sport Act 1987

Football (Offences and Disorder) Act 1999

Football (Disorder) (Amendment) Act 2002

Football Spectators Act 1989

Safety of Sports Grounds Act 1975

Sporting Events (Control of Alcohol etc) Amendment Act 1992

Water Resources Act 1991

(26) Tenants' associations

Housing Acts 1988–2004

Housing Associations Act 1985

Housing Grants, Construction and Regeneration Act 1996

Protection from Eviction Act 1977

Rent Act 1977

Rent (Amendment) Act 1985

(27) Welfare associations

Eg clubs for the disabled, Darby and Joan clubs, over-sixties clubs, youth clubs, leagues of friends of hospitals

Chronically Sick and Disabled Persons Acts 1970

Chronically Sick and Disabled Persons (Amendment) Act 1976

Disabled Persons Act 1981

Disabled Persons (Employment) Acts 1944 and 1958

Disabled Persons (Services, Consultation and Representation) Act 1986

Registered Homes Acts 1984

Registered Homes (Amendment) Act 1991

(28) Wine-and beer-making clubs

Alcoholic Liquor Duties Act 1979

Licensing Act 2003

Appendix 7

MODEL ARTICLES 2008 FOR PRIVATE COMPANIES LIMITED BY GUARANTEE

SI 2008/3229

Regulation 3:

Schedule 2

Index to the Articles

PART 1
INTERPRETATION AND LIMITATION OF LIABILITY

1 Defined terms

In the articles, unless the context requires otherwise –

"articles" means the company's articles of association;
"bankruptcy" includes individual insolvency proceedings in a jurisdiction other than England and Wales or Northern Ireland which have an effect similar to that of bankruptcy;
"chairman" has the meaning given in article 12;
"chairman of the meeting" has the meaning given in article 25;
"Companies Acts" means the Companies Acts (as defined in section 2 of the Companies Act 2006), in so far as they apply to the company;
"director" means a director of the company, and includes any person occupying the position of director, by whatever name called;
"document" includes, unless otherwise specified, any document sent or supplied in electronic form;
"electronic form" has the meaning given in section 1168 of the Companies Act 2006;
"member" has the meaning given in section 112 of the Companies Act 2006;
"ordinary resolution" has the meaning given in section 282 of the Companies Act 2006;
"participate", in relation to a directors' meeting, has the meaning given in article 10;
"proxy notice" has the meaning given in article 31;

"special resolution" has the meaning given in section 283 of the Companies Act 2006;

"subsidiary" has the meaning given in section 1159 of the Companies Act 2006; and

"writing" means the representation or reproduction of words, symbols or other information in a visible form by any method or combination of methods, whether sent or supplied in electronic form or otherwise.

Unless the context otherwise requires, other words or expressions contained in these articles bear the same meaning as in the Companies Act 2006 as in force on the date when these articles become binding on the company.

2 Liability of members

The liability of each member is limited to £1, being the amount that each member undertakes to contribute to the assets of the company in the event of its being wound up while he is a member or within one year after he ceases to be a member, for –

(a) payment of the company's debts and liabilities contracted before he ceases to be a member,
(b) payment of the costs, charges and expenses of winding up, and
(c) adjustment of the rights of the contributories among themselves.

PART 2
DIRECTORS

Directors' Powers And Responsibilities

3 Directors' general authority

Subject to the articles, the directors are responsible for the management of the company's business, for which purpose they may exercise all the powers of the company.

4 Members' reserve power

(1) The members may, by special resolution, direct the directors to take, or refrain from taking, specified action.

(2) No such special resolution invalidates anything which the directors have done before the passing of the resolution.

5 Directors may delegate

(1) Subject to the articles, the directors may delegate any of the powers which are conferred on them under the articles –

(a) to such person or committee;
(b) by such means (including by power of attorney);
(c) to such an extent;
(d) in relation to such matters or territories; and
(e) on such terms and conditions; as they think fit.

(2) If the directors so specify, any such delegation may authorise further delegation of the directors' powers by any person to whom they are delegated.

(3) The directors may revoke any delegation in whole or part, or alter its terms and conditions.

6 Committees

(1) Committees to which the directors delegate any of their powers must follow procedures which are based as far as they are applicable on those provisions of the articles which govern the taking of decisions by directors.

(2) The directors may make rules of procedure for all or any committees, which prevail over rules derived from the articles if they are not consistent with them.

Decision-Making By Directors

7 Directors to take decisions collectively

(1) The general rule about decision-making by directors is that any decision of the directors must be either a majority decision at a meeting or a decision taken in accordance with article 8.

(2) If –

(a) the company only has one director, and
(b) no provision of the articles requires it to have more than one director,

the general rule does not apply, and the director may take decisions without regard to any of the provisions of the articles relating to directors' decision-making.

8 Unanimous decisions

(1) A decision of the directors is taken in accordance with this article when all eligible directors indicate to each other by any means that they share a common view on a matter.

(2) Such a decision may take the form of a resolution in writing, copies of which have been signed by each eligible director or to which each eligible director has otherwise indicated agreement in writing.

(3) References in this article to eligible directors are to directors who would have been entitled to vote on the matter had it been proposed as a resolution at a directors' meeting.

(4) A decision may not be taken in accordance with this article if the eligible directors would not have formed a quorum at such a meeting.

9 Calling a directors' meeting

(1) Any director may call a directors' meeting by giving notice of the meeting to the directors or by authorising the company secretary (if any) to give such notice.

(2) Notice of any directors' meeting must indicate –

(a) its proposed date and time;
(b) where it is to take place; and
(c) if it is anticipated that directors participating in the meeting will not be in the same place, how it is proposed that they should communicate with each other during the meeting.

(3) Notice of a directors' meeting must be given to each director, but need not be in writing.

(4) Notice of a directors' meeting need not be given to directors who waive their entitlement to notice of that meeting, by giving notice to that effect to the company not more than 7 days after the date on which the meeting is held. Where such notice is given after the meeting has been held, that does not affect the validity of the meeting, or of any business conducted at it.

10 Participation in directors' meetings

(1) Subject to the articles, directors participate in a directors' meeting, or part of a directors' meeting, when –

(a) the meeting has been called and takes place in accordance with the articles, and

(b) they can each communicate to the others any information or opinions they have on any particular item of the business of the meeting.

(2) In determining whether directors are participating in a directors' meeting, it is irrelevant where any director is or how they communicate with each other.

(3) If all the directors participating in a meeting are not in the same place, they may decide that the meeting is to be treated as taking place wherever any of them is.

11 Quorum for directors' meetings

(1) At a directors' meeting, unless a quorum is participating, no proposal is to be voted on, except a proposal to call another meeting.

(2) The quorum for directors' meetings may be fixed from time to time by a decision of the directors, but it must never be less than two, and unless otherwise fixed it is two.

(3) If the total number of directors for the time being is less than the quorum required, the directors must not take any decision other than a decision –

(a) to appoint further directors, or

(b) to call a general meeting so as to enable the members to appoint further directors.

12 Chairing of directors' meetings

(1) The directors may appoint a director to chair their meetings.

(2) The person so appointed for the time being is known as the chairman.

(3) The directors may terminate the chairman's appointment at any time.

(4) If the chairman is not participating in a directors' meeting within ten minutes of the time at which it was to start, the participating directors must appoint one of themselves to chair it.

13 Casting vote

(1) If the numbers of votes for and against a proposal are equal, the chairman or other director chairing the meeting has a casting vote.

(2) But this does not apply if, in accordance with the articles, the chairman or other director is not to be counted as participating in the decision-making process for quorum or voting purposes.

14 Conflicts of interest

(1) If a proposed decision of the directors is concerned with an actual or proposedtransaction or arrangement with the company in which a director is interested, that director is not to be counted as participating in the decision-making process for quorum or voting purposes.

(2) But if paragraph (3) applies, a director who is interested in an actual or proposed transaction or arrangement with the company is to be counted as participating in the decision-making process for quorum and voting purposes.

(3) This paragraph applies when –

(a) the company by ordinary resolution disapplies the provision of the articles which would otherwise prevent a director from being counted as participating in the decision-making process;

(b) the director's interest cannot reasonably be regarded as likely to give rise to a conflict of interest; or

(c) the director's conflict of interest arises from a permitted cause.

(4) For the purposes of this article, the following are permitted causes –

(a) a guarantee given, or to be given, by or to a director in respect of an obligation incurred by or on behalf of the company or any of its subsidiaries;

(b) subscription, or an agreement to subscribe, for securities of the company or any of its subsidiaries, or to underwrite, sub-underwrite, or guarantee subscription for any such securities; and

(c) arrangements pursuant to which benefits are made available to employees and directors or former employees and directors of the company or any of its subsidiaries which do not provide special benefits for directors or former directors.

(5) For the purposes of this article, references to proposed decisions and decision-making processes include any directors' meeting or part of a directors' meeting.

(6) Subject to paragraph (7), if a question arises at a meeting of directors or of a committee of directors as to the right of a director to participate in the meeting (or part of the meeting) for voting or quorum purposes, the question may, before the conclusion of the meeting, be referred to the chairman whose ruling in relation to any director other than the chairman is to be final and conclusive.

(7) If any question as to the right to participate in the meeting (or part of the meeting) should arise in respect of the chairman, the question is to be decided by a decision of the directors at that meeting, for which purpose the chairman is not to be counted as participating in the meeting (or that part of the meeting) for voting or quorum purposes.

15 Records of decisions to be kept

The directors must ensure that the company keeps a record, in writing, for at least 10 years from the date of the decision recorded, of every unanimous or majority decision taken by the directors.

16 Directors' discretion to make further rules

Subject to the articles, the directors may make any rule which they think fit about how they take decisions, and about how such rules are to be recorded or communicated to directors.

Appointment Of Directors

17 Methods of appointing directors

(1) Any person who is willing to act as a director, and is permitted by law to do so, may be appointed to be a director –

- (a) by ordinary resolution, or
- (b) by a decision of the directors.

(2) In any case where, as a result of death, the company has no members and no directors, the personal representatives of the last member to have died have the right, by notice in writing, to appoint a person to be a director.

(3) For the purposes of paragraph (2), where 2 or more members die in circumstances rendering it uncertain who was the last to die, a younger member is deemed to have survived an older member.

18 Termination of director's appointment

A person ceases to be a director as soon as –

- (a) that person ceases to be a director by virtue of any provision of the Companies Act 2006 or is prohibited from being a director by law;
- (b) a bankruptcy order is made against that person;
- (c) a composition is made with that person's creditors generally in satisfaction of that person's debts;
- (d) a registered medical practitioner who is treating that person gives a written opinion to the company stating that that person has become physically or mentally incapable of acting as a director and may remain so for more than three months;
- (e) by reason of that person's mental health, a court makes an order which wholly or partly prevents that person from personally exercising any powers or rights which that person would otherwise have;
- (f) notification is received by the company from the director that the director is resigning from office, and such resignation has taken effect in accordance with its terms.

19 Directors' remuneration

(1) Directors may undertake any services for the company that the directors decide.

(2) Directors are entitled to such remuneration as the directors determine –

- (a) for their services to the company as directors, and
- (b) for any other service which they undertake for the company.

(3) Subject to the articles, a director's remuneration may –

(a) take any form, and
(b) include any arrangements in connection with the payment of a pension, allowance or gratuity, or any death, sickness or disability benefits, to or in respect of that director.

(4) Unless the directors decide otherwise, directors' remuneration accrues from day to day.

(5) Unless the directors decide otherwise, directors are not accountable to the company for any remuneration which they receive as directors or other officers or employees of the company's subsidiaries or of any other body corporate in which the company is interested.

20 Directors' expenses

The company may pay any reasonable expenses which the directors properly incur in connection with their attendance at –

(a) meetings of directors or committees of directors,
(b) general meetings, or
(c) separate meetings of the holders of debentures of the company, or otherwise in connection with the exercise of their powers and the discharge of their responsibilities in relation to the company.

PART 3
MEMBERS

Becoming And Ceasing To Be A Member

21 Applications for membership

No person shall become a member of the company unless –

(a) that person has completed an application for membership in a form approved by the directors, and
(b) the directors have approved the application.

22 Termination of membership

(1) A member may withdraw from membership of the company by giving 7 days' notice to the company in writing.

(2) Membership is not transferable.

(3) A person's membership terminates when that person dies or ceases to exist.

Organisation Of General Meetings

23 Attendance and speaking at general meetings

(1) A person is able to exercise the right to speak at a general meeting when that person is in a position to communicate to all those attending the meeting, during the meeting, any information or opinions which that person has on the business of the meeting.

(2) A person is able to exercise the right to vote at a general meeting when –

(a) that person is able to vote, during the meeting, on resolutions put to the vote at the meeting, and
(b) that person's vote can be taken into account in determining whether or not such resolutions are passed at the same time as the votes of all the other persons attending the meeting.

(3) The directors may make whatever arrangements they consider appropriate to enable those attending a general meeting to exercise their rights to speak or vote at it.

(4) In determining attendance at a general meeting, it is immaterial whether any two or more members attending it are in the same place as each other.

(5) Two or more persons who are not in the same place as each other attend a general meeting if their circumstances are such that if they have (or were to have) rights to speak and vote at that meeting, they are (or would be) able to exercise them.

24 Quorum for general meetings

No business other than the appointment of the chairman of the meeting is to be transacted at a general meeting if the persons attending it do not constitute a quorum.

25 Chairing general meetings

(1) If the directors have appointed a chairman, the chairman shall chair general meetings if present and willing to do so.

(2) If the directors have not appointed a chairman, or if the chairman is unwilling to chair the meeting or is not present within ten minutes of the time at which a meeting was due to start –

(a) the directors present, or
(b) (if no directors are present), the meeting, must appoint a director or member to chair the meeting, and the appointment of the chairman of the meeting must be the first business of the meeting.

(3) The person chairing a meeting in accordance with this article is referred to as "the chairman of the meeting".

26 Attendance and speaking by directors and non-members

(1) Directors may attend and speak at general meetings, whether or not they are members.

(2) The chairman of the meeting may permit other persons who are not members of the company to attend and speak at a general meeting.

27 Adjournment

(1) If the persons attending a general meeting within half an hour of the time at which the meeting was due to start do not constitute a quorum, or if during a meeting a quorum ceases to be present, the chairman of the meeting must adjourn it.

(2) The chairman of the meeting may adjourn a general meeting at which a quorum is present if –

(a) the meeting consents to an adjournment, or
(b) it appears to the chairman of the meeting that an adjournment is necessary to protect the safety of any person attending the meeting or ensure that the business of the meeting is conducted in an orderly manner.

(3) The chairman of the meeting must adjourn a general meeting if directed to do so by the meeting.

(4) When adjourning a general meeting, the chairman of the meeting must –

(a) either specify the time and place to which it is adjourned or state that it is to continue at a time and place to be fixed by the directors, and
(b) have regard to any directions as to the time and place of any adjournment which have been given by the meeting.

(5) If the continuation of an adjourned meeting is to take place more than 14 days after it was adjourned, the company must give at least 7 clear days' notice of it (that is, excluding the day of the adjourned meeting and the day on which the notice is given) –

(a) to the same persons to whom notice of the company's general meetings is required to be given, and
(b) containing the same information which such notice is required to contain.

(6) No business may be transacted at an adjourned general meeting which could not properly have been transacted at the meeting if the adjournment had not taken place.

Voting At General Meetings

28 Voting: general

A resolution put to the vote of a general meeting must be decided on a show of hands unless a poll is duly demanded in accordance with the articles.

29 Errors and disputes

(1) No objection may be raised to the qualification of any person voting at a general meeting except at the meeting or adjourned meeting at which the vote objected to is tendered, and every vote not disallowed at the meeting is valid.

(2) Any such objection must be referred to the chairman of the meeting whose decision is final.

30 Poll votes

(1) A poll on a resolution may be demanded –

(a) in advance of the general meeting where it is to be put to the vote, or
(b) at a general meeting, either before a show of hands on that resolution or immediately after the result of a show of hands on that resolution is declared.

(2) A poll may be demanded by –

(a) the chairman of the meeting;
(b) the directors;
(c) two or more persons having the right to vote on the resolution; or

(d) a person or persons representing not less than one tenth of the total voting rights of all the members having the right to vote on the resolution.

(3) A demand for a poll may be withdrawn if –

(a) the poll has not yet been taken, and
(b) the chairman of the meeting consents to the withdrawal.

(4) Polls must be taken immediately and in such manner as the chairman of the meeting directs.

31 Content of proxy notices

(1) Proxies may only validly be appointed by a notice in writing (a "proxy notice") which –

(a) states the name and address of the member appointing the proxy;
(b) identifies the person appointed to be that member's proxy and the general meeting in relation to which that person is appointed;
(c) is signed by or on behalf of the member appointing the proxy, or is authenticated in such manner as the directors may determine; and
(d) is delivered to the company in accordance with the articles and any instructions contained in the notice of the general meeting to which they relate.

(2) The company may require proxy notices to be delivered in a particular form, and may specify different forms for different purposes.

(3) Proxy notices may specify how the proxy appointed under them is to vote (or that the proxy is to abstain from voting) on one or more resolutions.

(4) Unless a proxy notice indicates otherwise, it must be treated as –

(a) allowing the person appointed under it as a proxy discretion as to how to vote on any ancillary or procedural resolutions put to the meeting, and
(b) appointing that person as a proxy in relation to any adjournment of the general meeting to which it relates as well as the meeting itself.

32 Delivery of proxy notices

(1) A person who is entitled to attend, speak or vote (either on a show of hands or on a poll) at a general meeting remains so entitled in respect of that meeting or any adjournment of it, even though a valid proxy notice has been delivered to the company by or on behalf of that person.

(2) An appointment under a proxy notice may be revoked by delivering to the company a notice in writing given by or on behalf of the person by whom or on whose behalf the proxy notice was given.

(3) A notice revoking a proxy appointment only takes effect if it is delivered before the start of the meeting or adjourned meeting to which it relates.

(4) If a proxy notice is not executed by the person appointing the proxy, it must be accompanied by written evidence of the authority of the person who executed it to execute it on the appointor's behalf.

33 Amendments to resolutions

(1) An ordinary resolution to be proposed at a general meeting may be amended by ordinary resolution if –

(a) notice of the proposed amendment is given to the company in writing by a person entitled to vote at the general meeting at which it is to be proposed not less than 48 hours before the meeting is to take place (or such later time as the chairman of the meeting may determine), and
(b) the proposed amendment does not, in the reasonable opinion of the chairman of the meeting, materially alter the scope of the resolution.

(2) A special resolution to be proposed at a general meeting may be amended by ordinary resolution, if –

(a) the chairman of the meeting proposes the amendment at the general meeting at which the resolution is to be proposed, and
(b) the amendment does not go beyond what is necessary to correct a grammatical or other non-substantive error in the resolution.

(3) If the chairman of the meeting, acting in good faith, wrongly decides that an amendment to a resolution is out of order, the chairman's error does not invalidate the vote on that resolution.

PART 4
ADMINISTRATIVE ARRANGEMENTS

34 Means of communication to be used

(1) Subject to the articles, anything sent or supplied by or to the company under the articles may be sent or supplied in any way in which the Companies Act 2006 provides for documents or information which are authorised or required by any provision of that Act to be sent or supplied by or to the company.

(2) Subject to the articles, any notice or document to be sent or supplied to a director in connection with the taking of decisions by directors may also be sent or supplied by the means by which that director has asked to be sent or supplied with such notices or documents for the time being.

(3) A director may agree with the company that notices or documents sent to that director in a particular way are to be deemed to have been received within a specified time of their being sent, and for the specified time to be less than 48 hours.

35 Company seals

(1) Any common seal may only be used by the authority of the directors.

(2) The directors may decide by what means and in what form any common seal is to be used.

(3) Unless otherwise decided by the directors, if the company has a common seal and it is affixed to a document, the document must also be signed by at least one authorised person in the presence of a witness who attests the signature.

(4) For the purposes of this article, an authorised person is –

(a) any director of the company;
(b) the company secretary (if any); or

(c) any person authorised by the directors for the purpose of signing documents to which the common seal is applied.

36 No right to inspect accounts and other records

Except as provided by law or authorised by the directors or an ordinary resolution of the company, no person is entitled to inspect any of the company's accounting or other records or documents merely by virtue of being a member.

37 Provision for employees on cessation of business

The directors may decide to make provision for the benefit of persons employed or formerly employed by the company or any of its subsidiaries (other than a director or former director or shadow director) in connection with the cessation or transfer to any person of the whole or part of the undertaking of the company or that subsidiary.

Directors' Indemnity And Insurance

38 Indemnity

(1) Subject to paragraph (2), a relevant director of the company or an associated company may be indemnified out of the company's assets against –

(a) any liability incurred by that director in connection with any negligence, default, breach of duty or breach of trust in relation to the company or an associated company,

(b) any liability incurred by that director in connection with the activities of the company or an associated company in its capacity as a trustee of an occupational pension scheme (as defined in section 235(6) of the Companies Act 2006),

(c) any other liability incurred by that director as an officer of the company or an associated company.

(2) This article does not authorise any indemnity which would be prohibited or rendered void by any provision of the Companies Acts or by any other provision of law.

(3) In this article –

(a) companies are associated if one is a subsidiary of the other or both are subsidiaries of the same body corporate, and

(b) a "relevant director" means any director or former director of the company or an associated company.

39 Insurance

(1) The directors may decide to purchase and maintain insurance, at the expense of the company, for the benefit of any relevant director in respect of any relevant loss.

(2) In this article –

(a) a "relevant director" means any director or former director of the company or an associated company,

(b) a "relevant loss" means any loss or liability which has been or may be incurred by a relevant director in connection with that director's duties or powers in relation to the company, any associated company or any pension fund or employees' share scheme of the company or associated company, and

(c) companies are associated if one is a subsidiary of the other or both are subsidiaries of the same body corporate.

Appendix 8

MODEL ARTICLES 2008 FOR PRIVATE COMPANIES LIMITED BY SHARES

SI 2008/3229

Regulation 2

Schedule 1

Index to the Articles

PART 1
INTERPRETATION AND LIMITATION OF LIABILITY

1 Defined terms

In the articles, unless the context requires otherwise –

"articles" means the company's articles of association;
"bankruptcy" includes individual insolvency proceedings in a jurisdiction other than England and Wales or Northern Ireland which have an effect similar to that of bankruptcy;
"chairman" has the meaning given in article 12;
"chairman of the meeting" has the meaning given in article 25;
"Companies Acts" means the Companies Acts (as defined in section 2 of the Companies Act 2006), in so far as they apply to the company;
"director" means a director of the company, and includes any person occupying the position of director, by whatever name called;
"distribution recipient" has the meaning given in article 31;
"document" includes, unless otherwise specified, any document sent or supplied in electronic form;
"electronic form" has the meaning given in section 1168 of the Companies Act 2006;
"fully paid" in relation to a share, means that the nominal value and any premium to be paid to the company in respect of that share have been paid to the company;
"hard copy form" has the meaning given in section 1168 of the Companies Act 2006;
"holder" in relation to shares means the person whose name is entered in the register of
members as the holder of the shares;
"instrument" means a document in hard copy form;
"ordinary resolution" has the meaning given in section 282 of the Companies Act 2006;
"paid" means paid or credited as paid;
"participate", in relation to a directors' meeting, has the meaning given in article 10;
"proxy notice" has the meaning given in article 45;
"shareholder" means a person who is the holder of a share;
"shares" means shares in the company;
"special resolution" has the meaning given in section 283 of the Companies Act 2006;
"subsidiary" has the meaning given in section 1159 of the Companies Act 2006;
"transmittee" means a person entitled to a share by reason of the death or bankruptcy of a shareholder or otherwise by operation of law; and
"writing" means the representation or reproduction of words, symbols or other information in a visible form by any method or combination of methods, whether sent or supplied in electronic form or otherwise.

Unless the context otherwise requires, other words or expressions contained in these articles bear the same meaning as in the Companies Act 2006 as in force on the date when these articles become binding on the company.

2 Liability of members

The liability of the members is limited to the amount, if any, unpaid on the shares held by them.

PART 2
DIRECTORS

Directors' Powers And Responsibilities

3 Directors' general authority

Subject to the articles, the directors are responsible for the management of the company's business, for which purpose they may exercise all the powers of the company.

4 Shareholders' reserve power

(1) The shareholders may, by special resolution, direct the directors to take, or refrain from taking, specified action.

(2) No such special resolution invalidates anything which the directors have done before the passing of the resolution.

5 Directors may delegate

(1) Subject to the articles, the directors may delegate any of the powers which are conferred on them under the articles –

(a) to such person or committee;
(b) by such means (including by power of attorney);
(c) to such an extent;
(d) in relation to such matters or territories; and
(e) on such terms and conditions;

as they think fit.

(2) If the directors so specify, any such delegation may authorise further delegation of the directors' powers by any person to whom they are delegated.

(3) The directors may revoke any delegation in whole or part, or alter its terms and conditions.

6 Committees

(1) Committees to which the directors delegate any of their powers must follow procedures which are based as far as they are applicable on those provisions of the articles which govern the taking of decisions by directors.

(2) The directors may make rules of procedure for all or any committees, which prevail over rules derived from the articles if they are not consistent with them.

Decision-Making By Directors

7 Directors to take decisions collectively

(1) The general rule about decision-making by directors is that any decision of the directors must be either a majority decision at a meeting or a decision taken in accordance with article 8.

(2) If –

(a) the company only has one director, and
(b) no provision of the articles requires it to have more than one director,

the general rule does not apply, and the director may take decisions without regard to any of the provisions of the articles relating to directors' decision-making.

8 Unanimous decisions

(1) A decision of the directors is taken in accordance with this article when all eligible directors indicate to each other by any means that they share a common view on a matter.

(2) Such a decision may take the form of a resolution in writing, copies of which have been signed by each eligible director or to which each eligible director has otherwise indicated agreement in writing.

(3) References in this article to eligible directors are to directors who would have been entitled to vote on the matter had it been proposed as a resolution at a directors' meeting.

(4) A decision may not be taken in accordance with this article if the eligible directors would not have formed a quorum at such a meeting.

9 Calling a directors' meeting

(1) Any director may call a directors' meeting by giving notice of the meeting to thedirectors or by authorising the company secretary (if any) to give such notice.

(2) Notice of any directors' meeting must indicate –

(a) its proposed date and time;
(b) where it is to take place; and
(c) if it is anticipated that directors participating in the meeting will not be in the same place, how it is proposed that they should communicate with each other during the meeting.

(3) Notice of a directors' meeting must be given to each director, but need not be in writing.

(4) Notice of a directors' meeting need not be given to directors who waive their entitlement to notice of that meeting, by giving notice to that effect to the company not more than 7 days after the date on which the meeting is held. Where such notice is given after the meeting has been held, that does not affect the validity of the meeting, or of any business conducted at it.

10 Participation in directors' meetings

(1) Subject to the articles, directors participate in a directors' meeting, or part of a directors' meeting, when –

(a) the meeting has been called and takes place in accordance with the articles, and
(b) they can each communicate to the others any information or opinions they have on any particular item of the business of the meeting.

(2) In determining whether directors are participating in a directors' meeting, it is irrelevant where any director is or how they communicate with each other.

(3) If all the directors participating in a meeting are not in the same place, they may decide that the meeting is to be treated as taking place wherever any of them is.

11 Quorum for directors' meetings

(1) At a directors' meeting, unless a quorum is participating, no proposal is to be voted on, except a proposal to call another meeting.

(2) The quorum for directors' meetings may be fixed from time to time by a decision of the directors, but it must never be less than two, and unless otherwise fixed it is two.

(3) If the total number of directors for the time being is less than the quorum required, thedirectors must not take any decision other than a decision –

(a) to appoint further directors, or
(b) to call a general meeting so as to enable the shareholders to appoint further directors.

12 Chairing of directors' meetings

(1) The directors may appoint a director to chair their meetings.

(2) The person so appointed for the time being is known as the chairman.

(3) The directors may terminate the chairman's appointment at any time.

(4) If the chairman is not participating in a directors' meeting within ten minutes of the time at which it was to start, the participating directors must appoint one of themselves to chair it.

13 Casting vote

(1) If the numbers of votes for and against a proposal are equal, the chairman or other director chairing the meeting has a casting vote.

(2) But this does not apply if, in accordance with the articles, the chairman or other director is not to be counted as participating in the decision-making process for quorum or voting purposes.

14 Conflicts of interest

(1) If a proposed decision of the directors is concerned with an actual or proposed ransaction or arrangement with the company in which a director is interested, that director is not to be counted as participating in the decision-making process for quorum or voting purposes.

(2) But if paragraph (3) applies, a director who is interested in an actual or proposed transaction or arrangement with the company is to be counted as participating in the decision-making process for quorum and voting purposes.

(3) This paragraph applies when –

(a) the company by ordinary resolution disapplies the provision of the articles which would otherwise prevent a director from being counted as participating in the decision-making process;
(b) the director's interest cannot reasonably be regarded as likely to give rise to a conflict of interest; or
(c) the director's conflict of interest arises from a permitted cause.

(4) For the purposes of this article, the following are permitted causes –

(a) a guarantee given, or to be given, by or to a director in respect of an obligation incurred by or on behalf of the company or any of its subsidiaries;
(b) subscription, or an agreement to subscribe, for shares or other securities of the company or any of its subsidiaries, or to underwrite, sub-underwrite, or guarantee subscription for any such shares or securities; and
(c) arrangements pursuant to which benefits are made available to employees and directors or former employees and directors of the company or any of its subsidiaries which do not provide special benefits for directors or former directors.

(5) For the purposes of this article, references to proposed decisions and decision-making processes include any directors' meeting or part of a directors' meeting.

(6) Subject to paragraph (7), if a question arises at a meeting of directors or of a committee of directors as to the right of a director to participate in the meeting (or part of the meeting) for voting or quorum purposes, the question may, before the conclusion of the meeting, be referred to the chairman whose ruling in relation to any director other than the chairman is to be final and conclusive.

(7) If any question as to the right to participate in the meeting (or part of the meeting) should arise in respect of the chairman, the question is to be decided by a decision of the directors at that meeting, for which purpose the chairman is not to be counted as participating in the meeting (or that part of the meeting) for voting or quorum purposes.

15 Records of decisions to be kept

The directors must ensure that the company keeps a record, in writing, for at least 10 years from the date of the decision recorded, of every unanimous or majority decision taken by the directors.

16 Directors' discretion to make further rules

Subject to the articles, the directors may make any rule which they think fit about how they take decisions, and about how such rules are to be recorded or communicated to directors.

Appointment Of Directors

17 Methods of appointing directors

(1) Any person who is willing to act as a director, and is permitted by law to do so, may be appointed to be a director –

(a) by ordinary resolution, or
(b) by a decision of the directors.

(2) In any case where, as a result of death, the company has no shareholders and no directors, the personal representatives of the last shareholder to have died have the right, by notice in writing, to appoint a person to be a director.

(3) For the purposes of paragraph (2), where 2 or more shareholders die in circumstances rendering it uncertain who was the last to die, a younger shareholder is deemed to have survived an older shareholder.

18 Termination of director's appointment

A person ceases to be a director as soon as –

(a) that person ceases to be a director by virtue of any provision of the Companies Act 2006 or is prohibited from being a director by law;
(b) a bankruptcy order is made against that person;
(c) a composition is made with that person's creditors generally in satisfaction of that erson's debts;
(d) a registered medical practitioner who is treating that person gives a written opinion to the company stating that that person has become physically or mentally incapable of acting as a director and may remain so for more than three months;
(e) by reason of that person's mental health, a court makes an order which wholly or partly prevents that person from personally exercising any powers or rights which that person would otherwise have;
(f) notification is received by the company from the director that the director is resigning from office, and such resignation has taken effect in accordance with its terms.

19 Directors' remuneration

(1) Directors may undertake any services for the company that the directors decide.

(2) Directors are entitled to such remuneration as the directors determine –

(a) for their services to the company as directors, and
(b) for any other service which they undertake for the company.

(3) Subject to the articles, a director's remuneration may –

(a) take any form, and
(b) include any arrangements in connection with the payment of a pension, allowance or gratuity, or any death, sickness or disability benefits, to or in respect of that director.

(4) Unless the directors decide otherwise, directors' remuneration accrues from day to day.

(5) Unless the directors decide otherwise, directors are not accountable to the company for any remuneration which they receive as directors or other officers or employees of the company's subsidiaries or of any other body corporate in which the company is interested.

20 Directors' expenses

The company may pay any reasonable expenses which the directors properly incur in connection with their attendance at –

(a) meetings of directors or committees of directors,
(b) general meetings, or

(c) separate meetings of the holders of any class of shares or of debentures of the company, or otherwise in connection with the exercise of their powers and the discharge of their responsibilities in relation to the company.

PART 3
SHARES AND DISTRIBUTIONS

Shares

21 All shares to be fully paid up

(1) No share is to be issued for less than the aggregate of its nominal value and any premium to be paid to the company in consideration for its issue.

(2) This does not apply to shares taken on the formation of the company by the subscribers to the company's memorandum.

22 Powers to issue different classes of share

(1) Subject to the articles, but without prejudice to the rights attached to any existing share, the company may issue shares with such rights or restrictions as may be determined by ordinary resolution.

(2) The company may issue shares which are to be redeemed, or are liable to be redeemed at the option of the company or the holder, and the directors may determine the terms, conditions and manner of redemption of any such shares.

23 Company not bound by less than absolute interests

Except as required by law, no person is to be recognised by the company as holding any share upon any trust, and except as otherwise required by law or the articles, the company is not in any way to be bound by or recognise any interest in a share other than the holder's absolute ownership of it and all the rights attaching to it.

24 Share certificates

(1) The company must issue each shareholder, free of charge, with one or more certificates in respect of the shares which that shareholder holds.

(2) Every certificate must specify –

(a) in respect of how many shares, of what class, it is issued;
(b) the nominal value of those shares;
(c) that the shares are fully paid; and
(d) any distinguishing numbers assigned to them.

(3) No certificate may be issued in respect of shares of more than one class.

(4) If more than one person holds a share, only one certificate may be issued in respect of it.

(5) Certificates must –

(a) have affixed to them the company's common seal, or
(b) be otherwise executed in accordance with the Companies Acts.

25 Replacement share certificates

(1) If a certificate issued in respect of a shareholder's shares is –

(a) damaged or defaced, or
(b) said to be lost, stolen or destroyed, that shareholder is entitled to be issued with a replacement certificate in respect of the same shares.

(2) A shareholder exercising the right to be issued with such a replacement certificate –

(a) may at the same time exercise the right to be issued with a single certificate or separate certificates;
(b) must return the certificate which is to be replaced to the company if it is damaged or defaced; and
(c) must comply with such conditions as to evidence, indemnity and the payment of a reasonable fee as the directors decide.

26 Share transfers

(1) Shares may be transferred by means of an instrument of transfer in any usual form or any other form approved by the directors, which is executed by or on behalf of the transferor.

(2) No fee may be charged for registering any instrument of transfer or other document relating to or affecting the title to any share.

(3) The company may retain any instrument of transfer which is registered.

(4) The transferor remains the holder of a share until the transferee's name is entered in the register of members as holder of it.

(5) The directors may refuse to register the transfer of a share, and if they do so, the instrument of transfer must be returned to the transferee with the notice of refusal unless they suspect that the proposed transfer may be fraudulent.

27 Transmission of shares

(1) If title to a share passes to a transmittee, the company may only recognise the ransmittee as having any title to that share.

(2) A transmittee who produces such evidence of entitlement to shares as the directors may properly require –

(a) may, subject to the articles, choose either to become the holder of those shares or to have them transferred to another person, and
(b) subject to the articles, and pending any transfer of the shares to another person, has the same rights as the holder had.

(3) But transmittees do not have the right to attend or vote at a general meeting, or agree to a proposed written resolution, in respect of shares to which they are entitled, by reason of the holder's death or bankruptcy or otherwise, unless they become the holders of those shares.

28 Exercise of transmittees' rights

(1) Transmittees who wish to become the holders of shares to which they have become entitled must notify the company in writing of that wish.

(2) If the transmittee wishes to have a share transferred to another person, the transmittee must execute an instrument of transfer in respect of it.

(3) Any transfer made or executed under this article is to be treated as if it were made or executed by the person from whom the transmittee has derived rights in respect of the share, and as if the event which gave rise to the transmission had not occurred.

29 Transmittees bound by prior notices

If a notice is given to a shareholder in respect of shares and a transmittee is entitled to those shares, the transmittee is bound by the notice if it was given to the shareholder before the transmittee's name has been entered in the register of members.

Dividends And Other Distributions

30 Procedure for declaring dividends

(1) The company may by ordinary resolution declare dividends, and the directors may decide to pay interim dividends.

(2) A dividend must not be declared unless the directors have made a recommendation as to its amount. Such a dividend must not exceed the amount recommended by the directors.

(3) No dividend may be declared or paid unless it is in accordance with shareholders' respective rights.

(4) Unless the shareholders' resolution to declare or directors' decision to pay a dividend, or the terms on which shares are issued, specify otherwise, it must be paid by reference to each shareholder's holding of shares on the date of the resolution or decision to declare or pay it.

(5) If the company's share capital is divided into different classes, no interim dividend may be paid on shares carrying deferred or non-preferred rights if, at the time of payment, any preferential dividend is in arrear.

(6) The directors may pay at intervals any dividend payable at a fixed rate if it appears to them that the profits available for distribution justify the payment.

(7) If the directors act in good faith, they do not incur any liability to the holders of shares onferring preferred rights for any loss they may suffer by the lawful payment of an interim dividend on shares with deferred or non-preferred rights.

31 Payment of dividends and other distributions

(1) Where a dividend or other sum which is a distribution is payable in respect of a share, it must be paid by one or more of the following means –

- (a) transfer to a bank or building society account specified by the distribution recipient either in writing or as the directors may otherwise decide;
- (b) sending a cheque made payable to the distribution recipient by post to the distribution recipient at the distribution recipient's registered address (if the distribution recipient is a holder of the share), or (in any other case) to an address specified by the distribution recipient either in writing or as the directors may otherwise decide;
- (c) sending a cheque made payable to such person by post to such person at such address as the distribution recipient has specified either in writing or as the directors may otherwise decide; or

(d) any other means of payment as the directors agree with the distribution recipient either in writing or by such other means as the directors decide.

(2) In the articles, "the distribution recipient" means, in respect of a share in respect of which a dividend or other sum is payable –

(a) the holder of the share; or
(b) if the share has two or more joint holders, whichever of them is named first in the register of members; or
(c) if the holder is no longer entitled to the share by reason of death or bankruptcy, or otherwise by operation of law, the transmittee.

32 No interest on distributions

The company may not pay interest on any dividend or other sum payable in respect of a share unless otherwise provided by –

(a) the terms on which the share was issued, or
(b) the provisions of another agreement between the holder of that share and the company.

33 Unclaimed distributions

(1) All dividends or other sums which are –

(a) payable in respect of shares, and
(b) unclaimed after having been declared or become payable,

may be invested or otherwise made use of by the directors for the benefit of the company until claimed.

(2) The payment of any such dividend or other sum into a separate account does not make the company a trustee in respect of it.

(3) If –

(a) twelve years have passed from the date on which a dividend or other sum became due for payment, and
(b) the distribution recipient has not claimed it,

the distribution recipient is no longer entitled to that dividend or other sum and it ceases to remain owing by the company.

34 Non-cash distributions

(1) Subject to the terms of issue of the share in question, the company may, by ordinary resolution on the recommendation of the directors, decide to pay all or part of a dividend or other distribution payable in respect of a share by transferring non-cash assets of equivalent value (including, without limitation, shares or other securities in any company).

(2) For the purposes of paying a non-cash distribution, the directors may make whatever arrangements they think fit, including, where any difficulty arises regarding the distribution –

(a) fixing the value of any assets;
(b) paying cash to any distribution recipient on the basis of that value in order to adjust the rights of recipients; and
(c) vesting any assets in trustees.

35 Waiver of distributions

Distribution recipients may waive their entitlement to a dividend or other distribution payable in respect of a share by giving the company notice in writing to that effect, but if –

(a) the share has more than one holder, or
(b) more than one person is entitled to the share, whether by reason of the death or bankruptcy of one or more joint holders, or otherwise,

the notice is not effective unless it is expressed to be given, and signed, by all the holders or persons otherwise entitled to the share.

Capitalisation Of Profits

36 Authority to capitalise and appropriation of capitalised sums

(1) Subject to the articles, the directors may, if they are so authorised by an ordinary esolution –

(a) decide to capitalise any profits of the company (whether or not they are available for distribution) which are not required for paying a preferential dividend, or any sum standing to the credit of the company's share premium account or capital redemption reserve; and
(b) appropriate any sum which they so decide to capitalise (a "capitalised sum") to the persons who would have been entitled to it if it were distributed by way of dividend (the "persons entitled") and in the same proportions.

(2) Capitalised sums must be applied –

(a) on behalf of the persons entitled, and
(b) in the same proportions as a dividend would have been distributed to them.

(3) Any capitalised sum may be applied in paying up new shares of a nominal amount equal to the capitalised sum which are then allotted credited as fully paid to the persons entitled or as they may direct.

(4) A capitalised sum which was appropriated from profits available for distribution may be applied in paying up new debentures of the company which are then allotted credited as fully paid to the persons entitled or as they may direct.

(5) Subject to the articles the directors may –

(a) apply capitalised sums in accordance with paragraphs (3) and (4) partly in one way and partly in another;
(b) make such arrangements as they think fit to deal with shares or debentures becoming distributable in fractions under this article (including the issuing of fractional certificates or the making of cash payments); and
(c) authorise any person to enter into an agreement with the company on behalf of all the persons entitled which is binding on them in respect of the allotment of shares and debentures to them under this article.

PART 4
DECISION-MAKING BY SHAREHOLDERS

Organisation Of General Meetings

37 Attendance and speaking at general meetings

(1) A person is able to exercise the right to speak at a general meeting when that person is in a position to communicate to all those attending the meeting, during the meeting, any information or opinions which that person has on the business of the meeting.

(2) A person is able to exercise the right to vote at a general meeting when –

(a) that person is able to vote, during the meeting, on resolutions put to the vote at the meeting, and
(b) that person's vote can be taken into account in determining whether or not such esolutions are passed at the same time as the votes of all the other persons attending the meeting.

(3) The directors may make whatever arrangements they consider appropriate to enable those attending a general meeting to exercise their rights to speak or vote at it.

(4) In determining attendance at a general meeting, it is immaterial whether any two or more members attending it are in the same place as each other.

(5) Two or more persons who are not in the same place as each other attend a general meeting if their circumstances are such that if they have (or were to have) rights to speak and vote at that meeting, they are (or would be) able to exercise them.

38 Quorum for general meetings

No business other than the appointment of the chairman of the meeting is to be transacted at a general meeting if the persons attending it do not constitute a quorum.

39 Chairing general meetings

(1) If the directors have appointed a chairman, the chairman shall chair general meetings if present and willing to do so.

(2) If the directors have not appointed a chairman, or if the chairman is unwilling to chair the meeting or is not present within ten minutes of the time at which a meeting was due to start –

(a) the directors present, or
(b) (if no directors are present), the meeting,

must appoint a director or shareholder to chair the meeting, and the appointment of the chairman of the meeting must be the first business of the meeting.

(3) The person chairing a meeting in accordance with this article is referred to as "the chairman of the meeting".

40 Attendance and speaking by directors and non-shareholders

(1) Directors may attend and speak at general meetings, whether or not they are shareholders.

(2) The chairman of the meeting may permit other persons who are not –

(a) shareholders of the company, or
(b) otherwise entitled to exercise the rights of shareholders in relation to general meetings, to attend and speak at a general meeting.

41 Adjournment

(1) If the persons attending a general meeting within half an hour of the time at which the meeting was due to start do not constitute a quorum, or if during a meeting a quorum ceases to be present, the chairman of the meeting must adjourn it.

(2) The chairman of the meeting may adjourn a general meeting at which a quorum is present if –

(a) the meeting consents to an adjournment, or
(b) it appears to the chairman of the meeting that an adjournment is necessary to protect the safety of any person attending the meeting or ensure that the business of the meeting is conducted in an orderly manner.

(3) The chairman of the meeting must adjourn a general meeting if directed to do so by the meeting.

(4) When adjourning a general meeting, the chairman of the meeting must –

(a) either specify the time and place to which it is adjourned or state that it is to continue at a time and place to be fixed by the directors, and
(b) have regard to any directions as to the time and place of any adjournment which have been given by the meeting.

(5) If the continuation of an adjourned meeting is to take place more than 14 days after it was adjourned, the company must give at least 7 clear days' notice of it (that is, excluding the day of the adjourned meeting and the day on which the notice is given) –

(a) to the same persons to whom notice of the company's general meetings is required to be given, and
(b) containing the same information which such notice is required to contain.

(6) No business may be transacted at an adjourned general meeting which could not properly have been transacted at the meeting if the adjournment had not taken place.

Voting At General Meetings

42 Voting: general

A resolution put to the vote of a general meeting must be decided on a show of hands unless a poll is duly demanded in accordance with the articles.

43 Errors and disputes

(1) No objection may be raised to the qualification of any person voting at a general meeting except at the meeting or adjourned meeting at which the vote objected to is tendered, and every vote not disallowed at the meeting is valid.

(2) Any such objection must be referred to the chairman of the meeting, whose decision is final.

44 Poll votes

(1) A poll on a resolution may be demanded –

(a) in advance of the general meeting where it is to be put to the vote, or
(b) at a general meeting, either before a show of hands on that resolution or immediately after the result of a show of hands on that resolution is declared.

(2) A poll may be demanded by –

(a) the chairman of the meeting;
(b) the directors;
(c) two or more persons having the right to vote on the resolution; or
(d) a person or persons representing not less than one tenth of the total voting rights of all the shareholders having the right to vote on the resolution.

(3) A demand for a poll may be withdrawn if –

(a) the poll has not yet been taken, and
(b) the chairman of the meeting consents to the withdrawal.

(4) Polls must be taken immediately and in such manner as the chairman of the meeting directs.

45 Content of proxy notices

(1) Proxies may only validly be appointed by a notice in writing (a "proxy notice") hich –

(a) states the name and address of the shareholder appointing the proxy;
(b) identifies the person appointed to be that shareholder's proxy and the general meeting in relation to which that person is appointed;
(c) is signed by or on behalf of the shareholder appointing the proxy, or is authenticated in such manner as the directors may determine; and
(d) is delivered to the company in accordance with the articles and any instructions contained in the notice of the general meeting to which they relate.

(2) The company may require proxy notices to be delivered in a particular form, and may pecify different forms for different purposes.

(3) Proxy notices may specify how the proxy appointed under them is to vote (or that the proxy is to abstain from voting) on one or more resolutions.

(4) Unless a proxy notice indicates otherwise, it must be treated as –

(a) allowing the person appointed under it as a proxy discretion as to how to vote on any ancillary or procedural resolutions put to the meeting, and

(b) appointing that person as a proxy in relation to any adjournment of the general meeting to which it relates as well as the meeting itself.

46 Delivery of proxy notices

(1) A person who is entitled to attend, speak or vote (either on a show of hands or on a poll) at a general meeting remains so entitled in respect of that meeting or any adjournment of it, even though a valid proxy notice has been delivered to the company by or on behalf of that person.

(2) An appointment under a proxy notice may be revoked by delivering to the company a notice in writing given by or on behalf of the person by whom or on whose behalf the proxy notice was given.

(3) A notice revoking a proxy appointment only takes effect if it is delivered before the start of the meeting or adjourned meeting to which it relates.

(4) If a proxy notice is not executed by the person appointing the proxy, it must be accompanied by written evidence of the authority of the person who executed it to execute it on the appointor's behalf.

47 Amendments to resolutions

(1) An ordinary resolution to be proposed at a general meeting may be amended by ordinary resolution if –

(a) notice of the proposed amendment is given to the company in writing by a person entitled to vote at the general meeting at which it is to be proposed not less than 48 hours before the meeting is to take place (or such later time as the chairman of the meeting may determine), and

(b) the proposed amendment does not, in the reasonable opinion of the chairman of the meeting, materially alter the scope of the resolution.

(2) A special resolution to be proposed at a general meeting may be amended by ordinary resolution, if –

(a) the chairman of the meeting proposes the amendment at the general meeting at which the resolution is to be proposed, and

(b) the amendment does not go beyond what is necessary to correct a grammatical or other non-substantive error in the resolution.

(3) If the chairman of the meeting, acting in good faith, wrongly decides that an amendment to a resolution is out of order, the chairman's error does not invalidate the vote on that resolution.

PART 5
ADMINISTRATIVE ARRANGEMENTS

48 Means of communication to be used

(1) Subject to the articles, anything sent or supplied by or to the company under the articles may be sent or supplied in any way in which the Companies Act 2006 provides for documents or information which are authorised or required by any provision of that Act to be sent or supplied by or to the company.

(2) Subject to the articles, any notice or document to be sent or supplied to a director in onnection with the taking of decisions by directors may also be sent or supplied by the means by which that director has asked to be sent or supplied with such notices or documents for the time being.

(3) A director may agree with the company that notices or documents sent to that director in a particular way are to be deemed to have been received within a specified time of their being sent, and for the specified time to be less than 48 hours.

49 Company seals

(1) Any common seal may only be used by the authority of the directors.

(2) The directors may decide by what means and in what form any common seal is to be used.

(3) Unless otherwise decided by the directors, if the company has a common seal and it is affixed to a document, the document must also be signed by at least one authorised person in the presence of a witness who attests the signature.

(4) For the purposes of this article, an authorised person is –

- (a) any director of the company;
- (b) the company secretary (if any); or
- (c) any person authorised by the directors for the purpose of signing documents to which the common seal is applied.

50 No right to inspect accounts and other records

Except as provided by law or authorised by the directors or an ordinary resolution of the company, no person is entitled to inspect any of the company's accounting or other records or documents merely by virtue of being a shareholder.

51 Provision for employees on cessation of business

The directors may decide to make provision for the benefit of persons employed or formerly employed by the company or any of its subsidiaries (other than a director or former director or shadow director) in connection with the cessation or transfer to any person of the whole or part of the undertaking of the company or that subsidiary.

Directors' Indemnity And Insurance

52 Indemnity

(1) Subject to paragraph (2), a relevant director of the company or an associated company may be indemnified out of the company's assets against –

- (a) any liability incurred by that director in connection with any negligence, default, breach of duty or breach of trust in relation to the company or an associated company,
- (b) any liability incurred by that director in connection with the activities of the company or an associated company in its capacity as a trustee of an occupational pension scheme (as defined in section 235(6) of the Companies Act 2006),
- (c) any other liability incurred by that director as an officer of the company or an associated company.

(2) This article does not authorise any indemnity which would be prohibited or rendered void by any provision of the Companies Acts or by any other provision of law.

(3) In this article –

(a) companies are associated if one is a subsidiary of the other or both are subsidiaries of the same body corporate, and
(b) a "relevant director" means any director or former director of the company or an associated company.

53 Insurance

(1) The directors may decide to purchase and maintain insurance, at the expense of the company, for the benefit of any relevant director in respect of any relevant loss.

(2) In this article –

(a) a "relevant director" means any director or former director of the company or an associated company,
(b) a "relevant loss" means any loss or liability which has been or may be incurred by a relevant director in connection with that director's duties or powers in relation to the company, any associated company or any pension fund or employees' share scheme of the company or associated company, and
(c) companies are associated if one is a subsidiary of the other or both are subsidiaries of the same body corporate.

Appendix 9

MODEL SHORT-FORM SET OF RULES FOR A MEMBERS' CLUB[1]

RULES OF THE BASSETSHIRE HOCKEY UMPIRES ASSOCIATION

1. **Name**
   The Association shall be called the Bassetshire Hockey Umpires Association ('the Association').
2. **Affiliation**
   The Association shall be affiliated to the Bassetshire Hockey Association and the Mid-Counties Hockey Umpires Association.
3. **Object**
   The object of the Association is to provide and promote high quality hockey umpiring through networking, development, training, grading, support, and opportunity for all the members and the teams which it serves.
4. **Membership**
   Membership shall be open to men and women over the age of 18 years, on a non-discriminatory basis, who are interested in the object of the Association, and the Association shall consist of Ordinary Members, Appointed Members, and Honorary Members.
5. **Election of members**
   (1) The election of each category of member shall be vested in the Committee. A person who wishes to be elected as an Ordinary Member shall fill in an application form provided by the Honorary Secretary. A person who wishes to be elected as an Appointed Member, if he is not already an Ordinary Member, shall fill in an application form provided by the Honorary Secretary; if he is already an Ordinary Member, he should informally approach the Honorary Secretary to make known his wish, who will pass on this information to the Committee.
   (2) The Committee may accept as a probationer any person requesting election as an Appointed Member. The Committee shall not elect any person as an Appointed Member unless it is satisfied that the candidate has the knowledge and ability to apply the rules of hockey and is suitable to be elected an Appointed Member of the Association. Active members of other hockey umpires associations may be elected Appointed Members of the Association.

---

1 Based on the actual rules of an umpiring association. The association will have no clubhouse or premises, so the rules do not have to cater for such topics as trusteeship of property or alcohol licensing, nor is there any call for bye-laws. The form and contents of the rules can be expressed in a straightforward manner, yet tailored to suit the needs of the association. These rules take account of all the basic rules set out in **2.15**.

(3) Appointed Members will be placed on either the Active List or the Non-Active List.

(4) The Committee may elect as Honorary Members those persons, not exceeding five in number, who in its opinion have rendered such service to the Association as to merit this status. Honorary Members shall be exempt from paying subscriptions and shall enjoy all the privileges of membership, save that they shall have no voting rights nor may they be elected to any office of the club.

6. **Communications with the Association**

Every member shall be under a continuing duty to notify the Hon. Secretary of his up-to-date postal address, his telephone number and his e-mail address. All notices in writing required to be given by the Association to the members under these rules may be sent by post and/or by electronic means, which shall include notices posted on the Association's website. All notices sent to the member at his notified address, whichever means of communication are used, shall be deemed to have arrived two days after despatch by the Association unless the contrary is shown. Neither the non-arrival nor late arrival of any notice sent by the Association nor the accidental omission to give due notice of the meeting to one or more members shall invalidate any meeting convened by the Association.

7. **Subscriptions**

A member's annual subscription shall be such sum as the members may determine at the AGM. All subscriptions shall become due on the 1 October in each year. Any member not paying his subscription by the due date may, at the Committee's discretion, be disqualified from umpiring any match where the appointment is made by the Association. If the subscription remains unpaid after two months of its due date, the Hon. Secretary will send to the member a written reminder of his arrears, and if the same remains unpaid after three months of its due date the member shall automatically cease to be a member of the Association.

8. **Resignation of members**

A member may resign from the Association by notifying the Secretary in writing of this fact. A member remains liable for his subscription for the year in which he resigned (a year for this purpose shall run from 1 October to the following 30 September).

9. **Suspension and expulsion of members**

(1) Complaints received by the Association concerning an umpiring member should be recorded in writing by the Honorary Secretary and then referred to the Committee for its consideration.

(2) The Committee shall have the power to stand down any member from umpiring pending the hearing of the case against him (including umpiring at non-appointed matches).

(3) The Committee shall have the power to suspend for a period not exceeding 12 months or to expel a member who infringes any of these rules or whose conduct, whether on or off the field, is in the opinion of the Committee injurious to the good name of the Association or renders him unfit for membership. No person shall be suspended or expelled without first being summoned before the Committee and full opportunity afforded to him to advance a defence to the allegations being made against him nor unless two-thirds of the Committee then present shall vote for his suspension or expulsion.

(4) No suspended member may be elected as an officer of the Association but he shall remain liable for his subscription.

10. **Officers of the Association**
The Association shall have the following officers, all of whom shall be elected at the annual general meeting: a Chair, a Vice-Chair, an Honorary Secretary, an Honorary Treasurer, two Appointment Secretaries (men/women); a Development Officer, two Regional Representatives (men/women) and a Publicity Officer. Upon election all officers shall hold office until the next AGM when their term of office shall expire but they may offer themselves for re-election.

11. **Management of the Association**
The management and control of all the affairs of the Association shall be vested in a committee of members ('the Committee'). The Committee shall consist of the Chair, the Vice-Chair, the Honorary Secretary, the Honorary Treasurer, and two other officers who shall be chosen from their own number. The Committee shall meet as and when appropriate. Any committee member who is absent without an accepted apology from three consecutive committee meetings shall be deemed to have vacated office. A quorum for meetings of the Committee shall be three members. The chair of any committee meeting shall have an additional casting vote. All resolutions or decisions taken by the Committee shall require a simple majority of those present at the meeting.

12. **Powers of the Committee**
For the avoidance of doubt the Committee shall have the following specific powers:
(1) to fill any vacancy amongst the officers until the next AGM;
(2) to appoint such sub-committees as it deems necessary. A sub-committee shall conduct its business in accordance with the directions of the Committee and shall periodically report its proceedings to the Committee for approval and ratification;
(3) to open a bank account with a High Street bank in the name of the Association and to arrange such facilities as may be necessary to carry on the activities of the Association, including the arrangement of a loan or overdraft provided that such loan or overdraft shall not exceed the sum of £2,000 without the prior approval of the members obtained at a general meeting;
(4) to retain and hold as property of the Association all sums of money coming into the Association and to bank the funds of the Association. All cheques drawn by the Association shall be signed by the Chair and the Honorary Treasurer, or by such other officers of the Association as may be duly authorised by the Committee, provided that all cheques are signed by two officers;
(5) to invest sums of money in any prudent manner which the Committee thinks will benefit the Association;
(6) to permit, unless a contrary direction is given, all officers to pay out-of-pocket expenses or fees authorised by the Committee;
(7) to arrange insurance cover for members in respect of all their umpiring activities, whether or not they are acting as appointed umpires;
(7) to assess on an on-going basis the performance of the Appointed Members and to re-grade them, higher or lower, as and when necessary;
(8) to appoint, at the request of any club or school affiliated to the Bassetshire Hockey Association, one or two Appointed Members as the umpires for any match, provided that the club or school shall pay (if so requested by the Association) the notified appointment fees and expenses, and provided that they agree to be bound by the rules of the Association as may be made from time to time.

13. **Annual General Meeting**

(1) The annual general meeting ('AGM') of the Association shall be held in June of each year for the purpose of receiving the reports of the Committee and any sub-committee in respect of the Association's activities since the previous AGM (including the election of any Honorary Member); receiving from the Honorary Treasurer and, if thought fit, approving the accounts in respect of the preceding financial year; electing the officers of the Association (including the appointment of any Honorary Auditor); fixing the subscriptions; and for the transaction of the general business of the Association.

(2) All categories of members shall receive 21 days' notice in writing of the date of such meeting, together with an agenda.

(3) No member, save with the permission of the chair of the meeting, may bring any matter before the meeting unless, before 15 May in that year, he has given notice in writing to the Honorary Secretary of the substance of the matter which he wishes to raise at the meeting.

14. **Special meetings**

A special meeting of the members shall be convened by the Honorary Secretary within 28 days of receipt by him of a direction by the Committee or of a requisition signed by not fewer than one-fifth of the total membership. All categories of members shall receive 14 days' notice in writing of such meeting. The notice will specify the purpose of the meeting and no other matter may be brought before such meeting.

15. **Quorum and voting at meetings**

(1) A general meeting (that is, an AGM or a special meeting) may proceed to business if 25 members are present within half an hour after the time fixed for the meeting; otherwise the meeting, if convened on the requisition of the members, shall be dissolved but, if convened by direction of the Committee, shall stand adjourned to the same time and place in the following week, save that the adjourned meeting may proceed to business whatever the number of members present.

(2) Only fully paid up members shall be allowed to vote at a general meeting. The chair of the meeting shall have an additional casting vote. Any motion to be carried shall require a simple majority of those entitled to vote and present at the meeting, save for any amendment of the rules or the dissolution of the Association which shall require a two-thirds majority of those entitled to vote and present at the meeting.

16. **Amendment of the rules**

These rules may be added to, altered or revoked by members at a special meeting or, if the amendment is proposed by the Committee, at an AGM. Any amendment to be proposed at the AGM must be contained in the notice of the AGM sent under Rule 13.

17. **Interpretation**

The reference in these rules to the masculine gender shall in all cases apply equally to the feminine gender. If any question or dispute arises as to the meaning or interpretation of these rules, the matter must be referred to the Committee for a ruling thereon.

18. **Dissolution of the Association**

In the event that the members pass a resolution to dissolve the Association, any property belonging to the Association shall not be distributed to the members if there is a surplus of assets over liabilities, but will be given or transferred to the Bassetshire Hockey Association or to such other body having similar objects to the Association as the members may decide upon.

Date of Rules: 12 June 2007

Amended: 24 November 2010

Appendix 10

MODEL FULL SET OF RULES FOR A MEMBERS' CLUB

RULES OF THE BASSET SPORTS CLUB

1. **Name**

   The club shall be called the Basset Sports Club ('the Club').

2. **Objects**

   The objects of the Club are:

   (1) to promote and provide for the benefit of members of the Club amenities for the pursuit of sporting activities and for social and recreational activities;

   (2) to promote fellowship amongst the members;

   (3) to foster links with, and to support and co-operate with other persons or organisations with similar objects as set out in this rule;

   (4) to do all things necessary for or incidental to or conducive to the attainment of the above-mentioned objects.

3. **Sports defined**

   The sports in which the Club is involved are cricket, tennis, hockey and athletics.

4. **Sporting rules**

   The rules of the sports carried on by the Club shall be those rules adopted from time to time by the governing body of the sport in question.

5. **Trustees**

   (1) All property and assets of the Club shall be vested in not less than two nor more than four trustees appointed from time to time by the Committee from membership of the Club [OR vested in a trust corporation[1]]. The trustees shall hold the same for and on behalf of the Ordinary Members and the Life Members of the Club. No member shall be appointed (or re-appointed) over the age of 75. Any trustee must have been a member of the Club for at least five years before the date of appointment.

   (2) Trustees shall be appointed for a term of five years but at the expiry of this period shall be eligible for re-appointment. The trustee's tenure of office will terminate on the resignation, retirement or death of the trustee. In addition, a trustee may be removed by a vote of two-thirds of the members present and entitled to vote at a special meeting.

   (3) The Committee shall have power to nominate a new trustee if a vacancy occurs by reason of one of the grounds set out in sub-rule (2) above. For the purpose of giving effect to such nomination the Committee is hereby

---

1 The professional trust corporation will involve the club in additional expenditure. See also footnote 81 in **8.25**.

nominated as the person to appoint a new trustee of the Club within the meaning of section 36 of the Trustee Act 1925.

(4) The trustees shall deal with the Club's property and assets as directed by the Committee from time to time. Without derogation from this obligation, the trustees shall have the general power of investment set out in section 3 of the Trustee Act 2000 on the basis that the statutory duty of care shall apply to the exercise of the trustees' powers. The trustees shall have power to insure the trust property; to sell the same; to borrow money; or to give security for borrowed money by mortgage or charge on the Club's property, provided always that the transaction in question does not involve a greater sum than £25,000. Any transaction involving a greater sum than £25,000 shall require the consent of two-thirds of the members (including proxies if applicable) present and entitled to vote at a general meeting of the Club.

(5) The trustees shall be indemnified against risk and expense out of the Club's funds.

6. **Membership**

Membership of the Club shall be open to all without EQA discrimination ('EQA discrimination' means discrimination which is unlawful under the Equality Act 2010). The membership shall consist of:

(1) Ordinary Members;
(2) Life Members;
(3) Honorary Members;
(4) Social Members;
(5) Junior Members;
(6) Temporary Members;
(7) Associate Members.

7. **Ordinary Members**

Ordinary Members shall be adults and full members of the Club, whose numbers shall not exceed 1,500. Ordinary Members are those who join the Club as playing members. When an Ordinary Member has retired from playing, he may continue as a full member but shall be treated as a Social Member for the purpose of his subscription.

8. **Life Members**

An Ordinary Member may pay a lump sum determined by the Committee from time to time to become a Life Member of the Club. Life Members shall have the full privileges of membership and full voting rights, but shall not be liable to pay any further subscription.

9. **Honorary Members**

An Ordinary Member of at least five years' standing may propose to the Committee a person for honorary membership. The Committee may elect as Honorary Members those persons, not exceeding 10 in number, who in the opinion of the Committee have for good or sufficient reason merited this status. Honorary Members shall be exempt from paying any entrance fee or subscription and shall be entitled to all the privileges of membership, save that they shall have no voting rights nor may they be appointed to any office or committee of the Club.

10. **Social Members**

Social Members are those who join the Club as non-playing members and whose number shall not exceed 375. Social Members shall be entitled to use all the social facilities of the Club. Social Members shall have the full privileges of membership and full voting rights, save that if a motion is put to the members at a general meeting which is or may be prejudicial to the interests of the playing members the Social Members shall not be entitled to vote on it.

11. **Junior Members**
Membership shall be open to boys and girls over the age of 8 years and under the age of 18 years. A parent or sponsor must countersign the application form of a Junior Member. No Junior Member shall be entitled to attend general meetings of the Club but may do so at the discretion of the Committee. If he or she does so attend, the Junior Member may not vote thereat nor shall his or her presence count towards any requisite quorum. A Junior Member wishing to be elected an adult member must follow the procedure laid down in Rule 14.

12. **Temporary Members**
Holiday residents staying at the South Bassetshire Camping and Caravan Park may apply to the Committee for temporary membership for the duration of their stay at the Park for a period not exceeding 14 days in any one year. The Committee shall have power to permit other Temporary Members for good or sufficient reason. Temporary Members are subject to the two-day rule set out in Rule 14(4). Temporary Members may introduce their guests into the club. Temporary Members shall be entitled to all the privileges of membership, save that they shall have no voting rights nor may they be appointed to any office or committee of the club.

13. **Associate Members**
(1) Members of the Basset Bowls Club may be admitted into the Club as Associate Members.
(2) Members of other clubs which are recognised clubs within the meaning of section 193 of the Licensing Act 2003 may be admitted into the Club as Associate Members provided the Committee has given its prior consent to such admission.

14. **Election and admission of members**
(1) The election and admission[2] of all categories of member shall be vested in the Committee.
(2) A candidate for Ordinary Membership or Social Membership must be proposed and seconded by at least two Ordinary Members of at least two years' standing at the date of the proposal.
(3) An application for Temporary Membership may be authorised, and only authorised, by three members of the Committee nominated by the Committee to carry out this task.
(4) Any application for membership (excluding Associate Membership) must be made on an application form provided by the Secretary. A candidate may not be admitted to membership (or, as a candidate for membership, be admitted to the privileges of membership) without an interval of at least two days between their nomination or application for membership and their admission as a member of the Club.
(5) Any potential member may be asked to demonstrate his playing ability in the sport in which he wishes to participate before his application is considered by the Committee. This demonstration may be required of an Associate Member.
(6) A candidate for Ordinary Membership or Social Membership who receives two adverse votes (provided they are not based on EQA

[2] 'Admission' here would include security considerations. It is increasingly common for clubs to insist on all members producing a membership card (with the associate member producing the membership card of his 'recognised club': see **9.34**) before being allowed on to the club premises, and the committee may give a direction to this effect as part of its managerial powers.

discrimination) shall not be elected a member. Any objection to an application for membership should be notified to and recorded by the chairman of the meeting before the election takes place. The objection is to be treated as confidential to the members of the Committee until after the election has taken place.[3]

(7) Upon election or admission the member will be notified accordingly and will be provided with a copy of these rules, together with a copy of the bye-laws. The member shall be bound by all rules and bye-laws which may be made from time to time.

(8) The elected or admitted member shall not be entitled to any privileges of membership until he has paid the entrance fee (if any) and the initial subscription.

15. **Communication with the Club**

Every member shall be under a continuing duty to notify the Secretary of his up-to-date postal address, his telephone number and his e-mail address. All notices in writing required to be given by the Club to the members under these rules may be sent by post and/or by electronic means, which shall include notices posted on the club's website. All notices sent to the member at his notified address, whichever means of communication are used, shall be deemed to have arrived two days after despatch by the Club unless the contrary is shown. Neither the non-arrival nor the late arrival of any notice sent by the Club nor the accidental omission to give due notice of the meeting to one or more members shall invalidate any meeting convened by the Club. Any member who wishes to be contacted by the Club via the postal service and not by other means must expressly notify the Secretary of this fact in writing. The club will not use the member's e-mail address for confidential or sensitive matters.

16. **Membership list**[4]

For the purposes of carrying on the activities of the Club, a list of members with suitable contact details shall be circulated annually to the membership. The list shall indicate who are officers of the club and who are members of the Committee. The contents of this list will be protected by the Data Protection Act 1998.

17. **Entrance fee**

Entrance fees (if any) for Ordinary Members and Social Members shall be such sum as the Committee shall recommend and the members approve at the annual general meeting.

18. **Subscriptions**

(1) ***Ordinary Members and Social Members*** The subscription shall be such sum as the Committee shall recommend and the members approve at the annual general meeting.

(2) All subscriptions shall become due and payable on 1st April in each year. If a member is elected after the 1st October, his first subscription shall be reduced by one-half.

(3) The Committee may authorise members to pay their subscriptions by up to four instalments payable not later than 15 March in the following year, provided that the instalments are paid by direct debit or standing order.

---

[3] Any objection based on discrimination prohibited under the Equality Act 2010 is not permissible: see **4.19**. Rejection of a candidate without any visible explanation may well lead to a finding by the court that unlawful discrimination has in fact occurred: see **4.26**.

[4] See **5.86** to **5.89** inclusive for guidance on this topic.

(4) If the subscription or any instalment is not paid within one calendar month of its due date, the member shall cease to enjoy the privileges of membership until payment is made. If the subscription or an instalment remains unpaid after two months of its due date, the Secretary will send to the member a written reminder of his arrears, and if the same remains unpaid after three months of its due date the member shall automatically cease to be a member of the Club. The committee shall have the power to affix a notice in the clubhouse to the effect that a particular person has ceased to be a member under this rule.

(5) ***Temporary Members*** The subscription shall be such sum as determined by the Committee.

(6) ***Associate Members*** The fees shall be such sums as determined by the Committee.

(7) ***Remission*** In special cases the Committee shall have power to remit the whole or any part of a member's subscription.

(8) ***Levy*** The members in general meeting shall have power to authorise that monies should be raised by a levy on the members. Life Members and suspended members shall be subject to this levy. Honorary Members, Temporary Members and Associate Members shall be exempt from this levy.

19. **Resignation**

A member may resign from the Club by notifying the Secretary in writing of this fact. If a resignation is received after 1st March in any year, the member shall remain liable to pay his subscription for the following year.

20. **Suspension and expulsion**

(1) The Committee shall have the power to suspend for a period not exceeding 12 months or to expel any member whose conduct, whether within the club premises or elsewhere, is in opinion of the Committee injurious to the good name of the Club or renders him unfit for membership of the Club.

(2) No member shall be suspended or expelled without first being summoned before the Committee and full opportunity given to him to advance an explanation or defence, nor unless two-thirds of the Committee then present shall vote for his suspension or expulsion. The Chairman of the Committee who hears the case shall not have a casting vote on this occasion.

(3) The Committee shall have the power to exclude the member from the club premises pending the hearing of the case against him.

(4) A suspended member shall cease to have any of the privileges of membership, nor may he be nominated for or hold office whilst suspended, but he shall remain liable for his subscription.

(5) A member who is suspended shall have the right of appeal to the Committee if he so requests in writing to the Secretary within 7 days of his suspension. The appeal shall take place within 14 days of the request. The composition of the appellant tribunal shall, if possible, comprise different members of the Committee from those who imposed the suspension. If this is not possible, the appellant tribunal shall be chaired by an independent, senior Ordinary Member of at least 10 years' standing, who shall be entitled to vote on the appeal.

(6) A member who is expelled shall have the right of appeal to the members at a special meeting if he so requests in writing to the Secretary within 7 days of his expulsion. The meeting shall be convened by the Secretary within 21 days of the expulsion. If at least two-thirds of the members

present and entitled to vote at the meeting are in favour of allowing the appeal, the member shall be automatically reinstated.

(7) If the member so requests, he may attend any hearing before the Committee or the special meeting of the members with a legal or other representative.

21. **Disciplinary proceedings**

(1) The Committee shall have the power to operate a system of disciplinary proceedings for dealing with complaints made in respect of any act or omission which in the opinion of the Committee is discreditable or prejudicial to the interests of the sporting world and which relates to or is connected with the member's conduct whilst participating in one of the sports referred to in Rule 3.[5]

(2) The conduct of the disciplinary proceedings shall be vested in the Committee who shall have power to delegate any investigation or hearing to a Disciplinary Sub-Committee ('DSC').

(3) No member shall be disciplined without first being summoned before the DSC and a proper opportunity given to him to advance an explanation or defence, nor unless two-thirds of the DSC then present shall vote for the member being disciplined. The chairman of the DSC who hears the case shall not have a casting vote on this occasion.

(4) If the complaint is upheld, the DSC acting on behalf of the Committee shall have power to impose one or more of the following sanctions:[6]

(a) to warn the member about his future conduct;
(b) to censure him;
(c) to fine him in a sum not exceeding £500;
(d) to disqualify him for a specified period not exceeding six months from taking part in any match, game or competition;
(e) to deprive him for a specified period not exceeding six months of some or all of his privileges of membership;
(f) to impose on him an order for costs.

The DSC must report forthwith to the Committee any decision made under this rule.

(6) A member who is disciplined shall have the same right of appeal as is described in Rule 20(5).

(7) If the DSC is of the opinion that the members' conduct merits the attention of the full Committee, it may refer the matter to the Committee to be dealt with under Rule 20, save that the Committee in this instance shall have the power to impose any of the sanctions set out in Rule 21(4) in addition to or in lieu of its powers in Rule 20. If the Committee suspends the member, he shall have the same right of appeal as described in Rule 20(5) and, if the Committee expels the member, he shall have the same right of appeal as described in Rule 20(6).

22. **Officers**

(1) The officers of the Club shall consist of a President; such Vice-Presidents as are elected in accordance with sub-rule (3) below; a Chairman of the Club;[7] two Captains (Men/Ladies); two Vice-Captains (Men/Ladies); an Honorary Secretary unless there is a paid secretary,[8] either being referred

---

5 A golf club will need to include here a reference to Rule 11.6 of the Council of National Golf Unions Regulations 2004 in order to give the disciplinary body jurisdiction to deal with the member's handicap.

6 In dealing with a junior member the club can make suitable adjustments e g by omitting sanctions (c) and (f).

7 In many clubs the Chairman is elected by the Committee from one of its own number: see **5.13**.

8 Some clubs have no Secretary but a (paid) Club Manager instead: see **5.10**.

to in these rules as 'the Secretary'; and an Honorary Treasurer. (Any paid secretary shall not be a member of the Club).

(2) The nominations for the office of President shall be presented by the Committee to the members at the annual general meeting, and upon election by the members the President shall serve for a term of three years, but shall be eligible for re-election at the end of each term.

(3) There shall from time to time be Vice-Presidents not exceeding three in number. The nominations for the office of Vice-President shall be presented by the Committee to the members at the annual general meeting, and upon election by the members the Vice-Presidents shall serve for a term of three years, renewable once only. After six years in office a Vice-President must stand down for a year before being eligible to be nominated as a Vice-President for a further term.

(4) All the other officers shall be elected annually at the annual general meeting. Nominations for the other officers must be signed by two members who are Ordinary Members of at least three years' standing or Life Members, and must be received in writing by the Secretary at least 15 days prior to the annual general meeting. All these other officers shall be eligible for re-election.

(5) The Secretary shall 14 days prior to the annual general meeting post the nominations for election of all officers on the Club's notice board and on the Club's website.

(6) In the event of there being more than one nomination for any particular office the election shall be decided by secret ballot, with the outcome of the vote being decided on a 'first-past-the-post' basis. In the event of a tie, the election shall be decided by lot.

(7) The duties of the Secretary shall include: keeping an up-to-date list of the names and addresses of the members and their contact numbers; collecting subscriptions; dealing with correspondence of the Club; organising and attending general meetings of the Club and preparing minutes thereof; liaising between the Committee and the sub-committees; and preparing a report on the club's activities since the last annual general meeting and circulating the same amongst the membership.

(8) The duties of the Honorary Treasurer shall include: [liaising with the finance sub-committee]; keeping the accounts of the Club in good order; banking without delay in the Club's name all monies received from the Secretary; preparing an audited statement of account (including a balance sheet and a profit and loss account) for the members at the annual general meeting and circulating the same amongst the membership; and being answerable to the Committee as to the state of the Club's finances during the year leading up the annual general meeting.

(9) The office of Vice-President may be combined with another office.

23. **Auditor**

There shall be an independent auditor appointed on an annual basis.

24. **Management of the Club**

(1) *Generally* The management and control of all the affairs of the Club (including the supply or sale of alcohol on the Club's premises)[9] shall be vested in an elected committee (referred to in these rules as 'the Committee').[10]

(2) *Bye-laws* The Committee shall have power to make, alter or revoke such bye-laws as it considers necessary for the good governance and well-being of the Club. All such bye-laws shall be published annually and a copy displayed in the clubhouse. [The Committee shall have power to fine any member up to a maximum of £100 for any breach of the bye-laws.]

(3) *Clubhouse* Any special provisions relating to the use of the clubhouse by members shall be set out in the bye-laws.

25. **The Committee**

(1) The Committee shall consist of the officers set out in Rule 22(1) (except the President and Vice-Presidents) plus four Ordinary Members and one Social Member. If the Secretary is a paid official, the number of Ordinary Members shall be increased to five.

(2) The Ordinary Members and the Social Member forming part of the Committee shall be elected annually at the annual general meeting. Nominations must be signed by two members who are Ordinary Members or Social Members of at least three years' standing or Life Members, and must be received in writing by the Secretary at least 15 days prior to the annual general meeting. All nominees shall be eligible for re-election.

(3) The Secretary shall 14 days prior to the annual general meeting post the nominations for election on the Club's notice board and on the Club's website.

(4) In the event of there being more nominations than vacancies the election shall be decided by secret ballot, with the outcome of the vote being decided on a 'first-past-the-post' basis. In the event of a tie, the election shall be decided by lot.

(5) The Committee shall be chaired by the elected Chairman of the Club. At its first meeting after the annual general meeting the Committee shall choose a Vice-Chairman from one of its own number who will undertake the duties of the Chairman in his or her absence.

(6) The Committee shall meet on a regular basis, and sufficiently often to carry out its duties efficiently. Any committee member who is absent without an accepted apology from three consecutive meetings shall be deemed to have vacated office.

(7) The quorum for a meeting of the Committee shall be four persons. The chairman of the Committee, whether it be the formally chosen person or an ad hoc choice, shall have an additional casting vote at any meeting. All resolutions or decisions taken by the Committee shall require a simple majority of those present at the meeting, save that any amendment of the bye-laws shall require a two-thirds majority of the Committee.

---

9 The detailed arrangements concerning matters arising under the Licensing Act 2003 are best dealt with in the bye-laws. Under the Licensing Act 1964 certain matters like the supply of intoxicating liquor to non-members or the club's permitted hours had to be dealt with in the rules themselves. This is no longer the case.

10 This may be one of the shortest rules in the rulebook but it is one of the most important.

(8) The Committee shall have power to appoint an Ordinary Member or a Social Member to fill any casual vacancy that may arise on the Committee and that member shall remain in office until the next annual general meeting. The Committee may also co-opt up to three additional members from the Ordinary or the Social Membership for such purposes and for such time as it thinks fit but not beyond the next annual general meeting. Appointed and co-opted members shall have the right to vote.

26. **Sub-committees**

(1) The Committee may from time to time appoint such sub-committees as it shall deem necessary or expedient to assist it in managing the affairs of the Club. Without derogation from the generality of this rule, there shall be a sub-committee attached to each defined sport whose remit is to look after the welfare of that sport in the Club.

(2) The composition of any sub-committee may include Ordinary Members and Social Members who are not members of the Committee. All sub-committees shall conduct their business in accordance with directions from the Committee and shall periodically report their proceedings to the Committee for approval or ratification.

(3) The Vice-Presidents shall be eligible to sit as ex-officio members of all the sub-committees, save that if they attend meetings in this capacity they shall have no voting rights.

(4) All members of sub-committees shall automatically retire on the date on which the annual general meeting is held but shall be eligible for re-appointment by the incoming Committee immediately following the annual general meeting.

(5) A sub-committee at its first meeting after the annual general meeting shall choose a chairman from one of its own number and shall decide on the quorum for any meeting of the sub-committee, and notify the Secretary accordingly. The chairman of a sub-committee, whether it be the formally chosen person or an ad hoc choice, shall have an additional casting vote at any meeting. All resolutions or decisions taken by a sub-committee shall require a simple majority of those present at the meeting.

(6) If for any reason a vacancy occurs during its period of appointment, the sub-committee shall so notify the Committee, who shall have power to appoint another member to fill that vacancy for the remainder of the period.

27. **Declaration of interest**

A member must disclose to the chairman of the Committee or any sub-committee on which he sits any interest which may conflict with the proper consideration of a matter under discussion. If the disclosing member is the chairman of the Committee or of the sub-committee, he shall disclose his interest to the next most senior person. A member disclosing an interest shall not be entitled to vote on the matter under discussion and the other members at the meeting shall decide whether the disclosing member may participate in the discussion.

28. **Club indemnity**

The members of the Committee, the officers of the Club, and the officials of the Club shall be indemnified by the Club out of club funds against any legal or monetary claim made against them by third parties in connection with the proper discharge of their duties.

29. **Annual General Meeting**

(1) There shall be an annual general meeting of the Club held on a date fixed by the Committee not later than 30 June in each year, provided that not more than 15 months shall elapse between each meeting.

(2) The purposes for which the meeting is convened shall be:

(a) to receive a report from the Secretary in respect of the Club's activities since the previous annual general meeting;

(b) to receive from the Honorary Treasurer and, if thought fit, to approve the Club's audited accounts in respect of the preceding financial year;

(c) to elect the President (if the office be vacant), the Vice-Presidents (if there be any vacancy), the officers of the Club and the members of the Committee;

(d) to appoint an auditor for the ensuing year;

(e) to discuss or decide any other matter of general business of the Club duly submitted to the meeting.

(3) All members shall receive 28 days' notice in writing of the meeting, together with the agenda of the meeting. No member, save with the consent of the chairman of the meeting, shall bring any matter before the meeting unless he has given notice of motion in writing to the Secretary not less than 14 days before the meeting (although points for discussion only may be received up to 48 hours before the meeting). A notice of agenda shall be posted in the clubhouse for at least 14 days prior to the meeting.

30. **Special meetings**

(1) A special general meeting shall be convened by the Secretary within 28 days of receipt by him of a direction of the Committee or of a requisition signed by not less than 30 members entitled to attend and vote at a general meeting or by one-fifth of such members (whichever is the smaller number). All members will receive not less than 14 days' notice in writing of the meeting. The notice shall specify the purpose of the meeting and no other business may be brought before the meeting.

(2) If the Secretary fails to convene a duly requisitioned meeting within the 28 day period, the requisitionists themselves may convene such meeting to be held not later than 56 days after the deposit of the requisition with the Secretary. The reasonable costs of the requisionists in convening this meeting shall be borne by the Club.

31. **Procedure at general meetings**

(1) A general meeting may proceed to business if 30 Ordinary Members and/or Life Members are present within half an hour after the time fixed for the meeting. If no quorum is then present and the meeting was convened by requisition of the members, it shall be dissolved; and if convened by direction of the Committee it shall stand adjourned to the week following on the same day and at the same time and place. If at the adjourned meeting there is still no quorum the meeting shall be dissolved.

(2) If a general meeting is adjourned for want of time, the members present at the meeting will be notified there and then of the adjourned date, if this is practicable. If not, and the matter is adjourned for more than 14 days, all the members shall receive notice in writing of the adjourned hearing; otherwise only those who attended the original meeting will be notified of the adjourned date.

(3) No member who is in arrear with the payment of his subscription shall be entitled to exercise his vote at a general meeting.

(4) Unless otherwise stipulated in these rules, any motion to be carried shall require the votes of a simple majority of the members present and voting at the meeting.

(5) Where a motion relates to an item of special business, the following shall apply:

(a) the vote shall be decided on a show of hands unless a poll is demanded under (b) or (c) below;

(b) a poll may be demanded in advance of the meeting;

(c) a poll may be demanded at the meeting either before the show of hands or immediately after the result of a show of hands;

(d) a poll may be demanded by the chairman of the meeting or by at least 10 Ordinary Members and/or Life Members;

(e) the poll must take place at the meeting;

(f) the poll shall include voting by proxy. The proxy forms shall be sent out with the notice of the meeting, and are to be returned to the Secretary by e-mail or post to arrive not later than three days before the meeting;

(g) all business shall be deemed special save those items appearing regularly on the AGM agenda.

(6) The chairman of any meeting shall be entitled to a casting vote in addition to his ordinary vote.

32. **Financial powers**

(1) The Committee shall have power to open a bank account with a High Street bank in the name of the Club and to arrange such facilities as may be necessary to carry on the activities of the Club including the arrangement of a loan or overdraft, whether on a secured or unsecured basis, provided that such loan or overdraft shall not exceed the sum of £10,000 without the prior approval of the members obtained at a general meeting;

(2) The Committee via the Trustees may in its discretion establish and maintain a sinking fund or a reserve fund for such purposes as it shall think fit.

(3) The Committee via the Trustees shall have power to invest the Club's funds in any prudent manner which in the reasonable opinion of the Committee will benefit the Club.

(4) The Committee shall have power to spend the Club's funds in furtherance of the objects set out in Rule 2 above, as well as in compliance with its duties of management under Rule 24(1).

(5) The Club shall have power to defray out of the Club's funds expenses wholly and necessarily incurred by members of the Committee or any sub-committee, or incurred by any member acting on the authority of the Committee, which relates to or is connected with carrying out their duties or responsibilities on behalf of the Club. For the avoidance of doubt, the Committee may arrange appropriate insurance cover in respect of the conduct of the Club's trustees, officers and members of the Committee.[11]

(6) All cheques drawn by the Club shall be signed by the Chairman of the Club and the Honorary Treasurer or by such other officers as may be authorised by the Committee, provided that all cheques are signed by two officers.

---

11 The rule relating to insurance cover can be expanded to include other members of the club where, for example, its members undertake refereeing or umpiring duties in such sports as boxing, rugby, football and hockey.

33. **Guests and visitors**
   (1) The Committee shall have power by way of bye-laws to regulate the admission of associate members, guests and visitors into any part of the Club's premises.
   (2) Members may personally introduce guests into the Club's premises, but must accompany such guests during their stay at the Club and shall be responsible for the good behaviour of such guests. The Committee shall have power in their absolute discretion to exclude any guest or visitor from the Club's premises.

34. **Interpretation of the rules**
   The reference in these rules to the masculine gender shall in all cases apply equally to the feminine gender. If any question or dispute arises as to the meaning or interpretation of these rules or of the bye-laws made thereunder, the matter must be referred to the Committee for a ruling thereon.

35. **Amendment of the rules**[12]
   (1) These rules may be added to, altered or revoked by the members at a special meeting or at the annual general meeting. Any amendment to be proposed at the annual general meeting must be sent out as part of the agenda referred to in Rule 29(3).
   (2) To be carried, any motion to amend the rules shall require the votes of two-thirds of the members (including proxies if applicable) present at the meeting and entitled to vote.
   (3) In the discussion of a motion to amend the rules, any proposed amendment to the motion may be carried by a simple majority of the members (including proxies if applicable) present and voting at the meeting.

36. **Dispute resolution**
   Any dispute between the Club and its members or between the members themselves which relates to these rules (or the bye-laws) or which concerns the affairs of the Club shall be referred to the arbitration of a sole arbitrator to be appointed in accordance with section 16(3) of the Arbitration Act 1996, the seat of such arbitration being hereby designated as London, England. In the event of failure of the parties to make the appointment pursuant to section 16(3), the appointment shall be made by the President of the Chartered Institute of Arbitrators. The arbitrator shall decide the dispute according to the laws of England and Wales. This rule does not prevent the dispute being referred to mediation for resolution prior to arbitration.

37. **Dissolution of the Club**
   (1) Any motion to dissolve the Club must be the subject matter of a special meeting.
   (2) To be carried, any motion to dissolve the Club shall require the votes of two-thirds of the members (including proxies if applicable) present at the meeting and entitled to vote thereat.
   (3) In the event that the members pass a resolution to dissolve the Club, any property or assets belonging to the Club shall not be distributed to the members if there is a surplus of assets over liabilities, but will be given or transferred to The Bassetshire Association for the Encouragement of

12 Alterations to the rules often need careful thought as to their practical and legal consequences and advice may be on hand for clubs from supporting organisations such as the National Golf Clubs' Advisory Association.

Sport or to such other club or entity having similar objects to the Club, or to a charitable organisation, as the members may decide upon.[13]

Date of Rules: 12 June 2007

Amended: 24 November 2010

[13] See **1.65** and **8.11** as to the need for or the desirability of this sub-rule.

Appendix 11

SPECIMEN NOTICE AND AGENDA FOR AN ANNUAL GENERAL MEETING (WITH PROXY FORM)

BASSETSHIRE HISTORICAL SOCIETY

Notice is hereby given that the seventy-fifth Annual General Meeting of the Society will be held at the Constitutional Club, Basset, BA1 3XA on Thursday 27 May 2010 at 7.30pm.

(Signed)
Daniel Whiddon
Honorary Secretary

27 April 2010

AGENDA

1. To receive apologies for absence.
2. To approve the minutes of the previous Annual General Meeting.
3. Matters arising.
4. To receive from the Honorary Secretary a report on the Society's activities since the previous Annual General Meeting.
5. To receive from the Honorary Treasurer and, if thought fit, to approve the Society's audited accounts for the preceding financial year ended 31 December 2009.
6. To elect for the forthcoming year the President, the Vice-President and the other officers of the Society and the members of the Committee, and also to appoint the Honorary Auditor.
7. To fix the subscriptions of the various categories of member.
8. To present to Professor Tom Cobley FBA an inscribed and illustrated Special Edition of the History of Basset in Roman Times in recognition of his exemplary work on behalf of the Society.
9. Any other business.

Note: A member who wishes to bring any other matter of general business before the Annual General Meeting must give notice in writing to the Hon Secretary of such matter by 13 May 2010 pursuant to Rule 15.

Special Business

10. To consider the recommendation of the Committee that a junior section of the Society be established in accordance with the motion referred to below.

Motion

(1) That this meeting resolves that membership of the Society be open to children between the ages of 10 and 18 years.
(2) That pursuant to the said resolution this meeting resolves that a new Rule 6A be added to the Rules of the Society as follows:

> '6A **Junior Membership** Membership shall be open to boys and girls over the age of 10 years and under the age of 18 years. A parent or sponsor must countersign the application form of a junior member. No junior member shall be entitled to attend general meetings of the Society but may do so at the discretion of the Committee. If he or she does so attend, the junior member may not vote thereat nor shall his or her presence count towards any requisite quorum. A junior member wishing to be elected an adult member must follow the procedure laid down in Rule 8.'

Note: as item (2) of the motion will entail amendment of the rules of the Society, a two-thirds majority of those present and entitled to vote will be required in accordance with Rule 20, if this item is to be passed at the Annual General Meeting.

Please see attached Proxy Voting Form on next page

BASSETSHIRE HISTORICAL SOCIETY

Proxy Voting Form

Special Business at the Annual General Meeting on Thursday 27 May 2010

Please complete in BLOCK CAPITALS

I, (name)..............................

of (address)...

being a member of the Bassetshire Historical Society, hereby appoint

.... (the proxy),

or in default the chairman of the meeting, to be my proxy to vote for me on my behalf at the Annual General Meeting of the Society to be held on 27 May 2010 and at any adjournment thereof.

This form is to be used as follows:

Resolution (1): FOR* AGAINST*

Resolution (2): FOR* AGAINST*

Unless otherwise instructed, the proxy may vote as he thinks fit or he may may abstain from voting.[1]

* Strike out whichever is not desired.

Signed....................................

Dated....................

This form should be returned by e-mail to the Hon. Secretary (daniel.whiddon@coolmail.co.uk) or posted to Mr Daniel Whiddon, The Gables, Basset BA4 9RP to arrive not later than Monday 24 May 2010.

---

1 This rider is commonly added to proxy forms since it gives the proxy leeway to vote in accordance with what he honestly believes would be the member's wishes where his instructions do not cover a particular situation, for example, an amendment to Resolution (1) is proposed at the meeting to put the age of admission of the Junior Member at 12 years instead of 10 years which was specified in the original motion. If in doubt as to those wishes and mindful of the best interests of the member he is representing, the proxy may decide to abstain from voting on the amendment.

Appendix 12

SPECIMEN MINUTES OF A COMMITTEE MEETING[1]

BASSET BOROUGH COUNCIL STANDARDS COMMITTEE

MONDAY 20 APRIL 2009

MEETING HELD AT THE BASSET TOWN HALL

Present: Cllr W Brewer (Vice-Chairman), Cllr J Stewer, Cllr P Gurney, Mr P Davey (independent member) and Mr D Whiddon (parish council representative).

In attendance: Cllr H Hawke (Council Leader) pursuant to Council Procedure Rule 9.34, and Mr T Cobley (Chief Solicitor in his capacity of Monitoring Officer).

Apologies for absence were received from Mr T Pearce (Independent Chairman) and Cllr Mrs F Widecombe.

Part 1 – Public

SC 09/08 **Appointment of Chairman of the Meeting**

The Vice-Chairman, Councillor Brewer, informed the meeting that the Chairman, Mr Pearce, was unable to attend due to ill-health. He reminded the Committee that under Article 19 of the Constitution of the Basset Borough Council meetings of the Standards Committee must be chaired by an independent member and proposed that Mr Davey be appointed to chair this meeting. Councillor Gurney seconded the proposal and it was:

Resolved: that Mr Peter Davey chair the meeting of the Standards Committee.

SC 09/09 **Declarations of Interest**

There were no declarations of interest made.

SC 09/10 **Minutes**

[1] Based on some actual minutes and commended for their clarity and conciseness.

Resolved: that the minutes of the meeting of the Standards Committee held on 20 January 2009 be approved as a correct record and signed by the Chairman.

SC 09/11 **Protocol on the Discharge of the Functions of the Monitoring Officer**

The Chief Solicitor presented a new protocol for the principal functions of the Monitoring Officer and the manner in which the Council could expect those functions to be discharged. The Committee was advised that the protocol had been drawn up by Mr East Devon, an expert on local government law, and customised to meet the needs of the Borough Council, and it was:

Resolved: that the protocol be approved and adopted.

SC 09/12 **Initial Assessment of Complaints**

The report of the Chief Solicitor set out details of the criteria to be applied by the Assessment Sub-Committee when conducting an initial assessment of allegations of failure by Members to observe the Code of Conduct. Concern was expressed about the process in respect of anonymous complaints and about the format of evidence to be submitted in support of complaints. Members requested that a future report should give guidance in respect of the three categories of complaint (namely, complainant's identity fully disclosed; fully anonymous; and semi-anonymous, that is to say, complainant's identity disclosed to the Monitoring Officer but withheld from the subject of the complaint).

Resolved: that the report be received and noted and, following amendment and clarification by the Chief Solicitor, be re-submitted to the next meeting of the Standards Committee.

SC 09/13 **Complaints Process**

The report of the Chief Solicitor set out details of the complaint form and guidance notes to be provided to complainants. In view of the previous resolution it was:

Resolved: that the report be withdrawn and, following clarification by the Chief Solicitor, an amended report be submitted to the next meeting of the Standards Committee.

SC 09/14 **Annual Report to the Standards Committee**

The report of the Chief Solicitor set out details of monitoring activity during 2008 and highlighted the arrangements for submitting information to the Standards Board for England in the Borough Council's Annual Return following the change of procedure dealing with complaints.

Resolved: that the report be received and noted.

Part 2 – Private

SC 09/15 **Exclusion of Press and Public**

The Chairman said that public discussion of the next item would involve disclosure of exempt information and must be discussed in private.

SC 09/16 **Appeal by the Basset North End Parish Councillors to the Adjudication Panel for England**

The Appeals Tribunal's decision in the above matter dated 20 February 2009 from the decision of the Standards Committee made on 21 December 2008 was put before the meeting. It was noted that the Tribunal had allowed the appeal in part by setting aside one of the sanctions imposed on the two councillors by the Hearings Sub-Committee, namely, the letter of apology. The members discussed the wisdom of this decision in the light of the facts of the case.

Resolved: that the appeal decision be noted.

THE MEETING ENDED AT 20:38 HOURS.

Appendix 13

TABLE OF COMPARISON OF SPORTS CLUBS' TAX REGIMES[1]

	No special status	Charitable status	CASC[2] status
Regulation			
1.	Little financial regulation other than to meet members' requirements	Charity Commission regulation and audit	HM Revenue & Customs regulation; generally a 'lighter' touch
2.	No definitions to meet	Sports clubs need to meet Charity Commission's definition of promoting community participation in sport for the benefit of the public	CASCs need to meet HMRC's definition of sport
3.	Can have restricted membership	Community participation (membership open to all members of the public)	Membership open to all members of the public
4.	No restrictions on sports pursued	Healthy sports including elements of strength/stamina/suppleness[3]	Sports drawn from Sports Council's lists
5.	No restrictions on activities	Significant social activity and trading e.g. a bar, to be kept separate from charitable activities	Social membership and trading e.g. a bar, generally permitted
6.	Prima facie no restriction on distribution of profits and assets to member	Cannot distribute profits or assets to members	Cannot distribute profits or assets to members
7.	No need to change club rules	Club will have to change its rules since its objects must be exclusively charitable, i.e. to promote community participation in healthy recreation/sport	Club will need to change its rules e.g. if it does not have a dissolution rule providing for its net assets to go to sport's governing body for community sport, another CASC or charitable purposes rather than to its members
8.	Players can be paid	Players cannot be paid unless for coaching; they can receive reimbursement of expenses for travel to away matches	Players cannot be paid unless they also coach; they can receive reimbursement of expenses to away matches
Incentives to give			
9.	No tax relief	Gift Aid on individual and company donations	Gift Aid on individual donations (no relief on company donations)
10.	No Payroll Giving	Payroll Giving allowed	No Payroll Giving

1 Table based on Community Amateur Sports Clubs – The Tax Options, published by Deloittes and Touche Sports, 2005 and kindly updated for this edition by Richard Baldwin, Tax Consultant and Chair of CASC Development Forum.

2 Community Amateur Sports Clubs.

3 This may therefore exclude such sports as angling, ballooning, crossbow, darts, flying, gliding, motor sports, parachuting, rifle and pistol shooting, and snooker.

	No special status	Charitable status	CASC[2] status
11.	No tax relief	Income and corporation tax relief for gifts of shares and property	No income or corporation relief for gifts of shares and property
12.	No tax relief	Inheritance tax relief on gifts	Inheritance tax relief on gifts
13.	No tax relief	Gifts of assets on 'no-gain no-loss' basis for capital gains	Gifts of assets on 'no-gain no-loss' basis for capital gains
Fund raising			
14.	Relief if gift constitutes business sponsorship	Business: relief on gifts or trading stock	Business: relief on gifts or trading stock
15.	Reliance on existing sources of funding	Grants may be available from other charities e.g. community foundations and other bodies supporting charities	No new sources of funding generally available
Direct taxes			
16.	Income from non-members taxable	Primary purpose trading income exempt from tax	Income from non-members taxable (but see 17.and18.)
17.	Fund-raising income taxable	Other fund raising income exempt from tax either by concession or by using a 'trading subsidiary'	Fund raising income exempt from tax where turnover less than £30,000 (if more, it is all taxable without marginal relief)
18.	Rental income taxable	All rental income exempt from tax	First £15,000 p a of rental income exempt from tax (if more, it is all taxable without marginal relief)
19.	Capital gains (subject to re-investment relief) and interest taxable	Capital gains and interest exempt from tax	Capital gains and interest exempt from tax
20.	Corporation tax on all taxable profits	Corporation tax on all taxable profits	Corporation tax on all taxable profits
21.	Discretionary rate relief (up to 100%)	80% mandatory rate relief; discretionary relief as to the remaining 20%	80% mandatory rate relief ; discretionary relief as to the remaining 20%
22.	Funds can be applied generally for any purpose within the rules	Corporate tax liabilities can arise if funds applied for non-qualifying purposes	Corporate tax liabilities can arise if funds applied for non-qualifying purposes

INDEX

References are to paragraph numbers.